Advances in Economics and Econometrics

This is the second of three volumes containing edited versions of papers and a commentary presented at invited symposium sessions of the Ninth World Congress of the Econometric Society, held in London in August 2005. The papers summarize and interpret key developments, and they discuss future directions for a wide variety of topics in economics and econometrics. The papers cover both theory and applications. Written by leading specialists in their fields, these volumes provide a unique survey of progress in the discipline.

Richard Blundell, CBE FBA, holds the David Ricardo Chair in Political Economy at University College London and is Research Director of the Institute for Fiscal Studies, London. He is also Director of the Economic and Social Research Council's Centre for the Microeconomic Analysis of Public Policy. Professor Blundell serves as President of the Econometric Society for 2006.

Whitney K. Newey is Professor of Economics at the Massachusetts Institute of Technology. A 2000–01 Fellow at the Center for Advanced Study in the Behavioral Sciences in Palo Alto, he is associate editor of *Econometrica* and the *Journal of Statistical Planning and Inference*, and he formerly served as associate editor of *Econometric Theory*.

Torsten Persson is Professor and Director of the Institute for International Economic Studies at Stockholm University and Centennial Professor of Economics at the London School of Economics. He was elected a Foreign Honorary Member of the American Academy of Arts and Sciences in 2001 and served as President of the European Economic Association in 2003.

Professors Blundell, Newey, and Persson are Fellows of the Econometric Society and served as Co-Chairs of the Program Committee of the Ninth World Congress of the Econometric Society, held in London in August 2005.

Econometric Society Monographs

Editors:

Andrew Chesher, University College London
Matthew Jackson, Stanford University

The Econometric Society is an international society for the advancement of economic theory in relation to statistics and mathematics. The Econometric Society Monograph Series is designed to promote the publication of original research contributions of high quality in mathematical economics and theoretical and applied econometrics.

Other titles in the series:

G. S. Maddala *Limited dependent and qualitative variables in econometrics*, 0 521 33825 5
Gerard Debreu *Mathematical economics: Twenty papers of Gerard Debreu*, 0 521 33561 2
Jean-Michel Grandmont *Money and value: A reconsideration of classical and neoclassical monetary economics*, 0 521 31364 3
Franklin M. Fisher *Disequilibrium foundations of equilibrium economics*, 0 521 37856 7
Andreu Mas-Colell *The theory of general equilibrium: A differentiable approach*, 0 521 26514 2, 0 521 38870 8
Truman F. Bewley, Editor, *Advances in econometrics – Fifth World Congress* (Volume I), 0 521 46726 8
Truman F. Bewley, Editor, *Advances in econometrics – Fifth World Congress* (Volume II), 0 521 46725 X
Herve Moulin *Axioms of cooperative decision making*, 0 521 36055 2, 0 521 42458 5
L. G. Godfrey *Misspecification tests in econometrics: The Lagrange multiplier principle and other approaches*, 0 521 42459 3
Tony Lancaster *The econometric analysis of transition data*, 0 521 43789 X
Alvin E. Roth and Marilda A. Oliviera Sotomayor, Editors, *Two-sided matching: A study in game-theoretic modeling and analysis*, 0 521 43788 1
Wolfgang Härdle, *Applied nonparametric regression*, 0 521 42950 1
Jean-Jacques Laffont, Editor, *Advances in economic theory – Sixth World Congress* (Volume I), 0 521 56610 X
Jean-Jacques Laffont, Editor, *Advances in economic theory – Sixth World Congress* (Volume II), 0 521 48460 X
Halbert White, *Estimation, inference and specification*, 0 521 25280 6, 0 521 57446 3
Christopher Sims, Editor, *Advances in econometrics – Sixth World Congress* (Volume I), 0 521 56610 X
Christopher Sims, Editor, *Advances in econometrics – Sixth World Congress* (Volume II), 0 521 56609 6
Roger Guesnerie *A contribution to the pure theory of taxation*, 0 521 23689 4, 0 521 62956 X
David M. Kreps and Kenneth F. Wallis, Editors, *Advances in economics and econometrics – Seventh World Congress* (Volume I), 0 521 58011 0, 0 521 58983 5
David M. Kreps and Kenneth F. Wallis, Editors, *Advances in economics and econometrics – Seventh World Congress* (Volume II), 0 521 58012 9, 0 521 58982 9
David M. Kreps and Kenneth F. Wallis, Editors, *Advances in economics and econometrics – Seventh World Congress* (Volume III), 0 521 58013 7, 0 521 58981 9
Donald P. Jacobs, Ehud Kalai, and Morton I. Kamien, Editors, *Frontiers of research in economic theory: The Nancy L. Schwartz Memorial Lectures, 1983–1997*, 0 521 63222 6, 0 521 63538 1
A. Colin Cameron and Pravin K. Trivedi, *Regression analysis of count data*, 0 521 63201 3, 0 521 63567 5
Steinar Strom, Editor, *Econometrics and economic theory in the 20th century: The Ragnar Frisch Centennial Symposium*, 0 521 63323 0, 0 521 63365 6
Eric Ghysels, Norman R. Swanson, and Mark Watson, Editors, *Essays in econometrics: Collected papers of Clive W. J. Granger* (Volume I), 0 521 77297 4, 0 521 80407 8, 0 521 77496 9, 0 521 79697 0

Continued on page following the index

Advances in Economics and Econometrics

Theory and Applications,
Ninth World Congress,
Volume II

Edited by

Richard Blundell
University College London

Whitney K. Newey
Massachusetts Institute of Technology

Torsten Persson
Stockholm University

CAMBRIDGE
UNIVERSITY PRESS

CAMBRIDGE UNIVERSITY PRESS
Cambridge, New York, Melbourne, Madrid, Cape Town, Singapore, São Paulo

Cambridge University Press
32 Avenue of the Americas, New York, NY 10013-2473, USA

www.cambridge.org
Information on this title: www.cambridge.org/9780521871532

First published 2006

Printed in the United States of America

A catalog record for this publication is available from the British Library.

Library of Congress Cataloging in Publication Data
Advances in economics and econometrics : theory and applications, Ninth World
Congress / edited by Richard Blundell, Whitney K. Newey, Torsten Persson.
     p. cm. – (Econometric Society monographs; no. 42)
  Edited versions of papers and a commentary presented at invited symposium sessions of
the ninth World Congress of the Econometric Society, held in London in 2005.
Includes bibliographical references and index.
     ISBN 0-521-87152-2 (hardback: v.1) – ISBN 0-521-69208-3 (pbk.: v.1)
     ISBN 0-521-87153-0 (hardback: v.2) – ISBN 0-521-69209-1 (pbk.: v.2)
     1. Econometrics – Congresses. 2. Economics – Congresses. I. Blundell, Richard.
II. Newey, Whitney K. III. Persson, Torsten. IV. Econometric Society.
World Congress (9th : 2005 : London, England) V. Title. VI. Series.
  HB139.A35   2005
  330–dc22   2006014485

ISBN-13   978-0-521-87153-2 hardback
ISBN-10   0-521-87153-0 hardback

ISBN-13   978-0-521-69209-0 paperback
ISBN-10   0-521-69209-1 paperback

100533780 1

Contents

Contributors

Joseph G. Altonji
Yale University

Mark Armstrong
University College London

Susan Athey
Harvard University

Steven Berry
Yale University

Colin F. Camerer
California Institute of Technology

Esther Duflo
Massachusetts Institute of Technology

Liran Einav
Stanford University

Glenn Ellison
Massachusetts Institute of Technology

Philip A. Haile
Yale University

Kenneth Hendricks
University of Texas at Austin

Costas Meghir
University College London

Aviv Nevo
Northwestern University

Ted O'Donoghue
Cornell University

Rohini Pande
Yale University

Fabien Postel-Vinay
University of Bristol

Matthew Rabin
University of California at Berkeley

Jean-Marc Robin
*Université de Paris 1 and
    University College London*

Ariel Rubinstein
*Tel Aviv University and
    New York University*

Elie Tamer
Northwestern University

Christopher Udry
Yale University

Introduction by the Editors

These volumes constitute the invited proceedings from the Ninth World Congress of the Econometric Society held on the campus of University College London on August 19–24, 2005.

As co-chairs of the Program Committee for the Congress, one of our most pleasant tasks was to select topics and authors for fifteen invited symposia – each organized around two papers. We chose topics for these invited papers that we thought were important, of current research interest, and where we could see a prospective long-run impact on the profession. All of the scholars that we first contacted agreed to contribute a paper. We encouraged them to write papers that would be of broad interest but would not necessarily be comprehensive literature surveys.

In the event, all symposia ran for two hours, during which the authors presented their papers and an invited discussant made comments on both of them. This book collects revised versions of the thirty papers presented in the fifteen invited symposia, as well as some of the comments by the discussants.

In all but one day of the congress, three invited symposia were run in parallel: one in economic theory, one in an applied field, and one in econometrics. The three volumes making up the book are organized by the same principle.

Volume I contains the papers on economic theory, broadly defined. In Chapter 1, "The Economics of Social Networks," Matthew Jackson discusses a central field of sociological study, a major application of random graph theory, and an emerging area of study by economists, statistical physicists, and computer scientists. The chapter provides an illuminating perspective on these literatures, with a focus on formal models of social networks, especially those based on random graphs and those based on game-theoretic reasoning. Jackson highlights some of the strengths, weaknesses, and potential synergies between these two network modeling approaches.

Chapter 2, "Multi-Contracting Mechanism Design" by David Martimort, surveys the literature on common agency. Martimort describes the features that make common-agency games special, reviews the tools needed to describe equilibrium allocations under common agency, and uses a set of simple examples to illustrate such equilibrium allocations – under complete as well as asymmetric information – and their efficiency properties. The chapter concludes that common agency might perform quite well, especially in the presence of collusion or limited commitment.

Chapter 3, by Philippe Jehiel and Benny Moldovanu, is entitled "Allocative and Informational Externalities in Auctions and Related Mechanisms." Such externalities arise naturally in models embedding (multi-object) auctions in larger economic contexts, e.g., when bidders interact downstream once the auction has closed. In such settings, traditional auction formats need no longer be efficient and may give rise to multiple equilibria and strategic nonparticipation. Jehiel and Moldovanu discuss which allocations are possible and impossible to achieve under different approaches to implementation and in different information environments.

In Chapter 4, "The Economics of Relationships," Larry Samuelson discusses recent work in the theory of repeated games, which provides the tools for studying long-run relationships. He examines folk theorems for games with imperfect public and private monitoring and new techniques for studying equilibria when folk theorems are not helpful because players are not sufficiently patient or well informed. The chapter illustrates a number of recent applications that have moved the literature on repeated games from technical questions to findings of economic relevance. It concludes with a discussion of outstanding problems.

Following these chapters on game theory are two chapters on economic design. Chapter 5, "Information in Mechanism Design," written by Dirk Bergemann and Juuso Välimäki, examines endogeneity of private information, and robustness to private information in mechanism design. The authors view information acquisition and robustness to private information as two distinct but related aspects of information management, which are important in many design settings. The chapter not only surveys the existing literature, but also points out directions for future work.

In Chapter 6, "Computational Issues in Economic Design," Ilya Segal argues that full revelation of privately held information about preferences may often be impractical or undesirable. He then asks what minimal information must be elicited from agents to achieve the social goals of the mechanism designer. Segal relates this question to the work on communication complexity in computer science and dimensionality of message space in economics, where communication is measured in bits and real numbers, respectively. He outlines existing results on the topic, a substantial body of related work, and some extensions.

The next two chapters deal with macroeconomic theory. Chapter 7, by Naryana Kocherlakota, is entitled "Advances in Dynamic Optimal Taxation." It surveys the recent literature concerning the structure of optimal taxes in dynamic economies. As in the literature following Mirrlee's path-breaking work on optimal static taxation, there are no restrictions on the available policy instruments, and the optimal tax schedules are designed subject only to the private information held by private agents about skills and effort. Kocherlakota illustrates and explains the major results achieved so far and suggests where the literature may go next.

In Chapter 8, "Quantitative Macroeconomic Models with Heterogeneous Agents," Per Krusell and Tony Smith review recent work on dynamic stochastic macroeconomic models with individual heterogeneity in income, employment status, and wealth, to approximate empirical models in the applied consumption and labor literatures. They focus on the properties of such models – especially so-called approximate aggregation – and the computational methods for analyzing them. The chapter also presents a simple two-period setting that serves as a useful laboratory to examine the implications of the distribution of income in different economic settings.

The final section of the volume concerns political economy. In Chapter 9, "Modeling Inefficient Institutions," Daron Acemoglu asks why inefficient institutions emerge and persist, and he develops a simple framework to provide some answers to this question. He illustrates how a group may want to pursue inefficient policies so as to increase their income and to directly or indirectly transfer resources from the rest of the society to themselves, and how the preferences over inefficient policies may translate into inefficient economic institutions. The chapter also provides a framework for the analysis of institutional change and institutional persistence.

While Acemoglu emphasizes the macro side of political economy, Chapter 10, "Whither Political Economy? Theories, Facts, and Issues," by Antonio Merlo emphasizes the micro side. Merlo reviews current research on four of the fundamental institutions of a political economy: voters, politicians, parties, and governments. He identifies and discusses salient questions posed in the literature, presents some stylized models and examples, and summarizes the main theoretical findings. Moreover, the chapter describes available data, reviews relevant empirical evidence, and discusses challenges for empirical research in political economy.

Volume I ends with a discussion of Chapters 9 and 10, by Tim Besley.

Volume II contains papers on applied economics and applied econometrics, again broadly defined. For example, the first six chapters present a broad review and evaluation of developments in modern industrial economics. There is then an assessment of behavioral economics. This is followed by a detailed review of progress in dynamic labor economics. The volume rounds up with two insightful chapters on progress and new ideas in empirical development economics.

In Chapter 1 of Volume II, "Empirical Models of Auctions," Susan Athey and Phil Haile review some of the most innovative of the recent empirical applications and present three key insights that underlie much of the progress in the econometrics of auction models. The first is the usefulness of casting the identification problem as one of learning about latent distribution functions based on observation of certain order statistics. The second is the observation that equilibrium can be thought of as a state of mutual best responses. The third is the value of additional variation in the data beyond the realizations of bids. Although observable variation in auction characteristics might initially seem to be minor nuisances to be dealt with they argue that these kinds of variation often can be exploited to aid identification. Chapter 2, "Identification in Models of Oligopoly Entry" by Steve Berry and Elie Tamer, reviews and extends a number of results on the identification of models that are used in the empirical literature. They present simple versions of both static and dynamic entry models. For simple static models, they show how natural shape restrictions can be used to identify competition effects. In the case of dynamic models, they examine existing results on the model with i.i.d. linear errors and then consider more realistic cases, such as when the distribution of fixed costs is unknown. Chapter 3, "Empirical Models of Imperfect Competition: A Discussion," by Liran Einav and Aviv Nevo, discusses the first two chapters of this volume. They note that in the empirical IO literature much progress has been made on identification and estimation of many different dimensions of firms' decisions. There are more flexible models of consumer demand and better methods to non-parametrically estimate bidder valuation in auctions, and significant progress has been made on estimating entry and dynamic games.

Chapter 4, "Recent Developments in the Economics of Price Discrimination" by Mark Armstrong, surveys the recent literature on price discrimination. The focus is on three aspects of pricing decisions: the information about customers available to firms; the instruments firms can use in the design of their tariffs; and the ability of firms to commit to their pricing plans. Armstrong notes that developments in marketing technology mean that firms often have access to more information about individual customers than was previously the case. The use of this information might be restricted by public policy toward customer privacy. Where it is not restricted, firms may be unable to commit to how they use the information. With monopoly supply, an increased ability to engage in price discrimination will boost profit unless the firm cannot commit to its pricing policy. Likewise, an enhanced ability to commit to prices will benefit a monopolist. With competition, the effects of price discrimination on profit, consumer surplus, and overall welfare depend on the kinds of information and/or tariff instruments available to firms. The paper shows that the ability to commit to prices may damage industry profit. Chapter 5, "Bounded Rationality in Industrial Organization" by Glenn Ellison, notes that three main approaches are found in the recent literature: rule-of thumb papers specify simple rules for behavior; explicit bounds papers consider agents who maximize payoffs net of cognitive costs; the psychology and economics approach typically cites experimental evidence to motivate utility-like frameworks. Common to each recent literature is a focus on consumer irrationalities that firms might exploit. The paper then discusses several new topics that have been opened up by the consideration of bounded rationality and new perspectives that have been provided on traditional topics. Chapter 6, "Price Discrimination and Irrational Consumers: A Discussion of Armstrong and Ellison" by Ken Hendricks, presents a discussion of these two chapters. In relation to the Armstrong paper he argues that one of the roles of theory is to classify the kinds of oligopoly markets where price discrimination is likely to occur, the form that it is likely to take, and the impact that it is likely to have on profits and welfare. He notes that the theme of firms exploiting consumers is also present in Ellison's chapter, which focuses primarily on irrational consumers. However, the main issues there are methodological, challenging the field to reexamine its traditional approach.

Chapters 7 to 9 turn to the field of behavioral economics. In Chapter 7, Colin Camerer shows how evidence from psychology and other disciplines has been used in behavioral economics to create models of limits on rationality, willpower, and self-interest and explores their implications in economic aggregates. The paper reviews the basic themes of behavioral economics: sensitivity of revealed preferences to descriptions of goods and procedures; generalizations of models of choice over risk, ambiguity, and time; fairness and reciprocity; non-Bayesian judgment; and stochastic equilibrium and learning. He argues that a central concern is what happens in equilibrium when agents are imperfect but heterogeneous. Camerer argues that neuroeconomics extends the psychological data use and suggests that it is likely to support rational choice theory in some cases, to buttress behavioral economics in some cases, and to suggest different constructs as well. In Chapter 8, "Incentives and Self-Control," Ted O'Donoghue and Matthew Rabin investigate the design of incentives for people subject to self-control problems in the form of a time-inconsistent taste for immediate gratification. They argue that because such present-biased people may not behave in their own long-run best interests, there is scope for firms, policymakers, friends and family, and the people themselves to create incentives for "better" behavior. They note that optimal incentive design, therefore, will attend to details that the conventional model would say are essentially irrelevant. The paper goes on to describe some general principles that have emerged in recent and ongoing research on incentives, highlighting the importance of heterogeneity among agents and providing for flexibility, and illustrating these principles with some simple examples. In his discussion presented in Chapter 9, Ariel Rubinstein argues that although there is no reason for economics to hide behind the traditional barriers, for behavioral economics to be a revolutionary program of research rather than a passing episode, it must become more open-minded and much more self-critical.

Turning to dynamic labor economics, in Chapter 10, "Dynamic Models for Policy Evaluation," Costas Meghir shows that the evaluation of interventions has become a commonly used policy tool, which is frequently adopted to improve the transparency and effectiveness of public policy. However, he argues that evaluation methods based on comparing treatment and control groups in small-scale trials are not capable of providing a complete picture of the likely effects of a policy and do not provide a framework that allows issues relating to the design of the program to be addressed. Meghir shows how experimental data from field trials can be used to enhance the evaluation of interventions and also illustrates the potential importance of allowing for longer-term incentive and general equilibrium effects. In Chapter 11, "Microeconometric Search-Matching Models and Matched Employer-Employee Data," Fabien

Postel-Vinay and Jean-Marc Robin suggest that the recent advent of matched employer-employee data has allowed significant progress in our understanding of individual labor earnings. He argues that viewing these empirical analyses through the lens of structural job search models can help clarify and unify some of its recurring findings. Among other things he shows how search frictions combined with a theoretically founded wage formation rule based on renegotiation by mutual consent can account for the widely documented dynamic persistence of individual wages. In his discussion of these two papers in Chapter 12, Joe Altonji argues that they provide useful analyses of developments in two important areas in labor economics and public finance. He examines the potential to utilize a continuum of models between a simple experimental or quasi experimental analysis on the one hand and a dynamic structural model on the other, even in complicated dynamic settings where reduced form analysis is difficult. He also supplements the research agenda in search/matching models and the application using matched employer/ employee data.

Volume II concludes with two key papers on advances in development economics. Chapter 13, "Field Experiments in Development Economics," by Esther Duflo, observes that over the last decade, the long tradition in development economics of collecting original data to test specific hypotheses has merged with an expertise in setting up randomized field experiments. This in turn has resulted in an increasingly large number of studies where an original experiment has been set up to test economic theories and hypotheses. The paper extracts some substantive and methodological lessons from such studies in three domains: incentives, social learning, and time-inconsistent preferences. It makes the case that we need both to continue testing existing theories and to start thinking of how the theories may be adapted to make sense of the field experiment results, many of which are starting to challenge them. In Chapter 14, "Institutions and Development: A View from Below," Rohini Pande and Christopher Udry argue the case for greater exploitation of synergies between research on specific institutions based on micro-data and the big questions posed by the institutions and growth literature. They suggest two research programs based on micro-data that have significant potential. The first uses policy-induced variation in specific institutions within countries to understand how these institutions influence economic activity. The second exploits the fact that the incentives provided by a given institutional context often vary with individuals' economic and political status. The chapter analyzes the way variations in individual responses to the same institution can be used to both identify how institutions affect economic outcomes and to understand how institutional change arises in response to changing economic and demographic pressures.

Volume III contains papers on econometrics. The first five chapters are about identification and estimation when unobserved heterogeneity has nonlinear effects. This work is motivated by economic models where the common assumption of additive disturbances is not satisfied. The three chapters that follow concern weak instruments and empirical likelihood. These methods provide alternatives to classical instrumental variables inference, which can be important in applications. The next three chapters are about econometrics for financial markets. They summarize powerful approaches to analyzing the time series behavior of asset markets. The last two chapters return to the subject of unobserved heterogeneity, now in the context of nonlinear models for panel data. They consider bias correction methods for fixed effects estimation, a promising method of controlling for unobserved heterogeneity in panel data.

In Chapter 1 of Volume III, "Identification of Nonadditive Structural Functions," Andrew Chesher reviews recent work on identification of structural models with disturbances that are not additively separable. This chapter focuses on the case where there are no more disturbances than endogenous variables. In the one-disturbance-per-equation case independence of the instrument and a conditional quantile of the disturbance can suffice for identification of the structural equation at a particular value of the disturbance. In the triangular model case, where the number of disturbances entering each equation is equal to the number of endogenous variables in that equation, local independence of instruments and disturbances suffices for identification of structural derivatives. Bounds are also given for the case with a discrete endogenous variable. In Chapter 2, "Nonadditive Models with Endogenous Regressors," Guido Imbens considers the case where the disturbance in the equation of interest can have any dimension. Identification and estimation with control functions are discussed, a control function being a variable that when conditioned on gives exogeneity. A control function for the triangular system is provided. Identification of certain policy effects is considered.

In Chapter 3, "Heterogeneity and Microeconometric Modeling," Martin Browning and Jesus Carro suggest that heterogeneity is more common in applications than usually allowed for, that how it is allowed for can often have large effects on results, and that it is difficult to allow for in a general way. They illustrate these suggestions with applied and theoretical examples. In particular, they consider a stationary first-order Markov chain model that allows for general heterogeneity, where they propose estimators and analyze their properties. Chapter 4, "Heterogenous Choice" by Rosa Matzkin, gives identification results for nonparametric choice models where disturbances enter nonlinearly. For models where choices are dependent variables, this paper describes very recent results on identification of demand models and discrete choice models that are important for understanding revealed preference with unobserved heterogeneity. For models where the choices are regressors, the paper gives control function and other identification results for structural effects. In Chapter 5, "Modeling Heterogeneity," Arthur Lewbel discusses the results from Chapters 3 and 4, showing that model interpretation depends critically on how the nonseparable disturbance enters.

Chapter 6, "Inference with Weak Instruments" by Donald Andrews and James Stock, reviews recent developments in methods for dealing with weak instruments (IVs) in IV regression models. The focus is more on tests (and confidence intervals derived from tests) than estimators. Power comparisons of the conditional likelihood ratio (CLR), Anderson-Rubin, and Lagrange multiplier tests are made. The paper also presents new testing results under "many weak IV asymptotics." Chapter 7, "Empirical Likelihood Methods in Econometrics: Theory and Practice" by Yuichi Kitamura, gives nonparametric maximum likelihood and generalized minimum contrast interpretations of the empirical likelihood estimator. This chapter presents an asymptotic optimality result for empirical likelihood under a large deviations optimality criterion. Monte Carlo results are given, illustrating substantial gains that can result. Also, the literature on higher-order properties of empirical likelihood is reviewed. Chapter 8, "Weak Instruments and Empirical Likelihood: A Discussion of Papers by D. W. K. Andrews and J. H. Stock and Yuichi Kitamura" by Richard Smith, considers inference for GMM with weak identification based on generalized empirical likelihood. It provides an asymptotic analysis for GMM that is a direct extension of the Andrews and Stock small sample analysis for IV. This chapter proposes a version of the CLR for GMM that is a precise analog to the IV case.

Chapter 9, "Estimating Continuous Time Models with Discretely Sampled Data" by Yacine Ait-Sahalia, starts with a familiar model and describes many of the most recent developments. It begins with identification and estimation of a univariate diffusion. This model is then progressively generalized to allow for different data generating processes (such as multivariate diffusions or jump processes), different observation schemes (such as incorporating market microstructure noise), and different sampling schemes (such as allowing for random time intervals). Chapter 10, "Variation, Jumps, and High Frequency Data in Financial Econometrics" by Neil Shephard and Ole Barndorff-Nielsen, describes the econometrics of realized volatility. This chapter focuses on quadratic variation and considers the detection of jumps. The impact of market frictions is considered. Chapter 11, "Discussion of Ait-Sahalia and Barndorff-Nielsen and Shephard" by Oliver Linton and Ilze Kalnina, considers an approach to allowing for market microstructure noise. It presents consistency results for estimation of quadratic variation in the presence of small measurement errors.

Chapter 12, "Understanding Bias in Nonlinear Panel Models: Some Recent Developments" by Manuel Arellano and Jinyong Hahn, describes and discusses the relationship among recently developed bias adjustments for nonlinear panel data models with fixed effects. These bias adjustments are used to reduce the bias order of fixed effect parameter and marginal effects as the number of time series observations grows with the number of cross-section observations. The paper shows that a wide variety of bias adjustments lead to similar results, including those based on profile likelihoods and those based on moment conditions. In Chapter 13, "Fixed and Random Effects in Nonlinear Panels: A Discussion of Arellano and Hahn" by Tiemen Woutersen, an alternative bias reduction approach is discussed. This approach, which predates many of the others, involves integrating the fixed effect over a prior distribution and produces bias reductions equivalent to the other methods.

We are grateful to Christina Lönnblad, Emma Hyman, and Emily Gallagher for assisting us in our work with putting the papers together into books. We would also like to thank all the authors, not only for writing such excellent papers, but also for delivering just in time for these books to appear less than a year after the Congress. Such prompt publication would, of course, not have been possible without the keen support of our Cambridge editor, Scott Parris.

London, Cambridge, and Stockholm, May 2006

Richard Blundell, Whitney Newey, and Torsten Persson

Advances in Economics and Econometrics

CHAPTER 1

Empirical Models of Auctions*
Susan Athey and Philip A. Haile

1   INTRODUCTION

Auctions have provided a fruitful area for combining economic theory with econometric analysis in order to understand behavior and inform policy. Early work by Hendricks and Porter (1988) and others made important contributions by testing the empirical implications of auction theory. This work provided convincing evidence of the empirical relevance of private information and confirmed the value of strategic models for understanding firm behavior. However, many important economic questions can be answered only with knowledge of the underlying primitive distributions governing bidder demand and information. Examples include the division of rents in auctions of public resources, whether reserve prices in government auctions are adequate, the effects of mergers on procurement costs, whether changes in auction rules would produce greater revenues, whether bundling of procurement contracts is efficient, the value of seller reputations, the effect of information acquisition costs on bidder participation and profits, whether bidders' private information introduces adverse selection, and whether firms act as if they are risk averse. Many of these questions have important implications well beyond the scope of auctions themselves.

Motivated by a desire to answer these questions, a more recent literature has developed that aims to estimate the primitives of auction models, exploiting restrictions from economic theory as part of the econometric model.[1] Typically, such a "structural" approach incorporates two types of assumptions: (a) economic assumptions, such as behavioral assumptions (e.g. Bayesian Nash equilibrium) and economically motivated restrictions on preferences (e.g., risk

* We thank Liran Einav, Jon Levin, Aviv Nevo and Whitney Newey for helpful comments and Ying Fan and Gustavo Soares for capable research assistance. Research support from the National Science Foundation (grants SES-0112047 and SES-0351500) and the Alfred P. Sloan Foundation is gratefully acknowledged. Any conclusions, findings, or opinions are those of the authors and do not necessarily reflect the views of any funding organization.

[1] A seminal paper in this literature is Paarsch (1992a), which builds on insights in Smiley (1979) and Thiel (1988).

neutrality), and (b) functional form assumptions, imposed either for convenience in estimation or because only a limited set of parameters can be identified. An attractive feature of the recent econometric literature on auctions is that often the second type of assumption can be avoided, both in principle and in practice. In particular, in many cases identification of economic primitives can be obtained without resorting unverifiable parametric assumptions, and nonparametric estimation methods have been developed that perform well in data sets of moderate size. Even when parametric estimation approaches are used in applications, the fact that the literature has provided definitive positive (and sometimes negative) identification results provides important guidance about how to interpret the results. This paper aims to review some of the highlights of this recent literature, focusing on econometric identification and empirical applications.

Fundamental to the structural approach is an interpretation of data through the lens of an economic model. Hence, we begin by defining notation, reviewing the rules of the most prevalent types of auctions, and deriving equilibrium conditions. Next, we discuss three key insights that underlie much of the recent progress in econometrics for auction models. The first is the usefulness of casting the identification problem as one of learning about latent distribution functions based on observation of certain order statistics (e.g., the highest bid or the second-highest valuation). This is a simple observation, but one that has helped to organize the attack on identification of auction models and, in several cases, has led to the discovery of connections between auction models and other familiar models in economics and statistics. The second is the observation that equilibrium can be thought of as a state of mutual best responses. This is again a seemingly trivial observation, but it has enabled economists to obtain surprisingly powerful results by re-casting equilibrium conditions (characterizing a fixed point) in terms of simpler optimality conditions for players facing a distribution (often observable) of equilibrium play by opponents. Finally, we discuss a third fundamental insight: the value of additional variation in the data beyond the realizations of bids. Observable variation in auction characteristics, in the realized value of the object, and in the number of bidders might initially seem to be minor nuisances to be dealt with, perhaps by conditioning or smoothing. In fact, these kinds of variation often can be exploited to aid identification.

Beyond these three central insights, we also discuss some extensions that have proved important for empirical applications. We describe how the econometric approaches can be generalized to account for endogenous participation and unobserved heterogeneity. In addition, we provide a brief discussion of specification tests that can help a researcher evaluate and select among alternative modeling assumptions.

Our discussion of applications begins with Hendricks, Pinkse and Porter's (2003) analysis of oil lease auctions, which exploits the availability of data on the market value of oil (and other minerals) realized ex post from each tract. Combined with data on bids, this enables the authors to quantify the magnitude of the winner's curse in their pure common values model. This work suggests that the subtle inferences required by bidders in common value auctions are economically important, and that they are in fact incorporated in bidding strategies.

We next discuss the working paper of Haile, Hong, and Shum (2003), who develop and apply tests to discriminate between common values and private values models in first-price auctions. They build on a simple idea: in a common values auction, an increase in the number of competing bidders amplifies the winner's curse. Since the winner's curse is present only in common values auctions, a test for rational responses by bidders to variation in the strength of the winner's curse offers an approach for testing. Equilibrium conditions enable them to isolate responses to the winner's curse, and they show how this idea can be used with several models of endogenous bidder participation. Their preliminary results suggest that common values may not be important, at least for some types of timber contracts.

Next, we discuss Haile and Tamer's (2003) bounds approach to analysis of ascending auctions. Because an actual ascending auction is typically a dynamic game with exceedingly rich strategy and state spaces, the theory of ascending auctions has relied on significant abstractions for tractability. Haile and Tamer (2003), concerned with the potential implications of estimating a misspecified model, propose an approach based on simple intuitive restrictions on equilibrium bidding that hold in a variety of alternative models. They show that these restrictions are sufficient to enable fairly precise inference on bidder demand and on the effects of reserve price policy. Addressing a policy debate regarding reserve prices in timber auctions, they show that actual reserve prices are likely well below the optimal levels, but that raising them would have only a small effect on expected revenues.

In another study of timber auctions, the working paper of Athey, Levin, and Seira (2004) uses variation in auction format (ascending versus first-price auctions) to a) test qualitative predictions of the theory of asymmetric auctions with endogenous participation and b) assess the competitiveness of ascending auctions, widely believed to be more susceptible to collusion. They show that observed bids and participation decisions identify the underlying distributions of bidder valuations and the costs of acquiring the information necessary to participate in an auction. Their preliminary estimates suggest that in several national forests, behavior in ascending auctions is less aggressive than would be consistent with a competitive theory, given a benchmark created using the distributions of valuations estimated from first-price auction data. Although the competitive theory explains part of the revenue gap, an alternative theory such as collusion at ascending auctions is required to rationalize the remainder.

The analysis by Jofre-Bonet and Pesendorfer (2003) of dynamics in procurement auctions provides an elegant generalization of prior approaches for static models. They consider situations in which bidders have capacity constraints, so that winning an auction affects valuations (or costs) in future auctions. Perhaps surprisingly, few additional assumptions are required for identification of the primitives in this kind of model. Their empirical analysis of highway construction auctions reveals significant asymmetries in bidding strategies resulting from asymmetric capacities of bidders at different points in time. They also find a fairly large gap between bids and values, half of which they attribute to bidders' recognition of the option value to losing a contract today: They may use their limited capacity for another contract in the future.

Finally, we discuss the working paper of Hortaçsu (2002), which takes an empirical tack on one of the oldest unresolved questions in the auction literature: whether to sell treasury bills by discriminatory or uniform price auction. The performance of these auctions has a substantial impact on the cost at which governments raise funds. Hortaçsu (2002) extends the econometric approaches of the prior literature to discriminatory multi-unit (share) auctions, building on the theoretical model of Wilson (1979). His preliminary estimates suggest that, for the Turkish treasury auctions he studies, switching to a uniform-price auction would not enhance revenues.

2   ESSENTIAL THEORY

The baseline theoretical framework is a generalization of Milgrom and Weber's (1982) affiliated values model, where a single indivisible good is sold to one of $n \in \{\underline{n}, \ldots, \bar{n}\}$ risk neutral bidders, with $\bar{n} \geq \underline{n} \geq 2$.[2] We denote random variables in upper case, their realizations in lower case, and vectors in boldface. We let $\mathcal{N} \subset \{\underline{n}, \ldots, \bar{n}\}$ denote the set of bidders, with N denoting the number of bidders. $\mathcal{N}_{-i}$ will denote the set of competitors faced by bidder i. The utility bidder i would gain by obtaining the good is given by U_i, which we refer to as i's "valuation" and assume to have common support (denoted supp U_i) for all i.

Bidder i's private information (his "type") consists of a scalar signal $X_i \in [\underline{x}_i, \bar{x}_i]$. We let $\mathbf{X} = (X_1, \ldots, X_n)$ and $\mathbf{X}_{-i} = \mathbf{X} \backslash X_i$. We assume that the random variables $(U_1, \ldots, U_n, X_1, \ldots, X_n)$ are affiliated, i.e., that higher realizations of one variable make higher realizations of the others more likely.[3] Signals are further assumed to be informative in the sense that the expectation

$$E[U_i | X_i = x_i, \mathbf{X}_{-i} = \mathbf{x}_{-i}]$$

is strictly increasing in x_i for all realizations $\mathbf{x}_{-i}$ of i's opponents' signals. Since signals play a purely informational role, it is without loss of generality to impose a normalization, e.g.,

$$X_i = E[U_i | X_i].$$

We will say that the model is *symmetric* if the indices $(1, \ldots n)$ may be permuted without affecting the joint distribution $F_{\mathbf{U},\mathbf{X}}(U_1, \ldots, U_n, X_1, \ldots, X_n)$ of bidders' valuations and signals; otherwise the model is *asymmetric*. The set

---

[2] We discuss an extension to multi-unit auctions in section 4.6 below.

[3] More formally, random variables $\mathbf{Y} = (Y_1, \ldots, Y_n)$ with joint density $f_{\mathbf{Y}}(\cdot)$ are affiliated if for all $\mathbf{y}$ and $\mathbf{y}'$, $f_{\mathbf{Y}}(\mathbf{y} \vee \mathbf{y}') f_{\mathbf{Y}}(\mathbf{y} \wedge \mathbf{y}') \geq f_{\mathbf{Y}}(\mathbf{y}) f_{\mathbf{Y}}(\mathbf{y}')$, where $\vee$ denotes the component-wise maximum, and $\wedge$ the component-wise minimum.

of bidders and the joint distribution $F_{\mathbf{U},\mathbf{X}}(\cdot;\mathcal{N})$ are assumed to be common knowledge among bidders.[4]

When we come to discuss estimation, we will generally assume a sequence of independent auctions indexed by $t = 1, \ldots, T$.[5] We will then add subscripts t to random variables (e.g., X_{it}, N_t) as needed. Asymptotic arguments will be based on $T \to \infty$. In practice a stronger assumption will often be required, e.g., that $T_n = \#\{t : N_t = n\} \to \infty$. In some cases we will imagine for simplicity that these auctions are not only independent but also identically distributed, i.e., that $F_{\mathbf{U}}(U_1, \ldots, U_n)$ is the same for every n-bidder auction. In practice this will rarely be the case, although there are a number of approaches available to account for observable (and to some degree, unobservable) differences across auctions t.

Within this general framework we will make a distinction between *private values* and *common values* auctions. The distinction concerns the nature of bidders' private information. In a private values auction, a bidder's private information concerns only factors idiosyncratic to that bidder; in a common values auction, each bidder's private information concerns factors that affect all bidders' valuations. More precisely,

Definition 2.1 *Bidders have **private values** if $E[U_i|X_1 = x_1, \ldots, X_n = x_n]$ $= E[U_i|X_1 = x_1]$ for all $x_1, \ldots, x_n$ and all i; bidders have **common values** if $E[U_i|X_1 = x_1, \ldots, X_n = x_n]$ strictly increases in x_j for all i, j, and x_j.*[6]

Common values models apply whenever information about valuations is dispersed among bidders.[7] They include the special case of *pure common values,* where the value of the good is the same (but unknown) for all bidders.[8] Note that the distinction between private and common values is separate from the question of whether bidders' information is correlated. Bidders may have highly correlated private values, or could have pure common values but independent signals. In addition, the distinction is separate from the question of whether bidders' valuations are affected by shared factors. For example, even in a private values model, bidder valuations might all be affected by characteristics of the good for sale that are known to all bidders, or be subject to future macroeconomic shocks, about which bidders have identical priors. In either

---

[4] See, e.g., Hendricks, Pinkse, and Porter (2003), Athey and Haile (2006), Song (2004), and Li and Zheng (2005) for applications relaxing the assumption that $\mathcal{N}$ is known by bidders.

[5] We discuss relaxation of the independence across auctions in section 4.5.

[6] Affiliation implies that $E[U_i|X_1 = x_1, \ldots, X_n = x_n]$ is increasing in x_j for all i, j, and x_j. For simplicity, our definition of common values rules out cases where strict monotonicity holds for some realizations of types but not others.

[7] Common values models include all environments in which a winner's curse arises – i.e., where winning an auction reveals to the winner new information about his own valuation for the object.

[8] Some authors (e.g., Krishna (2002)) use the term "interdependent values" to refer to the class of models we call "common values," motivated in part by inconsistencies in the literature in the use of the latter term.

case, because bidders have no private information about the shared factor, a private values model still applies.

We follow the literature and restrict attention to (perfect) Bayesian Nash equilibria in weakly undominated pure strategies, $\beta_i(\cdot; \mathcal{N}), i = 1, \ldots, n$, mapping each bidder's signal (and, implicitly, any public information) into a bid. In symmetric models we further restrict attention to symmetric equilibria, where $\beta_i(\cdot) = \beta(\cdot) \, \forall i$. We will denote a bidder i's equilibrium bid by B_i, with $\mathbf{B} = \{B_1, \ldots, B_n\}$.

In a first-price sealed-bid auction, bids are submitted simultaneously, and the good is awarded to the high bidder at a price equal to his bid (as long as this exceeds any reserve price, r).[9] For first-price auctions we make the following additional assumptions:

Assumption 1. *(First-Price Auction Assumptions) (i) For all i, U_i has compact, convex support denoted* $\mathrm{supp} U_i = [\underline{u}, \bar{u}]$. *(ii) The signals $\mathbf{X}$ are affiliated, with* $\mathrm{supp} \mathbf{X} = \times_{i=1}^n \mathrm{supp} X_i$. *(iii) $F_{\mathbf{X}}(\cdot)$ has an associated joint density $f_{\mathbf{X}}(\cdot)$ that is strictly positive on the interior of* $\mathrm{supp} \mathbf{X}$.

Under Assumption 1, there exists an equilibrium in nondecreasing bidding strategies, and in all models except the asymmetric common values model (which we will not discuss here), existence of an equilibrium in strictly increasing strategies has been established (see Athey and Haile (2006) for a more detailed discussion). We will restrict attention to equilibria in strictly increasing strategies and will derive the first-order conditions characterizing equilibrium bidding in Section 3.2 below. An important feature of equilibrium in first-price auctions is that bidders "shade" their bids by bidding less than their valuations; thus, a key step in developing econometric approaches to first-price auctions is estimation of the equilibrium bid functions that relate the observable bids to the latent primitives.

A second prevalent auction format is the oral ascending bid, or "English" auction. Ascending auctions are typically modeled following Milgrom and Weber (1982). In their model (sometimes referred to as a "clock auction" or "button auction" model) the price rises continuously and exogenously while bidders raise their hands or depress a button to indicate their willingness to buy at the current price. As the auction proceeds, bidders exit by lowering their hands or releasing their buttons. Exits are observable and irreversible, and the auction ends when only one bidder remains. This bidder wins the auction and pays a price equal to that at which the auction stopped, i.e., at his final opponent's exit price. Bids are synonymous with exits, so the auction ends at the second highest bid.

A bidding strategy in this model specifies a price at which to exit, conditional on one's own signal and on any information revealed by previous exits. If bidders

---

[9] This auction game is strategically equivalent to a Dutch (descending) auction. An important difference for empirical work, however, is the fact that only one bid could be observed, since only one bid (the winner's) is ever made.

use strategies that are strictly increasing in their signals, the price at which a
bidder exits reveals his signal to the others. This matters in a common values
auction, since the observed exit prices cause remaining bidders to update their
beliefs about their own valuations. The prices at which bidders plan to exit
thus change as the auction proceeds. In a private values auction there is no
such updating, and each bidder has a weakly dominant strategy to bid up to his
valuation, i.e.,

$$\beta_i(x_i; \mathcal{N}) = E[U_i \mid X_i = x_i] = x_i \equiv u_i. \tag{2.1}$$

With common values there are multiple equilibria, even with the restriction
to strictly increasing, weakly undominated strategies; however, in any such
equilibrium if i is one of the last two bidders to exit, his exit price b_i is equal to

$$E[U_i \mid X_i = x_i, \ X_j = x_i \ \forall j \notin \{i \cup \mathcal{E}_i\}, \ X_k = x_k \ \forall k \in \mathcal{E}_i], \tag{2.2}$$

where $\mathcal{E}_i$ denotes the set of bidders who exit before i (Bikhchandani, Haile, and
Riley (2002)).

In a private values ascending auction, the Milgrom-Weber model predicts
a trivial relation between a bidder's valuation and his bid. Even in this case,
however, identification can present challenges, due to the fact that the auction
ends before the winner bids. While bids directly reveal valuations in this model,
they do not reveal all of them. Furthermore, in many applications one may not
be comfortable imposing the structure of the Milgrom-Weber model. In many
ascending auctions, prices are called out by bidders rather than by the auctioneer,
and bidders are free to make a bid at any point, regardless of their activity (or
lack thereof) earlier in the auction. This raises doubts about the interpretation of
bids (e.g., the highest price offered by each bidder) as representing each bidder's
maximum willingness to pay. In Section 4.3 we will show that progress can still
be made in some cases using a relaxation of Milgrom and Weber's model.

3   FOUNDATIONS OF IDENTIFICATION

3.1   Bids as Order Statistics

A simple but important insight, made early in the literature (e.g., Paarsch
(1992a), Paarsch (1992b)), is that bid data can usefully be thought of in terms of
order statistics. In particular, many identification problems involve the recovery
of the latent distribution of a set of random variables from the distribution of a
limited set of observable order statistics. An order statistic of particular interest
is the transaction price (winning bid). This bid is the most commonly available
datum, and it is the only bid one could observe in a Dutch auction. Thus, an important question is whether (or when) the joint distribution of bidder valuations
can be recovered from the distribution of the winning bid alone.

We introduce some additional notation in order to discuss order statistics
more formally. Given any set of random variables $\{Y_1, \ldots Y_n\}$, let $Y^{(k:n)}$ denote
the kth order statistic, with $F_Y^{(k:n)}(\cdot)$ denoting the corresponding marginal CDF.

We follow the convention of indexing order statistics lowest to highest so that, e.g., $Y^{(n:n)} = \max \{Y_1, \ldots Y_n\}$.

Order statistics are particularly informative in the case of independent random variables. Independence reduces the dimensionality of the primitive joint distribution of interest. For example, the joint distribution $F_\mathbf{Y}(\cdot)$ of i.i.d random variables $\{Y_1, \ldots Y_n\}$ is the product of identical marginal distributions $F_Y(\cdot)$. This suggests that the distribution of a single statistic might be sufficient to uncover $F_\mathbf{Y}(\cdot)$. This is obviously correct in the case that one observes the maximum, $Y^{(n:n)}$, since $F_Y(y) = \left(F_Y^{(n:n)}(y) \right)^{1/n}$. In fact, it is well known that the distribution of any single order statistic from an i.i.d. sample of size n from an arbitrary distribution $F_Y(\cdot)$ has the distribution (see, e.g., Arnold, Balakrishnan, and Nagaraja (1992))

$$F_Y^{(k:n)}(s) = \frac{n!}{(n-k)!(k-1)!} \int_0^{F_Y(s)} t^{k-1}(1-t)^{n-k} \, dt \quad \forall s. \qquad (3.1)$$

It is easy to verify that the right-hand side is strictly increasing in $F_Y(s)$. Hence, for any k and n, we can define a function $\phi(F; k, n) : [0, 1] \to [0, 1]$ implicitly by the equation

$$F = \frac{n!}{(n-k)!(k-1)!} \int_0^\phi t^{k-1}(1-t)^{n-k} \, dt. \qquad (3.2)$$

Then $F_Y(y) = \phi \left(F_Y^{(k:n)}(y); k, n \right)$ for all y; i.e., knowledge of the distribution of a single order statistic uniquely determines the underlying parent distribution.

Athey and Haile (2002) point out that this observation is immediately useful for the standard model of the ascending auction in the symmetric independent private values setting, where each bidder's valuation is an independent draw from a CDF $F_U(\cdot)$. The equilibrium transaction price is equal to the second highest valuation, $u^{(n-1:n)}$. Since $F_U^{(n-1:n)}(u)$ uniquely determines $F_U(u)$ for all u (by (3.1)), $F_U(\cdot)$ is identified, even if one observes just the transaction price and the number of bidders. This identification result immediately extends to cases in which valuations are affected by auction-specific observables, which we denote $\mathbf{Z}$. In that case, (3.1) implies that the underlying parent distribution $F_U(\cdot|\mathbf{z})$ is uniquely determined by $F_U^{(n-1:n)}(\cdot|\mathbf{z})$ for all $\mathbf{z}$.

Independence is the key assumption. If the symmetry assumption is dropped but independence is maintained, $F_\mathbf{U}(\cdot)$ is again the product of n marginal distributions $F_{U_i}(\cdot)$, and one can show that when all U_i have the same support, observation of

$$\Pr \left(U^{n-1:n} \leq u, i \text{ is winner}; \mathcal{N} \right)$$

for each $i \in \mathcal{N}$ is sufficient to identify each $F_{U_i}(\cdot)$ in the standard ascending auction model (Athey and Haile (2002)). In an asymmetric model, identification requires having some information about which bidders' actions are observed; here, the identity of the winner is sufficient. Athey and Haile (2006) sketch the formal argument, which is based on results for an isomorphic model studied by Meilijson (1981).

In a first-price auction, the observations here regarding distributions of order statistics are not enough by themselves to demonstrate identification, since bids do not directly reveal bidders' private information. However a hint at their value can be seen by noting that the joint distribution of *bids* is identified from observation of a single order statistic of the bids when bidders' signals $(X_1, \ldots, X_n)$ are independent. This follows from the fact that each bid is a measurable function of the latent signal, which implies that bids are independent. We discuss this further below.

Note that these results require observation of n. This is easy to understand: In interpreting the second-highest bid (for example) it is essential to know whether this is the second highest of two bids or the second-highest of twenty-two bids! However, observation of an additional order statistic can eliminate this requirement (Song (2003)). Consider a symmetric independent private values ascending auction and suppose, for example, that in addition to the winning bid $(B^{(n:n)} = U^{(n-1:n)})$ the next highest bid (equal to $U^{(n-2:n)}$ in equilibrium) is also observed. The number of bidders n, however, is not known. Observe that, given $U^{(n-2:n)} = u'$, the pair $\left(U^{(n-1:n)}, U^{(n:n)}\right)$ can be viewed as the two order statistics $\left(\tilde{U}^{(1:2)}, \tilde{U}^{(2:2)}\right)$ for sample of two i.i.d random variables drawn from the truncated distribution

$$F_{\tilde{U}}\left(\cdot|u'\right) = \frac{F_U\left(\cdot\right) - F_U\left(u'\right)}{1 - F_U\left(u'\right)}.$$

Although $\tilde{U}^{(2:2)}$ is not observed, equation (3.1) implies that observation of the transaction price $\tilde{U}^{(1:2)}$ alone is sufficient to identify the parent distribution $F_{\tilde{U}}\left(\cdot|u'\right)$ for this sample. Identification of $F_U\left(\cdot\right)$ then follows from the fact that

$$\lim_{u' \downarrow \inf \mathrm{supp} U^{(n-2:n)}} F_{\tilde{U}}\left(\cdot|u'\right) = F_U\left(\cdot\right).$$

Note that as long as the distribution $F_U\left(\cdot\right)$ does not vary with n, this argument does require that n be fixed or have a particular stochastic structure.

When the independence assumption is dropped, Athey and Haile (2002) show that identification fails (even with symmetric private values) when one observes only a subset of bidders' valuations and the set of bidders, $\mathcal{N}$. This is particularly important in an ascending auction, where the winning bidder's valuation cannot be observed. Intuitively, without independence, the joint distribution of interest is n-dimensional, so data of lower dimension will not be adequate. To see this more precisely (following Athey and Haile (2002)), consider a symmetric n-bidder environment and suppose all order statistics of bidders' valuations are observed except $U^{(j:n)}$ for some j. Take a point $(u_1, u_2, \ldots, u_n)$ on the interior of the support of $F_U\left(\cdot\right)$, with $u_1 < \cdots < u_n$. Define a joint density function $\tilde{f}_{\mathbf{U}}\left(\cdot\right)$ by shifting mass δ in the true density $f_{\mathbf{U}}\left(\cdot\right)$ from a neighborhood of $\left(u_1, \ldots, u_j, \ldots, u_n\right)$ (and each permutation) to a neighborhood of the point $(u_1, \ldots, u_j + \epsilon, \ldots, u_n)$ (and each permutation). For small ϵ and δ, this change preserves symmetry and produces a valid pdf. Now note that the only order statistic affected in moving from $\tilde{f}_U(\cdot)$ to $f_U(\cdot)$ is $U^{(j:n)}$. Since $U^{(j:n)}$ is unobserved, the distribution of observables is unchanged.[10]

While this is an important negative result, it may suggest greater pessimism than is warranted for many applications. In many first-price auctions, for example, bids from all n bidders are observable, and we will see in the following section that identification often holds. Furthermore, even when the dimensionality of the bid data is less than n, there are often other observables that can enlarge the dimensionality of the data to match the dimensionality of $F_U(\cdot)$. We discuss this possibility in Section 3.3.

3.2   Equilibrium as Best Responses

Identification outside a second-price sealed-bid or ascending auction presents different challenges, since bids do not directly reveal the underlying private information of bidders. Even the problem of identifying the joint distribution of valuations $F_U(\cdot)$ in a private values auction in which bids are observed from all bidders seems quite challenging at first, since the equilibrium bid function relating the observed bids to the underlying valuations is a function of marginal distributions derived from the joint distribution $F_U(\cdot)$ itself. Smiley (1979) and Paarsch (1992a) proposed early approaches relying on special functional forms. Laffont, Ossard, and Vuong (1995) applied a simulation-based method applicable in symmetric independent private values models.

An important breakthrough, due to Guerre, Perrigne, and Vuong (2000), was the insight that the first-order condition for optimality of a bidder's best response can be rewritten, replacing distributions of primitives with equilibrium bid distributions. Consider a private values auction and let

$$G_{M_i|B_i}(m|b; \mathcal{N}) = \Pr\left(\max_{j \in \mathcal{N} \backslash i} B_j \leq m | B_i = b\right)$$

denote the equilibrium distribution function for the maximum equilibrium bid among a bidders i's opponents, conditional on his own equilibrium bid being b. Let $g_{m_i|B_i}(m|b; \mathcal{N})$ denote the corresponding density. This distribution represents i's equilibrium beliefs about competing bids. Conditioning on i's own equilibrium bid is merely a way of conditioning on i's private information (recall that bids are strictly increasing in types). This conditioning is necessary because bidders' own types may be correlated with those of their opponents, and therefore with the competing bids they face.

Underlying Guerre, Perrigne and Vuong's insight are two simple ideas: (a) equilibrium is achieved when each player best responds to the equilibrium

---

[10] Athey and Haile (2002) extend the non-identification results to common values ascending auctions, where we show that the underlying information structure is not identified even under strong assumptions, such as a pure common values model with independent signals.

distribution of opposing bids; and (b) when we assume the data are generated by the model, this equilibrium distribution of opposing bids is observable to the econometrician. For example, in a private values auction, the equilibrium bid of a bidder i with valuation u_i must solve

$$\max_{\tilde{b}} \int_{-\infty}^{\tilde{b}} \left(u_i - \tilde{b}\right) g_{M_i|B_i} \left(m|\beta\left(u_i;\mathcal{N}\right);\mathcal{N}\right) dm \tag{3.3}$$

which has first-order condition

$$u_i = b_i + \frac{G_{M_i|B_i}\left(b_i|b_i;\mathcal{N}\right)}{g_{M_i|B_i}\left(b_i|b_i;\mathcal{N}\right)}. \tag{3.4}$$

To interpret this expression, note that slightly rearranging (3.4) requires that the percentage "markdown" for bidder i, $(u_i - b_i)/b_i$, equal $\frac{G_{M_i|B_i}}{b_i \cdot g_{M_i|B_i}}$, the inverse of the elasticity of the probability of winning with respect to player i's choice of bid. Interchanging quantities and probabilities, we see that this is precisely the condition characterizing equilibrium pricing in standard oligopsony models, with the probability of winning replacing the residual supply curve. Just as in the oligopsony case, when considering an increase in the price he offers, a bidder here trades off the losses from paying a higher price conditional on winning against an increase in the chance of winning.

If the econometrician observes all bids in the auction as well as bidder identities, everything on the right-hand side of (3.4) is observable, while the left-hand side is the latent valuation associated with the bid b_i. Hence this equation demonstrates the identifiability of the valuations underlying each observed bid. When a bid is observed from each bidder, this immediately implies identification of the joint distribution $F_\mathbf{U}\left(\cdot\right)$, since

$$F_\mathbf{U}\left(\mathbf{u}\right) = \Pr\left(B_1 + \frac{G_{M_1|B_1}\left(B_1|B_1;\mathcal{N}\right)}{g_{M_1|B_1}\left(B_1|B_1;\mathcal{N}\right)} \leq u_1, \ldots, B_n + \frac{G_{M_n|B_n}\left(B_n|B_n;\mathcal{N}\right)}{g_{M_n|B_n}\left(B_n|B_n;\mathcal{N}\right)} \leq u_n\right).$$

Note that independence is not required. In fact, the conditions necessary for identification are only the conditions necessary for the theoretical model to have a unique equilibrium characterized by a first-order condition. [11]

This insight can be combined with those from Section 3.1 when bidders have independent types. For example in an independent private values environment, the distribution of the winning bid in a first-price sealed-bid or Dutch auction is $G_B^{(n:n)}\left(\cdot\right)$. As discussed previously, when bidders' valuations are independent, so are their equilibrium bids. Hence, using the results from Section 3.1, $G_B^{(n:n)}\left(\cdot\right)$ is sufficient to uniquely determine the underlying distributions $G_{B_i}\left(\cdot\right)$ for each i as long as the set of bidders and identity of the winner are observable to the econometrician (with symmetry, observation of the winning bid and n is

---

[11] See Athey and Haile (2006) for a detailed discussion of these conditions.

sufficient, since $G_B^{(n:n)}(b) = (G_B(b))^n$. Since

$$G_{M_i|B_i}(b|b;\mathcal{N}) = \prod_{j \in \mathcal{N} \backslash i} G_{B_i}(b)$$

under independence, the right-hand side of (3.4) is identified for each bid b_i, implying identification of each $F_{U_i}(\cdot)$ (Guerre, Perrigne, and Vuong (2000), Athey and Haile (2002)).

Of course, the independence assumption will not always be natural. As suggested in the discussion of identification failure in ascending auctions, observation of all n bids will be necessary to recover an arbitrary n-dimensional joint distribution $F_U(\cdot)$. However, in a sealed-bid auction, observation of bids from all n bidders is possible and common. Hence, despite the more complicated strategic bidding behavior in a first-price auction, one can often identify richer models than is possible in an ascending auction.

Even when all bids are observable, however, there are limits to what can be identified. In a common values auction, for example, if we let

$$v_i(x, y;\mathcal{N}) = E\left[U_i | X_i = x, \max_{j \in \mathcal{N} \backslash i} \beta_j(X_j;\mathcal{N}) = \beta_i(y;\mathcal{N})\right] \quad (3.5)$$

a bidder's optimization problem (the analog of (3.3)) can be written

$$\max_{\tilde{b}} \int_{-\infty}^{\tilde{b}} \left(v_i\left(x_i, \beta_i^{-1}(m);\mathcal{N}\right) - \tilde{b}\right) g_{M_i|B_i}\left(m|\beta_i(x_i);\mathcal{N}\right) dm$$

giving the first-order condition

$$v_i(x_i, x_i;\mathcal{N}) = b_i + \frac{G_{M_i|B_i}(b_i|b_i;\mathcal{N})}{g_{M_i|B_i}(b_i|b_i;\mathcal{N})}. \quad (3.6)$$

This looks encouraging, since the right-hand side again consists only of observables. However the left-hand side is not a primitive in a common values auction. By its definition in (3.5), the left-hand side depends on equilibrium bidding strategies. Furthermore, the primitive of interest for a common values auction is typically the joint distribution $F_{U,X}(\cdot)$. For example, this is the distribution needed to predict outcomes under alternative selling procedures, or to assess the division of surplus. A simple counting exercise again suggests the problem here: While the arguments above do imply that one can identify the joint distribution of the n random variables $(v_1(X_1, X_1;\mathcal{N}), \ldots, v_n(X_n, X_n;\mathcal{N}))$ for any given $\mathcal{N}$, the distribution of interest $F_{U,X}(\cdot;\mathcal{N})$ governs $2n$ random variables for each $\mathcal{N}$. It is easy to confirm that this intuition is correct: Without additional restrictions, observation of all bids is insufficient to identify $F_{U,X}(\cdot;\mathcal{N})$. A simple proof is to observe that whatever the true $F_{U,X}(\cdot;\mathcal{N})$, the model will be observationally equivalent to a private values model in which $U_i = X_i = v_i(X_i, X_i;\mathcal{N})$ (Laffont and Vuong (1996)).

While this is an important negative result, in many applications one observes more than just bids. As we discuss in the following section, such additional observables can help to overcome the limitations of bid data alone.

3.3   The Value of Data beyond Bids

3.3.1   Bidder Covariates

In Section 3.1 we saw that if the only observables are bids, identification fails in an ascending auction when the assumption of independent types is dropped. This problem can be overcome if there are bidder-specific covariates with sufficient variation. Indeed, observation of such variation and the transaction price alone can suffice.

Let W_i denote a scalar covariate (extension to the non-scalar case is straightforward) affecting bidder i's private value for the good – for example, his location relative to a construction site.[12] Each bidder i has a valuation given by

$$U_i = g_i(W_i) + A_i$$

where each $g_i(\cdot)$ is a function unknown to the econometrician, and the private stochastic components $(A_1, \ldots, A_n)$ are drawn from an arbitrary joint distribution $F_A(\cdot)$. Assume that $(A_1, \ldots, A_n)$ are independent of $\mathbf{W} = (\mathbf{W}_1, \ldots, \mathbf{W}_n)$.

To see the role of the bidder-specific covariates, suppose for the moment that each $g_i(\cdot)$ were known and that we could somehow observe the order statistic $U^{(n:n)}$ (the intended exit price of the winning bidder), but no other valuations/bids. Given $\mathbf{w}$, $U^{(n:n)}$ has cumulative distribution

$$\begin{aligned}
F_U^{(n:n)}(u|\mathbf{w}) &= \Pr(U^{(n:n)} \leq u|\mathbf{w}) \\
&= F_{\mathbf{U}}(u, \ldots, u|\mathbf{w}) \\
&= \Pr(g_i(w_i) + A_i \leq u \; \forall i) \\
&= F_{\mathbf{A}}(u - g_1(\mathbf{w}_1), \ldots, u - g_n(\mathbf{w}_n)).
\end{aligned}$$

Observing this probability reveals a great deal when there is sufficient independent variation in $(g_1(\mathbf{w}_1), \ldots, g_n(\mathbf{w}_n))$; indeed, such variation could "trace out" the joint distribution $F_A(\cdot)$ at every possible value of its arguments. So what about the assumption that $g_i(\cdot)$ is known? This is not necessary with sufficient variation in covariates: At sufficiently low values of $g_j(w_j) \; \forall j \neq i$, bidder i will have the largest valuation with probability arbitrarily close to one, so that variation in $\mathbf{w}_i$ and the point of evaluation u would trace out the function $g_i(\cdot)$.[13]

This is not to suggest that in practice we should hope to have a large number of observations at extreme realizations of covariate values. Rather, the point is that variation in covariates can enable even limited bid data to reveal significant information about the underlying structure – enough to construct finite sample estimates with valid asymptotic justifications.

---

[12] Extension to non-scalar covariates is straightforward.

[13] This argument is essentially that made by Heckman and Honoré (1989) and Heckman and Honoré (1990) for the nonparametric identification of competing risks models and the Roy model.

Of course in practice one cannot observe $U^{(n:n)}$ in an ascending auction, but given the analysis above one might hope that another order statistic would also suffice. Athey and Haile (2006) have shown that this is the case. They make the following assumptions, which, in particular, spell out sufficient conditions for the "sufficient variation in covariates" condition referred to above:

(i) $U_i = g_i(\mathbf{W}_i) + A_i$, $i = 1, \ldots, n$.
(ii) $\mathbf{A}$ has support $\mathbb{R}^n$ and a continuously differentiable density.
(iii) A_i and $\mathbf{W}_j$ are independent for all i, j.
(iv) $\operatorname{supp}(g_1(\mathbf{W}_1), \ldots, g_n(\mathbf{W}_n)) = \mathbb{R}^n$.
(v) For all i, $g_i(\cdot)$ is continuously differentiable and satisfies $\lim_{\mathbf{w}_i \to (\infty, \ldots, \infty)} g_i(\mathbf{w}_i) = \infty$ and $\lim_{\mathbf{w}_i \to (-\infty, \ldots, -\infty)} g_i(\mathbf{w}_i) = -\infty$.

Under these assumptions, $F_{\mathbf{A}}(\cdot)$ and each $g_i(\cdot)$, $i = 1, \ldots, n$, are identified up to a location normalization from observation of $U^{(j:n)}$ and $\mathbf{W}$, for any single value of $j \in \{1, \ldots, n\}$. Hence, for example, observation of the winning bid alone in an ascending auction is sufficient to identify an arbitrary joint distribution $F_{\mathbf{U}}(\cdot)$ under these assumptions.

3.3.2   Ex Post Values

Another source of variation in the data that can be particularly useful in a pure common values setting is the ex post realization of the good's value.[14] For example, data on ex post values have been collected for U.S. Forest Service timber auctions (Athey and Levin (2001)), auctions of real estate (McAfee, Quan, and Vincent (2002)), and U.S. offshore oil lease auctions (Hendricks, Pinkse, and Porter (2003)). In a pure common values auction, $U_i = U_0 \ \forall i$, so the joint distribution $F_{\mathbf{U},\mathbf{X}}(\cdot)$ (which we can rewrite $F_{U_0,\mathbf{X}}(\cdot)$) governs $n + 1$ random variables. Observation of bids from all n bidders as well as the realization of U_0, therefore, at least offers hope of identification.

Hendricks, Pinkse, and Porter (2003) have provided conditions under which this is the case. Consider a symmetric pure common values model in which, conditional on the realization of U_0, bidders' signals are independent draws from a distribution $F_X(\cdot|U_0)$.[15] Fixing the number of bidders, one can impose the normalization

$$E[U_i | X_i = \max_{j \neq i} X_j = x, n] = x \tag{3.7}$$

without loss of generality. In a first-price sealed-bid auction, the first-order

---

[14] Related possibilities include noisy ex ante estimates (e.g., Smiley (1979)) or noisy ex post estimates (e.g., Yin (2003)).

[15] In the literature this special case of a pure common values model is referred to as the symmetric "mineral rights model."

condition (3.6) then gives

$$E\left[U_0|X_i = \max_{j \neq i} X_j = x_i, n\right] = x_i = b_i + \frac{G_{M_i|B_i}(b_i|b_i;n)}{g_{M_i|B_i}(b_i|b_i;n)}. \quad (3.8)$$

As discussed in Section 3.2, observation of all bids identifies the right-hand side of (3.8) and, therefore, the realizations of X_i associated with each bid. Observation of U_0 for each auction then immediately enables identification of the joint distribution $F_{U_0,\mathbf{X}}(\cdot)$.

The use of data on ex post values can be extended to environments in which not all bids are observed, exploiting the independence of signals conditional on U_0. In the case of an ascending auction, however, bidders' ability to observe their opponents' bids presents a complication. In particular, there is no normalization like (3.7) that equates signals to bids for all bidders, since bidders update their beliefs about opponents' signals as the auction proceeds. In a two-bidder auction, this problem does not arise. In fact, with $n = 2$ there is no multiplicity of equilibria in weakly undominated strategies (Bikhchandani, Haile, and Riley (2002)) and for $i = 1, 2$

$$\begin{aligned} b_i &= \beta_i(x_i; 2) = E\left[U_0|X_1 = X_2 = x_i, N = 2\right] \\ &= E\left[U_0|\beta_1(X_1; 2) = \beta_2(X_2; 2) = \beta_i(x_i; 2), N = 2\right] \\ &\equiv \zeta(b_i, b_i, 2). \end{aligned}$$

Under the normalization (3.7), $B^{(1:2)} = X^{(1:2)}$ and, conditional on U_0, $X^{(1:2)}$ is an order statistic from a sample of independent draws from $F_{X|U_0}(\cdot)$. Exploiting equation (3.1), identification is then obtained for a symmetric two-bidder auction when the transaction price (lowest bid) and ex post value are observed. This approach, based on the lowest observed bid, can be extended to the case with $n > 2$, although relying on the assumption $B^{(1:n)} = U^{(1:n)}$ may be particularly questionable when $n > 2$ (see the discussion in Section 4.3 below).[16]

3.4 Important Extensions

The insights discussed in the preceding sections have been applied and extended in many different ways. We will discuss some of these in the context of individual applications below. Before doing so, however, we highlight several general topics that have received increasing attention in recent years – topics that are also particularly relevant for developing convincing empirical applications of the basic methods.

3.4.1 Endogenous Participation

Bidders will not participate in an auction unless they expect doing so to be profitable. In the baseline model, bidding is always profitable; however, a number of factors such as reserve prices, participation fees, or costly information

---

[16] See Athey and Haile (2006) for a variation.

acquisition can cause some potential bidders to stay out of an auction. The distinction between actual bidders (those who place a bid) and potential bidders (those who could in principle bid) has been emphasized throughout the literature on structural econometrics of auctions (e.g., Paarsch (1992b)). Indeed, a common goal of work in this literature has been to better inform mechanism design choices accounting for the endogeneity of participation (e.g., Paarsch (1997), Haile and Tamer (2003), Athey, Levin, and Seira (2004)).

Recently, more attention has been given to the variety of possible models of endogenous participation. Bidders may decide to participate based on exogenous randomization (mixed strategies) as in Li and Zheng (2005) or Athey, Levin, and Seira (2004); based on preliminary private signals of the object's value (e.g., Hendricks, Pinkse, and Porter (2003)); based on their idiosyncratic costs of acquiring information; or based on public information about the object that is observable or unobservable to the econometrician (e.g., Haile, Hong, and Shum (2003)). Each of these possibilities has implications that must be accounted for in interpreting bids. In addition, one lesson of the work thus far is that incorporating equilibrium participation decisions can often aid identification and estimation of the bidding model (see, e.g., Section 4.2 below). Furthermore, endogenous participation can have important implications for mechanism design choices, such as the auction format (Athey, Levin, and Seira (2004)). More work is needed in this area, for example to develop approaches for evaluating alternative assumptions on bidder participation.

3.4.2   Unobserved Heterogeneity

Unobserved heterogeneity is a concern in almost all empirical work. In auctions, one may often expect that there are characteristics of the object for sale that are observed by all bidders but not by the econometrician. Such unobservables can create significant challenges. In an ascending auction, unobserved heterogeneity generally leads to correlation in bidders' valuations, often causing identification to fail (see Section 3.1). In a first-price sealed-bid auction, suppose bidders have private values given by

$$U_i = V_0 + A_i \tag{3.9}$$

where V_0 is an auction-specific characteristic observed by all bidders and A_i is a private idiosyncratic factor affecting only bidder i's valuation. In this environment, bidders will use their knowledge of V_0 when constructing their beliefs about the competing bids they face. In particular, equilibrium bids will solve the first-order condition

$$u_i = b_i + \frac{G_{M_i|B_i}(b_i|b_i; v_0)}{g_{M_i|B_i}(b_i|b_i; v_0)} \tag{3.10}$$

where $G_{M_i|B_i}(b_i|b_i; v_0) = \Pr\left(\max_{j\neq i} B_j \leq b_i | B_i = b_i, V_0 = v_0\right)$. If the econometrician does not observe V_0, it is not clear how the the right-hand side of (3.10) could be consistently estimated.

Although this is a challenging problem, several fruitful ideas have recently been explored. One approach builds on insights from the econometrics literatures on measurement error with repeated measurements and duration models with multiple spells. These literatures consider multiple observations for each of many units, with observations within each unit reflecting both a common (unobserved) shock as well as idiosyncratic shocks. Using deconvolution methods (e.g., Kotlarski (1966)), these literatures have shown how to separate the unit-specific factors (V_0 in the auction example above) from the observation-specific factors (the A_i here). Krasnokutskaya (2004), for example, shows how to combine these techniques with the insights from Section 3.2 to obtain identification and consistent estimators for first-price sealed-bid auctions. The model of Athey, Levin, and Seira (2004), discussed in Section 4.4 below, builds on these ideas in an application to timber auctions.

Another possible approach is to utilize additional observables that control for the unobserved heterogeneity through another endogenous outcome. For example, suppose bidder participation is monotonic in the unobservable V_0, conditional on some set of observables, $\mathbf{Z}$; i.e.,

$$N = \phi(\mathbf{Z}, V_0)$$

with ϕ strictly increasing in V_0. In this case, conditioning on $(\mathbf{Z}, N)$ indirectly fixes the realization of V_0, making it possible to estimate the right-hand side of (3.10) (Campo, Perrigne, and Vuong (2003), Haile, Hong, and Shum (2003)). This can be thought of as using a set of observable outcomes as "control functions" for the unobservable.[17]

Each of these approaches requires assumptions on unobservables: independence and a separable structure like (3.9) in the case of the deconvolution approach; strict monotonicity of a participation equation (or some other relation) in the control function approach. Each set of assumptions has strengths and limitations. Given the importance of unobserved heterogeneity in practice, we suspect that other useful methods will be explored in the future.

3.4.3   Specification Testing

As mentioned in the introduction, a "structural" approach to empirical work typically incorporates two types of assumptions: (a) economic assumptions, such as behavioral assumptions (e.g., Bayesian Nash equilibrium) and economically motivated restrictions on preferences (e.g. risk neutrality), and (b) functional form assumptions, imposed either for convenience in estimation or because only a limited set of parameters can be identified. As we have seen, for some kinds of auction models, the second type of assumption is not essential. However, not all models are nonparametrically identified, and typically even those that are make assumptions like independence or separability on unobservables.

---

[17] Indeed, an alternative approach is to condition directly on an estimated residual from the participation equation, rather than on the observables $(\mathbf{Z}, N)$.

Because the conclusions one reaches in empirical work can be sensitive to such assumptions, it is desirable to test them when possible.

A natural approach to specification testing is to examine overidentifying restrictions. For example, in a model in which the winning bid alone is sufficient to identify the distribution of bidder valuations, observability of other bids (which would also identify this distribution on their own) provide overidentifying restrictions that can be tested. In other cases, it is possible to nest one model (e.g., symmetric private values) within another (asymmetric private values), leading to a testable restriction. Perhaps surprisingly, even without overidentifying restrictions (or even identifying restrictions), tests are sometimes possible. We will see an example in Section 4.2 below. Athey and Haile (2002) and Athey and Haile (2006) discuss a variety of testable restrictions that can be used to evaluate or decide between alternative specifications. More work is needed in this area, for example, to develop appropriate statistical tests.

4   APPLICATIONS

In the following sections we illustrate some of the ways the ideas above have been applied and extended to address important economic questions.

4.1   Assessing the Winner's Curse in Common Value First-Price Auctions

Since the early work of Capen, Clapp, and Campbell (1971), considerable attention has been given to U.S. Interior Department auctions of rights to drill for offshore oil and gas. One topic of particular interest is the "winner's curse" – the fact that, in a common values auction, winning bidders tend to be those who have overestimated the good's value. Some of the most influential early empirical work on auctions (e.g., Hendricks and Porter (1988)) explored implications of rational bidding in the presence of the winner's curse and provided compelling evidence of the empirical relevance of asymmetric information and strategic behavior. Recent developments in methods for structural empirical work on auctions have opened up opportunities for additional testing. This might be surprising, since sometimes empirical work is described as falling in one of two categories: structural estimation, or model testing. However, these are not mutually exclusive. Structure from economic theory often provides restrictions that enable one to test hypotheses that could not otherwise be considered. In auctions, for example, maintaining one set of restrictions (e.g., Bayesian Nash equilibrium bidding) often provides overidentifying restrictions that can be used to test other economic hypotheses that could not be examined without this structure.[18]

---

[18] Athey and Haile (2006) discuss a wide range of testable restrictions in auction models. Other examples from the literature include Haile (2001), Campo, Guerre, Perrigne, and Vuong (2002), and Haile, Hong, and Shum (2003), discussed in section 4.2 below.

Hendricks, Pinkse, and Porter (2003) take this approach to develop several tests of rational responses to the winner's curse in offshore "wildcat" sales in Texas and Louisiana. In these auctions, held between 1954 and 1970, leases of tracts in previously unexplored areas of the outer continental shelf were offered for sale. The auctions are conducted in first-price sealed-bid format, and all bids are recorded.

The authors make use of the fact that the actual volume of oil and other minerals extracted from each tract is metered to determine royalties and, therefore, observable ex post. If idiosyncratic determinants of costs are small, then a pure common values model may be appropriate, and the product of the realized volumes and market prices (less a measure of extraction costs) provides a measure of the ex post value, U_0.

Hendricks, Pinkse, and Porter (2003) apply the mineral rights model to these auctions (see Section 3.3.2 above)[19] and develop a sequence of tests of increasingly demanding implications of rational strategic bidding.[20]

Positive Average Rents. With rational bidding, winning bidders should make positive profits on average. That is, up to sampling variation,

$$\frac{1}{T} \sum_t \left[u_{0t} - b^{(n_t : n_t)} \right]$$

should be positive. Hendricks, Pinkse, and Porter (2003) find average rents of around \$3.7 million. Taking this further, not only should the actual winners obtain positive expected rents, but every observed bid should be consistent with a rational expectation of making positive profits in the event that the bid wins. This is a more subtle restriction, since conditioning on the (usually counterfactual) event that a bid wins the auction means conditioning on the implied (in equilibrium) information about opponents' signals, and therefore about U_0.

Let

$$\omega(b) \equiv E\left[U_0 | B_{it} = b, \max_{j \neq i} B_{jt} \leq b; n \right]$$

be the expected value of the object for bidder i conditional on his winning the auction with bid b. This expectation is identified directly from the data on ex

[19] They allow for two classes of bidders: "large" and "fringe," and for endogenous participation. Their analysis focuses on the large bidders, although bids from fringe bidders are included when they construct distributions of opposing bids. The model of participation offers a formal "purification" of a mixed strategy participation equilibrium. We abstract from both of these features for simplicity.

[20] Hendricks, Pinkse, and Porter (2003) use an estimate of the number of potential bidders (the number of firms ever to bid in a neighborhood of the tract in question) as a control for unobserved heterogeneity of tracts and perform the analysis below conditional on "high" and "low" values of this variable.

post values and bids. With symmetric strictly increasing equilibrium bidding strategies $\beta(\cdot; n)$, this is equivalent to

$$E\left[U_0 | X_{it} = \beta^{-1}(b; n), \max_{j \neq i} X_{jt} \leq \beta^{-1}(b; n); n\right].$$

Hendricks, Pinkse, and Porter (2003) propose testing the restriction

$$E_B\left[\omega(B) - B\right] > 0$$

where B represents the bid of a generic bidder.

Because each u_{0t} and all bids are observable, various parametric or non-parametric regression techniques could be used to estimate $\omega(b)$. Hendricks, Pinkse, and Porter (2003) employ local-linear regression (see, e.g., Loader (1999)), yielding estimates $\hat{\omega}(b_{it})$ for each observed bid b_{it}. They then examine whether

$$\frac{1}{T} \sum_t \sum_{i=1}^{n_t} [\hat{\omega}(b_{it}) - b_{it}] > 0.$$

They find an average expected margin of around \$3.7 million—essentially the same as the average rents to winning bidders. This compares to winning bids averaging \$3 to \$8 million. Using a block bootstrap to construct standard errors,[21] the hypothesis of zero average margins can be rejected in favor of positive margins.

Positive Expected Rents for All Bids. The tests of rationality above can be sharpened by asking whether inequalities hold for all bids, not just on average. For example,

$$E\left[U_0 | B_i = b\right] - b$$

should be positive for each observed bid b. Likewise, if bidders recognize that winning the auction is informative about others' signals, $\omega(b) - b$ should be positive for all observed bids b, not just on average. Again using local linear regression to estimate the conditional expectations, Hendricks, Pinkse, and Porter (2003) find support for both restrictions.

Equilibrium Bidding. The most demanding test uses the structural model, combining several of the ideas discussed in Sections 3.2, 3.3, and 3.4.3. Let

$$\zeta(b, m, n) = E\left[U_0 | B_i = b, \max_{j \neq i} B = m, n\right]. \tag{4.1}$$

---

[21] Blocking by auction is necessary since bids in this model will be correlated within auction.

With strictly increasing equilibrium bidding strategies

$$
E\left[U_0 | X_i = \max_{j \neq i} X_j = x_i, n\right]
$$

$$
= E\left[U_0 | \beta(X_i; n) = \max_{j \neq i} \beta(X_j; n) = \beta(x_i; n), n\right]
$$

$$
= E\left[U_0 | B_i = \max_{j \neq i} B_j = b_i, n\right]
$$

$$
= \zeta(b_i, b_i, n).
$$

The first-order condition (3.8) can then be written

$$
\zeta(b_i, b_i, n) = b_i + \frac{G_{M|B}(b_i | b_i; n)}{g_{M|B}(b_i | b_i; n)} \equiv \xi(b_i, n). \tag{4.2}
$$

Because the joint distribution of $(U_0, B_1, \ldots, B_n, N)$ is observable, $\zeta(b_i, b_i, n)$ is identified directly through equation (4.1). Indeed, $\zeta(b_i, b_i, n)$ is just a conditional expectation of the observable U_0 given that the observable bids satisfy $B_i = \max_{j \neq i} B_j = b_i$. Since $\xi(b_i, n)$ is also identified from the bidding data (without the ex post values) under the assumption of equilibrium bidding (recall Section 3.2), the overidentifying restriction $\zeta(b_i, b_i, n) = \xi(b_i, n)$ can be tested.

The right-hand side of (4.2) can be estimated using the kernel methods now standard in the literature on first-price auctions (see, e.g., Guerre, Perrigne, and Vuong (2000), Li, Perrigne, Vuong (2000), and Li, Perrigne, and Vuong (2002)). In particular, let

$$
\hat{G}_{M,B}(b, b; n) = \frac{1}{nT_n h_G} \sum_{t=1}^{T_n} \sum_{i=1}^{n} K\left(\frac{b - b_{it}}{h_G}\right) \mathbf{1}\{m_{it} < b, n_t = n\} \tag{4.3}
$$

$$
\hat{g}_{M,B}(b, b; n) = \frac{1}{nT_n h_g^2} \sum_{t=1}^{T_n} \sum_{i=1}^{n} \mathbf{1}\{n_t = n\} K\left(\frac{b - b_{it}}{h_g}, \frac{b - m_{it}}{h_g}\right) \tag{4.4}
$$

where M_{it} denotes $\max_{j \neq i} B_{jt}$, $K(\cdot)$ is a kernel, and h_G and h_g are appropriately chosen bandwidth sequences. Under standard conditions, $\frac{\hat{G}_{M,B}(b,b;n)}{\hat{g}_{M,B}(b,b;n)}$ is a consistent estimator of $\frac{G_{M|B}(b|b;n)}{g_{M|B}(b|b;n)}$, so that

$$
\hat{\xi}_{it} \equiv b_{it} + \frac{\hat{G}_{M,B}(b_{it}, b_{it}; n)}{\hat{g}_{M,B}(b_{it}, b_{it}; n)}
$$

is a consistent estimate of $\xi(b_i, n)$.[22] Using local linear regression to estimate the left-hand side of (4.2) and the bootstrap to construct critical values, Hendricks, Pinkse, and Porter (2003) fail to reject the null hypothesis of equality, providing support for the equilibrium bidding hypothesis.

How Large Is the Winner's Curse?   Hendricks, Pinkse, and Porter (2003) also suggest ways of illustrating the magnitude of the winner's curse based on the difference

$$E\left[U_0 | X_i = x_i, n\right] - E\left[U_0 | X_i = x_i, \max_{j \neq i} X_j \leq x_i, n\right]. \tag{4.5}$$

Under the pure common values assumption, this represents the adjustment a bidder must make to account for the information implied by winning the auction.[23] Exploiting the monotonicity of equilibrium bidding, this difference is equal to

$$E\left[U_0 | B_i = b_i, n\right] - E\left[U_0 | B_i = b_i, \max_{j \neq i} B_j \leq b_i, n\right] \tag{4.6}$$

and each of the expectations can be estimated using a variety of regression techniques. Using local linear regression, Hendricks, Pinkse, and Porter (2003) find that this difference is positive and larger on tracts with more potential bidders. On tracts with few potential bidders, the estimated difference is about $2 million for a tract receiving a bid of $1 million. For tracts with more potential bidders, the difference in (4.6) of $5 million (at a $1 million bid) is considerably larger. Hence, the magnitude of the winner's curse is significant. Moreover, it is larger when there is greater anticipated competition, as must be the case if the maintained assumption of symmetric pure common values is correct.

4.2   Discriminating between Private and Common Values

The distinction between private and common values models is fundamental and was, in fact, the motivation behind Paarsch's (1992a) early influential work on structural estimation of auction models. Discriminating between the two classes of models is subtle, however. Laffont and Vuong (1996) argued that they are empirically indistinguishable without a priori parametric assumptions. When data beyond bids are available, however, this is not always correct. For example,

---

[22] Hendricks, Pinkse, and Porter (2003) do not condition on the number of bidders n but on whether the auction is one with a large or small number of potential bidders, treating this as the information available to bidders.

[23] As pointed out by Hendricks, Pinkse, and Porter (2003), positive values for this difference (or even monotonicity of this difference in n) do not provide evidence against a private values assumption, since the interpretation of the ex post value data presumes pure common values. See Athey and Haile (2006) for additional discussion.

Hendricks, Pinkse, and Porter (2003) suggested a testing approach for auctions with binding reserve prices.[24]

Haile, Hong, and Shum (2003) have proposed another approach based on the fact that the winner's curse is present only in common values auctions and becomes more severe as the level of competition increases. In particular, while the expectation

$$v(x, x; n) = E[U_i | X_i = \max_{j \neq i} X_j = x; n] \qquad (4.7)$$

is invariant to n in a private values model, it strictly decreases in n in any common values environment.[25] This observation provides a testing approach that can be applied with or without binding reserve prices, and can allow for a range of models of endogenous participation.

The basic idea is simple: Estimate the right-hand side of (3.6) and compare estimates of $v(x, x; n)$ at different values of n.[26] Let

$$H_n(\check{v}) = \Pr(v(X_i, X_i; n) \leq \check{v}).$$

Under the null hypothesis of private values, $H_n(\check{v})$ should be invariant to n, while under the common values alternative,

$$H_n(\check{v}) < H_{n+1}(\check{v}) \qquad \forall \check{v}, n.$$

Tests of equal distributions against a one-sided alternative of stochastic dominance can then provide tests of the private values null against the common values alternative.[27] This testing problem is nonstandard, however, due to the fact that one cannot observe realizations of the random variable $v(X, X; n)$ but only estimates obtained through observed bids and the first-order condition (3.6). Haile, Hong, and Shum (2003) explore a variety of testing approaches. A consistent test demonstrating good finite-sample power and coverage properties in Monte Carlo simulations is a modified Kolmogorov-Smirnov test, using subsampling to construct critical values.

Haile, Hong, and Shum (2003) discuss details and apply this approach to two types of auctions held by the U.S. Forest Service (USFS). In all auctions, a contract to harvest all specified timber on a tract of land is sold to the high

---

[24] See Hendricks and Porter (forthcoming) or Athey and Haile (2006) for details.

[25] The idea of using variation in n to detect the winner's curse precedes the first precise statements, given in early drafts of Athey and Haile (2002) and Haile, Hong, and Shum (2003). However, the observation was often misinterpreted as providing a way to test for common values based directly on the relation between bids and n (see, e.g., Brannman, Klein, and Weiss (1987), Paarsch (1992a), Paarsch (1992b), Laffont (1997)). Pinkse and Tan (2005) showed that the relation of bids to n is indeterminate in both private and common values models.

[26] The approach described here uses all bids. Athey and Haile (2002) discuss a variation that could be applied when certain subsets of bids are observed, in either first-price or ascending auctions.

[27] As discussed in Athey and Haile (2006), there are several other hypotheses of interest in auction models that take the form of equality of estimated distributions.

bidder by first-price sealed-bid auction. Before each auction, the Forest Service conducts a "cruise" of the tract in order to publish detailed pre-auction estimates of timber volumes by species and other determinants of the contract's value. Under one type of contract, known as a lumpsum sale, the winning bidder simply pays its bid. Consequently, bidders frequently conduct their own cruises of the tract, providing a likely source of private information. While such information might be of a private or common values nature, intuition might suggest that these auctions might have a significant common values component. With the second type of contract, payments are not made until the timber is harvested, and the amount paid is based on the actual volume of timber harvested, not the ex ante estimates. Bids in these "scaled" sales are real unit prices that will be applied to the actual volumes. So although bidders may face considerable uncertainty over the volume of timber on the tract, this common uncertainty may have limited importance to the value of the tract. Consequently, bidders are less likely to conduct a private cruise for a scaled sale. Several prior empirical studies used these facts to motivate an assumption of private values.[28]

Several practical issues must be overcome to implement the testing approach in this application. One is that tracts are heterogeneous, as evidenced by the variation in tract characteristics published in the Forest Service cruise report. These characteristics could be conditioned on using standard nonparametric methods, but they are sufficiently numerous that this approach is impractical here. Haile, Hong, and Shum (2003) propose a semi-parametric alternative based on the observation that if valuations take an additively separable form

$$u_{it} = \gamma(\mathbf{z}_t) + \epsilon_{it}$$

then equilibrium bids have the same additively separable form

$$b_{it} = \gamma(\mathbf{z}_t) + \tilde{b}_{it}.$$

Here $\tilde{b}_{it}$ represents the equilibrium bid that bidder i *would have made* in auction t if $\mathbf{z}_t$ were such that $\gamma(\mathbf{z}_t) = 0$. Such a value of $\mathbf{z}_t$ need not actually exist and, of course, bids could be recentered at any other value of $\mathbf{z}_t$. This additive separability implies that the effects of covariates on bids can be controlled for using a first-stage regression of bids on covariates. In particular, subtracting the estimate $\hat{\gamma}(\mathbf{z}_t)$ from each b_{it} then gives a sample of "homogenized" bids. Haile, Hong, and Shum (2003) use linear regression for this step.

A second issue is the likelihood that the number of bidders is endogenous. Several models of endogenous participation exist in the literature, and it is fairly straightforward to extend the approach to allow for binding reserve prices, entry fees, and costly signal acquisition (see Haile, Hong, and Shum (2003) for details). A more difficult case is that in which participation is partially determined

---

[28] See e.g., Baldwin, Marshall, and Richard (1997), Haile (2001), Haile and Tamer (2003), and Athey, Levin, and Seira (2004). Baldwin (1995), Athey and Levin (2001), and Haile (2001) have provided evidence that a common value element is introduced to scaled sales through misestimation of timber volumes by the Forest Service, or by resale opportunities.

by unobservable factors that also affect the distribution of bidders' signals and valuations. Such a situation creates two problems. First, if the number of bidders is correlated with valuations, the expectation $v(x, x; n)$ would vary with n even in a pure private values model, or might fail to vary with n in a common values model. This is a familiar problem of an endogenous "treatment." The second problem is the problem discussed in Section 3.4.2: Unobserved heterogeneity threatens the identification of the distribution of $v(X, X; n)$.

Concerned that participation may be affected by unobserved heterogeneity,[29] Haile, Hong, and Shum (2003) propose an instrumental variables approach that combines an exclusion restriction with a monotonicity assumption: that, conditional on the observables, participation is strictly increasing in the unobservable.[30] Their approach requires an instrument, w, for the number of bidders, and they use counts of nearby sawmills and logging firms, following Haile (2001).

With this structure, bidders' conditional expectations of the value of winning the auction can be written

$$v(x, x; n, w) = E[U_i | X_i = \max_{j \neq i} X_j = x; n, w].$$

These expectations can be estimated using the first-order condition

$$v(x_i, x_i; n, w) = b_i + \frac{G_{M|B}(b_i, b_i; n, w)}{g_{M|B}(b_i, b_i; n, w)}$$

using the methods described above but conditioning on both the number of bidders and the value of the instrument w. The resulting estimates $\hat{v}(x, x; n, w)$ are then pooled over the realizations of n and compared across values of w, enabling a comparison of auctions with different levels of participation due to exogenous factors. Their preliminary results suggest that common values may not be empirically important, particularly in the case of scaled sales.

4.3 Bidder Demand and Reserve Price Policy for Ascending Auctions

Reserve price policy has been one source of tension for the USFS timber sales program. Critics of Forest Service policies have suggested that reserve prices are systematically too low, resulting in a loss of revenues and a subsidy to the timber industry. However, the USFS has a range of mandated objectives, including forest management goals and provision of a steady supply of timber, which lead to a desire to ensure that most tracts it offers for sale are actually harvested. The Forest Service has sometimes argued that historical data are

---

[29] Evidence that unobserved heterogeneity affects participation in other USFS timber auctions is given in Haile (2001).

[30] Recall Section 3.4.2. See Haile, Hong, and Shum (2003) for details. This approach is related to prior insights in Olley and Pakes (1996) and Campo, Perrigne, and Vuong (2003).

useless for guiding the trade-offs between these objectives and revenues:

> Studies indicate it is nearly impossible to use sales records to determine if marginal sales made in the past would have been purchased under a different [reserve price] structure. (U.S. Forest Service (1995))

Economic theory tells us that there is something to this view: The effects of reserve prices in a competitive environment are subtle and unlikely to be measured correctly with a descriptive empirical analysis. However, this is exactly the kind of policy question that structural empirical work on auctions has the potential to inform. Haile and Tamer (2003) explore this possibility using data from auctions in Washington and Oregon.

One immediate concern in studying ascending auctions with a structural model is the suitability of the standard "button auction" model, discussed in Section 2. Because bidders typically call out bids rather than indicating their participation continuously, researchers may have quite noisy measures of the prices at which each bidder actually drops out of an auction – the "bids" in the button auction model. For example, even a bidder with a relatively high valuation may appear to exit at a low price if active bidding by his opponents pushes the price beyond his willingness to pay while he stands by. Further concerns arise from the use of minimum bid increments and the prevalence of "jump bidding." Hence, in many applications there may be no observables that correspond to the equilibrium "bids" (exit prices) in the standard model.

A natural response to this problem would be to explore an alternative model better suited for interpreting observed bids. Capturing the free-form dynamics of a typical ascending auction, however, presents serious challenges. Haile and Tamer (2003) explore an alternative. They consider a symmetric independent private values environment and rely on only two behavioral assumptions. First, no bidder bids more than his valuation. Second, no bidder lets an opponent win at a price he would be willing to beat. More precisely, if we let $\Delta \geq 0$ denote the minimum bid increment,

Assumption HT1. $b_i \leq u_i \qquad \forall i.$

Assumption HT2. $u^{j:n} \leq b^{n:n} + \Delta \forall_{j<n}.$

The first assumption seems uncontroversial. The second reflects the defining characteristic of an ascending auction: the ability to observe and respond to the bids of competitors before the auction ends. These assumptions can be interpreted as axioms or as necessary conditions for equilibrium in a variety of models. While these assumptions permit bidding as in the dominant strategy equilibrium of the standard model, they do not require it: Bids need not be equal to valuations or even monotonic in valuations, and the price need not equal the second highest valuation.

While relying only on these two behavioral assumptions has some appeal in terms of the robustness of the estimates to the details of the true data generating process, this flexibility comes at a price. In particular, under these assumptions, typically only bounds on $F_U(\cdot)$ are identified. Identification of these bounds follows from an application of (3.1). In an n-bidder auction, Assumption HT1 implies $b^{(i:n)} \leq u^{(i:n)}$ for all i. Hence,

$$G_B^{(i:n)}(u) \geq F_U^{(i:n)}(u) \quad \forall i, n, u. \tag{4.8}$$

Applying the monotonic transformation $\phi(\cdot; i, n)$ defined in (3.2) to both sides gives

$$\phi\left(G_B^{(i:n)}(u); i, n\right) \geq F_U(u) \quad \forall i, n, u.$$

For each u, this actually provides as many upper bounds on $F_U(u)$ as there are combinations of i and n. The most informative bound (i.e., the smallest upper bound) is obtained by taking the minimum at each value of u:

$$F_U^+(u) = \min_{i, n} \phi\left(G_B^{(i:n)}(u); i, n\right). \tag{4.9}$$

To obtain a lower bound, let $G_\Delta^{(n:n)}(\cdot) = \Pr\left(B^{(n:n)} + \Delta \leq b\right)$ and observe that Assumption HT2 implies

$$G_\Delta^{(n:n)}(u) \leq F_U^{(n-1:n)}(u) \quad \forall n, u.$$

Applying $\phi(\cdot; n-1, n)$ to both sides gives

$$\phi\left(G_\Delta^{(n:n)}(u); n-1, n\right) \leq F_U(u) \quad \forall n, u.$$

As before, the most informative bound can be constructed by taking the point-wise maximum:

$$F_U^-(u) = \max_n \phi\left(G_\Delta^{(n:n)}(u); n-1, n\right). \tag{4.10}$$

Haile and Tamer (2003) point out that estimates obtained using the standard ascending auction model to interpret bids need not lie within these bounds, even asymptotically. For example, if there is no minimum bid increment and the econometrician assumes only that the transaction price equals $u^{(n-1:n)}$, the natural nonparametric estimator $\hat{F}_U(\cdot)$ satisfies $\text{plim} \hat{F}_U(u) \leq F_U^-(u) \, \forall u$. On the other hand, if $B^{(n:n)} = B^{(n-1:n)}$ (as implied by the button auction model), the bounds $F_U^-(\cdot)$ and $F_U^+(\cdot)$ collapse to the true distribution $F_U(\cdot)$, providing point identification.

To estimate the bounds, one can substitute the empirical distributions

$$\hat{G}_B^{(i:n)}(b) = \frac{1}{T_n} \sum_{t=1}^T \mathbf{1}\left\{n_t = n, b^{(i:n_t)} \leq b\right\}$$

and

$$\hat{G}_\Delta^{(n:n)}(b) = \frac{1}{T_n} \sum_{t=1}^T \mathbf{1}\left\{n_t = n, b^{(n_t:n_t)} + \Delta_t \leq b\right\}$$

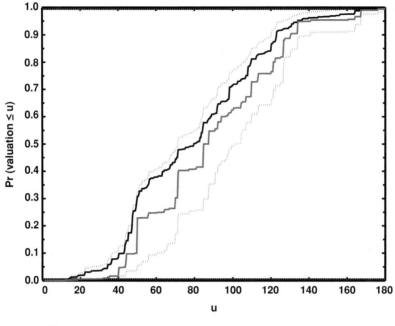

Figure 1.1.

for the corresponding population CDFs in (4.9) and (4.10).[31] It is straightforward to show consistency of these estimators, and Haile and Tamer (2003) suggest smooth approximations of the min and max functions in (4.9) and (4.10) to reduce finite sample bias – an approach that may be useful for other partially identified models based on multiple inequalities. They also demonstrate that the bootstrap can be used for inference.

The discussion above can be repeated conditioning on any vector of auction characteristics. Haile and Tamer (2003) condition on auction-specific covariates $\mathbf{Z}$, obtained from pre-sale assessments published by the Forest Service, using standard kernel smoothing methods. This leads to bounds on the conditional distribution function $F_U(u; \mathbf{z})$ for all $(u, \mathbf{z})$. They obtain fairly precise bounds on the effects of auction covariates on valuations and on the distribution of the idiosyncratic components of bidders' private values. Figure 1.1 shows the estimated bounds and 95 percent confidence bands for $F_U(\cdot; \mathbf{z})$ at the mean value of $\mathbf{Z}$.

Using bounds on $F_U(\cdot)$ to explore alternative reserve prices is straightforward. Assumptions HT1 and HT2 are sufficient to ensure that an ascending auction is revenue equivalent (Myerson (1981)) to a standard auction with the same reserve price. Since revenues are monotonic in $F_U(\cdot)$, one can simulate

---

[31] A variation on this estimation approach is applicable when one assumes the full structure of the button auction model. See Haile and Tamer (2002, 2003) or Athey and Haile (2006).

auction revenues using a standard (e.g., second-price sealed-bid) auction and valuations drawn from the bounds $F_U^-(\cdot)$ and $F_U^+(\cdot)$.

A more subtle problem is placing bounds on the profit-maximizing reserve price, defined by the equation[32]

$$r^* = c_0 + \frac{1 - F_U(r^*)}{f_U(r^*)} \tag{4.11}$$

where c_0 is the seller's valuation (or marginal cost) of the good. Since nondegenerate bounds on $F_U(\cdot)$ place no restriction on its derivative $f_U(\cdot)$ at any given point, it is not obvious how to proceed. Note, however, that r^* is also the solution to the (seemingly unrelated) problem

$$\max_r \pi(r)$$

where

$$\pi(r) = (r - c_0)(1 - F_U(r)).$$

Since $F_U(r)$ must lie between $F^-(r)$ and $F^+(r)$, $\pi(r)$ must lie between

$$\pi_1(r) = (r - c_0)\left(1 - F_U^+(r)\right) \quad \text{and} \quad \pi_2(r) = (r - c_0)\left(1 - F_U^-(r)\right).$$

Under the additional assumption that $\pi(r)$ is strictly quasi-concave in r (ensuring a unique solution to (4.11)), the functions $\pi_1(\cdot)$ and $\pi_2(\cdot)$ bounding $\pi(\cdot)$ can be used to place bounds on r^*. The idea is easily seen in Figure 1.2. Since $\pi(\cdot)$ must lie between $\pi_1(\cdot)$ and $\pi_2(\cdot)$, it must reach a peak of at least π_1^*. Such a peak cannot be reached outside the interval $[r^-, r^+]$, although prices arbitrarily close to either of these endpoints could be the true optimum r^*. Haile and Tamer (2003) provide a formal argument and propose consistent estimators of the resulting bounds on r^*.

Haile and Tamer (2003) apply this approach to USFS timber auctions, using a range of values for c_0 based on USFS estimates. While the estimated bounds on the optimal reserve price are quite wide, they are tight enough to determine that the actual reserve prices used by the Forest Service are likely well below the optimal levels. The important question, however, concerns not the difference between actual and optimal reserve prices, but the differences in revenues and probability of a sale under alternative policies. Their results indicate that, except when the actual reserve price is below c_0, the revenue gains from raising the reserve prices would actually be quite small. This suggests that getting the reserve price "right" may be relatively unimportant in these auctions, at least as long as it meets the minimal requirement of exceeding the opportunity cost c_0.

---

[32] See, e.g., Riley and Samuelson (1981) for a derivation. Haile and Tamer (2003) show that r^* remains optimal in their incomplete model if Assumptions 1 and 2 are interpreted as a partial characterization of equilibrium behavior in the true but unspecified auction mechanism.

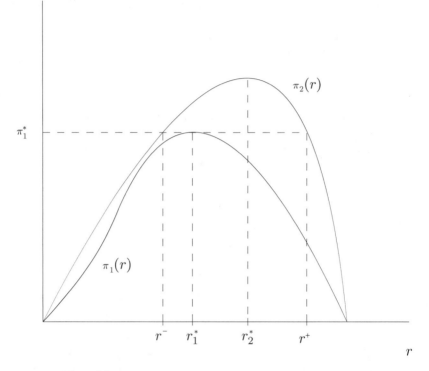

Figure 1.2.

4.4   Comparing Auction Formats: Entry, Revenue, and Competitiveness

The relative performance of ascending and first-price auctions is a central question in auction design. The Revenue Equivalence Theorem (Vickrey (1961)) implies that if bidders are risk-neutral, have independent and identically distributed values, and bid competitively, the two auction formats yield the same winner, the same expected revenue, and even the same bidder participation. However, if these assumptions are relaxed, auction choice becomes relevant, and the relative performance of alternative mechanisms depends both on details of the market and the objective (e.g., revenues or efficiency).

Athey, Levin, and Seira (2004) (ALS) study the impact of auction format using data from U.S. Forest Service timber program, which has historically used both ascending and sealed-bid auctions, sometimes randomizing. ALS maintain the independent private values assumption, but focus on two potentially important departures from Vickrey's assumptions: bidder asymmetry and collusion. Motivated by institutional features of the timber industry, ALS distinguish between two types of bidders, "mills" (firms with manufacturing capability) and "loggers." They highlight differences in participation patterns across auction formats that arise in the presence of bidder asymmetry, and they further explore the common hypothesis that collusion may be more likely in ascending auctions.

ALS analyze two distinct regions of the Forest Service during the 1980s. Auction format was determined in different ways in the two regions; however, in each region, ALS argue that conditional on the observable features of the tracts, auction format should be uncorrelated with unobserved sale characteristics. In the Northern region (comprised of Idaho and Montana) during the period of study, the selection of auction format was explicitly randomized for a subset of the tracts in the sample, where assignment to the randomization pool was based on observable characteristics in most cases. In California, the volume of the sale was the primary determinant of auction format. ALS compare outcomes across auction format in each region separately, and they control flexibly for the factors that influence the selection of auction format in the empirical analysis.

For the Northern region, ALS establish that controlling for auction characteristics, relative to ascending auctions, sealed bid auctions have the following features: (1) 10% more logger participants, (2) .4% more mill participants, (3) the fraction of sales won by loggers is 3.4% higher, and (4) 14% higher revenue.[33] The findings in California are similar, with the notable exception that revenue is almost identical in the first-price and ascending auctions. The large revenue difference in the Northern region is somewhat surprising, and it raises the question of whether a competitive model of equilibrium bidding can rationalize the gap.

ALS develop a model with several key features to reflect these facts. First, mills and loggers draw their valuations from different distributions (asymmetric independent private values). Second, a firm must choose whether to pay a cost to learn its valuation for each tract to be auctioned. Bidders make this decision based on expected profits, which differ by bidder type and auction format. Third, two models of conduct are considered: a baseline model in which bidders behave competitively, and a collusive alternative.

The timeline of the model is as follows. First, the auctioneer announces the auction format. Next, each firm i chooses whether to pay cost K to learn its valuation. Firms cannot bid unless they pay this cost. Third, bidder i draws private value U_i, where if i is a logger, $U_i \sim F_{U_L}(\cdot)$, and otherwise $U_i \sim F_{U_M}(\cdot)$. Fourth, participating bidders learn who else has made the information acquisition investment before bidding. Fifth, each bidder who acquired the information chooses a bid. For the purposes of the theory, ALS assume that $F_{U_M}(\cdot)$ dominates $F_{U_L}(\cdot)$ according to a conditional stochastic dominance order; this assumption is confirmed (not imposed) in the structural estimation.

Now consider the information acquisition equilibrium in this model, which may be in mixed or pure strategies. As in standard entry models in industrial organization, there will typically be multiple equilibria in the information

---

[33] In first-price auctions, the Forest Service records the identities of all bidders in each auction. In ascending auctions, all bidders who wish to participate must register in advance and place a deposit, and the Forest Service also records the identities of these bidders.

acquisition stage. To narrow the range of possibilities, ALS assume that all bidders of the same "type" (that is, mills or loggers) use the same entry strategies. They refer to such equilibria as *type-symmetric*. ALS provide a sufficient condition under which there is a unique type-symmetric equilibrium, and in this equilibrium either loggers never enter or mills enter with probability one. They verify that this condition is satisfied given the parameter values consistent with their bidding data. For simplicity, we assume for the rest of this discussion that the condition holds, and that parameters are such that loggers enter with positive probability (so that mills must enter with probability one).

Relative to ascending auctions, first-price auctions lead to inefficient allocations at the bidding stage. As established by Maskin and Riley (2000), when the set of participants is fixed, "strong" bidders (mills) bid less aggressively because when loggers and mills bid against one another, the competition for any logger is tougher than that for any mill. Anticipating this, in first-price auctions (relative to ascending auctions), (i) mill entry is the same, but the winning bidder is less likely to be a mill, while (ii) loggers enter (weakly) more often and the winning bidder is more likely to be a logger. In addition, (iii) the ascending auction equilibrium is socially efficient (subject to the type-symmetry constraint), while first-price auctions yield inefficient entry and bidding. Finally, the model does not generate unambiguous predictions about revenue. Since both participation and bidding vary with the auction format, a revenue comparison depends on all the primitives of the model (value distributions and entry costs). A goal of ALS is to estimate these primitives in order to assess the revenue gain (if any) from sealed bidding, as well as the efficiency distortion that sealed bidding induces in both entry and bidding.

Turning to the empirical work, ALS show that conditional on observable characteristics of an auction, bids are positively correlated within a first-price auction. To account for this correlation, ALS select a model of independent private values with unobserved heterogeneity. As described above, this model is not identified in data from ascending auctions; thus, ALS focus their structural estimation on first-price auctions and use their estimates of the underlying parameters of the model (value distributions and information acquisition costs K) to make out-of-sample predictions about outcomes at ascending auctions, predictions that can be compared to actual outcomes.[34]

---

[34] In addition to the issue of non-identification of the ascending auction model, there is another advantage to the approach of first estimating primitives from data on first-price auctions and then using these primitives to predict ascending auction outcomes. The empirical anomaly ALS wish to explain is that revenue is "too high" in the first-price auction relative to the ascending auction in the Northern region. By avoiding the use of a conduct assumption in ascending auctions for the estimation, it is possible to consider several alternative conduct assumptions for open auctions, including a model of collusion. In contrast, the conduct assumption of competition is imposed in the first-price auction. A competitive model of first-price auctions leads to implied valuations that are lower than with a collusive model, since in a collusive model there is a large gap between bids and valuations. In turn, it will generate a lower out-of-sample prediction about revenue in ascending auctions. This gives the best chance for the competitive model to rationalize the revenue gap.

Due to limitations in sample size, ALS use a parametric model to fit the bid distributions, where the bids are drawn from a Weibull distribution with Gamma-distributed heterogeneity. In this model, the hazard rate of the bid distributions is a multiplicative function of the unobserved heterogeneity. This allows the implied difference between equilibrium bids and values to vary across auctions.[35] Once the bid distributions have been estimated, they follow the approaches of Guerre, Perrigne, and Vuong (2000) and Krasnokutskaya (2004) to construct the value distributions implied by the estimated bid distributions. No parametric assumptions are imposed in this second step.

Now consider the identification of information acquisition (entry) costs.[36] Let $\tilde{\mathcal{N}}$ be a random set whose realization is $\mathcal{N}$, the set of participants. In any entry model that generates variation in $\tilde{\mathcal{N}}$ that is independent of valuations, our basic identification results for first-price auctions imply that a bidder's ex ante gross expected profit $\Pi_i(\mathcal{N})$ from entering the auction is identified. In particular,

$$\Pi_i(\mathcal{N}) = E_{U_i} \left[\left(U_i - \beta_i(U_i; \mathcal{N}) \right) \ G_{M_i | B_i} \left(\beta_i(U_i; \mathcal{N}) \mid \beta_i(U_i; \mathcal{N}); \mathcal{N} \right) \right]$$

with the right-hand side determined by the observed bid distribution and the first-order conditions for equilibrium bidding. Identification of $\Pi_i(\mathcal{N})$ requires no assumptions about the nature of the signal acquisition equilibrium (or equilibrium selection). Estimates of $\Pi_i(\mathcal{N})$ can then be used to calculate all equilibria of an entry game for given entry costs.

ALS also observe that for any firms that are indifferent about acquiring a signal (as in a mixed strategy equilibrium), the expected profit from entry must be zero. Thus, entry costs are identified by $\Pi_i(\mathcal{N})$ and the distribution of $\tilde{\mathcal{N}}$, which is directly observable. In particular, for any firm i that is indifferent about acquiring a signal, entry costs must be equal to

$$K = \bar{\Pi}_i = \sum_{\mathcal{N}: i \in \mathcal{N}} \Pr(\tilde{\mathcal{N}} = \mathcal{N} \mid i \in \tilde{\mathcal{N}}) \, \Pi_i(\mathcal{N}).$$

Thus, in contrast to much of the empirical industrial organization literature on entry,[37] which draws inferences solely from entry decisions, the level of entry costs can be inferred. Hence it is possible to conduct counterfactual simulations about changes in these costs on the competitiveness of markets and bidder rents.

With estimates of the value distributions and of K (both of which are allowed to vary with auction covariates $\mathbf{Z}$), it is possible to predict outcomes in an

---

[35] ALS assess the good fit of this model using a conditional Kolmogorov test due to Andrews (1997), showing that they cannot reject the Gamma-Weibull model against nonparametric alternatives.

[36] Li (2003) considers parametric estimation of value distributions in a symmetric entry model. Hendricks, Pinkse and Porter (2003) have also considered a variation on this model in a common values setting in which bidders choose whether to invest in a signal based on noisier preliminary estimates of their valuations. These papers do not provide an analysis of identification and estimation of entry costs.

[37] See, e.g., Bresnahan and Reiss (1987) or Berry (1992).

ascending auction. In particular, for each ascending auction tract, ALS calculate the information acquisition equilibrium (which generates a distribution over information acquisition behavior) and the expected revenue from the ascending auction. They then compare the actual outcomes in the ascending auction to those predicted by the model.

For California sales, ALS find that the competitive model can rationalize the bidding data: They cannot reject the hypothesis that the bids in ascending auctions are equal to those predicted using the primitives estimated from the first-price auction data. This is a striking finding, since the predictions are out-of-sample in two ways: First, the predictions are for tracts that were not used in the original estimation, and second, the predictions are for a different game. The actual revenue per unit of volume is \$119, while the structural model predicts \$115 with a standard error of \$9.

For Northern sales, the structural model predicts that if behavior in ascending auctions is competitive, sealed-bid auctions raise 8.4% more per unit of volume than ascending auctions. In contrast, the actual difference is 12%.[38] ALS can reject the hypothesis that the competitive model fits the ascending auction data. Thus motivated, they turn to consider an alternative, namely that ascending auctions are less competitive.[39] Bidder collusion has been a long-standing concern in timber auctions; the prevailing view is that ascending auctions are more prone to collusion because bidders are face-to-face and can respond immediately to opponents' behavior.[40] ALS extend the theory to allow for collusion by mills at ascending auctions. For simplicity, ALS consider a model where in ascending auctions, mills collude perfectly in bidding after independently gathering information. A convenient feature of this model of collusion is that it does not affect predictions about entry and allocation; the only effect of collusion on outcomes is to increase the predicted revenue difference between auction formats.

ALS find that this model of collusion can easily depress ascending auction prices below the observed levels. The actual ascending auction data can

---

[38] This is the gap without adjusting for covariates; the model includes the effect of covariates for the ascending auctions when it makes predictions.

[39] ALS argue that several factors that seem plausible in the context of timber auctions, but are omitted from their model, such as common values and bidder risk-aversion, are not good candidates to rationalize the findings.

[40] There is a small but growing empirical literature on collusion at auctions. A variety of approaches have been suggested to assess whether bidding data are consistent with models of competition or collusion. Examples include Porter and Zona (1993), Porter and Zona (1999), Bajari and Ye (2003), Pesendorfer (2000); see Bajari and Summers (2002) for a survey. Baldwin, Marshall, and Richard (1997) also analyze collusion in U.S. Forest Service timber auctions using data from open auctions; they argue that collusion provides a better fit than competition. Some of these approaches require prior knowledge about the existence and structure of a cartel, while others interpret departures from symmetric bidding behavior as evidence of collusion. The method of ALS differs in that they use behavior under one set of auction rules as a benchmark from which to evaluate the competitiveness of behavior under an alternative set of rules.

be rationalized with a model where mills collude in 25% of the ascending auctions.

Turning to the welfare differences between ascending and first-price auctions, ALS find that for a fixed set of participants (that is, ignoring the predicted differences in participation between ascending and first-price auctions), the calibrated model predicts relatively small discrepancies between sealed-bid auctions and competitive ascending auctions. Sealed-bid auctions raise more revenue and distort the allocation away from efficiency and in favor of loggers, but the effects are small (less than 1%). The differences are larger when accounting for equilibrium entry behavior: ALS predict that sealed bidding increases revenue by roughly 5% relative to a competitive ascending auction, at minimal cost to social surplus. Strikingly, even a mild degree of collusion by the mills at ascending auctions – the behavioral assumption most consistent with the observed outcomes in the Northern forests – results in much larger revenue differences (on the order of 20%). This suggests that susceptibility to collusion is an important consideration in the choice of auction format.

4.5   Dynamics in Procurement Auctions

Virtually all of the structural empirical literature has examined models of auctions as isolated games – one-time interactions between the bidders. This is obviously false in most applications. Moreover, significant intertemporal considerations seem likely to arise in many auction markets where the distribution of valuations changes as a function of observable auction outcomes.[41] One way this could arise is through learning-by-doing, where the winning firm expects to have higher valuations or lower costs in the future. In other settings, capacity constraints or diseconomies of scale may be important, causing a winning bidder to expect to have a lower valuation (or higher cost) in the future. In both cases, rational bidders will consider the effect of winning an auction on their continuation values when choosing participation and bidding strategies.

Jofre-Bonet and Pesendorfer (2003) consider this type of dynamic model in what, to our knowledge, is the first structural model of dynamic auctions with long-lived bidders and valuations that change as a function of auction outcomes. Despite the complexity of the dynamic problem, Jofre-Bonet and Pesendorfer (2003) establish that if the firms' discount factors are known to the econometrician, the distributions of bidder valuations are identified under very general conditions. The authors cleverly show how to combine the insights of Guerre, Perrigne, and Vuong (2000), outlined in Section 3.2 above, with those developed by Hotz and Miller (1993) for single-agent dynamic discrete choice models.

---

[41] There are other potentially interesting sources of dynamics. Even in a stationary environment, dynamic considerations arise if firms engage in collusion. In addition, bidders' valuation distributions may change over time in a way that is private information to each bidder. This can create dynamic links in bidder strategies.

A simplified version[42] of Jofre-Bonet and Pesendorfer (2003)'s model can be described as follows. Firms participate in a series of auctions taking place over an infinite horizon. They discount the future at rate δ, assumed to be known to the econometrician. In each period t, an item is sold by first-price auction to one of n bidders. For simplicity we ignore reserve prices and assume that all objects to be auctioned have the same observable characteristics. Capacities directly affect the distribution of bidder valuations. Conditional on capacities, bidder valuations are independent across bidders and over time. Let $c_{i,t}$ be bidder i's publicly observable capacity in period t, and let $F_U(\cdot|c_{i,t})$ be the conditional distribution of bidder i's valuation in period t.

The transition function for bidder capacities can be described as follows. Let k be the identity of the winning bidder in period t and let $\mathbf{c}_t$ be the vector of bidder capacities in period t. Then

$$c_{i,t+1} = \omega_i(\mathbf{c}_t, k).$$

The authors focus on Markov-perfect equilibrium with the vector of all bidders' capacities as the state variable. Bidders' equilibrium strategies depart from those in a static equilibrium because bidders anticipate that the identity of today's winner will affect future valuations of all bidders through changes in capacities. Hence, the distribution of outcomes in future auctions is affected by today's outcome too. Since bidders are symmetric except for differences induced by different capacities, Jofre-Bonet and Pesendorfer (2003) consider exchangeable strategies, which can be written $\beta(u_{i,t}, \mathbf{c}_t)$.[43]

The formal analysis begins by using dynamic programming to represent bidder payoffs. Suppress $\mathcal{N}$ in the notation. For a given vector of bidder capacities $\mathbf{c}$, let $G_{M_i}(\cdot|\mathbf{c})$ be the equilibrium distribution of the maximum opponent bid for bidder i. Let $\omega(\mathbf{c}, k) = (\omega_1(\mathbf{c}, k), \dots, \omega_n(\mathbf{c}, k))$. When opponent strategies are held fixed, the interim expected discounted sum of future profits for bidder i is given by

$$W_i(u_i, \mathbf{c}) = \max_{b_i} \left\{ (u_i - b_i)G_{M_i}(b_i|\mathbf{c}) + \delta \sum_{j=1}^{n} \Pr(j \text{ wins} \mid b_i, \mathbf{c}) \right.$$
$$\left. \times \int_{u_i'} W_i(u_i', \omega(\mathbf{c}, j)) \, f_{U_i}(u_i' \mid \omega_i(\mathbf{c}, j)) \, du_i' \right\}$$

where, given current capacities, the second term sums over the possible identities of the winner to form an expectation of the continuation value to player i.

---

[42] Their paper studies procurement auctions. In order to maintain consistency with the rest of this paper, we state the problem where bidders are buyers. We also make a further simplification, studying only long-lived bidders; they also consider "fringe bidders" who bid rarely and are myopic.

[43] Jofre-Bonet and Pesendorfer (2003) show that an equilibrium exists within the parametric framework they use for estimation, and they sketch a proof for the general case. Uniqueness is an open question.

The *ex ante* value function is then written

$$V_i(\mathbf{c}) = \int W_i(u_i, \mathbf{c}) \, f_{U_i}(u_i|\mathbf{c}) du_i$$

or, substituting,

$$V_i(\mathbf{c}) = \int \left\{ \max_{b_i} \left\{ (u_i - b_i) G_{M_i}(b_i|\mathbf{c}) + \delta V_i(\omega(\mathbf{c}, i)) \right. \right.$$

$$\left. \left. + \delta \sum_{j \neq i} \Pr(j \text{ wins} | b_i, \mathbf{c}) [V_i(\omega(\mathbf{c}, j)) - V_i(\omega(\mathbf{c}, i))] \right\} \right\} f_{U_i}(u_i|\mathbf{c}) du_i.$$

The second step of the analysis entails solving for the *ex ante* value functions in terms of observables, which requires a novel extension of the two-step indirect approach proposed by Guerre, Perrigne, and Vuong (2000). We begin by stating a bidder optimization problem in a given auction, letting $\bar{b}_j(\mathbf{c})$ and $\underline{b}_j(\mathbf{c})$ denote the largest and smallest equilibrium bid for bidder j when capacities are $\mathbf{c}$, respectively. Bidder i solves:

$$\max_{b_i} \left\{ (u_i - b_i) G_{M_i}(b_i|\mathbf{c}) + \delta V_i(\omega(\mathbf{c}, i)) \right.$$

$$+ \delta \sum_{j \neq i} \left(\int_{b_i}^{\bar{b}_j(\mathbf{c})} \prod_{k \neq i, j} G_{B_k}(b_j|\mathbf{c}) g_{B_j}(b_j|\mathbf{c}) db_j \right)$$

$$\left. \times [V_i(\omega(\mathbf{c}, j)) - V_i(\omega(\mathbf{c}, i))] \right\}$$

which has first-order condition

$$u_i = b_i + \frac{G_{M_i}(b_i|\mathbf{c})}{g_{M_i}(b_i|\mathbf{c})} + \delta \sum_{j \neq i} \frac{G_{M_i}(b_i|\mathbf{c})}{g_{M_i}(b_i|\mathbf{c})} \frac{g_{B_j}(b_i|\mathbf{c})}{G_{B_j}(b_i|\mathbf{c})} (V_i(\omega(\mathbf{c}, j))$$

$$- V_i(\omega(\mathbf{c}, i))). \tag{4.12}$$

If the inverse bidding strategy in (4.12) is substituted into the *ex ante* value function, a change of variables yields

$$V_i(\mathbf{c}) = \int_{\underline{b}_i(\mathbf{c})}^{\bar{b}_i(\mathbf{c})} \frac{G_{M_i}(b_i|\mathbf{c})}{g_{M_i}(b_i|\mathbf{c})} G_{M_i}(b_i|\mathbf{c}) dG_{B_i}(b_i|\mathbf{c})$$

$$+ \delta \sum_{j \neq i} V_i(\omega(\mathbf{c}, j)) \left\{ \int_{b_i}^{\bar{b}_j(\mathbf{c})} \prod_{k \neq i, j} G_{B_k}(b_j|\mathbf{c}) g_{B_j}(b_j|\mathbf{c}) db_j \right.$$

$$\left. + \int_{\underline{b}_i(\mathbf{c})}^{\bar{b}_i(\mathbf{c})} \frac{G_{M_i}(b_i|\mathbf{c})}{g_{M_i}(b_i|\mathbf{c})} \frac{g_{B_j}(b_i|\mathbf{c})}{G_{B_j}(b_i|\mathbf{c})} G_{M_i}(b_i|\mathbf{c}) dG_{B_i}(b_i|\mathbf{c}) \right\}.$$

This expresses each $V_i(\mathbf{c})$ as a linear function of $V_i(\cdot)$ evaluated at other capacity vectors. This linear function has coefficients that depend on the observable bid distributions, so that the equations can be solved explicitly and value functions can be expressed as functions of observables.

Given *ex ante* value functions, the first-order condition (4.12) can be used to establish identification of the distributions $F_U(\cdot|\mathbf{c})$. Since we have assumed that the discount factor δ is known, $F_{U_i}(\cdot|\mathbf{c})$ is identified from the distributions of observed bids (conditional on capacities).

The application of these techniques in Jofre-Bonet and Pesendorfer (2003) considers California highway construction contracts. They use a parametric estimation approach for parsimony, since there are a number of covariates to be included. They solve for the value functions by making discrete the set of possible capacities. Then, calculating the value functions entails solving a system of linear equations. They use a quadratic approximation to the value function in order to further simplify the estimation.

Jofre-Bonet and Pesendorfer (2003) assess the importance of private information, capacity constraints, and the inefficiencies that arise due to the asymmetries induced by capacity differences among bidders under the assumption of forward-looking equilibrium behavior. As usual, it is impossible to *test* whether bidders are forward-looking when the discount factor δ is assumed known. However, their results suggest that there is significant asymmetry in bidding behavior introduced by variation in capacities over time. Bidders with greater excess capacity, and thus higher valuations on average, bid less aggressively. Asymmetric bidding leads to inefficient allocations, since the highest-valuation bidder may not win the auction. In addition, their estimates imply that the average markup (that is, the average gap between bid and value) is equal to 40%, half of which they attribute to bidder recognition of the option value to losing a contract. The interpretation is that bidders recognize that they may use their limited capacity by winning another contract in the future.

4.6   Mechanism Choice for Treasury Bill Auctions

Most of the empirical literature on auctions focuses on the case of single-unit auctions. Recently, however, auctions of multiple units of identical goods ("multi-unit auctions") have gained increasing attention, in part because of the role they play in important public and private activities.[44] For example, multi-unit auctions have been used in restructured electricity markets to allocate electric power generation to different plants (see, e.g., Wolfram (1998), Borenstein, Bushnell, and Wolak (2002), or Wolak (2003)). Multi-unit auctions have long been used to allocate Treasury bills in the U.S. and elsewhere. Indeed, at least since Friedman (1960), economists have debated the optimal design of Treasury bill auctions. This question is potentially relevant to the design of markets for other types of securities as well. A number of complexities arise in the multi-unit auction case, including nonlinearities in cost functions and

---

[44] See Cantillon and Pesendorfer (2003) for a recent analysis of auctions of contracts that are not perfect substitutes but may be either substitutes or complements.

incentives to exercise market power by withholding demand. Thus, even when the choice is limited to standard *discriminatory* ("pay your bid") or *uniform-price* auctions, the revenue maximizing (or cost minimizing) design is typically ambiguous, depending on the primitives of the problem.

Here, we focus on the case of treasury auctions. In these auctions, a large number of identical securities is sold in a mechanism in which each bidder i offers a downward sloping schedule of price-quantity combinations (b_{ij}, q_j), where b_{ij} is the price he is willing to pay for his q_jth unit. This is typically referred to as i's "demand curve" even though this is a strategically chosen schedule that need not correspond to the usual notion of a demand curve in economics. The discriminatory format is the most common auction form in practice, although recently the U.S. adopted uniform-price auctions after conducting an experiment to evaluate alternative formats. In the discriminatory auction, each bidder who offers more than the market clearing bid for a unit receives that unit at the price he offered. Thus, different prices are paid for different units of the same security, even for the same bidder. In a uniform-price auction, the market clearing price is paid on all units sold. In addition to U.S. Treasury bill auctions, electricity auctions are typically uniform price, and some firms have used uniform-price auctions in initial public offerings.[45]

Of course, the auction format has an important effect on bidder strategies. Bidding one's true marginal valuation for each unit is not an equilibrium in either auction. In a discriminatory auction this is obvious, since such "truthful" bidding would lead to zero surplus for any bidder. In a uniform-price auction, bidders also have an incentive to shade bids below marginal valuations, since a bidder's own bid on a marginal unit may set the price for all inframarginal units.[46] The revenue ranking of the two mechanisms depends on the true distributions of bidder valuations (Ausubel and Cramton (2002)).

A working paper by Hortaçsu (2002) proposes to explore this question empirically by estimating the underlying distributions. He does this by developing a structural model of a discriminatory auction based on the "share auction" analysis of Wilson (1979).[47] Suppose that a fixed quantity, Q, of securities is to be offered. Each bidder i observes a signal X_i (possibly multi-dimensional)

---

[45] In the finance literature, these are often referred to as "Dutch auctions," conflicting with economists' use of this term for descending price single-unit auctions.

[46] Identification and estimation in uniform-price auctions has been explored recently by Wolak (2003) and Kastl (2005).

[47] Unfortunately, the theory of multi-unit auctions is not as complete as the theory of first-price auctions and ascending auctions. Swinkels, Jackson, Simon, and Zame (2002) and Jackson and Swinkels (forthcoming) establish existence of equilibrium in mixed strategies, but existence of pure strategy Nash equilibria in monotone strategies has been established for only a limited class of models, and there are examples with multiple equilibria (e.g., Back and Zender (1993)). Thus, most existing econometric approaches to these auctions require an explicit assumption about existence of equilibrium. In some cases, empirically verifiable properties of equilibrium bid distributions will guarantee that the assumptions of the econometric model are consistent with equilibrium behavior.

that determines his marginal valuations for all possible units of the good.[48] In particular his marginal valuation for a yth unit of the good is given by $v_i(y; x_i)$ for all $y \leq Q$.

Each bidder i's strategy specifies, for each possible value of his signal x_i and each potential price b, a demand function $q_i(b) = \varphi_i(b; x_i)$ giving the quantity demanded at price b. Hence, "actions" in this model are functions, and a strategy maps the realization of a signal into a demand function. Given a set of demand functions $q_1(\cdot), ..., q_n(\cdot)$, the market clearing price p^c is set by the seller to equate supply and demand, i.e.,

$$Q = \sum_i q_i(p^c).$$

Viewed differently, the market clearing price is that at which bidder i's demand curve intersects his *residual supply curve*

$$Q_{R_i}(p) = Q - \sum_{j \neq i} q_j(p).$$

Of course, the residual supply curve is stochastic and determined by the equilibrium bidding strategies of his competitors, as well as the realizations of their signals. Let

$$G_i(b, y) = \Pr\left(y \leq Q - \sum_{j \neq i} \varphi_j(b; X_j)\right) \tag{4.13}$$

so that $G_i(b, y)$ is the probability that, given equilibrium bidding by i's opponents, the market clearing price falls below b if i himself demands quantity y at price b.

When his type is x_i, bidder i's optimal strategy solves the problem

$$\max_{q_i(\cdot)} \int_0^\infty \left(\int_0^{q_i(p^c)} \left(v_i(y, x_i) - q_i^{-1}(y)\right) dy\right) \frac{\partial G_i(p^c, q_i(p^c))}{\partial p^c} dp^c.$$

The optimal bidding strategy can then be characterized by the Euler-Lagrange necessary condition

$$v_i(\varphi(b; x_i), x_i) = b + \frac{G_i(b, \varphi(b; x_i))}{\frac{\partial}{\partial b} G_i(b, \varphi(b; x_i))}.$$

This is similar to the first-order condition (3.4) used by Guerre, Perrigne, and Vuong (2000) to establish identification of the first-price sealed-bid auction, which can also be thought of as a single-unit discriminatory auction. Because

---

[48] Thus, this is a private values model. For parametric structural approaches to common values models, see the recent studies by Février, Préget, and Visser (2002) and Armantier and Sbaï (2003). Common values models may be appropriate for many securities auctions, although this is ultimately an empirical question – one for which testing approaches have not been developed. Hortaçsu (2002) motivates his assumption of private values using institutional details of the Turkish treasury bill auctions he studies.

the demand functions $q_j(b) = \varphi_i(b; x_j)$ are observable to the econometrician, $G_i(b, y)$ is identified from equation (4.13). For a given quantity y demanded at price b by bidder i, we can then express the marginal valuation of bidder i at quantity y as

$$v_i(y, x_i) = b + \frac{G_i(b, y)}{\frac{\partial}{\partial b} G_i(b, y)}.$$

Thus, the distributions of each $v_i(y, X_i)$ are identified; in particular, if for each quantity y we define B_i^y to be a (observable) random variable $\varphi_i^{-1}(y; X_i)$, $\Pr(v_i(y, X_i) \leq \tilde{v})$

$$\Pr(v_i(y, X_i) \leq \tilde{v}) = \Pr\left(B_i^y + \frac{G_i(B_i^y, y)}{\frac{\partial}{\partial b} G_i(b, y)\big|_{b=B_i^y}} \leq \tilde{v}\right) \forall \tilde{v}.$$

The distribution of the marginal valuation functions can then be used to do counterfactual experiments and evaluate policies.

Hortaçsu (2002) describes several different approaches to estimation. He also proposes a method for placing an upper bound on the revenue that could be obtained with a uniform price auction when one knows the underlying distributions of marginal valuations. This approach circumvents the difficult problem of solving for the equilibrium of the uniform-price auction by exploiting the fact that a bidder would not submit a bid function offering more than her marginal valuation for each unit. The revenue that would be obtained if bidders bid their marginal valuations for each unit in a uniform auction can then serve as an upper bound on the equilibrium revenue. Preliminary evidence shows that in the Turkish treasury bill auctions Hortaçsu (2002) studies, this upper bound on the uniform-price auction revenue is still lower than that from the actual discriminatory auction.

A number of authors have considered variants on the model of Hortaçsu (2002) in order to account for differences between theory and practice. In many applications, the demand functions bidders submit are restricted to be step functions. Recently, Wolak (2004), McAdams (2005), and Kastl (2005) have explored empirical models explicitly accounting for this discreteness.

5 CONCLUSION

We have discussed some of the key insights behind the recent methodological advances in the econometric analysis of auction data. In addition, we presented six extensions and empirical applications illustrating the range of economic questions now being addressed using these methods. We believe that the empirical analysis of auctions will remain a fruitful area for some time to come. The popularity of online auctions has generated a wealth of new data, and it has suggested new extensions to the theory and econometric methods to account for the institutional features of that environment (e.g., Song (2003), Song (2004)). Policy debates about natural resource auctions continue to arise (e.g., oil, timber), and the subtleties of procurement auctions have led to interesting theoretical extensions of standard models and new questions that can be asked of bidding data (e.g., Athey and Levin (2001), Asker and Cantillon (2004), Bajari, Houghton, and Tadelis (2004), Asker and Cantillon (2005)). The choice of auction design for treasury bills has changed in recent years, partly in response to academic arguments, although the issue is far from settled. Recent applications of multi-unit auctions to allocate goods (e.g., radio spectrum) that may be substitutes or complements have inspired new theory, experimental work, and empirical work (e.g., Cantillon and Pesendorfer (2003)).

References

ARMANTIER, O. AND E. SBAÏ (2003): "Estimation and Comparison of Treasury Auction Formats when Bidders Are Asymmetric," Working Paper (SUNY Stony Brook).

ANDREWS, D. (1997): "A Conditional Kolmogorov Test," *Econometrica*, 65, 1097–1128.

ARNOLD, B., N. BALAKRISHNAN, AND H. NAGARAJA (1992): *A First Course in Order Statistics*, New York: Wiley & Sons.

ASKER, J. AND E. CANTILLON (2004): "Properties of Scoring Auctions," Working Paper (New York University).

—— (2005): "Optimal Procurement when both Price and Quality Matter," Working Paper (New York University).

ATHEY, S. AND P. A. HAILE (2002): "Identification of Standard Auction Models," *Econometrica*, 70, 2107–2140.

—— (2006): "Nonparametric Approaches to Auctions," in *Handbook of Econometrics*, ed. by J. J. Heckman and E. Leamer, vol. 6, Elsevier.

ATHEY, S. AND J. LEVIN (2001): "Information and Competition in U.S. Forest Service Timber Auctions," *Journal of Political Economy*, 109, 375–417.

ATHEY, S., J. LEVIN, AND E. SEIRA (2004): "Comparing Open and Sealed Bid Auctions: Theory and Evidence from Timber Auctions," Working Paper (Stanford University).

AUSUBEL, L. M. AND P. CRAMTON (2002): "Demand Reduction and Inefficiency in Multi-Unit Auctions," Working Paper 96–07 (University of Maryland).

BACK, K. AND J. F. ZENDER (1993): "Auctions of Divisible Goods: On the Rationale for the U.S. Treasury Experiment," *Review of Financial Studies*, 6, 733–764.

BAJARI, P., S. HOUGHTON, AND S. TADELIS (2004): "Bidding for Incomplete Contracts," Working Paper (Duke University).

BAJARI, P. AND G. SUMMERS (2002): "Detecting Collusion in Procurement Auctions," *Antitrust Law Journal*, 70, 143–170.

BAJARI, P. AND L. YE (2003): "Deciding Between Competition and Collusion," *Review of Economics and Statistics*, 85, 971–989.

BALDWIN, L. H. (1995): "Risk Aversion in Forest Service Timber Auctions," Working Paper (RAND Corporation).

BALDWIN, L. H., R. C. MARSHALL, AND J.-F. RICHARD (1997): "Bidder Collusion in U.S. Forest Service Timber Sales," *Journal of Political Economy*, 105, 657–699.

BERRY, S. (1992): "Estimation of a Model of Entry in the Airline Industry," *Econometrica*, 60, 889–917.

BIKHCHANDANI, S., P. A. HAILE, AND J. G. RILEY (2002): "Symmetric Separating Equilibria in English Auctions," *Games and Economic Behavior*, 38, 19–27.

BORENSTEIN, S., J. B. BUSHNELL, AND F. A. WOLAK (2002): "Measuring Market Inefficiencies in California's Restructured Wholesale Electricity Market," *American Economic Review*, 92, 1376–1405.

BRANNMAN, L., J. D. KLEIN, AND L. W. WEISS (1987): "The Price Effects of Increased Competition in Auction Markets," *Review of Economics and Statistics*, 69, 24–32.

BRESNAHAN, T. AND P. REISS (1987): "Do Entry Conditions Vary Across Markets?" *Brookings Papers on Economic Activity: Microeconomics*, 833–871.

CAMPO, S., E. GUERRE, I. M. PERRIGNE, AND Q. VUONG (2002): "Semiparametric Estimation of First-Price Auctions with Risk Averse Bidders," Working Paper (Pennsylvania State University).

CAMPO, S., I. M. PERRIGNE, AND Q. VUONG (2003): "Asymmetry in First-Price Auctions with Affiliated Private Values," *Journal of Applied Econometrics*, 18, 197–207.

CANTILLON, E. AND M. PESENDORFER (2003): "Combination Bidding in Multi-Unit Auctions," Working Paper (London School of Economics and Political Science).

CAPEN, E. C., R. V. CLAPP, AND W. M. CAMPBELL (1971): "Competitive Bidding in High-Risk Situations," *Journal of Petroleum Technology*, 23, 641–653.

FEVRIER, P., R. PREGET, AND M. VISSER (2002): "Econometrics of Share Auctions," Working Paper (CREST).

FRIEDMAN, M. (1960): *A Program for Monetary Stability*, New York: Fordham University Press.

GUERRE, E., I. M. PERRIGNE, AND Q. VUONG (2000): "Optimal Nonparametric Estimation of First-Price Auctions," *Econometrica*, 68, 525–574.

HAILE, P. A. (2001): "Auctions with Resale Markets: An Application to U.S. Forest Service Timber Sales," *American Economic Review*, 91, 399–427.

HAILE, P. A., H. HONG, AND M. SHUM (2003): "Nonparametric Tests for Common Values in First-Price Sealed-Bid Auctions," NBER Working Paper 10105.

HAILE, P. A. AND E. T. TAMER (2003): "Inference with an Incomplete Model of English Auctions," *Journal of Political Economy*, 111, 1–52.

HECKMAN, J. J. AND B. E. HONORÉ (1989): "The Identifiability of the Competing Risks Model," *Biometrika*, 76, 325–330.

——— (1990): "The Empirical Content of the Roy Model," *Econometrica*, 58, 1121–1149.

HENDRICKS, K., J. PINKSE, AND R. H. PORTER (2003): "Empirical Implications of Equilibrium Bidding in First-Price, Symmetric, Common Value Auctions," *Review of Economic Studies*, 70, 115–145.

HENDRICKS, K. AND R. H. PORTER (1988): "An Empirical Study of an Auction with Asymmetric Information," *American Economic Review*, 78, 865–883.

——— (forthcoming): "An Empirical Perspective on Auctions," in *Handbook of Industrial Organization*, ed. by M. Armstrong and R. Porter, vol. 3, Elsevier.

HORTAÇSU, A. (2002): "Mechanism Choice and Strategic Bidding in Divisible Good Auctions: An Empirical Analysis of the Turkish Treasury Auction Market," Working Paper (University of Chicago).

HOTZ, V. J. AND R. MILLER (1993): "Conditional Choice Probabilities and the Estimation of Dynamic Models," *Review of Economic Studies*, 60, 497–531.

JACKSON, M. O. AND J. M. SWINKELS (forthcoming): "Existence of Equilibria in Single and Double Private Value Auctions," *Econometrica*.

JOFRE-BONET, M. AND M. PESENDORFER (2003): "Estimation of a Dynamic Auction Game," *Econometrica*, 71, 1443–1489.

KASTL, J. (2005): "Discrete Bids and Empirical Inference in Divisible Good Auctions," Working Paper (Northwestern University).

KOTLARSKI, I. (1966): "On Some Characterization of Probability Distributions in Hilbert Spaces," *Annali di Matematica Pura ed Applicata*, 74, 129–134.

KRASNOKUTSKAYA, E. (2004): "Auction Models with Unobserved Heterogeneity: Application to the Michigan Highway Procurement Auctions," Working Paper (University of Pennsylvania).

KRISHNA, V. (2002): *Auction Theory*, San Diego: Academic Press.

LAFFONT, J.-J. (1997): "Game Theory and Empirical Economics: The Case of Auction Data," *European Economic Review*, 41, 1–35.

LAFFONT, J.-J., H. OSSARD, AND Q. VUONG (1995): "Econometrics of First-Price Auctions," *Econometrica*, 63, 953–980.

LAFFONT, J.-J. AND Q. VUONG (1996): "Structural Analysis of Auction Data," *American Economic Review, Papers and Proceedings*, 86, 414–420.

LI, T. (2003): "Econometrics of First-Price Auctions with Entry and Binding Reservation Prices," Working Paper (Indiana University).

LI, T., I. PERRIGNE, AND Q. VUONG (2000): "Conditionally Independent Private Information in OCS Wildcat Auctions," *Journal of Econometrics*, 98, 129–161.

———— (2002): "Structural Estimation of the Affiliated Private Value Auction Model," *RAND Journal of Economics*, 33, 171–193.

LI, T. AND X. ZHENG (2005): "Procurement Auctions with Entry and an Uncertain Number of Actual Bidders: Theory, Structural Inference, and an Application," Working Paper (Indiana University).

LOADER, C. (1999): *Local Regression and Likelihood*, New York: Springer.

MASKIN, E. S. AND J. G. RILEY (2000): "Asymmetric Auctions," *Review of Economic Studies*, 67, 413–438.

McADAMS, D. (2005): "Identification and Testable Restrictions in Private Value Multi-Unit Auctions," Working Paper (MIT).

McAFEE, R. P., D. C. QUAN, AND D. R. VINCENT (2002): "Minimum Acceptable Bids, with Application to Real Estate Auctions," *Journal of Industrial Economics*, 50, 391–416.

MEILIJSON, I. (1981): "Estimation of the Lifetime Distribution of the Parts from the Autopsy Statistics of the Machine," *Journal of Applied Probability*, 18, 829–838.

MILGROM, P. R. AND R. J. WEBER (1982): "A Theory of Auctions and Competitive Bidding," *Econometrica*, 50, 1089–1122.

MYERSON, R. B. (1981): "Optimal Auction Design," *Mathematics of Operations Research*, 6, 58–73.

OLLEY, G. S. AND A. PAKES (1996): "The Dynamics of Productivity in the Telecommunications Equipment Industry," *Econometrica*, 64, 1263–1297.

PAARSCH, H. J. (1992a): "Deciding between the Common and Private Value Paradigms in Empirical Models of Auctions," *Journal of Econometrics*, 51, 191–215.

———— (1992b): "Empirical Models of Auctions and an Application to British Columbian Timber Sales," *Research Report 9212* (University of Western Ontario).

———— (1997): "Deriving an Estimate of the Optimal Reserve Price: An Application to British Columbian Timber Sales," *Journal of Econometrics*, 78, 333–57.

PESENDORFER, M. (2000): "A Study of Collusion in First-Price Auctions," *Review of Economic Studies*, 67, 381–411.

PINKSE, J. AND G. TAN (2005): "The Affiliation Effect in First-Price Auctions," *Econometrica*, 73, 263–277.

PORTER, R. H. AND J. D. ZONA (1993): "Detection of Bid Rigging in Procurement Auctions," *Journal of Political Economy*, 101, 518–538.

———— (1999): "Ohio School Milk Markets: An Analysis of Bidding," *RAND Journal of Economics*, 30, 263–288.

RILEY, J. G. AND W. F. SAMUELSON (1981): "Optimal Auctions," *American Economic Review*, 71, 381–392.

SMILEY, A. K. (1979): *Competitive Bidding Under Uncertainty: The Case of Offshore Oil*, Cambridge: Ballinger.

SONG, U. (2003): "Nonparametric Estimation of an eBay Auction Model with an Unknown Number of Bidders," Working Paper (University of Wisconsin).

——— (2004): "Nonparametric Identification and Estimation of a First-Price Auction Model with an Uncertain Number of Bidders," Working Paper (University of Wisconsin).

SWINKELS, J., M. JACKSON, L. SIMON, AND W. ZAME (2002): "Equilibrium, Communication, and Endogenous Sharing Rules in Discontinuous Games of Incomplete Information," *Econometrica*, 70, 1711–1740.

THIEL, S. E. (1988): "Some Evidence on the Winner's Curse," *American Economic Review*, 78, 884–895.

U.S. FOREST SERVICE. (1995): *Timber Program Issues*, Washington, DC: U.S. Forest Service, Department of Agriculture.

VICKREY, W. (1961): "Counterspeculation, Auctions, and Competitive Sealed Tenders," *Journal of Finance*, 16, 8–37.

WILSON, R. B. (1979): "Auctions of Shares," *Quarterly Journal of Economics*, 93, 675–689.

WOLAK, F. A. (2003): "Identification and Estimation of Cost Functions Using Observed Bid Data: An Application to Electricity Markets," in *Advances in Economics and Econometrics – Theory and Applications, Eighth World Congress*, ed. by M. Dewatripont, L. P. Hansen, and S. J. Turnovsky, Cambridge: Cambridge University Press, vol. 2, 115–149, Econometric Society Monographs.

——— (2004): "Quantifying the Supply-Side Benefits from Forward Contracting in Wholesale Electricity Markets," Working Paper (Stanford University).

WOLFRAM, C. D. (1998): "Strategic Bidding in a Multi-Unit Auction, An Empirical Analysis of Bids to Supply Electricity in England and Wales," *RAND Journal of Economics*, 29, 703–725.

YIN, P.-L. (2003): "Information Dispersion and Auction Prices," Working Paper (Harvard Business School).

CHAPTER 2

Identification in Models of Oligopoly Entry[*]

Steven Berry and Elie Tamer

Abstract

In the empirical study of markets, models of entry are often used to study the nature of firms' profits and the nature of competition between firms. Most of these estimated models have been parametric. In this paper, we review and extend a number of results on the identification of models that are used in the empirical literature. We study simple versions of both static and dynamic entry models. For simple static models, we show how natural shape restrictions can be used to identify competition effects. We consider extensions to models with heterogeneous firms, mixed-strategy equilibria and private information and provide insights that can be used in these settings to conduct inference. In the case of dynamic models, we review existing results on the model with i.i.d. linear errors, and then consider more realistic cases, such as when the distribution of fixed costs is unknown.

1 INTRODUCTION

In the empirical study of markets, models of entry are often used to study the nature of firms' profits and the nature of competition between firms. The idea of these models is that firms enter into a market only when they expect to operate profitably; therefore, entry decisions can be used as an indicator of a latent profit function.

The study of entry into oligopoly markets is complicated by strategic interactions between firms. This means that traditional ideas in the econometric literature on discrete choice models have to be modified somewhat to account for these strategic interactions.

Most of the empirical literature on entry models has focused on ideas for estimating models under various assumptions. This literature has typically relied on strong parametric assumptions and no formal approach to identification has

[*] Prepared for the World Congress Meeting of the Econometric Society, August 2005. We thank seminar participants at UT-Austin, Federal Reserve Board of Governors, CEPR-ESSET and ESWC 2005 conference, A. Nevo, and especially W. Newey for comments. Support from the Sloan Foundation (Tamer) and the National Science Foundation is gratefully acknowledged.

been well examined. In this paper, we review and extend a number of results on the formal identification of models that are used in the empirical literature, giving insights about the problem and new avenues to explore.

These identification results and ideas are interesting because they provide intuition on the role of various qualitative assumptions and of different sources of variation in the data, especially when estimating parametric models.

1.1   Why Study Entry Models?

There are a number of important economic problems that one can hope to solve by considering models of oligopoly entry.

These economic problems might include:

1. The prediction of equilibrium market structure under alternative hypothetical scenarios,
2. Determining the sources of firm profitability,
3. Identifying the "nature of competition."

The first two problems can sometimes be answered easily from the data, but the "nature of competition" is more subtle. Researchers have been interested in questions such as "How fast do profits decline in the number of firms?" and "To what degree do high and low quality firms compete?" Also, the problem of predicting equilibrium market structure can also be reasonably complicated. Predictions within the range of the observable data can often be made without inferring any "structural" parameters, but sometimes we want predictions about, for example, the effect of changes in the number of potential entrants (as might come about as a result of changes in regulatory structure). These latter predictions often require us to first uncover structural parameters.

1.2   Identification Ideas in Entry Models

We study identification of a set of entry models. These are typically binary (enter or not[1]) choice models with multiple decision makers and strategic interaction.

The identification strategy we follow is the following. We consider the economic model of entry based on the fact that a firm enters a market when entry is profitable. Heuristically, given a profit function containing both variable and fixed profits, one can obtain information on the choice probabilities predicted by the model. Hence, the identification question clarifies what can and cannot be learned about the parameters of the profits functions under a set of maintained assumptions, some plausible and others not. This is done by comparing the predicted choice probabilities under the maintained assumptions to the observed choice probabilities (the data).

---

[1] Even though the results will be tailored for the entry case, the insights carry over to models where the discrete outcome has larger support.

Naturally, using fewer assumptions (functional forms or stochastic restrictions) helps to ensure credibility and robustness of results. However, using fewer assumptions also puts strain on identification, whereby the econometric model becomes ineffectual, in that data are not helpful in distinguishing between different models (the mapping from parameters to data distribution is not one-to-one). So, one needs to delicately balance this tension between model assumptions and identification. Generally two approaches can be followed. The first is the top down approach where one starts with a complete parametric econometric model and then tries to study its robustness to the various assumptions made. Heuristically, this can be done by studying the sensitivity of the results to "peeling off" some of the parametric assumptions. The second is the bottom up approach where the analyst starts with the weakest assumptions (like monotonicity for example) and gradually moves "up" by adding restrictions. At every step, one examines the prediction of the model or set of models and sees how these change with the addition of further assumptions. This approach generally relies on starting with the necessary conditions that an economic model imply and seeing what restrictions these conditions impose (if any). In both approaches, one needs to clearly define the object of interest (a parameter of economic interest).

1.3   Outline of the Paper

We begin with a discussion of "static" entry models. These are models of equilibrium market structure where firms make a one-time decision to be in or out of the market. First, we review existing identification results for threshold-crossing models. We do this in the context of a simple "monopoly entry" model. We then turn to the the classic "Bresnahan and Reiss" (or BR) ordered-entry model, which has much in common with traditional threshold-crossing models. We use the threshold-crossing model results to show that identification of the parameter of interest (the "extent of competition" for example) depends critically on the underlying assumptions and is sometimes not identified at all.

One extension to the Bresnahan and Reiss models is to allow for firm heterogeneity. This makes the econometric model look more like models used in the multi-variate discrete choice literature, but the strategic interactions now prove to be a complicating problem. One problem is the possibility of multiple equilibria and mixed strategies. This complicates the identification problem and in many cases would lead us to consider inference in models that do not point identify the parameter of interest. We also discuss models with incomplete information and highlight the inferential problem and the role different assumptions play.

In the last part of the paper, we consider simple dynamic entry models with i.i.d. errors. We first review the existing identification results, which typically requires one to know the true distribution of fixed costs, and then suggest some alternative approaches that provide identification under different assumptions. These alternative approaches help to illustrate the role of different sources of variation in the data.

2   IDENTIFICATION IN STATIC ENTRY MODELS WITH COMPLETE INFORMATION

In this section, we study identification and inference strategies in static entry models of complete information. As a review, we begin with existing results for the "monopoly entry" (or more generally, "threshold-crossing") model. We then move on to the more interesting oligopoly set-up of the Bresnahan and Reiss model and then consider models with firm heterogeneity. We emphasize the role multiple equilibria play in these models and strategies to examine the practical implication of multiple equilibria on the parameters of interest. We also examine the impact of allowing for mixed strategies.

2.1   The Monopoly Entry, or Threshold-Crossing, Model

It is useful to review some existing results in discrete choice identification by considering the simple monopoly entry model, which takes the exact form of the traditional econometric threshold-crossing model. There are no new results in the section, just a review, using the language of entry models, of older results on the threshold-crossing model.

Consider a cross-section of markets, with one potential entrant in each market. Profits in market i are given by

$$\pi(x_i, F_i) = v(x_i) - F_i, \tag{2.1}$$

where v gives the deterministic part of profits, as a function of observable profit-shifters x, and F is the random component of profits, assumed to enter linearly. In many specific entry applications, we will think of v as "variable profits" and F as "fixed costs," although this strict interpretation may not be appropriate in some contexts.

The firm enters whenever $F_i \leq v(x_i)$. For purposes of identification, we treat the entry probabilities, $p(x)$, as being observed without error. The unknown objects of interest are the function $v(x)$ and the distribution of fixed costs, $\Phi(.)$, where we assume in the simplest case, that F is independent of x. We also consider the generalization to a limited dependence of F on x. For example, one traditional assumption (Manski (1988)) is to require that F is median independent of x and to treat the unknowns as the function v (which is typically known up to a finite dimensional parameter) and sometimes the (conditional) distribution of F. This allows, for example, for heteroskedasticity of unknown form (assumptions on other quantiles of the distribution of F can be handled in the same way).

We begin our analysis with the case where F is independent of x. The first classic problem is suggested by the threshold-crossing condition, $F < v(x)$. It is clear that a monotonic transformation of both sides of this equation will not change any entry probability. Thus, without further restrictions, the distribution of F and the function v are identified, at best, only up to a monotonic transformation.

For example, one can perfectly explain the data via a model where $v(x)$ is set equal to $p(x)$ and the distribution of F is uniform on $[0, 1]$. In this case, the entry probability is the probability of the threshold crossing condition $F \leq p(x)$, which is exactly $p(x)$, as required. Thus, with the assumption that F is independent of x, we learn that $v(x)$ is some monotonic transformation of $p(x)$, but we learn nothing more.

Now, knowing $v(x)$ up to a monotonic transformation is still useful. Simply from the data $p(x)$ we can answer some questions about predicted "market structure": i.e., we know the probability that a market is served by a firm. Also, knowing that $p(x)$ is a monotonic transformation of v, we learn the sign of $\partial v / \partial x$ and thereby can answer questions about the "sources of profitability." We can also note that for two different elements of x, say x^1 and x^2, the relative derivatives,

$$\frac{\partial v / \partial x^2}{\partial v / \partial x^1} = \frac{\partial p(x) / \partial x^2}{\partial p(x) / \partial x^1} \tag{2.2}$$

are also invariant with respect to monotonic transformations of v.

One way to proceed is to assume that we already know either $v(x)$ or the distribution of F. We might learn about $v(x)$ from using traditional data on prices, quantity demanded, production, and so forth. Once v is known, we learn about the distribution of F from $p(x) = \Phi(v(x))$. Alternatively, we might have prior knowledge of the true distribution of F. In practical empirical applications, auxiliary data relevant to the distribution of fixed costs seems much less common than data relevant to v. However, many authors have been willing to simply assume the distribution of $\Phi(F)$ (or that it is known up to a finite dimensional parameter), in which case it is trivial to solve for v.

Matzkin (1992) considers the case of identification of the threshold-crossing models, with i.i.d. errors (i.e., our F), under "qualitative" assumptions on the shape of the deterministic v. In particular, her theorem implies that if $v(x)$ is homogeneous of degree one in some subset of the x's, then both v and the distribution of F can be identified.

Result 1   (*Matzkin*[2]) *In the model above, if the function $v(x)$ is homogeneous of degree 1 and if there exists an x_0 such that $v_1(x_0) = 1$, then the functions $v(\cdot)$ and $\Phi(\cdot)$ are identified.*[3]

To illustrate the Matzkin argument in our context, consider the special case where v is homogeneous of degree one in exactly one variable. In particular, BR note that there are economic assumptions that generate a variable profit function that is proportional to population. In particular, assume that [i] demand

---

[2] A more precise statement of the result with all the needed assumptions and regularity conditions is given in Theorem 1 of Matzkin (1992) on page 244.

[3] Heuristically, what "identified" means here is that the functions $v(\cdot)$ and $\Phi(\cdot)$ can be recovered uniquely from $p(\cdot)$.

is proportional to population and that [ii] marginal cost is constant.[4] The first assumption implies that observed x's account for all the shifts in per-capita demand, so that we can model market demand as per-capita demand times population. The assumption on marginal cost is strong but considered to be approximately true in many markets (note that there are still economies of scale in the model, generated by the fixed costs).

Under the assumptions of the last paragraph, the first-order condition for profit maximization does not depend on population and profit in market i can be written as

$$z_i v(x_i) - F_i, \tag{2.3}$$

where v is per-capita profit and z is observed population. To set the units of profits, normalize $v(x_0) = 1$ for some arbitrary x_0. The probability of entry at z, x_0 is then

$$\begin{aligned} p(z, x_0) &= Pr(F < zv(x_0)) \tag{2.4} \\ &= Pr(F < z) \\ &= \Phi(z), \end{aligned}$$

where $p(\cdot, \cdot)$ is the observed entry probability.

If across the range of z, $p(z, x_0)$ takes on every value between zero and one, then (2.4) defines the entire function Φ. We can then trivially find $v(x)$ for other values of x and hence recover the function v on the support of x. This is a simple constructive version of Matzkin's proof, which works for a broader array of cases where the (normalized) v function is known along some ray or curve in the space of exogenous data.

Another example where Matzkin's proof applies is the partially linear model where $v(x) = x^1 + v(x^2)$. Here, v is linear in the variable x^1 and is an unknown function of the remaining variables $v(x^2)$. Some version of this partially linear model is frequently used in applied econometrics, although in the entry case under discussion, this partial linearity is harder to generate from qualitative economics assumptions such as the "proportional to population" model.

One criticism of Matzkin's approach is that it relies on the independence of F and x. Manski (1988) suggests the weaker assumption of median independence but requires that v be known up to a finite dimensional parameter ($v(x) = x\beta$ for example). Note that once we drop the full independence assumption and assume median independence (i.e., $Med(F|x) = 0$), an appropriate qualitative shape restriction (like linearity) identifies v (up to scale), given the appropriate support conditions on x. Moreover, once v is identified,[5] the (conditional) distribution of F can also be recovered using, for example, Horowitz's (1992) estimator. Recently, under the conditional quantile restriction, Khan (2004)

---

[4] The necessary assumption on demand is that market demand is equal to population times a per-capita demand function that can depend on x's other than population.

[5] One can use Manski's maximum score estimator to get v for example.

provided a method to get consistent estimates of both v and the distribution of F using sieve methods. A lot less is known about semiparametric models where F and x are allowed to be correlated. One approach is to first write down an economically coherent entry model where this correlation is generated from a well-defined optimizing framework and plausible economic restrictions (like the "proportional to population" restriction of BR) are imposed. Then at the inference stage, instead of looking for esoteric statistical assumptions that guarantee point identification, one can study the identified features of the class of models without making these typically non-plausible assumptions. The econometric structure, tightly linked to the economic model, admits consistent sets of parameters that rationalize the observed data. So appropriate inferential methods are required to handle, statistically, the possibility that the parameter of interest is a set.[6]

The monopoly model is, however, not typically of interest in the entry literature, which focuses on potential oligopolies. Questions of identification may become more subtle, and new questions start to arise about the nature of competition, the structure of information across firms and the nature of equilibrium. In these more complicated models, we might want to know further information about the shape of $v(x)$ and/or the distribution of F. We now take these results to one classic model of oligopoly entry, the Bresnahan and Reiss model.

2.2   Bresnahan and Reiss Models

We first examine the symmetric entry model of Bresnahan and Reiss (1991b),[7] in which we assume that a cross section of markets is available where in each market we observe the number of symmetric firms in the market and other market characteristics. This is the standard benchmark model of entry where all firms are similar. One object of interest in this kind of work is the shape of the variable profit function. Specifically, how do variable profits change with the number of firms in the market? This question is related to important questions about the nature of competition. But some researchers express skepticism about what exactly we can learn about the shape of variable profits from entry data alone. A more complete examination of the identification of the model might shed light on this debate.

The Bresnahan and Reiss model is a simple extension of the monopoly model with identical potential entrants. Variable profits v are assumed to decline in the number of firms, y: $v_y(x)$, where x is a vector of profit shifters.

Suppose that fixed costs, F, are *identical* across firms within a market and are distributed i.i.d. across markets with unknown distribution $\Phi(\cdot)$. If there are y_m firms in market m, then each firm operating in the market earns identical

---

[6] See Chernozhukov, Hong, and Tamer (2002) and Andrews, Berry, and Jia (2003) for some recent inference methods in these settings.

[7] See also presentations of the same model in Bresnahan and Reiss (1987), and Bresnahan and Reiss (1990).

profits of

$$\pi(y_m, x_m, F_m) = v_{y_m}(x_m) - F_m. \tag{2.5}$$

Entry is profitable for y firms when $v_y(x_m) \geq F_m$ and is profitable for no more than y firms when $v_y(x_m) < F_m$. The unique Nash equilibrium number of firms is the largest y for which entry is profitable. This implies that the probability distribution over the number of observed firms is given by:

$$\Pr(y = 0|x) = 1 - \Phi(v_1(x)) \tag{2.6}$$
$$\Pr(y = 1|x) = \Phi(v_1(x)) - \Phi(v_2(x))$$
$$\Pr(y = 2|x) = \Phi(v_2(x)) - \Phi(v_3(x)). \tag{2.7}$$

This implies that

$$\Phi(v_1(x)) = 1 - \Pr(y = 0|x) = G_1(x)$$
$$\Phi(v_2(x)) = 1 - \Pr(y = 1|x) - \Pr(y = 0|x) = G_2(x) \tag{2.8}$$
$$\Phi(v_3(x)) = 1 - \Pr(y = 3|x) - \Pr(y = 1|x) - \Pr(y = 0|x) = G_3(x).$$

The data identifies the choice probabilities, hence one can assume that the right-hand side (rhs) in (2.8), the Gs, are known. Taking the first equation in (2.8), we see that this is similar to identification in binary choice models.

BR make parametric assumptions on both $v(\cdot)$ and $\Phi(\cdot)$ and estimate the resulting model by MLE. One specific economic question that they want to ask is "What is the value of the ratio $\dfrac{v_2(x)}{v_1(x)}$?" This ratio is interesting under various benchmark models. In particular,

1. Given fixed prices, $\dfrac{v_2(x)}{v_1(x)} = 1/2$, while given

2. Cournot competition: $\dfrac{v_2(x)}{v_1(x)} \in (0, 1/2)$, and given

3. Homogeneous goods Bertrand: $\dfrac{v_2(x)}{v_1(x)} = 0.$

One can think of similar ratios for other $y > 2$. These ratios are the objects of economic interest for BR.

We can relate the BR model directly to the earlier threshold-crossing literature by converting it into a series of related threshold-crossing models. These ordered-probit style "entry probabilities" can be rewritten as follows:

$$\Pr(y \geq 1|x) = \Phi(v_1(x)) \tag{2.9}$$
$$\Pr(y \geq 2|x) = \Phi(v_2(x))$$
$$\cdots$$
$$\Pr(y \geq n|x) = \Phi(v_n(x)).$$

A very important point that follows directly from the previous section is that the ratios of variable profits that are of economic interest are not robust to monotonic transformations of v_y and F, so:

The economic parameter of interest is not non-parametrically identified in Bresnahan and Reiss models without shape restrictions.

It is easy to show that one can find a monotonic transformation that sets the relevant ratio to anything between 0 and 1. That is,

Result 2   *Let F be independent of x and $v_y(x)$ is unspecified except that it is weakly monotonic in y. Assume that we observe a random sample of i.i.d. markets. Then, the ratio $\frac{v_2(x)}{v_1(x)}$ can take any value in* [0, 1].

This seems like a negative result for the Bresnahan and Reiss model. However, the intuition for identification in BR depends very much on the use of the "proportional to population" restriction discussed in the prior subsection. By the same argument as in the prior subsection, restricting variable profits to be proportional to population **will identify** variable profits. Indeed, once we assume the $v_y(x, z) = zv_y(x)$, then for each number of firms n we can identify both v_n and Φ from the threshold condition $\Pr(y \geq n|x) = \Phi(zv_n(x))$. In particular, we have the following result:

Result 3   *Consider the symmetric game in (2.5) above. Then,*

1. *Suppose that there exists (x, x') such that $G_i(x') = G_j(x)$ for $i \neq j$, then $v_i(x') = v_j(x)$. For example, for (x, x') such that $G_1(x') = G_2(x)$ then $v_1(x') = v_2(x)$.*
2. *If $v_y(x) = zv_y(\tilde{x})$, and $x = (z, \tilde{x})$ and $x' = (z', \tilde{x})$ such that $G_2(x') = G_1(x)$, then the ratio of interest is identified:*
$$\frac{v_2(\tilde{x})}{v_1(\tilde{x})} = \frac{z}{z'}.$$
3. *If $v_y(x) = zv_y(\tilde{x})$ and $v_1(x_0) = a \equiv 1$, then*
$$\Phi(z) = G_1(z, x_0)$$
and the function $\Phi(\cdot)$ is identified on the support of z. Also, for all y,
$$v_y(\tilde{x}) = \frac{F^{-1}(G_y(z, \tilde{x}))}{z},$$
i.e., the function $v_y(\cdot)$ is identified on the support of x and z.

In part 1 of the result above, and without making any assumptions, we can match the choice probabilities (the Gs) from markets with different entrants, to recover regressor values for which the variable profits match. This matching allows one to examine how much one needs to change (or compensate) a regressor so that variable profits in a duopoly market are equal to variable profits in a monopoly market. The second part of the result above shows that the object of interest in BR is point identified in an oligopoly setting with the usual "proportional to population" assumption given variation in z and x. It is interesting to note, for example, that this ratio of interest is equal to a specific ratio of the populations.

In addition, if we normalize profits, we can recover the distribution of fixed costs and the variable per-capita profit function.

Actually, with the proportional-to-population assumption, we can even relax the model to allow for a different distribution, $\Phi_y(F)$, of fixed costs for every y. We then convert the model into a set of unrelated threshold-crossing models, one for each value of y. One economic motivation for the distribution of F to shift with the number of firms y would be the possibility of some fixed resource with an upward sloping supply curve. Indeed, BR includes a parametric shift in Φ for different y.

An even easier result is possible when there is additional data available that we can use to identify $v_y(x)$ exactly. There is a large literature in empirical industrial organization on how to use observed data on prices and quantities (and possibly product characteristics and/or direct information on inputs or costs) to identify the oligopoly and (possibly differentiated products) versions of the "supply and demand" models (see as examples Bresnahan (1989) and Berry, Levinsohn, and Pakes (1995)). In these cases, we may be able to learn about $v_y(x)$ without using the information on entry. It is then trivial to use the observed v's to back out the distribution of F from the relationship $\Pr(y \geq n|x) = \Phi(v_n(x))$. This idea is implemented in a parametric context in Reiss and Spiller (1989) and Berry and Waldfogel (1999). Also, recall from the discussion in section (2.1) that even when the "nature of competition" is not defined, other features of v that are subject to monotonic transformations will still be defined.

To summarize then, in the binary choice symmetric model of entry à la Bresnahan and Reiss, and without assumptions on the shape of the variable profit function or the distribution of fixed costs conditional on x, (point) identification is not possible. However, results from the threshold-crossing literature suggest that variable profits are point identified when one imposes shape restrictions like homogeneity. It is thus important to motivate the assumptions one uses. An example of such assumptions is the insight of BR to write the variable profit as per-capita profit multiplied by the size of the market. Or, alternatively, in some settings one has additional information on the variable portion of profits (such as a separate data set from which the form of variable profits can be ascertained) that can be used and so the problem becomes one on inference on the distribution of fixed costs.

2.3   Bivariate Game with Heterogenous Profits

We consider a richer version of the BR model by allowing firms' profits to be different, as in the work by Berry (1989), Bresnahan and Reiss (1991a), Berry (1992), and Ciliberto and Tamer (2003). In particular, consider the simple duopoly model with two firms and heterogenous fixed costs. Let the profit of firm i in market m be

$$\pi_{im}(x_{im}, y_{jm}, f_{im}) = v(y_{jm}, x_{im}) - f_{im} \tag{2.10}$$

$$= v_{0i}(x_{im}) + y_{jm}v_{1i}(x_{im}) - f_{im}, \tag{2.11}$$

where the second equality is without loss of generality since y_{jm} is a binary variable. The profit of firm j is similar. Again, we assume that a firm enters a market when it is profitable to do so, and hence firm i enters market m, $y_{im} = 1$, if and only if $\pi_{im}(x_{im}, y_{jm}, f_{im}) \geq 0$ (here non-entry profits are set to zero) and we also assume that both functions v_{1i} and v_{1j} are nonpositive. Notice that in the above, the effect of firm i on firm j's profits is different than the effect of firm j on firm i's profits. The objects of interest are the variable profits and the joint distribution of the fixed costs conditional on the regressors, $F_{f_i, f_j | x_i, x_j}$. The correlation among the unobservables is of interest since it allows one to see whether entry occurs because of unobserved profitability that is independent of the competition effect.

We assume that we have a random sample of observations on markets where every observation is an observable realization of an equilibrium game played between i and j. The sampling assumptions allows us to obtain the choice probabilities $\Pr(0, 0|x)$, $\Pr(1, 0|x)$, $\Pr(0, 1|x)$, and $\Pr(1, 1|x)$. To analyze identification, as usual, one needs to relate these quantities to their counterparts predicted by the model.

2.4   Pure Strategies

Here we study inference in the bivariate model above when we allow only pure strategy equilibria. With mixed strategies ruled out, we can focus on the $(0, 0)$ and $(1, 1)$ outcomes, the only 2 outcomes of the game that are observed only if they are pure strategy equilibria of the game.[8] The predicted choice probabilities for $(0, 0)$ and $(1, 1)$ are

$$\Pr(0, 0|x_{im}, x_{jm}) = \Pr(f_{im} \geq v_{0i}(x_{im}); f_{jm} \geq v_{0j}(x_{jm})|x_{im}, x_{jm})$$
$$\Pr(1, 1|x_{im}, x_{jm}) = \Pr(f_{im} \leq v_{0i}(x_{im}) + v_{1i}(x_{im}); f_{jm} \leq v_{0j}(x_{jm})$$
$$+ v_{1j}(x_{jm})|x_{im}, x_{jm}). \tag{2.12}$$

The strategy is to use the first equation above to identify the v_0's and the second equation to identify the v_1's (recall that the v_1 functions are assumed to be nonnegative). Without any further assumptions, the v's and F are not separately identified. One can then use sufficient conditions, mainly ones involving support conditions, to (point) identify the objects of interests. One example of sufficient conditions that involves support conditions is contained in the next result and discussed after the result.

Result 4   *Assume that the random vector (f_{im}, f_{jm}) is distributed independently of (x_{im}, x_{jm}) with a joint distribution F. Assume that only pure strategy equilibria are considered. Suppose that $v_{0i}(x_{im}) = z_{im}v_0(\tilde{x}_{im})$ and similarly*

---

[8]   What is meant here is that $(0, 0)$ and $(1, 1)$ are uniquely predicted as pure strategy equilibria by this model. If one allows for mixing, then these outcomes can show when players mix between entering and not entering. This will be examined in section 2.5 below.

for v_{0j}, $v_{0i}(x_0) = v_{0j}(x_0) = 1$ and that the $v_1(\cdot)$s are non-positive. Moreover, assume that $z_{im}|z_{jm}, x_{im}, x_{jm}$ has a distribution with support on $\mathcal{R}$ a.e. z_{jm}, x_{im}, x_{jm} and similarly for z_{jm}. Then, v_{0i}, v_{0j}, v_{1i}, v_{1j}, and F are identified.

To show the above result, and using the first equation in (2.12), we can recover the joint distribution F from the choice probabilities evaluated at the normalization point x_0. Then, again using the first equation, we can "push" z_{jm} far out so that effectively we can transform the problem into a simple threshold-crossing model with known distribution (marginal of F) and solve for v_{0i}. We can then use the second equation in (2.12) to get the v_1's. Notice that the sufficient conditions above impose exclusion restrictions: z_i with wide support is included in the payoff of firm i but not in firm j's, and vice versa for j. Notice also that we used only the two outcomes $(0, 0)$ and $(1, 1)$ to get identification (where we implicitly used the $(1, 1)$ choice probability to get the v_1 functions). These outcomes are observed if and only if they are pure strategy equilibria of the underlying game. This is a result of this being an entry model (negative v_1's) and the restriction to pure strategy equilibria.

Identification in more realistic games with a larger set of players is harder under the same conditions, especially if one maintains a rich correlation structure on the joint distribution of the unobservables (like allowing heterogeneity in the marginal distributions). Mazzeo (2002) allowed for types of firms, hence his model is a bivariate version of the BR model above. Berry (1992) introduced a more heterogenous model of entry in airline markets with potential entrants and player specific variables where the profit functions were specified up to a finite dimensional parameter. Berry showed there that the model predicts the *number* of players in a market uniquely, which allows one to reduce the identification into one similar to identification in nonlinear parametric method of moments model. Ciliberto and Tamer (2003) extended the Berry model by allowing for heterogeneity and player identities.

2.4.1   Variation in the Number of Potential Entrants

We will now consider another approach to identification in complete information entry games with heterogeneous firms: variation in the number or identity of potential entrants (from regulation or geographic variation). This idea is related to some intuition on identification found in Berry (1992).

We begin with the relatively simple case of independent draws on F and then consider the more complicated (and interesting) case of correlated fixed costs. Consider the simple case where the profits of firm i in market m, given y total firms in the market, are $v_y(x_m) - F_{im}$, which is a simplification from the earlier examples. (This form can be derived from examples with heterogeneity only in fixed costs.) We continue to assume that F is independent of x.

The basic idea is to return in part to the binary threshold identification literature by breaking the problem into two parts. First, we think of identifying certain threshold-crossing probabilities, such as the probability that a given firm would be profitable if that firm were (exogenously) made into a monopoly entrant. We will see that these probabilities can be useful for many exercises, such as predicting market share, or else considering "sources of profitability" (the relative effect of different x's on firm's profits). These can be derived under fairly weak assumptions – for example we don't need "shape" restrictions on the variable profit function. Second, if necessary for the question at hand, the threshold probabilities can be transformed into the underlying variable profit function $v_y(x)$ under the same conditions (e.g., shape restrictions) as discussed in section (2.1). Given an appropriate restriction, we can then discuss questions about the "nature of competition" as in BR.

Define, to begin, the probability that a firm would be profitable as a monopolist as

$$\mu(x) \equiv \Pr(F_{im} < v_1(x)) \tag{2.13}$$

and the probability that a firm would be profitable as a duopolist as

$$\delta(x) = \Pr(F_{im} < v_2(x)). \tag{2.14}$$

Note that these are not equilibrium probabilities but rather a simple, particular transformation of the model primitives. For example, $\delta(x)$ is the probability that a firm would be profitable if it was placed exogenously into a market with one rival firm already present.[9]

In the monopoly case of section (2.1), as in the BR case, $\mu(x)$ is just the probability of entry and so is directly observed in the data. In the case of heterogeneous firms, however, the threshold probabilities must be derived from the observed probabilities of a different market structure. The derivation is simple when the fixed costs F are independent across firms within a market, which is not a particularly interesting case but which provides a good starting point.

In the two-firm case with independent fixed cost, we have for $x = (x_1, x_2)$, the conditions

$$Pr(0, 0 \,|x) = (1 - \mu(x_1))(1 - \mu(x_2)) \tag{2.15}$$
$$Pr(1, 1 \,|x) = \delta(x_1)\delta(x_2), \tag{2.16}$$

and these equations can be used to express μ and δ as unique functions of the data probabilities. In particular, with $x_2 = x_2 \equiv x$ we have two equations in two unknowns and a unique solution for $\mu(x)$ and $\delta(x)$. This is a point-wise (in x) identification argument and, once μ and δ are identified for multiple x's, the model has testable restrictions for values of x_1 not equal to x_2.

---

[9] Note that μ and δ could be derived under somewhat weaker assumptions – for example that profits are a nonlinear (but monotonically increasing) function of the independent error F.

These probabilities are useful on their own account. For example, they can be used to solve for counterfactual predictions of market structure. If one of the potential firms goes bankrupt, what is the probability that a market will be served by the remaining firm? The answer is $\mu(x_i)$. Also, as in (2.1), we can identify the sign of the effect of a specific x on profits and we can identify the relative (but not absolute) effects of those x's.

Interestingly, the questions in Berry (1992) concern the sources of profitability, so they might have been answered without solving for the underlying v functions. However, if (as in BR), one has questions about the "nature of competition", then one needs to transform the μ's and δ's into the underlying v's using, e.g., the shape restrictions discussed in section (2.1). This approach is relatively easy to extend to more than 2 potential firms.

The advantages of solving for the threshold-crossing probabilities include:

1. Weak assumptions on underlying profit function,
2. Easy to state restrictions (polynomials),
3. The ability to make equilibrium predictions about market structure,
4. The ability to learn about "sources of profitability," and
5. The ability to learn, using stronger restrictions, about v and the distribution of F.

Disadvantages of the approach in this section include:

1. Not making use of stronger restrictions from the underlying profit model, and
2. Limited modeling of correlation (but see below).

2.4.2   Adding Market-Level Correlation

So far this subsection has not considered the realistic case of within-market correlation in the unobserved fixed costs (or, more generally, the unobserved profit shocks) of the firms. In particular, one thinks that some markets are more profitable (have lower fixed costs) than others. Say that ϵ_m is a market-level scalar random variable that shifts the distribution of fixed costs for all firms in the market.

The probability of being profitable as a monopolist is now $\mu(x, \epsilon)$ and the observed probabilities of market outcomes take forms like

$$Pr(0, 0 \,|x) = \int (1 - \mu(x_1, \epsilon))(1 - \mu(x_2, \epsilon))d\Gamma(\epsilon). \qquad (2.17)$$

Where $\Gamma(\cdot)$ is the distribution of market level unobservables, which are assumed to be independent of x. For discrete distributions of ϵ we can try to solve for the threshold-crossing probabilities $\mu(x, \epsilon)$, but one will typically need some additional variation in the data. As an example, assume that the market level shifter takes on two values, 0 and 1, with $Pr(\epsilon = 0) = \lambda$.

In the two potential entrant case, the probability of no firms is now:[10]

$$Pr(0, 0 \,|x) = \lambda(1 - \mu(x_1, 0))(1 - \mu(x_2, 0)) + \qquad (2.18)$$
$$(1 - \lambda)(1 - \mu(x_1, 1))(1 - \mu(x_2, 1)). \qquad (2.19)$$

Holding the number of potential entrants fixed, it is clear that there are not enough restrictions to uniquely get the monopoly threshold-crossing probabilities from this equation alone.

However, we get a further source of identification if there is variation in the number of potential entrants, as in Berry (1992).[11] In that paper, it was assumed (consistent with data) that the only potential entrants into an airline city-pair were those with some service out of at least one of the endpoints of the city-pair. Another example would be competition between retail chains that do not operate in all regions of the country. Or, consider a dataset that contains market outcomes before and after the entry or exit of a major rival.

To illustrate the possibilities, take even the simple case with $x = x_1 = x_2$, and let the number of potential entrants be K. With $K = 1$,

$$Pr(0 \,|x) = \lambda(1 - \mu(x, 0)) + (1 - \lambda)(1 - \mu(x, 1)),$$

whereas with $K = 2$,

$$Pr(0, 0 \,|x) = \lambda(1 - \mu(x, 0))^2 + (1 - \lambda)(1 - \mu(x, 1))^2,$$

and so forth for arbitrary K:

$$Pr(0, 0, \ldots \,|x) = \lambda(1 - \mu(x, 0))^K + (1 - \lambda)(1 - \mu(x, 1))^K.$$

Assume now that we observe market outcomes in markets with varying numbers of potential entrants, from $K = 1$ to $K = \bar{K}$. Then we have $\bar{K}$ polynomial equations in 3 unknowns: $\mu(x, 0)$, $\mu(x, 1)$ and the "correlation" term, λ. Hence the problem becomes one of finding solutions to (nonlinear) equations in 3 unknowns (that are probabilities). As $\bar{K}$ increases further, we will find multiple solutions for the unknowns only in degenerate cases and so we can likely solve uniquely for both the μ's and the discrete distribution of ϵ.

Once again, "shape restrictions" can be used to uncover variable profits, and the appropriate marginal distributions of F. In this example, we would be solving for the marginal distribution of F conditional on the appropriate value of the market-level shock ϵ. Since we also know the discrete distribution of ϵ, we also uncover the unconditional distribution of F.

---

[10] Note that the term $\mu(x, 0)$ has the interpretation of being the probability that a firm is profitable [i] as a monopolist [ii] when overall market profitability is "low."

[11] Another useful restriction comes from markets that share a value for x_1 but have a different x_2 (and vice-versa).

In this subsection, expanding on the suggestion of Berry (1992), we have sketched the possibilities of using the variation in number of entrants as a source of identification. We have also suggested an identification strategy that is different from most of the existing literature. First, we try to identify the probability that firms would be profitable if placed (exogenously) into various market structure. In the case of discrete market-level shocks, this involves a solution to a set of simple polynomial equations. Then, if necessary, these threshold probabilities can be transformed into the underlying variable profit function and fixed-cost distribution.

2.5 Multiple Equilibria and Mixed Strategies

Inference in static discrete games with complete information is complicated due to the presence of multiple equilibria and equilibria in mixed strategies. In the game of the previous section, one is able to derive a set of sufficient conditions for point identification without dealing with multiplicity. The reason for this is that the game, under pure strategies, predicts equilibria that are unique in the *number* of players (for example, identification was based on the choice probabilities of the $(0, 0)$ and $(1, 1)$, outcomes that are equivalent to no firms and two firms in the market while the third outcome is the union of $(1, 0)$ and $(0, 1)$ and represents the one firm equilibrium). Berry (1992) studied a more general class of entry games with more players in which the number of firms in a market is unique. It is worth noting that in games without mixed strategies, one need not specify (or model) any *equilibrium selection rules* since the game is transformed into one that predicts a unique feature (the number of players in the market).

Uniqueness in the number of firms across equilibria does not always hold. Ciliberto and Tamer (2003) extend the Berry setup to cover entry games with identity (or type) specific effects. For example, the effects on Americans' profits from having Southwest enter is different than if United enters. This heterogeneity in the effects leads the game to have multiple equilibria where different equilibria can differ in the number of firms, even when one is restricted to pure strategies. A simple two type example of such a game is illustrated in the appendix. Another example where uniqueness across equilibria does not hold is in games where one allows for mixed strategy equilibria. In the simple bivariate game studied in section 2.3, if we allow for mixed strategies then $(0, 0)$ is a potentially observable outcome of the mixed strategy equilibrium in which the players mix between entering a market and not since it lies on the support of the mixing distribution. Hence, when one observes $(0, 0)$, it is not clear whether this was because it is the unique pure strategy equilibrium or it was a result of the mixing. So, for some values of the unobservables, the econometric model can predict $(0, 0)$, $(1, 1)$, $(1, 0)$, and $(0, 1)$ as potential observables. Recently also, Bajari, Hong, and Ryan (2005) provide sufficient conditions based on exclusion restrictions that allow for identification in the presence of mixed strategies.

Below, we first consider a simple game that involves multiple equilibria and mixing and study its observable implication. This will illustrate in a clear way the insights needed to analyze these games and shows, in a simple example, that the data might contain informaton about selection. Then, we go back to the bivariate game of the previous section and study its empirical content in the presence of mixing and multiplicity.

Inference in a Game with Mixed Strategies and Multiple Equilibria

Consider the following simple 2×2 game

	0	1
0	0, 0	0, a
1	a, 0	a − 2, a − 2

where a is a binary random variable that takes the value of 3 with probability l and 1 with probability $1 - l$. The realization of a is not known to the econometrician but is observed by both players. This is a symmetric game with no exogenous regressors and no heterogeneity. The question that we want to ask is what is the observable implication of this game? The "data" we observe is a sample of observable outcomes each of which corresponds to a draw of the random variable a. Given a random sample assumption (say we observe an iid sample of N markets), we are able to consistently estimate the choice probabilities $P(0, 0)$, $P(0, 1)$, $P(1, 0)$, and $P(1, 1)$ as N increases. Next, we derive the choice probabilities implied by the model (i.e., as a function of the structural parameters of the model). When $a = 3$, $(1, 1)$ is the unique pure strategy equilibrium of the game (see the left-hand side (lhs) display in figure 2.1). On the other hand, when $a = 1$, the game has multiple equilibria. There are two pure strategy equilibria, $(1, 0)$ and $(0, 1)$, and one mixed strategy equilibrium $p = \frac{1}{2}$,

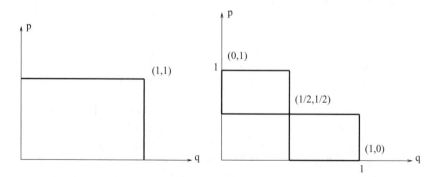

Figure 2.1. Equilibria for the case when $a = 3$ (left) and when $a = 1$ (right).

where p is the mixing probabilities for both players (see rhs of figure 2.1). Assuming only pure strategies are allowed, the choice probabilities derived by the model are

Predicted Probabilities without Mixed Strategies

$\Pr(0, 0) = 0$

$\Pr(1, 1) = \Pr(1, 1|a = 1) \Pr(a = 1) + \Pr(1, 1|a = 3) \Pr(a = 3)$

$\quad\quad\quad = \Pr(1, 1|a = 3) \Pr(a = 3) = l$

$\Pr(0, 1) = \Pr(0, 1|a = 1) \Pr(a = 1) + \Pr(0, 1|a = 3) \Pr(a = 3)$

$\quad\quad\quad = \Pr(0, 1|a = 1) \Pr(a = 1) = \Pr(0, 1|a = 1)(1 - l)$

$\Pr(1, 0) = \Pr(1, 0|a = 1) \Pr(a = 1) + \Pr(1, 0|a = 3) \Pr(a = 3)$

$\quad\quad\quad = \Pr(1, 0|a = 1) \Pr(a = 1) = \Pr(1, 0|a = 1)(1 - l).$

We have $\Pr(1, 1|a = 3) = 1$ since $(1, 1)$ is the unique equilibrium when $a = 3$ and $\Pr(1, 1|a = 1) = 0$ since when $a = 1$ and without allowing for mixed strategies, $(1, 1)$ is not a *potentially observable outcome of the game*. So the predicted choice probability by the model above for the $(1, 1)$ outcome is $\Pr(a = 3) = l$ (and hence l is point identified by looking at $(1, 1)$ markets). On the other hand, the predicted choice probability for the $(1, 0)$ outcome is $\Pr(0, 1) = \Pr(0, 1|a = 1) \Pr(a = 1) = \Pr(0, 1|a = 1)(1 - l)$ where here $\Pr(0, 1|a = 1)$ is the equilibrium selection rule. This selection rule is also identified (since l is identified from the $(1, 1)$ outcomes). So, as we can see in this simple game, the parameters of the game (l and the selection rule function $P(0, 1|a)$) are point identified.[12]

When we allow for mixed strategies, the predicted choice probabilities will change. When $a = 3$, the outcome $(1, 1)$ is the unique pure strategy equilibrium of the game and hence is the unique observable outcome. On the other hand when $a = 1$, the *potentially observable outcomes* are all 4: $(1, 0)$, $(0, 1)$, $(0, 0)$, and $(1, 1)$. In particular, $\Pr(0, 0|a = 1) \neq 0$ since $(0, 0)$ will appear as the *observable outcome* of the game if players coordinate on the mixed strategy equilibrium in which $(0, 0)$ will appear with probability $\frac{1}{4}$. So the predicted choice probabilities with mixed strategies are:

$\Pr(0, 0) = \Pr(0, 0|a = 1) \Pr(a = 1)$

$\Pr(1, 1) = \Pr(1, 1|a = 3) \Pr(a = 3) + \Pr(1, 1|a = 1) \Pr(a = 1)$

$\quad\quad\quad = l + \Pr(1, 1|a = 1) \Pr(a = 1)$

$\Pr(1, 0) = \Pr(1, 0|a = 1) \Pr(a = 1) + \Pr(1, 0|a = 3) \Pr(a = 3)$

$\quad\quad\quad = \Pr(1, 0|a = 1) \Pr(a = 1).$

Conditional on $a = 1$, let the random variable d denote the equilibrium selection

---

[12] The selection rule depends on unobservables. But since the support of a has only two points, the probabilities are tractable.

mechanism: $d = 1$ if $(1, 0)$ equilibrium is selected with probability P_1, $d = 2$ if the $(0, 1)$ equilibrium is chosen with probability P_2, and $d = 3$ if the mixed strategy equilibrium $\left(\frac{1}{2}, \frac{1}{2}\right)$ is chosen with probability $P_3 = 1 - P_1 - P_2$. Hence,

Predicted Choice Probabilities with Mixed Strategies

$$\Pr(0, 0|a = 1) = \sum_{i=1,2,3} \Pr(0, 0|a = 1, d = i) \Pr(d = i|a = 1)$$

$$= \Pr(0, 0|a = 1, d = 3) P_3 = \frac{1}{4} P_3$$

$$\Pr(1, 0|a = 1) = \sum_{i=1,2,3} \Pr(1, 0|a = 1, d = i) \Pr(d = i|a = 1)$$

$$= \Pr(1, 0|a = 1, d = 3) P_3 + \Pr(1, 0|a = 1, d = 1) P_1$$

$$= \frac{1}{4} P_3 + P_1$$

$$\Pr(1, 1|a = 1) = \sum_{i=1,2,3} \Pr(1, 1|a = 1, d = i) \Pr(d = i|a = 1)$$

$$= \Pr(1, 1|a = 1, d = 3) P_3 = \frac{1}{4} P_3.$$

This implies that

$$\Pr(0, 0) = \frac{1}{4} P_3 (1 - l)$$

$$\Pr(1, 0) = \left(\frac{1}{4} P_3 + P_1\right)(1 - l)$$

$$\Pr(0, 1) = \left(\frac{1}{4} P_3 + P_2\right)(1 - l)$$

$$\Pr(1, 1) = l + \frac{1}{4} P_3 (1 - l)$$

$$P_1 + P_2 + P_3 = 1$$

$$0 \leq l \leq 1.$$

The parameters of interest in this game are (P_1, P_2, P_3, l). The identification question in this game reduces to one of studying the set of solutions to the above system of equalities/inequalities. The game (or parameters) is point identified if there exists a unique solution and is set identified if the game restricts the parameters to a non-singleton set of parameters (and of course in case of no solutions, then the game is misspecified).

A simple insight that emerges from this example is the importance of pinpointing the set of *potentially observable outcomes* in a game. Heuristically, given a value for the exogenous variables, the set of potentially observable outcomes or POO is the set of outcomes that can be observed when the game is played. For example, when $a = 1$, the set of observable outcomes is $\{(0, 0), (1, 1), (1, 0), (0, 1)\}$. The POO consists of the pure strategy equilibria

Table 2.1. *Bivariate entry game*

	0	1
0	$0, 0$	$0, x_2\beta_2 - \epsilon_2$
1	$x_1\beta_1 - \epsilon_1, 0$	$x_1\beta_1 + \Delta_1 - \epsilon_1, x_2\beta_2 + \Delta_2 - \epsilon_2$

(which can be mapped one to one to a set of outcomes) and the set of outcomes that are on the support of the mixed strategy distribution.

The equilibrium selection mechanism plays a key role in forming the predicted choice probabilities. Usually, the economist has no information about equilibrium selection or is not willing to make assumptions on equilibrium selection. The reason is that it is not unusual that different equilibria can be chosen in otherwise "similar" markets. So, the key *practical* question becomes: What can we learn about the features of the model (like the variable profit functions and the joint distribution of unobserved fixed costs) without imposing any restrictions on equilibrium selection? In other words, is using an ad-hoc selection rule practically important? Another important issue is whether the model contains information about the selection mechanism. The simple game above shows that it does. So, the data does have identifying power regarding the selection mechanism (the data generally point identifies the selection rule in the simple game above).

2.5.1 Bivariate Entry Game: Inference, Multiplicity, and Mixed Strategies

Reconsider the bivariate entry game studied in section (2.3) above except that here and for simplicity we parametrize the profit functions as in Table 2.1. This game is similar to the one studied in Tamer (2003).

Again, we assume that Δ_1 and Δ_2 are negative. So, for $\epsilon_1 \in [x_1\beta_1 + \Delta_1, x_1\beta]$ and $\epsilon_2 \in [x_2\beta_2 + \Delta_2, x_2\beta]$ the game has multiple equilibria: $(0, 1)$ and $(1, 0)$ are pure strategy equilibria and there is a mixed strategy equilibrium. To study identification in this game in the presence of mixed strategies (and multiplicity), we follow the insights given in the simple game above.[13] Notice that, $(1, 1), (0, 0), (1, 0)$ and $(0, 1)$ are potentially observed outcomes in the case where the mixed strategy is an equilibrium. So, again we assume that we have a random sample of markets and that the vector (ϵ_1, ϵ_2) is independent of $x = (x_1, x_2)$ and has a known (up to some parameter) joint density with support

---

[13] Tamer (2003) studied identification in this game without allowing for mixed strategies. The inequalities based approach used in Ciliberto and Tamer (2003) can easily be extended to allow for mixing. Recently, also, Bajari, Hong, and Ryan (2005) introduce a model where mixed strategies are explicitly accounted for.

on the real plane.[14] We are interested in inference on the parameter vector $\theta = (\beta_1, \beta_2, \Delta_1, \Delta_2, \gamma)$, where γ is the parameter of the joint distribution of the ϵ's. Define the following sets. First, let

$$A_{(p,q)}^{x,\theta} = \{(\epsilon_1, \epsilon_2) : (p, q) \text{ is the unique equilibrium}\}.$$

In the case of multiplicity, define

$$M_C^{x,\theta} = \{(\epsilon_1, \epsilon_2) : C \text{ is a set of multiple equilibria}\}$$

where either set A or M can be empty. Similar definitions can be written for any discrete game in general, but we keep the specific definitions in this example for simplicity. For example, sets A are regions for the epsilons where the outcome $(p, q) \in [0, 1] \times [0, 1]$ is the unique equilibrium for a given value of x and θ. This equilibrium can either be in pure or in mixed strategies. For example $A_{(1,1)}^{x,\theta}$ is the set of epsilons where $(1, 1)$ is the unique pure strategy equilibrium. This region is $(\epsilon_1, \epsilon_2) \in [-\infty, x_1\beta_1 + \Delta_1] \times [-\infty, x_2\beta_2 + \Delta_2]$ for the game above. On the other hand, sets M are regions for the epsilons where the game predicts multiple equilibria (some of which can be in mixed strategies). In the above game for example, $M_{\{(1,0),(0,1),(p,q)\}}^{x,\theta} = \{(\epsilon_1, \epsilon_2) \in [x_1\beta_1 + \Delta_1, x_1\beta] \times [x_2\beta_2 + \Delta_2, x_2\beta]\}$. For a given x and θ, the game predicts the following choice probabilities:

$$\mathcal{P}(x; \theta, \pi) = \begin{pmatrix} \Pr((0, 0)|x, \theta, \pi) \\ \Pr((1, 1)|x, \theta, \pi) \\ \Pr((1, 0)|x, \theta, \pi) \\ \Pr((0, 1)|x, \theta, \pi) \end{pmatrix}$$

$$= \begin{pmatrix} \int \sum_{i \in C} \Pr((0, 0)|x, \theta, \pi, \epsilon, d = i) \Pr(d = i|\epsilon, x) dF_\epsilon \\ \int \sum_{i \in C} \Pr((1, 1)|x, \theta, \pi, \epsilon, d = i) \Pr(d = i|\epsilon, x) dF_\epsilon \\ \int \sum_{i \in C} \Pr((1, 0)|x, \theta, \pi, \epsilon, d = i) \Pr(d = i|\epsilon, x) dF_\epsilon \\ \int \sum_{i \in C} \Pr((0, 1)|x, \theta, \pi, \epsilon, d = i) \Pr(d = i|\epsilon, x) dF_\epsilon \end{pmatrix}$$

$$= \begin{pmatrix} \Pr(A_{(0,0)}^{x,\theta}) + \int_{M_{(0,0)}^{x,\theta}} (1 - \frac{x_1\beta_1 - \epsilon_1}{-\Delta_1})(1 - \frac{x_2\beta_2 - \epsilon_2}{-\Delta_2}) \Pr(d = 3|x, \epsilon_1, \epsilon_2) dF \\ \Pr\left(A_{(1,1)}^{x,\theta}\right) + \int_{M_C^{x,\theta}} \frac{x_1\beta_1 - \epsilon_1}{-\Delta_1} \frac{x_2\beta_2 - \epsilon_2}{-\Delta_2} \Pr(d = 3|x, \epsilon_1, \epsilon_2) dF \\ \Pr(A_{(1,0)}) + \int_{M_C^{x,\theta}} \Pr(d = 1|x, \epsilon_1, \epsilon_2) dF + \int_{M_C^{x,\theta}} \frac{x_1\beta_1 - \epsilon_1}{-\Delta_1}(1 - \frac{x_2\beta_2 - \epsilon_2}{-\Delta_2}) \\ \Pr(d = 3|x, \epsilon_1, \epsilon_2) dF \\ \Pr(A_{(0,1)}) + \int_{M_C^{x,\theta}} \Pr(d = 2|x, \epsilon_1, \epsilon_2) dF + \int_{M_C^{x,\theta}} (1 - \frac{x_1\beta_1 - \epsilon_1}{-\Delta_1}) \frac{x_2\beta_2 - \epsilon_2}{-\Delta_2} \\ \Pr(d = 3|x, \epsilon_1, \epsilon_2) dF \end{pmatrix}$$

$$(2.20)$$

where $C = \{(0, 1), (1, 0), (p, q)\}$ and $\pi = (\Pr(d = i|x, \epsilon_1, \epsilon_2), i = 1, 2, 3)$, $\sum_i \Pr(d = i|x, \epsilon_1, \epsilon_2) = 1$ is the equilibrium selection mechanism in the region of multiplicity. Notice, this equilibrium selection mechanism is left unspecified

---

[14] Identification in this game with unknown F is complicated and will not be dealt with here.

and can depend on market unobservables. The outcome $d = 1$ corresponds to "selecting" $(1, 0)$, $d = 2$ corresponds to selecting $(0, 1)$, and $d = 3$ corresponds to selecting the mixed strategy equilibrium. Examining the probability of $(0, 1)$ we find that

$$\Pr((1, 0)|x, \theta, \pi) = \underbrace{\Pr(A_{(1,0)}^{x,\theta})}_{(1)} + \underbrace{\int_{M_C^{x,\theta}} \Pr(d = 1|x, \epsilon_1, \epsilon_2)dF}_{(2)}$$

$$+ \underbrace{\int_{M_C^{x,\theta}} \overbrace{\frac{x_1\beta_1 - \epsilon_1}{-\Delta_1}(1 - \frac{x_2\beta_2 - \epsilon_2}{-\Delta_2})}^{(3a)} \Pr(d = 3|x, \epsilon_1, \epsilon_2)dF.}_{(3)}$$

The first term (1) is the probability of the region $A_{(1,0)}$ under F, i.e., $(1) = \Pr(\epsilon_1 \leq x_1\beta_1; \epsilon_2 \geq x_2\beta_2) + \Pr(\epsilon_1 \leq x_1\beta_1 + \Delta_1; x_2\beta_2 + \Delta_2 \leq \epsilon_2 \leq x_2\beta_2)$. This is the probability mass of the region where $(1, 0)$ is the *unique* equilibrium of game. Next, the region $M_C^{x,\theta}$ is the region of multiplicity, and in this model it is the "square" where $x_1\beta_1 + \Delta_1 \leq \epsilon_1 \leq x_1\beta_1$ and $x_2\beta_2 + \Delta_2 \leq \epsilon_2 \leq x_2\beta_2$. So, in (2) we calculate the probability that the outcome $(1, 0)$ is selected (i.e., $d = 1$), which is the weighted probability of selection integrated against F in the region of multiplicity. The third term (3) takes account of mixed strategies. If mixed strategies are allowed, all 4 outcomes are potentially observed. In particular, conditional on $d = 3$ (mixed strategy equilibrium), (3a) gives the (mixing) probability of observing $(1, 0)$.

As we can see, observing event $(1, 0)$ is a consequence of several distinct possibilities (three here): first, either that $(1, 0)$ is the unique equilibrium of the game (term (1)), $(1, 0)$ is an equilibrium of a game with multiplicity where it is a pure strategy equilibrium (term (2)), or it is on the support of a mixed strategy equilibrium (term (3)). So, without making equilibrium selection assumptions, the presence of multiple equilibria complicates the inferential problem by introducing nuisance parameters (selection probabilities). Moreover, with mixed strategies the model does not necessarily predict multiple equilibria that are unique in the number. So, here the observable implication of multiple equilibria is that $(1, 0)$ or $(1, 1)$ can show up, and hence these observables do not involve the same number of firms entering.

Common equilibrium selection assumptions are the requirements that the distribution of d conditional on x be independent of (ϵ_1, ϵ_2) and sometimes also the x's, i.e., one uses the same selection mechanisms in similar markets. One then usually parametrizes the probability (as in using a multinomial logit) and uses maximum likelihood for inference. See for example Bjorn and Vuong (1985) and more recently Bajari, Hong, and Ryan (2005).

Identification In this setup, identification is defined as follows. The *sharp* identified set Θ_I is

$$\Theta_I = \{\theta : \exists \pi \text{ such that } \Pr\left(\mathcal{P}(x) = \mathcal{P}(x; \theta, \pi)\right) = 1\}. \tag{2.21}$$

The set Θ_I is the sharp identified set, i.e., the set of parameters θ that are consistent with the data and the model. Heuristically, a $\theta \in \Theta_I$ if and only if there exists a (proper) selection mechanism $\pi = (P(d = i|x, \epsilon_1, \epsilon_2), \ i = 1, 2, 3)$ such that the induced probability distribution $\mathcal{P}(x; \theta, \pi)$ matches the choice probabilities $\mathcal{P}(x)$ for all x almost everywhere. So, the presence of multiple equilibria introduces nuisance parameters that are not specified and hence makes it harder to identify the parameter θ. In the case of point identification, Θ_I reduces to a singleton (this set is nonempty otherwise the model would be misspecified). When one models equilibrium selection (by specifying a consistent π), the identification problem reduces to one in a modified multivariate discrete choice model where sometimes, one is able to provide sufficient point identification conditions (usually involving large support). Under these conditions, the model identifies a unique parameter θ, which is associated with that particular selection mechanism. So, if one considers another consistent selection mechanism, the model would point identify another parameter θ. Hence, the set Θ_I collects the set of (structural) parameters that are consistent with a well-defined selection mechanism.

Allowing for mixed strategies adds an additional selection function (when $d = 3$) and so the set $\mathcal{C}$ increases in size. Hence, the observational implication of mixed strategies is that any outcome on the support of the mixing distribution is potentially observable. So, mixing, although qualitatively similar to multiplicity, complicates the identification problem (and thus makes the task of identification harder) since we require the data to identify more functions.

Remark   *In other models (like in the case where the Δ's have a different sign) it is possible that for some values of the ϵ's the game only admits an equilibrium in mixed strategies (the unique equilibrium is one in mixed strategies). So, it does not seem natural in those games to only allow pure strategies. Hence, one needs to pay special attention to the assumption of not allowing mixed strategy equilibria since it might lead to regions of the exogenous variables where the model does not predict any outcomes (this might not be a big problem in some entry models where unique equilibria in mixed strategies only, are less common).*

Inference on the set Θ_I based on definition (2.21) though theoretically attractive is not practically feasible since one needs to deal with infinite dimensional nuisance parameters (the π's).[15] A practical approach to inference in this class of models, follows the approach in Ciliberto and Tamer (2003) by exploiting the fact that the selection mechanism π is a probability and hence bounded between zero and one. Although this approach does not provide a sharp set, it is practically attractive. So, exploiting the fact that $\Pr(d = i|x, \epsilon_1, \epsilon_2) \in [0, 1]$

---

[15] Inference is more practical in settings where one discretizes the model, i.e., uses discrete x's and assumes that the epsilons take finitely many values with given probabilities. This makes it into a finite dimensional problem that is easier to handle.

for $i = 1, 2, 3$ we can get the following model with inequality restrictions on regressions:

$$
\begin{pmatrix} \Pr(A_{(0,0)}^{x,\theta}) \\ \Pr(A_{(1,1)}^{x,\theta}) \\ \Pr(A_{(1,0)}^{x,\theta}) \\ \Pr(A_{(0,1)}^{x,\theta}) \end{pmatrix} \leq \begin{pmatrix} \Pr(0, 0|x) \\ \Pr(1, 1|x) \\ \Pr(1, 0|x) \\ \Pr(0, 1|x) \end{pmatrix}
$$

$$
\leq \begin{pmatrix} \Pr(A_{(0,0)}^{x,\theta}) + \int_{M_{(0,0)}^{x,\theta}} (1 - \frac{x_1\beta_1 - \epsilon_1}{-\Delta_1})(1 - \frac{x_2\beta_2 - \epsilon_2}{-\Delta_2})dF \\ \Pr(A_{(1,1)}^{x,\theta}) + \int_{M_C^{x,\theta}} \frac{x_1\beta_1 - \epsilon_1}{-\Delta_1}\frac{x_2\beta_2 - \epsilon_2}{-\Delta_2}dF \\ \Pr(A_{(1,0)}) + \max \left(\Pr(M_C^{x,\theta}), \int_{M_C^{x,\theta}} \frac{x_1\beta_1 - \epsilon_1}{-\Delta_1}(1 - \frac{x_2\beta_2 - \epsilon_2}{-\Delta_2})dF \right) \\ \Pr(A_{(0,1)}) + \max \left(\Pr(M_C^{x,\theta}), \int_{M_C^{x,\theta}} (1 - \frac{x_1\beta_1 - \epsilon_1}{-\Delta_1})\frac{x_2\beta_2 - \epsilon_2}{-\Delta_2} \right) \end{pmatrix} .
$$

$$(2.22)$$

Notice here that the above inequalities represent a cube that consists of a superset of the feasible probabilities. This superset was generated by taking the extreme points of the selection probabilities equation by equations. For example the $(0, 0)$ probability in (2.20) can be as low as $\Pr(A_{(0,0)}^{x,\theta})$ and as high as $(A_{(0,0)}^{x,\theta}) + \int_{M_{(0,0)}^{x,\theta}} (1 - \frac{x_1\beta_1 - \epsilon_1}{-\Delta_1})(1 - \frac{x_2\beta_2 - \epsilon_2}{-\Delta_2})dF$. Then we repeat this exercise for every outcome. By transforming the predictions of the model into ones with *inequality restrictions*, we are able to bypass the specification of the selection probabilities. Note that in constructing the cube we have ignored the cross equation restrictions (basically that the selection probabilities sum to one). One can certainly exploit these restrictions, but we omit this for simplicity of description. The econometric structure of this model is a method of moments model with inequality restrictions. Inference in models with inequality restrictions is studied in Chernozhukov, Hong, and Tamer (2002) and Andrews, Berry, and Jia (2003) and applied in these settings by Ciliberto and Tamer (2003).

Are Multiple Equilibria and Mixed Strategies a Problem? As we can see from above, dealing with multiple equilibria and mixed strategy equilibria in games with complete information introduces functions that, if left unspecified, complicate the identification problem. In addition, policy analysis in the presence of multiplicity is complicated by the fact that the model is only able to predict uniquely in some regions of multiplicity. Motivated by practical convenience, another approach to inference in games is to make simple equilibrium selection assumption or/and pick an equilibrium on the support of a mixed strategy equilibrium using a predetermined rule. This will yield a complete (nonlinear) econometric model where methods for identifying the model can be studied. So the practical question of interest is whether parameters or policy functions can change significantly with different selection rules. One way to examine this question is to look for set estimates of the parameters of interest without making selection assumptions. The "size" of this set is an indicator of how important selection assumptions are. Finally, the framework above maintains parametric assumptions on the variable profits and the joint distribution of the unobservables. It is thus important to study identification in settings where these distributional assumptions are relaxed. In general, in multivariate discrete models, relaxing these complicates the identification problem (see Bajari, Hong, and Ryan (2005) for more on this). This is a largely unexplored area of research.

3 STATIC GAMES OF INCOMPLETE INFORMATION

In this section, we examine the question of inference in a discrete game under different informational assumptions. It is maintained that decision makers' profit functions contain a variable that is not observed by them. One may assume that an entrant does not observe another's fixed costs for example. Seim (2002) considers a model of endogenous entry and product positioning where she assumes that some "idiosyncratic sources of profitability are hard to observe by competitors." Another example is the paper by Sweeting (2004), which analyzes an incomplete information model of different radio stations' decisions to play a commercial break. Also, a recent paper by Aradillas-Lopez (2005) examines the identified feature in a game similar to the one in Table 2.1 above but with incomplete information and provides conditions for uniqueness under the assumptions that player belief can depend on variables that do not enter the variable profits function. Most of the work on empirical games with incomplete information[16] deal with the presence of multiple equilibria in two ways. In one way, they provide conditions for uniqueness of equilibria; usually, these are constraints on the shape of the profit function guaranteeing that the equilibrium correspondence admits a unique fixed point. Another way is that it is assumed that the same equilibrium is chosen in similar markets or that one uses the same equilibrium selection distribution in observationally similar markets. This equilibrium is the one that can be estimated from the data nonparametrically or using a parametric equilibrium selection mechanism. These assumptions rest on the underlying principle that "similar" equilibria are being played in markets that are observationally equivalent. Here we provide a different but complementary approach to inference by studying the inferential problem without making equilibrium selection assumptions. We relate our findings to results obtained in the complete information games. We illustrate our insights using a simple bivariate game where we derive the econometric restriction of this game and analyze its identification problem. The objective is to try and nest the different assumptions that are made under a more general framework.

Multiple Equilibria in a Simple Bivariate Game

The nature of equilibria in games with incomplete information is slightly different from the complete information counterpart. Strategies now are mappings

---

[16] Sweeting (2004) is an exception.

Table 2.2. *Bivariate game*

	0	1
0	$0,0$	$0, v_2(x_2) - \epsilon_2$
1	$v_1(x_1) - \epsilon_1, 0$	$v_1(x_1) + u_1(x_1) - \epsilon_1, \ v_2(x_2) + u_2(x_2) - \epsilon_2$

from players' types to actions where types are private to the players. We maintain throughout the assumption of common priors, i.e., that the distribution of signals or types is common knowledge to the players, and we also restrict ourselves to pure strategies, i.e., we do not allow for mixing. Again, we focus on the bivariate game below where we assume that players have imperfect information about the profit function of their opponent. The functions u_i and v_i for $i = 1, 2$ are left unspecified as is F, the distribution of the unobservables ϵ_1 and ϵ_2, which are assumed to be independent of the observable exogenous variables with F as their joint distribution. Both ϵ_1 and ϵ_2 are not observed by the econometrician, but ϵ_1 is private information to player 1 and similarly for player 2.

We fix $X = (x_1, x_2)$ and derive the observable implication of the game. It is easy to see that equilibrium mappings are going to be step functions that are decreasing in a threshold. So the Bayesian Nash equilibrium of the game in Table 2.2 is a pair of mappings $\left(1[\epsilon_1 \leq t_1], 1[\epsilon_2 \leq t_2]\right)$ where $T = (t_1, t_2)$ are threshold variables that are functions of $X, \theta = (v_1, v_2, u_1, u_2)$ and the common prior distributions. Player 1 believes that ϵ_2 has a distribution G_b^1 and similarly for player 2. These distribution functions can depend on X and θ.[17] So, T solves (assuming independence of players' private values) the following

$$(v_1(x_1) - t_1)(1 - G_b^1(t_2)) + (v_1(x_1) + u_1(x_1) - t_1)G_b^1(t_2) = 0$$
$$(v_2(x_2) - t_2)(1 - G_b^2(t_1)) + (v_2(x_2) + u_2(x_2) - t_2)G_b^2(t_1) = 0$$

where these represent the "zero-profit" conditions. Hence, the equilibrium thresholds T are fixed points of the following mapping

$$H_b(t_1, t_2) = \begin{bmatrix} v_1(x_1) + u_1(x_1)G_b^1(t_2) \\ v_2(x_2) + u_2(x_2)G_b^2(t_1) \end{bmatrix}.$$

For example, assuming that $G_b^1 \equiv G_b^2 \equiv G$ then we get that the equilibrium thresholds solve

$$t_1 = v_1(x_1) + u_1(x_1)G(t_2)$$
$$t_2 = v_2(x_2) + u_2(x_2)G(t_1). \tag{3.23}$$

---

[17] The belief distribution can also depend on other "excluded" variables Z as in Aradillas-Lopez.

The above map can have multiple solutions (equilibria), and so the set of solutions to the above system of equations, $\mathcal{E}$, is defined as

$$\mathcal{E}(X, \theta, G) = \{(t_1, t_2) : (t_1, t_2) \text{ solves } (3.23)\}.$$

The cardinality of this set is a function of X and (v_1, v_2, u_1, u_2). See the next section for an example where the belief distribution G is normal and the set $\mathcal{E}$ can be shown to have at most three solutions (three equilibria). It is possible to obtain distributions G with a continuum of equilibria (we assume that away below for simplicity). Now, we derive the model predicted probability $\mathcal{P}(X, \theta)$ where $t = (t_1, t_2) \in \mathcal{E}(X, \theta)$:

$$\mathcal{P}(X, \theta) = \begin{pmatrix} P_{(0,0)}(X, \theta, G) \\ P_{(1,1)}(X, \theta, G) \\ P_{(1,0)}(X, \theta, G) \\ P_{(0,1)}(X, \theta, G) \end{pmatrix}$$

$$= \begin{pmatrix} \sum_{t_i \in \mathcal{E}} \int_{v_1(x_1)+u_1(x_1)G(t_{1i})}^{+\infty} \int_{v_2(x_2)+u_2(x_2)G(t_{2i})}^{+\infty} P(t_i | x, \epsilon_1, \epsilon_2) \, dF \\ \sum_{t_i \in \mathcal{E}} \int_{-\infty}^{v_1(x_1)+u_1(x_1)G(t_{1i})} \int_{+\infty}^{v_2(x_2)+u_2(x_2)G(t_{2i})} P(t_i | x, \epsilon_1, \epsilon_2) \, dF \\ \sum_{t_i \in \mathcal{E}} \int_{-\infty}^{v_1(x_1)+u_1(x_1)G(t_{1i})} \int_{v_2(x_2)+u_2(x_2)G(t_{2i})}^{+\infty} P(t_i | x, \epsilon_1, \epsilon_2) \, dF \\ \sum_{t_i \in \mathcal{E}} \int_{v_1(x_1)+u_1(x_1)G(t_{1i})}^{-\infty} \int_{-\infty}^{v_2(x_2)+u_2(x_2)G(t_{2i})} P(t_i | x, \epsilon_1, \epsilon_2) \, dF \end{pmatrix}$$

$$(3.24)$$

where $\sum_{t_i \in \mathcal{E}} P(t_i | x, \epsilon_1, \epsilon_2) = 1$ for all x, ϵ a.e. Then, one can define identification constructively as we have done above. See (2.21). It is clear that without prior assumptions on the shape of G and the functions u and v that the identified set is not a singleton (and can be large). Note here that the joint distribution of ϵ's played no role in the cardinality or construction of the equilibria. What matters is the assumption of common priors, which we maintain,[18] and its distribution. In addition, there is the added complication that one has to "solve" for the set of equilibria for every "parameter" iteration. Notice that the above formulation in (3.24) is general and hence does not allow one to characterize the identified features of the model. The identification problem becomes less complicated if one imposes assumptions on $P(t | x, \epsilon_1, \epsilon_2)$. For example, one assumption is requiring that $P(t | x, \epsilon_1, \epsilon_2) \equiv P(t | x) = P_\lambda(t | x)$ where P_λ is a known probability distribution up to the parameter λ. This assumption requires that in markets with similar observables, the same equilibrium selection distribution is used. The presence of multiple equilibria introduces the unknown parameter λ, and so the inferential problem becomes one of trying to identify the parameters of interest in the presence of the "selection" parameter λ. A more

---

[18] In reality, it is not clear why a common prior assumption is usually made in these settings. In addition, even with this assumption, it is not clear why one would want to assume that the common distribution is known to the econometrician.

stringent assumption would require that $P(t|x, \epsilon_1, \epsilon_2)$ be degenerate at one of the equilibria. This would be the one that can be estimated from the data. If we also require that the the distribution $G \equiv F$ (i.e., the common prior distribution is the same as the distribution of the ϵ's) then the choice probabilities solve a fixed point theorem.

The presence of multiple equilibria here is of a different nature than in games with complete information in that one is not able to just focus on games where the outcome is uniquely predicted. So, to that extent it might appear that inference in this class of games is simpler. As we can see, this is so only if one makes equilibrium selection assumptions.

The nature of the data is important in models with incomplete information. For example, if one has a data set where the number of players goes to infinity from one market, then one can assume that the equilibrium that is being played is the "observed" equilibrium. This is usually done in "social interactions" models as in Brock and Durlauf (2001). However, in industrial organization it is more common to have a cross section of markets or games where each data "point" represents an observable outcome of a game. In this case, there is a subtle but crucial difference between the distribution of the data and the underlying economic model. For a given set of observable covariates, the distribution of the data provides an "aggregator" that tells us a summary of the observed outcomes. This data distribution in turn needs to be related to an economic model. In each market a different game (different equilibrium) might be played, since in the general case equilibrium selection depends on the unobservables. Hence, one has a single observation per game (market). So, the link between the observed data distribution and the underlying distribution of interest is complicated in the presence of multiplicity.[19] The statistical structure is similar to inference in a mixture model with unknown mixing distributions. It is possible to characterize the identified set in more parametric examples. See section 3.2 below. But basically, without making selection assumption, the characterizing identification can be complicated.

3.1   Complete vs Incomplete Information

The sharp econometric restrictions from a model with incomplete information (equations (3.24) above) look strikingly similar to the restrictions from a model with complete information (2.20). Basically, restrictions from both models share the same statistical structure due to the presence of unknown equilibrium selection probabilities. Both models are a version of a discrete mixture with an

---

[19] For example, in general games with multiple equilibria, standard descriptive statistics from the observed data are related in a nontrivial way to the underlying statistics from the economic model. For example, the average number of entrants in observationally similar markets is an average with respect to a mixture where the mixing distributions correspond to different equilibria. For more on this point, see Echenique and Komunjer (2005).

unknown mixing distribution. So, methods for inference in games with incomplete information without selection assumptions can be used to analyze models with complete information. This mixture framework is similar to one studied by Honoré and Tamer (2005). There the incompleteness in the model is a result of the ambiguity regarding the initial condition in a single agent dynamic discrete choice model. In cases with discrete x's and discrete ϵ's, the identified regions for these models can be characterized as solutions to linear programming problems. So, this strategy of discretizing the data and the distribution of equilibrium selection will transform the structure of the problem of inference in both complete and incomplete information games into one of solving a linear (and sometimes nonlinear) programming problem. We leave this connection to future work. Finally, it is also worth mentioning that the approach to inference above requires that one is able to solve for the equilibria of the game repeatedly, which increases the computational burden.

3.2   A Parametric Example

Consider again the example of Table 2.2 above where now we assume that player i does not observe player $1 - i$'s fixed costs ϵ_{1-i} for $i = 0, 1$. Assume that ϵ_1, ϵ_2 are independent of x with a joint distribution F and also that the common belief distribution G is the normal CDF Φ_θ with mean μ and variance σ^2 (normality is assumed here without loss of generality). Then to examine multiplicity one needs to look at the map

$$
\begin{aligned}
t_1 &= x_1\beta_1 + \Delta_1\Phi_\theta(t_2) \\
t_2 &= x_2\beta_2 + \Delta_2\Phi_\theta(t_1).
\end{aligned}
\tag{3.25}
$$

For some values of x, θ and $(\beta, \Delta) = (\beta_1, \beta_2, \Delta_1, \Delta_2)$, this map has multiple solutions. An example is illustrated in Figure 2.2. It can be shown that in the case of normal beliefs we can have at most 3 equilibria in this model:

$$
\mathcal{P}(X, \theta, \beta, \Delta) = \begin{pmatrix}
\sum_{i=1}^{2} \int_{x_1\beta_1+\Delta_1\Phi_\theta(t_{1i})}^{+\infty} \int_{x_2\beta_2+\Delta_2\Phi_\theta(t_{2i})}^{+\infty} P(t_i|x, \epsilon_1, \epsilon_2)\, dF \\
\sum_{i=1}^{2} \int_{-\infty}^{x_1\beta_1+\Delta_1\Phi_\theta(t_{1i})} \int_{+\infty}^{x_2\beta_2+\Delta_2\Phi_\theta(t_{2i})} P(t_i|x, \epsilon_1, \epsilon_2)\, dF \\
\sum_{i=1}^{2} \int_{-\infty}^{x_1\beta_1+\Delta_1\Phi_\theta(t_{1i})} \int_{x_2\beta_2+\Delta_2\Phi_\theta(t_{2i})}^{+\infty} P(t_i|x, \epsilon_1, \epsilon_2)\, dF \\
\sum_{i=1}^{2} \int_{x_1\beta_1+\Delta_1\Phi_\theta(t_{1i})}^{-\infty} \int_{-\infty}^{x_2\beta_2+\Delta_2\Phi_\theta(t_{2i})} P(t_i|x, \epsilon_1, \epsilon_2)\, dF
\end{pmatrix}.
\tag{3.26}
$$

The restrictions in (3.24) can be adapted here (we restrict ourselves to the two stable equilibria for simplicity), where for some values of the parameters the equilibrium is unique, and the set $\mathcal{E}$ is a singleton. The presence of the selection mechanisms $P(t_i|\epsilon_1, \epsilon_2)$ for $i = 1, 2$ complicate the identification. But, for example, assume that x_{11} has large support conditional on the other regressors with a nonzero positive coefficient β_{11}. Then, for example, by looking at the

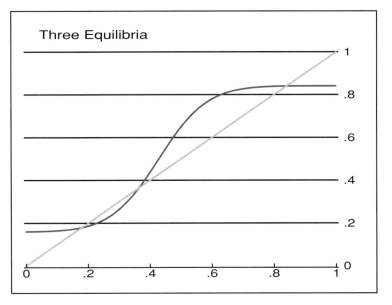

Figure 2.2. Equilibria for some value of X and θ when $F = \Phi$.

second equation in (3.25) above, we see that as x_{11} becomes large for a given value of the other regressors, t_1 becomes large, and hence t_2 becomes close to $x_2\beta_2 + \Delta_2$, and the equilibrium correspondence is unique. For these values of x_{11}, the model becomes a standard bivariate discrete choice model where one can use usual methods for identification. Another way to make inference in this model without making equilibrium selection assumptions is to use the requirement that the function P is a probability and is hence between zero and one. This implies that

$$
\begin{pmatrix}
\min\left(P(0,0|x,\beta,\Delta,t_1),\, P(0,0|x,\beta,\Delta,t_2)\right) \\
\min\left(P(1,1|x,\beta,\Delta,t_1),\, P(1,1|x,\beta,\Delta,t_2)\right) \\
\min\left(P(1,0|x,\beta,\Delta,t_1),\, P(1,0|x,\beta,\Delta,t_2)\right) \\
\min\left(P(0,1|x,\beta,\Delta,t_1),\, P(0,1|x,\beta,\Delta,t_2)\right)
\end{pmatrix}
$$

$$
\leq
\begin{pmatrix}
\Pr(0,0|x) \\
\Pr(1,1|x) \\
\Pr(1,0|x) \\
\Pr(0,1|x)
\end{pmatrix}
$$

$$
\leq
\begin{pmatrix}
\max\left(P(0,0|x,\beta,\Delta,t_1),\, P(0,0|x,\beta,\Delta,t_2)\right) \\
\max\left(P(1,1|x,\beta,\Delta,t_1),\, P(1,1|x,\beta,\Delta,t_2)\right) \\
\max\left(P(1,0|x,\beta,\Delta,t_1),\, P(1,0|x,\beta,\Delta,t_2)\right) \\
\max\left(P(0,1|x,\beta,\Delta,t_1),\, P(0,1|x,\beta,\Delta,t_2)\right)
\end{pmatrix}
\tag{3.27}
$$

where

$$
\begin{pmatrix}
P(0,0|x,\beta,\Delta,t_i) \\
P(1,1|x,\beta,\Delta,t_i) \\
P(1,0|x,\beta,\Delta,t_i) \\
P(0,1|x,\beta,\Delta,t_i)
\end{pmatrix}
=
\begin{pmatrix}
\int_{x_1\beta_1+\Delta_1\Phi_\theta(t_i)}^{+\infty} \int_{x_2\beta_2+\Delta_2\Phi_\theta(t_i)}^{+\infty} dF \\
\int_{-\infty}^{x_1\beta_1+\Delta_1\Phi_\theta(t_i)} \int_{+\infty}^{x_2\beta_2+\Delta_2\Phi_\theta(t_i)} dF \\
\int_{-\infty}^{x_1\beta_1+\Delta_1\Phi_\theta(t_i)} \int_{x_2\beta_2+\Delta_2\Phi_\theta(t_i)}^{+\infty} dF \\
\int_{x_1\beta_1+\Delta_1\Phi_\theta(t_i)}^{-\infty} \int_{-\infty}^{x_2\beta_2+\Delta_2\Phi_\theta(t_i)} dF
\end{pmatrix}
$$

and t is the solution to the set of equations in (3.25). If this equilibrium fixed point relation has a unique solution, then the inequalities in (3.27) become equalities. This system of *inequality restrictions* is not sharp but is more practically feasible to use. Similarly to games with complete information where one needs to solve the equilibria of the game at each parameter value and for each market, here one needs to solve the fixed point problem at each iteration.[20]

4   SOME THOUGHTS ON IDENTIFICATION IN DYNAMIC ENTRY GAMES

There has been a set of mostly methodological papers exploring the inferential properties of dynamic models with multiple decision makers. A summary of these papers is contained in Ackerberg, Benkard, Berry, and Pakes (2006). Most of the recent papers[21] build on existing results in the single agent dynamic optimization models as explored in Rust (1994) and further studied in Hotz and Miller (1993). In this paper, we extend the identification framework we explored earlier to a dynamic setting. Most of the discussion will be a review of existing work with some emphasis on some of the subtle details. In the first section, we examine a simple monopoly entry model and show how the model can be identified under a set of assumptions, some of which are strong and suspect. For example, we show that if the distribution of fixed costs is known (up to a finite dimensional parameter), then one can identify variable profits under the assumptions that the fixed costs are iid over time and markets, and that the same equilibrium is played in observationally similar markets. Then we can examine the reverse question, i.e., what can we learn about the distribution of fixed costs if one observes variable profits? Here, we see that under some support conditions one can identify the distribution of fixed costs. But that

---

[20] We can take a transformation of both sides in (3.25) to get

$$
\Phi_\theta(t_1) = \Phi_\theta\big(x_1\beta_1 + \Delta_1\Phi_\theta(t_2)\big)
$$
$$
\Phi_\theta(t_2) = \Phi_\theta\big(x_2\beta_2 + \Delta_2\Phi_\theta(t_1)\big).
$$

One can solve for $\Phi_\theta(t_i)$ as a fixed point of the above mapping (as opposed to t_i). This is easier since solving for Φ can be done using a grid search method on [0, 1].

[21] The papers are Pakes, Ostrovsky, and Berry (2005), Bajari, Benkard, and Levin (2005), Aguiregabiria and Mira (2004), and Pesendorfer and Schmidt-Dengler (2004). For a summary of these papers see Ackerberg, Benkard, Berry, and Pakes (2006).

generally, this distribution is partially identified. In the last section we provide some heuristics about dealing with multiplicity in dynamic models.

4.1   Identification in a Simple Dynamic Exit Game

Consider the problem of a monopolist operating in a market and facing the choice of staying the next period or exiting. Once out, the monopolist receives zero profits and stays out forever. At the beginning of every period, the monopolist observes ϵ, a random variable representing fixed cost of staying an extra period. This random variable is not observed by the economist and is the only unobservable in the model. The crucial assumption is that ϵ is independent and identically distributed over time and markets, which restricts the presence of unobserved market heterogeneity that can affect profits. The economist observes the sequence of exit decisions by monopolists in an independent cross section of markets. As usual, the objective of the problem is to see what we can learn about variable profits and the distribution of fixed costs under a set of assumptions. The data identifies the choice probability of exit $P_0(x)$ (or entry $P_1(x) = 1 - P_1(x)$) as a function of the state variable x. The question becomes one of relating these choice probabilities to the underlying parameters of interest. To start with, this simple setup, which can be generalized to oligopoly cases, imposes strong assumptions that are unlikely to hold in practice. These assumptions though provide a benchmark for analysis (and are used by most of the recent papers) and are a natural starting point for studying identification.

The Bellman equation for the model above is

$$v(x, \epsilon) = \max \left\{ u(x) - \epsilon + \beta \int v(x', \epsilon')\gamma(x', \epsilon'|x, \epsilon)d\epsilon'dx', 0 \right\}$$

where $u(\cdot)$ is variable period profit and is an object of interest. Moreover, $\gamma(x', \epsilon'|x, \epsilon) = \gamma(x'|x)\gamma(\epsilon')$ is the equilibrium transition probability that we assume here is the same across markets and hence $\gamma(x'|x)$ can be consistently estimated. The expected Bellman equation is

$$v(x) = \int v(x, \epsilon)dF = P_1(x)\{u(x) + E[\epsilon|\epsilon \leq \delta(x)] + \beta \int v(x')\gamma(x'|x)dx'\}$$
$$= P_1(x)\{\delta(x) + E[\epsilon|\epsilon \leq \delta(x)]\}$$

$$(4.28)$$

where

$$\delta(x) = u(x) + \beta \int v(x')\gamma(x'|x)dx' \qquad (4.29)$$

is the deterministic part of present and future returns. In addition, the choice probabilities are related to $\delta(\cdot)$ in the obvious manner,

$$P_1(x) = F(\delta(x)) \qquad (4.30)$$

where $F(\cdot)$ is the distribution function of ϵ. Without strong assumptions on

$F(\cdot)$ or $\delta(\cdot)$, one can use results from the binary choice literature by Matzkin to identify both these functions up to some homogeneity and normalizations. Assuming that F is known (up to a finite dimensional θ) and is sufficiently smooth, we have $\delta(x) = F^{-1}(P_1(x))$ and so we can "solve" for v by substituting δ from (4.30) into (4.28). This will give us a functional space map $v = \Psi(F)$ (this is the map that Aguiregabiria and Mira use). Notice here, that other than support conditions and smoothness on F, all we require to get the conditional expected value function is knowledge of F. To solve for $u(x)$ we use the equation for δ to back out u as a function of the discount parameter β. We summarize identification in the following lemma.

Result 5   *Let the model above hold. Assume that ϵ has a continuous density on the real line with distribution F with finite mean.*

1. *If F is known, then $v(\cdot)$ is identified on the support of x. In addition, if β is known, then $u(\cdot)$ is also identified on the support of x. If β is not known, then if there exists an $\bar{x}$ such that $u(\bar{x}) = a$ where a is known, then β and $u(\cdot)$ can be identified.*

2. *If F is known up to a finite dimensional parameter θ and β is an unknown parameter, then we can get v_θ and $u_{\theta,\beta}$ on the support of x. The identified set Θ_I is defined as*

$$\Theta_I = \big\{(\theta, \beta) : \Pr\big[x : P_1(x) = F_\theta(u_{\theta,\beta}(x)$$
$$+ \beta \int F_\theta^{-1}(P_1(x'))\gamma(x'|x)dx'\big] = 1\big\}.$$

Notice here, that we do not require discrete support on the x's. In addition, the results above can be extended to multinomial models. For more on this see Magnac and Thesmar (2002), Hotz and Miller (1993), and Aguiregaberia and Mira. Of course identification is easier (the set Θ_I is "smaller") if one makes more parametric assumptions on the variable profit function $u(\cdot)$. The question of point identification thus focuses on conditions under which the set Θ_I shrinks to a singleton. Those are not simple to obtain, especially in nonlinear models like the one above.

4.2   Identification of the Fixed Costs Distribution

Pakes, Ostrovsky, and Berry (2005) note that we often have information about variable profits from the analysis of data on prices, demand, costs and so forth. Entry data is called on to learn about the distribution of fixed costs. This is the reverse of the question we asked above, i.e., given that we know $u(\cdot)$ what can we learn about $F(\cdot)$. We know from above that given F, we can get v through the map $v = \Psi(F)$. Given that we know v (and u), we can get $\delta(x)$ through (4.29). Then, this allows us to get F on the support of $\delta(x)$ through $P_1(x) = F(\delta(x))$. Hence, one can define the map $F = \Phi(v)$. Sufficient conditions for point identification of F (on the support of δ) can be obtained by analyzing the fixed points of the following map

$$\begin{bmatrix} F \\ v \end{bmatrix} = \begin{bmatrix} \Phi(v) \\ \Psi(F) \end{bmatrix}.$$

Sufficient conditions for uniqueness of fixed points in Banach exist, but in general, those are hard to satisfy. Below, we characterize solutions to the fixed point map in two cases. The first case provides necessary conditions for local solutions to the value function $v(\cdot)$, which then allows one to construct the fixed cost distribution (modulo measurability). The second case constructs a consistent fixed costs distribution in the case where x takes discretely many values.

Case 1: Continuous x

Interestingly, one can provide a necessary condition for a value function $v(x)$ to be a solution to the above problem in the case F is unknown. In this analysis we deliberately omit exact conditions for differentiability, and measurability for the sake of simplicity. Start with the fact that

$$P_1(x)E[\epsilon | \epsilon \le \delta(x)] = \int^{\delta(x)} \epsilon f(\epsilon) d\epsilon.$$

This means that from (4.28),

$$v(x) = \delta(x)P_1(x) + \int^{\delta(x)} \epsilon f(\epsilon) d\epsilon.$$

Taking a derivative with respect to x (examining $v(x)$ locally), we get

$$\begin{aligned} v'(x) &= \big(\delta(x)P_1(x)\big)' + \delta(x)f(\delta(x))\delta'(x) \\ &= \big(\delta(x)P_1(x)\big)' + \delta(x)P_1'(x) \qquad\qquad (4.31) \\ &= \delta'(x)P_1(x) + 2\delta(x)P_1'(x). \end{aligned}$$

The second equality follows from $P_1(x) = F(\delta(x))$, which implies that $P_1'(x) = f(\delta(x))\delta'(x)$. Hence, replacing $\delta(x) = u(x) + \beta \int v(x')\gamma(x'|x)$ we get a non-linear differential equation in v and v' where methods can be used to examine existence and uniqueness of solutions. Given a solution v, that will give us the function $\delta(x)$, which in turn gives us $F(\cdot)$ on the support of $\delta(x)$. Another avenue for identification is making parametric assumptions on $v(\cdot)$. Conditions for identifications can then be obtained more easily (of course, making assumptions on $v(\cdot)$ is a little tenuous since v is not a model primitive).

Case 2: Discrete x

We present insights about an interesting case where x has discrete support. In particular, let $x \in \{x_1, \ldots, x_K\}$. Moreover, let the order be such that

$\delta(x_1) < \ldots < \delta(x_K)$. We know this order since $P_1(x) = F(\delta(x))$ (here, the strict inequality is without loss of generality since one can only learn $F(\cdot)$ on the support of δ) and $P_1(x)$ is known. We construct a distribution function that is consistent with the model and the data. Consider a distribution function F_L that takes K values and has support on $\delta(x_1), \ldots, \delta(x_K)$ with probability $P_1(x_1)$, $P_1(x_2) - P_1(x_1)$, $P_1(x_3) - P_1(x_2)$, $\ldots$, $P_1(x_K) - P_1(x_{K-1})$. By construction, this distribution is consistent with the empirical evidence (in fact, this provides a lower bound on the true underlying $F(\cdot)$). What remains is to derive the implied function $v(\cdot)$. The implied conditional expectation is

$$
\begin{aligned}
E[\epsilon | \epsilon \le \delta(x_i)] &= \frac{\sum_{j<i} \delta(x_j)(P_1(x_j) - P_1(x_{j-1}))}{P_1(x_i)} \\
&= \frac{\sum_{j<i} \left(u(x_j) + \beta \sum_{i=1}^{K} v(x_i) \gamma(x_i | x_j) \right) (P_1(x_j) - P_1(x_{j-1}))}{P_1(x_i)}.
\end{aligned}
$$

(4.32)

Using a discrete version of the optimized Bellman equation we have

$$
v(x) = P_1(x) \Big\{ u(x) + E[\epsilon | \epsilon \le \delta(x)] + \beta \sum_{i=1}^{K} v(x_i) \gamma(x_i | x) \Big\}. \tag{4.33}
$$

Substituting for $E[\epsilon | \epsilon \le \delta(x)]$ from (4.32) above, one can set up a system of equations to obtain information about $v(\cdot)$ given that we know $u(\cdot)$. Another distribution function that is consistent with the empirical evidence is F_U in the figure below. This distribution obeys (4.30). One can then derive the function v, which in turns gives us the "support" functions (the δ's).

4.3   Multiple Equilibria in a Simple Dynamic Model

In this section, we provide insights about the effect of multiple equilibria on inference in a simple dynamic game. In the above, we have always assumed

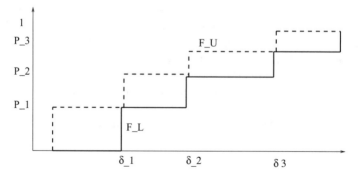

Figure 2.3. Two Discrete Distributions F.

that one knows (or can consistently estimate) the transition probability function $\gamma(\cdot|\cdot)$. In most existing papers this function is replaced by its empirical counterpart. What rationalizes this is a common equilibrium assumption, i.e., that conditional on observables the same equilibrium is played across markets. If one allows for multiple equilibria in different markets then the empirical transition probability (the empirical analog of $\gamma(\cdot)$) will have no particular structural meaning but rather it aggregates observations across markets that come from potentially different equilibria. In this section we provide simple insights about cases when one drops this equilibrium selection assumption.

Consider the entry decision of two firms 1 and 2. Firm 1 makes profit $u(1, y_2) - \epsilon_1$ from entry where ϵ_1 are the fixed costs of staying next period. If firm 1 decides to stay out next period, it gets zero profits forever. The same holds for firm 2. In this example, all markets are identical to the econometrician (no x's). The belief for firm 1 about firm 2's actions next period are $P_1^b(y_2'|y_1, y_2)$ where y_2' is player 2's decision to enter next period. The objective function for player 1 (similarly for player 2) is to enter next period if

$$\epsilon_1 \leq u(1, y_2) + \beta \sum_{y_2'} W(1, y_2') P_1^b(y_2'|y_1, y_2)$$

$$= u(1, y_2) + \beta\big((W(1, 1) - W(0, 1))P_1^b(1|y_1, y_2) + W(0, 1)\big)$$

where W is the value function that depends on (y_1, y_2). Again as in the static game with incomplete information the equilibrium here is a threshold $(\bar{\epsilon}_1, \bar{\epsilon}_2)$ for the ϵ's at which the firms are indifferent between dropping out and staying in. These thresholds are solutions to the following fixed point map:

$$\bar{\epsilon}_1 = u(1, y_2) + \beta\big((W(1, 1) - W(1, 0))F^b(\bar{\epsilon}_2|y_1, y_2) + W(1, 0)\big)$$

$$\bar{\epsilon}_2 = u(y_1, 1) + \beta\big((W(1, 1) - W(0, 1))F^b(\bar{\epsilon}_1|y_1, y_2) + W(0, 1)\big)$$

where F^b is the common prior belief distribution. This map can have multiple solutions. This depends on F^b and the other parameters u, W, and β. One can immediately see that without further assumptions the model adds an equilibrium selection function that can depend on the unobservables. For example, instead of the moment condition in (4.30), we have the following

$$P_1(x) = \sum_i \int^{\delta_i(x)} P(t_i|\epsilon, x) dF_\epsilon$$

where $P(\cdot)$ is the equilibrium selection function and the index i runs over the set of equilibria (assumed discrete here). Then, identification in these settings involves the set of variable profits and fixed cost distributions that obey the Bellman equation and the above modified choice probability map. This is further complicated by the fact that the above map involves solving for the equilibria of the game at each iteration. As we can see, without further assumptions, identification in dynamic Markov games while allowing for players to play different equilibria in observationally similar markets is hard. There are other avenues that one might want to consider. One avenue might be one where one knows ex-ante that there are two types of markets and that in one type one equilibrium is played and another is played in the other market. We leave this and other identification results for dynamic games as a topic for further research.

5   CONCLUSION

In this chapter, we review and study the identification question in parametric and nonparametric models of entry. We find, for example, that combinations of economic insights into the nature of competition coupled with results from the binary choice literature help clarify what can and cannot be learned from the data. We also pay particular attention to the role multiple equilibria and mixed strategies play. The common econometric specification to both models of complete and incomplete information is the mixture model with unknown mixing distributions. We also provide some insights for identification in dynamic models. But, in general, there has not been much work on identification in dynamic discrete games that clarifies the role different assumptions (especially ones related to selection functions) play.

References

Ackerberg, D., L. Benkard, S. Berry, and A. Pakes (2006): "Econometric Tools for Analyzing Market Outcomes," Handbook of Econometrics Vol 6, forthcoming.

Aguirregabiria, V., and P. Mira (2004): "Sequential Estimation of Dynamic Games," Working Paper.

Andrews, D., S. Berry, and P. Jia (2003): "On Placing Bounds on Parameters of Entry Games in the Presence of Multiple Equilibria," Working Paper.

Aradillas-Lopez, A. (2005): "Semiparametric Estimation of a Simultaneous Game with Incomplete Information," Working Paper, Princeton University.

Bajari, P., L. Benkard, and J. Levin (2005): "Estimating Dynamic Models of Imperfect Competition," Working Paper.

Bajari, P., H. Hong, and S. Ryan (2005): "Identification and Estimation of Discrete Games of Complete Information," Working Paper.

Berry, S. (1992): "Estimation of a model of entry in the airline industry," *Econometrica*, 60(4), 889–917.

Berry, S., J. Levinsohn, and A. Pakes (1995): "Automobile Prices in Market Equilibrium," *Econometrica*, 63, 841–890.

Berry, S., and J. Waldfogel (1999): "Free Entry and Social Inefficiency in Radio Broadcasting," *Rand Journal of Economics*, 70(3), 397–420.

Berry, S. T. (1989): "Entry in the Airline Industry," Ph.D. thesis, University of Wisconsin–Madison.

Bjorn, P., and Q. Vuong (1985): "Simultaneous Equations Models for Dummy Endogenous Variables: A Game Theoretic Formulation with an Application to Labor Force Participation," Caltech Working Paper 537.

Borzekowski, R., and A. Cohen (2004): "Estimating Strategic Complementarities in Credit Unions' Outsourcing Decisions," Fed Working Paper.

Bresnahan, T. (1989): "Empirical Studies of Industries with Market Power," in *Handbook of Industrial Organization*, ed. by R. Schmalensee and R. Willig, vol. 2. North-Holland.

Bresnahan, T., and P. Reiss (1987): "Do Entry Conditions Vary Across Markets," *Brookings Papers on Economic Activity: Microeconomics*, pp. 833–871.

——— (1990): "Entry in Monopoly Markets," *Review of Economic Studies*, 57, 531–553.

——— (1991a): "Empirical Models of Discrete Games," *Journal of Econometrics*, 48, 57–81.

——— (1991b): "Entry and Competition in Concentrated Markets," *Journal of Political Economy*, 99, 977–1009.

Brock, W., and S. Durlauf (2001): "Discrete Choice with Social Interactions," *The Review of Economic Studies*.

Chernozhukov, V., H. Hong, and E. Tamer (2002): "Inference in Incomplete Econometric Models," Department of Economics, Princeton University.

Ciliberto, F., and E. Tamer (2003): "Market Structure and Multiple Equilibria in Airline Markets," Working Paper.

Echenique, F., and I. Komunjer (2005): "Testing Models with Multiple Equilibria by Quantile Methods," UC San Diego Working Paper.

Honoré, B., and E. Tamer (2005): "Bounds on Parameters in Panel Dynamic Discrete Choice Models," Working Paper, forthcoming in *Econometrica*.

Horowitz, J. (1992): "A Smoothed Maximum Score Estimator for the Binary Response Model," *Econometrica*, 60(3).

Hotz, J., and R. Miller (1993): "Conditional Choice Probabilities and the Estimation of Dynamic Models," *Review of Economic Studies*, 60, 397–429.

Khan, S. (2004): "Distribution Free Estimation of Heteroskedastic Binary Response Models Using Probit Criterion Functions," Rochester Working Paper.

Magnac, T., and D. Thesmar (2002): "Identifying Synamic Discrete Decision Processes," *Econometrica*, 70(2), 801–816.

Manski, C. F. (1988): "Identification of Binary Response Models," *Journal of the American Statistical Association*, 83.

Matzkin, R. (1992): "Nonparametric and Distribution-Free Estimation of the Binary Threshold Crossing and The Binary Choice Models," *Econometrica*, 60(2), 239–270.

Mazzeo, M. (2002): "Product Choice and Oligopoly Market Structure," *Rand Journal of Economics*, 33(2), 1–22.

Pakes, A., M. Ostrovsky, and S. Berry (2005): "Simple Estimators of the Parameters in Discrete Dynamic Games (with entry/exit)," Working Paper.

Pesendorfer, M., and P. Schmidt-Dengler (2004): "Identification and Estimation of Dynamic Games," Working Paper.

Reiss, P., and P. Spiller (1989): "Competition and Entry in Small Airline Markets," *Journal of Law and Economics*, 32, S179–S202.

Rust, J. (1994): "Structural Estimation of Markov Decision Processes," in *Handbook of Econometrics, Vol. 4*, ed. by D. McFadden and R. Engle. Elsevier Science.

Seim, K. (2002): "An Empirical Model of Firm Entry with Endogenous Product-Type Choices," Working Paper, Stanford Business School.

Sweeting, A. (2004): "Coordination Games, Multiple Equilibria, and the Timing of Radio Commercials," Working Paper.

Tamer, E. T. (2003): "Incomplete Bivariate Discrete Response Model with Multiple Equilibria," *Review of Economic Studies*, 70, 147–167.

APPENDIX 1:   ENTRY GAME WITH TWO TYPES: AN ILLUSTRATION

This example shows that in games with heterogenous effects, multiple equilibria occur that are not unique in the number. Applications to these games are studied in Ciliberto and Tamer (2003). Here, consider an entry game similar to the BR baseline model in (2.5) above, but where we allow for two types, type 1 and 2 with the following profits functions:

$$\pi_1(y_{1m}, y_{2m}, x_m, f_{1m}) = v_1(y_{1m} + y_{2m}, x_m) - f_{1m}$$
$$\pi_2(y_{1m}, y_{2m}, x_m, f_{2m}) = v_2(y_{1m}, y_{2m}, x_m) - f_{2m}.$$

We assume that the variable profits for type 1 firms do not depend on the types of firms in the market but only on the total number of firms in the market while the profits for type 2 firms depend on the number of type 1 and type 2 firms. In addition, assume that $v_2(1, 1, x_m) < v(0, 2, x_m)$ for all x a.e. (this is not essential). We will also make a set of assumptions that simplify the model. First, assume that

$$v_1(y_1 + y_2, x) = \alpha_0 + \alpha_1(y_1 + y_2) + \alpha_2 x - f_1$$

$$v_1(y_1 + y_2, x) = \beta_0 + \beta_1 y_1 + \beta_2 y_2 + \beta_3 x - f_2$$

where β_2, β_1 and α_1 are strictly negative and $\beta_2 > \beta_1$ (profits for type 2 firms will decrease by a larger amount if a type 1 firm enters the market vs a type 2 firm). Second, assume that only 4 firms, two of each type, can be in any market (just for simplicity). One can then easily write down the probability of all the outcomes. For example,

$$\Pr(0, 0|x) = \Pr(f_1 > \alpha_0 + \alpha_1 + \alpha_2 x; f_2 > \beta_0 + \beta_2 + \beta_3 x)$$
$$\Pr(1, 0|x) = \Pr(\alpha_0 + \alpha_1 + \alpha_2 x \geq f_1 \geq \alpha_0 + 2\alpha_1 + \alpha_2 x;$$
$$\beta_0 + \beta_1 + \beta_2 + \beta_3 x \leq f_2)$$
$$\Pr(0, 2|x) = \Pr(f_1 \geq \alpha_0 + 3\alpha_1 + \alpha_2 x; f_2 \leq \beta_0 + 2\beta_2 + \beta_3 x|x).$$

It is easy to see that if (f_1, f_2) has wide support, then there is region for which $(1, 0)$ and $(0, 2)$ are multiple pure strategy equilibria of the game if $\beta_2 > \beta_1$. This heterogeneity in the effect on type 2 variable profits of the two types of firms entering causes the model to have multiple equilibria, where each equilibrium involves a *different number* of firms. Looking at Figure 2.4, we see that $(1, 2)$ and $(2, 0)$ can also appear as equilibria of the game. Finally, we assume that we are going to restrict ourselves to games with pure strategies only. So, given a random sample of markets, where in each market m we observe its configuration in terms of the number of type 1 and type 2 firms and a vector of regressors x_m (that can be type specific), we can relate the (conditional) distribution of the total number of firms to the predictions of the model. For example, Borzekowski and Cohen (2004) study a technology adoption game with network effects where the decision of a credit union to adopt a particular

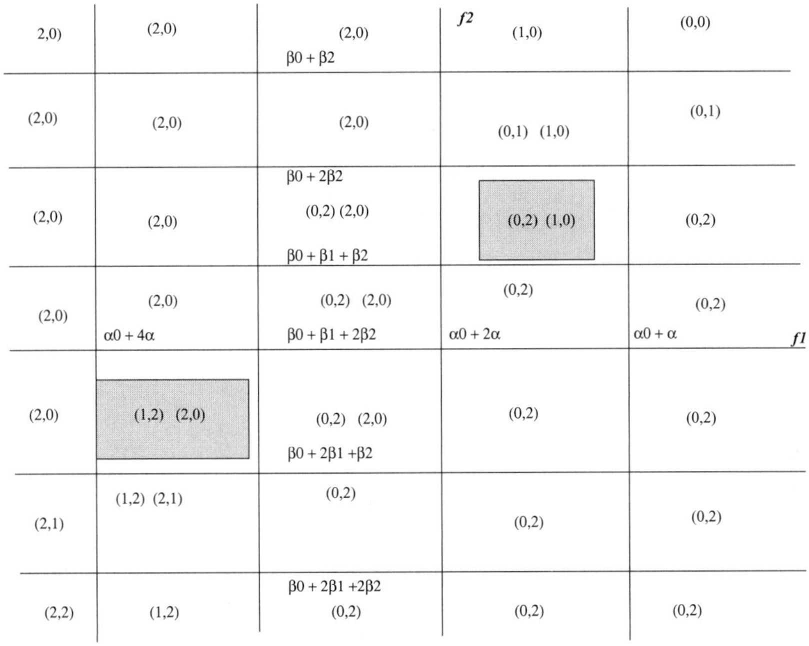

2,0)	(2,0) β0 + β2	(2,0)	*f2* (1,0)	(0,0)
(2,0)	(2,0)	(2,0)	(0,1) (1,0)	(0,1)
(2,0)	(2,0)	β0 + 2β2 (0,2) (2,0) β0 + β1 + β2	(0,2) (1,0)	(0,2)
(2,0) α0 + 4α	(2,0)	(0,2) (2,0) β0 + β1 + 2β2	(0,2) α0 + 2α	(0,2) α0 + α *f1*
(2,0)	(1,2) (2,0)	(0,2) (2,0) β0 + 2β1 +β2	(0,2)	(0,2)
(2,1)	(1,2) (2,1)	(0,2)	(0,2)	(0,2)
(2,2)	(1,2)	β0 + 2β1 +2β2 (0,2)	(0,2)	(0,2)

Figure 2.4. Equilibrium Maps for a Two-Type Game.

technology depends on the the number of other credit unions that adopt the technology. Strategies for identification in these models is similar to ones we highlighted in section 3 above. To relate the observed choice probabilities to ones predicted by the model, one can use Figure 2.4. For example, for values of (f_1, f_2) when $(0, 0)$ is the unique equilibrium, $\Pr((0, 0)|x; A_0) = 1$ and so

$$\Pr((0, 0)|x) = \int_{A_0} dF_{f_1; f_2} \equiv \Pr(A_0)$$

where $A_0 = \{f_1, f_2 : v(1, x) \le f_1; v_2(0, 1, x) \le f_2\}$ since $(0, 0)$ is a potentially observable outcome in cases when it is a unique equilibrium of a game (assuming no mixing). On the other hand, to write down the the probabilities of observing $(1, 2)$ predicted by the model, one needs a selection mechanism as in section 2 above. In general though, entry models with types reduces the dimension of the problem and makes inference more practically feasible since instead of dealing with whether a particular firm enters, now we deal with the number of firms of a given type that enter.

CHAPTER 3

Empirical Models of Imperfect Competition: A Discussion[*]
Liran Einav and Aviv Nevo

1 INTRODUCTION

The field of Industrial Organization (IO) studies the behavior of firms and the interaction among them. In the last 25 years, IO studies have increasingly focused on single industries, using a combination of economic theory and statistics to analyze strategic interaction between firms. The focus on a particular industry allows the researcher to develop a model that takes into account the specific details of the industry. IO economists then use the model to derive comparative statics and test them in the data, and often estimate the structural parameters of the model using state-of-the-art econometric methods.

IO studies a broad array of decisions made by firms, starting from long-run decisions, such as those of entry into particular markets or those that relate to product design and development, medium-run decisions, such as contractual relationships and production, and short-run decisions, such as pricing and bidding in auctions. As each of these decisions is somewhat distinct from others in various aspects (the nature of the decision, the relevant policy questions, the typical data sets available to the empirical researcher, and so on), the literature of recent years can be classified according to which decision it analyzes.

Two issues of particular interest have been entry and exit decisions that determine market structure and price competition. These issues are the focus of the two excellent surveys by Athey and Haile, and Berry and Tamer. Athey and Haile survey the key principles guiding the studies of auction markets, while the paper by Berry and Tamer addresses recent work and identification in empirical models of strategic entry. While the papers and the topics are quite different, they share several themes. First, they exploit the assumption that agents are acting optimally (i.e., maximizing profits or utility) and that the data is generated by equilibrium behavior in order to infer unobserved quantities from observed

[*] We wish to thank Ignacio Esponda, Igal Hendel, and Jon Levin for comments. Einav gratefully acknowledges financial support from the National Science Foundation and the hospitality of the Hoover Institution. Nevo gratefully acknowledges financial support from the National Science Foundation and the Sloan Foundation.

variables. Second, by building complete economic models and estimating their parameters, the work surveyed here permits counterfactual policy experiments. For example, in studies of auctions, data on bids are used to infer unobserved valuations, which can be used to assess, say, counterfactual revenues from alternative auction formats. Similarly, in entry models, observed entry behavior is used to back out fixed costs and intensity of competition, which can then be used to assess the change in market structure in response to various government interventions. Third, both papers emphasize the importance of non-parametric identification by addressing the question of how much can be learned from data without specific functional form assumptions. Both papers suggest that even if eventually the model is estimated parametrically, non-parametric identification is important; it provides the researcher the assurances that with enough data the parametric assumptions required for estimation could be relaxed.

The papers contain a vast amount of material in them, making it impossible to comment in detail on every section. Therefore, our plan in this discussion is to re-iterate some of the key principles the papers emphasize, and to try to place them within a greater context of the field. We hope to achieve two goals in this discussion. The first goal (Section 2) is to survey the main issues and developments in some of the main areas of study, primarily targeting readers who have not followed the field carefully. We briefly summarize both auctions and entry literatures, as well as the demand/pricing literature; the latter is useful as background for our subsequent discussion.

The second goal (Section 3) is to offer a conceptual framework that encompasses the different aspects of firms' behavior. In particular, we emphasize a conceptual distinction between the way modeling of auction markets (and, to a similar extent, entry) evolved, compared to the empirical models used to study price competition in differentiated product oligopoly. A simple conceptual framework may be appealing for readers outside of IO who care less about the details of particular IO problems but want to learn more generally about the key features of empirical IO. In addition, we think that active IO researchers may also benefit from thinking along the lines we sketch in Section 3; to the extent that different areas of research within IO evolve somewhat separately, it is useful to step back and ask whether there is a scope for "arbitrage."

2 SUMMARY OF SEVERAL AREAS OF STUDY IN IO

2.1   Empirical Models of Price Setting

A large literature in empirical IO over the past 25 years has studied short-term, price or quantity, competition in a variety of industries (Porter, 1983; Bresnahan, 1987; Berry, Levinsohn, and Pakes, 1995; Nevo, 2001; and many others). The main goal of this literature is to study the form of competition, understand firm behavior, generate a counterfactual, such as the likely effect of a merger, or quantify welfare gains from, say, the introduction of a new product. Although this literature was not discussed in either of the papers in the session, we describe it as background for the discussion in Section 3.

The typical data set will include a cross section, time series, or panel of markets. For each market the researcher observes the quantity sold, the price charged, and possibly advertising for each product. In addition, both market and product characteristics are observed, and in some cases consumer level data are available.

The main challenge is to infer unobserved marginal costs. The solution is to use quantity and price data to recover demand, and use the demand estimates jointly with the optimality conditions for pricing to back out implied marginal costs. For example, consider a market where single product firms with constant marginal costs set prices to solve

$$\max_{p_i}(p_i - c_i)D_i(p_i, p_{-i}). \tag{1}$$

Consequently, in a Nash equilibrium this choice satisfies the following first order condition:

$$c_i = p_i + \left(\frac{\partial D_i(p_i, p_{-i})}{\partial p_i}\right)^{-1} D_i(p_i, p_{-i}). \tag{2}$$

Given estimates of the demand function $D_i(p_i, p_{-i})$ and $(\partial D_i(p_i, p_{-i})/\partial p_i)^{-1}$ can be computed and used to back out the implied marginal costs. These costs can then be used to test the supply model, as inputs into simulation of a counterfactual, or to fit a marginal cost function.

One important issue in this literature is the specification of the demand function, given the large number of products present in most markets, and the need for a flexible demand model. There are several solutions for the dimensionality problem in the literature. Multi-level demand systems (Hausman, Leonard and Zona, 1994; Hausman, 1997) solve the problem by a-priori separating the products into segments and allowing for flexible functional forms within and across segments. The functional forms can be flexible because the number of products within a segment and the number of segments are relatively small. Discrete choice models (McFadden, 1973; Berry, Levinsohn, and Pakes, 1995) provide an alternative that solves the dimensionality problem by projecting products onto a characteristics space. Thus, the relevant dimension becomes the number of characteristics and not the number of products. Several discrete choice models that allow for flexible substitution patterns across products have been suggested in the literature.

A second important issue is the endogeneity of prices, and potentially other product characteristics, in the estimation of demand. Unless accounted for, this endogeneity may bias the estimated parameters due to possible correlation between prices and unobserved product attributes. The issue arises because firms are assumed to have more information than the researcher. To address this potential problem researchers have formulated the model so that the econometric error term, usually unobserved product characteristics, enters the estimated equation linearly. This makes standard instrumental variable techniques readily applicable. Common instrumental variables include the characteristics of products, which proxy for the degree of competition (Bresnahan, 1981; Berry, Levinsohn, and Pakes, 1995), or prices in other markets, which are correlated through common shocks to marginal costs and are valid due to an independence assumption on the demand error term (Hausman, 1997; Nevo, 2001).

Recent developments in this area include alternative models of demand, estimation using a combination of individual-level and market-level data (Berry, Levinsohn, and Pakes, 2004), and estimation of dynamic demand (Hendel and Nevo, 2005). Applied work has focused on a variety of questions, including estimation of market power and testing for collusion, simulation of the effects of mergers on prices, regulations and trade constraints, valuation of new goods, computation of price indices, quantifying network effects, vertical relations, and many more.

2.2   Empirical Studies of Auctions

The main goal of the auction literature surveyed by Athey and Haile is to recover the distribution of bidder valuation (or costs) in order to study the form of competition, understand bidding behavior, and compute the optimal auction design (e.g., the format of the auction or the optimal reserve price). Typical data come from a sequence of similar auctions and include the winning bids and possibly the number of bids, all bids, and/or characteristics of bidders and auctions. A main problem is to infer the unobserved valuations or costs from the observed bids. The solution is to use the known rules of the auction, the optimality of bidding behavior, and the estimated probability of winning in order to back out the unobserved valuations.

Athey and Haile discuss three key ideas in this literature. First, when signals are independent the distribution of a single order static determines the parent distribution. Suppose a researcher observes the winning bid and the number of bidders in an ascending independent private values auctions. Assuming optimal bidding, and that the researcher observes several auctions with the same distribution of valuations, then the distribution of the order statistic can be observed and the distribution of valuations can be recovered non-parametrically.

Second, the parameters of the model can be estimated without the need to solve for the equilibrium bidding strategies, which is often difficult. One possible strategy for estimation would be to compute, for given parameter values, the equilibrium bidding behavior and then choose the parameter values that minimize the distance between observed and predicted behavior. Alternatively, one can avoid computing equilibrium behavior and instead recover it from the data. For example, in a first-price sealed-bid auction with independent private values (IPV) bidders place bids to solve

$$\max_{b_i}(v_i - b_i)\Pr(b_j \le b_i \forall j \ne i). \tag{3}$$

Consequently, in equilibrium this choice satisfies the following first order condition:

$$v_i = b_i + \left(\frac{\partial \Pr(b_j \leq b_i \forall j \neq i)}{\partial b_i} \right)^{-1} \Pr(b_j \leq b_i \forall j \neq i). \tag{4}$$

The key insight of Guerre, Perrigne, and Vuong (2000) is that if the econometrician observes all the information available to bidders about their competitors, the markdown factor, $\partial \Pr(b_j \leq b_i \forall j \neq i)/\partial b_i)^{-1} \Pr(b_j \leq b_i \forall j \neq i)$, can be estimated from observed bids in the same and/or other similar auctions. The observed bids and the first order condition in equation (4) can then be used to recover the unobserved valuation. The recovered valuations can in turn be used to estimate the distribution of valuations.[1]

The third principle discussed by Athey and Haile is the value of additional information. This can be in the form of bidder or auction covariates, or information regarding ex-post valuation.

Athey and Haile touch briefly on some of the recent developments in this area, including application of set identification (Haile and Tamer, 2003), incorporating unobserved heterogeneity (Krasnokutskaya, 2003), dynamics and the importance of capacity constraints (Jofre-Bonet and Pesendorfer, 2003), multi-unit auctions and bundling (Cantillon and Pesendorfer, 2004), and auction participation (Athey, Levin, and Seira, 2004). Applied work has addressed questions such as the optimal reserve price, the detection of collusion, testing between private and common value models, and the value of seller reputation.

2.3   Empirical Studies of Entry

The paper by Berry and Tamer discusses identification in models of strategic entry. The focus of this literature is on the entry and location decisions of firms. The typical data set includes market characteristics, the number of firms, and potentially firm identities for a cross section of local markets. The goal is to recover the distribution of fixed costs, and the properties of the variable profit function, if data is not available to estimate the variable profit function directly. Applied questions analyze the determinants of firm (or product) entry and exit, the optimal market structure under different scenarios, the speed at which variable profits decline with the number of firms, and the degree of competition and substitution between different market segments.

The basic idea is to back out profitability from entry and location decisions. Firms enter only if it is more profitable than staying out of the market, and in choosing location they choose the most profitable one. There are several unique issues to this literature that stem from the discreteness of the action space in such settings. First, joint non-parametric identification of the distribution of costs and

---

[1] If computing equilibrium bidding strategies is feasible, one could imagine iterating the process in order to gain efficiency.

variable profits is difficult. Berry and Tamer provide an excellent discussion of the identification issue, presenting the relevant results from the literature, and extending them as needed. Second, multiplicity of equilibria introduces additional econometric difficulties. In principle, multiple equilibria could arise in both the auctions and the price-setting games previously discussed. In both these cases, however, the estimation is usually based on first order conditions that hold in all equilibria. With discrete controls, as in the entry literature, multiple equilibria are common but restrictions that hold in all equilibria may not exist without further assumptions. Therefore, it is often the case that there is no unique mapping from the observed and unobserved variables to market outcomes. In other words, the model does not generate a unique prediction that can be used for estimation (for example, to compute the likelihood of the data).

Several solutions to the problem of multiple equilibria have been offered in the literature. First, one could search for outcomes that hold in all equilibria, such as the number of firms rather than their identities (Bresnahan and Reiss, 1990; Berry, 1992). This often requires firms to be symmetric in their (post-entry) competitive effect on rivals. A second alternative is to modify the structure of the game so that a unique (potentially probabilistic) prediction is obtained. This can be done by specifying an equilibrium selection mechanism (Mazzeo, 2002), by assuming a sequential (rather than simultaneous) order of moves (Berry, 1992), by moving from a complete information game to one of incomplete information (Seim, 2005), or by a combination of both (Einav, 2003). A third solution (Ciliberto and Tamer, 2004; Andrews, Berry, and Jia, 2004) is to leave the model incomplete and focus on set identification.

A recent development in this area has been the explicit consideration of dynamics. Most of the earlier work has focused on reduced form variable profit functions. These reduced form profit functions can be used to recover the distribution of entry costs and to possibly learn some general features of the entry decision, but they cannot be used to distinguish between fixed and sunk costs, or to simulate counterfactual experiments that might change the shape of the reduced form relation. In addition, the explicit modeling of the variable profit function helps with the identification problems discussed by suggesting a framework that can bring in additional information. For example, the variable profit function can be computed from the estimates of the studies discussed above in Sections 2.1 and 2.2.

3   A CONCEPTUAL FRAMEWORK

In this section we provide a unified conceptual framework for all the areas of research mentioned above. Our goal is to highlight the difference in the nature of the econometric error term as an important distinction between these areas. In what follows we first describe the framework, and then discuss how the literatures relate to it.

3.1 The Setup

Consider N players interacting with each other by making choices about a continuous control variable. The econometrician observes two quantities for player i: y_i is player i's control variable, and z_i is an outcome variable. We introduce two unobserved (by the econometrician) mean-zero stochastic variables, η_i and ξ_i, which are associated with player i. For simplicity, suppose that both η_i and ξ_i for all i are known to all players.

Player i chooses y_i in order to maximize his objective function given knowledge (or beliefs) about his opponents' choices, namely to solve

$$\max_{y_i} E\left[\pi_i(y_i, y_{-i}, \eta_i, \xi_i, \xi_{-i}) | \{\eta_i, \xi_i\}_{i=1}^N\right]. \tag{5}$$

Equation (5) provides the key conceptual distinction between the two stochastic elements η_i and ξ_i. While both of them affect player i's choices, only the latter directly affects player i's opponents' payoffs. This is shown in equation (5) because ξ_{-i} enters the equation but η_{-i} does not. Thus, player i does not care about η_{-i} directly. He only uses η_{-i} to form beliefs about y_{-i}. In contrast, ξ_{-i} directly affects player i's payoffs in addition to its role in helping player i in forming beliefs about y_{-i}. Consequently, we will loosely call ξ_i a "strategic error term" while η_i a "non-strategic error term."

To identify both error terms in the same model, we will need the outcome observation z_i, which for example may be a direct observation of $\pi_i(y_i, y_{-i}, \eta_i, \xi_i, \xi_{-i})$. The system can then be inverted so that there would be a one-to-one mapping between $\{(y_i, z_i)\}_{i=1}^N$ and $\{(\eta_i, \xi_i)\}_{i=1}^N$. Note, however, that in order to establish that this mapping exists and is unique, the function $\pi_i(y_i, y_{-i}, \eta_i, \xi_i, \xi_{-i})$ should satisfy certain regularity conditions.

In contrast, suppose now that z_i is not observed. Then, it is clear that the one-dimensional observations cannot identify a two-dimensional error term without further functional form or distributional assumptions. Suppose then that the strategic error term is assumed away. In such a case, equation (5) simplifies to

$$y_i = \arg\max \pi_i(y_i, y_{-i}, \eta_i) \tag{6}$$

which can be easily inverted, for each player separately, as long as $\pi_i(y_i, y_{-i}, \eta_i)$ is monotone in η_i.

Example *As an example, consider the empirical studies of pricing, discussed in Section 2.1. Here p_i is the control variable and $q_i = D_i(p_i, p_{-i})$ is the outcome variable. To fix ideas further, consider the example of a simple logit discrete-choice demand model. The utility for consumer h from product i is given by $u_{hi} = \delta_i - \alpha p_i + \varepsilon_{hi}$ where δ_i is the average quality of product i, p_i is its price, and ε_{hi} is an idiosyncratic taste preference, distributed type I extreme value, which is i.i.d across consumers and products. The mean utility from the outside good (good 0) is normalized to zero. If the number of consumers* *in the market is M, this specification gives rise to the well-known logit demand function:*

$$D_i(p_i, p_{-i}) = M \frac{\exp(\delta_i - \alpha p_i)}{1 + \sum_{j \in J} \exp(\delta_j - \alpha p_j)}. \tag{7}$$

This demand function satisfies the restriction that δ_i is a sufficient statistic for player i, so all heterogeneity across firms can be summarized by a one-dimensional parameter. One can think of the unobserved firm-specific marginal cost c_i as the non-strategic error term in the conceptual model above and of δ_i as the strategic error term. If we only observe prices, we will not be able to determine whether the price of a certain product is higher because of higher marginal costs (high c_i) or because of higher quality (high δ_i). Clearly, separating these two cases is important for any counterfactual analysis. The latter case, because of its strategic implication, is the one that introduces the problem of price endogeneity in empirical pricing models.

The literature solves the indeterminacy problem by exploiting an additional source of data. We typically observe quantities, as well as prices. Quantities identify the δ_i's, and therefore prices can identify the marginal costs, c_i. Without quantity data, however, the system is not identified unless we know (or make assumptions about) the product qualities, δ_i's. Even with quantity data, in order to identify the δ_i's we need to assume that δ_i is one-dimensional sufficient statistic for player i and that the distribution of ε_{hi} is either known or restricted by certain parametric assumptions.

3.2 Discussion

There are several parallels between the empirical auctions literature and the empirical studies of price setting games. Both are focused on recovering an unobserved primitive, bidder valuation or marginal costs, from observed behavior, bids or prices. Indeed, even the mathematical structure of the problem is similar, as can be seen from the similarity between the structure of equation (4) and equation (2). The similarity is, of course, not incidental; after all, one way of thinking about IPV auctions is as an incomplete information version of a Bertrand price competition with homogeneous products. Despite this similarity in the nature of the problem, the two literatures evolved in very different directions. Much of the auction literature emphasizes non-parametric identification and non-parametric estimation techniques, while the demand literature concentrates on parametric ways to deal with endogeneity of prices.

One common belief is that studies of auctions tend to have better data. While there might be a sense in which this is true, it is not obvious. Normally, a researcher interested in estimating demand will have quantities and all prices, while a researcher studying an auction might only observe the winning bid (price). This makes the question even more relevant: What is it that allows the empirical auction literature to focus on non-parametric methods while the literature studying price and quantity competition is mostly parametric?

Part of the answer has to do with the fact that in auctions the rules of the game are known and in many cases sufficient for estimation. For example, suppose that we wanted to study a pricing game similar to an ascending IPV "button" auction. Namely, suppose that firms sell a homogenous good, get private independent draws of marginal costs, which are drawn from an identical distribution, and compete in prices. The object of interest is the distribution of cost, which can be recovered from the observed prices. So in a setting where one believes this is the right model the methods of auctions can be used.

One objection to the setup offered in the previous paragraph for many industries is that products are differentiated. This alone is not enough to explain the difference between the two literatures. For example, suppose one observes a sequence of markets with differentiated products. In each market the products receive independent identical shocks to marginal costs, and there are no other unobserved shocks. If products are symmetric then the demand for a product, as a function of its price, can be recovered non-parametrically even with a large number of products because only the number of competitors matters (but not their identities). Alternatively, if products are not symmetric but are present in all markets, then the demand for each product can be recovered even with a large number of products because the shocks to marginal costs are i.i.d. across markets. As the setup becomes more complicated, because, say, products vary in unobserved (to the econometrician) dimensions across markets and some products are better substitutes than others, or if the shocks to marginal costs are not independent across markets, then non-parametric estimation will not be feasible with reasonably sized data sets. Thus, the use of parametric models for price competition is not driven by the dimensionality per se, but rather by the combination of the dimensionality, symmetry assumptions, and a wedge between the information available to the econometrician and that available to the players.

We believe that the key difference between the price-setting and auction literatures relates to the conceptual framework presented earlier. For simplicity, consider an IPV procurement auction. A quick comparison of equation (3) and equation (1) reveals that one can think of the probability of winning as the demand function. If bidders are ex-ante symmetric (or can be a-priori mapped into a finite set of types), the auction model does not give rise to a strategic error term. Since in such a setting the idiosyncratic shocks are private information, they cannot enter opponents' considerations, and therefore are similar to the η_i's in the conceptual framework.

One should note, however, that strategic error terms in auction environments may exist by allowing a richer structure of unobserved heterogeneity. As an example, they may show up when there exist differences among bidders, which are *common knowledge* to all participants (but not to the econometrician). Common knowledge differences are strategic: They make one bidder's expectation about his probability of winning, given a bid, be different from those expectations of other bidders, given the same bid. Cost variation, which is *private information*, is non-strategic: By construction, it does not enter the opponent's optimization problem.

There may be various reasons why the auction literature has evolved in this way. First, symmetry and exchangeability assumptions are reasonable approximations in many auction settings but may be less credible approximations in product markets. Second, the parallel to quantity data (i.e., the probability of winning) is, of course, not observable, so identification of a strategic error-term with typical auction data sets and without more parametric assumptions is impossible. At the same time, the absence of "quantity" data does not allow the researcher to falsify the modeling assumptions, as the model is just identified. It may be interesting to analyze whether auxiliary information about outcome variables (e.g., the ex-post resale value of an object, or the cost of a project), which are emphasized by Athey and Haile, may help in testing the typical empirical models, and in identifying richer models, which allow for strategic error terms.

The entry literature may also fit into the conceptual framework. The entry literature does not typically model a strategic error term. The stochastic term is in the sunk cost of entry, which (conditional on the entry decision) does not affect the profitability of opponents. One can imagine a strategic error term here; namely, it is reasonable to think that firms are more likely to enter a market because of lower entry cost or because of better productivity. The latter is strategic, as better productivity will make such firms more profitable after entry, and their opponents less. In fact, such an additional (strategic) error term may be identified from post-entry price and quantity data, which can often be available in applications of entry models.

4 CONCLUDING REMARKS

The empirical IO literature has evolved quite rapidly over the last few years. As the papers in the session demonstrated, much progress has been made on identification and estimation of many different dimensions of firms' decisions. For example, we have more flexible models of consumer demand, better methods to non-parametrically estimate bidder valuation in auctions, and significant progress has been made on estimating entry and dynamic games. Given these important methodological advances it is time to apply these methods. Through systematic application to different industries we will be able to learn about the economy and about how to even further improve our methods.

References

[1] Andrews, D., S. Berry, and P. Jia (2004), "Confidence Regions for Parameters in Discrete Games with Multiple Equilibria, with an Application to Discount Store Locations," manuscript, Yale University.

[2] Athey, S., J. Levin, and E. Seira (2004), "Comparing Open and Sealed Bid Auctions: Theory and Evidence from Timber Auctions," manuscript, Stanford University.

[3] Berry, S. (1992), "Estimation of a Model of Entry in the Airline Industry," *Econometrica*, 60, 889–917.

[4] Berry, S., J. Levinsohn, and A. Pakes (1995), "Automobile Prices in Market Equilibrium," *Econometrica*, 63(4), 841–890.

[5] Berry, S., J. Levinsohn, and A. Pakes (2004), "Differentiated Products Demand Systems from a Combination of Micro and Macro Data: The New Car Market," *Journal of Political Economy*, 112(1), 68–105.

[6] Bresnahan, T. (1981), "Departures from Marginal-Cost Pricing in the American Automobile Industry," *Journal of Econometrics*, 17, 201–227.

[7] Bresnahan, T. (1987), "Competition and Collusion in the American Automobile Market: The 1955 Price War," *Journal of Industrial Economics*, 35(4), 457–482.

[8] Bresnahan, T., and P. C. Reiss (1990), "Entry into Monopoly Markets," *Review of Economic Studies*, 57(4), 531–553.

[9] Cantillon, E., and M. Pesendorfer (2004), "Combination Bidding in Multi-Unit Auctions," manuscript, Harvard Business School.

[10] Ciliberto, F., and E. Tamer (2004), "Market Structure and Multiple Equilibria in the Airline Industry," manuscript, Northwestern University.

[11] Einav, L. (2003), "Not All Rivals Look Alike: Estimating an Equilibrium Model of the Release Date Timing Game," manuscript, Stanford University.

[12] Guerre, E., I. Perrigne, and Q. Vuong (2000), "Optimal Nonparametric Estimation of First-Price Auctions," *Econometrica*, 68, 525–574.

[13] Haile, P., and E. Tamer (2003), "Inference with an Incomplete Model of English Auctions," *Journal of Political Economy*, 111(1), 1–51.

[14] Hausman, J. (1997), "Valuation of New Goods Under Perfect and Imperfect Competition," in Bresnahan and Gordon (eds.), *The Economics of New Goods*, NBER Studies in Income and Wealth, 58, 209–237.

[15] Hausman, J., G. Leonard, and J. D. Zona (1994), "Competitive Analysis with Differentiated Products," *Annales d'Economie et de Statistique*, 34, 159–180.

[16] Hendel, I., and A. Nevo (2005), "Measuring the Implications of Sales and Consumer Inventory Behavior," *Econometrica*, forthcoming.

[17] Jofre-Bonet, M., and M. Pesendorfer (2003), "Estimation of a Dynamic Auction Game," *Econometrica*, 71(5), 1443–1489.

[18] Krasnokutskaya, E. (2003), "Identification and Estimation in Highway Procurement Auctions under Unobserved Auction Heterogeneity," manuscript, University of Pennsylvania.

[19] Mazzeo, M. J. (2002), "Product Choice and Oligopoly Market Structure," *RAND Journal of Economics*, 33(2), 1–22.

[20] McFadden, D. (1973), "Conditional Logit Analysis of Qualitative Choice Behavior," in P. Zarembka (ed.), *Frontiers of Econometrics*, New York: Academic Press.

[21] Nevo, A. (2001), "Measuring Market Power in The Ready-to-Eat Cereal Industry," *Econometrica*, 69(2), 307–342.

[22] Porter, R. (1983), "A Study of Cartel Stability: The Joint Economic Committee, 1880–1886," *Bell Journal of Economics*, 14, 301–314.

[23] Seim, K. (2005), "An Empirical Model of Firm Entry with Endogenous Product-Type Choices," *RAND Journal of Economics*, forthcoming.

CHAPTER 4

Recent Developments in the Economics of Price Discrimination[*]

Mark Armstrong

Abstract

This paper surveys the recent literature on price discrimination. The focus is on three aspects of pricing decisions: the information about customers available to firms; the instruments firms can use in the design of their tariffs; and the ability of firms to commit to their pricing plans. Developments in marketing technology mean that firms often have access to more information about individual customers than was previously the case. The use of this information might be restricted by public policy towards customer privacy. Where it is not restricted, firms may be unable to commit to how they use the information. With monopoly supply, an increased ability to engage in price discrimination will boost profit unless the firm cannot commit to its pricing policy. Likewise, an enhanced ability to commit to prices will benefit a monopolist. With competition, the effects of price discrimination on profit, consumer surplus and overall welfare depend on the kinds of information and/or tariff instruments available to firms. The ability to commit to prices may damage industry profit.

1 INTRODUCTION

This paper surveys, in a highly selective manner, recent progress that has been made in the economic understanding of price discrimination. One can say that price discrimination exists when two "similar" products with the same marginal cost are sold by a firm at different prices.[1] There are many forms of price

---

[*] Much of this paper reflects joint work and discussions with John Vickers. In preparing this paper I have greatly benefited from consulting the earlier and more comprehensive survey by Lars Stole (2006), and the reader is referred to that survey for a more complete account of the important contributions to this topic. Thanks for comments and criticisms are due to V. Bhaskar, Richard Blundell, Jan Bouckaert, Yongmin Chen, Drew Fudenberg, Ken Hendricks (my excellent discussant), Paul Klemperer, Marco Ottaviani, Barry Nalebuff, Pierre Regibeau, Patrick Rey, John Thanassoulis, Frank Verboven, Nir Vulkan, Mike Waterson, and Mike Whinston. The support of the Economic and Social Research Council (UK) is gratefully acknowledged.

[1] Stigler (2004) suggests a definition that applies to a wider class of cases: Discrimination exists when two similar products are sold at prices that are in different ratios to their marginal costs.

discrimination, including: charging different consumers different prices for the same good (third-degree price discrimination); making the marginal price depend on the number of units purchased (nonlinear pricing); making the marginal price depend on whether other products are also purchased from the same firm (bundling); making the price depend on whether this is the first time a consumer has purchased from the firm (introductory offers; customer "poaching").

In broad terms, this paper is about what happens to profit and consumer surplus when firms use more ornate tariffs to sell their products. There are two reasons why a firm might be able to tune its tariff more finely: It might obtain more detailed *information* about its potential customers, or it might be able to use additional *instruments* in its tariff design.

A firm can become better informed about its potential customers if it purchases customer data from a marketing company or from another firm. It can use this data to send personalized price offers to new customers (an example of third-degree price discrimination).[2] Alternatively, a firm might keep records of its customers' past purchases and use this information to update its future prices or the range of products offered to those customers. Firms' access to better information is affected by public policy towards consumer privacy (for instance, whether firms are permitted to pass information about their customers to other firms). It is also constrained by a consumer's ability to "anonymise" contact with firms and to pretend to be a new customer.

Examples of the use of more tariff instruments include: using two-part tariffs instead of linear prices; charging different identifiable consumer groups different prices instead of a common price; offering a discount if two products are jointly purchased; or making the price for an item depend on whether a customer has previously purchased similar items from the firm.[3] Public policy towards price discrimination affects the range of instruments that firms can use. Firms are also constrained in their range of instruments by the possibility of arbitrage and resale between consumers.

A third theme of the paper, in addition to the effects of more information and instruments, is how the ability of firms to *commit* to their pricing plans affects outcomes. Recent advances in marketing techniques may mean that the commitment problem has become more severe. The finely tuned customer data that

---

(This definition makes more sense when discussing "versioning," where slightly different versions of a product – such as hardback and paperback books – are offered for sale at very different prices.) Which of these definitions we use makes no difference for the purposes of this paper. An alternative definition might be that price discrimination is present when a similar product is sold to different consumers at different prices. However, this definition rules out cases of "intra-personal" discrimination, which are sometimes relevant, as discussed in section 4.1 below.

[2] See Taylor (2004, section 1) for a summary of the market for customer information. For instance, he reports that a good customer mailing list can sell for millions of dollars on its own.

[3] *Pure* bundling – where two products are made available only as a joint purchase – is not a more ornate tariff compared to separable prices, but rather just a different kind of tariff. However, mixed bundling, where individual products as well as the bundle are offered for sale, is a more ornate tariff compared to either pure bundling or separable prices.

firms often possess permits the use of personalized prices. Such prices are often "secret" rather than public, and it is unlikely that firms can commit to such prices. Moreover, even if firms could commit, the complexity of the linkages between consumer actions and future prices may be too complicated for many consumers to comprehend. A related theme is the impact of consumer naivete or sophistication on firms' policies. Most forms of personalised pricing make a customer's future prices depend upon her past actions, often in a way that is not explicitly stated by firms. Sophisticated consumers – or consumers who have been active in a market for some time – may be able to predict the effect their actions will have on their subsequent deals, and adjust their behavior accordingly. Naive consumers – or consumers in a new market – may not adequately take this linkage into account, however, and firms may be in a position to exploit this myopia.[4]

A summary of the main results presented in the paper is as follows. With monopoly supply, except when commitment problems arise, the use of more ornate tariffs must lead to higher profits. When the firm has access to more detailed information about its customers or can use a wider range of instruments in its tariff, it can do no worse than before and generally it can do better. With competition, though, the effects of using more ornate tariffs are less clear cut. In particular, in section 3 a Hotelling example is used to argue that the impact of more information on profits and prices depends crucially on the *kind* of information that becomes available. Some information will cause firms to make higher profits in equilibrium, whereas other kinds of information will cause all prices to fall compared to the situation with uniform pricing. An important factor for predicting the impact of more information is whether firms agree about which consumers are "strong" and which are "weak."[5] If firms agree about the effect of a specific kind of information on the incentive to set a higher or lower price (the case of "best-response symmetry"), some prices will rise and others will fall, and profit will typically rise, when price discrimination is practiced. However, if firms obtain information about a consumer which suggests to one firm that its price to that consumer should rise and suggests to the other firm that its price should fall ("best-response asymmetry"), the outcome may well be that all prices fall in equilibrium. In such cases, this competition-intensifying effect of price discrimination benefits all consumers. Finally, in section 3.4, the incentives of firms to acquire and to share information with rivals is considered. In cases of best-response symmetry, a firm typically wishes to acquire and to share its private information about consumers. With best-response asymmetry we show that a firm can sometimes be made worse off if it unilaterally acquires customer data.

The availability of an additional tariff instrument also has ambiguous effects on profit and consumer surplus in oligopolistic settings (see section 4). Competing multiproduct firms often make less profit when they practice mixed

---

[4] See Ellison (2006) for further discussion of the effects of (firm and consumer) bounded rationality.
[5] In the price discrimination literature, a market is said to be "strong" ("weak") if a firm wishes to raise (lower) its price there compared to the situation where it must charge a uniform price across all markets.

bundling than when they sell their products separately, while consumers benefit. In contrast, in a one-stop shopping framework where consumers buy all relevant products from one firm, the effect of more ornate tariffs in competitive markets is often to boost profit and harm consumers. Unfortunately, the underlying economic reasons for why some tariff instruments are profit-enhancing, while other instruments damage profit, is currently unclear.

In a dynamic context, a monopolist's ability to commit to future prices raises its profit, since this ability can only widen the range of tariffs that the firm can offer (see section 2.2). With monopoly supply, profit is also higher if consumers are naive. Once a consumer has made a purchase, he typically reveals himself to be likely to purchase at the same price (or higher) subsequently, while consumers who do not initially purchase reveal that they are likely to be unwilling to pay a high price in the future. A firm that cannot commit (or which faces naive consumers) will price to these distinct consumer groups accordingly. In such situations, a policy that forbids price discrimination can act to restore commitment power, to the detriment of consumers. The same pattern of prices prevails in competitive settings, where firms price low to try to poach their rival's past customers. As with monopoly, consumers often benefit from this form of price discrimination. However, in duopoly the ability to set long-term contracts can be damaging to profit, and firms can also be worse-off if they face naive consumers (see section 5).

The welfare effects of allowing price discrimination is ambiguous, both with monopoly and with oligopoly supply. Price discrimination can lead to efficient pricing (see section 2.1). When firms offer different prices to their loyal customers and to their rival's previous customers this can make competition more intense, but it can also induce socially excessive switching between firms (section 5). By contrast, multiproduct firms might induce excessive loyalty, or one-stop shopping, when they offer bundling discounts (section 4.2). In a one-stop shopping framework, the effect of firms using more ornate tariffs is often welfare-enhancing, at least in highly competitive markets. Price discrimination also allows a firm to target price reductions more accurately at market segments where competition is most intense. Doing so can harm rivals and deter entry, and as such can harm consumers compared to the case where discrimination is banned (section 4.3). In sum, sensible policy towards price discrimination needs to be founded on a good economic understanding of the market in question.

2   MONOPOLY SUPPLY

2.1   Information and Instruments

With monopoly supply, the use of more ornate tariffs will boost profit, at least if commitment is not a problem. If the firm has access to more detailed information about its customers or to a wider range of tariff instruments, it can do no worse than before and usually it can do better. In addition, the ability to commit to future prices can only enhance the monopolist's profit, since the firm with such an ability can always choose to implement the non-commitment price if it so chooses. (We will see later in the paper that these easy conclusions for monopoly do not easily carry over to competitive situations.)

In many cases, the efficiency losses caused by monopoly power are due to the firm being unable to offer sufficiently ornate tariffs. In some circumstances, allowing firms to engage in price discrimination can implement efficient prices, in which case welfare is unambiguously improved. One familiar example is first-degree discrimination, where a monopolist has perfect information about each consumer's valuation for its products and has the ability to set personalized prices. To be concrete, suppose there is a population of consumers, each of whom wishes to consume a unit of the firm's product. A consumer's valuation for this unit is denoted v and this varies among consumers according to the distribution function $F(v)$. Suppose the firm has unit cost c. If price discrimination is not possible (e.g., because the firm does not have the necessary information, cannot prevent arbitrage between consumers, or is not permitted to engage in discrimination), the firm will choose a uniform price p to maximize profit $(p - c)(1 - F(p))$. Clearly, this uniform price will be above cost, and total surplus is not maximized. (It is efficient to serve those consumers with $v \geq c$, but only those with $v \geq p > c$ are served.) If the firm can observe each consumer's v and is permitted to discriminate on that basis, it will charge the type-v consumer $p = v$, provided this price covers its cost of supply. In other words, an efficient outcome is achieved. However, the firm appropriates the entire gains from trade and consumers are left with nothing.

There are also situations when price discrimination can lead to *approximately* efficient prices, even when the monopolist has relatively little information about consumer tastes.[6] A supermarket, say, supplies a large number of products. Consumers have a wide variety of preferences over these products – some people prefer tea to coffee, and so on. Suppose consumer valuations for the various products are independently distributed product by product (so the fact a consumer likes coffee, say, gives no guidance about whether she also likes potatoes). For a given list of prices, the "law of large numbers" implies that each consumer's total surplus is approximately the same, even though consumers differ significantly in their individual purchases. Therefore, the firm can extract almost all this total surplus without excluding many consumers. In these circumstances the firm can obtain approximately the first-best profit level by setting its marginal prices equal to marginal costs and extracting the resulting consumer surplus by means of a lump-sum fee.[7] The key insight is that a multiproduct firm can better predict a consumer's total surplus than it can predict a consumer's surplus derived from any individual product. As with exact first-degree price discrimination, the efficient outcome is approximately achieved and the firm extracts almost all the gains from trade.

---

[6] See Armstrong (1999), Bakos and Brynjolfsson (1999), and Geng, Stinchcombe, and Whinston (2005) for this analysis.

[7] As emphasized by Bakos and Brynjolfsson (1999), if marginal costs are zero (as with electronic distribution of software and other information), this profit-maximizing outcome is implemented by pure bundling.

Monopoly first-degree price discrimination is merely an extreme form of a fairly common situation. Lack of information about consumer tastes (or an inability to set suitably finely tuned prices) in combination with market power leads to welfare losses as the firm faces a trade-off between volume of demand and the profit it makes from each consumer. In many cases, if the firm obtains more detailed information about its consumers (or if it is permitted to price discriminate when it was not previously) this will enable the firm to extract consumer surplus more efficiently, and this will often lead to greater overall welfare. However, it is consumers' private information that protects them against giving up their surplus to a monopoly. Therefore, there will often be a reduction in consumer surplus when the monopolist can use more ornate tariffs.

2.2   Dynamic Pricing with Monopoly

A topic that has received much recent attention is dynamic price discrimination.[8] There are many aspects to this phenomenon. A publisher sets a high price for a new (hardback) book, then subsequently the price is reduced. Or a retailer might use information it has obtained from its previous dealings with a customer to offer that customer a special deal (or, as we will see, sometimes a bad deal). This latter form of discrimination, sometimes termed "behavior-based" price discrimination, could be highly complex. If a supermarket has sufficient information, it could offer those customers who have purchased, say, nappies, a voucher offering discounts to a particular brand of baby food. If a customer regularly spends £80 per shopping trip, the supermarket might send the customer a discount voucher if he spends more than £100 next time. Or if the consumer appears to have starting shopping elsewhere recently, the supermarket will send a generous discount voucher to attempt to regain that consumer.

Here and in section 5 the focus is on only simple forms of dynamic price discrimination. Specially, I assume that consumers have unit demand for a single product per period, and that there is no scope for firms to tailor their products to what they judge to be a consumer's particular tastes.[9] I will focus on the case where firms are able, where policy and technology permit, to make their price depend on whether or not the consumer has already purchased from the firm.[10]

---

[8] See Fudenberg and Villas-Boas (2005) for a more detailed survey of this material, covering both monopoly and oligopoly supply.

[9] For instance, someone might return to the same hairdresser since that hairdresser knows how best to cut his/her hair. Or Amazon suggests new books that you might like, given your past purchases. See Acquisti and Varian (2005) for a fuller account of the various ways in which a monopolist might use a customer's history to tailor its current deal.

[10] Another form of dynamic price discrimination, not discussed further in this survey, involves a firm experimenting with different prices over time in order to obtain information about aggregate consumer demand, See Rothschild (1974) and the subsequent literature. That analysis focuses on a very different motive for "discriminatory" pricing than I present in this survey, namely the desirability of using time-varying prices in order to try to learn the aggregate demand function (at which point no price discrimination is practiced).

The reader might ask: what is the difference between dynamic discrimination and static multi-product discrimination such as mixed bundling (discussed in section 4.2)? There are two chief differences. First, unlike the static case, consumers might not know their preferences for future consumption at the time of their initial dealings with a firm. And second, firms might be unable to commit to their future price policy at the time of their initial dealings with consumers. It is perhaps especially plausible that firms cannot commit when they offer personalized discounts (such as the supermarket examples just mentioned). In the following discussion I will focus on this second aspect of the dynamic interaction.

In more detail, suppose there is a diverse population of consumers, each of whom potentially wishes to buy a single unit of the firm's product in each of two periods. A consumer's valuation of the unit v is uniformly distributed on $[0, 1]$, and this valuation is the same in the two periods. Suppose production is costless, and the firm and consumers share the discount factor $\delta \leq 1$. In general, the firm chooses three prices: p_1, the price for a unit in the first period; p_2, the price in the second period if the consumer did not purchase in the first period; and $\hat{p}_2$, the price for a unit in the second period if the consumer also purchased in the first period. In this framework there are two forms of price discrimination possible: (i) the firm can base its second-period price on whether the consumer purchased in the initial period (i.e., $p_2 \neq \hat{p}_2$), or (ii) the firm sets the same price the second period, but this common price is different from the initial price ($p_2 \neq p_1$). Case (i) might be termed "behavior-based" discrimination, while case (ii) could be termed "inter-temporal" discrimination.

Three settings are discussed in this section: the case where consumers are sophisticated and the firm can commit to its pricing plans; the case where consumers are naive and do not foresee the firm may react strategically to their initial choices; and the case where consumers are sophisticated but the firm cannot commit to its pricing plans.

Sophisticated Consumers and Commitment

Suppose the firm announces its three prices $\{p_1, p_2, \hat{p}_2\}$ at the start of period 1, and the firm cannot alter these prices in the light of a consumer's first-period decision. In this case, the profit-maximizing policy is to reproduce the optimal static policy over the two periods, so that[11]

$$p_1 = p_2 = \hat{p}_2 = \frac{1}{2}. \tag{1}$$

---

[11] See Hart and Tirole (1988) and Acquisti and Varian (2005). More generally, it is a standard result in principal-agent theory that when the agent's private information does not change over time, the optimal dynamic incentive scheme simply repeats the optimal static incentive scheme. (See section 8.1 of Laffont and Martimort (2002) and the references therein.) If consumer valuations are imperfectly correlated over time, then even with commitment the firm will wish to practice behavior-based price discrimination. For instance, see Baron and Besanko (1984) for this analysis in the context of regulation.

When the firm can commit to its second-period prices, it is optimal not to price discriminate (in either sense).[12] Clearly, this is also the outcome when the firm is unable to practice price discrimination.

Naive Consumers

Suppose next that consumers do not take into account the effect that their initial purchasing decision has on the second-period prices they will face.[13] This framework might be relevant for a new market, for instance, where consumers have not yet learned the firm's pricing strategy. If the firm chooses the first-period price p_1, naive consumers will purchase in the first period whenever $v \geq p_1$, in which case the firm makes profit in the first period equal to $p_1(1 - p_1)$. In the second period, the firm knows whether a consumer's valuation lies in the interval $[0, p_1]$, if the consumer did not purchase in period 1, or $[p_1, 1]$, if the consumer did purchase in period 1, and will choose its second-period prices accordingly. In the low-value segment it will set the price $p_2 = \frac{1}{2}p_1$, and in the high-value segment it sets the higher price $\hat{p}_2 = max\{\frac{1}{2}, p_1\}$. In particular, the firm views its previous customers as its strong market in the second period, while new customers constitute the weak market. (This will continue to hold in oligopolistic settings in section 5.)

The static profit-maximizing price in the first period is $p_1 = \frac{1}{2}$. However, the firm will wish to raise its price above this level, since this strategy renders its customer information in the second period more valuable.[14] If it chooses the initial price $p_1 \geq \frac{1}{2}$, its discounted profit is

$$p_1(1 - p_1) + \delta \left[p_1(1 - p_1) + \frac{1}{4}p_1^2 \right],$$

and so the profit-maximizing initial and subsequent prices are

$$p_1 = \hat{p}_2 = \frac{1 + \delta}{2 + \frac{3}{2}\delta} > \frac{1}{2} \; ; \; p_2 = \frac{1}{2}p_1 \; . \tag{2}$$

Thus, consumers face an unchanged price in the second period if they purchase in the first period, while the offered price is halved if they did not initially

---

[12] If the model is modified so that either consumers have different discount factors or consumers as a whole have a different discount factor to the firm, then it can be optimal to engage in price discrimination. In addition, Crémer (1984) presents a model with commitment where the price declines over time. At the time of their first purchase consumers are uncertain about their valuation for the product. In this setting it is optimal to set the second-period price equal to marginal cost, since that maximizes a consumer's "option value" from future consumption. All the monopolist's profit is therefore extracted in the first period.

[13] Alternatively, we could think of consumers as simply being myopic. However, the stated "behavioral" assumption seems more plausible.

[14] The period-1 price, which generates the highest period-2 profit is $p_1 = \frac{2}{3}$.

purchase. Here, discounted consumer surplus is lower compared to when the firm cannot practice price discrimination.[15]

Sophisticated Consumers and No Commitment

When consumers are sophisticated, the price plan in (1) (or (2)) is not feasible when the firm cannot commit to its future prices. Once those consumers with $v \geq \frac{1}{2}$ have purchased in the first period, the firm is left with an identifiable pool of low-value consumers. Given this, in the second period the profit-maximizing policy is to set $p_2 = \frac{1}{4}$ to those consumers who have not already purchased. Sophisticated consumers foresee the firm will behave in this opportunistic manner, and some consumers (with v slightly greater than $\frac{1}{2}$) will strategically delay their purchase in order to receive the discounted price next period.

The non-commitment price policy is calculated as follows. Suppose in the first period the price is p_1. What must the time-consistent second-period prices be? Given p_1, suppose those consumers with value $v \geq v^*$ choose to buy in the first period, where the threshold v^* is to be determined. The firm will optimally choose the second-period price for consumers who did not purchase in the first period to be

$$p_2 = \tfrac{1}{2}v^* . \tag{3}$$

The second-period price for those who did buy in the first period depends on v^*: if $v^* < \frac{1}{2}$ then $\hat{p}_2 = \frac{1}{2}$ whereas if $v^* > \frac{1}{2}$ then $\hat{p}_2 = v^*$. In either case, the consumer who is indifferent between buying in the first period and buying only in the second period, v^*, satisfies

$$v^* - p_1 = \delta(v^* - p_2) ,$$

and so from expression (3) it follows that $v^* = 2p_1/(2 - \delta)$. If $v^* \geq \frac{1}{2}$ (as will happen in equilibrium) the firm's discounted profit is

$$p_1(1 - v^*) + \delta \left\{ v^*(1 - v^*) + \left(\tfrac{1}{2}v^* \right)^2 \right\} .$$

After substituting $v^* = 2p_1/(2 - \delta)$ and maximizing this expression with respect to p_1, equilibrium prices are shown to be

$$p_1 = \frac{4 - \delta^2}{2(4 + \delta)} ; \ p_2 = \frac{2 + \delta}{2(4 + \delta)} ; \ \hat{p}_2 = v^* = \frac{2 + \delta}{4 + \delta} . \tag{4}$$

Notice that $p_2 \leq p_1 \leq \frac{1}{2} \leq \hat{p}_2$. Therefore, when the firm cannot commit to future prices, it will set a relatively low first-period price ($p_1 \leq \frac{1}{2}$), followed by a high second-period price for those consumers who purchased in the first period ($\hat{p}_2 \geq \frac{1}{2}$) and an even lower second-period price aimed at those who

---

[15] Discounted consumer surplus with the prices in (2) is equal to $\frac{1}{2} \left(5\delta + 2\delta^2 + 4 \right) (\delta + 1)/ (3\delta + 4)^2$. This is lower than the case without price discrimination, when prices are given by (1) and discounted consumer surplus is $\frac{1}{8}(1 + \delta)$.

did not purchase in the first period ($p_2 \le p_1$). In this example, the second-period price for consumers who previously purchased from the firm is twice the price for those consumers who did not already purchase.[16] All consumers are better off when the firm cannot commit, compared to the price plan (1), while the firm is obviously worse off.[17] Total welfare is also higher, despite the restricted consumption in the first period ($v^* > \frac{1}{2}$) and the high price for repeated sales compared to the commitment regime.[18]

The effect of a ban on price discrimination in this case is to restore the firm's commitment power, to the detriment of all consumers.[19] (By contrast, when consumers are naive, a ban on price discrimination will make consumers in aggregate better off.) All that is needed to restore commitment power is to forbid behavior-based discrimination, i.e., to require $p_2 = \hat{p}_2$. When second-period prices are constrained to be equal, a consumer has no incentive to behave strategically in the first period (i.e., he will buy if $v \ge p_1$), and the firm has no incentive to lower the second-period price below the commitment level. If the firm could commit not to practice behavior-based discrimination, for instance by being seen not to invest in consumer tracking technology, its profits would rise.[20]

---

[16] Of course, this form of discrimination is not feasible if past consumers can pretend to be new customers, for instance by deleting their computer "cookies" or using another credit card when they deal with an online retailer.

[17] With commitment prices (1), the total discounted payment for two units is $(1 + \delta)/2$. With the no-commitment prices (4), if a consumer buys two units the total discounted payment $p_1 + \delta\hat{p}_2$ is less than $(1 + \delta)/2$, and so all consumers must be better off when the firm cannot commit. (Some consumers will be even better off if they choose to consume only in the second period.)

[18] One can also consider a plausible form of *partial* commitment, where the firm can commit to long-term contracts but not to its future price for those consumers who did not initially purchase. Thus, a consumer who buys in the first period is promised a specified second-period price, but the price aimed at new consumers in the second period is determined in a time-consistent manner (i.e., the firm announces its prices p_1 and $\hat{p}_2$ at the start of period 1, while p_2 is chosen at the start of period 2). However, one can show that the no-commitment prices in expression (4) remain optimal in this regime of partial commitment. (The balance of prices p_1 and $\hat{p}_2$ is indeterminate, but the prices in (4) are among the set of prices which are optimal.) Thus, in this example at least, the commitment problem that harms profit lies with the inability to commit to p_2 rather than $\hat{p}_2$, and the ability to commit to $\hat{p}_2$ brings no benefit to the firm (nor does it harm consumers). The firm's damaging temptation is to target low-valuation consumers in the future, not to exploit consumers who have revealed themselves to have high valuations.

[19] A similar feature is seen in the related model of "secret deals" in vertical contracting. Suppose an upstream monopolist offers contracts for an essential input to two competing downstream firms. If these contracts are secret, in the sense that one downstream firm does not observe the other downstream firm's deal, then the monopolist cannot help but choose marginal-cost prices for the input. This harms its profit but benefits final consumers. If public policy prevented price discrimination and forced the monopolist to offer the same contract to the two downstream firms, this restores the monopolist's commitment power, and harms consumers. See Rey and Tirole (2006) for a survey of this literature.

[20] Villas-Boas (2004) analyzes a related model with an infinitely lived firm facing a sequence of (sophisticated) two-period consumers arranged in overlapping generations. The firm's prices depend on whether a consumer has previously purchased, but it cannot determine whether a

Taylor (2004) analyzes a related model where one firm sells a product in period 1, and a separate firm sells a related product in period 2.[21] The first firm is able to sell its information about which consumers purchased from it in the first period to the second firm. The second firm is willing to pay for this information, since it provides the basis for behavior-based price discrimination towards its consumers. Since the first firm can fully extract the second firm's benefit from the information, the scenario is essentially the same as when an integrated firm supplies in both periods and cannot commit to its second-period price. Taylor also distinguishes between sophisticated and naive consumers. If consumers are naive, in the sense that they do not foresee their decisions with one firm might affect their offers from the subsequent firm, the first firm has an incentive to raise its price above the monopoly level in order to boost the value of information to the second firm (just as in expression (2) above). Public policy towards privacy might prohibit the passing of consumer information between firms, and this would make naive consumers better off and reduce the level of industry profit. On the other hand, when consumers are sophisticated, a ban on information transfer will surely increase profit.

3 THE EFFECTS OF MORE INFORMATION IN OLIGOPOLY

The discussion to this point has focused on monopoly, and argued that consumers are protected from having their surplus extracted when (i) they possess private information about their tastes and/or (ii) the firm is unable to commit to its pricing plans. Competition between suppliers provides a third means by which consumers are protected against surplus extraction. Even if firms know everything about a consumer's tastes and can commit to any price plan, competition ensures the consumer will still be left with positive surplus. A question of current policy concern (for instance, in discussions about the impact of e-commerce) is whether the availability of more detailed customer information to firms is likely to benefit or to harm consumers, firms or overall welfare. This is a subtle question, as we will see in this section.[22]

---

new consumer is "young" or whether she is "old" but chose not to consume in her first period. An interesting result in this richer framework is that there can be cycles in the pattern of prices offered to new consumers. In addition, as in the two-period framework presented in the text, the firm is better off if it is unable to practice behavior-based price discrimination.

[21] In Taylor's model, consumer valuations are binary and are not perfectly correlated for the two products. See Calzolari and Pavan (2005) for a related and more general model.

[22] In general, however, when a fixed set of competing firms are *fully* informed about consumer tastes, (one) equilibrium necessarily involves the efficient outcome. See Spulber (1979) for this analysis. Bernheim and Whinston (1986) provide related analysis in a more general context. Also, notice that not all equilibria need be efficient. Consider two firms that each supply one of two perfectly complementary products. Suppose that consuming one unit of each product yields utility 2 to the consumer, while consuming two units of each product yields utility 3. Suppose production is costless. If both firms offer the nonlinear tariff such that $p_1 = 1$ and $p_2 = 3$

Many of the extra effects that appear with competition can be illustrated using a simple symmetric Hotelling duopoly example.[23] A consumer wishes to buy a single unit from either firm A or firm B, and if he buys from firm $i = A, B$ his net surplus is

$$u^i = v - p^i - t d^i,$$

where v is the consumer's valuation for the unit (which is the same at either firm), p^i is firm i's price, d^i is the distance the consumer travels to firm i, and t is the transport cost per unit of distance incurred. The two firms are situated at each end of the unit interval $[0, 1]$ and consumers are uniformly located along this interval. A consumer located at $x \in [0, 1]$ is a distance $d^A = x$ from firm A and $d^B = 1 - x$ from firm B. A consumer's preferences are then defined by three parameters: v is the consumer's valuation for the product, x represents his relative preference for firm B over firm A, and t represents his "choosiness," i.e., how much he dislikes buying his less preferred brand.

The parameters (v, x, t) are distributed among consumers in some way. In the various examples that follow, I assume for simplicity that all consumers choose to buy from one firm or the other. This assumption largely, but not entirely, eliminates the ability to compare welfare with or without price discrimination, but it does hugely simplify the calculations. In addition, I assume the parameters (v, x, t) are independently distributed. (I will in the following sections suppose that each of the three parameters in turn is observable to the firms, and I do not wish to consider whether observing v, say, allows firms to obtain a signal about (x, t).) Suppose that production costs are normalised to zero. The consumer with preferences (v, x, t) will buy from A rather than B if his surplus u is higher there. Since his valuation of the product v is the same from either firm, he will buy from the firm with the lower total cost of purchase, and he will buy from firm A if

$$p^A + xt \le p^B + (1 - x)t. \tag{5}$$

3.1   Discriminating on Valuation: Profit Neutrality

Suppose that firms each observe a consumer's valuation v and can target a personalized price to that consumer. Does this information affect prices and

---

(where p_i is the firm's price for buying i units), the consumer will choose to buy just one unit of each product, which is inefficient. Nevertheless, neither firm has a profitable deviation. Bhaskar and To (2004) show in a free entry model that, even when firms possess full information about the market and can use the full range of tariff instruments, there is a socially excessive number of firms in the market.

[23] A similar exercise was performed in the pioneering paper by Borenstein (1985). He analyzes a free entry model rather than a duopoly, and so also considers the effect of permitting price discrimination on the equilibrium number of firms. He does not consider the effect of discriminating on the basis of brand preference. See Stole (1995) for related analysis in the context of nonlinear pricing.

profits in equilibrium? Clearly, with monopoly supply the ability to observe valuations would be valuable – see section 2.1 – but in this particular competitive environment it actually has no effect. For simplicity, suppose all consumers have the same choosiness parameter t.[24] Given v, if firms' prices are p^A and p^B, expression (5) shows that a type-x consumer will buy from A when $x \le \frac{1}{2} - \frac{p^A - p^B}{2t}$. Therefore, firm i's profit from the type-v segment is

$$\pi^i = \left(\frac{1}{2} - \frac{p^i - p^j}{2t} \right) p^i$$

and it is straightforward to show that the equilibrium price in this segment is $p^A = p^B = t$. Since the equilibrium price does not depend on v, whether or not v is observable has no effect on outcomes. Notice that this is true even with asymmetric information: If firm B has no information about v while A does, A has no incentive to use its superior information in its pricing decisions. Therefore, a marketing firm with customer data about v would, in this setting, be unable to sell this data to one or both duopolists.

This example extends to situations where consumers buy multiple units and multiple products, and where consumers' preferences over these various units is private information.[25] Suppose that a type-θ consumer obtains gross utility $u(\theta, q)$ if she buys the vector of quantities q from a firm, excluding his transport cost and the price he must pay. The net surplus obtained by a type-θ consumer located at x if he purchases quantities q^A from firm A in return for total payment P^A is

$$u(\theta, q^A) - P^A - tx,$$

while his net surplus if he purchases q^B from firm B in return for payment P^B is

$$u(\theta, q^B) - P^B - t(1 - x).$$

In particular, we assume brand preferences (or transport costs) do not depend on the quantities purchased.[26] Suppose first that firms can observe the type θ of each consumer (but not the location x), and that θ is distributed independently from the brand preference parameter x. Then the most profitable way for a firm to attract a consumer is to set its marginal prices equal to marginal costs and to extract profit by means of a fixed charge. If each firm's marginal cost for

---

[24] The argument works just as well with unobserved heterogeneity in t, provided all consumers participate.

[25] For this analysis see Armstrong and Vickers (2001, section 4) and Rochet and Stole (2002). This analysis presumes a one-stop-shopping framework where consumers purchase all products from a single firm. Rochet and Stole show that this "no discrimination" result is not robust to a number of changes to the model, including: firms having different costs, brand preference x being correlated with the vertical taste parameter θ, or the total market size being affected by the contracts offered.

[26] See Spulber (1989), Stole (1995) and Yin (2004) for models of nonlinear pricing when transport costs do depend on the quantities purchased.

supplying product i is c_i, each firm will set marginal price $p_i \equiv c_i$ and the fixed charge t. This cost-based two-part tariff does not depend on θ. Therefore, this two-part tariff remains an equilibrium even when firms cannot observe the taste parameter θ. If firm B offers the cost-based two-part tariff $T(q) = t + \sum_i c_i q_i$, then the same tariff is firm A's best response if A does not observe θ (since it is also A's best response when it can observe θ).[27]

In sum, information about "vertical" taste parameters (v or θ in the previous discussion) has no effect on outcomes in these models of competitive price discrimination.

3.2   Discriminating on Choosiness: Best-Response Symmetry

Now return to the unit demand Hotelling framework and suppose consumers differ in their choosiness parameter t. Suppose that t is distributed on the interval $[t_L, t_H]$ according to some probability distribution, and that location x is independently and uniformly distributed on the unit interval $[0, 1]$. Assume $t_L > 0$, so that no consumers view the firms' services as perfect substitutes. If firms were able to observe t but not x, the equilibrium price to the type-t consumers is $p_t = t$, as in section 3.1. This reveals a major difference between discrimination based on choosiness t and based on valuation v: in the latter case firms could not extract anything extra from high-value consumers due to competitive pressure, but when a consumer is known to be choosy, firms can extract high profit. Industry profit when firms price discriminate in this way is $\bar{t}$, the mean of t.

If firms cannot price discriminate, they will set uniform prices p^A and p^B. From (5), a type-(x, t) consumer will buy from A if $x \leq \frac{1}{2} - \frac{p^A - p^B}{2t}$. When prices are not too different, the number of such consumers is[28]

$$\frac{1}{2} - \frac{p^A - p^B}{2\hat{t}},$$

where $\hat{t}$ is the harmonic mean of t (so $\hat{t} = (E\{1/t\})^{-1}$). Therefore, the equilibrium non-discriminatory price (and equilibrium industry profit) is $\hat{t}$.[29] Since the

---

[27] Miravete and Röller (2004) fit a model of duopoly competition in nonlinear tariffs to data from cellular telephone markets. (The model assumes that consumers buy services from both firms, in contrast to the one-stop shopping framework used in the text.) They estimate that if firms were restricted to offer two-part tariffs rather than fully nonlinear tariffs, in equilibrium they would obtain 94% of the equilibrium profits with unrestricted tariffs.

[28] The condition for this to be the correct formula for A's demand is that $\left| p^A - p^B \right| < t_L$, so that no firm has a monopoly over even the most price-sensitive of consumers.

[29] One important issue not discussed here is when a pure strategy equilibrium exists. If some consumers view the two firms as very close substitutes then no pure strategy equilibrium exists, as in Varian (1980), for instance. If t_L is close to zero the candidate equilibrium price $\hat{t}$ is also close to zero, and it will be worthwhile for a firm to deviate from the candidate equilibrium, and instead to set a high price, which targets the choosier consumers. For instance, take the special case where there are just two values of t, t_L and t_H, which are equally likely. One can show

harmonic mean is necessarily lower than the (arithmetic) mean, it follows that industry profits rise when firms can discriminate according to choosiness. Since total welfare is not affected by price discrimination in this full-participation framework,[30] aggregate consumer surplus decreases with this form of discrimination, although clearly the more price-sensitive consumers are better-off with price discrimination.[31]

In this example a firm will raise some prices and lower others if it is permitted to engage in price discrimination. That is to say, the non-discriminatory price is an "average" of the discriminatory prices (in this case it is the harmonic mean). In the remainder of this section we investigate in more detail when this phenomenon occurs.

First, consider the straightforward case of monopoly supply. Suppose a monopolist serves two markets, 1 and 2, which have independent consumer demands. The firm's profit in market i when it sets the price p_i in that market is denoted $\pi_i(p_i)$. Then the profit-maximizing discriminatory prices are characterized by $\pi'_i(p_i) = 0$, while the profit-maximizing uniform price $\bar{p}$ satisfies $\pi'_1(\bar{p}) + \pi'_2(\bar{p}) = 0$. Except in the fluke case where there is no gain from discrimination, it follows that in market 1, say, we have $\pi'_1(\bar{p}) > 0$ and in market 2 we have $\pi'_2(\bar{p}) < 0$. Assuming profit functions are single-peaked, it follows that if the firm can price discriminate it will raise its price in market 1 (the strong market) and lower its price in market 2.[32]

---

that the candidate equilibrium, where price equals the harmonic mean of t, is an equilibrium provided $p_L/p_H > 0.093$.

[30] As ever, one should be wary of reaching policy conclusions on the basis of these unit demand models since prices have little role to play in welfare terms. If consumers had elastic multi-unit demands in each period, the price reductions to the low-t consumers, as well as the high prices charged to high-t consumers, would have a welfare impact. A similar remark applies at several points in this survey.

[31] This example is closely related to Proposition 4 (part (i)) in Armstrong and Vickers (2001), specialized to the case of inelastic demand. Similar effects are seen if the model of "tourists and locals" in Varian (1980) is extended to allow for price discrimination. Local consumers are assumed to know the full range of prices offered by the competing firms and to buy from the lowest price firm. Tourists are assumed to know nothing, and randomly choose a firm. If firms cannot price discriminate between these two groups, Varian shows that firms choose prices according to a mixed strategy. However, if firms can distinguish between the two groups, they would charge a price equal to marginal cost to the local consumers and a price equal to the reservation value to tourists. Therefore, as in the example in the text, the choosy group (here, the ignorant group) is treated badly by price discrimination. In Varian's model, however, industry profit is unchanged when price discrimination is practiced.

[32] This discussion concerns third-degree discrimination. At least in the case of monopoly, the typical case with other forms of discrimination is also that some prices rise while others fall. For instance, when a multiproduct monopolist practices mixed bundling, in many cases it will raise its prices for individual purchase, and lower its price for joint purchase, compared to the case where the firm sets a separable price for each product. Similarly, if a firm offers a two-part tariff instead of a linear price, the typical case is that the overall payment increases for consumers who buy little but falls for high-volume consumers.

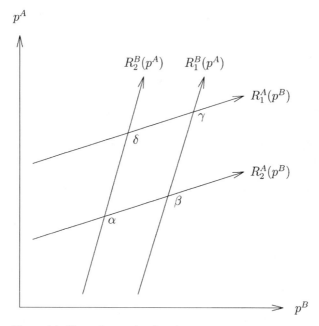

Figure 4.1. Duopoly reaction functions.

Matters are more complicated when there are competing firms, as discussed in Corts (1998). The chief aspect that differs from monopoly is that a market might be strong for one firm but weak for its rival.[33] For now, though, suppose firms do not differ in their judgement of which markets are strong. Corts uses the term "best-response symmetry" for such cases. This case of price discrimination based on choosiness is an example of best-response symmetry.

Suppose there are two markets, 1 and 2, and two firms, A and B. Suppose there are no cross-price effects across the two markets, and that firm A's profit in market i is $\pi_i^A(p_i^A, p_i^B)$ if it sets the price p_i^A while its rival sets the price p_i^B. If discrimination is allowed, write $p_i^A = R_i^A(p_i^B)$ for firm A's profit-maximizing price in market i if its rival sets the price p_i^B. (Similar notation is used for firm B's reaction functions.) In reasonable situations these reaction functions are upward sloping. Suppose that both firms view market 1, say, as the strong market, in the sense that

$$R_1^A(p^B) > R_2^A(p^B) \, ; \; R_1^B(p^A) > R_2^B(p^A) \, .$$

See Figure 4.1 for a depiction of this situation.

---

[33] This basic insight is also found in Stole (1995, page 530): "Of fundamental importance, horizontal preferences are naturally incongruous across firms – a strong preference for one firm implies a weaker preference for the others. Vertical preferences, in contrast, are harmonious across firms – a customer with a high marginal valuation of quality for one firm will have similar preferences for other firms as well; all firms prefer these customers."

When firms can price discriminate, the equilibrium prices in market 1 are at γ on the figure, and the prices in market 2 are at α. Now suppose that firms cannot price discriminate. As in the monopoly case just described, if the profit functions are single-peaked, firm A's best response to a uniform price p^B from its rival will lie between its pair of reaction functions on the figure. Similarly, firm B's response function, if it cannot discriminate, lies between its two reaction functions. We can deduce that the equilibrium prices when discrimination is not possible lie inside the diamond $\alpha\beta\gamma\delta$. In particular, the comparison between discriminatory and non-discriminatory prices is clear: Permitting discrimination increases the prices in market 1 (the strong market) and decreases the prices in market 2 (the weak market).

3.3   Discriminating on Brand Preference: Best-Response Asymmetry

Now return to the specific Hotelling example, and suppose for simplicity that all consumers have the same choosiness parameter t.[34] Suppose that firms can observe a consumer's location x and price accordingly. Consider firm A's best response to its rival's price p_x^B when a consumer has brand preference parameter x. Firm A can profitably serve this consumer segment provided that

$$tx < p_x^B + t(1-x),$$

in which case it will offer the limit price that just prevents the consumer from being tempted by the rival offer p_x^B, so that $p_x^A + tx = p_x^B + t(1-x)$, or

$$p_x^A = p_x^B + t(1-2x).$$

Thus, firm A prices high to those consumers who prefer its product but prices low to consumers who prefer its rival's product, so that small x consumers are the strong market for firm A. Similarly, those consumers who prefer firm B's product are that firm's strong market. A firm sets a high price to consumers with a strong brand preference for its product to exploit those consumers' distaste for the rival product. We deduce that one firm's strong market is the other's weak market. Corts terms this situation "best-response asymmetry."

With this form of price discrimination, the equilibrium price paid by a consumer located at x is

$$p_x = \begin{cases} (1-2x)t & \text{if } x \leq \frac{1}{2} \\ (2x-1)t & \text{if } x \geq \frac{1}{2} \end{cases}. \tag{6}$$

Consumers will obtain the product from the closer (preferred) firm, which is efficient, and those consumers closer to the middle will obtain the best deal (even when account is taken of their greater transport costs).

---

[34] This analysis is due to Thisse and Vives (1988).

Suppose next that firms must set a uniform price to consumers. If consumers are uniformly distributed along the interval then the equilibrium uniform price is $p = t$. This uniform price is above all the discriminatory prices in expression (6). Thus, this is an example where *all* prices fall when firms have access to more customer information.[35,36] Price discrimination has no impact on total welfare since all consumers just wish to buy a single unit, and they buy this unit from the closer firm with either pricing regime. All consumers clearly benefit from price discrimination. Firms make lower profits – in fact, in this example they make precisely *half* the profit – when they engage in this form of price discrimination compared to when they must offer a uniform price.

The fact that firms might be worse off when they practice price discrimination is one of the key differences between monopoly and competition. Ignoring issues of commitment, a monopolist is better off when it can price discriminate. In the same way, an oligopolistic firm is always better off if it can price discriminate, for *given* prices offered by its rivals. However, once account is taken of what rivals too will do, firms in equilibrium can be worse off when discrimination is used. Firms then find themselves in a classic prisoner's dilemma.

A closely related model, which is also useful for understanding models of dynamic price discrimination in section 5, is by Bester and Petrakis (1996).[37] Instead of being able to condition prices on a consumer's precise location, here a firm merely observes whether a consumer has a brand preference for its product or its rival's product. That is to say, firms observe whether a consumer has location $x \leq \frac{1}{2}$ or location $x \geq \frac{1}{2}$. (For instance, firms might target different prices to consumers in different regions by placing targeted coupons, which promise a discount if the consumer brings the coupon to the store, in different regional newspapers.) When consumers are uniformly located along the interval one can show the equilibrium discriminatory prices are

$$\hat{p} = \tfrac{2}{3}t \; ; \; p = \tfrac{1}{3}t \; . \tag{7}$$

Here, $\hat{p}$ is a firm's price to a consumer on that firm's "turf" (i.e., when the consumer is known to prefer that firm), and p is a firm's price to a consumer on the rival's turf. Thus, each consumer is offered two prices: a low price from the less-preferred firm and a high price from the preferred firm. However, as in the Thisse-Vives model, these prices are both below the equilibrium uniform price ($p = t$). Those consumers close to the middle of the interval, who have little preference for one firm over the other, will clearly choose the low price

---

[35] In this framework it is perfectly possible that some prices increase with discrimination. Suppose that instead of following a uniform distribution, the density of x on $[0, 1]$ is $f(x) = 6x(1 - x)$, a density which puts more consumers located close to the mid-point. Then one can show that the equilibrium uniform price is $p = \frac{2}{3}t$, which is lower than discriminatory prices for those consumers close to the ends of the interval.

[36] See Wallace (2004) for an extension of the Thisse-Vives framework to allow firms to make customer-specific investments, which adds quality to the product they supply to a customer. He finds that locational price discrimination can then increase equilibrium profit.

[37] See also Shaffer and Zhang (1995).

from the (slightly) more distant firm. This is inefficient, since consumers should buy from their preferred firm regardless of prices. Consumers with a strong brand preference will buy from the preferred firm despite the high price. Again, a prisoner's dilemma emerges, and both firms are better off without this form of price discrimination even though each would individually like to discriminate.[38]

Thus, there are competitive situations where price discrimination causes all prices to fall.[39] In such cases, discrimination acts to intensify competition. The analysis in section 3.2 indicates that, at least in the case of third-degree discrimination, this situation can only occur when firms differ in their view of which markets are strong and which are weak. In the early literature on competitive price discrimination it was not always made clear that the crucial feature that can cause discrimination to intensify competition is best-response asymmetry. For instance, Thisse and Vives (1988, page 134) wrote that "denying a firm the right to meet the price of a competitor on a discriminatory basis provides the latter with some protection against price attacks. The effect is then to weaken competition [. . .]" And Anderson and Leruth (1993, page 56), in the context of mixed bundling, argue that price discrimination reduces profits since "firms compete on more fronts." The example of discrimination based on choosiness in section 3.2 above, illustrates that it is not the number of fronts on which firms compete which is relevant. (In that example, price discrimination raises equilibrium profit.) Rather, in the case of third-degree price discrimination what matters is whether firms have divergent views about which markets are strong and which are weak.[40]

3.4   Private Information

Until this point the discussion has considered situations in which information is either freely available to all firms or it is not available to any firm. In this section we discuss the impact of firms possessing information about consumers that is not necessarily available to rival firms. To this end, consider a variant

---

[38] Notice that industry profit with discrimination in the Thisse-Vives model ($\frac{1}{2}t$) is lower than that in the Bester-Petrakis model (which can be calculated to be $\frac{5}{9}t$). Liu and Serfes (2004) propose a model that encompasses these two as extremes. They show that equilibrium profits are U-shaped in the precision of information about brand preferences: profit is lowest when the firms have information that is less precise than the perfect information in the Thisse-Vives framework.

[39] Price discrimination might also cause all prices to fall when there is monopoly supply. Nahata, Ostaszewski, and Sahoo (1990) show that if the profit functions are not single-peaked then all prices might decrease, or all might increase, when a monopolist engages in third-degree price discrimination. In addition, as discussed in Coase (1972), when a monopolist sells a durable good over time and cannot commit to future prices, all prices might fall compared to the case where the firm can commit to future prices.

[40] Nevo and Wolfram (2002) present evidence consistent with the hypothesis that price discrimination via coupons in the breakfast cereal market exhibits best-response asymmetry, and that the introduction of coupons leads to a fall in all prices. They also document how firms allegedly colluded to stop the use of coupons. Odlyzko (2003) discusses how competing railway companies may have welcomed tariff regulation in order to avoid profit-destroying price discrimination.

of the Bester and Petrakis (1996) model where firms have private information about brand preferences. Perhaps each firm purchases customer data from a different marketing company, for example. If a consumer prefers firm A (i.e., $x \leq \frac{1}{2}$) suppose firm i receives the signal $s^i = s_L$ with probability $\alpha \geq \frac{1}{2}$ and the signal $s^i = s_R$ with probability $1 - \alpha$.[41] Similarly, if a consumer prefers firm B then firm i receives a signal $s^i = s_R$ with probability α and the signal $s^i = s_L$ with probability $1 - \alpha$. Conditional on a consumer's location x, the signals s^A and s^B are independently distributed. A symmetric equilibrium will consist of a firm choosing the price $\hat{p}$ for those consumers they believe prefer their product and choosing price p when they think the consumer is likely to prefer their rival's product. (Specifically, if firm A observes the signal $s^A = s_L$ it will set the price $\hat{p}$, while if it sees the other signal it will set the price p. Firm B will follow the reverse strategy.)

Then Appendix A shows that equilibrium prices are

$$\hat{p} = \frac{t}{\alpha + \frac{1}{2}} \; ; \; p = \frac{t}{\alpha + 2\alpha^2} . \tag{8}$$

When $\alpha > \frac{1}{2}$ it follows that $\hat{p} > p$ and firms charge more to those consumers they consider likely to have a brand preference for them. When $\alpha = \frac{1}{2}$ (i.e., when the signal has no informational content) it follows that $\hat{p} = p = t$, just as in the standard Hotelling model without information. When $\alpha = 1$ (i.e., the signal is perfectly accurate), the prices are as given in expression (7). More generally, the availability of the private signal causes both prices to fall compared to the case when the signal is not available. Finally, one can show that equilibrium industry profit falls monotonically as the accuracy of the private signal rises.

One can perform the same exercise when signals instead give information about a consumer's choosiness t. In this case, industry profit is increasing in the precision of the signal. More interesting, though, is to present an asymmetric variant of this model, which is suited to discussing whether a firm has an incentive to acquire and/or share information with its rival. Suppose there are two consumer segments: a consumer has choosiness parameter $t = t_L$ with probability $\frac{1}{2}$ and choosiness parameter $t = t_H$ with probability $\frac{1}{2}$. Suppose that firm A knows each consumer's choosiness precisely, but firm B knows nothing. Does A have an incentive to share its private information with its rival? Without information sharing, firm A sets the two prices, p_L^A and p_H^A, respectively to the type-t_L and the type-t_H consumers, but firm B is constrained to choose a uniform price, p^B. One can show equilibrium prices are

$$p_L^A = \frac{3t_L t_H + t_L^2}{2t_L + 2t_H}; \; p_H^A = \frac{3t_L t_H + t_H^2}{2t_L + 2t_H}; \; p^B = 2\frac{t_L t_H}{t_L + t_H}.$$

---

[41] This model is a variant of chapter 2 of Esteves (2004).

Here, $p_L^A \leq p^B \leq p_H^A$, and so the better-informed firm has the greater market share in the price-sensitive market but the smaller share of the choosy market.[42] With these equilibrium prices, one can show that the profits of firms A and B are respectively

$$\pi_I = \frac{14t_L t_H + t_L^2 + t_H^2}{16(t_L + t_H)} \; ; \; \pi_U = \frac{t_L t_H}{t_L + t_H} \leq \pi_{INF}, \tag{9}$$

so that the better-informed firm makes higher profit.[43] (Here, "I" stands for informed and "U" for uninformed.) Firm B's profit is the same as if firm A were not informed. Therefore, in this example, an uninformed firm is indifferent about whether or not its rival has the ability to practice price discrimination. Firm A obtains higher profit compared to the case in which it was not informed and so has an incentive unilaterally to acquire this information.

Suppose now that firm A shares its information with its rival. In this case, both firms' equilibrium prices are $p_L = t_L$ in the price-sensitive segment and $p_H = t_H$ in the choosy segment. Firms share each segment equally, and so firm A obtains profit $\frac{1}{4}(t_L + t_H)$. One can verify that this profit is higher than π_I in expression (9) except when $t_L = t_H$. Thus, the well-informed firm has an incentive to provide its rival with its information (and the rival is willing to accept this information). In this example, when a firm is uninformed about a consumer's choosiness it will price low, and this low price disadvantages the well-informed firm. Welfare also rises when there is sharing of information, since in this framework welfare is maximized when firms share the markets equally. The effect of information sharing on consumers appears to be ambiguous in this framework.[44]

Finally, we can investigate a firm's incentive to acquire and share information about brand preference.[45] Specifically, suppose all consumers have the same choosiness parameter t, and firm A knows whether $x < \frac{1}{2}$ or $x > \frac{1}{2}$ while firm B knows nothing. Suppose firm A sets the price $\hat{p}^A$ to those consumers it knows prefer its product and the price p^A to those consumers who prefer B's product, while firm B sets the uniform price p^B. Then one can show the equilibrium prices are

$$\hat{p}^A = \tfrac{3}{4}t \; ; \; p^A = \tfrac{1}{4}t \; ; \; p^B = \tfrac{1}{2}t.$$

---

[42] One can also show neither market is cornered by one firm with these prices. Interestingly, firm B's price is the same as when firm A is not informed. When neither firm is informed, section 3.2 above shows that each firm sets the uniform price $2\frac{t_L t_H}{t_L + t_H}$.

[43] It is unclear whether it is a general result that a better-informed firm makes higher profit than its rival.

[44] However, if t_L and t_H are not too different then information sharing is bad for consumers in aggregate.

[45] See also section III of Thisse and Vives (1988) and section 3 of Chen (2006). These authors assume that when one firm chooses to discriminate while the other does not, the non-discriminating firm acts as a Stackleberg price leader.

With these prices, the central 25% of consumers buy from their less-preferred firm. The profits of firms A and B are respectively

$$\pi_I = \tfrac{5}{16}t \; ; \; \pi_U = \tfrac{1}{4}t \; .$$

Suppose instead that neither firm has information. In this case, firms set the uniform price $p = t$ and each makes profit $\tfrac{1}{2}t$. Therefore, firm A is actually made worse off by its private information about consumer tastes.[46,47] Clearly, if firm A could *secretly* obtain the information (so that firm B continued to set the price $p^B = t$) then it is made better off by its information. However, so long as it is common knowledge that firm A has this information (and will surely use it), firm A is worse off once B's aggressive response is considered. If firm A has this information, it would like to commit not to price discriminate. Another way to think about this is to suppose that the Bester-Petrakis model is extended to a two-stage interaction, where firms first (simultaneously) decide whether or not to "invest" in the technology or information gathering procedures needed to be able to price discriminate, and in the second stage they choose their price(s). In this two-stage game, one equilibrium is for neither firm to choose to be able to price discriminate in the first period. Thus, the prisoner's dilemma aspect of the Bester-Petrakis model falls away in this dynamic setting.[48,49]

4   THE EFFECTS OF MORE INSTRUMENTS IN OLIGOPOLY

4.1   One-Stop Shopping

The model presented in Armstrong and Vickers (2001, section 3) provides an initial framework in which to discuss the effects of increasing the range of

---

[46] If firm A gives firm B this information, we are in the Bester-Petrakis situation where each firm makes profit $\tfrac{5}{18}t$. This means that firm A's profits decrease, and it has no incentive to share its information.

[47] Somewhat related analysis is in Cooper (1986), who presents a model of repeated Bertrand duopoly where, before competition starts, firms can publicly commit to set constant prices over time (a kind of commitment not to price discriminate). He shows that it can be unilaterally profitable for a firm to make such a commitment, even if the rival does not.

[48] There is also another, lower profit, equilibrium where both firms choose to be able to discriminate in the first period. Thus, there is a complementarity in the firms' decisions about whether to price discriminate, and a firm's incentive to discriminate is higher if its rival also discriminates. A similar feature is seen in Ellison (2005).

[49] A related issue is whether firms choose to compete in (i) "posted prices" or by (ii) "secret deals." For instance, one might envisage a two-stage interaction in which each firm chooses its pricing strategy in the first stage and then chooses its actual prices in the second stage. With (i) a firm knows nothing about its individual consumers and posts a uniform price. With (ii) a firm might learn about the consumers from the negotiation process and price accordingly, and moreover the firm might take the rival's posted price as given if the rival chooses strategy (i). Thus, when one firm chooses (i) and the other chooses (ii), the former acts as a Stackleberg price leader (as in section III of Thisse and Vives (1988)).

tariff instruments. Suppose there are two firms, A and B. Suppose that firm i's maximum profit per consumer is $\pi_i(u)$ when the firm offers each of its consumers the surplus u. For this function to be well behaved, assume that firms have constant-returns-to-scale technology in serving consumers, so profit per consumer does not depend on the number of consumers served. Assume consumers are homogeneous in the sense that the relationship $\pi_i(u)$ is the same for each consumer. Assume further that consumers choose to purchase all relevant products from one firm. The shape of $\pi_i(u)$ embodies the firm's cost function, the demand function of consumers, and – most important for the current purpose – the kinds of tariffs the firm can employ. In particular, when a firm has access to a wider range of tariff instruments its profit function $\pi_i(\cdot)$ is necessarily shifted upward.

If consumers choose their supplier according to a Hotelling specification with homogeneous transport cost parameter t, firm i's profit is

$$\Pi_i = \left(\frac{1}{2} + \frac{u_i - u_j}{2t} \right) \pi_i(u_i) , \tag{10}$$

where u_i is its chosen consumer surplus and u_j is its rival's consumer surplus. Let $\bar{u}_i$ denote the maximum level of consumer surplus that allows firm i to break even. In most natural cases, this is the level of consumer surplus associated with marginal-cost pricing, a pricing policy that is assumed to be feasible for either firm. Assume firms are symmetric except possibly for the range of tariff instruments they employ. This implies that each firm delivers the same consumer surplus with marginal-cost pricing, and so $\bar{u}_A = \bar{u}_B = \bar{u}$, say. Moreover, since pricing at marginal cost maximizes total per-consumer surplus $(u + \pi_i(u))$, it follows that $\pi_i'(\bar{u}) = -1$ for each firm. In sum, it is natural to assume

$$\pi_A(\bar{u}) = \pi_B(\bar{u}) = 0 ; \ \pi_A'(\bar{u}) = \pi_B'(\bar{u}) = -1. \tag{11}$$

The analysis in Appendix B shows that in competitive markets (t small), firm i's equilibrium consumer surplus (u_i), firm i's total profit (Π_i), and total welfare (W) are approximately:

$$u_i \approx \bar{u} - t - \frac{t^2}{6} \left(2\pi_i''(\bar{u}) + \pi_j''(\bar{u}) \right) \tag{12}$$

$$\Pi_i \approx \frac{t}{2} + \frac{t^2}{6} \left(2\pi_i''(\bar{u}) + \pi_j''(\bar{u}) \right) \tag{13}$$

$$W \approx \bar{u} - \frac{t}{4} + \frac{t^2}{4} \left(\pi_A''(\bar{u}) + \pi_B''(\bar{u}) \right) . \tag{14}$$

Next, suppose there are two possible profit functions, $\pi(\cdot)$ and $\hat{\pi}(\cdot)$, where $\pi(\cdot) \leq \hat{\pi}(\cdot)$. Therefore, $\hat{\pi}$ is the profit function when a firm has access to a wider range of instruments when designing its tariff compared to the situation associated with profit function $\pi(\cdot)$. (For instance, π might be the profit function when a firm uses linear prices, while $\hat{\pi}$ is the corresponding profit function when a firm uses two-part tariffs. Alternatively, π could be the profit function if the firm is constrained to set uniform linear prices for similar products, while $\hat{\pi}$ is the profit function that corresponds to third-degree price discrimination.) Since the two profit functions satisfy (11) and $\hat{\pi} \geq \pi$, it follows that $\hat{\pi}''(\bar{u}) \geq \pi''(\bar{u})$, with strict inequality except in knife-edge cases. Using expressions (12)–(14) we can then draw the following conclusions for competitive markets.

Suppose the market environment changes so that both firms have access to more instruments in their tariff design. This can be modeled by supposing that both firms use the profit function $\hat{\pi}(\cdot)$ instead of $\pi(\cdot)$. In this case consumer surplus falls, profit rises, and total welfare rises.[50] Thus, this model exhibits the same qualitative features as monopoly first-degree price discrimination discussed in section 2.1: The use of more instruments enables the industry to better extract consumer surplus, which causes profits and welfare to rise but consumer surplus to decline. Moreover, there is no prisoner's dilemma in this setting, and a firm wishes to use the more ornate tariff even if its rival does not.[51] In sum, in this framework we predict that firms will use whichever tariff instruments they can, and the result is that profit and welfare rise (compared to a situation where less ornate tariffs are employed), while consumers suffer.

This result seems sometimes to be at odds with casual observation. Firms in many industries do not use two-part tariffs, for instance, even though such tariffs could be offered. (Supermarkets do not generally offer two-part tariffs, for example.) That is to say, there is sometimes *too little* price discrimination observed compared to what simple theory suggests. It seems, then, that this framework fails to capture an important aspect of many real-world markets. One possibility is that consumers have an aversion to fixed charges, say, for psychological reasons, which is not captured in the model. Another possibility is that arbitrage between consumers renders the use of some instruments infeasible. Alternatively, the presence of substantial consumer heterogeneity might overturn the result, and a firm perhaps might be made worse off by unilaterally choosing to compete with two-part tariffs, say, given the response this induces from its rivals.[52] A fourth aspect of some real-world markets that this model

---

[50] This is part (i) of Proposition 3 in Armstrong and Vickers (2001). For instance, from expression (12) $u_i \approx \bar{u} - t - \frac{1}{2}t^2\pi''(\bar{u})$ if $\pi(\cdot)$ is used, but $u_i \approx \bar{u} - t - \frac{1}{2}t^2\hat{\pi}''(\bar{u})$ if $\hat{\pi}(\cdot)$ is used, and so consumers are worse off in the latter case. Expression (13) shows the firms' benefit from using more ornate tariffs is approximately twice the loss that consumers then suffer.

[51] From expression (13), it is a dominant strategy for a firm to use the profit function $\hat{\pi}$ instead of π. In this case, (12) shows that the firm that uses the more ornate tariff will obtain a smaller market share in equilibrium.

[52] However, Armstrong and Vickers (2006) suggest it is hard to find models where industry profit falls with the use of competitive nonlinear pricing, which indicates that this is unlikely to be an important factor in many settings. Armstrong and Vickers (2006) investigate a one-stop model with lump-sum transport costs where consumers are heterogeneous in their demands. If firms can practice nonlinear pricing, the unique symmetric equilibrium is the cost-based two-part tariff reported in section 3.1 above. A comparison of this outcome with the situation where firms

ignores is that consumers often make purchases from more than one supplier. This extension is pursued in the next section, where it is seen that the use of more ornate tariffs can then depress equilibrium profit.

4.2 Mixed Bundling

In addition to the case of discrimination based on brand preference (section 3.3), a second situation in which price discrimination can intensify competition is competitive bundling. Consider for instance the following two-dimensional Hotelling model.[53] Two firms, A and B, each offer their own brand of two products, 1 and 2. Consumer preferences are determined by the parameters $(x_1, x_2) \in [0, 1]^2$. Here, x_1 represents a consumer's distance from firm A's brand of product 1 and x_2 represent a consumer's distance from the same firm's brand of product 2. Transport cost (or choosiness) is t_1 for product 1 and t_2 for product 2.

In general, each firm sets three prices. Let p_1^i denote firm i's price for its product 1, let p_2^i be its price for its product 2, and let p_{12}^i be its total price when a consumer buys both of its products. For simplicity, suppose that conditions in the market are such that all consumers buy both products.[54] A type-(x_1, x_2) consumer's total cost if he buys both products from firm A is $p_{12}^A + t_1 x_1 + t_2 x_2$, his total cost if he buys both products from B is $p_{12}^B + t_1(1 - x_1) + t_2(1 - x_2)$, and his total cost if he buys product i from A and product $j \neq i$ from B is $p_i^A + p_j^B + t_i x_i + t_j(1 - x_j)$. The consumer will choose the option from among these four possibilities that involves the smallest outlay. Whenever firms offer discounts for joint purchase ($p_{12}^i \leq p_1^i + p_2^i$), the pattern of demand is as shown in Figure 4.2.

Suppose that production is costless and consumer preferences (x_1, x_2) are uniformly distributed on the unit square. Consider first the case where firms cannot use the instrument of discounts for joint consumption. That is to say, firms must choose separable tariffs, so that $p_{12}^i \equiv p_1^i + p_2^i$. In this case firms compete product-by-product, the equilibrium price for product i from each firm is $P_i = t_i$, and each firm makes profit $\frac{1}{2}(t_1 + t_2)$.

Next suppose firms offer discounts for joint consumption (i.e., firms can set $p_{12}^i < p_1^i + p_2^i$). By calculating the areas of the regions depicted in Figure 4.2,

---

can only set linear prices shows that firms are always better off when they practice nonlinear pricing.

[53] The following model is very similar to Matutes and Regibeau (1992). (See Anderson and Leruth (1993) for related analysis using a Logit model of consumer demand.) There are two main differences between Matutes and Regibeau (1992) and the analysis presented here: (i) Matutes and Regibeau do not assume that all consumers buy and (ii) they restrict attention to situations where the two products are symmetric, whereas the analysis here allows the two products to differ in their substitutability.

[54] This assumption implies that the two products could equally well be taken to be perfect complements, so that each consumer needs to buy both products if he is to gain any utility, as is assumed in the more general model with partial consumer participation in Matutes and Regibeau (1992).

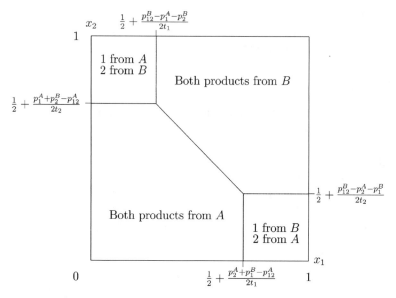

Figure 4.2. Pattern of consumer demand with duopoly bundling.

when $t_1 \neq t_2$ intricate calculations show the symmetric equilibrium prices are

$$p_{12} = \tfrac{1}{2}t_1 + \tfrac{1}{2}t_2 + \tfrac{1}{6}\sqrt{9t_1^2 + 9t_2^2 - 14t_1t_2} \tag{15}$$

$$p_1 = \tfrac{11}{16}t_1 + \tfrac{3}{16}t_2$$
$$+ \tfrac{1}{48}\frac{1}{t_1 - t_2}\left((5t_1 + 3t_2)\sqrt{9t_1^2 + 9t_2^2 - 14t_1t_2} - 16t_1t_2\right) \tag{16}$$

$$p_2 = \tfrac{11}{16}t_2 + \tfrac{3}{16}t_1$$
$$+ \tfrac{1}{48}\frac{1}{t_2 - t_1}\left((5t_2 + 3t_1)\sqrt{9t_1^2 + 9t_2^2 - 14t_1t_2} - 16t_1t_2\right). \tag{17}$$

The prices p_1 and p_2 are well behaved as $t_1 \to t_2$, and by L'Hôpital's rule the above prices reduce to

$$p_{12} = \tfrac{4}{3}t \; ; \; p_1 = p_2 = \tfrac{11}{12}t \tag{18}$$

when $t_1 = t_2 = t$.[55,56] Notice also that when there is no product differentiation

---

[55] These prices are not the only equilibrium, and when $t_1 = t_2 = t$, one can check that the prices $p_{12} = t$, $p_1 = p_2 = \infty$ also form a symmetric equilibrium. With these prices, all consumers buy both products from one firm or the other, and there is pure bundling. With these prices, profit is lower than with the prices in (18), and so the discussion is focused on the equilibrium prices in (18).

[56] Even more strenuous calculations yield the equilibrium mixed bundling tariff with three products. If consumer locations (x_1, x_2, x_3) are uniformly distributed on the unit cube $[0, 1]^3$, and if each

for one product (say $t_2 = 0$), then bundling plays no role: $p_{12} = p_1 = t_1$ and $p_2 = 0$, just as when there is no bundling. This has the interpretation that a firm has no incentive to bundle a product over which it enjoys market power with a perfectly competitive product. In other cases, though, one can show that $p_1 + p_2 > p_{12}$, so that firms offer discounts for joint purchases. One can also show that with the prices in (15)–(17) there are always some "two-stop shoppers" who choose to buy a single item from both firms.

Next, compare prices with and without bundling. (Recall that without bundling each firm sets the price $P_i = t_i$ for product i.) From (15) we see that $P_1 + P_2 \geq p_{12}$, with strict inequality unless some $t_i = 0$. Thus, the bundle price is always lower than the sum of the two prices when bundling is not practiced. Next, it is possible to show that the stand-alone prices also fall when bundling is practiced, provided that the two products are not too asymmetric.[57] Thus, as with expression (18), whenever the two products are not too asymmetric all three prices fall when firms practice mixed bundling. When products are very asymmetric, however, the more differentiated product's stand-alone price rises when mixed bundling is practiced.

One can also show that a firm's equilibrium profit is smaller with bundling than without (except if one $t_i = 0$ when profit is unchanged). For instance, in the symmetric case (18), each firm's profit is approximately $0.7 \times t$ compared to profit of t when the bundling instrument is not employed. And all consumers are better off when mixed bundling is practiced.[58] Thus, although it is not necessarily the case that all individual prices fall when bundling is used, consumers are nevertheless offered better overall deals. However, there is excessive one-stop shopping: Too many consumers buy both products from the same firm than is efficient, and welfare falls with this form of discrimination. (The efficient pattern of consumption requires there be no bundling discounts, so that $p_{12} = p_1 + p_2$.) These are *exactly* the opposite comparative statics to those obtained in the one-stop shopping model in section 4.1.[59]

Similarly to the model in section 3.3, firms play a prisoner's dilemma: Given a rival's prices, a firm is always better off if it has the flexibility to engage in mixed bundling, but in equilibrium profit is reduced when this extra instrument is employed by both firms. As discussed in section 3.4, though, in some

---

product's transport cost is normalized to $t = 1$, by calculating the volumes of the relevant regions in the three-dimensional version of Figure 4.2, one can show that the equilibrium price for any single item from a firm is (approximately) 0.85, the price for any two items from the same firm is 1.43, and the price for all three items from the same firm is 1.67.

[57] The precise condition is that the smaller of $\{t_1, t_2\}$ is at least $\frac{5}{9}$ the size of the larger.

[58] The easiest way to see this is to notice that the sum of the stand-alone prices $p_1 + p_2$ in (16)–(17) is always lower than the sum of the non-bundling prices, which is $P_1 + P_2 = t_1 + t_2$. Since consumers are assumed always to purchase each product, when bundling is practiced one possible consumer strategy is to buy the product from her preferred firm for each product. At worst, this entails the outlay $p_1 + p_2$, which is less than when firms do not engage in bundling.

[59] Closely related comparison of the two situations is contained in Thanassoulis (2006).

circumstances it is natural to model the firms' interaction as a two-stage game, where firms first decide whether to compete using separable prices or using mixed bundling, and then in the second stage they choose their prices. Suppose in the second stage of this interaction that firm A can practice mixed bundling whereas B cannot. In the case where the two products are symmetric ($t_1 = t_2 = t$), one can show the equilibrium prices are

$$p_1^A = p_2^A = \tfrac{13}{12}t \; ; \; p_{12}^A = \tfrac{3}{2}t \; ; \; p_1^B = p_2^B = \tfrac{3}{4}t \; .$$

Firm A's equilibrium profit in this case is approximately $0.82 \times t$, while firm B's profit is $\tfrac{3}{4}t$. (Thus, the firm with more tariff instruments makes higher profit.) Recall that if neither firm chooses to compete using mixed bundling each will make profit t. Therefore, in the first stage a firm has no incentive unilaterally to price discriminate in this manner if its rival does not. If firm A has the ability to bundle, this induces such an aggressive response from B that A's profits fall. Moreover, even if its rival chooses to bundle, it is still in a firm's interest to choose not to bundle. Therefore, in this extended two-stage game it is no longer an equilibrium to practice bundling, and it is a dominant strategy for a firm to commit to price its products separably.[60]

The economic reason for why bundling depresses profit is not easy to come by. Some intuition is available if one restricts attention to a choice between separable pricing and *pure* bundling.[61] Take the symmetric situation mentioned in footnote 55 where $p_{12}^A = p_{12}^B = t$, and firms each make profit of just $\tfrac{1}{2}t$. Thus, with pure bundling the profit *halves*. As Nalebuff (2000, page 328) puts it: "The price of the entire bundle is reduced to the prior price of each of the single components. In hindsight, the intuition is relatively straightforward. Cutting price brings the same number of incremental customers as when selling individual components. So the bundle price must equal the individual price in a symmetric equilibrium." This competition-intensifying impact of pure bundling becomes more pronounced as the number of component products increases, and a "large number" effect comes into play. This effect – that bundling has a homogenizing effect on consumer valuations – is essentially the same as discussed in the monopoly context of section 2.1. Equilibrium prices are determined as a balance between building market share and exploiting infra-marginal consumers. If there are many marginal consumers compared to consumers overall (as is the case with homogeneous consumers), then equilibrium prices are close to cost. With monopoly, when consumers become more homogeneous because

---

[60] Gans and King (2006) consider a variant of this model, where there are four separate firms each offering one of the four product variants. They show that it can be profitable for two firms to agree to set a discount for joint purchase of their two products. (The authors assume that the two firms commit to the size of the discount, which they agree to fund equally, and subsequently set their prices non-cooperatively.) If both pairs of firms do this, then there is no effect on profit compared to the case where neither pair of firms offers bundling discounts (although there is again socially excessive bundling).

[61] See Matutes and Regibeau (1988), Economides (1989), and Nalebuff (2000) for this analysis.

of bundling, the firm can extract more consumer surplus. With competition, though, when bundling makes consumers more homogeneous this leads to more aggressive competition and low prices.[62,63]

Exogenous Shopping Costs

The discussion about bundling has so far assumed that consumers do not incur any exogenous additional costs when they buy from more than one firm. Rather, when firms offered a discount for joint purchase this gave consumers an endogenous, "tariff mediated," shopping cost, which generated a tendency towards one-stop shopping. It is worthwhile to extend this analysis to allow consumers to face an exogenous shopping cost, and to see how this might affect firms' incentives to bundle. To this end, keep everything as in the previous analysis except suppose all consumers face an additional cost z if they buy from two firms rather than just one.[64] In this case, Figure 4.2 is modified as shown in Figure 4.3.

For simplicity, suppose the two products are symmetric, so that $t_1 = t_2 = t$. Suppose further that $z < t$ (otherwise all consumers will choose to buy both products from a single firm). When firms do not practice bundling, one can show that they will each set the price

$$P = \frac{t^2}{t+z} \qquad (19)$$

for each product. This price decreases from the usual Hotelling price $P = t$ when $z = 0$ to the price $P = \frac{1}{2}t$ when $z = t$. (This latter price corresponds to the case of pure bundling, when the price of the bundle is t.) Therefore, the presence of the shopping cost acts to make the market more competitive, in just the same way as firms selling their products as a bundle did so.

---

[62] Nalebuff (2000) shows that as the number of products which can be bundled together becomes large, the profit obtained with pure bundling becomes an ever smaller proportion of the profit obtained with separable pricing. If there are n products, Nalebuff shows that profits with pure bundling increase at the rate $\sqrt{n}$, while profits with separable pricing increase at the rate n.

[63] The fact that (pure) bundling can make firms price aggressively appears in a different context in Whinston (1990). There, a multiproduct firm faces competition from a single-product rival. In certain conditions, when the multiproduct firm commits to bundle its products together before prices are chosen, it will choose a lower effective price in the rival's market compared to when it prices its products separately. Therefore, a commitment to bundle can act to deter single-product entry. (See section 4.3 below for a related model in a more conventional price discrimination framework.) In other circumstances, however, when the multiproduct firm commits to bundle its products, this can act to *relax* subsequent competition with a single-product rival. In such cases, an incumbent might wish to commit to price its products separately to convince potential entrants that it will be aggressive in the event of entry. See Carbajo, De Meza, and Seidman (1990), Whinston (1990), Chen (1997a), and section III.E of Nalebuff (2004) for further details.

[64] Section 4.1 in effect assumed that z was so large that all consumers choose to buy from a single firm. See Klemperer (1992) for further analysis of the effects of shopping costs.

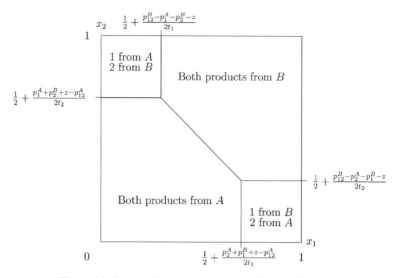

Figure 4.3. Pattern of consumer demand with bundling and shopping cost z.

Suppose next that firms can offer a discount for joint purchase. One can show that the equilibrium mixed bundling tariff is given by

$$p_{12} = \frac{4t^2}{3t + z} \; ; \; p_1 = p_2 = \frac{11t^2 - 2tz - z^2}{12t + 4z} .$$ (20)

(These prices reduce to (18) when $z = 0$.) The discount for joint purchase is

$$p_1 + p_2 - p_{12} = \tfrac{1}{2}(t - z) ,$$

which is decreasing in z. In this sense, the shopping cost reduces the equilibrium incentive to offer bundling discounts. Nevertheless, in this example firms still have an incentive to offer a discount ($p_1 + p_2 > p_{12}$). Comparing (20) with (19) shows the bundle price is always lower than the sum of the non-bundling prices. However, the stand-alone price with bundling in (20) is higher than the non-bundling price (19) unless the shopping cost z is small.[65] Whenever z is not too small, then, the "two-stop shoppers" (those consumers with a strong preference for one firm's product 1 and strong preference for the other firm's product 2) will be worse off when firms engage in bundling.

Firms continue to receive lower profits with bundling compared to non-bundling (unless $z = t$, in which case both regimes involve pure bundling), and welfare too is lower since the discount for joint consumption continues to induce excessive one-stop shopping.

---

[65] The stand-alone price with bundling is above the non-bundling price if $z > (\sqrt{5} - 2)t$.

4.3   Selective Price Cuts

This section discusses a more asymmetric situation in which a firm that operates in several markets faces a rival that is (potentially) active in just one market.[66] Price discrimination can enable a multi-market firm to target price cuts selectively in those markets where competition is present. The ability to make selective price cuts is therefore likely to have an adverse effect on a single-market firm's profits.

To see this formally, suppose firm A serves two independent markets, 1 and 2. Market 1 is monopolized by firm A, whereas in market 2 there is a rival firm B. Firm A's (linear) prices in the two markets are p_1^A and p_2^A, while firm B's price in market 2 is p_2^B. In market 1, firm A's profit function is $\pi_1(p_1^A)$ whereas in market 2 the firm's profit function given its rival's price is $\pi_2^A(p_2^A, p_2^B)$. Similarly, firm B's profit function is $\pi_2^B(p_2^A, p_2^B)$. If firm A can price discriminate, in the sense that it may set different prices in the two markets, it will set the monopoly price p_1^M in market 1 (where this price maximizes $\pi_1(\cdot)$) and in market 2 prices will be determined by the intersection of reaction functions. In market 2, let $p_2^A = R_2^A(p_2^B)$ be firm A's best response to firm B's price when price discrimination is allowed, and let $p_2^B = R_2^B(p_2^A)$ be firm B's best response to A's price. These two reaction functions are depicted on Figure 4.4, and the equilibrium prices in market 2 are at β on the figure.

Next suppose that firm A cannot set different prices in the two markets. Suppose further that for all relevant prices set by B, firm A prefers to set a higher price in the monopoly market than in the competitive market, so that $p_1^M > R_2^A(p_2^B)$. In other words, the captive market is firm A's strong market, which seems plausible in a variety of contexts. With single-peak assumptions on firm A's profit functions, it follows that when it must set a common price in the two markets, firm A's best response to its rival's price, $R_{ND}^A(p_2^B)$ say, is shifted upward, so that $R_{ND}^A(p_2^B) > R_2^A(p_2^B)$. (See Figure 4.4.) It follows that market 2 prices when price discrimination is permitted are lower than the corresponding prices when A must set a uniform price (denoted γ on the figure). Therefore, the effect of a ban on price discrimination is to reduce price in the captive market, and to raise both prices in the competitive market. The profit of the single-market rival clearly increases with such a ban, while the effect on firm A's overall profit is not clear cut in general.[67]

---

[66] This discussion is loosely based on Armstrong and Vickers (1993). That paper also argues that the effect of allowing price discrimination on the incumbent's response to entry is exacerbated when the multiproduct firm is regulated and operates under an average-price constraint. (If it reduces its price in the competitive market it is then allowed to raise its price in the captive market.)

[67] Dobson and Waterson (2005) present a related model where a national retailer operates in a number of markets, in some of which it is the sole supplier and in the remainder of which it faces a single local competitor. They show that it is possible for the chain store to benefit if it commits to a national pricing policy (i.e., it does not price differently depending on competitive conditions in each local market).

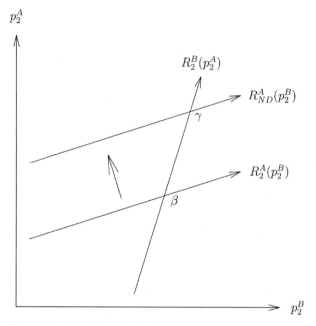

Figure 4.4. The effect of banning price discrimination.

Of course, if firm B has not yet entered the market, firm A's ability to engage in price discrimination has implications for B's incentive to enter. If the entrant has a fixed cost of entry, it will enter only if it expects its post-entry profit to cover its entry cost. There are then three cases to consider. If the entry cost is large, entry will not take place regardless of whether the incumbent can price discriminate. In this case, the social desirability of price discrimination is exactly as in the standard monopoly case (which is ambiguous in general). Similarly, if the entry cost is small, entry will take place regardless of policy towards price discrimination. The interesting case is when the cost of entry lies in the intermediate range where entry is profitable only if the incumbent is not permitted to make selective price cuts. In such cases, a ban on price discrimination acts to induce entry. Then a ban on price discrimination will cause prices in *both* markets to fall: If discrimination is possible, there will be no entry and the incumbent will charge monopoly prices in each market; if the incumbent must charge a common price in the two markets, this will bring in the entrant, which causes both prices to fall from monopoly levels.

The general principle, as in the Thisse-Vives quote in section 3.3, is that denying an incumbent the right to meet the price of a competitor on a discriminatory basis provides the latter with some protection against price attacks. While the effect of a ban on price discrimination is indeed to weaken competition if the entrant is already in the market, once *ex ante* incentives to enter are considered, the effect of a ban on price discrimination might be pro-competitive. However, the welfare effect of a ban on price discrimination in this context is not clear cut. For instance, since the incumbent is reluctant to cut its profits in the captive market by meeting its rival's price in the competitive market, even a highly inefficient entrant might prosper. While preventing an incumbent from engaging in selective price cuts is likely to be a powerful means with which to assist entry, as with many forms of entry assistance the danger of inefficient entry is rarely far away.[68]

5   DYNAMIC PRICING IN OLIGOPOLY

This section extends the discussion of behavior-based price discrimination in section 2.2 to competitive situations. Two kinds of models are discussed. First, situations in which firms react *ex post* to previous consumer decisions are presented. In these models, firms learn about a consumer's relative preference for the firms' future offerings from her initial choice of firm, and prices are chosen accordingly. Firms do not announce or commit to future prices or discounts in these situations. As will be seen, in these situations, firms attempt to "poach" their rival's previous customers by offering those customers low prices, and the market typically exhibits excessive switching between firms (or two-stop shopping). Second, the case where firms announce explicit loyalty schemes *ex ante* is considered. This corresponds to the case where firms can fully commit to their future prices. This situation is similar to the previous discussion of mixed bundling in section 4.2, and here the danger is rather that there is excessive loyalty (or one-stop shopping). In both kinds of situation, the typical outcome is that profit is reduced when behavior-based price discrimination is used, while consumers benefit.

5.1   *Ex Post* Price Discrimination and Customer Poaching

Here, two distinct models are presented, one by Fudenberg and Tirole (2000) and the other by Chen (1997b).[69] In the first model, consumers have a stable brand preference for one of the two firms. If a consumer buys from firm A in the first period, she prefers to buy from firm A in the second period as well, all else equal, and both firms will price accordingly. In the second model, consumers initially view the two firms as perfect substitutes, but in the second period they incur a switching cost if they wish to change supplier. In each model, the second period closely resembles the static model of Bester and Petrakis

---

[68] See section 2.2 of Vickers (2005) for an account and analysis of recent policy towards selective price cuts.

[69] Although it does not specifically address the issue of price discrimination, the analysis of switching costs in Klemperer (1988) shares several of the features in the following analysis. For instance, Klemperer's model involves the firm with the larger initial market share pricing less aggressively than its rival in the second period. In addition, Klemperer compares the cases of sophisticated and naive consumers, and shows that the initial market is less competitive with sophisticated consumers. (A similar feature is seen in the model of price discrimination in Fudenberg and Tirole (2000), as I will discuss.)

(1996) discussed in section 3.3: When price discrimination is permitted, firms will price low to poach their rival's previous customers and price high to their own previous customers. Each firm regards its previous customers as its strong market, and there is again best-response asymmetry. Therefore, the models will share the feature that second-period prices are all lower than they would be if behavior-based discrimination were not feasible.

Stable Brand Preferences

First, consider Fudenberg and Tirole's (2000) model with stable brand preferences. Suppose there are two periods, and consumers wish to buy a single unit from one of two firms in each period. Consumer preferences are as specified in the Hotelling framework, and a consumer located at $x \in [0, 1]$ incurs total cost $p^A + tx$ if she buys from firm A at the price p^A, and she incurs total cost $p^B + t(1 - x)$ if she buys the unit from B at the price p^B. Assume that a consumer's brand preference parameter x is the same in the two periods. For simplicity, suppose production is costless.

Suppose that firms cannot commit to future prices, in which case the model is analyzed by working back from period 2. In the second period we have, in general, an asymmetric version of the Bester and Petrakis (1996) model. Specifically, suppose firm A managed to attract a fraction $\frac{1}{2} + \gamma$ of consumers in the first period. That is to say, firm A's turf is the interval $[0, \frac{1}{2} + \gamma]$, while firm B's turf is the remaining $[\frac{1}{2} + \gamma, 1]$. On firm A's turf one can show the equilibrium second-period prices are[70]

$$\hat{p}_2^A = \tfrac{2}{3}t(1 + \gamma) \; ; \; p_2^B = \tfrac{1}{3}t(1 + 4\gamma) \, . \tag{21}$$

Similarly, the prices aimed at firm B's turf are

$$\hat{p}_2^B = \tfrac{2}{3}t(1 - \gamma) \; ; \; p_2^A = \tfrac{1}{3}t(1 - 4\gamma) \, . \tag{22}$$

These prices generalize expression (7) above.[71] Perhaps surprisingly, with these prices the two firms make the same profit in the second period, and this common profit is

$$\left(\frac{5}{18} + \frac{10}{9}\gamma^2 \right) t \, . \tag{23}$$

Thus, each firm's second-period profit is minimized when firms share the first-period market equally. Intuitively, an equal initial market share generates the

---

[70] For these prices to be valid the initial market shares cannot be too asymmetric, and we require that $-\tfrac{1}{4} \leq \gamma \leq \tfrac{1}{4}$. For more asymmetric market shares, the firm with the larger share will set a price of zero to its distant market.

[71] Notice that in very asymmetric situations, where one firm has more than two-thirds of the first-period consumers, the smaller firm sets a *higher* price on its rival's turf than on its own. Related issues are explored in Shaffer and Zhang (2000).

most informative outcome in the second period, and, in this setting with best-response asymmetry, more information destroys profit. When initial market shares are very asymmetric, on the other hand, little is learned about most consumers' brand preferences.[72]

Consider next the choice of first-period prices. Here, the outcome depends on the sophistication of consumers. Suppose first that consumers are sophisticated and anticipate the effect of initial market share on future prices in expressions (21)–(22). Notice that the larger "turf" faces higher second-period prices, which implies that, all else equal, a sophisticated consumer would prefer to purchase from the firm with fewer consumers in the first period. When both firms choose the same initial price p_1 say, they will share the market equally in the first period (so $\gamma = 0$). Suppose instead that firm A slightly undercuts its rival in the first period, and chooses price $p_1 - \varepsilon$. How many more consumers will it attract in the first period? Let us say that the marginal consumer in period 1 is located at $x = \frac{1}{2} + \gamma$. When a consumer lies near the midpoint between the two firms (γ small), she will surely switch firms in the second period in order to take advantage of the poaching discount. Therefore, the marginal consumer is indifferent between buying from A-then-B or buying from B-then-A. Given the second-period prices in (21)–(22), γ satisfies

$$p_1 - \varepsilon + \left(\tfrac{1}{2} + \gamma\right)t + \delta\left[\tfrac{1}{3}t(1 + 4\gamma) + \left(\tfrac{1}{2} - \gamma\right)t\right]$$
$$= p_1 + \left(\tfrac{1}{2} - \gamma\right)t + \delta\left[\tfrac{1}{3}t(1 - 4\gamma) + \left(\tfrac{1}{2} + \gamma\right)t\right],$$

and so

$$\gamma = \frac{\varepsilon}{2t\left(1 + \tfrac{1}{3}\delta\right)}.$$

We deduce that sophisticated consumers react less sensitively to price reductions in the first period than they would in a static model of this kind (when $\gamma = \varepsilon/(2t)$). The reason is that if a firm cuts its price in the first period, that brings a direct benefit to a consumer in the first period, but a disadvantage to the marginal consumer at that firm in the second period, since her poaching price is raised. It follows that the first-period price is[73]

$$p_1 = t(1 + \tfrac{1}{3}\delta) \tag{24}$$

---

[72] This is especially clear in the variant of the Fudenberg-Tirole model presented in chapter 3 of Esteves (2004). Esteves assumes that consumer preferences follow a binary distribution, and half the consumers prefer A by a fixed amount and half the consumers prefer B by the same fixed amount. If firms set similar prices in the first period, they will share the market and consumer tastes are fully revealed in the second period. If firms set significantly different first-period prices then one firm attracts all consumers, and so nothing is learned in the second period and subsequent profit is high.

[73] In fact, if a firm undercuts it rival in the first period this will affect its equilibrium profit in the second period (which from (23) will rise). However, this effect is second-order for small deviations, at least for this particular example, and so it plays no role in the calculation of the equilibrium first-period price.

while the second-period prices are as in (7) above:

$$\hat{p}_2 = \tfrac{2}{3}t \; ; \; p_2 = \tfrac{1}{3}t. \tag{25}$$

These second-period prices imply that the middle third of consumers switch firms in the second period.

The sophisticated reasoning of the consumers in this model when there is behavior-based discrimination might sometimes be implausible, especially in new markets where consumers have not yet grasped the firms' pricing incentives. Suppose instead consumers are naive and do not foresee that when they buy from the low price firm in the first period they will face higher prices in the second period. Then, competition in the first period is just as in a standard static model, and the first-period price is $p_1 = t$ instead of the price in (24). Second-period prices are unaffected. Therefore, if consumers are naive this improves their position compared to when they are sophisticated. By contrast, in the monopoly situation of section 2.2, when consumers are naive they are treated less favourably.

If the instrument of behavior-based price discrimination is not available, a firm's price in each period is $p_1 = p_2 = \hat{p}_2 = t$. This implies that the first-period price is reduced (or unchanged with naive consumers) while second-period prices are raised compared to the situation with discrimination. Just as with the Bester-Petrakis model, behavior-based price discrimination is socially inefficient, since in the second period a third of consumers buy from the less-preferred firm. When consumers are sophisticated, total discounted profit is lower with discrimination.[74] (When consumers are naive, firms are even worse off with discrimination.) Therefore, when firms cannot commit to future prices, the ability to engage in behavior-based price discrimination reduces their profit. All consumers are at least weakly better off with discrimination.[75] (And if consumers were naive, they would be even better off with discrimination.) In sum, a ban on this form of price discrimination makes consumers worse off, regardless of their presumed sophistication.[76] (By contrast, in the monopoly analysis of section 2.2, a ban on discrimination makes naive consumers better off.)

---

[74] Industry profit with discrimination is $(1 + \tfrac{8}{9}\delta)t$ and without discrimination it is $(1 + \delta)t$.

[75] Without discrimination, a consumer pays a total discounted charge $(1 + \delta)t$ for the two units. With discrimination, a consumer can buy a unit from the same firm in each period, in which case expressions (24)–(25) imply that the total discounted charge is the same $(1 + \delta)t$. However, some consumers will be strictly better off by switching firms in the second period.

[76] Villas-Boas (1999) presents related analysis when long-lived firms face overlapping generations of short-lived consumers. One important difference with the Fudenberg-Tirole model is that a firm only knows whether or not a consumer has previously purchased from it, and cannot distinguish between its rival's previous consumer and consumers who are new to the market. He finds that, at least for patient firms and consumers, behavior-based discrimination causes all prices to fall.

Finally, a richer model would consider the impact of imperfect correlation of brand preference over time. If the first-period choice of firm was only an imperfect signal of second-period brand preference, the temptation to set low prices in the second period would be mitigated. In the extreme case where consumer brand preference was uncorrelated over time, a consumer's initial choice of firm would give no useful information about her subsequent preferences, and there would be no scope for behavior-based price discrimination. In general, we expect that when firms price discriminate, profit is decreasing in the extent of correlation of brand preference, while consumers benefit from higher correlation.

Switching Costs

Second, consider Chen's (1997b) model of switching costs. Again, there are two firms each selling a product over two periods and consumers wish to purchase a single unit in each of the two periods. If a consumer wishes to change supplier in the second period, she must incur a switching cost s. This cost varies across consumers, and suppose s is uniformly distributed on the interval $[0, t]$. Thus, if firm A sets the second-period price $\hat{p}_2^A$ to its first-period customers, and if firm B sets the poaching price p_2^B to the same group of customers, a customer will switch to B whenever $\hat{p}_2^A > p_2^B + s$. If firms can price discriminate in the second period, one can show the equilibrium prices are just as in the brand loyalty model in (25). (These are the prices regardless of market shares in the first period.) Just as in the Fudenberg-Tirole model, a third of consumers switch suppliers in the second period, which is inefficient. If the number of firm A's first-period customers is denoted n^A (and the number of firm B's customers is $n^B = 1 - n^A$), then firm A's second-period profit is[77]

$$\tfrac{2}{3}n^A \hat{p}_2 + \tfrac{1}{3}n^B p_2 = \tfrac{1}{3}t(\tfrac{1}{3} + n^A) . \tag{26}$$

Consider next the equilibrium first-period price. Since second-period prices are the same for the two firms, a consumer will choose her initial supplier purely on the basis of the lowest initial price. (The sophistication or otherwise of consumers plays no role here.) Since each first-period consumer brings with her a second-period profit of $\tfrac{1}{3}t$ (see expression (26)), which is discounted by δ, the equilibrium first-period price is $p_1 = -\tfrac{1}{3}\delta t$, which is below cost. This feature is common in models of switching costs, where firms compete hard to attract new consumers, anticipating consumers will generate high profit subsequently. Therefore, we see a major difference between the two models of Fudenberg-Tirole and Chen: In the former, prices start high and then decrease, whereas here the reverse is seen.

---

[77] Thus, in contrast to the Fudenberg-Tirole model, here the firm with the larger initial market share makes a higher profit in the second period compared to its rival.

By contrast, consider the situation where firms must charge a uniform price in the second period. Unlike the case of price discrimination, the equilibrium second-period prices will here depend on initial market shares (as well as the assumed sophistication of consumers). If firms divide the market equally in the first period, the equilibrium price in the second period is $p_2 = t$. If firms have different market shares in the first period, the larger firm will choose the higher price in the second period since it has a greater number of "captive" consumers. More precisely, the uniform prices in the second period given firm A's initial market share $n^A \geq \frac{1}{2}$ are

$$p^A = \frac{1 + n^A}{3n^A} t \; ; \; p^B = \frac{2 - n^A}{3n^A} t \leq p^A \; . \tag{27}$$

Both prices here are lower than when firms share the market equally ($n^A = \frac{1}{2}$), and so second-period competition is intensified when firms have asymmetric initial market shares. Second-period profits of the two firms are

$$\pi_2^A = \frac{(1 + n^A)^2}{9n^A} t \; ; \; \pi_2^B = \frac{(2 - n^A)^2}{9n^A} t \; , \tag{28}$$

and the firm with the larger market share obtains higher second-period profit. However, the profit of both firms is decreasing in the larger firm's market share and both firms are better off in the second period if they share the first-period market equally.

From (27), in the first period sophisticated consumers may not react sensitively to price reductions since they know that if they buy from the larger firm they will face a higher price in the second period. (Somewhat confusingly, this is the same mechanism as occurs in the Fudenberg-Tirole model *with* price discrimination.) A more important factor, which applies equally if consumers are naive, is that a firm has a strong incentive to set the same price as its rival in the first period: From (28) a firm makes less second-period profit if it obtains a higher or a lower market share in the first period, compared to when the two firms share the initial market equally. As a result, there are multiple symmetric first-period prices that can be equilibria.[78] Chen shows that firms are always better off when behavior-based price discrimination is not possible, and it is ambiguous whether consumers are better or worse off.[79]

---

[78] Take for instance the situation where consumers are naive (which is not considered by Chen), and in the first period consumers simply buy from the firm with the lower price (and the initial market is equally divided if firms choose equal prices). If a firm undercuts its rival in the first period it will attract all consumers and so make less profit in the second period (see (28)). Similarly, if a firm sets a negative price in the first period, its rival may be unwilling to choose a higher price because if it does so it will lose all its initial consumers and so make small profits in the second period. One can show that any initial price in the range $-\frac{7}{9}\delta t \leq p_1 \leq \frac{1}{9}\delta t$ can be an equilibrium in this context.

[79] See Taylor (2003) for an extension to Chen's analysis in a number of important directions, for instance to more than two periods and more than two firms. When there are more than

5.2   *Ex Ante* Price Discrimination and Customer Loyalty

Finally, suppose firms can commit to all future prices.[80] This setting, where firms commit to explicit rewards for consumer loyalty, seems broadly applicable to frequent flyer programes and the like. Consider the Fudenberg-Tirole setting of repeated sales to consumers with Hotelling preferences between the two firms' products. For simplicity, consider the extreme case in which a consumer's brand preferences are independently distributed over the two periods. Suppose further that consumers know their second-period preferences at the time of their initial choice of firm. In this situation, the mixed bundling model discussed in section 4.2 applies immediately. Therefore, equilibrium prices are given in expression (18), which in the current notation become

$$p_1 = p_2 = \tfrac{11}{12}t \; ; \; \hat{p}_2 = \tfrac{5}{12}t \; ,$$

and a repeat buyer receives a discount of $\tfrac{1}{2}t$ on her second unit. Here, compared to the case where this form of *ex ante* dynamic pricing is not possible, firms suffer from the profit-destroying impact of mixed bundling while consumers benefit. Welfare is reduced since there is excessive customer loyalty.

Both kinds of price discrimination involve welfare losses, but of a different form. *Ex ante* pricing involves excessive loyalty (one-stop shopping) while *ex post* pricing induces excessive switching (two-stop shopping). The key difference between the two models is that with *ex post* pricing the low price is aimed at the rival's past customers, whereas with explicit *ex ante* loyalty schemes the low price is aimed at a firm's own past customers. This analysis suggests that explicit loyalty schemes have the potential to be pro-consumer, just like the customer poaching schemes of the previous section.[81]

---

two periods, the fact that a consumer switched supplier in the second period indicates that the consumer has low switching costs, and this could generate more intense competition for him in future periods.

[80] One issue is the realistic extent of commitment in this dynamic oligopoly context. For instance, can firms commit to their second-period "poaching" price p_2^i? This seems less plausible than to suppose firms can commit to their repeat price to loyal consumers, $\hat{p}_2^i$. (One can say the same for the monopoly analysis of section 2.2 – see footnote 18.) Section 5 of Fudenberg and Tirole (2000) analyzes the use of long-term contracts where firms have the opportunity to poach their rival's customers in the second period at prices that are determined only in the second period. Compared to when short-term contracts are employed, they show in the uniform example that the use of long-term contracts reduces profit, reduces switching (which improves efficiency) and boosts consumer surplus.

[81] For related analysis in the case where consumers do not know their future preferences at the time of the initial choice, see Caminal and Matutes (1990), section 6 of Fudenberg and Tirole (2000), and Caminal and Claici (2005). See Kim, Shi, and Srinivasan (2001) for an analysis of reward programs as a price discrimination device to segment the high-volume and low-volume markets. This paper also shows that firms might commit to use inefficient reward schemes (e.g., free gifts instead of price reductions), since that can sometimes act to soften subsequent price competition.

6 CONCLUDING COMMENTS

This paper has surveyed the recent literature on price discrimination, with a focus on the effects on industry outcomes when firms: (i) have access to more information about their potential customers; (ii) can use more instruments when choosing their tariffs; and (iii) cannot commit to their pricing policy. The paper argued that the importance of each of these three factors has been increased due to developments in marketing and e-commerce.

The analysis reported here is more suggestive than definitive, and was largely presented through a series of worked examples. (Many of the papers from which this analysis was taken share this feature.) In particular, it is important to extend the analysis beyond the examples presented here, which involved a relentless use of Hotelling demand specifications with unit demands and uniform distributions. For instance, when consumers have inelastic demand there is no welfare benefit when price discrimination causes prices to fall, and such a benefit would be present in a richer model.[82]

Economic intuition seems to be better developed for the impact of more detailed information than it is for the effects of more tariff instruments. For instance, the concept of best-response symmetry is a useful tool for predicting the outcome of better information on profits and consumer surplus. However, there is as yet no such tool or intuition which can explain why competing firms are (i) typically better off using two-part tariffs than linear prices (see section 4.1) but (ii) typically worse off if they use bundling rather than separable prices (see section 4.2). There is plenty more work to be done in this exciting area.

TECHNICAL APPENDIX

A PRIVATE INFORMATION

Here, the equilibrium prices in expression (8) are derived. Suppose that firm B sets the price $\hat{p}$ when it sees the signal s_R and the price p when it sees the signal s_L. First consider the case when firm A sees the signal $s^A = s_L$ for a consumer. What price should firm A offer this consumer? There are four relevant events: (i) the consumer is near to firm A and the rival firm also receives the signal $s^B = s_L$ and so sets the price p; (ii) the consumer is near to firm A but the rival firm receives the 'wrong' signal $s^B = s_R$ and so sets the high price $\hat{p}$; (iii) the consumer is far from A and the rival firm also receives the signal $s^B = s_L$ and so sets the price p; and (iv) the consumer is far from A and the rival firm receives the 'correct' signal $s^B = s_R$ and so sets the price $\hat{p}$. Conditional on firm A seeing the signal $s^A = s_L$, the respective probabilities of the four events are $\alpha^2, \alpha(1 - \alpha), (1 - \alpha)^2, \alpha(1 - \alpha)$. If firm A sets a price $\hat{q}$ to this consumer

---

[82] See Armstrong and Vickers (2006) for some preliminary work on this extension.

(which lies in the range $p \le \hat{q} \le \hat{p}$) then it will make the sale with probability

$$\alpha^2 \left(1 + \frac{p - \hat{q}}{t} \right) + \alpha(1 - \alpha) + \alpha(1 - \alpha)\frac{\hat{p} - \hat{q}}{t} .$$

(With case (ii) firm A will surely make the sale whenever it sets a price $\hat{q} \le \hat{p}$; with case (iii) it will surely not make the sale when $\hat{q} \ge p$.)

Suppose next that firm A observes signal $s^A = s_R$. In the same way, if it sets the price q (which lies in the range $p \le q \le \hat{p}$) its probability of making the sale is

$$\alpha^2 \frac{\hat{p} - q}{t} + \alpha(1 - \alpha)\left(1 + \frac{p - q}{t} \right) + (1 - \alpha)^2 .$$

One can then show that symmetric equilibrium prices are given by expression (8).

B   EFFECT OF MORE INSTRUMENTS

Here, the results reported in section 4.1 are derived. Let $\pi_A(u)$ and $\pi_B(u)$ be two profit-as-a-function-of-utility functions which satisfy (11). Firm i will choose u_i to maximize expression (10), and so equilibrium utilities $\{\hat{u}_A(t), \hat{u}_B(t)\}$ satisfy the first-order conditions

$$\pi_i(\hat{u}_i(t)) + (t + \hat{u}_i(t) - \hat{u}_j(t))\pi_i'(\hat{u}_i(t)) = 0 , \tag{29}$$

where $\hat{u}_i(t)$ denotes the equilibrium utility offered by firm i when transport cost is t. We wish to investigate the equilibrium in competitive markets, i.e., when $t \approx 0$. Clearly, $\hat{u}_i(0) = \bar{u}$. Differentiating (29) yields

$$\pi_i'\hat{u}_i' + (1 + \hat{u}_i' - \hat{u}_j')\pi_i' + (t + \hat{u}_i - \hat{u}_j)\pi_i''\hat{u}_i' \equiv 0 .$$

Setting $t = 0$ here yields $\hat{u}_A'(0) = \hat{u}_B'(0) = -1$. Differentiating (29) once more yields

$$\pi_i''(\hat{u}_i')^2 + \pi_i'\hat{u}_i'' + (\hat{u}_i'' - \hat{u}_j'')\pi_i' + 2(1 + \hat{u}_i' - \hat{u}_j')\pi_i''\hat{u}_i'$$
$$+ (t + \hat{u}_i - \hat{u}_j)(\pi_i'''(\hat{u}_i')^2 + \pi_i''\hat{u}_i'') = 0 .$$

When $t = 0$ this simplifies to

$$\hat{u}_j''(0) - 2\hat{u}_i''(0) = \pi_i''(\bar{u}) .$$

Solving this pair of simultaneous equations yields

$$\hat{u}_i''(0) = -\frac{2\pi_i''(\bar{u}) + \pi_j''(\bar{u})}{3} ,$$

which leads to expression (12).

The equilibrium market share of firm i is approximately

$$n_i = \frac{1}{2} + \frac{u_i - u_j}{2t} \approx \frac{1}{2} + \frac{1}{12}(\pi_j''(\bar{u}) - \pi_i''(\bar{u}))t .$$

Aggregate consumer surplus in equilibrium is approximately equal to

$$U(t) \approx \bar{u} - \frac{5t}{4} - \frac{t^2}{4}(\pi''_A(\bar{u}) + \pi''_B(\bar{u})) \, . \tag{30}$$

The per-consumer profit for firm i is

$$\pi_i(\hat{u}_i(t)) \approx t + \left(\frac{5}{6}\pi''_i(\bar{u}) + \frac{1}{6}\pi''_j(\bar{u})\right) t^2 \, .$$

Therefore, the total profit of firm i (i.e., $n_i \times \pi_i$) is given by expression (13). Industry profit is therefore

$$\Pi(t) \approx t + \frac{t^2}{2}(\pi''_A(\bar{u}) + \pi''_B(\bar{u})) \, .$$

Finally, from (30), total welfare ($W = \Pi + U$) is given by expression (14).

References

Acquisti, A., and H. Varian (2005): "Conditioning Prices on Purchase History," *Marketing Science,* 24(3), 367–381.

Anderson, S., and L. Leruth (1993): "Why Firms May Prefer Not to Price Discriminate via Mixed Bundling," *International Journal of Industrial Organization,* 11(1), 49–61.

Armstrong, M. (1999): "Price Discrimination by a Many-Product Firm," *Review of Economic Studies,* 66(1), 151–168.

Armstrong, M., and J. Vickers (1993): "Price Discrimination, Competition and Regulation," *Journal of Industrial Economics,* 41(4), 335–360.

—— (2001): "Competitive Price Discrimination," *Rand Journal of Economics,* 32(4), 579–605.

—— (2006): "Competitive Nonlinear Pricing and Bundling," mimeo.

Bakos, Y., and E. Brynjolfsson (1999): "Bundling Information Goods: Pricing, Profits, and Efficiency," *Management Science,* 45(12), 1613–1630.

Baron, D., and D. Besanko (1984): "Regulation and Information in a Continuing Relationship," *Information Economics and Policy,* 1(4), 267–302.

Bernheim, D., and M. Whinston (1986): "Menu Auctions, Resource Allocation, and Economic Influence," *Quarterly Journal of Economics,* 101(1), 1–31.

Bester, H., and E. Petrakis (1996): "Coupons and Oligopolistic Price Discrimination," *International Journal of Industrial Organization,* 14(2), 227–242.

Bhaskar, V., and T. To (2004): "Is Perfect Price Discrimination Really Efficient? An Analysis of Free Entry," *Rand Journal of Economics,* 35(4), 762–776.

Borenstein, S. (1985): "Price Discrimination in Free-Entry Markets," *Rand Journal of Economics,* 16(3), 380–397.

Calzolari, G., and A. Pavan (2005): "On the Optimality of Privacy in Sequential Contracting," *Journal of Economic Theory,* forthcoming.

Caminal, R., and A. Claici (2005): "Are Loyalty-Rewarding Pricing Schemes Anti-Competitive?," mimeo.

Caminal, R., and C. Matutes (1990): "Endogenous Switching Costs in a Duopoly Model," *International Journal of Industrial Organization,* 8(3), 353–373.

Carbajo, J., D. De Meza, and D. Seidman (1990): "A Strategic Motivation for Commodity Bundling," *Journal of Industrial Economics,* 38(3), 283–298.

Chen, Y. (1997a): "Equilibrium Product Bundling," *Journal of Business,* 70(1), 85–103.

——— (1997b): "Paying Customers to Switch," *Journal of Economics and Management Strategy,* 6(4), 877–897.

——— (2006): "Marketing Innovation," *Journal of Economics and Management Strategy,* 15(1), 101–123.

Coase, R. (1972): "Durability and Monopoly," *Journal of Law and Economics,* 15(1), 143–149.

Cooper, T. (1986): "Most-Favored-Customer Pricing and Tacit Collusion," *Rand Journal of Economics,* 17(3), 377–388.

Corts, K. (1998): "Third-Degree Price Discrimination in Oligopoly: All-Out Competition and Strategic Commitment," *Rand Journal of Economics,* 29(2), 306–323.

Crémer, J. (1984): "On the Economics of Repeat Buying," *Rand Journal of Economics,* 15(3), 396–403.

Dobson, P., and M. Waterson (2005): "Chain-Store Pricing Across Local Markets," *Journal of Economics and Management Strategy,* 14(1), 93–119.

Economides, N. (1989): "The Desirability of Compatibility in the Absence of Network Externalities," *American Economic Review,* 71(5), 1165–1181.

Ellison, G. (2005): "A Model of Add-on Pricing," *Quarterly Journal of Economics,* 120(2), 585–637.

——— (2006): "Bounded Rationality in Industrial Organization," in *Advances in Economics and Econometrics: Theory and Applications: Ninth World Congress,* ed. by R. Blundell, W. Newey, and T. Persson. Cambridge University Press, Cambridge, UK.

Esteves, R. B. (2004): "Competitive Behaviour-Based Price Discrimination," PhD thesis, Oxford University.

Fudenberg, D., and J. Tirole (2000): "Customer Poaching and Brand Switching," *Rand Journal of Economics,* 31(4), 634–657.

Fudenberg, D., and M. Villas-Boas (2005): "Behaviour-Based Price Discrimination and Customer Recognition," in *Handbook on Economics and Information Systems,* ed. by T. Hendershott. North-Holland, Amsterdam, forthcoming.

Gans, J., and S. King (2006): "Paying for Loyalty: Product Bundling in Oligopoly," *Journal of Industrial Economics,* 54(1), 43–62.

Geng, X., M. Stinchcombe, and A. Whinston (2005): "Bundling Information Goods of Decreasing Value," *Management Science,* 51(4), 662–667.

Hart, O., and J. Tirole (1988): "Contract Renegotiation and Coasian Dynamics," *Review of Economic Studies,* 55(4), 509–540.

Kim, B.-D., M. Shi, and K. Srinivasan (2001): "Reward Programs and Tacit Collusion," *Marketing Science,* 20(2), 99–120.

Klemperer, P. (1988): "The Competitiveness of Markets with Switching Costs," *Rand Journal of Economics,* 18(1), 138–150.

——— (1992): "Equilibrium Product Lines: Competing Head-to-Head May be Less Competitive," *American Economic Review,* 82(4), 740–755.

Laffont, J.-J., and D. Martimort (2002): *The Theory of Incentives: The Principal-Agent Model.* Princeton University Press, Princeton, NJ.

Liu, Q., and K. Serfes (2004): "Quality of Information and Oligopolistic Price Discrimination," *Journal of Economics and Management Strategy,* 13(4), 671–702.

Matutes, C., and P. Regibeau (1988): "Mix and Match: Product Compatibility without Network Externalities," *Rand Journal of Economics,* 19(2), 221–234.

―――― (1992): "Compatibility and Bundling of Complementary Goods in a Duopoly," *Journal of Industrial Economics,* 40(1), 37–54.

Miravete, E., and L.-H. Röller (2004): "Competitive Nonlinear Pricing in Duopoly Equilibrium: The Early U.S. Cellular Telephone industry," mimeo.

Nahata, B., K. Ostaszewski, and P. Sahoo (1990): "Direction of Price Changes in Third-Degree Price Discrimination," *American Economic Review,* 80(5), 1254–1258.

Nalebuff, B. (2000): "Competing Against Bundles," in *Incentives, Organization, and Public Economics,* ed. by G. Myles and P. Hammond. Oxford University Press.

―――― (2004): "Bundling as an Entry Barrier," *Quarterly Journal of Economics,* 119(1), 159–188.

Nevo, A., and C. Wolfram (2002): "Why do Manufacturers Issue Coupons? An Empirical Analysis of Breakfast Cereals," *Rand Journal of Economics,* 33(2), 319–339.

Odlyzko, A. (2003): "Privacy, Economics, and Price Discrimination on the Internet," *ICEC2003: Fifth International Conference on Electronic Commerce,* pp. 355–366.

Rey, P., and J. Tirole (2006): "A Primer on Foreclosure," in *Handbook of Industrial Organization: Volume III,* ed. by M. Armstrong and R. Porter. North-Holland, Amsterdam, forthcoming.

Rochet, J.-C., and L. Stole (2002): "Nonlinear Pricing with Random Participation," *Review of Economic Studies,* 69(1), 277–311.

Rothschild, M. (1974): "A Two-Armed Bandit Theory of Market Pricing," *Journal of Economic Theory,* 9, 185–202.

Shaffer, G., and J. Zhang (1995): "Competitive Coupon Targeting," *Marketing Science,* 14(4), 395–415.

―――― (2000): "Pay to Switch or Pay to Stay: Preference-Based Price Discrimination in Markets with Switching Costs," *Journal of Economics and Management Strategy,* 9(3), 397–424.

Spulber, D. (1979): "Noncooperative Equilibrium with Price Discriminating Firms," *Economics Letters,* 4, 221–227.

―――― (1989): "Product Variety and Competitive Discounts," *Journal of Economic Theory,* 48(2), 510–525.

Stigler, G. (1987): *Theory of Price.* Macmillan, New York.

Stole, L. (1995): "Nonlinear Pricing and Oligopoly," *Journal of Economics and Management Strategy,* 4(4), 529–562.

―――― (2006): "Price Discrimination and Imperfect Competition," in *Handbook of Industrial Organization: Volume III,* ed. by M. Armstrong, and R. Porter. North-Holland, Amsterdam, forthcoming.

Taylor, C. (2003): "Supplier Surfing: Competition and Consumer Behavior in Subscription Markets," *Rand Journal of Economics,* 34(2), 223–246.

―――― (2004): "Consumer Privacy and the Market for Customer Information," *Rand Journal of Economics,* 35(4), 631–650.

Thanassoulis, J. (2006): "Competitive Bundling and Mixed Consumer Surplus," mimeo.

Thisse, J.-F., and X. Vives (1988): "On the Strategic Choice of Spatial Price Policy," *American Economic Review,* 78(1), 122–137.

Varian, H. (1980): "A Model of Sales," *American Economic Review,* 70(4), 651–659.

Vickers, J. (2005): "Abuse of Market Power," *Economic Journal,* 115(504), F244–F261.

Villas-Boas, J. M. (1999): "Dynamic Competition with Customer Recognition," *Rand Journal of Economics,* 30(4), 604–631.

———— (2004): "Price Cycles in Markets with Customer Recognition," *Rand Journal of Economics,* 35(3), 486–501.

Wallace, R. (2004): "Preference-Based Discrimination and Profit: On the Profitability of Discriminatory Spatial Policy," *Journal of Economics and Management Strategy,* 13(2), 351–369.

Whinston, M. (1990): "Tying, Foreclosure and Exclusion," *American Economic Review,* 80(4), 837–859.

Yin, X. (2004): "Two-Part Tariff Competition in Duopoly," *International Journal of Industrial Organization,* 22(6), 799–820.

CHAPTER 5

Bounded Rationality in Industrial Organization*

Glenn Ellison

Abstract

This paper discusses the use of bounded rationality in industrial organization. There is a long tradition of such work: Literatures from various decades have discussed irrationalities by firms and consumers. Three main approaches are found in the recent literature: Rule-of-thumb papers specify simple rules for behavior; explicit bounds papers consider agents who maximize payoffs net of cognitive costs; the psychology and economics approach typically cites experimental evidence to motivate utility-like framworks. Common to each recent literature is a focus on consumer irrationalities that firms might exploit. I discuss several new topics that have been opened up by the consideration of bounded rationality and new perspectives that have been provided on traditional topics.

1 INTRODUCTION

In the last few years there has been a surge of interest in bounded rationality in industrial organization. The field has attracted the attention of a remarkable collection of top young researchers from industrial organization and behavioral economics. Much of the recent interest has been spurred by developments in psychology and economics, but there is also a long-standing tradition of such work in industrial organization. Although the field is not yet as coherent and advanced as most fields surveyed at an Econometric Society World Congress, the fact that diverse strands of research and diverse researchers are coming together seemed to me to make it a topic for which a discussion could be useful.

The terms "boundedly rational" and "behavioral" have been used by different groups of economists over the years to describe different styles of work. The

* This paper was supported by NSF grant SES-0219205. Tom Chang and Moshe Cohen provided valuable research assistance. I thank Richard Blundell, Ken Hendricks, and many World Congress attendees for their comments.

"bounded rationality" in my title is interpreted broadly, and includes work from three different traditions. One tradition I call the rule-of-thumb approach. These papers typically assume directly that consumers or firms behave in some simple way, rather than deriving behavior as the solution to a maximization problem. A second tradition is what I call the "explicit bounded rationality" approach. In this literature, cognition is costly, and agents adopt second-best behaviors taking these costs into account. The third tradition examines what happens in industrial organization settings when consumers are subject to behavioral biases identified in the psychology and economics literature.

The primary motivation for boundedly rational analysis is common across three traditions: In many situations the "rational" model does not seem plausible or has a hard time incorporating factors that seem important. There are also other motivations. One is that after twenty years of dominance of the game-theoretic paradigm, boundedly rationality explanations have been much less worked over. Another is that boundedly rational models are sometimes more tractable than rational models and make it feasible to enrich one's analysis in other dimensions.

Although rational game-theoretic approach has dominated IO for the past twenty-five years, the idea of using bounded rationality is far from new. This World Congress coincides with the 50th anniversary of Simon's (1955) call to replace the rational economic man with a boundedly rational counterpart. This year is the 50th anniversary of Strotz's (1956) seminal work on time inconsistency. The rule-of-thumb approach is even older. The application of these ideas to industrial organization has waxed and waned, but by now it amounts to a substantial literature.

I begin this essay with a discussion of several old literatures. I do this both because I think it is useful to recount what happened before 1990, and because it provides an opportunity to explain what the different boundedly rational approaches are, what are their strengths and weaknesses, and where they have been most successful. I think all three methodologies are useful and that anyone interested in boundedly rational industrial organization should be fluent with each of them.

I then turn to the more recent literature on boundedly rational IO. Here, I see the literature as having divided into two main branches. The first is growing out of the industrial organization literature. Papers in this branch typically begin with one of two observations: the IO literature on some topic is unsatisfying because aspects of the existing rational models aren't compelling; or the IO literature has had little to say about some topic (perhaps because rational modeling would have been awkward). They then propose models with some boundedly rational elements and discuss how they add to the literature on the topic. The second branch is growing out of the psychology and economics literature. Papers in this branch typically start by noting that the psychology and economics literature has shown that consumers depart from rationality in some particular way. They then explore how a monopolist would exploit such a bias, what the effects would be under competition, etc. I provide overviews of each of these literatures and discuss some general themes.

Readers of this survey will note that the literatures I discuss remain sparse. Most topics in IO have little or no boundedly rational work on them. Most behavioral biases have received little or no consideration in IO, and even when they have been discussed it is only the most basic IO questions that have been asked. This makes it an exciting time to work in the field.

2   EARLY HISTORY

It is impossible to identify the beginnings of bounded rationality in industrial organization. Throughout the period when the neoclassical profit-maximizing model was being developed there were spirited debates between proponents and opponents of "marginal revenue = marginal cost" as a foundation for firm behavior. Hall and Hitch (1939), for example, take direct aim at economists who "assume the general relevance of the simple analysis in terms of marginal cost and marginal revenue" and "that production is carried out to the point where this elasticity is equal to the ratio $\frac{P}{P-MC}$." They report that interviews of 38 business executives

> ... casts doubt on the general analysis of price and output policy in terms of marginal cost and marginal revenue . . . they are thinking in altogether different terms; that in pricing they try to apply a rule of thumb we call "full cost."

Hall and Hitch were mostly concerned with debating the modeling of firm behavior, but other papers from the 1920s, 1930s, and 1940s were more directly focused on industrial organization implications. Rothschild (1947) is a delightful example that in many ways is quite like modern behavioral IO papers. It assumes that a firm's "desire for secure profits" is a second objective as important as the desire for maximum profits and discusses various implications in oligopoly settings. For example, it argues that this can lead to price rigidity, to varying contractual terms-of-trade, to price wars, to political actions, etc. He sees the firms in his paper as practicing full cost pricing beause they are rational with a different objective function rather than irrational, but would rather throw out rationality than full-cost pricing if his rationalization proves incorrect: "If business behaviour were really irrational, this would not serve as an excuse for the neglect of such behavior. Irrationality would then have to become one of the premises of oligopolistic price theory." Analytically, of course, the paper is quite different from modern work. The conclusions are drawn from very loose verbal arguments. Rothschild is, however, prescient in recognizing this limitation. He explains that "A completely novel and highly ingenious general theoretical apparatus for such a solution of the oligopoly problem has recently been created by John von Neumann and Oskar Morganstern . . . Unfortunately, at the time of writing this article I had no opportunity of obtaining a copy of this important book."

One tends to think that there was a long era of neoclassical dominance between the death of this old literature and the birth of interest in post-rationality bounded rationality. In this light, I find it noteworthy that less than a decade separates the publication of Rothschild's paper and the publication of Simon's (1955) "A Behavioral Model of Rational Choice." Simon is clearly writing for an audience steeped in rationality and sells his bounded rationality as an enhancement of the prevailing paradigm:

> The task is to replace the global rationality of economic man with a kind of rational behavior that is compatible with the access to information and the computational capacities that are actually possessed by organisms.

Simon discusses the various challenges involved in optimization. His critiques and visions for a new framework are compelling. The progress he makes toward this goal is less satisfying. He mostly ends up emphasizing a "satisficing" model in which agents search for actions until they find one that achieves a payoff that provides them with at least some aspiration level.

Cyert and March (1956) is an early application to industrial organization. In the modern style, they start by citing interesting papers from the psychology literature to justify their assumptions about deviations from profit-maximization.[1] Among the implications of satisficing they discuss are that firms are most likely to expand sales when profits are low and costs high, and that dominant firms may tend to lose market share over time. The analytic methodology, of course, is still far from modern: Other than one set of diagrams using Stigler's dominant firm model, the analysis is completely informal. They do present empirical data related to their hypotheses.

One aspect of this literature that is striking in contrast to the current literature is that the focus is almost exclusively on firms' deviations from profit-maximization rather than on consumer irrationality. Indeed, consumers are rarely mentioned. Their presence is, of course, implicit in the assumption that the firm is facing a specified demand curve. Perhaps this is why consumer irrationality was not discussed. Whether the demand curve reflects the aggregation of utility-maximizing decisions or some other consumer behavior would not really affect the analysis.

3 BOUNDED RATIONALITY AT THE TIME OF THE GAME-THEORETIC REVOLUTION

The late 1970s and early 1980s is usually thought of as the beginning of the game-theoretic revolution in Industrial Organization. It was also a time when several distinct "boundedly rational" or "behavioral" approaches were being developed.

---

[1] For example, the notion that people satisfice is supported by the experiments showing that subjects who are asked to throw darts as close to the center of a target as possible are more accurate when the target is smaller.

3.1   The Rule-of-Thumb Approach

Consider the simple problem a consumer faces on every trip to the supermarket: should he buy any of the dozens of relatively new products he has never tried or should he continue to buy what he habitually buys? To make a rational decision the consumer must start with a prior over the quality of the unknown goods, he must also have a prior over how quality covaries with cost and think through what this implies about the signals inherent in the price of the good and the amount of shelf space the store has devoted to the product. Whether by observing other shoppers or talking to friends, the consumer will also learn something about the popularity of the product. Correctly accounting for this signal requires a correct prior over the set of possible social processes by which popularity has been achieved. How long has the product been on the shelf before I noticed it? Are the previous consumers people who have used the good before or people trying it for the first time? How many previous customers did they talk to before trying it? What did they know about where those customers got their information and how they used it? Recent models by Banerjee (1992), Bikhchandani, Hirshleifer, and Welch (1992), Banerjee and Fudenberg (2004), and Bose, Orosel, Ottaviani, and Vesterlund (2006) provide remarkable analyses showing that the rational approach can be made tractable in some such situations.

Despite my admiration for these papers, when I think about consumers' making such decisions dozens of times in the course of an hour-long shopping trip I have the same reaction that Smallwood and Conlisk (1979) had when contemplating this problem twenty-five years ago:

> . . . a would-be optimizing consumer who took account of market popularities would be involved in a massive game theory problem with all other consumers. Is it really plausible that he could solve the game?

The approach of the rule-of-thumb literature is to simply posit rules of thumb that consumers are assumed to follow. One can think of this as similar to the game-theoretic approach, but skipping the part of the argument in which one posits utility functions and derives the behaviors as optimizing choices. Proponents of the rule-of-thumb approach see it as having two advantages. First, in some models it seems implausible that consumers would do the "rational" calculations. A desiderata for choosing a rule-of-thumb is that the explicitly assumed consumer behavior should be more believable than the behavior implicitly assumed in the obvious rational alternatives. Second, rule-of-thumb papers tend to provide more analysis of robustness. One reason is inherent: The analysis of rule-of-thumb models is simpler, making it possible to analyze more variants in the same amount of time. Another is probably sociological: Rule-of-thumb authors recognize that they will be subject to more scrutiny than their "rational" peers and must head off critiques about the conclusions being nonrobust to changes in the ad hoc assumptions.

Smallwood and Conlisk's (1979) model of the effect of product quality on market share remains a beautiful example of the rule-of-thumb approach.

Consider a market in which consumers choose between K brands at $t = 0, 1, 2, \ldots$. Suppose that a consumer of product i in period t experiences a "breakdown" with probability b_i. This could be a literal breakdown of a durable good or just a disappointing experience with an ordinary consumable.

In this environment, Smallwood and Conlisk examine what happens when consumers follow particular rules of thumb. Specifically, they assume each consumer continues to use the same product until he experiences a breakdown. When a breakdown occurs he considers switching and ends up choosing product i with probability proportional to $m_i(t)^\sigma$, where $m_i(t)$ is the market share of product i. By varying the parameter σ the assumption can encompass a range of behaviors. For example, $\sigma = 0$ is purely random choice, and $\sigma = 1$ models consumers who ask one randomly selected friend which brand they used and purchase that product.

The first theorems in the paper explore the connection between behavior at the consumer level and the efficiency of product adoption. For example, they show that when $\sigma < 1$, higher quality products eventually become more popular regardless of the initial conditions, but all products have positive market shares in the long run. When $\sigma > 1$ this is not true and an inferior product can come to dominate the market if its initial market share is sufficiently high. A particularly interesting feature of the model is that when $\sigma = 1$ the highest quality product (or products) always dominates in the long run. In this sense, we see that limited rationality at the individual level – recall that $\sigma = 1$ means copying the decision made by one randomly chosen user without using any information about their satisfaction – can make product adoption socially optimal in the long run. When this happens, it makes the rule-of-thumb assumption all the more palatable: There is no strong incentive to deviate to some more complex behavior.

The Smallwood-Conlisk paper has other features that presage future developments in boundedly rational IO. Stylistically, it includes a quick reference to some work by Tversky to motivate the assumption of bounded rationality. More substantively, the second half of the paper pairs irrational consumers with strategic firms to endogenize the product qualities:

> Firms, unlike consumers, will be assumed to solve optimization problems in choosing their $b_i(t)$. A rationale is that firms are better able to compute optima and are penalized more if they do not (through the force of competition).

In the recent psychology and economics–motivated literature, the rational firm–irrational consumer assumption has become the norm, and the question of what firms do to exploit irrationality is often the primary focus.

When the game-theoretic revolution swept through industrial organization, much of rule-of-thumb literature could not withstand the onslaught. For example, Schmalensee (1978) used a rule-of-thumb approach to analyze a model in which higher quality products were more costly to produce and firms chose advertising levels. He argues for the rule-of-thumb approach over the rational approach on the grounds that "it seems implausible to assume that households actually compute optimal solutions to a large number of difficult game-theoretic and information-theoretic problems." Part of his argument for this contention is that "buyers' optimal use of the signals transmitted by firms' choices of advertising levels would depend on the strategies being employed by all sellers." Within just a few years, the mechanics of solving such signalling problems had become so routine that I am sure few economists presented with this latter quote would have guessed that it was meant as a critique of signalling theory rather than as an exposition of how to solve signalling problems.

3.2   Explicit Bounded Rationality

Although Simon's initial motivation of bounded rationality leaned very heavily on limited human capacity for computation, the theory mostly developed along lines that had little to do with this. Agents were assumed to satisfice rather than to maximize, but there was little attempt to formalize why this might be easier than maximizing or to provide criterion on which to assess the feasibility of other behaviors.

One place in which computational limitations were made explicit was in team theory.[2] In the canonical model of this literature, a firm is modeled as a group of agents sharing a common objective. The firm needs to choose a vector-valued action. Which action is optimal depends on an unknown state of nature. Each employee has some information. The problem of choosing an optimal action is complicated by the presence of two additional costs: Each agent may incur a cost of gathering information; and there may be costs of communicating information across agents. Given these information costs, it will generally not be optimal to gather all the available information, nor to convey what has been gathered to a single decision maker. Instead, the firm may want to decentralize decision-making and have agents or groups of agents choose components of the vector-valued action independently.

Making decisions according to the optimal decentralized procedure is, of course, the fully rational thing to do in this model if one takes all costs into account. It can thus be seen as providing a rational analysis of why firms are organized as they are. Team theory models can also, however, be seen as a tool for looking at a range of industrial organization problems. The idea is that team theory provides information-cost-based microfoundations that can guide our choice of rules of thumb. The traditional analysis of monopoly and oligopoly problems ignores information costs. Hence, what we call "rational" models are really rule-of-thumb models that assume firms use a particular rule of thumb: Behave as if information costs were not present. If team theory gives us some general insights into how information costs affect firm behavior, then analyzing IO problems by using rules of thumb suggested by team theory should be superior to the "rational" approach as it is conventionally applied.

[2] See Marschak and Radner (1972).

Radner's (1975) model of cost-reduction by satisficing managers connects with both the explicit bounds and the rule-of-thumb literatures. He examines the problem of a firm that has only limited managerial attention to devote to minimizing its costs. Analytically, Radner takes a rule-of-thumb approach. He defines procedures for the manager to follow and examines the consequences.

3.3 Empiricism as "Behavioral Economics"

The 1970s also featured a third "behavioral" approach to industrial organization that would not normally be thought of as behavioral today. Joskow's (1973) "Pricing Decisions of Regulated Firms: A Behavioral Approach," is a good example. What Joskow does in this paper is simply to estimate a probit model. The dependent variable is an indicator for whether a utility applied to the New York Public Service Commission for an increase in its electric rate. He assumes that they apply for a rate hike if and only if $X_i\beta + \epsilon_i > 0$ and estimates the parameter β. The right-hand side variables X_i include things like the firm's earnings growth.

Economists today will wonder why this would have been called "behavioral." Today, the probit model would be thought of simply as a method for estimating the firm's profit function. If the firm is rational and profits are of the form $\pi_i = X_i\beta + \epsilon_i$, with ϵ_i a normally distributed component of profits that is unobserved by the econometrician, then the probit model provides a consistent estimate of β. Suppose, however, that profits are not actually linear. In the rational paradigm one assumes that firms fully understand the nonlinearities, but in many cases it would be equally plausible to assume that firms are unaware of the nonlinearities and follow an irrational rule of thumb of applying for a rate hike whenever $X_i\beta + \epsilon_i > 0$. In this case, the probit regression no longer estimates for profits, but it remains a consistent estimator of behavior. Whether the behavior we estimate is profit-maximizing or derived from a rule of thumb is irrelevant in many applications.[3]

It is because empirical work often involves directly estimating behavior (rather than utility or profit) that one can think of empirical economics as a behavioral approach. The empirical literature then becomes a place where "boundedly rational" industrial organization has quietly carried on for decades. Consider, for example, my empirical work with Judy Chevalier (1997) on risk-taking by mutual funds. We start by estimating the relationship between a mutual fund's performance in year t and how much new business it attracts in year $t + 1$. The main focus is then on how fund companies distort their investment decisions in order to attract new business. It may be possible to provide a plausible rational explanation for the precise form of the relationship between investment returns and the inflow of new business, although my prior would be

---

[3] One notable exception is papers doing welfare analyses.

that it is not.[4] For the main question of interest, however, why consumers choose between mutual funds as they do simply doesn't matter. The initial estimates of consumer behavior tell us everything about consumers that we need to know to think about the firm's optimization problem.

A similar argument could in fact be made for much of empirical industrial organization. Consider, for example, a classic "rational" paper, Porter's (1983) study of price wars in a railroad cartel. Porter estimates a structural econometric model in which demand is assumed to be of the form $\log(Q_t) = \alpha_0 - \alpha_1 \log(P_t) + \alpha_2 Lakes_t + u_t$ and firms' supply decisions are of the form predicted by the Green-Porter model of collusion with imperfect monitoring. Again, to answer his main questions about what the firms are doing, it does not matter whether the demand curve comes from a population of consumers who are optimizing some utility function or a population of boundedly rational consumers. By focusing on consumer behavior as an empirically estimable object, the approach is robust.

Discussing the whole field of empirical industrial organization is obviously far beyond what is possible in this format. For the remainder of this paper, I will treat work that is behavioral in the sense that Joskow's paper was behavioral as outside the scope of my talk.

3.4   Psychology and Economics

Psychology and economics was also developing rapidly in the late 1970s and early 1980s. Kahneman and Tversky had published their work on prospect theory in *Econometrica* in 1979, and many new areas were opening up. Developments in psychology and economics have had a huge impact on the new boundedly rational IO. Many other surveys of psychology and economics are available (including two in this volume), so I won't survey developments in psychology and economics that are not focused on industrial organization.

4   DEVELOPMENTS IN THE THEORY OF BOUNDED RATIONALITY

In the 1980s the game theoretic revolution in industrial organization seems to have been all-consuming. One can find slight departures from rationality in quite a few papers, but most seem to be unintentional or desired shortcuts.

In the field of economic theory the situation was somewhat different. The 1982 volume of *Econometrica* is a remarkable illustration of the progress in game theory in the early 1980s: Rubinstein's bargaining paper, Kreps and Wilson's sequential equilibrium paper, Milgrom and Weber's auction paper, and Crawford and Sobel's cheap talk paper are just some of the well-known papers in that volume. By the time Tirole's *The Theory of Industrial Organization*

---

[4] See Lynch and Musto (2003) and Berk and Green (2004) for more on this.

appeared in 1988, however, theorists were already looking beyond the rational agent–equilibrium paradigm. In this section I will discuss a couple of the late 1980s developments in theory that have been important in the growth of boundedly rational industrial organization.

4.1   Learning

Fudenberg-Kreps's (1988) draft monograph "A Theory of Learning, Experimentation, and Equilibrium in Games," promoted a rule-of-thumb approach to the question of whether we should expect players to play the equilibrium of a game. Again, a two-fold argument can be made for this approach. First, a fully rational approach to the problem of how players learn to play the equilibrium of a game is unappealing – it essentially replaces the assumption that agents play the equilibrium of some simple game with the assumption that they don't know enough to do this but somehow know enough to play the equilibrium of some horribly complicated game in which agents with different information are all simultaneously learning from one another. Second, a boundedly rational approach can provide an enlightening discussion of which rules would and wouldn't lead to equilibrium play. One way to do this is to examine a variety of behavioral assumptions. Fudenberg and Kreps advocated another: They ask the reverse-engineering question of what assumptions about behavior are needed to get to particular conclusions about the outcome of the learning process.

By the early 1990s boundedly rational learning models were clearly the hot topic in game theory. Most of this literature was directed at game theorists, but several of the classic papers included little industrial-organization stories. For example, Kandori, Mailath, and Rob (1993) motivated their model using the example of a group of students buying computers in a world with network externalities.

The nicest example I know of a paper addressing a real industrial organization problem by such methods is Möbius's (2001) examination of the rise and fall of competition in local telephone service in the U.S. in the early 20th century. The basic facts about telephone competition are striking. AT&T was a monopolist in the U.S. telephone market until key patents expired in 1893/4. Eight years later, three thousand firms had built separate networks not connected to AT&T's and taken approximately half of the rapidly growing market. The entrants continued to do well for another decade or so as the market quadrupled in size. But a period of consolidation followed, and by the mid 1920s competition had essentially ended.

Möbius provides an explanation for this pattern using a rule-of-thumb learning model. In his model, consumers and businesses are connected by social networks. The network consists of many "islands," each containing several consumers and one business. Everyone interacts disproportionately with others in their island, but consumers also benefit from interactions with businesses on other islands. The behavior rules that describe how consumers and businesses decide between competing noninterconnected telephone networks are similar to those in Kandori, Mailath, and Rob (1993), Young (1993), and Ellison (1993). In each period most consumers take others' actions as given and choose myopically between having no phone or buying service from firm A or firm B to maximize their current period utility. Firms' decision rules are similar, but firms may also want to get two telephones so as to be accessible to consumers on both networks. A small fraction of consumers are assumed to adopt randomly in each period. Essentially, what Möbius has done with these few assumptions is to describe a Markov process governing telephone adoption. What remains is just to analyze the behavior of the process. Using both analytic results and simulations he shows how the model can account for the growth and decline of independents. Roughly speaking, what happens in the early period is that each network grows by adding new subscribers within the islands in which they are dominant. Later, the "duplication" effect becomes important. Businesses in islands dominated by the minority telephone network start to get a second phone to communicate with consumers from other islands. Once this happens, the minority network has only a weak hold on the islands it dominates and can easily lose a whole island in a chain reaction if a few friends randomly decide to switch to the majority system. He presents empirical evidence consistent with this mechanism.

Thinking about the methodology, what makes the boundedly rational approach so useful here is more related to the second advantage mentioned above. The relative tractability of making direct assumptions about behavior allows Möbius to enrich his model in a way (incorporating the social network) that would have made it too complex to analyze had he insisted on assuming consumer rationality.

4.2   Computational Complexity

Explicit concern for computational complexity entered game theory at about the same time. Rubinstein (1986) and Abreu and Rubinstein (1988) discussed complexity in the context of repeated games. In particular, they discussed the concept of strategies' being implementable by finite automata and used the number of states of an automaton as a measure of its complexity. Standard repeated game equilibria can be implemented by automata, but they note that a conundrum appears if one thinks of agents as trying both to maximize the payoffs they receive in the repeated game and to minimize costs inherent in constructing a more complex automata: Agents will be tempted to leave off any states that are not reached on the equilibrium path, and this may render the kinds of off-path threats necessary to support cooperation infeasible.

Fershtman and Kalai (1993) examine some IO questions using a similar complexity notion. They consider a multimarket monopoly and single- and multimarket duopoly competition. Implicit in the complexity notion is a diseconomy of multimarket operation. If there are two possible states of demand in each market, then there are 2^n possible states for the n market combination, and a fully optimizing monopolist would therefore need a plan with 2^n

contingencies. They note that monopolists may want to avoid entering some markets to reduce complexity and discuss the complexity of dynamic collusion.

The models of Rubinstein (1993) and Piccione and Rubinstein (2003) discussed below develop alternate approaches to complexity. Rubinstein (1998) provides a nice survey of old and new work in this vein.

5 THE NEW BEHAVIORAL IO: BOUNDED RATIONALITY AS PART OF THE IO TOOLBOX

In the 1980s it seems to have been extremely important that IO theory papers be fully rational. Today, being less than fully rational is much more acceptable. Indeed, I'd guess that at the top general interest journals an IO paper now has a better chance of being accepted if it sells itself as being "behavioral" or "boundedly rational."[5] A bias in either direction is unfortunate, but the opening of journals to boundedly rational papers is a very good thing: The legitimization of boundedly rational modeling provides an opportunity to explore new explanations for old phenomena and opens up whole new topics.

In this section and the one that follows, I'll discuss recent work in boundedly rational industrial organization. The division into two sections reflects a divide I perceive in the literature in the way in which authors approach their topics. The papers I discuss in this section are topic-focused. Many grow out of existing rational IO literatures and look to bounded rationality as a complementary way to think about some phenomenon. Others discuss topics that had received little attention. In most cases, the papers have an easy time making the case that less than fully rational behavior seems implausible and that bounded rationality can provide additional insights.

I organize my discussion in this section by the IO topic being addressed.

5.1   Technology Adoption

At least since Griliches's (1957) work on hybrid corn and Mansfield's (1968) work on industrial technologies there has been a recognition in industrial organization that the slow pace of technology adoption may have significant welfare consequences. Sociologists often explain slow s-shaped adoption patterns as resulting from heterogeneity in individuals' attitudes toward new technologies.

---

[5] One anecdote to this effect is that the *Journal of Political Economy* (which I've always thought of as the ultimate proponent of rational explanations) recently explained that it was rejecting a paper not because of anything the referees said but because the editor's "gut feeling is that most of the time, forgetfulness, confusion, or other types of bounded rationality play a much more crucial role." I would hypothesize that the fact that IO is a relatively small field makes it more likely to be subject to such whims than other fields. The top general interest journals always have a macroeconomist coeditor to handle the many macro submissions but usually get by with someone outside the field handling IO submissions. People outside the field will have a harder time selecting the papers that are most important in the field and may be more likely to follow popular trends.

Rational explanations based on long machine lifetimes are also plausible for many industrial technologies. It is also clear, however, that information is important – it is not easy to know what technologies really are cost-effective – and this is an area where rationality is easy to critique. It is awkward to assume that consumers have correct priors over the set of new products that might be invented and even more awkward to assume that they fully understand the social processes by which some products achieve popularity. Ellison and Fudenberg (1993) build on the Smallwood-Conlisk approach to explore whether dispersed information about product quality will be aggregated at the population level and come to be reflected in adoption decisions.

We identify two mechanisms by which such "social learning" can occur. In one, information is aggregated via agents paying attention to popularity. In the other it is aggregated by geography. In both models, there are two technologies f and g. The payoffs are random variables related by $u_t^g - u_t^f = \theta + \epsilon_t$ with ϵ_t uniformly distributed on $[-\sigma, \sigma]$. Boundedly rational players observe $u_t^g - u_t^f$ but don't know the full history of payoff realizations. The popularity model looks at a homogeneous population in which there is inertia and in which players who do switch are more likely to use more popular actions: Players choose g if $u_t^g - u_t^f > k(m_t(f) - m_t(g))$, where k is a positive constant and $m_t(f)$ is the market share of technology f at time t. In this model, we show that with no popularity weights ($k = 0$) both technologies get positive shares in the long run. With $k > \sigma$ there can be herding on an inferior technology. With $k = \sigma$ full learning occurs in the long run and all consumers eventually adopt the superior technology.

In the geographic model, players are arrayed on a line (which could be a physical location or a position in some social network or taste space). There is no longer a single best technology – which technology is superior depends on the location. Players observe the technology choices of those in a neighborhood around them and also observe the average payoff of any technology used in their neighborhood. In this model, we show that social learning occurs via a geographic mechanism: The dividing point between the f-adopters and the g-adopters shifts over time and a law-of-large-numbers mechanism keeps it close to the optimum when the observation neighborhood is small. There is a tradeoff between the speed of adoption and its long-term efficiency.

Ellison and Fudenberg (1995) consider a model closely related to the non-spatial model described above. There are two primary differences: There is a random idiosyncratic component to the payoff each agent receives in each period; and we consider rules of thumb in which an agent asks k randomly selected members of the population about the payoffs they received in the current period and chooses the technology that provided the highest payoff in this random sample (with the proviso that an agent never adopts a technology that was used by no one in his sample). We focus on the question of how the structure of information flows affects the learning process.

Considering first the case where the two technologies are equally good, we show that the value of k affects whether we see "herding" on one technology or "diversity" with both technologies retaining a positive market share in the long run. Intuitively, when agents rely on small samples, they are unlikely to hear about unpopular technologies, which makes it more likely that these technologies will die out. We then introduce differences in average payoffs across the technologies and show that long-run efficient social learning will occur for a range of values of the sample size k. When k is smaller, herding on an inefficient technology may be possible, and when k is larger both technologies may survive in the long run. Intuitively, there is a degree of popularity-weighting implicit in the assumption that agents don't adopt technologies not being used in their random sample, and this can support social learning as in the earlier model.

Spiegler (2004) introduces price-setting into a related model. There are N firms. Each firm has a distinct (albeit equally good) technology that provides random payoffs that are independent and identically distributed both over time and across individuals: Each technology gives a payoff of one with probability α and zero with probability $1 - \alpha$. There is also an $N + 1$st technology that provides this same payoff at no charge. (Spiegler discusses unscientific medical practices as a potential application and refers to the firms as quacks.)

Consumers are assumed to use a rule of thumb that involves finding one person using each technology, treating the payoff, v_i, that person received as if it were the expected payoff of technology i, and choosing the technology for which $v_i - p_i$ is maximized. This is similar to the decision rule of Ellison and Fudenberg (1995), with the main difference being that each technology is sampled once rather than a popularity-influenced random number of times. Spiegler notes that the rule of thumb can also be motivated as an extreme form of Rabin's (2002) model of "believers in the law of small numbers" or as an application of a solution concept in Osborne and Rubinstein (1998).

The pricing game between the firms turns out to have a unique mixed strategy Nash equilibrium (not unlike the equilibria one sees in search-based models of price dispersion). In this equilibrium, expected prices are inversely related to the common product quality. Industry profits are nonmonotone in the number of firms. Industry profits initially increase in N because there is more likelihood that consumers' samples will contain at least one firm success but decline as N becomes large because the price competition becomes more intense.

5.2   Models of Sales

The classic models of sales by Varian (1980) and Sobel (1984) are described by their authors as rational models. The papers could also have been sold as boundedly rational or behavioral: Varian's model features some "high search cost" consumers who are ignorant of the prices each store offers and end up going to one store chosen at random; and Sobel's features some infinitely impatient consumers who buy immediately regardless of the potential gain from waiting for a good to go on sale. In each case, a very rough intuition for why there are sales is that firms want to price discriminate and give discounts to the more sophisticated shoppers.

Rubinstein (1993) and Piccione and Rubinstein (2003) develop formal approaches to modeling cognitive abilities and use these frameworks to provide models of sales in which the discounts-for-sophisticated-consumers intuition is more formally grounded. In Rubinstein (1993), cognitive complexity is captured by the order of the "perceptron" needed to implement a strategy. Some agents can only implement very simple strategies (buying if price is above a threshold), whereas others can implement nonmonotone strategies involving two or more cutoffs. He writes down a model in which a monopolist wants to charge high-cognitive-ability agents a lower price in some states, and in which the monopolist can achieve this by randomly choosing prices in a manner that makes it unprofitable for low cognitive-ability customers to also buy in this state. Piccione and Rubinstein (2003) introduce an alternate form of differential cognitive ability: They assume that agents differ in the length m of the price history they can recall. They again consider an environment in which the firm would like to charge high-cognitive-ability agents a lower price and show how this can be done by alternating between regular and sale prices in a manner that high-ability agents can recognize (letting them buy only when the item is on sale) and low ability agents cannot (forcing them to pay the time-average price).

Kahneman, Knetsch, and Thaler (1986) had proposed much earlier that sales might have a different irrational origin. They conduct a survey, and find that many subjects say that it is "unfair" for firms to raise prices when demand goes up and speculate that this may give firms an incentive to hold sales rather than reducing "regular" prices: If firms lower regular prices when demand is low, they will be branded as unfair if they raise prices back to normal when demand returns to normal. Rotemberg (2005) proposes a more complex fairness-based model to account both for firms' occasional use of sales and for the stickiness of prices within and across non-sale periods. In his model, consumers have reciprocal-altruism preferences and punish firms discontinuously if their estimate of the firm's altruism crosses a threshold. The model also relies on the firms' objective function being a concave function of profits and on consumers feeling regret. He argues that similar assumptions can also help explain how firms adjust prices in response to demand shocks and inflation.

5.3   Price Dispersion

The IO literature developed a number of search-cost–based explanations for price discrimination in the early 1980s.[6] These models are compelling for many real-world applications, but Baye and Morgan (2004) note that dispersion seems to occur even in enviroments where it is less plausible that substantial search

---

[6] Baye and Morgan (2004) provide an excellent survey.

costs exist: It is common for products listed for sale on Internet price search engines; and it even occurs in laboratory experiments in which a computer plays the buyer's role to perfectly recreate a Bertrand duopoly.[7]

Baye and Morgan propose that one reason why this occurs may be that the equilibrium of the Bertrand competition game is somewhat nonrobust to departures from rationality. Suppose that firms are ϵ-optimizers rather than being fully rational, i.e., they may pick any action that earns profits that are within ϵ of the maximum possible profit. One might think at first that the Bertrand model is fairly robust to such a change because in any *pure strategy* ϵ-equilibrium industry profits would be at most ϵ. Baye and Morgan note, however, the Bertrand game also has mixed strategy ϵ-equilibria with much higher profits. For example, for any $x \in (0, \pi^m)$, suppose firms use the mixed strategy with CDF

$$F^x(p) = \begin{cases} 0 & \text{if } p < \underline{p} \\ 1 - x/pD(p) & \text{if } p \in [\underline{p}, p^m) \\ 1 & \text{if } p \geq p^m \end{cases}$$

where $\underline{p}$ is such that $\underline{p}D(\underline{p}) = x$. In the Bertrand duopoly game with zero costs, the maximum gain from deviating from this profile is $x^2/2\pi^m$. If we set this to ϵ, we find that a firm can earn at least $\sqrt{2\epsilon\pi^m} - \epsilon$ in an ϵ-equilibrium. This is a strikingly large number for reasonable values of ϵ. For example, if ϵ is one percent of the monopoly profit, the aggregate industry-profits in an ϵ-equilibrium can be approximately 26% of the monopoly profit.[8]

5.4   Obfuscation

One of the most basic results on the economics of information disclosure is that firms will disclose all relevant information to consumers if the information is costless to disclose and disclosures are credible (either because the facts are evident or because truth-in-advertising laws provide a guarantee) (Grossman 1981; Milgrom 1981). The simple intuition is that the firm with the highest possible quality will always want to disclose its information to increase consumers' willingness to pay. Given that the best-news firm is disclosing its information, the firm with the next best news will also gain from separating from any firms that are pooling on nondisclosure, and so on.

Ellison and Ellison (2005) note that there are big differences between this theoretical prediction and what we see in many real-world environments. For example, mattress manufacturers put different model names on products sold through different stores and provide sufficiently few technical specifications so as to make it very difficult to compare prices across stores. Credit cards are

---

[7] See Dufwenberg and Gneezy (2000).

[8] Note, however, that the play is ϵ-suboptimal only in an *ex ante* sense. When the realization of the randomization calls for setting $p = p^m$, play is $O(\sqrt{\epsilon})$ inefficient in an *ex post* sense.

another good example: It is also hard to imagine that the complex fee schedules in small print on the back of credit card offers could not be made simpler. Our empirical work examines a group of small retailers selling computer parts over the Internet via the PriceWatch search engine. The most basic observation of the paper is that many of the firms have clearly adopted pricing practices that make it time-consuming and difficult for consumers to understand what exactly a firm is offering and at what price. For example, products are described incompletely and consumers may have to go through many pages to learn all of the nonstandard aspects of the offer: the restocking fee that will apply if the product is returned, how much extra the consumer will need to pay for a warranty, etc. A second interesting empirical observation is that retailers appear to obtain substantial markups over marginal cost even though there is easy entry, minimal product differentiation, and minimal inherent search costs.

The combination of these two facts – there appears to be a great deal of obfuscation; and obfuscation appears to affect markups – makes obfuscation a natural topic for IO economists to study. The emphasis of the current IO literature on product differentiation as the source of markups may well be fully justified empirically, but another reason for the absence of any mention of obfuscation in Tirole (1988) may be that it would have been an awkward topic to discuss in the rational paradigm.

The most straightforward way to think about obfuscation using standard IO tools would be to regard it as increasing search costs in a model with a costly search like Stahl (1989). One would want, however, to extend the standard models to allow the search costs to vary by firm (instead of just across consumers). Even then, we would have a fairly black-box model. A nicer bounded rationality augmentation would be to derive search costs as a special case of costly computation.

More direct bounded rationality approaches are also appealing. Gabaix and Laibson (2004) suggest a very simple formalization: One could regard obfuscation as increasing the variance of the random evaluation error ϵ_i in a model in which consumers have noisy estimates of the utility they will receive from consuming a product – they think they will get utility $\delta_i + \epsilon_i$ from consuming product i when they actually get utility δ_i. Such a model is formally equivalent (from the firm's perspective) to a model in which firms can invest in product differentiation. Firms will invest in obfuscation just as they invest in differention to raise markups. The equilibrium markups for a given error distribution can be derived as in Perloff and Salop (1985).[9] Gabaix and Laibson derive new results on the asymptotic rate at which markups decline as the number of firms

---

[9] Perloff and Salop is an exception to my earlier remark about departures from rationality in 1980s' IO papers being unintended or unwanted. They have a brief section in the back of their paper noting that the ϵ's in their model could capture "'spurious' as well as actual product differentiation." They mention Chamberlin and Galbraith as among those who had previously discussed spurious differentiation and point to blind taste tests as providing empirical support for its importance.

increases and emphasize that for some error distributions adding firms to the market will drive down prices very slowly.

Spiegler (2006) discusses another rule-of-thumb model. In his model, products inherently have a large number of dimensions. Boundedly rational consumers evaluate products on one randomly chosen dimension and buy the product that scores most highly on this dimension. In this model, consumers would evaluate the products correctly if products were designed to be equally good on all dimensions. Spiegler shows that this will not happen, however. Essentially, firms randomize across dimensions, making the product very good on some dimensions and not so good on others. He thinks of this cross-dimensional variation as intentional obfuscation. The comparative statics of the model may help us understand why there is more obfuscation in some markets than in others: Obfuscation increases when there are more firms in the market and when the outside option is more attractive.

5.5   Add-On Pricing

In many industries, it is common to sell high-priced add-ons. Hotels charge high prices for dry cleaning, telephone calls, minibar items, and restaurant meals. Credit cards have high late-payment fees. Upgrading to a larger hard drive and adding more memory adds substantially to the advertised price of a Dell computer.

Ellison (2005) notes that we can think of high add-on prices in a couple ways. One is that we may simply be seeing the outcome of a standard multi-good price discrimination model. Suppose that consumers who are more price-sensitive when choosing between firms ("cheapskates") also have a lower willingness to pay for quality-improving add-ons.[10] Then, in a standard imperfect competition/price discrimination model in which firms simultaneously announce prices for low- and high-quality goods and all consumers are perfectly informed and rational, firms will charge higher markups on higher quality goods.

A second way to think about high prices for add-ons is as in Lal and Matutes (1994). If add-on prices are not observed by consumers when choosing between firms, then add-ons will always be priced at the ex post monopoly price.[11] In such a model, of course, the profits earned on the add-on may be competed away in the form of lower base-good price. Lal and Matutes's "loss leader" model is an example in which the price cut on the base good exactly offsets the profits

---

[10] I would argue that this assumption is the most natural one to make. Note, however, that it does differ from what is assumed in most papers discussed in Armstrong (2006) and Stole (2005). The standard assumption has been that brand preferences and quality preferences are independent.

[11] Lal and Matutes's explanation is a version of Diamond's (1971) classic argument about search costs leading to monopoly pricing. It can also be thought of as a version of Klemperer's (1987) switching cost model: One can think of the add-on being sold at a later date, with the inability of consumers to see add-on prices being equivalent to assuming the firm can't commit to future prices.

earned on the add-on. The second main observation of Ellison (2005) is that this no longer holds in models with cheapskates. In such an environment, firms that rely on sales of add-ons for a large part of their profits face a severe adverse selection problem: Price cuts disproportionately attract cheapskates who don't buy add-ons. This adverse selection problem discourages price-cutting. As a result, the joint adoption of add-on practices raises equilibrium profits.

An interesting question raised by the profitability of the joint adoption of add-on pricing in this second conceptualization is whether it is individually rational for firms to adopt add-on pricing. Typically, consumers would be able to buy a more efficient bundle if add-ons were priced closer to cost. If firms could commit to setting such prices and costlessly inform consumers via advertising, then firms in a rational-consumer model would typically want to do this.[12] Hence, advertising costs, tacit collusion, or some other modification is needed to account for why add-on pricing is practiced.[13]

Gabaix and Laibson (2005) develop a boundedly rational explanation for why add-on prices often are not advertised. Proceeding along lines suggested in Ellison (2005), they develop a model with two types of consumers: rational consumers and irrational consumers. In such an environment, the profits earned serving rational consumers are increased by advertising a higher base-good price and a lower add-on price. Profits obtained by serving irrational consumers are reduced, however. They describe the reason why this occurs as the "curse of debiasing." Irrational consumers are assumed to be unaware of the add-on's existence unless they see an advertisement listing a price for it. Once informed, they realize that they can take steps to avoid purchasing the add-on. This has the effect of reducing their willingness to pay for the advertising firm's product. If the fraction of irrational consumers is sufficiently high, then the losses on them can outweigh the gains on the rational consumers.

Papers on oligopoly behavior-based price discrimination, e.g., Chen (1997) and Fudenberg and Tirole (2000), consider a similar problem. They also, however, allow consumers to buy the add-on from the firm that did not supply them with the base good (although this is inefficient). In models without commitment, add-on prices are determined by the second-period oligopoly competition. As Armstrong (2006) notes, this would make the effect of naive consumers very different. The fact that consumers don't think about second period prices until the second period won't make second-period prices any higher, and would actually lower first-period prices by eliminating the effect that makes first-period behavior less sensitive to price differences. See Fudenberg and Villas-Boas (2005) for an insightful discussion of the mechanics of these models.

The paper of Spiegler (2006) I mentioned earlier can also be thought of as providing an explanation for add-on prices. One can think of the differences

---

[12] See, for example, Shapiro (1995).

[13] Note that this only applies to the second model of why add-ons are expensive, not to the first. The price discrimination model is a standard pricing game where add-on prices are high when optimally set and observed by all consumers.

in product quality on different dimensions as representing both pure quality differences and differences in add-on fees charged in various circumstances.

5.6   Performance Standards

How well an individual or firm has performed (or will perform) typically has a multidimensional answer. Performance assessments, however, often ultimately result in a zero or one decision. Should a student be admitted to this college? Should a student be given an A or a B? Should a job applicant be hired? Should a paper be published? Should a professor be granted tenure? These decisions establish performance standards. Two questions about standards are of primary interest: How will multiple dimensions be weighted? and How high will the overall hurdle be?

In some applications, one could try to develop fully rational models of performance standards, e.g., a firm should hire a worker if and only if the firm's profits are higher with the worker than without. In many other applications, no clear objective function is available, e.g., are colleges supposed to admit the students who will perform best in classes, those who will add most to campus life, those who will benefit most from the education, those who will go on to accomplish great things, or those who will eventually donate the most money to the college? Even when there is a clear objective, I would argue that the fully rational model is usually implausible because judges will typically lack the understanding necessary to maximize the objective, e.g., a firm will not know how a student's GPA in math classes and her experience at the school newspaper determine her incremental contribution to the firm's profits. As a result, the way that many such decisions are made is to compare the current candidate with past candidates, and to use relative performance to judge whether to admit the candidate.

Sobel (2000, 2001) uses a rule-of-thumb approach to explore how various factors affect whether standards tend to rise or fall. In these papers, candidates are assumed to choose a level of costly effort and to direct this effort to achieve a multidimensional vector of accomplishments. In the two-dimensional case, for example, the candidate's achievements are described by a pair (q, r). Candidates are then judged relative to the pool of recent successful candidates.

In Sobel (2000) the way the judging is done is that a single judge aggregates the multiple dimensions using a function $v(q, r)$ and deems the tth candidate successful if $v(q_t, r_t) \geq z_t$. It is assumed that the standard z_t is set so that a fraction τ of the previously successful candidates would meet the standard. When the function v is held fixed and there is no randomness in the achievement process, this model predicts a bunching of performance. Starting from any initial condition, candidates who are able to do so exert exactly the effort necessary to achieve the $1 - \tau^{th}$ percentile level of performance, and eventually the entire pool of recent sucessful candidates has achieved exactly this performance level. The most interesting results concern what happens when weighting functions change over time, e.g., shifting from v to v'

and back to v again. Such shifts cause standards to decline. Intuitively, when standards shift from v to v', the performance level of the earlier candidates (measured in terms of v') can be achieved at lower cost by tailoring effort to v'. Hence, equilibrium effort declines. When the standards shift back to v, candidates can again achieve a performance that grades as highly as the performance of the candidates who had worked toward v' with less effort. Comparing the first and third cohorts of agents, performance will have unambiguously declined.

Sobel (2001) considers institutions involving voting by a panel of judges. Each judge has a different v function. As in the earlier paper, judges vote to accept a candidate if the candidate's performance is in the top τ of recent successful candidates. What happens in this model depends both on the voting rules and the dimensionality of the performance space. When votes from only a small fraction of the judges are sufficient for admission, standards decline. When near unanimity is required, standards increase over time. In intermediate cases the results are more nuanced.

Ellison (2002) focuses on the weighting of different dimensions rather than the overall level of the standard. It is motivated by changes in the standards of academic journals over the last thirty years. There are several clear trends in economics (and other fields) over that period: Papers have been getting longer; they have longer introductions, more references and discuss more extensions; authors are required to carry out more extensive revisions before papers are published. I argue that all of these changes can be thought of as reflecting a shift in quality standards. Think of an academic paper as having a two-dimensional quality (q, r), where q reflects the importance of a paper's main contributions and r reflects other dimensions that can be improved with incremental effort, e.g., improving the exposition, generalizing and extending results, and performing robustness tests. The observed trends can be thought of as caused by or reflecting an increased weight being placed on r-quality, i.e., if articles are judged acceptable if $v(q, r) = \alpha q + (1 - \alpha)r \geq z$, then we may be seeing a decrease in α.

One way to account for such a trend would be to use the comparative statics of a rational model in which α is chosen to optimize some social welfare function. One can compute how the distribution of paper qualities is affected by α in equilibrium, and one could argue that the distribution produced by a lower α is now preferable because of some exogenous change in the profession. Such changes are hard to identify, however, and it is also hard to find any evidence that changes in standards were intentional. This motivates the search for explanations in which the shift is an unconscious by-product of rule-of-thumb behavior.

My model focuses on the behavior of referees. Referees are assumed to try to faithfully apply the profession's standards (rather than imposing their own preferences over quality dimensions). They do not, however, inherently know what values of (α, z) to apply. They try to learn these by seeing what parameters best fit the data they get in the form of seeing decisions made on papers they refereed, seeing papers in journals, and seeing decisions on their own papers. In each period authors work to maximize their chance of acceptance given their current understanding of the norm, referees apply the standard they currently believe in, editors accept the fraction τ of papers that referees rate most highly, and beliefs are updated given the acceptance decisions.

When referees are unbiased, this model has a continuum of equilibria. Given any weight α, there is a corresponding achievement level $z(\alpha)$ that yields an equilibrium. I then introduce a small behavioral perturbation, combining the rule-of-thumb and psychology-and-economics approaches. Players are assumed to be overconfident about the quality of their own work and think that it is ϵ higher in quality than it truly is. This destabilizes the former equilibria: Players will be puzzled about why it is that their papers are being rejected. The first effect that this would have on players is to make them think that z must be higher than they had thought. This hypothesis, however, also cannot fully explain the data: It cannot account for why marginal papers by others are being accepted. The result of players' continuing struggles to reconcile inherently contradictory data is a slow, gradual evolution of beliefs about the social norm in the direction of decreasing α. At the most abstract level, the idea of the paper is that one way to explain a long trend is to perturb a model with a continuum of equilibria. A slight perturbation of such a model can have a unique equilibrium and the disequilibrium dynamics can feature a slow evolution along the near equilibrium set.

6 THE NEW BEHAVIORAL IO: BIASES FROM PSYCHOLOGY AND ECONOMICS

The recent surge of interest in bounded rationality in industrial organization comes on the heels of a bigger and slightly less recent surge of interest in psychology and economics. This literature has by now documented a plethora of ways in which real consumers depart from the rational self-interested ideal: They discount in a nonexponential manner, exhibit loss aversion; care about fairness; have self-serving biases; fail to update in a fully Bayesian manner, etc. More importantly, it has developed a number of simple models that can be adopted as representations of agents subject to such biases. Exactly how portable such models are is subject to debate, but at least in principle one can construct the behavioral-bias counterpart of a given rational model by replacing the utility maximization assumption with the assumptions of one's favorite representation of consumers subject to this behavioral bias.

The initial papers in this branch of the behavioral IO literature have tended to focus on how firms will choose prices and product characteristics to exploit behavioral biases and whether competition will eliminate the exploitation. Combining the IO and psychology and economics literatures, however, naturally gives many more than just one paper topic per bias – we can get a whole matrix of paper topics. Think of the set of behavioral biases as the column headings, and put all of the standard models in IO as the row headings: how will a monopolist price, how will a monopolist selling durable goods price; how will a monopolist price discriminate; how will oligopolists selling differentiated goods set prices; how will some action be distorted to deter or accomodate entry, etc. It takes little knowledge or imagination to come up with literally thousands of paper topics: Tirole's (1988) text has hundreds of IO models, each of which could be combined with dozens of behavioral-bias models.

	Hyperbolic Discounting	Loss Aversion	Fairness	Self-Serving	Imperfect Bayesian
Monopoly pricing	DellaVigna Malmendier	Heidhues-Koszegi			
Price discrimination			Rotemberg		
Durable goods					
Static oligopoly					
Dynamic oligopoly					
Entry deterrence					
Innovation					

Will this lead to thousands of behavioral IO papers in the next few years? I am pretty sure (and hope) the answer is no. The problem is that most combinations will not produce observations that are sufficiently deep or interesting to warrant their being published. For example, Hossain and Morgan (2006) conduct field experiments on eBay and find that auctioning goods with a high (but not too high) shipping charge raises more revenue than using an equivalent minimum bid and making shipping free. It's a striking fact and they've written a very nice psychology and economics paper around it that discusses how the results can be explained by mental accounts with loss aversion (or other explanations). The companion how-should-firms-price paper, in contrast, is too obvious to write: If consumers behave this way then firms should use high shipping charges.

I would argue, nonetheless, that most boxes in this matrix are worth exploring. Without doing so, it is hard to know whether they will yield interesting alternate explanations for previously noted phenomena, provide potential explanations for facts about particular industries that are hard to square with existing models, or help us think about when consumer irrationality does and doesn't matter.

In this section I'll discuss two behavioral IO papers that build on the psychology and economics literature. Each belongs to the monopoly pricing and bias X row of my matrix. I will then discuss some general lessons.

6.1 Monopoly Pricing with Hyperbolic Discounting

Della Vigna and Malmendier's (2004, 2005) work on selling goods with delayed benefits (or delayed costs) to time-inconsistent consumers nicely exhibits the potential of behavioral IO. Their motivating example is pricing at health clubs: They think of consumers as incurring a short-run disutility when visiting a club and enjoying a delayed reward in the form of better health.

The model uses a theoretically appealing (and practically relevant) degree of generality in pricing. Consumers are initially offered a two-part tariff with an upfront payment of L and an additional per visit charge of p. If consumers accept this offer, they learn the disutility d that they will incur if they visit the club, and then decide whether to visit (which costs p and gives a delayed benefit b). Note that the decision to accept the two-part tariff is made under symmetric information, so in a rational model the health club would extract all consumer surplus via the fixed fee.

Consumers are assumed to have (β, δ) quasi-hyperbolic discounting preferences: From the perspective of period 0, payoffs in period t are discounted by $\beta\delta^t$. They consider both naive hyperbolic consumers who don't realize that they have a commitment problem, and sophisticated hyperbolic consumers who are fully aware of their time inconsistency.

In this model, one can think of two reasons why a health club will want to distort p away from marginal cost. First, sophisticated rational consumers would like to commit themselves to go to the health club more often. The health club can help them to do this by setting p below cost. Second, naive rational consumers will overestimate the number of times that they will go to the club. Reducing p and increasing L widens the gap between the surplus that the consumer expects to receive from accepting the contract and what the consumer actually receives. Hence, distorting the contract in this way makes the contract more appealing to these consumers. The two effects go in the same direction, so regardless of what type of hyperbolic consumers we have, we reach the same conclusion: Visits will be priced below marginal cost.

Is this distortion bad? In the case of sophisticated consumers it is not. Essentially, one can view the health club as selling a commitment device that allows the consumer to overcome his or her self-control problem and achieve the first-best. In the case of naive hyperbolic consumers, things are less clear cut. The low per-visit price does get consumers to visit the gym more often than they would with marginal cost pricing. Consumers' misperception of the value they will get from the contract, however, leads to their receiving negative total surplus.

One notable limitation of Della Vigna and Malmendier's work is that consumers are assumed to be *ex ante* homogeneous. This makes the paper less complete as an applied model – it can't explain why real-world health clubs offer a menu of contracts – and also eliminates any possible insights that might come from analyzing conflicts between rent extraction and surplus maximization.

Della Vigna and Malmendier's (2005) empirical study lends credence to the view that time-inconsistency is an important factor in health-club pricing. The health clubs they surveyed offer contracts in which the per-visit charge is set below marginal cost, and most consumers take them. In fact, they take these two-part tariffs even though the clubs also offer contracts with a higher per-visit charge that would be cheaper for most consumers. Clearly, people either must value the commitment or must overestimate their future usage. Survey data suggest that overestimation is at least part of the story.

6.2   Monopoly Pricing with Loss Aversion

Heidhues and Koszegi (2004) explore pricing to consumers who experience loss aversion.[14] The formal specification of consumer behavior follows Koszegi-Rabin (2005). Consumers have reference-dependent utility functions that depend not only on the number of units x of the good they consume and on the amount of money m they have left over, but also on reference levels r_x and r_m, which are their *ex ante* expectations: $u_t(x, m; r_x, r_m) = xv_t + m + \mu(x - r_x) + \mu(m - r_m)$. Loss aversion comes in via the function μ, which is assumed to be have a kink at the origin. Note that consumers feel a loss both if they are unable to buy a product they expected to buy and if they pay more than they expected to pay.

Heidhues and Koszegi consider a world in which demand and cost are both random and time-varying. In the base model, firms are assumed to be able to commit to a distribution of prices. Some interesting effects arise because this commitment allows the firm to manage consumer expectations. One observation is that prices will be sticky and firms may set a constant price (or choose prices from a discrete set) even when cost shocks are continuously distributed. The disutility that loss-averse consumers feel when they pay more than they were expecting is greater than the utility they derive from paying symmetrically less than they were expecting. This provides an incentive to keep prices constant. A related observation is that markups are countercyclical. Another fundamental conclusion is that there is substantial scope for indeterminacy: As in Koszegi-Rabin (2005), the purchase decision contingent on the price is not necessarily unique because the consumer has a higher valuation when he expects to buy, and even apart from this there can be multiple pricing equilibria when the firm lacks commitment power.

6.3   Some Thoughts

In this section I discuss some basic principles relating to how firms "distort" pricing to exploit behavioral biases and some challenges that the psychology and economics–motivated literature will face going forward.

---

[14] Schlag (2004) is another paper examining pricing to boundedly rational consumers. His consumers follow a regret-minimization strategy.

6.3.1 Will Monopolists Exploit Biases?

Consider a standard quality-selection problem as in Spence (1975). Suppose that there is a population of consumers with unit demands. A consumer of type θ is willing to pay at most $v(s;\theta)$ to obtain one unit of a good of quality s. Assume θ is uniformly distributed on $[0, 1]$ and that $\partial v/\partial\theta < 0$ so that if q units are sold then the consumers will be those with $\theta \in [0, q]$.

Suppose that a monopolist must choose a single quality level s for its product. Assume that the good is produced under constant returns to scale, with a quality s good having a unit production cost $c(s)$. The monopolist's problem is

$$\max_{q,s,p} \quad q(p - c(s))$$
$$\text{s.t.} \quad v(s;\theta) - p \geq 0 \ \text{ for all } \theta \in [0, q].$$

Conditional on the quantity sold being q and the quality being s, the highest price that can be charged is $v(s;q)$, so this reduces to

$$\max_{q,s} \ q(v(s;q) - c(s)).$$

The first-order condition for the monopolist's quality choice s^m is

$$\frac{\partial c}{\partial s}(s^m) = \frac{\partial v}{\partial s}(s^m, q^m).$$

The marginal cost of providing higher quality is equal to the marginal benefit for the marginal consumer.

The social planner's problem would be

$$\max_{q,s} \int_{\theta=0}^{q} v(s;\theta)d\theta - qc(s).$$

The first-order condition for the first-best quality choice s^{FB} is

$$\frac{\partial c}{\partial s}(s^{FB}) = \frac{1}{q^{FB}} \int_{\theta=0}^{q^{FB}} \frac{\partial v}{\partial s}(s^{FB}, \theta)d\theta.$$

The marginal cost of providing higher quality is equal to the marginal benefit for the average consumer.

Spence emphasized that monopolists typically will not provide optimal quality: The marginal and average consumer can have different valuations for quality, and the pool of customers served by the monopolist differs from the pool the social planner would want to serve. One case in which the monopolist's quality choice is optimal, however, is when the population is homogeneous. In this case, both the monopolist and the social planner will serve all consumers, and there is no difference between the marginal and average consumer. Hence, the monopolist provides optimal quality.

The quality-selection model is relevant to the question of how firms respond to behavioral biases because one can regard many decisions a monopolist makes as quality choices. For example, in Della Vigna and Malmendier's health-club application, the per-visit charge a health club imposes is a product characteristic that determines the quality of a club membership. A contract with a lower per-visit fee is a higher quality product.

The optimal quality result of Spence's model implies that a monopolist facing an *ex ante* homogenous unit-demand customer population will choose to sell the product s that maximizes $v(s) - c(s)$. When I developed the model I said $v(s; \theta)$ was the willingness to pay of the type θ consumer. In a rational model this is the amount of money that offsets the utility the consumer receives from consuming the product. Spence's result applies equally well in irrational models, however. One just has to keep in mind that the appropriate $v(s)$ is the willingness to pay for a quality s good at the moment at which the consumer makes the purchase decision.

In Della Vigna and Malmendier's sophisticated hyperbolic model, just like in the rational model, the willingness to pay of the time-zero agent is the expected utility that the time-zero consumer receives (in equilibrium) if she signs up for the health club. Hence, the outcome is that the health club chooses the contract that is optimal for the time-zero agent. In a naive hyperbolic model, willingness to pay is the time-zero agent's (incorrect) forecast of his equilibrium utility. Hence, the contract is also designed to increase the difference between the forecast utility and the true utility.

The same basic intuition will apply to other behavioral biases: Monopolists will distort product characteristics along whatever dimensions increase irrational consumers' willingness-to-pay. What these distortions are under alternate behavioral specifications, of course, still needs to be worked out. What makes Della Vigna and Malmendier (2004) successful is not that they show that a monopolist will exploit boundedly rational consumers, but rather that the exploitation is a compelling explanation for something we see in the world (low per-visit fees). A challenge for future authors is to find other applications where exploitation takes an interesting form.

6.3.2   Does Competition Eliminate Exploitation?

Another question that behavioral economists have raised is whether competition eliminates the exploitation of behavioral biases. The question can be asked either in the imperfect competition models that are common in industrial organization or in a perfect competition framework.

In the homogeneous population case, the answer is obviously no. Competitive firms will behave just like monopolists and make product-design choices s so as to maximize $v(s) - c(s)$. The only difference is that the surplus will be returned to consumers in the form of lower fixed fees.

In heterogeneous population models, the precise choices of monopolists and competitive firms will differ. How this will work depends on whether firms are or are not assumed to be able to offer multiple quality levels.

For some applications one would want to suppose that only a single quality level will be produced. The monopolist will design its product to appeal to its marginal consumer. Firms engaged in imperfect competition a la Hotelling will design their products to appeal to the consumer who is on the margin between the two firms. Although the monopoly and competitive product designs will be different because the marginal consumers are different, one imagines that qualitative conclusions about the direction in which product designs are distorted will usually be similar.

For other applications it will be better to assume that firms can introduce multiple products at different quality levels and use them to price discriminate. In a monopoly model, the type $\overline{\theta}$ with the highest willingness to pay is typically sold a product of the "optimal" quality, which here means maximizing $v(s; \overline{\theta}) - c(s)$. Other types will be sold products of quality lower than that which maximizes $v(s; \theta) - c(s)$. Whether this adds to or offsets the distortion that comes from exploiting the difference between v and utility will depend on the application. In competitive price discrimination models, the pattern of quality distortions depends on the joint distribution of preferences for quality and preferences for firm 1 versus firm 2. Hence, comparisons with the monopoly case will depend on how preference heterogeneity is specified.

7 CONCLUDING REMARKS

In this essay I've tried to give some perspective on the burgeoning field of boundedly rational industrial organization. It's a hard literature to summarize because one can depart from rationality in so many ways. The irrational actors can be the firms or the consumers. Several approaches to modeling irrationality can be taken: One can specify rules of thumb, behavior can be derived as the maximizer of something other than utility/profits; or one can explicitly introduce cognitive bounds. I've stressed two advantages of boundedly rational approaches: Boundedly rational behavior seems more realistic in some applications; and the tractability of boundedly rational models can sometimes allow researchers to incorporate additional features into a model. For the next few years at least there is probably also a third important advantage: After twenty-five years of focusing on rational models, the questions rational models are best suited to address have been much more thoroughly explored than questions best addressed in boundedly rational models.

I've noted that the current literature on boundedly rational industrial organization seems to be proceeding along two different branches. One easy way to give advice for the literature is to suggest that each branch adopt attractive features of the other. In many papers in the IO branch, the particular form of the departures from rationality is motivated by little more than the author's intuition that the departure is plausible. More reliance on empirical and experimental evidence could be a significant improvement. A relative weakness of the psychology and economics branch is that the papers are less informed by the existing IO literature on the topic and don't live up to existing IO norms in terms of incorporating consumer heterogeneity, imperfect competition, price discrimination, etc.

Which of the branches of boundedly rational IO is likely to be most successful in the coming years? Let me say first that I think in the long run the two branches will come together. Until they do, I think that having both is valuable. My answer to the question of which will be more successful in the next few years depends on the meaning of successful. If successful means advancing the IO literature I think the answer is the first branch. Delving into the IO literature and focusing on topics where the existing explanations are lacking is the most efficient way to improve a literature. If success is measured by publications or citations, I think the answer is the second branch. I noted earlier that an attractive feature of the psychology and economics literature is that the models developed in papers like Laibson (1997), Fehr and Schmidt (1999), and Eyster and Rabin (2005) are mechanically very much like rationality and can be grafted into just about any model. This creates many obvious opportunities for making contributions. When these opportunities do yield insights they should be easy to publish: The mechanics of these models make it easy to fill out an idea into a 35-page paper containing the kinds of fixed-point calculations referees are used to seeing.

To conclude, I'd like to make one last set of remarks on the shift that has taken place from focusing on irrational firms to focusing on irrational consumers. For many reasons this is very appealing. There is a great deal of experimental evidence on consumer behavioral biases. Firms can hire consultants to advise them on how to maximize profits and market competition may tend to eliminate firms that don't maximize profits. I agree with all these points but nonetheless think there are good reasons to keep the boundedly rational firm literature alive too.

Slight departures from traditional assumptions about consumer rationality can have a very large impact on economic models. Diamond's (1971) search model is a striking example in which prices go all the way from the competitive level to the monopoly level if consumers have an ϵ search cost. The evolving standards model of Ellison (2002) is another example how an ϵ behavioral bias can have a big impact. In other models, however, this sensitivity is not there: If all consumers ϵ-optimize or an ϵ fraction of consumers are irrational, then there will just be an $O(\epsilon)$ shift in firm strategies.

I noted above that Baye and Morgan (2005) have shown that the outcome of the Bertrand competition game is quite sensitive to whether firms are ϵ-optimizers. Although the mixed equilibrium they exhibit immediately strikes one as being a very special feature of this particular game, it is not clear that the sensitivity they are showing is at all unusual. As Akerlof and Yellen (1985) have noted, in smooth models, the derivative of a firm's profits with respect to its action is zero at the Nash equilibrium. If a firm changes its action by ϵ, profits will be within ϵ^2 of the best-response profits. A change in one firm's action does have a first-order effect on consumers and on the other firms' profits. Hence, in an ϵ-equilibrium, profits can be of order $\sqrt{\epsilon}$. For example, in the simplest Cournot duopoly with $D(p) = 1 - p$ and zero costs, any (q_1, q_2) with $q_i \in [1/3 - 2\sqrt{\epsilon}/3, 1/3 + 2\sqrt{\epsilon}/3]$ is an ϵ-equilibrium. This includes the monopoly outcome if $\epsilon > 1/64$, which is approximately 6% of the monopoly profit level.

In such examples, small departures from rationality on the part of firms can be as important as much larger departures from rationality on the part of consumers.

I look forward to seeing the literature on boundedly rational IO develop in the years to come.

References

Abreu, Dilip and Ariel Rubinstein (1988), "The Structure of Nash Equilibria in Repeated Games with Finite Automata," *Econometrica*, 56, 1259–1282.

Armstrong, Mark (2006), "Recent Developments in the Economics of Price Discrimination," in *Advances in Economics and Econometrics: Theory and Applications, Ninth World Congress* (ed. by Richard Blundell, Whitney Newey, and Torsten Persson), Cambridge: Cambridge University Press.

Banerjee, Abhijit V. (1992), "A Simple Model of Herd Behavior," *Quarterly Journal of Economics*, 107, 797–817.

Banerjee, Abhijit and Drew Fudenberg (2004), "Word-of-Mouth Learning," *Games and Economic Behavior*, 46, 1–22.

Baye, Michael and John Morgan (2004), "Price Dispersion in the Lab and on the Internet," *RAND Journal of Economics*, 35, 449–466.

Baye, Michael, John Morgan, and Patrick Scholten (2005), "Information, Search, and Price Dispersion," *Handbook on Economics and Information Systems*, Elsevier.

Berk, Jonathan B. and Richard C. Green (2004), "Mutual Fund Flows and Performance in Rational Markets," *Journal of Political Economy*, 112, 1269–1295.

Bikhchandani, Sushil, David Hirshleifer, and Ivo Welch (1992), "A Theory of Fads, Fashion, Custom, and Cultural Change as Informational Cascades," *Journal of Political Economy*, 100, 992–1026.

Bose, Subir, Gerhard Orosel, Marco Ottaviani, and Lise Vesterlund (2006), "Dynamic Monopoly Pricing and Herding," *RAND Journal of Economics*, forthcoming.

Burdett, Kenneth and Kenneth L. Judd (1983), "Equilibrium Price Dispersion," *Econometrica*, 51, 955–969.

Chevalier Judith, and Glenn Ellison (1997), "Risk-Taking by Mutual Funds as a Response to Incentives," *Journal of Political Economy*, 105, 1167–1200.

Chen, Yongmin (1997), "Paying Customers to Switch," *Journal of Economics and Management Strategy*, 6, 877–897.

Cyert, R. M. and James G. March (1956), "Organizational Factors in the Theory of Oligopoly," *Quarterly Journal of Economics*, 70, 44–64.

Della Vigna, Stefano and Ulrike Malmendier (2004), "Contract Design and Self-Control: Theory and Evidence," *Quarterly Journal of Economics*, 119, 353–402.

Della Vigna, Stefano and Ulrike Malmendier (2005), "Paying Not to Go to the Gym," *American Economic Review*, forthcoming.

Diamond, Peter (1971), "A Model of Price Adjustment," *Journal of Economic Theory*, 3, 156–168.

Dufwenberg, Martin and Uri Gneezy (2000), "Price Competition and Market Concentration: An Experimental Study," *International Journal of Industrial Organization*, 18, 7–22.

Ellison, Glenn (1993), "Learning, Local Interaction and Coordination," *Econometrica*, 61, 1047–1071.

Ellison, Glenn (2002), "Evolving Standards for Academic Publishing: A q-r Theory," *Journal of Political Economy*, 110, 994–1034.

Ellison, Glenn (2005), "A Model of Add-on Pricing." *Quarterly Journal of Economics*, 120, 585–637.

Ellison, Glenn and Drew Fudenberg (1993), "Rules of Thumb for Social Learning," *Journal of Political Economy*, 612–643.

Ellison, Glenn and Drew Fudenberg (1995), "Word-of-Mouth Communication and Social Learning," *Quarterly Journal of Economics*, 110, 93–125.

Ellison, Glenn and Sara Fisher Ellison (2005), "Search, Obfuscation, and Price Elasticities on the Internet," mimeo.

Eyster, Erik and Matthew Rabin (2005), "Cursed Equilibrium," *Econometrica*, forthcoming.

Fehr, Ernst and Klaus M. Schmidt (1999), "A Theory of Fairness, Competition, and Cooperation," *Quarterly Journal of Economics*, 114, 817–868.

Fershtman, Chaim and Ehud Kalai (1993), "Complexity Considerations and Market Behavior," *RAND Journal of Economics*, 24, 224–235.

Fudenberg, Drew and David Kreps (1988), "A Theory of Learning, Experimentation and Equilibrium in Games," mimeo.

Fudenberg, Drew and Jean Tirole (2000), "Customer Poaching and Brand Switching," *RAND Journal of Economics*, 31, 634–657.

Fudenberg, Drew and Miguel Villas-Boas (2005), "Behavior-Based Price Discrimination and Customer Recognition," *Handbook on Economics and Information Systems*, Elsevier, forthcoming.

Gabaix, Xavier and David Laibson (2004), "Competition and Consumer Confusion," mimeo.

Gabaix, Xavier and David Laibson (2005), "Shrouded Attributes, Consumer Myopia, and Information Suppression in Competitive Markets," *Quarterly Journal of Economics*, forthcoming.

Griliches, Zvi (1957), "Hybrid Corn: An Exploration in the Economics of Technological Change," *Econometrica* 25, 501–522.

Grossman, Sanford J. (1981), "The Role of Warranties and Private Disclosure about Product Quality," *Journal of Law and Economics*, 24, 461–483.

Hall, R. L. and C. J. Hitch (1939), "Price Theory and Business Behavior," *Oxford Economic Papers*, 2, 12–45.

Heidhues, Paul and Botond Koszegi (2004), "The Impact of Consumer Loss Aversion on Pricing," mimeo.

Hossain, Tanjim and John Morgan (2006), ". . . Plus Shipping and Handling: Revenue (Non)Equivalence in Field Experiments on eBay," *Advances in Economic Analysis & Policy*, 6, Article 3.

Joskow, Paul (1973), "Pricing Decisions of Regulated Firms: A Behavioral Approach," *The Bell Journal of Economics and Management Strategy*, 4, 118–140.

Kahneman, Daniel, Jack L. Knetsch, and Richard Thaler (1986), "Fairness as a Constraint on Profit Seeking: Entitlements in the Market," *American Economic Review*, 76, 728–741.

Kandori, Michihiro, George Mailath, and Rafael Rob (1993), "Learning, Mutation and Long Run Equilibria in Games," *Econometrica*, 61, 29–56.

Klemperer, Paul (1987), "Markets with Consumer Switching Costs," *Quarterly Journal of Economics*, 102, 375–394.

Koszegi, Botond and Matthew Rabin (2005), "A Model of Reference-Dependent Preferences," mimeo.

Laibson, David (1997), "Golden Eggs and Hyperbolic Discounting," *Quarterly Journal of Economics*, 112, 443–477.

Lal, Rajiv and Carmen Matutes (1994), "Retail Pricing and Advertising Strategies," *Journal of Business*, 67, 345–370.

Lynch, Anthony W. and David Musto (2003), "How Investors Interpret Past Fund Returns," *Journal of Finance*, 58, 2033–2058.

Mansfield, Edwin (1968), *The Economics of Technological Change*. New York: Norton.

Milgrom, Paul (1981), "Good News and Bad News: Representation Theorems and Applications," *Bell Journal of Economics* 12, 380–391.

Möbius, Markus (2001), "Death Through Success: The Rise and Fall of Local Service Competition at the Turn of the Century," mimeo.

Osborne, Martin and Ariel Rubinstein (1998), "Games with Procedurally Rational Players," *American Economic Review*, 88, 834–849.

Perloff, Jeffrey M. and Steven C. Salop (1985), "Equilibrium with Product Differentiation," *Review of Economic Studies*, 52, 107–120.

Piccione, Michele and Ariel Rubinstein (2003), "Modeling the Economic Interaction of Agents with Diverse Abilities to Recognize Equilibrium Patterns," *Journal of the European Economic Association*, 1, 212–223.

Porter, Robert H. (1983), "A Study of Cartel Stability: The Joint Executive Committee, 1880–1886," *Bell Journal of Economics*, 14, 301–314.

Rabin, Matthew (2002), "Inference by Believers in the Law of Small Numbers," *Quarterly Journal of Economics*, 117, 775–816.

Radner, Roy (1975), "A Behavioral Model of Cost Reduction," *Bell Journal of Economics*, 6, 196–215.

Rotemberg, Julio (2005), "Fair Pricing," mimeo.

Rothschild, K. W. (1947), "Price Theory and Oligopoly," *Economic Journal*, 57, 299–320.

Rubinstein, Ariel (1993), "On Price Recognition and Computational Complexity in a Monopolistic Model," *Journal of Political Economy*, 101, 473–484.

Rubinstein, Ariel (1998), *Modeling Bounded Rationality*. Cambridge: MIT Press.

Schlag, Karl (2004), "Competing for Boundedly Rational Consumers," mimeo.

Schmalensee, Richard (1978), "A Model of Advertising and Product Quality," *Journal of Political Economy*, 86, 485–503.

Shapiro, Carl (1995), "Aftermarkets and Consumer Welfare: Making Sense of Kodak," *Antitrust Law Journal* 63, 483–511.

Simon, Herbert A. (1955), "A Behavioral Model of Rational Choice," *Quarterly Journal of Economics*, 69, 99–118.

Smallwood, Dennis E. and John Conlisk (1979), "Product Quality in Markets where Consumers Are Imperfectly Informed," *Quarterly Journal of Economics*, 93, 1–23.

Sobel, Joel (1984), "The Timing of Sales," *Review of Economic Studies*, 51, 353–368.

Sobel, Joel (2000), "A Model of Declining Standards," *International Economic Review*, 41, 295–303.

Sobel, Joel (2001), "On the Dynamics of Standards," *RAND Journal of Economics*, 32, 606–623.

Spence, A. Michael (1975), "Monopoly, Quality, and Regulation," *Bell Journal of Economics*, 6, 417–429.

Spiegler, Ran (2004), "The Market for Quacks," mimeo.

Spiegler, Ran (2006), "Competition over Agents with Boundedly Rational Expectations," *Theoretical Economics*, forthcoming.

Stahl, Dale O. (1989), "Oligopolistic Pricing with Sequential Consumer Search." *American Economic Review*. 79, 700–712.

Stole, Lars (2005), "Price Discrimination and Imperfect Competition," in *Handbook of Industrial Organization*. North Holland.

Strotz, R. H. (1956), "Myopia and Inconsistency in Dynamic Utility Maximization," *Review of Economic Studies*, 23, 165–180.

Varian, Hal (1980), "A Model of Sales," *American Economic Review*, 70, 651–659.

Young, H. Peyton (1993), "The Evolution of Conventions," *Econometrica*, 61, 57–84.

CHAPTER 6

Price Discrimination and Irrational Consumers: A Discussion of Armstrong and Ellison

Kenneth Hendricks

1 OVERVIEW

I have the formidable task of commenting on two outstanding surveys of two important literatures. Armstrong (2005) examines developments in the theory of price discrimination, and Ellison (2005) examines the use of bounded rationality in industrial organization. Most of the recent work on price discrimination is concerned with oligopoly markets. The main issues in Armstrong's survey are: does competition eliminate price discrimination and, if not, what is the impact of a ban on price discrimination? General results on these questions are difficult to obtain. Thus, one of the roles of theory is to classify the kinds of oligopoly markets where price discrimination is likely to occur, the form that it is likely to take, and impact that it is likely to have on profits and welfare. Armstrong describes the progress that has been made on developing this taxonomy. I will highlight what I view are the main insights and make a couple of comments on outstanding issues.

The theme of firms exploiting consumers is also present in Ellison's survey, which focuses primarily on irrational consumers. However, the main issues are methodological. The rational game-theoretic approach has dominated theoretical and empirical work in IO for the past twenty years. Indeed, the literature on bounded rationality in IO is so sparse that Ellison's survey is in part a discussion of the potential of bounded rationality approaches for the field. A leading theorist recently told me that he thought that IO economists are so heavily invested in the rational game-theoretic approach that we are unwilling to consider other approaches. We either ignore behavior that is inconsistent with the paradigm or we build complicated, rational game-theoretic models (typically incorporating private information) to explain it. Ellison's very thoughtful, and possibly prophetic, essay challenges the field to reexamine its traditional approach. I try to meet his challenge in my remarks.

2   PRICE DISCRIMINATION

Armstrong's basic approach is to use a simple, parameterized Hotelling model to present the main insights of the recent work and the intuition behind them. Two firms are located at either end of a unit interval. Marginal costs of production are zero. Consumers have unit demands, and their preferences are indexed by three parameters: v, the consumer's utility from consuming the unit; x, the consumer's location in the unit interval; and t, the transport cost per unit of distance. Here v can also be interpreted as a measure of quality; x is a measure of the consumer's relative preference for the product of the firm that is located at the left-end point, and t represents how much he cares about the difference between the products – what Armstrong calls his level of "choosiness." The three parameters are independently distributed among consumers according some distribution.

One important result is that competition eliminates price discrimination on product dimensions where firms have no comparative advantage. In the Hotelling model, firms are symmetric in their ability to supply quality. Fixing t and assuming x is not observable, this symmetry implies that the location of the marginal consumer at any pair of prices does not depend on v, and the equilibrium is uniform pricing (i.e., $p = t$). This result is a special case of the cost-plus-fixed-fee result of Armstrong & Vickers (2001) and Rochet and Stole (2002). It suggests, for example, that as firms in the U.S. cell phone market become more symmetric in their capacity to provide quality service, their calling plans will simplify to two-part tariffs. Indeed, the two-part tariff was the standard tariff schedule in the U.S. during the 1980s when the cell phone markets were more local and arguably more symmetric.

Each firm has a comparative advantage supplying customers who prefer their product. Thus, when firms observe t or x, or a signal about them, they will charge personalized prices in much same way as a monopolist would. In these cases, the question is whether price discrimination increases equilibrium profits relative to uniform pricing. The answer turns out to depend upon what is observable. If firms observe t, the consumer's "choosiness" level, or signals about t, price discrimination softens competition and leads to higher profits. Moreover, firms will want to share their information about consumers. On the other hand, if firms observe x, the consumer's location, or a signal about x, then price discrimination intensifies competition, profits fall, and firms will prefer to keep their information private.

What is the difference between these two cases? Corts (1998) shows that the key issue is whether the firms' best replies shift across market segments in the same direction (best response symmetry) or in opposite directions (best response asymmetry). When firms discriminate on t, or a signal about t, their best replies shift in the same direction, since the high t segment is a stronger market for both firms than the low t segment. By contrast, when firms discriminate on x, or a signal about x, their best replies shift in opposite directions, since each firm's strong market (i.e., consumers who prefer its product) is the other firm's weak market. Best response symmetry/asymmetry is clearly an important new theoretical tool for studying competition in differentiated markets.

The possibility that profits fall when firms practice price discrimination distinguishes oligopoly markets from monopoly markets. Mixed bundling by multi-product firms is another case discussed by Armstrong where discriminating firms are worse off. These cases raise the question of whether firms can commit not to engage in price discrimination. Armstrong surveys a number of papers that model this issue as a two-stage game in which firms in effect choose the space of pricing strategies for the second stage. But, it is not always clear what actions firms can credibly and visibly take that make it prohibitively costly for them to charge personalized prices or bundled discounts. The commitment issue also arises in models of inter-temporal price discrimination. Despite the apparent absence of explicit commitment mechanisms, firms nevertheless frequently adopt uniform pricing rules when theory would imply price discrimination. For example, CD prices do not vary much across artists or over time. One possible mechanism is reputation but I am not aware of any papers that have explored the circumstances under which firms can build reputations for uniform pricing.

As Armstrong mentions, the development of scanner technologies and online markets has made it easier for firms to obtain information about consumer preferences from their purchase histories. These developments can enhance consumer welfare insofar as firms use this information to make consumers aware of other products. The worry, however, is that firms will use personal information to charge their customers higher prices. Armstrong's review of the literature on this issue shows, however, that price discrimination in oligopoly markets may mitigate this concern. Firms compete more aggressively when they can offer lower prices to their rivals' customers than their own customers. Furthermore, price discrimination across periods means that any rents earned by a firm on its customers in subsequent periods will be reflected in its initial offer. Thus, consumers may be able to earn back some or all of these rents when she becomes a customer of the firm. In fact, competition for new customers may force firms to commit to sharing customer information, forgoing the rents from private information. For example, credit agencies agree to share information on their consumers' credit histories. These results have important implications for antitrust policy on price discrimination.

3 BOUNDED RATIONALITY

Ellison distinguishes three kinds of bounded rationality in IO models: agents who use simple rules to make choices; agents who find it costly to make decisions; and agents who exhibit behavioral biases. The first two are closely related since agents with high decision or information costs typically find it optimal to adopt simple rules of thumb. Both of these approaches have a long tradition in IO. The last approach is new and originates in the recent work of psychologists and behavioral economists. Papers in this literature retain the maximizing calculus of the rational game-theoretic models but replace the utility functions with objective functions that incorporate a behavioral bias. The models are then solved using standard game-theoretic solution concepts.

Most IO economists would probably view the rule-of-thumb approach as complementary to the rational, game-theoretic approach. For example, in Varian's (1980) model of sales, some consumers use a simple rule of randomly selecting one supplier. The rule is rationalized by assuming these consumers have high search costs, but the costs can easily represent other kinds of frictions. The important issue is the impact of these consumers on the equilibrium pricing behavior of firms. Firms charge different prices for the same good, and the price dispersion is substantial with the support of the price distribution including the monopoly price. The theme here is a familiar one: a small amount of friction at the individual level can have big impact on outcomes. Another example is reputation models. A small probability of an incumbent firm being unwilling to accommodate entry has a dramatic effect on entry decisions in a multi-market, sequential entry model; a small probability that a supplier is committed to providing high quality service has a dramatic effect on the behavior of suppliers who find it costly to provide high quality service. In each of these cases, the goal is to explain behavior that is not consistent with equilibrium in a fully rational, game-theoretic model. But, instead of modifying the solution concept (e.g., ε-equilibrium), the approach has been to incorporate the "irrational" behavior directly into the model in the form of player types and then solve the game using standard solution concepts. I view this form of bounded rationality as basically a perturbation of the rational, game-theoretic model.

The behavioral bias approach represents a more fundamental shift in modeling. Della Vigna and Malmendier's (2004, 2005) fascinating work on health club memberships illustrates the main issues. They assume that health club members have quasi-hyperbolic discounting preferences. Members incur a short-run disutility with each exercise visit and obtain a long-term reward in the form of better health. The hyperbolic discounting implies that consumers will prefer a higher visitation rate ex ante than they will actually choose ex post. D&M show that the monopolist's optimal two-part tariff contract for these kinds of consumers involves a per-usage fee that is below marginal cost. The low fee helps consumers overcome their self-control problems and increases their willingness to pay for the membership, which the club extracts with the membership fee. The empirical prediction is that the usage rates of members on the monthly plan, where visits are free, are often so low that they would have been better off ex post using the per visit plan. D&M find that this is indeed the case for the majority of members in their sample. However, the hyperbolic discounting model fails to explain the delays in contract cancellation. To account for this feature of the data, D&M assume that some of the members are overconfident of their degree of self-control and consistently overestimate their usage rate.

One issue is the portability of the model. It is interesting to contrast D&M findings for health clubs to those obtained by Miravete (2003) for calling plans. He finds that most consumers on monthly metered and flat rate plans had ex post usage rates that justified their choice of plan. Furthermore, when this is not the case, consumers often responded to the potential savings by switching plans quickly. One possible explanation for the difference in results is that calling plans is a choice environment where consumers incur short-run benefits and delayed costs.

A second issue is that models of self-control problems are not necessarily inconsistent with the rational, game-theoretic approach. The traditional choice model in economics takes preferences as the primitive and utility functions as representations. Gul and Pesendorfer (2001) formulate a model of self-control preferences and provide a representation theorem. (See also Fudenberg and Levine (2005) for a game-theoretic approach to self-control problems.) The real issue here may be one of functional form rather than rationality. The parameterized hyperbolic discounting function is obviously a highly tractable way of modeling self-control problems.

The third issue is more troubling. The naïve consumers in the DM model are clearly bounded rational agents. They do not know their true preferences, are not aware that they do not know, and fail to learn even though actual play reveals their true discount rate. Other behavioral bias models (e.g., Gabaix and Laibson (2005)) also rely upon a substantial fraction of consumers who are naïve, unaware, and learn slowly, if at all, to explain behavior. This feature of the models is a fundamental challenge to the traditional rules. In the past, researchers would have been required to model the perception bias by assuming that consumers are uncertain about their preferences, are aware of their uncertainty, and update their beliefs in response to actual play. Today, I think the rules are less clear. It is difficult to know what to make of statements such as "This fact is consistent with a large share of naïve consumers." What constitutes an explanation of behavior? What does it mean for a model to be coherent if some players take actions based on expectations that are not consistent with the outcomes generated by those actions? Finally, when objective functions do not represent a preference ordering or incorporate misperceptions, how does one conduct welfare analysis?

In his paper, Ellison presents an interesting matrix that lists standard IO models as rows and different biases as columns. This matrix will undoubtedly be taught in many graduate IO courses over the next few years, and filling in the boxes is likely to become a major focus of researchers in IO. I think that this research strategy is on firm and fertile ground when it imports nonstandard preferences into monopoly and game-theoretic IO models. The D&M study of the effects of hyperbolic discounting on pricing in health club markets and Heidhues and Koszegi (2004) study on pricing in oligopoly markets when consumers experience loss aversion are excellent examples of what can be achieved. But, I am skeptical of models that rely on consumers with persistent perception biases to explain behavior.

Finally, I agree with Ellison that the recent shift from focusing on irrational firms to focusing on irrational consumers is an advance. As Ellison's example of a trip to the supermarket illustrates, consumers have much larger choice sets, make many more purchasing decisions, and in far smaller quantities, than most firms. As a result, decision and information costs are likely to matter more for consumers than for firms. The billions of dollars spent on image advertising targeted mostly at consumers also suggest that consumers are more easily influenced than firms. The challenge is to move beyond description and show how incorporating these frictions into a model of consumer choice can generate new insights into phenomena such as image advertising.

References

Armstrong, M. (2005): "Recent Developments in the Economics of Price Discrimination."

Armstrong, M and J. Vickers (2001): "Competitive Price Discrimination, " Rand Journal of Economics, 32(4), 579–605.

Corts, K. (1998): "Third-Degree Price Discrimination in Oligopoly: All-Out Competition and Strategic Commitment," Rand Journal of Economics, 29(2), 306–323.

Della Vigna, S. and U. Malmendier (2004): "Contract Design and Self-Control: Theory and Evidence," Quarterly Journal of Economics, 119 (2), 353–402.

Della Vigna, S. and U. Malmendier (2005): "Paying Not to Go to the Gym," American Economic Review, forthcoming.

Ellison, G. (2005): "Bounded Rationality in Industrial Organization."

Fudenberg, D. and D. Levine (2005): "A Dual Self Model of Impulse Control," mimeo.

Gabaix, X. and David Laibson (2005): "Shrouded Attributes, Consumer Myopia, and Information Suppression in Competitive Markets," Quarterly Journal of Economics, forthcoming.

Gul, F. and W. Pesendorfer (2001): "Temptation and Self-Control," Econometrica, 69, 1403–1436.

Heidhues, P. and B. Koszegi (2004): "The Impact of Consumer Loss Aversion on Pricing," mimeo.

Miravete, E. (2003): "Choosing the Wrong Calling Plan? Ignorance and Learning," American Economic Review, 93(1), 297–310.

Rochet, J-C., and L. Stole (2002): "Nonlinear Pricing with Random Participation," Review of Economic Studies, 69(1), 277–311.

CHAPTER 7

Behavioral Economics*

Colin F. Camerer

Abstract

Behavioral economics uses evidence from psychology and other disciplines to create models of limits on rationality, willpower and self-interest, and explore their implications in economic aggregates. This paper reviews the basic themes of behavioral economics: sensitivity of revealed preferences to descriptions of goods and procedures; generalizations of models of choice over risk, ambiguity, and time; fairness and reciprocity; non-Bayesian judgment; and stochastic equilibrium and learning. A central issue is what happens in equilibrium when agents are imperfect but heterogeneous; sometimes firms "repair" limits through sorting, but profit-maximizing firms can also exploit limits of consumers. Frontiers of research include careful formal theorizing about psychology and studies with field data. Neuroeconomics extends the psychological data use to inform theorizing to include details of neural circuitry. It is likely to support rational choice theory in some cases, to buttress behavioral economics in some cases, and to suggest different constructs as well.

1 THE THEMES AND PHILOSOPHY OF BEHAVIORAL ECONOMICS

Behavioral economics applies models of systematic imperfections in human rationality, to the study and engineering of organizations, markets and policy. These imperfections include limits on rationality, willpower and self-interest (Rabin, 1998; Mullainathan and Thaler, 2000), and any other behavior resulting from an evolved brain with limited attention. The study of individual differences in rationality and learning is also important for understanding whether social interaction and economic aggregation minimize effects of rationality limits.

In one sense, behavioral economics is the inevitable result of relaxing the assumption of perfect rationality. Like perfect competition and perfect

* This paper was prepared for the World Congress of the Econometric Society, London August 18–24, 2005. Thanks to audience members and Ariel Rubinstein for comments, and to Joseph Wang for editorial help.

information, the assumption of perfect agent rationality is a useful limiting case in economic theory. Generalizing those assumptions to account for imperfect competition and costly information was challenging, slow, and proved to be powerful; weakening the assumption of perfect rationality will be too.

One property of models of human rationality, which largely distinguishes them from studies of economic competition, is that other social sciences have cumulated a lot of ideas and empirical facts about human rationality. The approach to behavioral economics that I will describe chooses to pay careful attention to those constructs and facts. In this empirically driven approach to behavioral economics, assumptions are chosen to fit what is known from other sciences. This approach can be thought of as scientifically humble, or it can be thought of as efficient and respectful of comparative advantage across disciplines.

Other than trying to "get the psychology right" in choosing assumptions, the empirically driven approach to behavioral economics shares the methodological emphases of other kinds of analysis: The goal is to have simple formal models and themes that apply across many domains, which make predictions about naturally occurring data (as well as experimental data).

The behavioral economics approach I describe in this essay is a clear departure from the "as if" approach endorsed by Milton Friedman. His "F-twist" argument combines two criteria:

1. Theories should be judged by the accuracy of their predictions;
2. Theories should not be judged by the accuracy of their assumptions.

The empirically driven approach to behavioral economics agrees with criterion 1 and rejects criterion 2. In fact, criterion 2 is rejected *because of* the primacy of criterion 1, based on the belief that replacing unrealistic assumptions with more psychologically realistic ones should lead to better predictions. This approach has already had some success: This paper reports many examples of how behavioral theories grounded in more reasonable assumptions can account for facts about market outcomes, which are anomalies under rational theories. More empirical examples are emerging rapidly.

The empirically driven approach to behavioral economics combines two practices: (i) explicitly modeling limits on rationality, willpower and self-interest; and (ii) using established facts to suggest assumptions about those limits. A different, "mindless," approach (Gul and Pesendorfer, 2005) follows elements of practice (i) but not (ii) – modeling limits but ignoring most empirical details of psychology. The argument for the mindless approach is Friedmanesque: Since theories that infer utility from observed choices were not originally intended to be tested by any data other than choices,[1] evidence about assumptions does not count.

But theories are not copyrighted. So neuroscientists, for example, are free to assume that utilities are actually numbers that correspond to the magnitude

---

[1] The doctrine that choices are the only possible data is a modern one, however (see footnote 3 below).

of some process in the brain (e.g., neural firing rates) and search for utilities using neuroscientific methods (knowing full well their results will be ignored by "mindless"-type economists). Such a search doesn't 'misunderstand economics,' it just takes the liberty of defining economic variables as neural constructs. The hope is also that new neural constructs will be discovered that are most gracefully accommodated only if the standard language of preference, belief, and constraint is stretched by some new vocabulary.

Before proceeding, let me clarify two points. First, the discussion above should make clear that behavioral economics is *not* a distinct subfield of economics. It is a style of modeling, or a school of thought, which is meant to apply to a wide range of economic questions in consumer theory, finance, labor economics and so on. Second, while the psychological data that fueled many developments in behavioral economics are largely experimental, behavioral economics is an *approach* and experimental economics is a *method*. It is true that in early modern behavioral economics, experiments proved to be useful as a way of establishing that anomalies were not produced by factors that are hard to rule out in field data – transaction costs, risk-aversion, confusion, self-selection, etc. – but are easy to rule out with good experimental control. But the main point of these experiments was just to suggest regularities that could be included in models to make predictions about naturally occurring field data.

Section II is a brief digression reminding us that behavioral economics is something of a return to old paths in economic thought that were not taken. Section III reviews the tools and ideas that are the current canon of what is best established (see also Conlisk, 1996; Camerer, Loewenstein, and Rabin, 2004). Section IV is a reminder that aggregate outcomes – behavior in firms, and markets – matter and considers how imperfections in rationality cumulate or disappear at those levels. Section V discusses "franchises" of behavioral economics in applied areas and some examples of growth in theory and field empirics. Section VI discusses neuroeconomics and section VII concludes.

2 BEHAVIORAL PATHS NOT TAKEN

Why did behavioral economics not emerge earlier in the history of economic thought? The answer is that *it did*: Jeremy Bentham, Adam Smith, Irving Fisher, William Jevons and many others drew heavily on psychological intuitions. But those intuitions were largely left behind in the development of mathematical tools of economic analysis, consumer theory and general equilibrium (e.g., Ashraf, Camerer and Loewenstein, 2005; Colander, 2005).

For example, Adam Smith believed there was a disproportionate aversion to losses, which is a central feature of Kahneman and Tversky's prospect theory. Smith wrote (1759, III, *ii*, pp. 176–7):

> Pain . . . is, in almost all cases, a more pungent sensation than the opposite and correspondent pleasure. The one almost always depresses us much more

> below the ordinary, or what may be called the natural state of our happiness, than the other ever raises us above it.

Smith (1759, II, ii, *ii*, p. 121) also anticipates Thaler's (1980) seminal[2] analysis of the insensitivity to opportunity costs compared to out-of-pocket costs:

> ... breach of property, therefore, theft and robbery, which take from us what we are possessed of, are greater crimes than breach of contract, which only disappoints us of what we expected.

Why did behavioral insights like these get left out of the neoclassical revolution? A possible answer, suggested by Bruni and Sugden (in press), is that Vilfredo Pareto won an argument among economists in the early 1900s about how deeply economic theories should be anchored in psychological reality. Pareto thought ignoring psychology was not only acceptable, but was also necessary. In an 1897 letter he wrote:

> It is an empirical fact that the natural sciences have progressed only when they have taken secondary principles as their point of departure, instead of trying to discover the essence of things.... Pure political economy has therefore a great interest in relying as little as possible on the domain of psychology.

Pareto advocated divorcing economics from psychology by simply *assuming* that unobserved Benthamite utility ("the subjective fact") is revealed by choice ("the objective fact"). He justifies this equation (in modern terms, that choices necessarily reveal true preferences) by restricting attention "only [to] repeated actions," so that consistency results from learning.

The Paretian equation of choice and true preference is neither a powerful proof nor a robust empirical regularity. It is a philosophical stance, pure and simple. And because Pareto clearly limits the domain of revealed preference to "repeated actions" in which learning has taught people what they want, he leaves out important economic decisions that are rare or difficult to learn about from trial-and-error (e.g., Einhorn, 1982) – corporate mergers, fertility and mate choice, partly irreversible education and workplace choices, planning for retirement, buying houses, and so forth.

Could economic theory have taken another path? Many economists such as Edgeworth, Ramsey, and Fisher speculated about how to measure cardinal utility directly but lacked modern tools and gave up.[3] What seemed an impossible

---

[2] Many people regard Thaler's 1980 paper as the starting point of behavioral economics per se, since it drew on psychology but was clearly focused on the economics of consumer choice (see Thaler, 1999 for an update on the same topic).

[3] Colander (2005) notes that Edgeworth described a "hedonimeter" that would measure momentary fluctuations in pleasure and eventually provide a basis for utilitarian adding-up across people. Irving Fisher also speculated about how to measure utility in his 1892 dissertation. Ramsey wrote about a "psychogalvanometer." It is interesting to speculate about whether at least some economists might have taken a different path in the early 20th century if fMRI, genetic methods, single-unit recording, and other tools were available, which allowed more optimism about measuring utility directly. Would any of them have become neuroeconomists? Even if most did

task a hundred years ago might be possible now, given developments in experimental psychology, neuroscience, and genetics. So this is a good time in history to revisit the ideas of Adam Smith and others and the paths not taken by neoclassical economists due to Pareto's bold move.

3 THE BASIC IDEAS AND TOOLS OF BEHAVIORAL ECONOMICS

Much of behavioral economics emerged as the study of deviations from rational-choice principles. (The fact that clear deviations are permitted is one way the rational-choice approach is powerful.) Deviations and anomalies are not merely counterexamples, which any simplified theory permits; they are clues about new or more general theories.[4] I prefer alternative theories, which includes rational-choice as a limiting special case. These generalizations provide a clear way to measure the parametric advantage of extending the theory. They also make it easy to search empirically for conditions under which rational-choice principles hold.

Table 7.1 lists some central rational-choice modeling principles in economic theory, emerging behavioral alternative models, and some representative citations (see McFadden, 1999, for a longer list). I will describe each briefly, and highlight domains in which competing alternatives are emerging.

Complete preferences: Completeness and transitivity of preference (which implies that choices can be represented by real-valued utilities) is an extremely powerful simplification. But the power comes precisely from excluding the many variables that a good's utility could depend upon. Thinking of choice as a result of cognition suggests obvious ways in which completeness of preference will be violated (e.g., Kahneman, 2003). The way in which choices are described, or "*framed*," can influence choice by directing attention to different features. The psychophysics of adaptation suggests that changes from a point of reference (*reference-dependence*) are likely to be a carrier of utility. A long-standing empirical problem is what the natural point of reference is (and how reference points change). Koszegi and Rabin (in press) suggest a resolution that should charm game theorists: The point of reference is the expectation of actual choice (which determines choice recursively, since preferences depend on utilities relative to the reference point).[5] This approach creates multiple equilibria,

---

not, it is hard to believe that *none* of them would have, given the curiosity evident in all their writing.

[4] Lucas (1986) notes because rational expectations often permit multiple equilibria, theories based on limited rationality might actually be <u>more</u> precise than theories based on full rationality. This is also true in game theory, where theories with rationality limits can be more precise than equilibrium theories (e.g., Camerer, Ho, and Chong 2004). So if the goal is precision, behavioral alternatives may prove <u>even better</u> than rational theories in some cases.

[5] Denote the reference point by r (which may be probabilistic). Koszegi and Rabin assume utility depends on a combination of absolute outcomes, m(x) and a function $\mu(m(x)-m(r))$, which is reference-dependent, depending on the difference m(x)–m(r) between consumption utility and

Table 7.1. *Some rational-choice principles and behavioral economics alternatives*

Rational (or Simplifying) Assumption	Behavioral Alternative Model	Representative Citation
Complete preferences		
description-invariance	Framing, reference-dependence	Kahneman-Tversky, 1979; Koszegi-Rabin, in press
procedure-invariance	Contingent weighting	Slovic-Lichtenstein, 1968; Grether-Plott, 1979
context-independence	Comparative utility	Tversky-Simonson, 1992
separable u(x)	Regret, disappointment	Loomes- Starmer-Sugden, 1989; Gul, 1991
Choice over		
Risk	Prospect theory	Kahneman-Tversky, 1979
Ambiguity	Nonadditive decision weight	Schmeidler, 1989
Time	Hyperbolic β-δ discounting	Laibson, 1997
Self-interest	Inequality-aversion, fairness	Rabin, 1993; Fehr-Schmidt, 1999
Bayesian judgment	Overconfidence	Odean, 1998
	Encoding bias	Rabin-Schrag, 1999
Equilibrium	Learning	Erev-Roth, 1998; Camerer-Ho, 1999
	Quantal response, cognitive hierarchy	McKelvey-Palfrey, 1998; Camerer-Ho-Chong, 2004

which permits a supply-side role for marketing, advertising, and sale prices to influence preferences by creating reference points (e.g., Koszegi and Heidhues, 2005). This approach also provides a language in which to understand how small changes in instructions or repeated trading experience could change behavior – namely, through the reference point.[6]

Slovic and Lichtenstein (1968) were the first to notice that *reversals of expressed preference* could result when people choose between two gambles, relative to pricing the gambles separately, a violation of procedure-invariance (see also Grether and Plott, 1979). This insight lays the groundwork for

the reference utility. When goods have deterministic utility and the reference point is the same as the bundle chosen, then x = r, so the second term disappears, and the model reduces to standard consumer theory.

[6] List (2003) finds that experienced sports-card dealers do not exhibit an "endowment effect" (while novice traders do). A natural interpretation is that dealers do not expect to hold on to goods they receive. Since their reference point does not include the goods, they do not feel less of a loss when selling them. Kahneman, Knetsch and Thaler (1990:1328) clearly anticipated this effect of experience, noting that "there are some cases in which no endowment effect would be expected, such as when goods are purchased for resale rather than for utilization."

using pricing institutions (such as different auctions) to influence expressions of preference.

Human perception and cognition is heavily influenced by contrast. A circle looks larger when surrounded by smaller circles than when it is surrounded by larger circles (the Titchener illusion). Since choices undoubtedly involve basic perceptual and cognitive neural circuitry, it would be surprising if choice evaluation were not sensitive to contrast as well. Indeed, there is ample evidence that the appeal of choices depends on the set of choices they are part of (e.g., Simonson and Tversky, 1992; Shafir, Osherson and Smith, 1989). Similarly, psychological comparison of outcomes with unrealized outcomes (disappointment) or with outcomes from foregone choices (regret) imply that the utility of a gamble is not separable into a sum of its expected component utilities, but there are workable formal models of these phenomena (e.g., Gul, 1991; Loomes, Starmer and Sugden, 1989).

Choice over risk: Many applications in economics require a specification of preferences over gambles, which have probabilistic risk, when probabilities may be subjective and when costs and benefits are spread over time. Independence axioms assume that people implicitly cancel common outcomes of equal probability in comparing risky choices (contrary to gestalt principles of perception, which resist cancellation), which leads mathematically to expected utility (EU) and subjective expected utility.

In contrast to EU, prospect theory assumes reference-dependence and diminishing psychophysical sensitivity, which together imply a "*reflection*" of risk preferences around the reference point (i.e., since the hedonic sensation of loss magnitude is decreasing at the margin, the utility function for loss is convex). Many other non-EU theories have been proposed and studied (Starmer, 2000), but prospect theory is more clearly rooted in psychology than most other theories, which are generally based on ingenious ways of weakening the independence axiom. Prospect theory also survives well in careful empirical comparisons among many theories aggregating many different studies, and adjusting for degrees of freedom (Harless and Camerer, 1994; cf. Hey and Orme, 1994).

The other components of prospect theory are disproportionate disutility for losses (compared to equal-sized gains) – "*loss-aversion*" – and nonlinear sensitivity to probability, probably due to nonlinearity in attention to low probabilities (e.g., Prelec, 1998).[7] Coefficients of loss-aversion[8] λ – the ratio of marginal loss

---

[7] The one-parameter version of Prelec's axiomatically derived weighting function is $\pi(p) = 1/\exp(\ln(1/p)^\gamma)$ (where $\exp(x) = e^x$). In this remarkable function, the ratio of overweighting $\pi(p)/p$ grows very large as p becomes very small, as if there is a quantum of attention put on *any* probability, no matter how low. For example, with $\gamma = .7$ (an empirical estimate from experiments), $\pi(1/10) = .165$, $\pi(1/100) = .05$, and $\pi(1/1,000,000) = .002$. This type of extreme relative overweighting of very low probabilities is useful for explaining overreaction to rare diseases (mad cow disease) and the huge popularity of high-prize Powerball lotteries.

[8] The coefficient of loss-aversion is defined as the ratio of the limits of marginal utilities at the reference point, where marginal utilities approach from below and above, respectively. This

to gain utilities around zero – have been estimated from a wide variety of data to fall in a range around 2 (see Table 7.2). The striking feature of the table is that the studies cover such a wide range of types of data and levels of analysis.

Choice over ambiguity: Subjective expected utility (SEU) assumes that subjective (or, in Savage's term, "personal") probabilities are revealed by the willingness to bet on events. However, as Ellsberg's famous 1961 paradox showed (following Keynes and Knight), bet choices could depend both on subjective likelihood and the "weight of evidence," or confidence one has in the likelihood judgment; when bets are "ambiguous" decision weight is lower. In SEU, subjective probabilities are a slave with two masters – likelihood and willingness to bet (or decision weight). As Schmeidler (1989) pointed out, a simple resolution is to assume that decision weights are *nonadditive*. Then the nonadditivity is a measure of "reserved belief," or the strength of the unwillingness to bet on *either* of two events in the face of missing relevant information. Mukerji and Tallon (2004) describe many theoretical applications of ambiguity-aversion models to contracting, game theory and other domains.

Choice over time: If choices are dynamically consistent, then the discount weight put on future utilities must be exponential (δ^t). While dynamic consistency is normatively appealing, it seems to be contradicted by everyday behavior like procrastination and succumbing to temptations created by previous choices.[9] To understand these phenomena, Laibson (1997) borrowed a two-piece discounting function from work on intergenerational preference. His specification puts a weight of 1 on immediate rewards, and weights $u(x_t) = \beta \delta^t$ on rewards at future times t. This "quasi-hyperbolic" form is a close approximation to the mountains of evidence that animal and human discount functions are hyperbolic, $d(t) = 1/(1+kt)$, and is easy to work with analytically. (Rubinstein, 2003, suggests an alternative based on temporal similarity.) The β-δ model has been calibrated to explain regularities in aggregate savings and borrowing patterns (Angeletos, Laibson, and Tobacman, 2001), and applied to the study of procrastination and deadlines by O'Donoghue and Rabin (2001).

Self-interest: The idea that people only care about their own monetary or goods payoff is not a central tenet of rational choice theory, but it is a common simplifying assumption. Economists also tend to be skeptical that people will sacrifice to express a concern for the payoffs of others. As Stigler (1981) wrote, "When self-interest and ethical values with wide verbal allegiance are in conflict, much of the time, most if the time in fact, self-interest theory ... will win."

Despite skepticism like Stigler's, there is a long history of models that attempt to formalize when people trade off their own payoffs for payoffs of others

---

definition allows a "kink" at the reference point, which exhibits "first-order risk-aversion" (i.e., the utility loss from a gamble is proportional to the standard deviation, so that agents dislike even small-stakes gambles; Segal and Spivak, 1990).

[9] See also Gul and Pesendorfer, 2001, who model a distaste for flexibility when choice sets include tempting goods.

Table 7.2. *Evidence of loss-aversion from different studies using field and experimental data*

Economic Domain	Citation(s)	Type of Data	Estimated λ
Instant endowment effects for goods	Kahneman, Knetsch, and Thaler, 1990	Field data (survey), goods experiments	2.29
Choices over money gambles	Kahneman and Tversky, 1992	Choice experiments	2.25
Asymmetric price elasticities for consumer product increases & decreases	Putler, 1992; Hardie-Johnson and Fader, 1993	Consumer purchases (supermarket scanner data)	2.40, 1.63
Loss-aversion for goods relative to money	Bateman et al., 2005	Choice experiments	1.30
Loss-aversion relative to initial seller "offer"	Chen, Lakshminarayanan, and Santos, 2005	Capuchin monkeys trading tokens for stochastic food rewards	2.70
Reference-dependence in two-part distribution channel pricing	Ho and Zhang, 2005	Bargaining experiments	2.71
Aversion to losses from international trade	Tovar, 2004	Non-tariff trade barriers, US 1983	1.95–2.39
Surprisingly few announcements of negative EPS and negative year-to-year EPS changes	DeGeorge, Patel, and Zeckhauser, 1999	Earnings per share (EPS) changes from year to year for US firms	
Disposition effects in housing	Genesove and Mayer, 2001	Boston condo prices 1990–97	
Disposition effects in stocks	Odean, 1998	Individual investor stock trades	
Disposition effects in stocks	Weber and Camerer, 1998	Stock trading experiments	
Daily income targeting by NYC cab drivers	Camerer, Babcock, Loewenstein, and Thaler, 1997	Daily hours-wages observations (three data sets)	
Equity premium puzzle	Benartzi and Thaler, 1995	US stock returns	
Consumption: Aversion to period utility loss	Chua and Camerer, 2004	Savings-consumption experiments	

(e.g., Edgeworth, 1881; "equity theory" in social psychology; and Loewenstein, Bazerman and Thompson, 1989).

Sensible models of this type face a difficult challenge: Sometimes people sacrifice to increase payoffs of others, and sometimes they sacrifice to lower the payoffs of others. The challenge is to endogenize when the weights placed on payoffs of others switch from positive to negative. A breakthrough paper is Rabin's (1993), based on psychological game theory, which includes beliefs as a source of utility. In Rabin's approach, players form a judgment of kindness or meanness of another player based on whether the other player's action gives the belief-forming player less or more than a reference point (which can depend on history, culture, etc.). Players prefer to reciprocate in opposite directions, acting kindly toward others who are kind, and acting meanly toward others who are mean. As a result, in a coordination game like "chicken," there is an equilibrium in which both players expect to treat each other well, and they actually do (since doing so gives higher utility, but less money). But there is another equilibrium in which players expect each other to act meanly, and they also do. Rabin's model shows the thin line between love and hate. Falk and Fischbacher (2006) and Dufwenberg and Kirchsteiger (2004) extend it to extensive-form games, which is conceptually challenging.

A different approach is to assume that players have an unobserved type (depending on their social preferences), and their utilities depend on their types and how types are perceived (e.g., Levine, 1998; Rotemberg, 2004). These models are more technically challenging but can explain some stylized facts.

Simpler models put aside judgments of kindness based on intentions and just assume that people care about both money and inequity, either measured by absolute payoff deviations (Fehr and Schmidt, 1999) or by the deviation between earnings shares and equal shares (Bolton and Ockenfels, 2000). Charness and Rabin (2002) introduce a "Rawlsitarian" model in which people care about their own payoff, the minimum payoff (Rawlsian), and the total payoff (utilitarian). In all these models, self-interest emerges as a special case when the weight on one's own payoff swamps the weights on other terms.

These models are *not* an attempt to invent a special utility function for each game. They are precisely the opposite. The challenge is to show that the same general utility function, up to parameter values, can explain a wide variety of data that vary across games and institutional changes (e.g., Fischbacher, Fong and Fehr, 2003).

Bayesian statistical judgment: The idea that people's intuitive judgments of probability obey statistical principles, and Bayes' rule, is used in many applied microeconomics models (e.g., in games of asymmetric information). Tversky and Kahneman (see Kahneman, 2003) used deviations between intuitive judgments and normative principles ("biases") to suggest heuristic principles of probability judgment. Their approach is explicitly inspired by theories of perception, which use optical illusions to suggest principles of vision (Tversky and Kahneman, 1982), without implying that everyday visual perception is badly maladaptive. Similarly, heuristics for judging probability (like availability of examples and representativeness of samples to underlying processes) are not necessarily maladaptive. The point of studying biases is just to illuminate the heuristics they reveal, not to indict human judgment. Thus, their original view is consistent with the critique that heuristics can be ecologically rational.

The Bayesian approach is so simple and useful that is has taken some time to craft equally simple formal alternatives, which are consistent with the heuristics Kahneman and Tversky suggested. An appealing way to do this is to use the Bayesian framework but assume that people misspecify or misapply it in some way. Rabin and Schrag (1999) give a useful model of "confirmation bias." They define confirmation bias as the tendency to overperceive data as more consistent with a prior hypothesis than they truly are. The model is fully Bayesian, except for the mistake in encoding of data. Rabin (2002) models representativeness as the (mistaken) expectation that samples are drawn without replacement and shows some fresh implications of that model (e.g, perceiving more skill variation among managers than truly exists). Barberis, Shleifer and Vishny (1998) show how a similar misperception among stock investors – that corporate earnings which actually follow a random walk either exhibit momentum or mean-reversion – can generate short-term underreaction ("earnings drift") and long-term overreaction in stock returns.

Another principle implicit in Bayesian reasoning is informational irreversibility – if you find out a piece of evidence is mistaken, the brain should reverse its impact on judgment. (For example, juries are instructed to ignore certain statements after they have been heard.) But the brain is an organ, as is human skin. When skin is grafted onto skin, the old and new merge and eventually it is impossible to undo the graft. Information in the brain is probably organically irreversible in a similar way. For example, when people find out that an event occurred, it is hard to resist a "hindsight bias," which biases recollection of ex ante probability in the direction of new information (Fischhoff and Beyth, 1975; Camerer, Loewenstein, and Weber, 1989).

Equilibrium: Moving beyond the level of individual choice and judgment, behavioral economics has also contributed to a shift in the study of equilibrium at the market or game-theoretic level. Game theorists, in particular, have been uncomfortable with simply assuming that beliefs and choices are in equilibrium – i.e., that players correctly anticipate what others will do – without clearly specifying mechanisms that generate equilibration. Evolutionary game theory (e.g., Weibull, 1995; Samuelson, 1997) and the sensible extension to the study of imitation (e.g., Schlag, 1998), are important approaches that show how equilibria might emerge from limited rationality and selection pressures.

Empirical models of learning in games have also been carefully calibrated on many different types of experimental data. One approach is reinforcement of chosen strategies (Arthur, 1991; Erev and Roth, 1998). A seemingly different approach is updating of beliefs based on experience, as in fictitious play (e.g., Fudenberg and Levine, 1998). However, Camerer and Ho (1999) noted that fictitious play is simply a generalized kind of reinforcement in which unchosen strategies are reinforced as strongly as chosen strategies are. That recognition inspired a hybrid "dual process theory" (EWA), in which reinforcement of actual and foregone outcomes can differ, nesting choice reinforcement and fictitious play as boundary cases. The hybrid model tends to fit about as well as each of the boundary cases, and sometimes fits substantially better when one of the models misses a central feature of the data. Ho, Camerer and Chong (2005) introduce a "self-tuning" version of their hybrid theory in which the key parameters adjust flexibly to experience, which economizes on parameters and allows changes in the rate of learning after "surprise."[10]

Another approach to game-theoretic equilibrium maintains the assumption of equilibrium beliefs but substitutes stochastic choice for best-response, creating "quantal response equilibrium" (QRE) models (McKelvey and Palfrey, 1998). Weakening best-response explains many of the experimental deviations from Nash equilibrium, but also approximates Nash play in games where the Nash equilibrium tends to be accurate (Goeree and Holt, 2001).

An alternative non-equilibrium approach, rooted in principles of limited cognition, assumes a "cognitive hierarchy" (CH) in which more thoughtful players best-respond to their perceptions that others do less thinking (Nagel, 1995; Stahl and Wilson, 1995; Costa-Gomes, Crawford, and Broseta, 2001). These CH approaches are more precise than Nash equilibrium because they always predict a single statistical distribution of play and are generally more accurate than equilibrium in predicting behavior in one-shot games.

Before proceeding, note that the rational principles that are listed in Table 7.1 are *normative*. They describe behavior of an idealized agent with unlimited cognitive resources and willpower. As we are beginning to understand (e.g., Robson, 2001), it is unlikely that evolution would have sculpted us to satisfy these principles for all important economic decisions. As a result, it is a scientific error in judgment to always privilege normative principles in the search for the best descriptive principles across all decisions people make (see also Starmer, 2004). Normative principles are, of course, useful in raising our children, teaching students, and as limiting cases of how some people behave or learn to behave. Or normative principles might be enforced by aggregation of decisions and market discipline, a crucial topic we consider next.

4   AGGREGATION: FROM INDIVIDUALS TO FIRMS AND MARKETS

The previous section described behavioral economics' alternatives to rational-choice microfoundations. But the central question is: What happens in a political economy where agents have limited rationality (e.g., Camerer and Fehr, 2006)?

Asking about market and political outcomes forces behavioral economics to confront two classes of questions that have not been the central focus of research so far: First, how heterogeneous are agents? and How detectable is heterogeneity? (This question is important because heterogeneity drives the division of labor in organizations, the development of expertise and human capital, and market interaction of rational and limitedly-rational agents.) And second,

---

[10] The self-tuning approach is similar to Erev, Bereby-Meyer and Roth's (1999) use of "payoff variability;" and Marcet and Nicoli's (2003) theory of regime-shifts in response to hyperinflation. Self-tuning also creates shift in parameter values, as if players are switching rules throughout the game, akin to direct learning across rules (cf. Stahl, 2000, on "rule learning").

how do institutions sort heterogeneous agents, supply market substitutes for individual irrationality, and create organizational outcomes on the supply side?

Early theory: Some early papers tackled the issue of market aggregation theoretically. A pioneering paper is Thaler and Russell (1985)[11] who emphasized constraints that prevent rationality limits from being erased. Haltiwanger and Waldman (1989) noted that whether individual mistakes would be erased or magnified depends on whether behaviors are strategic *substitutes* or strategic *complements*. When behaviors are complements, a small proportion of irrational traders can force others to behave irrationally (as Keynes wrote about the stock market). The "limits to arbitrage" literature in finance is an extension of this general theme (e.g., Shleifer, 2000).

Sorting and constraint: Aggregation issues are central in labor economics. The fact that workers have different skills leads to sorting (self-selection and firms' allocation of workers to jobs), specialization, and division of labor.

Recent evidence shows substantial effects of basic intelligence on the tendency to make the kind of judgment mistakes documented in the heuristics literature, and on risk-aversion and immediacy preference (Benjamin and Shapiro, 2005; Frederick, 2005). This kind of evidence invites the possibility that "smarter" people will be sorted into jobs where their decisions minimize or repair mistakes by others. In a magazine interview, Gary Becker opined that "division of labor . . . 'strongly attenuates if not eliminates' any effects caused by bounded rationality" (Stewart, 2005).[12]

Becker's conjecture should be explored theoretically and empirically. The power of division of labor to necessarily produce organizational efficiency may be limited by various factors. First of all, large organizations demand some skills or traits at a very high level (e.g., extreme honesty when there are huge opportunities for theft). A limited supply of agents with enough skill will then limit the size of the firm.

Second, the sorting process requires a human resources department or other mechanism to identify talent. If the ability to spot talent is itself a scarce talent, or self-selection is limited by optimism (for example), those forces will limit how much talent is spotted.

Third, what happens if managers are biased in one dimension but excellent at another? Hard-driving CEOs, for example, may be superb at motivating people and creating an inspiring vision, precisely *because* they are wildly optimistic and genuinely convinced they can't fail. So it is possible that the sorting process of managerial selection actually *selects* for optimism rather than selects for realism. The organizational challenge is to design job structure that harnesses a CEO's optimism as motivation but keeps that optimism from making bad investments.

---

[11] See also the correction in Thaler and Russell (1987).

[12] Becker conjectures that "it doesn't matter if 90 percent of people can't do the complex analysis required to calculate probabilities. The 10 percent of people who can will end up in jobs where it's required." A good example is insurance actuaries or analysts who price derivative assets.

Finally, note that sorting is difficult to study in the field, but it is *easy* to study experimentally – because agents' characteristics can be measured, and self-selection can be measured too (e.g., Lazear, Malmendier, and Weber, 2005).

Organizational repairs: An interesting supply-side response to managerial rationality limits is what Heath, Larrick and Klayman (1998) call "organizational repairs." They suggest that some organizational practices can be seen as responses to managerial errors. Microsoft had a hard time getting its programmers to take customer complaints seriously (despite statistical evidence from customer help-lines) because the programmers thought the software was easy to use and couldn't believe that customers found it difficult (a "curse of knowledge"). So Microsoft created a screening room with a one-way mirror, so programmers could literally see for themselves how much trouble normal-looking consumers had using software. The trick was to use one judgment bias – the power of visually "available" evidence, even in small samples – to overcome another bias (the curse of knowledge).

Experiments on rationality aggregation: Experiments are ideally suited to studying how rationality aggregates. In an experiment, one can measure the degree of individual bias and market-level bias and compute whether biases in market prices or quantities is smaller than the average (or dollar-weighted) individual bias. Anderson and Sunder (1995), and Camerer (1987) studied errors in abstract Bayesian judgments designed to test whether traders would overreact to likelihood evidence (and underweight priors) when a small sample of balls drawn from a bingo cage was "representative" of the cage's contents. They found small biases in market prices, which were reduced by hours of trading, but not eliminated. Ganguly, Kagel, and Moser (2000) found much larger pricing errors when the event was a hypothetical word problem rather than a bingo cage draw. Camerer, Loewenstein and Weber (1989) studied the "curse of knowledge" (mistakenly assuming other subjects have your private information), and Kluger and Wyatt (2004) studied the famous "Monty Hall" three-door problem. Both found that market trading reduced, but did not eliminate, mistakes. Maciejovsky and Budescu (2005) found that markets for information in Wason 4-card logic problems do guide agents toward rational solutions.

The rationality tug-of-war between consumers and firms: Suppose you struggle with a gambling problem and type "pathological gambling" into the Google search engine looking for help.[13] When I did this in April 2005, one of the entries on the first page is shown in Figure 7.1 (leading to http://www.casinolasvegas.com/currency-us-dollars/lang-en/skins/noscript.html).

This exercise illustrates the rationality tug-of-war between consumers and firms: If heterogeneity and sorting enables firms to weed out poorly suited workers, is the result a larger supply of products and techniques for taking *advantage* of limited consumer rationality, or a larger supply of products that *help* consumers?

---

[13] Thanks to George Loewenstein's office door for this example.

---

1. **GAMBLING PROBLEMS** - TOP RATED ONLINE CASINO SITES. FREE KENO MASSAGE
    SANDALS BONUS 🔁

    ... is licensed and **gambling problems** regulated ! Here you will find **gambling problems** more information
    about all ...

    www.casino-startup.com/**gambling-problems**.html - 17k - <u>Cached</u> - <u>More from this site</u> - <u>Save</u> - <u>Block</u>

Figure 7.1. A first-page entry in an April 2005 Google search for "pathological gambling".

Whether markets will correct rationality depends on factors like whether consumers know their own limits (and hence are receptive to advice), and whether there is more profit in protecting consumers or taking advantage of them. The result for any particular rationality limit is likely to depend sensitively on self-awareness, industrial structure, regulation and law, the role of education in educating consumers, household dynamics between spouses, and many other factors.

One result might be an arms race in which consumer protection and exploitation *both* increase. For example, in the recent rise of obesity among Americans, industries selling cheap caloric food (such as pizzas with cheese *inside the crust*) have flourished. But healthier food, diet books, personal training, plastic surgery, and eating disorders have flourished too.

A simple example of how to analyze the impact of consumer rationality on markets is Gabaix and Laibson's (2006) model of products with "add-ons." Add-ons are typically marginal goods or services whose prices can be easily hidden or "shrouded" (like bank transaction fees or the cost of printer ink cartridges). If enough consumers don't think about the shrouded add-on price, then in a competitive market, firms will compete by offering very low prices on base goods (below marginal cost) and will charge high markups on add-ons. Sophisticated consumers who know the add-on price, but can cheaply substitute away from the add-ons (avoiding bank ATM fees, for example), will *prefer* products with expensive add-ons because they benefit from the low base-good price produced by competition. (The myopic consumers who don't think about the add-on cost are subsidizing the sophisticated consumers.) As a result, competition does not theoretically lead to revealing the add-on price because a firm that reveals its add-ons will not attract either myopic consumers (who will mistakenly think the price-revealing firm is too expensive) *or* sophisticates (who benefit from the below-cost base-good price). This paper is a good example of why careful analysis is needed to be able to make sharp conclusions about whether markets will erase or exploit limits on consumer rationality. Two other examples are Della Vigna and Malmendier's (2006) analysis of gym memberships, and Grubb's (2005) analysis of overconfident planning of cell phone usage of minutes and pricing of packages.

5   SOME FRONTIERS OF BEHAVIORAL ECONOMICS

This section is about some new frontiers in behavioral economics: franchising (applying behavioral economics to traditional subfields, like finance and labor); formal foundations; field studies; and importing different kinds of psychology.

5.1   The Franchising of Behavioral Economics

Much of the power of economic analysis comes from models used in different application areas that rely on shared general principles – consistent preferences and equilibrium – but are customized to the special questions in different application areas. A thriving part of behavioral economics is similar – the application of basic ideas to various subfields, or "franchising." Besides the areas discussed in more detail below, other franchises have been established in law (Jolls, Sunstein and Thaler, 1998; Jolls, in press) and development (Mullainathan, in press).

Finance: The central hypothesis in financial economics for the last thirty years is that stock markets are informationally efficient. Faith in this claim comes from a simple argument: Any semi-strong-form inefficiency (detectable using cheaply acquired data) would be noticed by wealthy investors and erased. Market efficiency was therefore thought to provide a stiff challenge to models, which assume investors have limited rationality. But "behavioral finance" based on rationality limits has emerged rapidly and might be the clearest empirical franchise success for behavioral economics (e.g., Barberis and Thaler, 2004). One advantage is that theories of asset pricing often provide sharp predictions. Another big advantage is that there are many cheaply available data that can be used to test theories.

Behavioral finance got its biggest early boost from DeBondt and Thaler's (1985) discovery that portfolios of "loser" stocks (stocks whose market value had dropped the most in the previous year) outperformed portfolios of winners in subsequent years. Their paper was published in the proceedings of the *Journal of Finance* and immediately drew attention and counterargument. Note that DeBondt and Thaler *predicted* this anomaly, based on the idea that investors would be surprised by reversion to the mean in unusually high- and low-performing firms (an application of the "representativeness heuristic").

An important theoretical attack on market efficiency was showing that if investors have limited horizons (due to quarterly evaluation of institutional portfolio managers, for example) then even if prices wander away from fundamental values, investors might not have enough aggregative incentive to trade prices back to the fundamentals, which allows mispricing to persist. (As Keynes purportedly noted, markets might stay irrational longer than you can stay liquid.)

A central point here is that an attack on the proposition that prices would fully reveal information caused the finance profession to carefully examine the microstructural and institutional reasons why such revelation might, or might not occur. So the behavioral critique, whether right or wrong, did lead to a sharper focus on institutional details, which eventually led to better financial economics.

A recent trend is extending some of these ideas to corporate finance – how companies raise and spend financing from capital markets (see Baker, Ruback, and Wurgler, 2004). Behavioral influences might be even stronger here than in asset pricing because large decisions are made by individuals or small groups, and discipline is only exerted by boards of directors, career concerns, sorting for talented decision makers, and so forth. So it is possible that very large corporate mistakes are made by a combination of limitedly rational managers and weak governance.

An interesting feature of the evolution of academic finance is how some early behavioral ideas, which were largely dismissed, are now taken seriously. For example, Miller (1977) suggested that divergence of opinion, combined with restrictions on short-selling, could lead to inflated stock valuations. Miller's paper was rarely cited at first, but roughly the same idea was used, twenty-five years later, to explain the American dot-com bubble (Ofek and Richardson, 2003). Similarly, Modigliani and Cohn (1979) advanced the radical idea that stock market investors did not distinguish between nominal and inflation-adjusted ("real") rates of return. Decades later, their radical theory is consistent with tests by Cohen, Polk and Vuolteenaho (2005), and Campbell and Vuolteenaho (2004).

Game theory: Game theory is a taxonomy of canonical strategic interactions and a collection of mathematical theories of how players with varying degrees of rationality are likely to play in games as they are perceived. Since many of the games are complicated, and equilibrium theories often assume a high degree of mutual rationality and complicated Bayesian inference, game theory is ripe for introduction of behavioral alternatives that weaken equilibrium assumptions in a disciplined way. Many theoretical papers have explored the implications of weakened assumptions of rationality. Many predictions of game theory depend delicately on what players commonly know and on assumptions about the utility derived from outcomes. As a result, experiments that carefully control strategies, information, and payoffs have been unusually helpful in clarifying conditions under which equilibrium predictions are likely to hold or not (Crawford, 1997; Camerer, 2003).

Two central contributions of behavioral game theory are worth mentioning. One is the study of limits on strategic thinking. One type of theory studies how finite automata that implement strategies with limited calculation and memory will behave (e.g., Rubinstein, 1998). Empirically driven theories posit some distribution of steps of thinking (the cognitive hierarchy theories discussed in section III). The other important contribution is precise theories of how monetary payoffs to one player and others map onto the focal player's utility (also discussed in section III).

Behavioral game theory has largely been shaped by experimental observation of educated people playing games in experiments for money. Here, equilibrium predictions do not always fare well compared to learning theories, or to QRE and cognitive hierarchy approaches. But equilibrium theory might apply at other levels of analysis, especially low and high levels, such as animal behavior sculpted by evolution (e.g., optimal foraging), and decisions of firms and nation-states, which are widely deliberated and analyzed carefully.

Labor and organizational economics: Labor economics is certainly ripe for behavioral analysis (see Camerer and Malmendier, in press). Most workers do not have much chance to learn from experience before making important decisions with irreversibility – choosing education, and a first job that often determines a career track. The goods that workers sell – their time – is also likely to involve more social comparison, optimism, emotion, and identity than when firms sell cars or iPods. In many cases, workers appear to care about a range of nonpecuniary incentives besides money, such as fair treatment and being appreciated.

Inside the firm, evaluation of worker performance is imperfect in all but the simplest organizations in which piece rates can be tied to individual productivity (like fruit-picking and auto glass installation); imperfect evaluation leads to scope for biases in judgment. For example, hindsight bias – the tendency to think, ex post, that outcomes were more ex-ante predictable than they actually were – creates second-guessing and complicates implementation of the idealized contracts in agency theory.

Many experiments have studied reciprocity (or gift-exchange) in simple versions of labor markets. In the simplest case, firms prepay a wage and workers then choose effort, which is costly for them but valuable for firms. If there is an excess supply of workers and no scope for reputation-building,[14] self-interested workers should be happy to get jobs but should also shirk; firms should anticipate this and offer a minimum wage. Empirically, however, when effort is very valuable to firms and not too costly to workers, firms pay wages far above the minimum, and workers reciprocate by exerting more effort when they were paid a higher wage. When workers are identified to firms, and firms can repeatedly hire good workers, Brown, Falk and Fehr (2004) show how a "two-tier" insider-outsider economy can emerge experimentally.

Data like these are a reminder that intrinsic motivations like reciprocity matter and can be quite strong. Furthermore, adding extrinsic incentives can be harmful if they "crowd out" intrinsic incentives (a phenomenon long-studied in psychology) so that standard models get the sign wrong in predicting effects of extrinsic incentive changes. Benabou and Tirole (2003) approach crowding out in a different way. They show that higher incentives can induce lower effort because high wages signal that a job is very hard, or a worker is unskilled.

---

[14] Healy (2004) shows that the amount of reciprocity by workers is sensitive to the shared gains from effort. Charness, Frechette and Kagel (2004) show that framing of the instructions can lower reciprocity. Healy also shows in a simple model how a perception of correlation of reciprocal worker types can induce gift exchange even when the wage-effort game is repeated only finitely. His important insight is that type correlation induces "group reputation."

Public finance: Behavioral public finance asks how limits on consumer and voter rationality influence taxation and public spending. Two pioneering examples are Krishna and Slemrod (2003) and McCaffrey's (1994) paper on cognitive psychology and taxation. The central principle is that some taxes are more visible than others. Politicians exploit these differences in searching for ways to increase tax receipts. A full theory of taxation and spending therefore depends on a good account of which types of taxes are easy and hard to impose (well-organized interest group competition will matter too, of course), and how astute revenue-seeking politicians are at understanding investor tax psychology.

Behavioral public economics is also likely to be the franchise that most squarely confronts issues of welfare analysis in behavioral economics. In the standard theory, what consumers choose is taken as a tautological definition of welfare (i.e., if consumers are rational, then what they choose is also what is best for them). Thinking about psychology permits the possibility that private choices do not maximize welfare. For example, Berridge and Robinson (2003) suggest that separate brain areas control "wanting" – choice – and "liking" – hedonic evaluation. If liking is true welfare, then neural separability of these processes implies that it is possible for choice and welfare to be different. The obvious places to look are decisions by adolescents and addicts (e.g., Bernheim and Rangel, 2004), and potential mistakes in rare decisions, or when it is difficult to learn from experience.

5.2   Formal Foundations

The goal of behavioral economics is not just to create a list of anomalies. The anomalies are used to inspire and constrain formal alternatives to rational-choice theories. Many such theories have emerged in recent years; a few of them were mentioned in section III.

Tremendous progress has been made in going from deviations and anomalies to general theories, which are mathematical and can be applied to make fresh predictions. The general theories that economists are justifiably proud of only emerged over many decades of careful attention and refinement. Behavioral economics theories will become refined, and more general and useful, now that it has attracted the attention of an army of smart theorists and graduate students.

Excluded from Table 7.1, and from the discussion of basic ideas in section III, are a rapidly emerging variety of formal "dual system" models, drawing on old dichotomies in psychology. These models generally retain optimization by one of the systems and make behavior of another system automatic (or myopic) and nonstrategic so that extensions of standard tools can be used. (Intuitively, think of part of the brain as optimizing against a new type of constraint – an internal constraint from another brain system, rather than a budget constraint or an external constraint from competition.) In Kahneman (2003) the systems are intuitive and deliberative systems ("systems 1 and 2"). In Loewenstein and O'Donoghue (2004) the systems are deliberative and affective; in Benhabib and Bisin (2005) the systems are controlled and automatic; in Fudenberg and

Levine (2005) the systems are "long-run" (and controlling) and "short-run"; in Bernheim and Rangel (2005) the systems are "hot" (automatic) and "cold." In Brocas and Castillo (2005) a myopic "agent" system has private information about utility, so a farsighted "principal" (who cares about the utility of all agents) creates mechanisms for the myopic agents to reveal their information.

These models are more alike than they are different. In the years to come, careful thought will probably sharpen our understanding of the similarities and differences among models. More thought will probably point to more general formulations that include models like those above as special cases, narrowing the focus of attention. And of course, empirical work is needed to see which predictions of different models hold up best, presumably inspiring some refinements that might eventually lead to a single model that could occupy a central place in microeconomics.

Herbert Simon was a towering figure in the development of behavioral economics. Simon coined the terms "bounded rationality" and "procedural rationality" and sowed the seeds for the analyses of rationality bounds that are the substance of this paper. Despite the influence of Simon's language, he had in mind a style of theorizing that has not caught on in economics. Influenced by cognitive science and the information processing model of human decision making, Simon thought good theories might take the form of algorithms, which describe the procedures that people and firms use.

The economist in modern times who carries Simon's methodological torch is Ariel Rubinstein (e.g., see his 1998 book). Rubinstein's models are often stylized to a particular economic application and describe the mathematical result of particular algorithms, which embody rationality limits. While these models are widely known, in many cases they have not led to a sustained program of research, as his seminal work on bargaining has. Rubinstein's frustration with inattention to models driven by similarity judgment, a central concept in psychology, is evident in his 2003 discussion of models of time preference.

5.3   Field Studies

Many new studies look for the influences of rationality limits in naturally occurring field data. A good example that highlights interest in time preference is Della Vigna and Malmendier's (2006) study of health club memberships. The health clubs they study allow people to spend a fixed sum for an annual membership or pay for each visit separately. People who discount hyperbolically, but are "naïve" about their future hyperbolic preferences, will sign up for large-fee annual plans with per-visit fees that are below marginal cost (typically free). They find that even though per-visit fees average $10, the typical consumer who bought the annual-fee package ended up going rarely enough that the per-visit cost was $19. They also show theoretically that this contract is optimal for firms: Naïve hyperbolics like it because they misforecast how often they will go (they don't realize they are choosing a suboptimal contract), and "sophisticated" hyperbolic consumers like it because the low per-visit fee provides external self-control (which they know they will need).

An early example of a field study inspired by behavioral economics is Camerer, Babcock, Loewenstein and Thaler's (1997) study of cab driver labor supply. New York City cab drivers typically rent their cabs by the day, for a fixed fee, keep all the revenues they earn, and can drive up to 12 hours. The standard theory of upward-sloping labor supply, and intertemporal substitution, predicts that drivers will drive longer on high-wage days. But suppose drivers take a short horizon, e.g., one day at a time, and have an aspiration level or reference point they dislike falling short of (i.e., they are averse to a perceived revenue "loss" relative to their reference point or daily target). Myopic target-driven drivers will drive more hours on low-wage days, the opposite of the standard prediction. (This is a case where behavioral economics made a clear prediction of a new phenomenon, rather than just explaining an established anomaly.) Camerer et al. found that inexperienced drivers appear to have a negative labor supply elasticity – they drove more hours on low-wage days – and the elasticity of experienced drivers was around zero. Farber (2004) replicated this study with a smaller sample using a hazard rate model of hourly quitting decisions. He found no evidence of daily targeting in general but found modest targeting by three of five drivers for whom there are a lot of data. A subsequent study (Farber, 2005) finds effects of targeting that are significant but small in magnitude.

Conlin, O'Donoghue and Vogelsang (2005) estimate how often items ordered from mail-order catalogues are returned. Their study is motivated by evidence of "projection bias" – the idea that one's current emotional state exerts too much influence on a projection of one's future state (e.g., people buy more groceries when they are hungry). They show theoretically that returns of cold-weather items (e.g., jackets or gloves) on a particular day depends on whether the return-day weather is warm, and also depends on weather the ordering-day weather was cold. (The intuition is that people who order on a cold day mistakenly forecast it will be equally cold in the future, so they are systematically surprised.) Their result is striking because people are well aware of seasonality in weather (most people can tell you whether a day is unseasonably warm or cold). It is not as if they are misforecasting their tastes for exotic novelties like sea urchin or funnypunk music.

A booming and important area of field study is experimentation in field settings. Field experiments can range (Harrison and List, 2004) from abstract simple experiments done outside university labs, to measurement of treatment effects in field sites where those effects are of special interest (see Cardenas and Carpenter, 2005). These studies combine the value of measuring an effect directly in a population of interest with the gain from experimental control. The gain comes from randomized assignment of treatments, which avoids self-selection effects that are challenging to control econometrically in field data.[15]

---

[15] Tanaka, Camerer and Nguyen (2006) is one study that measures multiple dimensions of time, risk, and trust preferences corresponding to models in Table 7.1.

5.4   Importing 'New' Psychology

The workhorse models in Table 7.1 draw on a narrow range of cognitive psychology, mostly from decision research. Other psychological concepts, which are hardly new in psychology but new to economists, are starting to be applied as well (such as memory; see Wilson, 2004).

Attention is perhaps the ultimate scarce cognitive resource. A few studies have started to explore its implications for economics. Odean and Barber (2005) show that attention-getting events – abnormal trading volumes or returns, or news events – correlate with purchases by individual investors. Della Vigna and Pollett (2005) find that markets react less to earnings announcements made on Fridays than on other days; firms seem to know this and are more likely to release bad news on a Friday. Falkinger (2005) develops a rich model in which firms must choose signal strength for their products to get the attention of consumers.

Attribution theory describes how people intuitively infer causes from effects. Many studies indicate systematic misattributions, such as the tendency to overattribute cause to personal actions rather than exogeneous structural features (Weber et al., 2001). For example, Bertrand and Mullainathan (2001) find that oil company executives are rewarded when oil prices go up, but are not penalized equally when prices go down. Einav and Yariv (2006) note that authors of economics papers whose names come earlier in a list of authors benefit disproportionately by various measures, even though the order is almost always alphabetical.

Categorization refers to the way in which the brain forms categories. Mullainathan (2002) shows how categorization can generate non-Bayesian effects. An important property of categories is that likelihood evidence that is weak can tip interpretations from one category to another, producing large effects from small causes. Fryer and Jackson (2004) develop a model of optimal categorization and discuss its application to labor market discrimination.

5.5   Neuroeconomics

Neuroeconomics is the grounding of microeconomics in details of neural functioning. It is natural to be skeptical about whether economists need to know precisely where in the brain computations occur to make predictions about economic behavior – such as responses to prices. But keep in mind that the revealed preferences approach which deliberately avoided "trying to discover the essence of things" (in Pareto's phrase) was adopted about a hundred years ago. At that time it really *was* impossible to make all the measurements and causal interventions that can be made today, with PET, TMS, MEG, pharmacological and hormone changes, genetic testing in all species and gene knockouts in mice (actually engineering the genes), and fMRI. The fact that there are so many tools means that limits of one method can be compensated for by strengths of other methods (they are complements). Technological substitution from 100 years ago to now suggests economists might learn something from these new measurements about determinants of choices.

Some basic facts about the brain can guide economic modeling (and already have, in "dual-process" models). The brain is divided into four lobes – frontal, parietal, occipital, and temporal. Regions of these lobes are interconnected and create specialized "circuits" for performing various tasks.

The human brain is a primate brain with more neocortex. To deny this important fact is akin to creationism. The fact that many human and animal brain structures are shared means that human behavior generally involves interaction between "old" brain regions and more newly evolved ones. The descent of humans from other species also means we might learn something about human behavior from other species. For example, rats become addicted to all drugs that humans become biologically addicted to, which implies that old reward circuitry shared by rat and human brains is part of human addiction.

While we often think of complex behavior as deliberate, resources for "executive function" or "cognitive control" are rather scarce (concentrated in the cingulate). As a result, the brain and body are very good at delegating components of complex behavior into automatic processes. For example, a student driver is overwhelmed by visual cues, verbal commands, memory required for navigation, and mastery of motor skills. Many accidents result during this learning process. But within a few years, driving becomes so effortless that drivers can eat and talk (perhaps on a cell phone) while driving safely.[16]

Methodologically, neuroeconomics is not intended to test economic theory in a traditional way (particularly under the view that utilities and beliefs are only revealed by choices). Instead, the goal is to establish the neural circuitry underlying economic decisions, for the eventual purpose of making better predictions.

Seen this way, neuroeconomics is likely to produce three types of findings: evidence for rational-choice processes; evidence supporting behavioral economics processes and parameters (as in Table 7.1); and evidence of different types of constructs that do not fit easily into standard modeling categories.

Results consistent with rational choice: In choice domains where evolution has had a long time to sculpt pan-species mechanisms that are crucial for survival (food, sex, and safety), neural circuits, which approximate Bayesian rational choice, have probably emerged. For example, Platt and Glimcher (1999) find neurons in monkey lateral intraparietal cortex (LIP) that fire at a rate that is almost perfectly correlated with the expected value of an upcoming juice reward, triggered by a monkey eye movement (saccade). Monkeys can also learn to approximate mixed-strategies in games, probably using generalized EWA-type reinforcement algorithms (Lee, McGreevy and Barraclough, 2005). Neuroscientists are also finding neurons that appear to express values of choices

---

[16] However, as activities become automatic, they often become harder to remember and difficult to teach to others, an important fact for the division of labor in large firms where learning-by-doing creates automaticity.

(Padoa-Schioppa and Assad, 2005) and potential locations of "neural currency" that create trade-offs (Shizgal, 1999).

Results consistent with behavioral economics: Other neural evidence is already vaguely consistent with behavioral economics ideas like those in Table 7.1. McClure et al. (2004) find evidence of two systems involved in time discounting, consistent with a quasi-hyperbolic β-δ theory. Sanfey et al. (2003) find that low offers in ultimatum games (compared to near-equal offers) differentially activate emotional areas (insula), planning and evaluation areas (dorsolateral prefrontal cortex, DLPFC) and conflict resolution areas (anterior cingulate). Relative activity in the insula and DLPFC predicts whether offers will be rejected or not. This result is consistent with social preferences models in which money and distaste for unfairness or inequality are traded off (by the cingulate). Hsu et al. (2005) compared decisions under ambiguity and risk (using Ellsberg-paradox examples). Ambiguity differentially activates the orbitofrontal cortex (OFC, just above the eye sockets) and the amygdala, a "vigilance" area, which responds rapidly to fearful stimuli and is important in emotional processing and learning. The fact that OFC activity is stronger and longer-lasting for ambiguous choices implies that people with damage to the OFC might not exhibit typical patterns of ambiguity-aversion. Indeed, Hsu et al. find that they do not.

New constructs and ideas: The biggest impact of neuroeconomics will probably not come from adjudicating debates between rational-choice and behavioral economics. Instead, it will come from establishing a detailed empirical basis for constructs that are new in economics (although some of them could be defined in familiar terms).

For example, in game theory, players are in equilibrium when their beliefs about what other players will do are accurate, and they choose best responses given those accurate beliefs. A neural analogue of this mathematical definition is that brain activity in equilibrium will be highly overlapping when players are making their own choices, compared to when they are forming beliefs about choices of others, because creating accurate beliefs requires them to simulate choices by others. Indeed, Bhatt and Camerer (2005) found very little difference in brain activity between choosing and guessing in periods in which players' choices and beliefs were in equilibrium. Thus, game-theoretic equilibrium is a "state of mind" as well as a restriction on belief accuracy and best response.

Causing **preferences:** *Some* areas in the brain are active during economic decision making. So what is learned from knowing precisely *where* those regions are? The answer is that regions develop at different rates across the life cycle, are different across species, use different neurotransmitters, have different types of neurons, and participate in decisions that might seem superficially different. (For example, the insula, which is activated by low ultimatum offers, is also activated by bodily discomforts like pain and disgust; so when a person says an offer is "disgustingly low" they may be speaking rather literally.)

Knowing which regions are part of the neural circuit for a particular decision enables us to use other knowledge about specialization to make new types of predictions. Valuation of a good – a utility, which is often thought of as basic preference, might actually be the *middle* phase of a biological process. Valuations are an *input* to a more complex downstream process, which incorporates prices, budget constraints, and possibly social concerns (e.g., peer pressure or rational conformity). But valuations are also the *output* of an earlier upstream process, which should perhaps be considered the "primitive" in modeling preferences.

A behavioral way to demonstrate an understanding of the process that creates expressed preferences is to show how changing variables can cause or influence preferences. In standard economic terms, preferences are "state-dependent," where the states are internal biological states (that can also be changed exogeneously). Then the important questions are: What are those states? and Does an executive cortical process understand how the state-dependence works, and either influences it or compensates for exogeneous shocks?

For example, the oxytocin hormone is involved in social bonding and is implicated in studies of trust games (Zak et al, 2005). It follows that if oxytocin can be increased exogeneously, and the brain does not undo the effect of the exogeneous change, then adding oxytocin might *create* trust. Kosfeld et al (2005) showed exactly this effect. They administered synthetic oxytocin to subjects, which increased the amount those subjects invested in a trust game. The capacity to change behavior (traditionally interpreted as revelation of preferences) is routine for neuroscientists. Direct stimulation of single neurons is conjectured to create preferences for one choice or another, by intervening upstream.

This approach suggests a general recipe for causing changes in behavior. As noted earlier in section B, most dual-process models posit two processes: (1) A controlled, long-run, deliberative, or "cold" process, which accepts inputs and tries to constrain or override another (2) process that is automatic, short-run, affective, or "hot." The recipe for changing behavior is to either stimulate the second process directly and see whether the first type of deliberative process undoes the exogeneous change, or to place cognitive overload on the first process (tying up its scarce resources) and see whether its ability to constrain the second process suffers. Lerner, Small and Loewenstein (2004) stimulate the second process. They induced emotional states that affected how people priced goods they were endowed with (reversing the typical "endowment effect" in which owned goods are valued more highly). Shiv and Fedorikhin (1999) constrained the first (controlled) process. They asked subjects to remember either simple (2-digit) or difficult (7-digit) strings of numerical digits as they walked by foods that were tempting (potato chips) or virtuous (fruit). Overloading the controller system with the more taxing 7-digit memory task led to more consumption of the tempting foods. The simplest language of preference theory would say that the difficult 7-digit memory task "changed preferences." A more detailed view, and a more useful one, is that resistance to temptation requires scarce cognitive resources; multitasking, which consumes these resources, lowers resistance and leads people to eat more chips.

6 CONCLUSIONS

Empirically driven behavioral economics uses evidence from psychology and other disciplines to inform models of limits on rationality, willpower, and self-interest to explain anomalies and make new predictions. This approach deliberately rejects the "F-twist" premise that theories should not be judged by their assumptions on the grounds that models based on more realistic assumptions will make better predictions.

Many concepts have already been proposed, which generally add one or more parameters to models of choice, including risk, ambiguity, and time (Table 7.1).

This essay highlights a few areas of active research. A central question is the market implications of limits on rationality, willpower, and self-interest. While experience and sorting might weaken the impact of limited individual rationality on firm behavior, these firms also supply goods to a demand side of the market where institutional and social forces are not as strong as erasing the effects of limits. Whether market forces therefore limit the impact of mistakes, or exaggerate them (by creating hyper-rational firms that are optimized to exploit consumer limits), is therefore an open question.

Important trends in behavioral economics include "franchising" of ideas to application areas (such as finance and labor economics), development of theoretical models, field studies, and including new types of psychology (such as attention, attribution, categorization, and limited memory). Another small emerging field is "neuroeconomics," a subfield of behavioral economics that uses details of neural activity to inform microfoundations. Some of these studies are likely to show neural evidence consistent with rational choice, others have already shown circuitry consistent with behavioral economics constructs, and still others will point to constructs that indicate state-dependence of preference (where the states are internal brain states).

References

Anderson, M. J. and S. Sunder (1995). "Professional Traders as Intuitive Bayesians." Organizational Behavior and Human Decision Processes 64(2): 185–202.

Angeletos, G.-M., D. Laibson, A. Repetto, J. Tobacman and S. Weinberg (2001). "The Hyperbolic Consumption Model: Calibration, Simulation, and Empirical Evaluation." Journal of Economic Perspectives 15(3): 47–68.

Arrow, K. J. (1963). Social Choice and Individual Values. New Haven, Yale University Press.

Arthur, W. B. (1991). "Designing Economic Agents that Act like Human Agents: A Behavioral Approach to Bounded Rationality." American Economic Review 81(2): 353–359.

Ashraf, N., C. F. Camerer and G. Loewenstein (2005). "Adam Smith, Behavioral Economist." Journal of Economic Perspectives 19(3): 131–145.

Baker, M. P., R. S. Ruback and J. Wurgler (2004). Behavioral Corporate Finance: A Survey, NBER.

Barberis, N., A. Shleifer and R. Vishny (1998). "A Model of Investor Sentiment." Journal of Financial Economics 49(3): 307–343.

Barberis, N. and R. Thaler (2004). A Survey of Behavioral Finance. Handbook of the Economics of Finance. G. Constantinides, M. Harris and R. Stulz. Vol. 1B. ch. 18.

Bateman, I., D. Kahneman, A. Munro, C. Starmer and S. Robert (2005). "Is There Loss Aversion in Buying? An Adversarial Collaboration." Journal of Public Economics 89(8): 1561–1580.

Bateman, I., A. Munro, B. Rhodes, C. Starmer and R. Sugden (1997). "A Test of the Theory of Reference-Dependent Preferences." Quarterly Journal of Economics 112(2): 479–505.

Benabou, R. and J. Tirole (2003). "Intrinsic and Extrinsic Motivation." Review of Economic Studies 70: 489–520.

Benartzi, S. and R. H. Thaler (1995). "Myopic Loss Aversion and the Equity Premium Puzzle." Quarterly Journal of Economics 110(1): 73–92.

Benhabib, J. and A. Bisin (2005). "Modeling Internal Commitment Mechanisms and Self-Control: A Neuroeconomics Approach to Consumption-Saving Decisions." Games and Economic Behavior 52(2): 460–492.

Benjamin, D. J. and J. M. Shapiro (2005). Who is "Behavioral"? Cognitive Ability and Anomalous Preferences. University of Chicago.

Bernheim, B. D. and A. Rangel (2004). "Addiction and Cue-Triggered Decision Processes." American Economic Review 94(5): 1558–1590.

Bernheim, B. D. and A. Rangel (2005). Behavioral Public Economics: Welfare and Policy Analysis With Fallible Decision-Makers. Economic Institutions and Behavioral Economics. P. Diamond and H. Vartiainen. Princeton, Princeton University Press.

Berridge, K. C. and T. E. Robinson (2003). "Parsing Reward." Trends in Neurosciences 26(9): 507–513.

Bertrand, M. and S. Mullainathan (2001). "Are CEOs Rewarded for Luck? The Ones Without Principals Are." Quarterly Journal of Economics 116(3): 901–932.

Bertrand, M. and S. Mullainathan (2004). "Are Emily and Greg More Employable than Lakisha and Jamal? A Field Experiment on Labor Market Discrimination." American Economic Review 94(4): 991–1013.

Bhatt, M. and C. F. Camerer (2005). "Self-Referential Thinking and Equilibrium as States of Mind in Games: fMRI Evidence." Games and Economic Behavior 52(2): 424–459.

Bolton, G. E. and A. Ockenfels (2000). "ERC: A Theory of Equity, Reciprocity, and Competition." American Economic Review 90(1): 166–193.

Brocas, I. and J. Carrillo (2005). The Brain as a Hierarchical Organization, University of Southern California.

Brown, A., C. Camerer and E. Chua (2006). Learning and Visceral Temptation in Savings Experiments, Caltech.

Brown, M., A. Falk and E. Fehr (2004). "Relational Contracts and the Nature of Márket Interactions." Econometrica 72(3): 747–780.

Bruni, L. and R. Sugden (in press). "The Road Not Taken. Two Debates on Economics and Psychology?" Economic Journal forthcoming.

Camerer, C., L. Babcock, G. Loewenstein and R. Thaler (1997). "Labor Supply of New York City Cabdrivers: One Day at a Time." Quarterly Journal of Economics 112(2, In Memory of Amos Tversky (1937–1996)): 407–441.

Camerer, C. and T. H. Ho (1999). "Experience-Weighted Attraction Learning in Normal Form Games." Econometrica 67(4): 827–874.

Camerer, C., G. Loewenstein and M. Weber (1989). "The Curse of Knowledge in Economic Settings – an Experimental-Analysis." Journal of Political Economy 97(5): 1232–1254.

Camerer, C. F. (1987). "Do Biases in Probability Judgment Matter in Markets – Experimental-Evidence." American Economic Review 77(5): 981–997.

Camerer, C. F. (2003). Behavioral Game Theory: Experiments on Strategic Interaction. Princeton, Princeton University Press.

Camerer, C. F. and E. Fehr (2006). "When does Economic Man Dominate Social Interaction?" Science.

Camerer, C. F., T. H. Ho and J. K. Chong (2004). "A Cognitive Hierarchy Model of Games." Quarterly Journal of Economics 119(3): 861–898.

Camerer, C. F., G. F. Loewenstein and M. Rabin (2004). Advances in Behavioral Economics. Princeton, Princeton University Press.

Camerer, C. F. and U. Malmendier (in press). Behavioral Organizational Economics. Yrjo Jahnsson Foundation 50th Anniversary Conference on Economics Institutions and Behavioral Economics. P. Diamond and H. Vartiainen. Princeton, Princeton University Press.

Campbell, J. Y. and T. Vuolteenaho (2004). "Inflation Illusion and Stock Prices." American Economic Review 94(2): 19–23.

Cardenas, J. C. and J. P. Carpenter (2005). Experiments and Economic Development: Lessons from Field Labs in the Developing World, Middlebury College.

Charness, G., G. R. Frechette and J. H. Kagel (2004). "How Robust Is Laboratory Gift Exchange?" Experimental Economics 7(2): 189–205.

Charness, G. and M. Rabin (2002). "Understanding Social Preferences with Simple Tests." Quarterly Journal of Economics 117(3): 817–869.

Chen, K., V. Lakshminarayanan and L. Santos (2005). How Basic are Behavioral Biases? Evidence from Capuchin-Monkey Trading Behavior, Yale University.

Cochrane, J. (1989). "The Sensitivity of Tests of the Intertemporal Allocation of Consumption to Near-Rational Alternatives." American Economic Review 79(3): 319–337.

Cohen, R. B., C. Polk and T. Vuolteenaho (2005). "Money Illusion in the Stock Market: The Modigliani-Cohn Hypothesis." Quarterly Journal of Economics 120(2): 639–668.

Colander, D. (2005). Neuroeconomics, the Hedonimeter, and Utility: Some Historical Links, Middlebury College.

Conlin, M., T. O'Donoghue and T. Vogelsang (2005). Projection Bias in Catalog Orders, Cornell University.

Conlisk, J. (1996). "Why Bounded Rationality?" Journal of Economic Literature 34(2): 669–700.

Costa-Gomes, M., V. P. Crawford and B. Broseta (2001). "Cognition and Behavior in Normal-Form Games: An Experimental Study." Econometrica 69(5): 1193–1235.

Coy, P. (2005). Why Logic Often Takes a Backseat. BusinessWeek, March 28, 2005.

Crawford, V. P. (1997). Theory and Experiment in the Analysis of Strategic Interaction. Advances in Economics and Econometrics: Theory and Applications. D. Kreps and K. Wallis. Cambridge, Cambridge University Press: 1–52.

De Bondt, W. F. M. and R. Thaler (1985). "Does the Stock-Market Overreact." Journal of Finance 40(3): 793–805.

Degeorge, F., J. Patel and R. Zeckhauser (1999). "Earnings Management to Exceed Thresholds." Journal of Business 72(1): 1–33.

Della Vigna, S. and U. Malmendier (2006). "Paying Not to Go to the Gym." American Economic Review 96(3): 694–719.

Della Vigna, S. and J. Pollet (2005). Investor Inattention, Firm Reaction, and Friday Earnings Announcements, University of California, Berkeley. NBER Working Paper No. 11683, issued Oct. 2005.

Dufwenberg, M. and G. Kirchsteiger (2004). "A Theory of Sequential Reciprocity." Games and Economic Behavior 47: 268–298.

Edgeworth, F. Y. (1881). Mathematical Psychics: An Essay on the Application of Mathematics to the Moral Sciences.

Einav, L. and L. Yariv (2006). "What's in a Surname? The Effects of Surname Initials on Academic Success." Journal of Economic Perspectives 20(1): 175–188.

Einhorn, H. J. (1982). Learning from Experience and Suboptimal Rules in Decision Making. Judgement under Uncertainty: Heuristics and Biases. D. Kahneman, P. Slovic and A. Tversky, Cambridge University Press.

Erev, I., Y. Bereby-Meyer and A. E. Roth (1999). "The Effect of Adding a Constant to All Payoffs: Experimental Investigation, and Implications for Reinforcement Learning Models." Journal of Economic Behavior & Organization 39(1): 111–128.

Erev, I. and A. E. Roth (1998). "Predicting How People Play Games: Reinforcement Learning in Experimental Games with Unique, Mixed Strategy Equilibria." American Economic Review 88(4): 848–881.

Falk, A. and U. Fischbacher (2006). "A Theory of Reciprocity." Games and Economic Behavior 54(2): 293–315.

Falkinger, J. (2005). Limited Attention as the Scarce Resource in an Information-Rich Economy, IZA Discussion Papers.

Farber, H. (2004). Reference-Dependent Preferences and Labor Supply: The Case of New York City Taxi Drivers, Princeton University.

Farber, H. (2005). "Is Tomorrow Another Day? The Labor Supply of New York City Cabdrivers." Journal of Political Economy 113(1): 46–82.

Fehr, E. and K. M. Schmidt (1999). "A Theory of Fairness, Competition, and Cooperation." Quarterly Journal of Economics 114(3): 817–868.

Fischbacher, U., C. M. Fong and E. Fehr (2003). Fairness, Errors and the Power of Competition, IEW Working Paper No. 133, University of Zurich.

Fischhoff, B. and R. Beyth (1975). "I Knew it Would Happen: Remembered Probabilities of Once-Future Things." Organizational Behavior and Human Performance 13: 1–16.

Frederick, S. (2005). "Cognitive Reflection and Decision Making." J. Economic Perspectives 19(4): 25–42.

Fryer, R. and M. Jackson (2004). A Categorical Model of Cognition and Biased Decision-Making, California Institute of Technology.

Fudenberg, D. and D. Levine (1998). Theory of Learning in Games. Cambridge, MA, MIT Press.

Fudenberg, D. and D. Levine (2005). A Dual Self Model of Impulse Control, Harvard.

Gabaix, X. and D. Laibson (2006). "Shrouded Attributes, Consumer Myopia, and Information Suppression in Competitive Markets." Quarterly Journal of Economics 121(2): forthcoming.

Ganguly, A. R., J. H. Kagel and D. V. Moser (2000). "Do Asset Market Prices Reflect Traders' Judgment Biases?" Journal of Risk and Uncertainty 20(3): 219–245.

Genesove, D. and C. Mayer (2001). "Loss Aversion and Seller Behavior: Evidence from the Housing Market." Quarterly Journal of Economics 116(4): 1233–1260.

Goeree, J. K. and C. A. Holt (2001). "Ten Little Treasures of Game Theory and Ten Intuitive Contradictions." American Economic Review 91(5): 1402–1422.

Grether, D. M. and C. R. Plott (1979). "Economic Theory of Choice and the Preference Reversal Phenomenon." American Economic Review 69(4): 623–638.

Grubb, M. (2005). Screening Overconfident Consumers, Stanford University.

Gul, F. (1991). "A Theory of Disappointment Aversion." Econometrica 59(3): 667–686.

Gul, F. and W. Pesendorfer (2001). "Temptation and Self-Control." Econometrica 69(6): 1403–1435.

Gul, F. and W. Pesendorfer (2005). The Case for Mindless Economics, Princeton University.

Haltiwanger, J. and M. Waldman (1989). "Limited Rationality and Strategic Complements: The Implications for Macroeconomics." Quarterly Journal of Economics 104(3): 463–483.

Hardie, B. G. S., E. J. Johnson and P. S. Fader (1993). "Modeling Loss Aversion and Reference Dependence Effects on Brand Choice." Marketing Science 12(4): 378–394.

Harless, D. W. and C. F. Camerer (1994). "The Predictive Utility of Generalized Expected Utility Theories." Econometrica 62(6): 1251–1289.

Harrison, G. W. and J. A. List (2004). "Field Experiments." Journal of Economic Literature 42(4): 1009–1055.

Healy, P. J. (2004). Group Reputations and Stereotypes as a Contract Enforcement Device, Caltech.

Heath, C., R. P. Larrick and J. Klayman (1998). "Cognitive Repairs: How Organizational Practices Can Compensate for Individual Shortcomings." Review of Organizational Behavior 20(1): 1–38.

Hey, J. D. and C. Orme (1994). "Investigating Generalizations of Expected Utility Theory Using Experimental Data." Econometrica 62(6): 1291–1326.

Hines, J., James R. and R. Thaler (1995). "Anomalies: The Flypaper Effect." Journal of Economic Perspectives 9(4): 217–226.

Ho, T., C. F. Camerer and J.-K. Chong (2005). "Self-Tuning Experience-Weighted Attraction Learning in Games." Journal of Economic Theory forthcoming.

Ho, T. H., N. Lim and C. F. Camerer (2006). "Modeling the Psychology of Consumer and Firm Behavior Using Behavioral Economics." Journal of Marketing Research forthcoming.

Ho, T.-H. and J.-J. Zhang (2005). Does the Format of Pricing Contracts Matter?, UC-Berkeley.

Hsu, M., M. Bhatt, R. Adolphs, D. Tranel and C. F. Camerer (2005). "Neural Systems Responding to Degrees of Uncertainty in Human Decision-Making." Science 310: 1680–1683.

Jolls, C., C. R. Sunstein and R. Thaler (1998). "A Behavioral Approach to Law and Economics." Stanford Law Review 50(5): 1471–1550.

Jolls, C. M. (in press). Behavioral Law and Economics. Yrjo Jahnsson Foundation 50th Anniversary Conference on Economics Institutions and Behavioral Economics. P. Diamond and H. Vartiainen. Princeton, Princeton University Press.

Kahneman, D. (2003). "Maps of bounded rationality: Psychology for Behavioral Economics." American Economic Review 93(5): 1449–1475.

Kahneman, D., J. L. Knetsch and R. H. Thaler (1990). "Experimental Tests of the Endowment Effect and the Coase Theorem." Journal of Political Economy 98(6): 1325–1348.

Kahneman, D. and A. Tversky (1979). "Prospect Theory – Analysis of Decision under Risk." Econometrica 47(2): 263–291.

Kahneman, D. and A. Tversky (1982). On the Study of Statistical Intuitions. Judgment under Uncertainty: Heuristics and Biases. D. Kahneman, P. Slovic and A. Tversky. Cambridge, Cambridge University Press.

Kluger, B. D. and S. B. Wyatt (2004). "Are Judgment Errors Reflected in Market Prices and Allocations? Experimental Evidence Based on the Monty Hall Problem." Journal of Finance 59(3): 969–998.

Kosfeld, M., M. Heinrichs, P. J. Zak, U. Fischbacher and E. Fehr (2005). "Oxytocin Increases Trust in Humans." Nature 435(7042): 673–676.

Koszegi, B. and P. Heidhues (2005). The Impact of Consumer Loss Aversion on Pricing, University of California, Berkeley.

Koszegi, B. and M. Rabin (forthcoming). "A Model of Reference–Dependent Preferences." Quarterly Journal of Economics forthcoming.

Krishna, A. and J. Slemrod (2003). "Behavioral Public Finance: Tax Design as Price Presentation." International Tax and Public Finance 10(2): 189–203.

Laibson, D. (1997). "Golden Eggs and Hyperbolic Discounting." Quarterly Journal of Economics 112(2, In Memory of Amos Tversky (1937-1996)): 443–477.

Lazear, E. P., U. Malmendier and R. Weber (2005). Sorting in Experiments with Application to Social Preferences, Stanford University. NBER Working Paper No. 12041.

Lee, D., B. P. McGreevy and D. J. Barraclough (2005). "Learning and Decision Making in Monkeys During a Rock-Paper-Scissors Game." Cognitive Brain Research 25(2): 416–430.

Lerner, J., D. A. Small and G. Loewenstein (2004). "Heart Strings and Purse Strings: Carryover Effects of Emotions on Economic Decisions " Psychological Science 15(5): 337–341.

Levine, D. K. (1998). "Modeling Altruism and Spitefulness in Experiments." Review of Economic Dynamics 1(3): 593–622.

List, J. A. (2003). "Does Market Experience Eliminate Market Anomalies?" Quarterly Journal of Economics 118(1): 41–71.

Loewenstein, G. and T. O'Donoghue (2004). Animal Spirits: Affective and Deliberative Influences on Economic Behavior, Carnegie Mellon University.

Loewenstein, G. F., M. H. Bazerman and L. Thompson (1989). "Social Utility and Decision-Making in Interpersonal Contexts." Journal of Personality and Social Psychology 57(3): 426–441.

Loomes, G., C. Starmer and R. Sugden (1989). "Preference Reversal: Information-Processing Effect or Rational Non-Transitive Choice?" Economic Journal 99(395): 140–151.

Lucas, R. E., Jr. (1986). "Adaptive Behavior and Economic Theory." Journal of Business 59(4, Part 2: The Behavioral Foundations of Economic Theory): S401–S426.

Maciejovsky, B. and D. V. Budescu (2005). Is Cooperation Necessary? Learning and Knowledge Transfer in Cooperative Groups and Competitive Auctions, University of Illinois, Urbana-Champaign.

Marcet, A. and J. P. Nicolini (2003). "Recurrent Hyperinflations and Learning." American Economic Review 93(5): 1476–1498.

McCaffery, E. J. (1994). "Cognitive Theory and Tax." UCLA Law Review 41(7): 1861–1947.

McClure, S. M., D. I. Laibson, G. Loewenstein and J. D. Cohen (2004). "Separate Neural Systems Value Immediate and Delayed Monetary Rewards." Science 306(5695): 503–507.

McFadden, D. L. (1999). "Rationality for Economists?" Journal of Risk and Uncertainty 19(1–3): 73–105.

McKelvey, R. D. and T. R. Palfrey (1998). "Quantal Response Equilibria for Extensive Form Games." Experimental Economics 1(1): 9–41.

Miller, E. M. (1977). "Risk, Uncertainty, and Divergence of Opinion." Journal of Finance 32(4): 1151–1168.

Modigliani, F. and R. Cohn (1979). "Inflation, Rational Valuation, and the Market." Financial Analysts Journal 35(3): 24–44.

Mukerji, S. and J. M. Tallon (2004). An Overview of Economic Applications of David Schmeidler's Models of Decision Making Under Uncertainty. Uncertainty in Economic Theory: A Collection of Essays in Honor of David Schmeidler's 65th Birthday. I. Gilboa, Routledge.

Mullainathan, S. (2002). Thinking Through Categories, MIT.

Mullainathan, S. (in press). Psychology and Development Economics. Yrjo Jahnsson Foundation 50th Anniversary Conference on Economics Institutions and Behavioral Economics. P. Diamond and H. Vartiainen. Princeton, Princeton University Press.

Mullainathan, S. and R. Thaler (2000). Behavioral Economics. In International Encyclopedia of the Social and Behavioral Sciences, Massachusetts Institute of Technology.

Nagel, R. (1995). "Unraveling in Guessing Games: An Experimental Study." American Economic Review 85(5): 1313–1326.

Odean, T. (1998). "Are Investors Reluctant to Realize Their Losses?" Journal of Finance 53(5): 1775–1798.

Odean, T. and B. M. Barber (2005). All that Glitters: The Effect of Attention and News on the Buying Behavior of Individual and Institutional Investors, University of California, Berkeley.

O'Donoghue, T. and M. Rabin (2001). "Choice and Procrastination." Quarterly Journal of Economics 116(1): 121–160.

Ofek, E. and M. Richardson (2003). "DotCom Mania: The Rise and Fall of Internet Stock Prices." Journal of Finance 58(3): 1113–1138.

Padoa-Schioppa, C. and J. Assad (2005). Neuronal Processing of Economic Value in Orbitofrontal Cortex, Harvard Medical School.

Platt, M. L. and P. W. Glimcher (1999). "Neural Correlates of Decision Variables in Parietal Cortex." Nature 400 (6741): 233–238.

Prelec, D. (1998). "The Probability Weighting Function." Econometrica 66(3): 497–527.

Rabin, M. (1993). "Incorporating Fairness into Game-Theory and Economics." American Economic Review 83(5): 1281–1302.

Rabin, M. (1998). "Psychology and Economics." Journal of Economic Literature 36(1): 11–46.

Rabin, M. (2002). "Inference by Believers in the Law of Small Numbers." Quarterly Journal of Economics 117(3): 775–816.

Rabin, M. and J. L. Schrag (1999). "First Impressions Matter: A Model of Confirmatory Bias." Quarterly Journal of Economics 114(1): 37–82.

Robson, A. J. (2001). "The Biological Basis of Economic Behavior." Journal of Economic Literature 39(1): 11–33.

Rotemberg, J. J. (2004). Minimally Acceptable Altruism and the Ultimatum Game, Harvard Business School.

Rubinstein, A. (1998). Modelling Bounded Rationality. Cambridge, MA, MIT Press.

Rubinstein, A. (2003). "Economics and Psychology"? The Case of Hyperbolic Discounting." International Economic Review 44(4): 1207–1216.

Russell, T. and R. Thaler (1985). "The Relevance of Quasi Rationality in Competitive Markets." American Economic Review 75(5): 1071–1082.

Russell, T. and R. Thaler (1987). "The Relevance of Quasi Rationality in Competitive Markets: Reply." American Economic Review 77(3): 499–501.

Samuelson, L. (1997). Evolutionary Games and Equilibrium Selection. Cambridge, MIT Press.

Sanfey, A. G., J. K. Rilling, J. A. Aronson, L. E. Nystrom and J. D. Cohen (2003). "The Neural Basis of Economic Decision-Making in the Ultimatum Game." Science 300(5626): 1755–1758.

Schlag, K. H. (1998). "Why Imitate, and If So, How?: A Boundedly Rational Approach to Multi-armed Bandits." Journal of Economic Theory 78(1): 130–156.

Schmeidler, D. (1989). "Subjective Probability and Expected Utility without Additivity." Econometrica 57(3): 571–587.

Segal, U. and A. Spivak (1990). "First Order Versus Second Order Risk Aversion." Journal of Economic Theory 51(1): 111–125.

Shafir, E., D. N. Osherson and E. E. Smith (1989). "An Advantage Model of Choice." Journal of Behavioral Decision Making 2(1): 1–23.

Shiv, B. and A. Fedorikhin (1999). "Heart and mind in conflict: The Interplay of Affect and Cognition in Consumer Decision Making." Journal of Consumer Research 26(3): 278–292.

Shizgal, P. (1999). On the Neural Computation of Utility: Implications from Studies of Brain Reward. Well-Being: The Foundations of Hedonic Psychology. D. Kahneman, E. Diener and N. Schwarz: 502–526.

Shleifer, A. (2000). Inefficient Markets. Oxford, Oxford University Press.

Simonson, I. and A. Tversky (1992). "Choice in Context – Tradeoff Contrast and Extremeness Aversion." Journal of Marketing Research 29(3): 281–295.

Slovic, P. and S. Lichtenstein (1968). "Importance of Variance Preferences in Gambling Decisions." Journal of Experimental Psychology 78: 646–654.

Smith, A. (1759/1892). The Theory of Moral Sentiments. Indianapolis, Liberty Fund.

Stahl, D. O., and P. Wilson, W. (1995). "On Players' Models of Other Players: Theory and Experimental Evidence." Games and Economic Behavior 10(1): 218–254.

Stahl, D. O. (2000). "Rule Learning in Symmetric Normal-Form Games: Theory and Evidence." Games and Economic Behavior 32(1): 105–138.

Starmer, C. (2000). "Developments in Non-Expected Utility Theory: The Hunt for a Descriptive Theory of Choice under Risk." Journal of Economic Literature 38(2): 332–382.

Starmer, C. (2004). Friedman's Risky Methodology, University of Nottingham.

Stewart, S. A. (2005). Can Behavioral Economics Save Us from Ourselves? University of Chicago Magazine. 97.

Stigler, G. (1981). Economics or Ethics? Tanner Lectures on Human Values. S. McMurrin. Cambridge, Cambridge University Press.

Tanaka, T., C. F. Camerer and Q. Nguyen (2006). Politics, Poverty and Preferences: Field Experiments and Survey Data from Vietnam, California Institute of Technology.

Thaler, R. (1980). "Toward a Positive Theory of Consumer Choice." Journal of Economic Behavior & Organization 1(1): 39–60.

Thaler, R. H. (1999). "Mental Accounting Matters." Journal of Behavioral Decision Making 12(3): 183–206.

Thompson, L. and G. Loewenstein (1992). "Egocentric Interpretations of Fairness and Interpersonal Conflict." Organizational Behavior and Human Decision Processes 51(2): 176–197.

Tovar, P. (2004). The Effects of Loss-aversion on Trade Policy and the Anti-trade Bias Puzzle, University of Maryland.

Tversky, A. and D. Kahneman (1992). "Advances in Prospect-Theory – Cumulative Representation of Uncertainty." Journal of Risk and Uncertainty 5(4): 297–323.

Weber, M. and C. F. Camerer (1998). "The Disposition Effect in Securities Trading: An Experimental Analysis." Journal of Economic Behavior & Organization 33(2): 167–184.

Weber, R., C. Camerer, Y. Rottenstreich and M. Knez (2001). "The Illusion of Leadership: Misattribution of Cause in Coordination Games." Organization Science 12(5): 582–598.

Weibull, J. (1995). Evolutionary Game Theory. Cambridge, MA, MIT Press.

Wilson, A. (2004). Bounded Memory and Biases in Information, University of Chicago.

Zak, P. J., K. Borja, W. T. Matzner and R. Kurzban (2005). "The Neuroeconomics of Distrust: Sex Differences in Behavior and Physiology." American Economic Review 95(2): 360–363.

CHAPTER 8

Incentives and Self-Control*
Ted O'Donoghue and Matthew Rabin

> The problem sets should have been graded. I had no incentive to do them, and as a result did poorly on the exams.
> — comment from anonymous teacher evaluation, undergraduate game theory course

Abstract

We investigate the design of incentives for people subject to self-control problems in the form of a time-inconsistent taste for immediate gratification. Because such present-biased people may not behave in their own long-run best interests, there is scope for firms, policymakers, friends and family, and the people themselves to create incentives for "better" behavior. Moreover, whereas for standard agents only ultimate well-being from different courses of action matter, for present-biased people the detailed structure of incentives becomes of critical importance. Optimal incentive design, therefore, will attend to details that the conventional model would say are essentially irrelevant. We describe some general principles that have emerged in recent and ongoing research on incentives, highlighting the importance of heterogeneity among agents and providing for flexibility, and illustrate these principles with some simple examples.

1 INTRODUCTION

Ever since receiving the above comment, one of us (Rabin) has presented it to students on the first day of class as the first exercise for his microeconomics courses: In the above situation, find the incentive! This exercise is a good – albeit somewhat easy – introductory economics question. If the student wanted to do well on the exams, and if doing the problem sets would have helped him to do well on the exams, then he should have had incentive enough to do the problem sets. For this student, however, wanting to do well on the exams was apparently not sufficient motivation to prepare for the exams by

* For helpful comments, we thank Torsten Persson, Paige Skiba, and Ariel Rubinstein. For financial support, we thank the National Science Foundation (grants SES-0214043 and SES-0214147).

doing the problem sets. Indeed, this student believed that, had an additional constraint been added in the form of graded problem sets, he would have been better off.

While it is possible that the student just didn't comprehend the basics of incentives, we believe that this comment reflects two related features of human nature that are missing from the conventional economic approach to incentives. First, people have self-control problems in the form of a *present bias*: Our short-term inclinations of what to do – watching TV rather than studying – often don't accord with our own assessment of what is in our long-term best interests – studying rather than watching TV. The point is *not* that watching TV is necessarily a worse way to spend one's time than studying game theory.[1] Rather, the point is that there is a meaningful sense in which people may wish they would study rather than watch TV, and yet they watch TV. Although pursuit of immediate gratification over future gratification is often the sensible thing to do, there are situations in which people by their own assessment tend to over-pursue immediate gratification.

Second, the comment also reflects that incentives cannot be understood solely by the total payoffs associated with different actions. The details matter. Two incentive schemes A and B may each yield the same aggregate payoffs associated with two courses of action x and y, yet, depending on the details, a person may choose x under scheme A but y under scheme B. Students may study for 100 hours and get a good grade rather than study for 50 hours and get a bad grade if induced by problem sets, but study the 50 hours for the bad grade rather than the 100 hours for a good grade if no problem sets are graded – even if all they care about is their total hours of effort and their grades.

In this paper, we investigate the design of incentives when people have present bias. Our main themes correspond to the two features above. First, because present-biased people may not behave in their own long-run best interests, there is scope for firms, policymakers, friends and family, and perhaps even the people themselves to create incentives for "better" behavior.[2] Second, whereas the standard economic model says that only ultimate payoffs matter, for present-biased people the detailed structure of incentives becomes of critical importance. Hence, optimal incentive design must pay attention to – and can sometimes efficiently use – details that the standard model would say are essentially irrelevant.

Casual evidence suggests that people vary a great deal in their degree of self-control problems, their degree of awareness of self-control problems, and (of course) in their intrinsic tastes for different activities. This heterogeneity of course complicates incentive design because incentives that help some

---

[1] That assessment would depend on the TV show being watched and the game-theoretic solution concept being studied.

[2] There is also scope for firms or opportunistic individuals to design incentives to exploit people's present bias. While our main focus will be beneficial incentives, we occasionally discuss exploitative incentives as well.

types – e.g., people with significant present bias – often harm other types – e.g., people with little or no present bias. Moreover, even individual agents themselves will typically face uncertainty about their own future tastes, needs, outside options, and constraints. If so, then optimal incentives may need to permit some flexibility to agents, and may even need to deal with heterogeneity in the need for flexibility. Hence, a third major theme will be the importance of heterogeneity and flexibility in designing incentives.

In Section 2, we describe the simple model of (what we call) present bias that was adopted in the seminal work of Laibson (1997) and has been widely used by many researchers ever since. We then discuss a variety of reasons why we believe the study of present bias is important for economics and also describe recent empirical papers that conclude that present bias may provide better explanations of many observed economic behaviors than does the standard model.

In Sections 3 and 4, we move to our main topic: the design of incentives when (some) people have present bias. The optimal design of incentives will, of course, depend on the details of the particular environment under consideration. Even so, existing research on how present-biased people react to natural incentives, as well as emerging research on designing incentives in specific contexts, suggests some general principles. In Section 3, we describe these general principles and then analyze a series of examples that illustrate these principles. In Section 4, we address more directly the roles of heterogeneity and flexibility. We describe how recent research has started to deal with heterogeneity and the need for flexibility, suggest some principles that have been missing from this literature, and illustrate these principles by discussing some examples of how to combat procrastination.

In Section 5, we discuss some broader issues and conclude. In particular, while our analysis focuses on the effects of incorporating present bias into the standard economic model, we discuss how similar conclusions might arise from other recent attempts to improve the standard economic model. We also discuss how market forces might influence incentive design when some consumers have present bias.

2 PRESENT-BIASED PREFERENCES AND ECONOMICS

Most economic models, intuitions, and policy prescriptions assume that people's short-run preferences match their long-run preferences. More precisely, most economists assume that preferences are time-consistent: As long as no new information is revealed, people have the same preferences now over future behavior as they will have when the future arrives. Hence, economists have traditionally assumed that if today we prefer to start spending less and saving more tomorrow, tomorrow we'll want to start spending less and saving more immediately; if today we prefer to quit smoking tomorrow, then tomorrow we'll want to quit smoking immediately; if today we prefer to diet tomorrow, tomorrow we'll want to diet immediately; and if today we prefer to work on our dissertation and prepare our taxes, and clean house tomorrow, tomorrow we'll want to do these things immediately.

Evidence suggests, however, that such assumptions are wrong, and more than just being wrong, they are wrong in a systematic direction: People have a bias towards immediate gratification. When thinking about two future dates, people care roughly equally about well-being on those two dates, but when the future arrives and the first of these dates becomes "today," we care more about that first date than about the second date. We buy more, smoke more, eat more, and work less tomorrow than we wish our tomorrow selves to do.[3]

Although the stuff of literature, philosophy, and everyday folk wisdom, economists have mostly ignored this general human tendency. There have over the years been a few exceptions. Strotz (1956) provided the first formal analysis of time-inconsistent preferences and suggested that the relevant form of time inconsistency was a preference for immediate gratification. But the literature that built upon Strotz chose to focus on general theoretical issues that arise with time-inconsistent preferences – most notably, the existence of a "sophisticated path." With the exception of a few researchers (e.g., Thomas Schelling, Richard Thaler, and George Akerlof), Strotz's suggestion to focus on a preference for immediate gratification was lost.[4] Fortunately, it was given a rebirth due to the neo-seminal work of Laibson (1997).

In order to formally analyze the implications of present bias, Laibson adopted a simple model that Phelps and Pollak (1968) used to study intergenerational altruism, to instead study intrapersonal intertemporal choice. Specifically, a person's intertemporal preferences at time t are given by

$$U^t(u_t, \ldots, u_T) \equiv u_t + \beta \sum_{\tau=t+1}^{T} \delta^{\tau-t} u_\tau,$$

where u_τ is her instantaneous utility in period τ. This two-parameter model is a simple modification of the standard exponential-discounting model. The parameter δ represents standard time-consistent impatience; for $\beta = 1$ these preferences reduce to exponential discounting. The parameter β represents a time-inconsistent preference for immediate gratification, where $\beta < 1$ implies an extra bias for now over the future.[5]

---

[3] For evidence that most humans do indeed have such a tendency, see Ainslie (1991, 1992), Ainslie and Haslam (1992a, 1992b), Loewenstein and Prelec (1992), Thaler (1981), and Thaler and Loewenstein (1989). For a recent overview, see Frederick, Loewenstein, and O'Donoghue (2002). This tendency is often referred to as "hyperbolic discounting" or "quasi-hyperbolic discounting."

[4] See, for instance, Schelling (1978, 1984), Thaler and Shefrin (1981), and Akerlof (1991).

[5] This model is a generalization of standard exponential discounting – that is, exponential discounting is a special case that imposes the restriction that $\beta = 1$. Moreover, virtually every paper that applies this model, whether theoretical or empirical, makes explicit how the implications for $\beta < 1$ differ from the implications for $\beta = 1$ in the particular context being studied. Hence, unlike the vast majority of papers in economics that *a priori* impose exponential discounting, this literature permits a careful comparison of the relative merits of exponential discounting vs.

The general feature of present bias is of course more general than the simple β, δ model. Indeed, psychologists who estimate discount functions often focus on a one-parameter hyperbolic functional form wherein a person puts weight $a/(a + d)$ on payoffs that are received with delay d – hence the label "hyperbolic discounting." We suspect that most qualitative and quantitative predictions of the β, δ model will hold for more nuanced forms of present bias, but this remains to be seen.

As discussed by Strotz (1956) and Pollak (1968), the behavior of people with time-inconsistent preferences depends on their beliefs about their own future behavior. Two extreme assumptions have appeared in the literature: *Sophisticated* people are fully aware of their future self-control problems and therefore correctly predict how their future selves will behave, and *naive* people are fully *un*aware of their future self-control problems and therefore believe their future selves will behave exactly as they currently would like them to behave.

Much of the research on present bias has followed Laibson in assuming sophistication – perhaps reflecting economists' natural inclination to assume people have "rational expectations." In our own work (beginning with O'Donoghue and Rabin (1999a)), we have emphasized both sophistication and naivete, in part to emphasize that many observed behaviors may be better understood in terms of naivete. Indeed, to demonstrate that many behaviors we believe reflect naivete need not reflect 100% naivete, we have developed and analyzed a model of *partial naivete*, wherein a person is aware that she has future self-control problems, but she underestimates their magnitude (see O'Donoghue and Rabin 2001).[6] In this paper, we will focus for simplicity on the two extreme types. But many intuitions that arise under both complete naivete and complete sophistication also apply under partial naivete.

While there is little formal evidence on the distribution of types, casual evidence certainly suggests that not everyone has present bias, and that people with present bias differ in their degree of sophistication. We suspect, for instance, that there are many activities – e.g., drinking alcohol – which many people engage in optimally, but which non-trivial numbers of people overdo because of present bias. We emphasize, however, that the heterogeneity in observed behavior, and the harm from this behavior, may be due even more to heterogeneity in underlying tastes for different activities than to differences in present bias or awareness of present bias, and that the implications of present bias depend on

---

incorporating present bias. Of course, permitting $\beta < 1$ is not the only direction for generalizing economic models, and we, like many researchers studying this model, are quite inclined to explore other generalizations. Nonetheless, the model as it stands is clearly less narrow and specialized than the model of time preference it is replacing.

[6] Formally, we let $\hat{\beta}$ be a person's beliefs about her future self-control problems, by which we mean that the person believes that in the future she will behave like a sophisticated person with self-control problem $\hat{\beta}$. With this formulation, a fully sophisticated person has perceptions $\hat{\beta} = \beta$ because she knows exactly her future self-control problems; a fully naive person has perceptions $\hat{\beta} = 1$ because she believes she will not have future self-control problems; and a partially naive person has perceptions $\hat{\beta} \in (\beta, 1)$.

these underlying tastes. If you don't like smoking or drinking or eating potato chips, present bias does not induce you to over-indulge in consuming these things. Although many papers that explore the implications of present bias assume for simplicity that there is no heterogeneity (or more to the point, explore behavior as a function of type), a more complete study of incentive design must account for heterogeneity. We address this issue in Section 4.

A major theme in the literature on present bias is that present bias can generate inefficient behavior – that is, can lead people not to behave in their own best interests. This theme will play a particularly prominent role in our discussion on designing incentives. Of course, such a claim requires a criterion for how to measure welfare. Economists have sometimes been perplexed about how to conduct welfare analysis when people have time-inconsistent preferences, since the person has different preferences at different points in time. One response has been to apply a Pareto criterion, where one outcome is deemed better than another if and only if the person views it as better at all points in time. But we view the Pareto criterion as too agnostic and have instead encouraged using people's "long-run preferences" to measure welfare, where long-run preferences are given by

$$U^0(u_t, \ldots, u_T) \equiv \sum_{\tau=t}^{T} \delta^{\tau-t} u_\tau.$$

A person's long-run preferences reflect her preferences when asked from a prior perspective when she has no option to indulge immediate gratification – hence why U^0 does not depend on β. We prefer this welfare criterion for several reasons. First, the Pareto criterion is clearly too agnostic about when one outcome is better than another. Indeed, it is not even close to the welfare criterion economists apply when studying standard exponential discounters. It does not, for instance, allow us to say that providing someone (or someone providing himself) with a large immediate benefit at a very small future cost is necessarily a good thing; we have, after all, made the current self better off at the cost of his future self. Second, we view the present bias as an "error." Consider, for instance, the person's present bias that applies on March 1, 2008. On every other day of her life, the person is upset with this present bias, and it is only at that moment that she is at peace with it. Hence, we believe that her present bias on March 1, 2008, or on any other day, should be given no normative weight. Third, if we were to consider a person who is choosing future incentives for herself, she would make this choice using exactly her long-run preferences. In fact, we will discuss many such examples below.

Hence, whenever we discuss welfare below, we will be using long-run preferences as our welfare measure, and this perspective is starting to take hold in the literature. Even so, it is worth making one final comment: Most instances of "bad behavior" that we discuss below and in the broader literature are bad by essentially any definition. As a practical matter, especially in applied work, conceptual difficulties over how to measure welfare within the present-bias framework often simply do not matter.

A great deal of research has built off of Laibson's initial model of (what we call) present-biased preferences. Much of the initial work has been theoretical in nature, investigating the implications of present bias both for behavior and for welfare in a variety of economic contexts.[7] More recently, a nascent empirical research program has begun to test present-biased preferences vs. exponential discounting in economic field data (as we discuss below).

There are several reasons why present bias is important for economics. Perhaps the simplest and most straightforward has been, we feel, insufficiently emphasized: without it, economists have no coherent model of short-term impatience. Most economists wouldn't bat an eye if someone suggested that people care 1% more about today than tomorrow – it's just discounting. But under the standard model of exponential discounting, such seemingly reasonable short-term impatience implies manifestly unrealistic long-term impatience. Specifically, because $.99^{365} \approx .0255$, such discounting implies that people care roughly 40 times more about now than a year from now – which none of us do. Without assuming transparently counterfactual and extreme long-term discounting, the exponential model is inconsistent with any noticeable taste for immediate gratification. Even an unrealistically low yearly discount factor of 0.7 (which says, counterfactually, that people care 6 times more about their well-being 10 years from now than 15 years from now) implies that people care only 0.1% more about today vs. tomorrow. Hence, not only does exponential discounting imply that people's current preferences over future behavior accord with their future preferences, but for any plausible discounting it further implies our desired behavior tomorrow is virtually identical to our desired behavior today. In practical terms, then, exponential discounting implies that, if today we prefer to quit smoking, diet, and study tomorrow, then we prefer to quit smoking, diet, and study *today*.

There are two related implications of this logic. First, the strong emphasis in the literature on proving present bias by finding time inconsistency via preference reversals has been misplaced. Finding short-term impatience is sufficient. Second, present bias is *not* a theory of long-term impatience. Economists sometimes seem to associate present bias with extreme myopia. This view is incorrect. Indeed, an important feature of the present-bias model is that it permits the study of immediate gratification without assuming insane myopia. It allows, for instance, that people might care 5% more about today than tomorrow, 10% more about today than a year from now, and 5% more about a year from now than two years from now – which holds in the β, δ model above if $\beta = .95$ and $\delta^{365} = .95$. This distinction is, in fact, a major theme in recent empirical research. We often observe the same people exhibiting long-run planning (committing to retirement plans or to attend college) *and* short-term indulgence (procrastination, credit-card borrowing). Whereas exponential discounting has a hard time accounting for this combination, present bias provides a natural explanation.

---

[7] See, for instance, Laibson (1997, 1998), O'Donoghue and Rabin (1999*a*, 1999*b*, 2001), Carrillo and Mariotti (2000), Benabou and Tirole (2002), and Gruber and Koszegi (2001, 2004).

A second – and more important – reason why present bias is so important for economics is that many real-world economic behaviors seem to clearly indicate short-term impatience. Topics now or soon to be studied with the perspective that present-biased preferences matter include: general savings rates, credit-card borrowing, cigarette consumption, welfare enrollment, procrastination in personal investment, unemployment and procrastination in employment search, purchase quantities under non-linear pricing for "virtue" vs. "vice" products, the effects of payday timing on monthly consumption patterns, food stamps, the effects of coupons and rebates on demand for products, organizational incentives, retirement timing, finishing school, returning to school for G.E.D.s, unsafe sex and AIDS and pregnancy, procrastination in seeking medical attention, compliance with medical prescriptions, alcohol consumption, unhealthy eating, exercise, obesity, procrastination in research, and seeing too few Johnny Depp movies.

Is all pursuit of immediate gratification in these domains "irrational"? Of course not. As all economists understand, rational behavior often involves pursuing immediate gratification at future expense. If chocolate or a cigarette brings you immediate gratification, it may be optimal to consume these items despite possible future health costs; if watching TV brings you immediate gratification, it may be optimal to watch despite possible future costs of poor grades; and if having unprotected sex brings you immediate gratification, it may be optimal to do so despite possible future costs to health or life or family. None of these activities should be deemed mistakes *per se*. The point of this paper and of the broader literature is that it is worth investigating whether, in some cases, people engage in these activities against their *own* long-run preferences due to an *over*-pursuit of immediate gratification.[8]

Indeed, in many situations, we feel the evidence seems to clearly implicate self-harm. Consider, for instance, a major facet of U.S. economic activity: credit-card borrowing.[9] There are roughly 1.2 billion credit cards in use in the United States, with an average annual interest rate of 18.9%. About 60% of active credit-card accounts are not paid off monthly. The average credit-card debt among all American households is $8,400, with an average card debt of $9,205 among people who have at least one card. A typical American family today pays about $1200 annually in credit-card interest.[10] Although further research

---

[8] Of course, many of these activities may also generate negative externalities on neighbors and taxpayers. While such externalities are and should be the topic of economic research, this research is to some extent orthogonal to research on the self-harm caused by over-pursuit of immediate gratification.

[9] We discuss credit-card borrowing and "fringe borrowing" in the context of U.S. consumers because we are more familiar with the data for the U.S. and because the amount and potential maladaptation of consumer debt seems to be greatest in the U.S. But problems with consumer debt have recently been growing in other countries as well – indeed, this international variation is itself a worthy topic for study.

[10] These particular estimates are from Bannister (2004), but the general scale of the estimates broadly match other sources.

is needed, it is hard to see how the lower "steady-state" consumption *and* lower financial security that result from common credit-card behavior can be optimal. Hence, while economists often debate whether Americans save enough for retirement, we feel an equally important question is whether Americans' steady-state consumption throughout their lives is too low due to the credit-card debts that they carry.

In fact, a smaller – but still worryingly large – proportion of Americans borrow with instruments that are far more costly than credit cards. This "fringe" set of financial institutions is even less studied by economists than the credit-card industry. There is a massive industry of pawn shops – putting household items into store as collateral for extremely high-interest loans – in the U.S. and in many other countries (this institution dates back millennia and is described by some as the second oldest profession in the world). And many Americans buy household items such as furniture on a "rent-to-own" plan: Instead of paying money to buy a couch, people rent it on a per-month basis, and after a while are given ownership, typically paying three times the price they could have paid initially.

And most dramatically in terms of recent growth, massive numbers of employed (and pensioned) people in U.S. have taken out one or more payday loans – borrowing against their next pay check. A typical transaction is that a person borrows $300 using his or her paycheck or social-security check as collateral, and pays back $354 when this check arrives. This is 18% interest for a month or, more commonly, *two weeks*. The size of this rapidly growing industry is hard to firmly establish. Stephens Incorporated Investment Bankers (2004) estimate that 9 to 14 million U.S. households – 8.5% of households – took out payday loans in 2002, from 22,000 payday-loan outlets. In a *New York Times* article, Henriques (2004) reports that 26% of military households took out such loans in the same year. The Stephens Incorporated report estimates that the total volume of payday loans in 2003 in the U.S. was $40 billion. It appears that most who take out such payday loans do so repeatedly, so that it doesn't appear to be solely as a source for one-time emergencies.

Most of this behavior seems to us hard to reconcile with full rationality as economists model it. People should buffer themselves with some savings to avoid all this borrowing. No matter how bad their situation, to repeatedly borrow at exorbitant rates puts people in worse situations. And the logic of present bias can readily predict that those facing both higher immediate temptation to consume and higher cost of doing so are particularly prone to overconsume. Because the very poor are more often in this situation than the not very poor, they are more prone to damaging overconsumption even if (as we believe probable) they do not have an intrinsically higher tendency to overconsume.

Beyond such examples that compel speculation about present bias, over the past decade a number of researchers have indeed empirically demonstrated ways in which present bias can explain economic field data better than exponential discounting. Laibson (1997, 1998) demonstrates theoretically that hyperbolic discounting could account for many well-known empirical anomalies in the saving-consumption literature – that is, it could account for many empirical findings that were difficult to understand when viewed with the maintained hypothesis of exponential discounting. For instance, whereas evidence suggests that there is too much income-consumption comovement in household consumption data to be consistent with the standard life-cycle/permanent-income model, Laibson demonstrates that hyperbolic discounting can generate such comovement because hyperbolic discounters often find themselves liquidity constrained. Similarly, whereas evidence suggests a large drop in consumption at retirement that is inconsistent with exponential discounting, hyperbolic discounting can generate such a drop.

In follow-up work, Laibson and his collaborators have conducted more explicit empirical tests of hyperbolic discounting vs. exponential discounting in saving-consumption data. Laibson, Repetto, and Tobacman (1998) and Angeletos, Laibson, Repetto, Tobacman, and Weinberg (2001) simulate a buffer-stock saving-consumption model for both an exponential economy and a hyperbolic economy. Importantly, they incorporate in the model the existence of an illiquid asset and the existence of credit-card borrowing, two features that are important for hyperbolic discounters. They calibrate the model to match the distribution of pre-retirement wealth across households in their observed population, and then compare their simulated data to actual data on other dimensions. They find that the hyperbolic economy performs significantly better at matching the data, particularly on the dimensions of amount of wealth held in liquid assets, amount of credit-card borrowing, and income-consumption comovement. More recently, Laibson, Repetto, and Tobacman (2005) have used the same data to estimate the discounting parameters. In their benchmark specification, they find a yearly $\beta \approx 0.7$ and a yearly $\delta \approx 0.96$, with both tightly estimated.

The key pattern in the data that drives these conclusions is that the same households that accumulate significant wealth by their pre-retirement years also accumulate a lot of credit-card debt when they are young. The fact that households accumulate significant pre-retirement wealth suggests a relatively low long-term discount rate, while the fact that they accumulate significant credit-card debts suggests a relatively high short-term discount rate. Because exponential discounting imposes the same discount rate for both the long term and the short term, it has a hard time generating the observed pattern. In contrast, present bias involves exactly this feature of high short-term and low long-term discount rates.

Recently, researchers have tested for hyperbolic discounting in other environments. DellaVigna and Paserman (2005) test for hyperbolic discounting in job-search decisions. They first develop a model in which unemployed people face two types of decisions: (i) they must decide each day how intensely to search for a job, and (ii) when they search and receive a wage offer, they must decide whether to accept that wage. In this framework, impatience (of whatever form) makes people less prone to search and more prone to accept lower wage offers. In principle, then, the impact of impatience on exit rates from unemployment is ambiguous – being less prone to search decreases exit rates, while being willing to accept lower wages increases exit rates. The authors demonstrate, however, that under exponential discounting with plausible discount rates, the wage effect dominates, hence increased impatience should lead to increased exit rates from unemployment. In contrast, under β, δ preferences, if the increased impatience comes in the form of short-term impatience (smaller β), then the search effect dominates and hence increased impatience should lead to decreased exit rates from unemployment. DellaVigna and Paserman use data from the National Longitudinal Survey of Youth (NLSY) and from the Panel Study of Income Dynamics (PSID) to test the relationships between proxies for impatience and exit rates from unemployment, and conclude that the evidence supports the hyperbolic model. In follow-up work, Paserman (2004) estimates a structural model of job search of this form (using males in the NLSY) and finds support for $\beta < 1$.

Shui and Ausubel (2004) find evidence of hyperbolic discounting in credit-card borrowing. They have access to data in which consumers were randomly assigned to receive credit-card offers with different features. They find that consumers are more prone to accept offers with a low introductory interest rate for a short duration, even when, given actual borrowing behavior, consumers would have been better off accepting offers with a larger introductory interest rate that lasts for a longer duration. Moreover, consumers seem reluctant to switch balances even after the introductory rate expires. Shui and Ausubel demonstrate that these findings are inconsistent with exponential discounting but consistent with hyperbolic discounting.

Fang and Silverman (2004) use the NLSY to test for hyperbolic discounting in welfare vs. work decisions among unmarried women with children. They develop a dynamic structural model in which women choose each period whether to work, stay home and take welfare, or stay home and not take welfare, where they incorporate the welfare rules that the women face (which differ across states). Their estimates for β are significantly different from 1; however, a puzzling aspect of their analysis is that it yields a surprisingly low estimate of short-term impatience – a yearly β on the order of .3.

DellaVigna and Malmendier (2006) find evidence suggestive of hyperbolic discounting in health-club data that tracks members' usage over time. They find that, among those who sign up for a monthly contract, people pay an average price per visit of about $17 over the first six months, despite that fact that they could have chosen instead to pay $10 per visit by purchasing daily passes rather than the monthly contract. Moreover, the monthly contract has an automatic-renewal feature – the person's credit card is automatically charged every month unless the person cancels either by mail or by visiting the club – and they find evidence of procrastination in cancellation in the form of a significant duration (2.29 months) between last use and cancellation. Finally, they find that the average price paid per visit in initial months is positively correlated with the cancellation lag. They argue that these findings are suggestive of naive present bias: People sign up for the monthly contract naively expecting to use the health club frequently and then later naively procrastinate cancellation.

Ariely and Wertenbroch (2002) provide experimental evidence on present bias and procrastination. They studied executive-education students who had to write three short papers for a class. For one group of students, each student chose a deadline for each of the three papers, while for a second group, evenly spaced deadlines were exogenously imposed. Students in the first group chose to impose deadlines on themselves, instead of making all papers due at the end of the term. But the deadlines that they chose allowed for more delay than the evenly spaced deadlines, and by various performance measures – e.g., their grades for the class – they fared worse than the students with exogenously imposed, evenly spaced deadlines. They interpret these results as being driven by partially naive present bias. The fact that people choose to make commitments implies that they are worried about future misbehavior; however, the fact that these commitments seem to allow too much delay implies that people underestimate their need for commitment.

Gruber and Mullainathan (2005) find a different form of evidence of present bias. Their starting point is to recognize that models of hyperbolic discounting predict that people might smoke despite preferring not to smoke, and hence might be made better off by cigarette taxes. They attempt to directly test this proposition by investigating how survey measures of subjective well-being depend on local cigarette taxes. Using both U.S. and Canadian data, they indeed find that cigarette taxes seem to increase happiness among those prone to smoke. (As a reliability check, they also test whether other types of excise taxes have similar effects, and confirm that they do not.)

Finally, Shapiro (2005) examines consumption patterns among food-stamp recipients. He finds that over the month between food-stamp deliveries, caloric intake declines by about 10-15 percent. He demonstrates that this behavior is inconsistent with exponential discounting and any plausible discount factor. After ruling out several other explanations, he argues that present bias seems to be the best explanation and demonstrates that the evidence is roughly consistent with people having a daily $\beta \approx 0.9$ and a daily $\delta \approx 1$.

3   INCENTIVES AND PRESENT BIAS

We now move to the main topic of this article: the design of incentives when (some) people have present bias. In particular, our interest is how principals faced with present-biased people are likely to set up incentives, and how these incentives are likely to differ from the incentives that would be used when facing exponential discounters.

There are at least four categories of designed incentives, differing by who is the principal and what is the principal's motive. Perhaps the most obvious category is when benevolent third parties – parents, teachers, friends, or the government – seek to achieve better outcomes for present-biased people. Because this category revolves around attempting to help the present-biased, it is often referred to as designing "paternalistic" incentives.[11] The second category is closely related: Present-biased people sometimes design their own future incentives in an attempt to achieve better outcomes for themselves. This category revolves around sophisticated attempts at self-control through commitment devices.[12]

The third category of designed incentives is when profit-seeking firms or individuals attempt to exploit present-biased people by designing incentives that lead to outcomes that the individuals don't really want or (in the case of naifs) expect. This might take the form of pricing schemes designed to sell more output or to sell output at a higher per-unit price. Alternatively, this might take the form of hiring workers with incentive schemes that lead to low per-unit wages. Such exploitation is of interest and may underlie many incentive structures that we see in the world. Even so, in many cases even profit-seeking firms will be motivated to seek efficient exchange for the usual mutual-gains-of-trade reasons. For instance, if a firm employs a procrastinator, it might attempt to bilk that person of money or extract extra work out of that person, but it is perhaps more likely to want to induce the worker to efficiently perform the tasks she was hired to do. Hence, the fourth category of designed incentives is when profit-seeking firms attempt to induce efficient exchange.

Whichever the category, the optimal design of incentives will depend on the nature of the particular environment under consideration. Even so, existing research on how present-biased people react to the natural incentives that they face in the environment around them, as well as emerging research on designing incentives in specific contexts, suggests some general principles for incentive design. In this section, we describe some general principles we have identified and then illustrate them with a series of examples.

Principle #1: For exponential discounters, only gestalt incentives matter.
For standard exponential discounters, all that matters are the overall costs and benefits of the available options. Hence, when designing incentives, altering details in a way that doesn't change gestalt incentives will have little effect on exponential discounters.

Principle #2: For present-biased people, the details of incentives matter.
Because of their focus on immediate payoffs, many intricacies of incentives that would be irrelevant for exponential discounters can become quite important for present-biased people. In particular, they are sensitive to the exact timing of when costs and benefits are experienced. In addition, they are

[11] The exploration of paternalism often sparks strong resistance among economists, on various grounds. Although we certainly concur that much further research is needed before advocating paternalism in practice, we feel it is a useful task to explore the nature of paternalistic incentives. Indeed, one interesting use of such analyses is that they might enable us to identify the motives behind real-world incentives – e.g., to assess whether they reflect a desire to help or a desire to exploit.

[12] The study of commitment devices has a special place in the history of the study of self-control problems (as the term "self-control" suggests), since the most blatant evidence that the conventional economic model isn't quite right is the existence of efforts to commit oneself.

sensitive to exactly how decisions are made – e.g., choosing in advance vs. in the moment.

Principle #3: There often exist changes in incentives that influence present-biased people without much affecting exponential discounters. A direct implication of the first two principles is that by focusing on altering details without changing gestalt incentives, we can alter the behavior of present-biased people without changing the behavior of exponential discounters. We emphasize this principle because it will be important for dealing with heterogeneity in the world. In particular, even if we cannot identify who is and is not present-biased, it is often possible to modify incentives so as to help (or exploit) the present-biased without much affecting the efficiency of behavior by exponential discounters.

Principle #4: For present-biased people, it can be useful to "magnify" future costs or rewards. Because present-biased people put too little weight on future payoffs, behavior can often be improved by magnifying future costs or rewards.

Principle #5: For present-biased people, it can be useful to encourage prospective choice. When all consequences of a decision are sufficiently far in the future, present bias is not a problem. Hence, if it is possible to induce people to make decisions now about future behavior, we may be able to induce better behavior. For instance, by putting restrictions on when people have access to a good (e.g., limited buying hours), people are forced to decide in advance whether they want to consume that good. Even more attractive, we can sometimes use prospective voluntary restrictions.

To illustrate these principles, we begin with a simple example that is a variant of the one-activity model that we studied in O'Donoghue and Rabin (1999a). Suppose there is an activity that a person must complete exactly once during the next 7 days. Completion of this activity generates both a reward and a cost as described in Table 8.1.

Table 8.1 reflects the gestalt reward and cost as a function of when the activity is completed; in this example, the reward and the cost both increase over time, with the net benefit peaking at Day 4. But the exact timing of when the person *experiences* the reward and the cost might vary depending on the type of activity under consideration. If this pattern of rewards and costs is generated by an onerous activity, such as completing a school assignment, the cost is incurred immediately while the reward is received in the future. For instance, if she completes the problem set on Day 3, then she incurs a cost of 5 on Day

Table 8.1. *Reward and cost as a function of completion day*

Completion Day	Day 1	Day 2	Day 3	Day 4	Day 5	Day 6	Day 7
Reward	5	9	17	33	33	33	33
Cost	5	5	5	5	9	17	33
Net benefit	0	4	12	28	24	16	0

3, and receives a reward of 17 sometime after Day 3. If instead this pattern of rewards and costs is generated by a pleasurable activity, such as eating a tempting food, the reward is received immediately while the cost (e.g., health cost) is incurred in the future. For instance, if she eats the food on Day 3, then she receives a reward of 17 on Day 3, and incurs a cost of 5 sometime after Day 3.

In this example, an exponential discounter with $\delta = 1$ will complete the activity on Day 4 regardless of the type of activity. This example highlights how exponential discounters focus solely on the gestalt rewards and costs of their available actions; the timing of rewards and costs is (virtually) irrelevant to their decision.[13]

Now consider a present-biased person with $\delta = 1$ and $\beta = 1/2$. From a prior perspective (or even from a Day-1 perspective), the person would most like to complete the activity on Day 4, regardless of the timing of rewards and costs. The person's actual behavior, however, depends crucially on this timing. In particular, if it is an onerous activity, the person is prone to procrastinate, incurring the immediate cost and hence delays beyond Day 4. In contrast, if it is a pleasurable activity, the person is prone to preproperate – grab the reward too soon – and hence does the activity before Day 4. Exactly how much the person procrastinates or preproperates depends on whether she is sophisticated or naive. If it is an onerous activity, naifs procrastinate until Day 7 while sophisticates complete the activity on Day 5. If it is a pleasurable activity, naifs do it on Day 3, while sophisticates do it on Day 1.

In addition to demonstrating how the timing matters for present-biased people in a way that is irrelevant for exponential discounters, this example also illustrates the potential value of prospective choice. It is only because present-biased people are making day-to-day, in-the-moment decisions that they end up not doing the activity in Day 4. If instead the person were forced in advance to commit to a day, people would choose Day 4 irrespective of sophistication and irrespective of the timing of rewards and costs. Indeed, even if the person were merely forced each day to commit to tomorrow's behavior (wait vs. do it), the activity would always be performed on Day 4.

Finally, this example illustrates some simple principles with regard to voluntary prospective commitments. As discussed above, if the person commits in advance, she'll commit to Day 4. But would the person want to make such a commitment? The answer depends on whether the person is sophisticated. Sophisticates correctly predict their behavior, and so they would see value to making a commitment. Hence, sophisticates would even be willing to pay for the ability to commit. More generally, sophisticates are often on the lookout for ways to commit their future behavior and are sometimes even willing to pay for such opportunities. In contrast, naifs incorrectly think that they will behave

---

[13] If exponential discounters are impatient, the timing of rewards and costs can matter somewhat. The more general point, however, is that exponential discounters are influenced by only the overall present discounted value of costs and benefits – that is, holding their present discounted value constant, altering the timing cannot alter their behavior.

themselves in the future, and so they see no value in making a commitment. But note that this does not mean that naifs won't make commitments. If making a commitment is costly, either directly or indirectly via reduced flexibility, they will turn it down, as would an exponential discounter. If, however, there were some incentive to commit – perhaps we offer to pay the person $1 if they commit in advance to a day – then they would take it. More generally, naifs, like sophisticates, can benefit from commitment, but since they themselves don't see the need, principals need to create incentives for them to make commitments.

We move next to a somewhat richer context that captures a common situation that we call "cumulative procrastination." Consider a student who must read P pages in T days – that is, she must choose a path $(p_1, \ldots, p_T)$, where p_t is the number of pages read on day t, such that $\sum_{t=1}^{T} p_t = P$. On any given day, her disutility is equal to the number of hours spent reading – that is, $u_t = -h_t$. The number of hours required to read p pages is p^α for some $\alpha > 1$ – that is, $h_t = (p_t)^\alpha$. The key feature of this situation is that, because there are increasing marginal costs to reading on any given day, efficiency calls for the person to spread out her work regularly rather than doing it all in a few days.

First consider *June Mae*, an exponential discounter with $\delta = 1$. How will she react to these circumstances? The answer is simple by the construction: June Mae will read the same amount on every day, which means reading P/T pages per day and therefore $(P/T)^\alpha$ hours per day.

Now consider *April Mae*, a naive person with $\delta = 1$ and $\beta < 1$. What will she do? On day 1, she expects to read the same amount on all remaining days beginning tomorrow. Specifically, she expects that if she reads p_1 pages today, then she'll read $(P - p_1)/(T - 1)$ pages on each of the $T - 1$ remaining days. Hence, on day 1 she'll choose p_1 to minimize

$$(p_1)^\alpha + \beta \left[(T - 1) \left(\frac{P - p_1}{T - 1} \right)^\alpha \right].$$

It follows that on day 1 April Mae will choose

$$p_1 = \frac{\beta^{1/(\alpha-1)}}{T - 1 + \beta^{1/(\alpha-1)}} P.$$

Iterating this logic, one can show that on day $t > 1$ April Mae will choose

$$p_t = \left(\prod_{n=1}^{t-1} \frac{T - n}{T - n + \beta^{1/(\alpha-1)}} \right) \frac{\beta^{1/(\alpha-1)}}{T - t + \beta^{1/(\alpha-1)}} P.$$

Table 8.2 uses this equation to present how the two types behave for some specific examples.

Consider the first example, where students must read 30 pages in 30 days. June Mae spreads out this work evenly, and hence reads 1 hour per day and a total of 30 hours. On Day 1, April Mae plans to spread out her work evenly, but her preference for immediate gratification leads her to choose to read less

Table 8.2. *Behavior in cumulative-procrastination example*

	$T = 30, P = 30, \alpha = 2$		$T = 30, P = 60, \alpha = 1.7$	
	June Mae	April Mae with $\beta = 1/2$	June Mae	April Mae with $\beta = 3/4$
h_1	1 hour	$15\frac{1}{2}$ minutes	$3\frac{1}{4}$ hours	99 minutes
h_2	1 hour	16 minutes	$3\frac{1}{4}$ hours	101 minutes
$\vdots$	$\vdots$	$\vdots$	$\vdots$	$\vdots$
h_{T-1}	1 hour	5.9 hours	$3\frac{1}{4}$ hours	9.6 hours
h_T	1 hour	23.76 hours	$3\frac{1}{4}$ hours	19.25 hours
Total Hours	30 hours	51 hours	$97\frac{1}{2}$ hours	108 hours

today and more on all future days. Specifically, on day 1 she reads for 15 1/2 minutes, planning to read for 62 minutes on each of the remaining 29 days. Hence, when she makes this decision to indulge immediate gratification, she has decided to increase total hours by 13 1/2 minutes.

Unfortunately for April Mae, on Day 2 she changes her mind and decides to indulge immediate gratification once again, this time reading for 16 minutes and planning to read for 64 minutes on each of the remaining 28 days. Indeed, she repeatedly revises her plans to indulge immediate gratification, and as a result she ends up reading for many hours just before the deadline – nearly 6 hours on day 29, and 23 3/4 hours on day 30 – an "all-nighter." Overall, whereas June Mae reads for a total of 30 hours, April Mae reads for a total of 51 hours.[14]

Notice in this example that April Mae did not plan to pull an all-nighter on Day 30. Rather, due to a series of decisions to indulge immediate gratification, she kept backloading more and more work, and ended up forced to do an all-nighter. This example illustrates the more general point that people with present bias do not choose optimal life courses in the way that exponential discounters do. For people who are (to some extent) naive, eventual life courses can be the result of a series of revisions of plans and look very different from the person's initial plan. Even for fully sophisticated people, who never deviate from their plans, to the extent that they cannot control their future behavior, they also do not choose optimal life courses.

We next explore the role of incentives in this example, and in particular how some micro-details that would have small effects for exponential discounters can have significant impact on a naive person with present bias, like April Mae. Consider first a minor modification of this environment: People experience a small bit of enjoyment from studying with their friends – specifically, whereas $u_t = -h_t$ if a person studies alone, $u_t = -.99h_t$ if the person studies with a

---

[14] If we were to consider *September "Sally" Mae* who is sophisticated with $\delta = 1$ and $\beta = 1/2$, we'd find (as the solution to a fairly tedious problem) that Sally Mae reads for a total of 39 hours.

friend. Suppose further, however, that studying together requires scheduling a day *in advance*, and that the cost of backing out from planned studying is significant. For exponential discounters, this modification would have no effect on hours worked, although students would now work together. For naifs like April Mae, however, the enjoyment of studying together would serve as a serendipitous commitment. In particular, they would always plan in advance to work the optimal one hour per day, and hence end up working 30 hours instead of 51 hours.

If, like April Mae, the person were completely naive, then it is important that she enjoy studying with friends. If instead she had a slight distaste for studying with friends, April Mae would never do so, and end up again with the 51 hours total. For people who are (to some degree) sophisticated, they might make use of a friend as a commitment device even if they had a slight (or even significant) distaste for studying with friends.

If a teacher wanted to help April Mae study more efficiently, what might he do? Taking the model literally, there is an obvious answer: just require a page every day. Such a policy will induce April Mae to choose the efficient one hour per day. Moreover, this policy would have no effect on June Mae. Hence, here we have an example of a policy that can have big benefits for people with present bias that does not affect standard exponential discounters.

A problem with this simple solution is that we probably shouldn't take the model literally. It is more realistic to assume day-to-day variation in the costs of reading, in which case the optimal strategy would involve more reading on low-cost days, less reading on high-cost days, and some "precautionary reading" early on to protect against high-cost days. If so, then requiring a page a day would likely make June Mae worse off. Even so, there is a natural compromise: Impose interim but not too micro-managed incentives. For instance, requiring 5 pages every 5 days in the certainty case would reduce April Mae's reading from 51 hours to about 39 hours and, even with uncertainty, leaves June Mae some flexibility.

In fact, an even better way to help April Mae with limited harm to June Mae is to use voluntary restrictions. Instead of requiring 30 pages in 30 days, as in our benchmark example, suppose the teacher offers students *at the start of the month* a choice between two sets of requirements. If they like, they can read 31 pages in 30 days, without any interim deadlines. Alternatively, they can be required to read at least 10 pages after 10 days, at least 20 pages after 20 days, and 30 pages after 30 days. Why the extra page in the former case? Because adding this extra work creates a small incentive to choose the interim deadlines. As a result, if the interim deadlines are too costly in terms of reducing flexibility, all types will choose the former option. But if the interim deadlines are not a big deal, everybody – naifs, sophisticates, and exponential discounters – will all choose the interim incentives.[15]

---

[15] As we discussed in Section 2, Ariely and Wertenbroch (2002) provide an experimental study of voluntary interim incentives.

Finally, there is a way to employ magnification here with a mechanism that we see quite a lot (largely for other reasons, but partly for present bias): Give people false deadlines. This raises perceived benefits of reading more now. A teacher can induce more efficient reading early on by people with present bias by saying that the 30 pages must be read in 15 days rather than 30 days – indeed, in our benchmark example, this would induce an hour of reading on day 1. Then, after a few days, the teacher can tell students that they really have 20 days to do the reading, and so forth. If students believed the teacher (which they shouldn't, and for credibility, moral, and other reasons, this is not a wise place to use false deadlines) the teacher could, even with uncertainty, greatly improve efficiency. (But unlike our other schemes, this *would* harm exponential discounters significantly.)

For our third example, we leave the realm of procrastination and consider instead overconsumption of harmful goods – specifically, whether people develop and maintain "bad habits." For both classically addictive substances and for all sorts of activities like diet, exercise, and lifestyle, researchers have started to pay more attention to the role of habit formation. We consider here in highly stylized form, an example of a bad habit. Suppose your happiness on day t is given by:

$$u_t \equiv \begin{cases} \rho_L \ln(x_t + 1) - px_t & \text{if } x_{t-1} = 0 \\ \rho_H \ln(x_t + 1) - px_t - (\Gamma + \gamma \ln(x_{t-1} + 1)) & \text{if } x_{t-1} > 0, \end{cases}$$

where p is the price of the addictive good, $x_t \geq 0$ is consumption of the addictive good on day t, and $\rho_L, \rho_H, \Gamma, \gamma > 0$ are taste parameters, with $\rho_H > \rho_L \geq \gamma$. This formulation reflects that the person allocates current income between the addictive good and a composite good – specifically, $-px_t$ reflects that expenditures on the addictive good reduce funds available for consumption of the composite good.

This formulation assumes a highly stylized version of addiction: If a person didn't consume at all last period, then she is unaddicted, whereas if she consumed any positive amount, she is addicted. But the model incorporates the two essential components of bad habits that have been much discussed in the economics literature. First, current consumption imposes a negative cost in the future – as reflected by the fact that if the person consumes x now, then she will incur a utility cost of $\Gamma + \gamma \ln(x + 1)$ next period.[16] Second, current consumption creates habit formation in the sense that it increases the benefits from future consumption – as reflected by the fact that consuming now raises the benefits from next period's consumption from $\rho_L \ln(x + 1)$ to $\rho_H \ln(x + 1)$.

It could be optimal to develop a bad habit, and whenever it is, people with self-control problems do so, although their steady-state consumption is suboptimally

---

[16] Herrnstein, Loewenstein, Prelec, and Vaughan (1993) labeled such effects "negative internalities."

large. Here, we focus on an example where it is not optimal to develop a bad habit. Specifically, we suppose that

$$
u_t \equiv \begin{cases} 15\ln(x_t + 1) - x_t & \text{if } x_{t-1} = 0 \\[2mm] 20\ln(x_t + 1) - x_t - (20 + 10\ln(x_{t-1} + 1)) & \text{if } x_{t-1} > 0. \end{cases}
$$

Consider how an exponential discounter with $\delta \approx 1$ would behave in this example. Because the incentive to consume is stronger when addicted than when unaddicted, this person would choose either an unaddicted steady state or an addicted steady state. In the unaddicted steady state, the person consumes $x_t = 0$ every period, and hence her instantaneous utility in all periods is 0. In the addicted steady state, she consumes $x_t = 9$ every period, and hence her instantaneous utility in all periods is $20\ln 10 - 9 - (20 + 10\ln 10) = -5.97$.[17] Because the unaddicted steady state is clearly better, an exponential discounter with $\delta \approx 1$ will choose the unaddicted steady state. Notice that this conclusion would hold even if the person started out addicted. For example, even if she had formed the habit in her youth, she would immediately stop consuming.

Consider next a naive hyperbolic discounter with $\beta = .8$ and $\delta \approx 1$. When thinking about the future, the naif, like the exponential discounter, views the unaddicted steady state as clearly better than the addicted steady state, and hence plans and expects never to consume in the future. Even so, her preference for immediate gratification might lead her to choose short-term consumption. In this example, if she starts out unaddicted, then she will not consume. Given the relatively small temptation to consume when unaddicted, she is not willing to incur the future costs even given her preference for immediate gratification.[18]

But suppose instead that she starts out with the habit – again, perhaps because she had consumed in her youth. If she thought her choice was to quit now or never, then she would quit, because she views the unaddicted steady state as clearly (essentially infinitely) better than the addicted steady state, and so no short-term temptation would lead her to choose a long-term addiction. But her choice is not to quit now or never. Rather, she also has the option to consume now and then quit tomorrow, and her preference for immediate gratification combined with the higher temptation when addicted in fact makes this her preferred option.[19] Moreover, because she feels this way on every day of her life, she would naively spend her entire life planning to quit in the near future.

Note several features of this example. First, once again we see that details that are irrelevant for standard exponential discounters matter for people with

---

[17] When addicted and consuming, optimal consumption x maximizes $20\ln(x + 1) - x - \delta 10\ln(x + 1) \approx 10\ln(x + 1) - x$, which yields $x = 9$.

[18] When unaddicted, the best x for short-term consumption maximizes $15\ln(x + 1) - x - \beta\delta 10\ln(x + 1) \approx 7\ln(x + 1) - x$, which yields $x = 6$. But since $15\ln(7) - 6 - \beta\delta[20 + 10\ln(7)] < 0$, the person prefers $x = 0$ to $x = 6$.

[19] When addicted, the best x for short-term consumption maximizes $20\ln(x + 1) - x - \beta\delta 10\ln(x + 1) \approx 12\ln(x + 1) - x$, which yields $x = 11$. And since $20\ln(12) - 11 - \beta\delta[20 + 10\ln(12)] > 0$, the person indeed prefers $x = 11$ to $x = 0$.

present bias. Here, initial conditions – whether a person starts out unaddicted or addicted – is irrelevant to exponential discounters. While this conclusion is not true for any example, it reflects that, for a reasonably patient exponential discounter, unless short-term transition costs are very large, the person will choose the best steady state. In contrast, because a person with present bias might naively procrastinate initiating the transition to a different steady state, initial conditions can determine lifetime outcomes.

Second, notice the distinction between people's choices and their life courses. Initially addicted naifs end up with a lifetime addiction, but they never chose this life course. Rather, on each day they are choosing merely one more day of addiction. But the end result is that they maintain a lifelong addiction despite the fact that on every day of their life they'd prefer quitting immediately.

Third, notice the power of prospective choice: If by market technology or by government regulation, she had to decide ahead of time – just a day ahead of time would be enough – whether to consume, then no matter the initial conditions she would end up choosing the unaddicted steady state.[20]

Our example suggests that people may be over-prone to maintain (and more generally to develop) bad habits. A natural policy response would be to tax such goods, because by raising the market price we can induce less consumption. Such a policy is a nice example of magnification: Because agents are prone to underweight the future costs of consumption, we might be able to help them to behave better by raising the monetary cost of consumption. Although such "sin" taxes might hurt those who consume optimally, Gruber and Koszegi (2004) and O'Donoghue and Rabin (2003, forthcoming) investigate this trade-off and demonstrate that sin taxes can often be welfare-improving; we'll return to this point in the next section.

It is also worth considering richer forms of incentives. For instance, sin licenses (or tax vouchers) may be a useful technique to induce people to make prospective decisions. Specifically, suppose we set a high presumptive tax but then let people buy in advance a license that exempts them from the tax this year. By setting the license fee equal to, say, the tax that would be paid on 100 cigarette packs, we can induce people to assess whether they plan to purchase more or less than 100 packs this year. Moreover, for those who choose not to buy the license, the high presumptive tax provides a motivation not to buy in the moment.

Consider a somewhat more speculative proposal. Suppose we impose a "clean-living" surcharge: anybody unhooked on this habit at any point pays $2 a day, and anybody hooked pays nothing. In addition, we offer a "quitting bonus" of $100 to anybody hooked who quits. How would people react? Un-hooked people, whether an exponential discounter or a naif, will choose to

---

[20] Extrapolating from our example, this type of framework generates implications for how people might react to quantity discounts, which are quite prevalent in the market (cartons of cigarettes vs. packs, big bags of chips vs. small). Such reactions can provide a hint as to whether people want or expect to consume the good in the future, and indeed Wertenbroch (1998) has documented that people tend to buy "vice" goods in smaller quantities than "virtue" goods.

become an addict only if being an addict is not very bad – less bad than paying $2 a day. And they might choose constantly starting and stopping, but only if doing so is worth $49 a day.

What about those who are addicted? First note that an exponential discounter, no matter her utility function, would not plausibly quit in response to this policy. For any plausible impatience, it would never be worth receiving a one-time $100 payment in return for having to pay $2 for the rest of her life. Hence, any rational addict will not be influenced by this policy. In contrast, naifs might quit in response to this policy. The reason is *not* because they are tempted by the $100 now in exchange for $2 every day for life – like exponential discounters, for plausible impatience they view that as a bad deal. The reason is rather that naive addicts might already be *planning* to quit soon, and so they expect to be paying the $2 per day for life in any event. If so, their choice boils down to choosing between $100 and pain of quitting now vs. $100 and pain of quitting tomorrow, and the former might be better.

4   HETEROGENEITY AND FLEXIBILITY

A central theme in the emerging literature on incentives for present-biased people is the importance of accommodating heterogeneity among agents and facilitating flexibility in behavior. Casual evidence suggests that people vary a great deal in their degree of self-control problems, their degree of awareness of self-control problems, and (of course) in their intrinsic tastes for different activities. This heterogeneity complicates incentive design because, as we highlighted in Section 3, optimal incentives differ for different types. Moreover, even individual agents will typically face uncertainty about their own future tastes, needs, outside options, and constraints. As a result, optimal incentives may need to permit some flexibility to agents.

Researchers have begun to address both issues. Heterogeneity has been most discussed in the recent literature on designing paternalistic incentives where there is concern that interventions designed to help people who make errors might cause significant harm to people who do not make errors. One strand of literature has dealt with this issue by identifying non-intrusive interventions that would combat errors while attempting to impose little or no harm on fully rational people. This basic approach has been put forth by various authors under various labels: "cautious paternalism" (O'Donoghue and Rabin 1999*c*), "asymmetric paternalism" (Camerer, Issacharoff, Loewenstein, O'Donoghue, and Rabin 2003), "libertarian paternalism" (Sunstein and Thaler 2003*a*, 2003*b*), and "benign paternalism" (Choi, Laibson, Madrian, and Metrick 2003). Although this approach has been applied to a broad set of errors, present bias is a common focus, and principles #1, #2, and #3 from Section 3 are particularly pertinent for this goal.

In O'Donoghue and Rabin (2003, forthcoming), we directly address heterogeneity by deriving optimal policy as a function of the distribution of types in the population. Specifically, we investigate consumption of goods that generate immediate consumption utility but future health costs, where people differ both in terms of their degree of present bias and in terms of their tastes for the good. We show that taxing such goods can yield significant benefits for present-biased people by inducing them to reduce over-consumption, while at the same time such taxes may have very little effect on the utility of fully rational people. Moreover, if tax proceeds are returned to consumers as a uniform lump sum, then there is a net redistribution from present-biased people to fully rational people, and as a result such taxes can sometimes end up making everybody better off – that is, they can create a Pareto improvement.

Heterogeneity is also relevant for firms concerned with either efficiency or exploitation – e.g., incentives designed to exploit people with present bias might end up losing revenue on those without it. Indeed, DellaVigna and Malmendier (2004) derive optimal two-part tariffs for a monopolist facing present-biased consumers, and they show that the optimal contract may look very different for people with sophisticated present bias, people with naive present bias, and those without present bias. They do not, however, consider the screening problem. More recently, Eliaz and Spiegler (forthcoming) investigate a contracting model in which a firm attempts to screen sophisticates from naifs so as to promote efficient exchange (efficient commitment) with sophisticates while at the same time exploiting naifs.[21]

Researchers have also started to address the need for flexibility. In many analyses, it has been implicit. For instance, O'Donoghue and Rabin (1999*b*) investigate incentives to combat procrastination when agents face day-to-day uncertainty in the opportunity cost of engaging in an activity. In such an environment, it is typically not optimal to impose an immediate deadline because the agent should be permitted some flexibility to find a good time to complete the task. Recently, Amador, Werning, and Angeletos (2006) explicitly investigate the optimal trade-off between commitment and flexibility in a savings-consumption model. (They find, for instance, that imposing a minimal level of savings is always a part of the optimal solution.)

An important aspect, in our view, that is missing from existing research is the use of more subtle, "voluntary" screening devices. If our goal is to implement a policy that combats present bias, but we are worried that this policy might hurt people who don't have present bias, why not let people voluntarily select in

---

[21] Formal analyses of heterogeneous populations are important to advance research on present bias. Demonstrating, for instance, the extent to which proposed incentives to combat present bias are robust to the existence of vast numbers of fully self-controlled agents will highlight that the merits of such incentive schemes do not rely on an assumption that virtually everyone is present-biased. It is also our hope that research acknowledging and investigating the prevalence of different degrees of self-control problems will help to rebut the over-frequent supposition among doctors, preachers, and laypeople that certain activities reflect purely unwarranted pursuit of immediate gratification. Research that incorporates self-control problems and carefully identifies those instances when consumption is actually optimal presumably has a better chance of persuading skeptics that such instances are indeed optimal than does research that a priori assumes that whatever a person does is optimal.

advance whether to be subject to the policy. If everyone were fully sophisticated, such a scheme can be very effective because we can count on all agents to choose whatever incentives are best for them. A problem arises, however, when there are naive agents because they may not see the value of the policy. Even so, we can deal with this problem by providing an ex ante incentive to volunteer – perhaps framed in reverse where the default is being subject to the policy but for a small price people can buy out the restrictions. We suspect this technique will play a prominent role as the literature evolves.

Voluntary incentives may be particularly important as a means to deal with the need for flexibility. Perhaps the most important aspect of the need for flexibility is heterogeneity in this need. For some agents, flexibility is quite important, while for others it is not. Much as for heterogeneity more generally, we suspect that the best way to deal with heterogeneity in the need for flexibility is via voluntary commitments. In our cumulative-procrastination example, for instance, we discussed how we could let people choose between having slightly more total work and lots of flexibility vs. slightly less total work but reduced flexibility. If uncertainty is high and thus flexibility is valuable, people will choose the former; if they have relatively little value for flexibility, they will choose the latter.

Indeed, procrastination is a useful context in which to make these ideas even more concrete. Our examples in Section 3 illustrate the usefulness of deadlines for combating procrastination. Deadlines are perhaps most important for "optional" tasks. People face many tasks in their lifetime that are on net beneficial but need not be done. These might be mundane tasks – such as building shelves in the garage or investing in a better technology for mowing the lawn – or they might be more economically relevant tasks – such as investing in human capital or improving one's portfolio of financial investments. Because such tasks have no inherent deadline, procrastination can lead to infinite delay – that is, present-biased people may never complete the task even when they would prefer to complete the task early on rather than never. In such cases, imposing *any* not-too-long-away deadline can yield significant benefits.

A major worry with any final deadline, however, is the need for flexibility – with a final deadline, if due to bad luck a person misses the deadline, she has lost the opportunity to ever do the task. To address this worry, there is another type of deadline that makes use of the difference between the nature of procrastinatory delay and that of rational delay. To the extent that procrastination is driven by a naive belief that a task will be completed in the near future, putting limits on the frequency with which one can carry out tasks can help to combat procrastination. If a person can take a job-certification course on any day for the rest of her life, then she might repeatedly delay based on a daily belief that she'll do it tomorrow or within a few days. If instead the job-certification course is offered, say, only once per month, then the person can no longer justify delay based on a naive belief that she'll do it soon. Rather, she'll be forced to recognize that delay now means at least a one-month delay, and if the consequences of a one-month delay – e.g., lower wages for the next 30 days – are sufficiently large, she won't delay.[22]

While this technique solves the final-deadline problem, it can still be critiqued for lack of flexibility – if it turns out that a person cannot make the course on the night it is offered, she must wait a month before her next opportunity. Here, voluntary incentives can be used as a means to address this concern. For instance, we might offer people two choices for a job-certification course. For an upfront fee of $100, they can take the course on any day they like; but for an upfront fee of $90, they can take the course only on the first of any given month (and we do not permit people to switch from their initial choice). People who face significant day-to-day uncertainty and thus put a high value on flexibility will choose the former option; people who face less day-to-day uncertainty will choose the latter option.

In addition to flexibility, we should also be worried about heterogeneity in the propensity to procrastinate, due either to heterogeneity in present bias or heterogeneity in how unpleasant a person finds the task. There are in fact other ways to combat procrastination that deal with such heterogeneity. One technique is to create direct incentives (rewards) for people to accelerate their plans. Suppose, for instance, that $20 vouchers are given to heroin addicts who maintain clean urine tests for a month. Heroin addicts who rationally prefer to remain heroin addicts presumably will not be influenced much by such vouchers – if they are influenced, it is either because they barely preferred to remain heroin addicts or because temporary restraint is not very costly. But among heroin addicts who had been planning to commence withdrawal, such small financial rewards can lead them to immediately initiate such plans when they otherwise would have procrastinated. Similarly, small vouchers, especially dated ones, by commercial enterprises that encourage people to sign up for a service are much more likely to have an effect on people planning to join such a service than those that never plan to.

A second technique is to focus less on combating procrastination and more on limiting the harm from procrastination. In particular, in many cases, policymakers or firms get to specify default outcomes that are implemented unless people opt out. By choosing these defaults wisely, it can be possible to implement better outcomes. A nice example of such defaults are in the Save More Tomorrow (SMART) Plan that has recently been marketed by Thaler and Benartzi (2004). They operate under the presumption that people want to initiate savings plans (for retirement), but have difficulty initiating those plans. To overcome this tendency, they offer people the option to set their default outcome to increased saving beginning in the future, with regular increases in the amount saved up to some limit, all implemented via automatic withdrawals

---

[22] Even better – to the extent it is possible – the course could be offered every day, but certifications for the month are processed only on, say, the last day of the month. Then the person could still take the course on any day, but the last day of the month would loom large as a deadline to receive the benefits for the upcoming month.

from one's paycheck. They document that many people indeed choose to sign up for such plans and end up saving more than those who do not sign up for the plan.

A third technique is to promote "active choice" – to the extent possible, force people to actually make a decision, or at least make them perceive that they are forced to make a decision. This technique was first proposed by Choi, Laibson, Madrian, and Metrick (2004), who studied a firm whose 401(k) plan unintentionally set up such a situation. Specifically, new employees were given the enrollment form for the company's 401(k) plan as part of a package of forms that needed to be filled out within 30 days. While some of these forms really were required, the 401(k) enrollment form was not – if the employee failed to turn it in, the employee just wasn't enrolled in the plan. Even so, employees seem to have viewed it as a requirement, and as a result more employees signed up for the 401(k) plan relative to what happened when the company later moved to an online system that permitted enrollment on any day.

5   DISCUSSION AND CONCLUSION

In this section, we discuss some broader issues and conclude. We have described how people seem to have a time-inconsistent taste for immediate gratification, and we have explored how this taste can lead to different reactions to incentives than does the standard economic model of choice. Present bias is, however, only one improvement in how to conceptualize people's behavior. Researchers have started to investigate other improvements, and these also can lead to different reactions to incentives.

In the realm of intertemporal choice, a related improvement is "temptation utility," as formulated by Gul and Pesendorfer (2001), wherein people find it unpleasant to have unchosen tempting options. In our example of a bad habit, for instance, if consuming the good is more tempting than not consuming, then a person may prefer to consume the good so as to avoid the temptation disutility that she would experience while not consuming. Moreover, even if she would be able to resist the temptation, she might in advance attempt to eliminate her access to the good so as to eliminate the temptation disutility that she would feel while not consuming. Because the details of incentives can influence the extent to which people experience temptation disutility, then, much as for present bias, more than just gestalt incentives matter.[23] Another related improvement in the realm of intertemporal choice is "projection bias," as formulated by Loewenstein, O'Donoghue, and Rabin (2003), wherein people underappreciate

---

[23] Indeed, a few recent papers have studied the design of incentives when people experience tempta-tion utility – see for instance Amador, Werning, and Angeletos (2006), and Esteban, Miyagawa, and Shum (2005). Temptation utility and (fully sophisticated) present bias are sometimes dis-cussed as mutually exclusive models, in part because they often yield similar predictions. In our view, however, these models reflect two distinct psychological phenomena that might both influence behavior.

taste changes – specifically, perceived future tastes are in between actual future tastes and current tastes. In our example of a bad habit, if an unaddicted person underappreciates the negative cost associated with being addicted, she might choose to become an addict even when she shouldn't. Again, because the details of incentives can influence both current and future tastes, more than just gestalt incentives matter.

It is instructive to compare the implications for incentive design of these different ways to improve the standard economic model. The models of temptation utility and of fully sophisticated present bias share two features: (i) people correctly predict their future behavior, and (ii) people's ex ante preferences correspond to their normative preferences. Two implications follow. First, from the perspective of designing incentives to promote better outcomes, we can never do better than eliciting from individuals what they view as their optimal commitments. Second, from the perspective of designing exploitative incentives, the best we can do is to create temptations and to undermine commitments. Contrast these conclusions with the models of projection bias and of naive present bias, where people might incorrectly predict future behavior. For such problems, designing incentives becomes more difficult. For incentives designed to produce better outcomes, it may be necessary, as we have discussed for naive present bias, to create incentives to encourage reluctant agents to take on commitments. And for exploitative incentives, it may be possible to induce people to pay for things that they will end up not valuing.

Indeed, there exist real-world examples that seem naturally interpreted as exploitation of naivete, where firms offer long-term contracts that take advantage of naive mispredictions. For instance, DellaVigna and Malmendier (2006) argue that health clubs may encourage long-term contracts to take advantage of people's naive beliefs that they will frequently use the health club. Shui and Ausubel (2004) describe how consumers seem to underpredict future credit-card borrowing, and hence are too sensitive to the introductory interest rate and pay too little attention to the long-term (post-introductory) interest rate. If so, then we might expect credit-card companies to take advantage of this propensity by pushing cards with low introductory rates and high long-term rates (although it is unclear how competition will affect their ability to make money in this way). More generally, there seems to be numerous examples of firms attempting to make the default outcome continued subscription to some service. The health club studied by DellaVigna and Malmendier, for instance, used the common approach of having a monthly membership that is automatically renewed by credit card, and they found evidence of significant procrastination in cancelling the membership – specifically, people continued to pay for the membership long after their last use of the health club.

We have emphasized throughout how the existence of present bias creates a need for incentives to promote better outcomes. An important issue is to what extent will the market provide such incentives. Researchers have long discussed how sophisticates would demand commitment devices, and have pointed to the existence of Christmas clubs, fat farms, and other commitment devices provided by the market as evidence that people have self-control problems. One might further infer from these examples that the market is an effective provider of commitment devices, and hence there is limited need for any "paternalistic" interventions.

Recently, however, economists have demonstrated that markets might, in fact, undermine the scope for commitment devices. In particular, a commitment device will work only to the extent that another firm doesn't come along offering ways to undo that commitment. For instance, Laibson (1997) demonstrates how illiquid savings instruments that tie up people's wealth in the short term can be a valuable commitment device to combat under-saving due to present bias. But he then discusses how the rapid expansion of the credit-card industry in the early 1990s might have undermined this commitment device by giving people the ability to borrow against that illiquid wealth. DellaVigna and Malmendier (2004) and Koszegi (forthcoming) explore more systematically the types of situations in which the market is likely to be able or unable to provide commitment devices. They show, for instance, that for investment goods for which the optimal commitment involves low per-unit prices (below marginal cost), there is little scope for other firms to undermine this commitment, whereas for indulgent goods for which the optimal commitment involves high per-unit prices (above marginal cost), there is significant scope for other firms to undermine this commitment.

Researchers are only beginning to study incentive design when people have present bias (and other behavioral phenomena). For such people, the usual intuitions still apply – e.g., in a standard moral-hazard model, the principal still faces the usual trade-off between insurance and incentives. But new intuitions also arise, and in particular details that would be mostly irrelevant to standard agents can become quite important. We hope that by describing some general principles, and by highlighting the importance of heterogeneity and flexibility, this paper will help lay the groundwork for this emerging literature.

References

AINSLIE, G. (1991): "Derivation of 'Rational' Economic Behavior from Hyperbolic Discount Curves," *American Economic Review*, 81, 334–340.

———— (1992): *Picoeconomics: The Strategic Interaction of Successive Motivational States Within the Person*. New York: Cambridge University Press.

AINSLIE, G. AND N. HASLAM (1992a): "Self-Control," in *Choice Over Time*, ed. by G. Loewenstein and J. Elster. New York: Russell Sage Foundation, 177–209.

———— (1992b): "Hyperbolic Discounting," in *Choice Over Time*, ed. by G. Loewenstein and J. Elster. New York: Russell Sage Foundation, 57–92.

AKERLOF, G. (1991): "Procrastination and Obedience," *American Economic Review*, 81, 1–19.

AMADOR, M., I. WERNING, and G.-M. ANGELETOS (2006): "Commitment vs. Flexibility," *Econometrica*, 74, 365–396.

ANGELETOS, G.-M., D. LAIBSON, A. REPETTO, J. TOBACMAN, AND S. WEINBERG (2001): "The Hyperbolic Buffer Stock Model: Calibration, Simulation, and Empirical Evaluation," *Journal of Economic Perspectives*, 15, 47–68.

ARIELY, D. AND K. WERTENBROCH (2002): "Procrastination, Deadlines, and Performance: Self-Control by Precommitment," *Psychological Science*, 13, 219–224.

BANNISTER, P. (2004): "25 Fascinating Facts About Personal Debt," September 20, 2004 (http://www.bankrate.com/brm/news/debt/debtguide2004/debt-trivial.asp).

BENABOU, R. AND J. TIROLE (2002): "Self-Confidence and Personal Motivation," *Quarterly Journal of Economics*, 117, 871–915.

CAMERER, C., S. ISSACHAROFF, G. LOEWENSTEIN, T. O'DONOGHUE, AND M. RABIN (2003): "Regulation for Conservatives: Behavioral Economics and the Case for 'Asymmetric Paternalism'," *University of Pennsylvania Law Review*, 151, 1211–1254.

CARRILLO, J. AND T. MARIOTTI (2000): "Strategic Ignorance as a Self-Disciplining Device," *Review of Economic Studies*, 67, 529–544.

CHOI, J., D. LAIBSON, B. MADRIAN, AND A. METRICK (2003): "Optimal Defaults," *American Economic Review (Papers and Proceedings)*, 93, 180–185.

——— (2004): "Optimal Defaults and Active Decisions," Unpublished Manuscript, Harvard University.

DELLAVIGNA, S. AND U. MALMENDIER (2004): "Contract Design and Self-Control: Theory and Evidence," *Quarterly Journal of Economics*, 119, 353–402.

——— (2006): "Paying Not to Go to the Gym," *American Economic Review*, 96, 694–719.

DELLAVIGNA, S. AND M. D. PASERMAN (2005): "Job Search and Impatience," *Journal of Labor Economics*, 23, 527–588.

ELIAZ, K. AND R. SPIEGLER (forthcoming): "Contracting with Diversely Naive Agents," *Review of Economic Studies*.

ESTEBAN, S., E. MIYAGAWA, AND M. SHUM (2005): "Nonlinear Pricing with Self-Control Preferences," Unpublished Manuscript, Pennsylvania State University.

FANG, H. AND D. SILVERMAN (2004): "Time-Inconsistency and Welfare Program Participation: Evidence from the NLSY," Unpublished Manuscript, Yale University and University of Michigan.

FREDERICK, S., G. LOEWENSTEIN, AND T. O'DONOGHUE (2002): "Time Discounting and Time Preference: A Critical Review," *Journal of Economic Literature*, 40, 351–401.

GUL, F. AND W. PESENDORFER (2001): "Temptation and Self-Control," *Econometrica*, 69, 1403–1435.

GRUBER, J. AND B. KOSZEGI (2001): "Is Addiction 'Rational'? Theory and Evidence," *Quarterly Journal of Economics*, 116, 1261–1303.

——— (2004): "Tax Incidence When Individuals are Time-Inconsistent: The Case of Cigarette Excise Taxes," *Journal of Public Economics*, 88, 1959–1987.

GRUBER, J. AND S. MULLAINATHAN (2005): "Do Cigarette Taxes Make Smokers Happier?" *B.E. Journals: Advances in Economic Analysis & Policy*, 5, Article 4.

HENRIQUES, D. B. (2004): "Seeking Quick Loans, Soldiers Race Into High-Interest Traps," *New York Times*, December 7, 2004.

HERRNSTEIN, R., G. LOEWENSTEIN, D. PRELEC, AND W. VAUGHAN, JR. (1993): "Utility Maximization and Melioration: Internalities in Individual Choice," *Journal of Behavioral Decision Making*, 6, 149–185.

KOSZEGI, B. (forthcoming): "On the Feasibility of Market Solutions to Self-Control Problems," *Swedish Economic Policy Review*.

LAIBSON, D. (1997): "Hyperbolic Discounting and Golden Eggs," *Quarterly Journal of Economics*, 112, 443–477.

―――― (1998): "Life-Cycle Consumption and Hyperbolic Discount Functions," *European Economic Review*, 42, 861–871.

LAIBSON, D., A. REPETTO, AND J. TOBACMAN (1998): "Self-Control and Saving for Retirement," *Brookings Papers on Economic Activity*, 1, 91–196.

―――― (2005): "Estimating Discount Functions from Lifecycle Consumption Choices," Unpublished Manuscript, Harvard University.

LOEWENSTEIN, G. AND D. PRELEC (1992): "Anomalies in Intertemporal Choice: Evidence and an Interpretation," *Quarterly Journal of Economics*, 107, 573–597.

LOEWENSTEIN, G., T. O'DONOGHUE, AND M. RABIN (2003): "Projection Bias in Predicting Future Utility," *Quarterly Journal of Economics*, 118, 1209–1248.

O'DONOGHUE, T. AND M. RABIN (1999*a*): "Doing It Now or Later," *American Economic Review*, 89, 103–124.

―――― (1999*b*): "Incentives for Procrastinators," *Quarterly Journal of Economics*, 114, 769–816.

―――― (1999*c*): "Procrastination in Preparing for Retirement," in *Behavioral Dimensions of Retirement Economics*, ed. by H. Aaron. Washington DC and New York: Brookings Institution Press and Russell Sage Foundation, 125–156.

―――― (2001): "Choice and Procrastination," *Quarterly Journal of Economics*, 116, 121–160.

―――― (2003): "Studying Optimal Paternalism, Illustrated by a Model of Sin Taxes," *American Economic Review (Papers and Proceedings)*, 93, 186–191.

―――― (forthcoming): "Optimal Sin Taxes," *Journal of Public Economics*.

PASERMAN, M. D. (2004): "Job Search and Hyperbolic Discounting: Structural Estimation and Policy Evaluation," Unpublished Manuscript, Hebrew University.

PHELPS, E. S. AND R. A. POLLAK (1968): "On Second-Best National Saving and Game-Equilibrium Growth," *Review of Economic Studies*, 35, 185–199.

POLLAK, R. A. (1968): "Consistent Planning," *Review of Economic Studies*, 35, 201–208.

SCHELLING, T. C. (1978): "Egonomics, or the Art of Self-Management," *American Economic Review*, 68, 290–294.

―――― (1984): "Self-Command in Practice, in Policy, and in a Theory of Rational Choice," *American Economic Review*, 74, 1–11.

SHAPIRO, J. M. (2005): "Is There a Daily Discount Rate? Evidence from the Food Stamp Nutrition Cycle," *Journal of Public Economics*, 89, 303-325

SHUI, H. AND L. M. AUSUBEL (2004): "Time Inconsistency in the Credit Market," Unpublished Manuscript, University of Maryland.

STEPHENS INCORPORATED INVESTMENT BANKERS (2004): "Stephens Payday Loan Industry Report, 2004."

STROTZ, R. H. (1956): "Myopia and Inconsistency in Dynamic Utility Maximization," *Review of Economic Studies*, 23, 165–180.

SUNSTEIN, C. AND R. H. THALER (2003*a*): "Libertarian Paternalism," *American Economic Review (Papers and Proceedings)*, 93, 175–179.

―――― (2003*b*): "Libertarian Paternalism Is Not An Oxymoron," *University of Chicago Law Review*, 70, 1159–1202.

THALER, R. H. (1981): "Some Empirical Evidence on Dynamic Inconsistency," *Economic Letters*, 8, 201–207.

THALER, R. H. AND S. BENARTZI (2004): "Save More Tomorrow: Using Behavioral Economics to Increase Employee Saving," *Journal of Political Economy*, 112, 164–187.

THALER, R. H. AND G. LOEWENSTEIN (1989): "Anomalies: Intertemporal Choice," *Journal of Economic Perspectives*, 3, 181–193.

THALER, R. H. AND H. M. SHEFRIN (1981): "An Economic Theory of Self-Control," *Journal of Political Economy*, 89, 392–406.

WERTENBROCH, K. (1998): "Consumption Self-Control by Rationing Purchase Quantities of Virtue and Vice," *Marketing Science*, 17, 317–337.

CHAPTER 9

Discussion of "Behavioral Economics"

"Behavioral Economics" (Colin Camerer) and "Incentives and Self-Control" (Ted O'Donoghue and Matthew Rabin)

Ariel Rubinstein*

1 WHAT IS THE BEHAVIORAL ECONOMICS "REVOLUTION"?

For me, economics is a collection of ideas and conventions that economists accept and use to reason with. Namely, it is a culture. Behavioral economics represents a transformation of that culture. Nonetheless, as pointed out by Camerer and Loewenstein (2003), its methods are pretty much the same as those introduced by the game theory revolution. At the core of most models in behavioral economics there are still agents who maximize a preference relation over some space of consequences and the solution in most cases still involves standard equilibrium concepts. However, the behavioral economists are not committed to what is usually referred to as rational motivations. An economic fable (or a model, as we would call it) that has at its core fairness, envy, present-bias and the like, is by now not only permitted but even preferred.

Why now? Perhaps, economists have finally realized that orthodox economic models are too unrealistic and dogmatic. And perhaps it is the result of our constant search for new directions in research. One might also ask why other ideas (such as those of bounded rationality) are less welcome than those of behavioral economics. I think that this is because the profession prefers progress in small steps. The models of behavioral economics are not that different from those of applied economics and thus are not perceived as a threat.

The extent of this transformation may go beyond the topics discussed in this session. For example, behavioral economics may influence the way economics is applied to political issues. It also reintroduces ideological questions such as to what extent governments should paternalistically "repair" biases and fallacies.

* I would like to thank Rani Spiegler for the many discussions we had on behavioral economics during the last few years. I could not imagine writing this essay without the benefit of his comments, insights, ideas and criticism.

2   THEORETICAL BEHAVIORAL ECONOMICS

A paper in behavioral economics typically begins with a description of a real life phenomenon that cannot easily be explained by the standard rational man paradigm. To support the case, references are brought from research in psychology and sometimes even studies of animal behavior. In O'Donoghue and Rabin's discussion all that is borrowed from psychology is the idea that *some* people, in *some* cases, have *some* present-bias. I doubt we need psychological justification in order to make that assumption. Each of us can think of situations in which we exhibit present-bias. However, it is also easy to think of situations where we have *future*-bias. For example, say I have one piece of expensive chocolate. Whenever I am about to eat it, I think to myself: Why not leave it for the future and enjoy the feeling of expectation? The outcome: I leave it so long that it is no longer edible. The psychology literature tries to understand the circumstances where a phenomenon exists. But, in order to just assume that present-bias often exists, it is sufficient to cite casual observation as is done in other fields of economics.

The typical paper in this field then moves on to modeling the bias. The basic framework used to model present-bias is not new and goes back to Strotz (1956). What is new is that time inconsistency is being applied to a variety of economic settings. Ten years ago it was difficult to publish a paper in the QJE which included a "present-bias" assumption. These days it is almost impossible to publish a paper in that same journal that ignores present-bias, let alone one which criticizes the approach.

O'Donoghue and Rabin adopted the $\beta, \delta = 1$ model. They repeatedly make the point that the standard time consistent model is wrong and that the β, δ model is correct. I agree that the β, δ model is a very interesting example of an analytically convenient functional form, but I find the claim that these models are more accurate and realistic to be misleading. Note that the introduction of time inconsistency requires the addition of strong assumptions about the way that different selves interact. In order to complete the model, behavioral economists resort to the standard assumptions. Usually these involve either naive or sophisticated agents. Naivete is not realistic since agents never learn. Sophistication is unrealistic since it suffers from the problems of subgame perfection. An agent is super-rational in the sense that he perfectly anticipates his future selves and arrives at equilibrium between them. Present-bias is a realistic phenomenon, but the combination of the β, δ preferences with naivete or sophistication assumptions makes the model even more unrealistic than time consistency models.

O'Donoghue and Rabin go out of their way to beat, if I may use their own phrase, the "dead parrot" of full rationality. Of course there are many facts that are hard to reconcile with full rationality. But the psychology and economics literature has replaced a dead parrot with one that is equally dead. If the "time consistent" model is wrong, then the β, δ model is equally wrong. It can easily be disproved experimentally (see Rubinstein (2003, 2004a)), but the β, δ fans apparently prefer to ignore experimental evidence that does not go their way.

The typical paper in this field then moves on to demonstrate that a particular standard economic result is not robust to the introduction of psychological bias. I cannot be more sympathetic to this research agenda and, in fact, I myself have been involved in research of a similar nature. In particular, I found O'Donoghue and Rabin's question regarding the design of incentive schemes to overcome time biases to be so interesting that it would remain of interest even if the authors add some modest reservations to their claims.

A major drawback of the behavioral economics models is that they lack both the elegance and generality that characterize the literature of general equilibrium and game theory. The typical paper is messy and terribly long. Simple ideas are lost in poorly formulated models and numerical examples.

If I were the authors, I would have presented the issue using the following simple model:

You bring your child to a street fair to buy him a toy. It is available in two versions – G and B. You are unable to assess the quality of the toy and rely on your child's judgement. There are T stands in a row and you plan to walk with your child from one edge of the row to the other. Each stand sells one of the versions and you assign probability 0.5 to the possibility that a particular stand sells G.

Both you and your child prefer to buy the G version rather than the B version. However, your child is a $\beta, \delta = 1$ type. He is present-biased and will settle for the B version even if he expects to find the G version with very high probability at another stand. Without your intervention, the trip will end at the first stand and the child will buy whatever version the first stand is selling. You are not happy about this and seek a way to trick your child into making the right choice.

You have $1 in your pocket. Your child prefers $G + \$1$ in the future over B today. On the other hand, he prefers G right away to $G + \$1$ in the future. A strategy determines, for every t, whether or not to pay the child a dollar if he buys the toy at the t'th stand. Your aim is to maximize the probability that your child buys G.

If the child is naive and T is large, an optimal strategy would be to promise to pay the dollar if the child buys the toy during the last K periods where K is relatively small. The reason is that when facing B in the first phase, the naive agent expects to obtain $G + \$1$ in the second phase with very high probability. Thus, he will pass over B in the first phase in anticipation of receiving $G + \$1$ in the second phase. The result is that he will almost always buy G in the first $T - K$ periods without the parent having to actually pay the $1.

As for the sophisticated child, it is not difficult to see that you can at most increase the probability that he buys G to $3/4$ by promising the $1 if the child buys the toy at the second stand.

This simple example has every advantage over Rabin's presentation: it is simple, non-trivial and avoids the long calculations.

Comment: One criticism made of behavioral economics is the arbitrariness of the welfare criterion. If an agent is a collection of selves, then why should the utility of the first self be the basis for welfare considerations? If an agent's utility is also affected by disappointment or envy, why should a utility function devoid of psychological effects serve as the welfare measure? Gul and Pesendorfer (2005) refer to several functional forms used in behavioral economics that have a psychological element. Gul and Pesendorfer point out that the behavior in a typical behavioral economics paper is consistent with many utility functions that have the assumed functional form and therefore welfare considerations cannot be derived from an agent's behavior. Since they only accept economic entities that are rooted in behavior, they are led to fundamentally reject the behavioral economics methodology.

I disagree with them. Behavioral economics makes it clear that one must make assumptions about the relation between the preferences that explain behavior and the preferences used in the welfare criterion. Even when an agent is perfectly rational in the sense that he systematically maximizes some function, it is not at all obvious that the utility function that explains his behavior should be inserted into the welfare considerations. An extreme case would be an agent who is acting against what he perceives to be his own best interests. That is, he maximizes the function $-v$, where v represents his own perceived interests. It would be absurd to use the function $-v$ as a positive component in the welfare analysis. More generally, once psychological effects enter into the calculus, there is no escape from separating welfare and behavior. The behavioral economics literature uses specific functional forms to state a particular relation between behavior and welfare.

3 "RELYING ON EVIDENCE"

The "behavioral economics" literature relies heavily on evidence from experiments, animal behavior and neuroeconomics. I am not happy with the way it is done and would like to comment on each in turn.

(i) Experiments

An experiment in economics starts from a basic intuition. Anybody can do an experiment but doing a good one that exposes a psychological phenomenon in a crystal clear manner is an art. If there is value in doing experiments, rather than making do with casual empiricism, it is only when they are done and assessed very carefully. It is my impression that intuitive and "sexy" results are gladly accepted by behavioral economists without sufficient criticism.

Let me illustrate the point with the well-known paper by Gneezy and Rustichini (2000). Camerer describes the paper in the following words: "To discourage parents from picking their children up late, a day-care center instituted a fine for each minute that parents arrived late at the center. The fine had the perverse effect of *increasing* parental lateness. The authors postulated that the fine eliminated the moral disapprobation associated with arriving late and replaced it with a simple monetary cost that some parents decided was worth incurring. Their results show that the effect of price changes can be quite different than in economic theory when behavior has moral components that wages and prices alter." Gneezy and Rustichini (2000) is indeed based on a very appealing intuition. The behavioral economics literature has wholeheartedly adopted the paper. Camerer, Loewenstein and Rabin (2003) included this paper in their impressive collection of selected papers and Levitt and Dubner (2005) discussed it in Chapter 1 of their new best seller *Freakonomics*.

Being a skeptic, I found it difficult to believe that the experiment could have been carried out as described. I know Israel quite well. It is a country where rules are rarely enforced. It is hard for me to believe that teachers would really fine a parent who is ten minutes late. In my experience, any excuse for lateness is accepted. Furthermore, it is impossible for me to imagine that Israeli teachers would have kept even roughly accurate records of late arrivals with noisy parents crowding around the entrance of the school to take home their screaming kids.

Therefore, I at least want to know what the procedure was for collecting data. The paper does not provide such details. In correspondence, one of the authors claimed that professional standards had been maintained. Apparently, an RA went to the schools once a week and asked the assistant teacher who was late the previous week. There was no attempt to control the accuracy of the RA's records. Oddly, I was not allowed to talk with the teachers.

The authors claim that their findings are "statistically significant." But, as always, the statistical calculations do not take into account the reliability of the collected data. What is the probability that teachers actually implemented the incentive scheme and that assistant teachers accurately reported late arrivals?

Again, I do not doubt the truth and originality of the conclusion that introducing a small fine might be counterproductive. In fact, Heyman and Arieli (2004) even demonstrated the point experimentally. But I am in doubt as to whether the conclusions were indeed confirmed experimentally in Haifa kindergartens.

Who is to blame? The overly motivated authors; the refereeing process, which puts too much trust in authors' data; myself, since I knew about the faulty procedure and did not bother to write a comment (which would probably have been rejected); and what is most relevant to the current discussion – those behavioral economists who gave the paper wide exposure without critical assessment.

Comment: The reader is encouraged to read Gneezy and Rustichini's response (see http://arielrubinstein.tau.ac.il/papers/WC05/GR.pdf). The fact that the authors feel that all standard professional rules were kept strengthens my argument (which is not directed at any particular experimenter) regarding the uncritical way in which experimental results are accepted.

I should clarify that, at the time, one of the authors agreed that he should delay publication until a new experiment with better monitoring of data collection was conducted. Eventually, the paper was published as is.

I was pleased to learn that the authors decided to redo the experiment more carefully and that a draft of the paper reporting the new results is available (see http://arielrubinstein.tau.ac.il/papers/WC05/GR1.pdf). The burden of proof is on the authors, and I cannot dismiss my doubts about the method of data collection in both experiments. Although the authors report that they are still working on the data and that they have asked the teachers for permission to be interviewed by me, the author who directed the experiment has just informed me that he has lost the names of the kindergarten teachers who participated in the experiment.

(ii) Animal Behavior

The behavioral economics literature often quotes results from animal behavior to support an assumption. Laibson (1986) quotes results on pigeon behavior (see Ainslie (1992)) as support for the β, δ model. Glimcher, Dorris and Bayer (2005) cite Harper's (1982) ducks who reach Nash equilibrium in an allocation game in a pond at Cambridge. Camerer quotes Dorris and Glimcher (2004) who claim that: "Monkeys can also learn to approximate mixed strategies in games."

Why is animal behavior relevant? I have no idea. If the behavioral economists are trying to say that the behavior of human beings is rooted in their physical nature, I imagine they are right. Indeed, we are just flesh, blood, and neurons. Even if we consider these experimental results relevant, a skeptical approach is recommended here as well.

Recently, I attended Colin's lecture on Neuroeconomics. I was impressed by a video of Chen's monkey experiment ($n = 3$), which Colin presented (see Chen, Lakshminarayanan and Santos (2005)). In each set of this experiment, a monkey was given 12 tokens. Each of two experimenters held either one piece of apple or one piece of candy. The monkey would then choose to which experimenter it gives a token for what he was holding in return. This process was repeated 12 times until the monkey had spent all its tokens. It is truly amazing to watch a monkey pay for food. It would only be more amazing to watch a monkey following a Wall Street ticker tape and trading options.

The experimenters report that they waited until the monkey's behavior stabilized (no data on this phase was made available) and then the average of the monkey's performance over a week was calculated. The monkeys clearly satisfied Walras' Law. No wonder, they were hungry. Then, the experimenters doubled the number of apple pieces the monkey could get for one token. The number of tokens was adjusted so that his previous average bundle was on his new budget curve. The three monkeys, on average, increased their apple consumption. Two of them spent more tokens on apples. Chen et al. make the following claim: "We show that standard price theory does a remarkably good job of describing capuchin purchasing behavior; capuchin monkeys react rationally to both price and wealth shocks." Camerer praises the result. National Public Radio concludes that "Humans Ape Monkey Market Decisions."

In correspondence with one of the authors, I found out a few things that were not reported in the paper.

First, the monkey was eating what he "bought" immediately. Thus, he was not selecting a bundle. He was actually involved in a series of binary choices interpreted only by the authors as a choice of bundles. The fact that a series of such choices is very different from a one-time choice is in fact something Simonson

(1990) demonstrated in a beautiful experiment which Camerer, Loewenstein and Rabin (2003) themselves refer to. When having to choose between the same two snacks day after day, children usually chose the same snack. When they had to plan in advance, they diversified much more. Thus, there is no reason to link successive choices to the choices made in the standard consumer model.

Second, the authors state that they are reporting on average consumption following the stabilization of choice (the allocation of the 12 tokens). On my first reading, I presumed that the stability of choice was maintained once achieved. The paper only presents average consumption without the raw data itself. When I obtained the data, I in fact did not find any stability in the choices following the "stabilization."

Thus, the most one can say is that when faced with a sequence of choices between a piece of apple and a piece of candy, the three monkeys chose the slice of apple with frequencies of 47%, 42% and 51% respectively; and when faced with a sequence of choices between two pieces of apple and one piece of candy they chose the slices of apple with frequencies 69%, 64% and 50% respectively. Not remarkable, nothing to do with prices and budget sets, nothing to quote. Just a story about three poor monkeys, three overly motivated researchers and some non-critical behavioral economists.

(iii) Neuroeconomics

I am sure that Neuroeconomics will be the subject of one of the sessions at the next World Congress. However, here again we have a field that oversells itself.

Consider, as an example, the fMRI study by Sanfey et al. of the ultimatum game with $10. Camerer, Leowenstein and Perlec (2005) refer to it as "one of the most striking neuroscientic findings about game theory." It is claimed that the activity in an area in the brain that is associated with negative feelings (in a statistical sense) is greater when an individual considers an offer of $2 than when he considers an offer of $5. It is also greater among individuals who accept a $2 offer than among those who reject it. Sanfey et al.'s interpretation of the observation is that in response to an unfair offer, the brain struggles to resolve the conflict between the desire to accept a monetary reward and the "insult" of being treated unfairly. I bet they are right! What other considerations can cross the mind of a player who is offered $2 out of $10? If confirmed by fMRI studies, it would be a cause for celebration among fMRI researchers. But the results themselves are not that clear.

Problems: If there are two centers in the brain that express conflicting emotional and cognitive motives, which brain center resolves the conflict? Does the increase in brain activities come before the subject's discussion or does it reflect his feeling after he made up his mind? If the finding is correct, would one not expect the time response of those who accept an insultingly low offer to be shorter than that of those who reject it? In fact, I found (among 3700 subjects) the distributions of response time of those who accept the offer and those who reject it to be amazingly similar (see Rubinstein (2004b)). In any case, the findings far from justify the title "The Neural Basis of Economic Decision-Making in the Ultimatum Game."

Of course, brain studies are fascinating, probably more so than even, say, economics. I would not be surprised if brain studies eventually change our view of decision making. However, I have yet to come across a single relevant insight produced by these studies. The popularity of brain studies might have to do with the obsession among many economists of becoming scientists.

How can serious researchers draw such hasty conclusions from so little data? Well, without the support of fMRI studies, I dare say economists are human beings with ordinary emotions and aspirations. Once I asked a researcher in the field whether he feels comfortable about making conclusions from such a small sample and relying on statistical inferences which are not well understood. He said, "Yes I know, but if I don't do it someone else will and I will not be the first."

4 FINAL NOTE

To conclude, some of us (see Rubinstein (2001), Harrison (2005) and Shaked (2005)) have already voiced our dismay with the rhetorics of behavioral economics. It is nice that economic research gets on the cover of *Newsweek*, is quoted by the *Economist* and is given airtime by NPR. There is no reason for economics to hide behind the traditional barriers. We should widen the range of economic discourse but not by lowering our standards. For behavioral economics to be a revolutionary program of research rather than a passing episode, it must become more open-minded and much more critical of itself.

References

Ainslie, G. (1992). *Picoeconomics*, Cambridge: Cambridge University Press.

Camerer, C., G. Loewenstein (2003). "Behavioral Economics: Past, Present, Future", in Camerer, C., G. Loewenstein, and M.Rabin, *Advances in Behavioral Economics*, Princeton University Press.

Camerer, C., G. Loewenstein, and D. Prelec (2005). "Neuroeconomics: How Neuroscience Can Inform Economics", *Journal of Economic Literature*, 43, 9–64.

Camerer, C., G. Loewenstein, and M. Rabin (2003). *Advances in Behavioral Economics*, Princeton University Press.

Chen, M.K., V. Lakshminarayanan and L. Santos (2005). "The Evolution of our Preferences: Evidence from Capuchin-Monkey Trading Behavior", mimeo.

Dorris, M.C. and P.W. Glimcher (2004). "Activity in Posterior Parietal Cortex is Correlated with the Subjective Desirability of an Action", *Neuron,* 44, 365–378.

Glimcher, P.W., M.C. Dorris and H.M. Bayer (2005). "Physiological Utility Theory and the Neuroeconomics of Choice", *Games and Economic Behavior*, 52, 213–256.

Gneezy, U. and A. Rustichini (2000). "A Fine Is a Price", *Journal of Legal Studies*, 29, 1–18.

Gul, F. and W. Pesendorfer (2005). "The Idea of Neuroeconomics", a lecture in the Nemmers conference.

Harrison, G.W. (2005). "Book Review: Advances in Behavioral Economics", *Journal of Economic Psychology*, 25, 793–795.

Harper, D.G.C. (1982). "Competitive Foraging in Mallards: 'Ideal Free' Ducks", *Animal Behavior,* 30, 575–584.

Heyman, J. and D. Ariely (2004). "Effort for Payment: A Tale of Two Markets", *Psychological Review*, 15, 787–793.

Laibson, D. (1996) "Hyperbolic Discount Functions, Undersaving, and Savings Plans", NBER Working Paper 5635.

Levitt, S. and S. Dubner (2005). *Freakonomics: A Rogue Economist Explores the Hidden Side of Everything*, William Morrow (a HarperCollins imprint).

Rubinstein, A. (2001). "A Theorist's View of Experiments", *European Economic Review,* 45, 615–628.

Rubinstein, A. (2003). "Economics and Psychology? The Case of Hyperbolic Discounting", *International Economic Review*, 44, 1207–1216.

Rubinstein, A. (2004a). "Dilemmas of An Economic Theorist", mimeo.

Rubinstein, A. (2004b). "Instinctive and Cognitive Reasoning: A Study of Response Times", mimeo.

Sanfey, A.G., J.K. Rilling, J.A. Aronson, L.E. Nystrom, and J.D. Cohen (2003). "The Neural Basis of Economic Decision-Making in the Ultimatum Game", *Science*, 300, 1755–1758.

Shaked, A. (2005). "The Rhetoric of Inequity Aversion", mimeo.

Simonson, I. (1990). "The Effect of Purchase Quantity and Timing on Variety Seeking Behavior", *Journal of Marketing Research*, 27, 150–162.

Strotz, R. H. (1956). "Myopia and Inconsistency in Dynamic Utility Maximization", *Review of Economic Studies,* 23, 165–180.

CHAPTER 10

Dynamic Models for Policy Evaluation
Costas Meghir*

Abstract

The evaluation of interventions has become a commonly used policy tool, which is frequently adopted to improve the transparency and effectiveness of public policy. However, evaluation methods based on comparing treatment and control groups in small scale trials are not capable of providing a complete picture of the likely effects of a policy and do not provide a framework that allows issues relating to the design of the program to be addressed. The longer term effects relate to decisions by individuals to change aspects of their life-cycle behavior not directly targeted by the intervention, so as to best take into account its presence. They also relate to possible changes in prices that may change or even reverse the incentives designed by the program. In this paper we show how experimental data from field trials can be used to enhance the evaluation of interventions, and we illustrate the potential importance of allowing for longer term incentive and General Equilibrium effects.

1   INTRODUCTION

The evaluation of interventions has become a commonly used policy tool. This has led to a better understanding of the overall benefits and costs of interventions, and of their distributional impact. It has also improved transparency in policy making and led to choices that are founded in fact rather than political prejudice. Recent examples of policy-influential evaluations are the Job Training Partnership act in the USA (see Heckman, Ichimura, and Todd, 1997) or the evaluation of the Education Maintenance allowance in the UK – a conditional cash transfer, incentivising 16-year-old children to stay on at school in

* Acknowledgements: I thank my co-authors, Orazio Attanasio, Richard Blundell, Monica Costa-Dias, Giovanni Gallipoli, Ana Santiago, and Gianluca Violante for allowing me to use material from our joint work as well as for stimulating discussions. I also thank Joe Altonji for his comments at the World Congress in London as well as Ken Judd and seminar participants at the Cowles lunchtime seminar in Yale.

the UK (see Dearden, Emmerson, Frayne, and Meghir, 2005), the PROGRESA program in Mexico, discussed below, and many others. A large body of research has further stimulated its use and has addressed important intellectual challenges.[1] The standard basis for evaluations has been field trials where a policy is implemented in a small scale and its effects measured by comparing outcomes to a suitably chosen comparison group. The gold standard in this approach is a randomized trial where the unit of randomization may by an individual or a community, however defined. Other than that, a large number of alternative methods have been developed, or adapted from standard econometric techniques, based on observational data. These include matching and quasi-experimental methods such as Instrumental Variables and Difference in Differences.[2] However there are many reasons why this set of approaches can only offer limited answers to the question of policy design and need to be complemented with further methods of analysis. First, long-term implementation of a program may induce changes in behavior by individuals that cannot be measured by a simple comparison of the treated and control group in the short run. Thus a program that subsidizes wages may indeed increase employment of the client group relative to a comparison grouping in some isolated labor market; however, it may also change the incentives to invest in human capital (see Heckman, Lochner, and Cossa (2003), and Adda, Dustmann, Meghir, and Robin (2005)), an effect that will occur a few years down the road. Second, the program may have more wide-ranging impacts affecting individuals who are not explicitly targeted by the policy, including changing behavior to become a member of the targeted group and thus obtaining the benefits of the program. In certain cases, field trials can be designed to measure such effects, as distinct from the main effects of the program; this is, however, difficult in practice and requires a large amount of resources to be expended. Thirdly, while a small field trial may not affect prices because the changes in supply and demand of say human capital that it induces are negligible, the same cannot necessarily be said of a broad implementation of a successful program (see Heckman, Lochner, and Taber (1998a)). In this case, the effects of the program can be seriously mitigated to the extent that they are almost neutralized.

There are two main themes that we address in this paper. First, we discuss the use of randomized field experiments to estimate structural economic models that can then be used to improve on the design of interventions. We argue that this approach reinforces the usefulness of experiments in that it allows, given the model assumptions, us to go beyond the simple conclusions that can be drawn by a comparison of means. Moreover, economic models can be used to guide the way we design experiments in the first place, so as to get the most out of them and be able to identify important aspects of behavior. In this sense we pursue the ideal set forth by Orcutt and Orcutt (1968) where experiments on incentives are

---

[1] Rosenbaum and Rubin (1983), LaLonde (1986), Heckman, Ichimura, and Todd (1997, 1998) Heckman and Robb (1985), Imbens and Angrist (1994) to name but a few.

[2] Effectively an instrumental variables method in itself.

used to learn about structural parameters in an economic model. Thus, our first example draws from the paper by Attanasio, Meghir, and Santiago (2005) where data from a field trial in Mexico (PROGRESA) was combined with a structural model of education choice to produce a model that at the same time challenges the results obtained by conventional observational data and provides a framework for thinking of better ways to redesign the program or compare with alternative policies.

The next theme of the paper addresses longer term evaluation questions that cannot be dealt with based on field experiments. Two issues arise requiring structural economic models. First, interventions may have longer run incentive effects along dimensions not intended. For example a program designed to boost employment by wage subsidies may reduce human capital accumulation. This issue has been addressed empirically by Heckman, Lochner, and Cossa (2003), Blundell, Costa-Dias, and Meghir (2003) and more recently by Adda, Dustmann, Meghir, and Robin (2005). These papers consider different forms of wage subsidy interventions and show that these can substantially affect Human Capital accumulation. Second, as discussed in Heckman, LaLonde, and Smith (1999) and illustrated empirically in Heckman, Lochner, and Taber (1998b) large scale interventions may have important consequences for prices and hence for outcomes, at least in some settings where factor price equalization internationally is somehow prevented. In this case these General Equilibrium (GE) effects can be very large and can often neutralize or sometimes reinforce the effects of policy.[3] More recently the notion of using empirical GE models to evaluate policy interventions and to understand trends in the labor market is becoming more prevalent. Examples of such work include Alonso-Borrego, Fernandez-Villaverde, and Galdon-Sanchez (2004), who look at the impact of short-term employment contracts and find that they decrease employment, and Lee and Wolpin (2005), who use a GE model to understand the evolution of wages and employment in the services sector.

Here we examine the potential importance of dynamic incentive and General Equilibrium effects by summarizing the results of two papers. The first is the paper by Gallipoli, Meghir, and Violante (2005) and the second by Blundell, Costa-Dias, and Meghir (2003). In these models, risk-averse life-cycle consumers choose education, labor supply and consumption in a world with uninsurable idiosyncratic risk. The economy is stationary and consists of overlapping generations. Output is produced by a production function, which is constant returns to scale in capital and three types of labor characterized by the level of formal education – less than high school, high school and some college. The models are capable of addressing the issues of dynamic incentives and endogenous prices. They thus allow for interactions between individuals due to a number of mechanisms: the government budget constraint, used to fund the intervention, the dynamic incentives created by the program and the

---

[3] For an example of the latter see (Gallipoli and Fella, 2005).

endogeneity of prices.[4] Using these models we consider the impact of tuition subsidies and of temporary wage subsidies, similar to those offered by the UK New Deal – an active labor market program introduced in 1998.

2 SCHOOL SUBSIDIES AND EDUCATION CHOICES IN MEXICO

Our first example is based on the paper by Attanasio, Meghir, and Santiago (2005) and illustrates the use of experimental data for fitting an economic model, with which it is then possible to address questions of design in a partial equilibrium framework.

2.1   The PROGRESA Program and the Evaluation Data

In 1997, the Mexican government started a large program to reduce poverty in rural Mexico by focusing on increasing education using subsidies ("conditional cash transfers") and improving health and nutrition. The program known as PROGRESA[5] was first implemented in a randomly chosen set of village communities out of a population of eligible ones, for the purposes of evaluation. Data was collected both from the communities that were randomized into the program and those randomized out. The program was implemented in all communities with a delay of 1.5 years. Greater details of the program can be found in (Schultz, 2003) and (Attanasio, Meghir, and Santiago, 2005).

Once a locality qualifies for the program, individual households within it could qualify or not, depending on a single indicator of poverty. The largest component of the program is the education one. Beneficiary households with school-age children receive grants conditional on school attendance. The size of the grant increases with the grade and, for secondary education, is slightly higher for girls than for boys. In Table 10.1, we report the grant structure as it was at the start of the program. To keep the grant, children have to attend at least 85% of classes. Upon not passing a grade, a child is still entitled to the grant for the same grade. However, if the child fails the grade again, the child loses eligibility.[6] In addition to the bimonthly payments, beneficiaries with children in school receive a small annual grant for school supplies.

The randomized trial offers the opportunity to obtain unbiased estimates of the average impact of the program on any desired outcome non-parametrically, simply by comparing the estimated mean outcomes between treatment and

---

[4] There is a real issue here relating to the possibility of factor price equalization. This is a controversial topic we have not addressed. In our illustrations we take prices as endogenous. However, even if prices were exogenous the other issues relating to dynamic incentives over the life-cycle would remain.

[5] The Spanish acronym for 'Health, Nutrition and Education.'

[6] All the figures are in current pesos, and can be converted to US dollars at approximately an exchange rate of 10 pesos per dollar.

Table 10.1. *PROGRESA Bimonthly Monetary Benefits, in Pesos*

Type of benefit	1998
Nutrition support	190
Primary school	
3	130
4	150
5	190
6	260
Secondary school	
1st year	
boys	380
girls	400
2nd year	
boys	400
girls	440
3rd year	
boys	420
girls	480
Maximum support	1,170

control villages. The results can also be broken down by characteristics that are exogenous or determined pre-program. However, there are a number of intricate aspects to the design of the program or deeper questions that cannot be answered directly by the randomized trial. For example, the policymakers in increasing the grant by grade are responding to the fact that the school drop out rates increase quite dramatically during the teenage years. But whether the best use of funds has been made in this direction cannot be addressed by the randomized trial. While it would be possible and scientifically desirable to design a field trial with many directions of variation by age this is not always practical. To proceed further, an economic model can be fitted to the observed responses by combining the exogenous source of variation induced by the experiment by other sources of variation that can be considered conditionally exogenous. This combines the experiment with reasonable assumptions to further enhance our understanding and the scope of the data. Within this context it will also be possible to test whether the experimental data would lead to the same conclusions as those obtained by a model estimated solely on observational data.

The analysis is based on the evaluation data, whose collection began in 1997 and followed the start of the year in 1998. This is a household based panel, which collects information on schooling, work patterns, earnings and income as well as on consumption and household assets.

Table 10.2 provides the difference in differences estimates of the effects of the policy for the eligible individuals drawn from Attanasio, Meghir, and Santiago (2005). These are obtained by comparing the growth of school attendance between baseline and after the program started in treatment and control

Table 10.2. *Experimental results October 1998*

Post-Program Differences in Educational Attendance Between Treatment and Control Communities

Age group	Eligible
6–17	0.034
	(0.012)
6–9	0.003
	(0.005)
10–13	0.032
	(0.011)
14–17	0.084
	(0.031)

Standard errors in parentheses are clustered at the locality level.
Source: Attanasio et al. (2005).

villages. While a simple post-program comparison between treatment and control would have provided an unbiased estimate, in this context the difference improves precision. The key conclusion from this table, which refers to boys, is that the program has little or no impact on young children, since they nearly all attend in the first place. However, it has a substantial impact on the 14–17 age group. To go beyond this result to questions relating to the design of the program, we need a model, or alternatively a much more elaborate experiment.

2.2   The Model and Its Estimation

We consider the choice of attending school versus work for boys from age 11 to 16. The trade-off is between current earnings in the labor market and future increased earnings. These are set against other schooling costs, such as travel, equipment, etc. The choice takes place in an environment of idiosyncratic risk: First, the child may not pass the grade and will have to repeat; second the costs of schooling may change – we model this latter aspect as a shock to preferences. The monetary opportunity cost of schooling is the local wage. We assume that children have the possibility of attending school up to age 17. All formal schooling ends by that time. In our model, schooling is taken as an investment. The parents are assumed to act in the best interest of the individual child and hence do not trade off welfare between children.

When the grant is offered conditional on attending school, it should have the same effect as a reduction in schooling costs or alternatively a reduction in the wage that the individual would earn if she worked. The implication is that it should be possible to estimate the effect of the grant on school participation by learning about the sensitivity of individual schooling choices to wages. This is the traditional approach to public policy analysis and dates back at least to Marschak and Andrews (1944). For example, learning about the implication of a tax rate on demand can be achieved by looking for a price increase under similar conditions at some other historical moment or point in space. For the PROGRESA case, Todd and Wolpin (2003) use this idea to examine whether a model estimated on non-experimental data and relying on wage variation can predict the impact of the policy; the latter can be estimated in an unbiased way because of the experimental design.

We take a different tack in Attanasio, Meghir, and Santiago (2005). We specify a dynamic model of education choice and include the grant as one of the current benefits of schooling. Subject to suitable scaling, we can then test whether the wage has the same effect (but in opposite direction) to the grant. However, our model is more than just a testing vehicle. It provides a framework to simulate changes in the design that would improve targeting and further increase school participation, at the same overall cost.

The heart of the model is the schooling flow utility function, which we specify to be a function of school availability in the village, distance from school, and direct costs of schooling. These variables either determine the cost of attending school or are direct components of the cost, such as fees, shoes, etc. In addition, we condition on parental education and ethnic background to capture indirect or "psychic" costs of schooling that may be driven by the support that the child gets at home. Finally, we condition on whether the household is program eligible in the sense of being below the poverty threshold defined by the intervention, as well as living in an eligible village. These variables account for permanent differences between eligible and ineligible households allowing for the human capital differences that could occur because of different income levels. They also control for pre-program differences that were identified among the ineligible households. Going to school may build a habit and a taste for this, as pupils learn to learn and create social networks. We thus include the past level of attainment as an additional component in the flow utility. Beneficiary households receive the grant, which is also included among the variables – its value for boys varies by grade. The final component on the flow utility of schooling is an unobserved component. This consists of a permanent effect and an iid shock. The former reflects unobserved tastes for schooling or factors such as risk aversion that are not explicitly modeled here, since we do not include consumption in a nonlinear way. The latter is an iid stochastic shock to schooling costs that can be interpreted as transitory factors affecting attendance, such as health for instance. Finally, when he is working, the flow utility is proportional to the wage he can earn.

The decision to attend school depends on comparing the expected discounted flows under the two alternatives, allowing for optimal decisions in the future. In both cases we assume that beyond 17, the individual will be working and earning wages commensurate to their educational attainment. Before that, individuals either obtain the (possibly negative) utility cost of schooling when they attend or earnings from the labor market, depending on their age and qualification. In simple, within village regressions the returns to schooling are as low as 1% for a year of education. However the relevant return is the one obtained when working in the urban centers. This is of the order of 10%. In other words, individuals who obtain education are probably committing themselves to moving out to seek better work opportunities.

To model schooling choice we need a forward-looking dynamic model. The model we consider is dynamic for three reasons. First, the fact that one cannot attend regular school past age 17 means that going to school now provides the option of completing some grades in the future. This source of dynamics becomes particularly important when we consider the impact of the PROGRESA grants because to take full advantage of the subsidy one has to attend continuously and pass the grade. Second, we allow for state dependence: The number of years of schooling affects the utility of attending in this period. State dependence is important because it may be a mechanism that reinforces the effect of the grant. Third, education choices when young affect future earnings and probably mobility choices.

The model contains two sources of uncertainty. We have already mentioned the iid shock to the cost of schooling. This implies that the costs of schooling are not known in future periods and consequently the individual has to take into account that in future these may be higher or lower. The other source of uncertainty originates from the possibility that one may not pass a grade. This may affect the value of attending. In our model we do not allow for an endogenous supply of effort to affect the probability of passing. While this is a potentially important source of program impact, we need to leave this for future work; this will have to allow for the fact that the composition of those attending and hence whose grade performance is observed are different in the treatment and control group.

Solving the model involves computing the value of the two alternatives – school and work, given the state variables, namely the current level of education, and the wage and given the set of observed and unobserved characteristics (at each point of the support of their distribution). This solution assumes future optimal decisions and accounts for the impact of current choices on future ones. Solving this model is straightforward because of the logistic assumption on the iid school cost shock.

The randomized availability of the program provides an important source of exogenous variation for the identification of the structural economic model and should increase our confidence in using it. While this is an important source of variation, it is not sufficient to identify all key parameters.[7] First, the model includes the actual amount of the grant, a quantity that does not vary randomly. Second, the model also includes the wage for the child, which reflects the opportunity cost of schooling.

To identify the impact of the grant we use the way it is designed to vary with the grade. The lack of perfect correlation of grade and age generates the

---

[7] See (Attanasio, Meghir, and Santiago, 2005) for a full discussion of identification issues.

required variation. Wages do vary from locality to locality, and this variation is used to identify the wage effect on schooling. This requires one to assume that the variability is due to different labor demand conditions, rather than changes in labor supply induced by unobserved factors. In addition, we use the adult wage as an instrument for predicting wages. This controls for measurement error and for missing wages caused by the choice to attend school.[8]

The experiment plays an important role in identifying the model. However, it is also true that identification would benefit from a richer experimental field trial. For example, randomizing the amounts received across villages as well as randomizing the age gradient of the grant would have been particularly useful. In this sense, thinking more broadly about the information that we would wish to extract from an experiment, other than the simple quantification of a particular design, is very important when coming up with the design of an evaluation. It is thus possible to come up both with a richer set of experimental results and create the conditions for estimating economic theory–based models with fewer statistical and functional form assumptions, which tend to have no foundation in economic theory.

The model we described can be estimated quite straightforwardly using maximum likelihood. The likelihood function is based on the distribution of ε, which is assumed to be logistic. Unobserved heterogeneity is then integrated out using a discrete mixture as in Heckman and Singer (1984).

2.3   Results and Policy Design

The estimated model fits very well with the experimental results, which is quite remarkable for such a parsimonious specification. However, its value lies in its ability to guide policy choices. In fact, it provides a tool both for redesigning the grant structure to obtain stronger attendance results and possibly to compare the relative merits of such a conditional cash transfer to other infrastructure-type policies; this would exploit the school availability variables and distance to school, both of which are included.

A further potentially important contribution is in its ability to test whether the evaluation results of the experiment were similar to those that would be predicted using observational data and relying on wage variation alone. It turns out that the effect of the grant is three times higher than the wage, when this is scaled up to represent lost earnings from school attendance. Although this points to the importance of running the experiment and collecting the evaluation database, one should not dismiss the underlying economic model on the basis of this finding: First wages may not be measured well enough leading to an attenuating effect. Beyond this simple statistical explanation the grant and earnings may have different effects because of who receives each of them. Thus

---

[8] There is also an important initial conditions problem, which causes an identification problem. This issue and its solution are discussed in Attanasio, Meghir, and Santiago (2005).

intrahousehold allocations may play an important role here, implying that the source of income, and to whom it is paid, may have important effects in itself. This point emphasizes the usefulness of the field trial; even within the context of a structural model, the information obtained from the trial can be of critical importance in understanding how the policy works.

Using these estimates, we can also address the question of redesigning the program. The grant is provided to all children over the age of 6. Our model fits behavior from 10 onwards. The impact of the grant is very small at earlier ages. In this policy experiment we consider redesigning the grant so as to make it zero up to and including age 11 and redistribute the grant equally beyond that age, keeping the overall cost of the program the same. We show that this simple redesign can almost double the effect of the policy on participation at 15 and even more than double them at 16 – all this at no extra financial cost (see Attanasio, Meghir, and Santiago (2005)). This simulation takes the sole aim of getting children into school. It may well be that the grant before 12 was considered a pure transfer, conveniently handed out via the school, because most children attend anyway. However, if school participation is the sole intention, and because the program has no effect on younger children, a properly targeted unconditional transfer for this group may be more efficient at alleviating poverty.

Our aim in this section has been to illustrate the power of combining experimental data with economic modeling. We illustrated how this can help understand potential failings when using observational data and how the model can enhance the use of the experiment in a policy context. We gave one example, but with the possibility of comparing this policy to alternative options, such as improvements in infrastructure – the scope of such an approach is very broad. We now proceed to consider wider issues with general equilibrium models.

3 POLICY INTERVENTIONS, LONG-TERM INCENTIVES AND GENERAL EQUILIBRIUM

The example we detailed in the previous section did not consider longer term incentives of the program and was set in a partial equilibrium context where prices remain constant. In the longer run, a number of changes can occur that will alter the impact of the program in important ways.

First, individuals may change their work and/or consumption behavior to become eligible for the benefits. This point is well understood in economics, and there is a vast literature on the work-disincentive effects of welfare benefits. However, their magnitude needs to be measured if the program is to be designed to achieve effectively its aims.

Second, beyond these longer term incentive effects, large-scale programs that successfully alter the supply of human capital may well affect prices. Thus an increase in educated individuals may compress educational differentials, or an increase in re-employment rates may put a downward pressure on wages.

This in itself may partly overturn the effects of the program as estimated from some limited field trial. This point has been eloquently made by Heckman, LaLonde, and Smith (1999); Heckman, Lochner, and Taber (1998a) and Lee (2001) have provided a quantification of the magnitude of the effects in quite different contexts. These papers show quite clearly that results can differ substantively, depending on the particular setup of the model and the choices faced by individuals. They also illustrate the potential importance for policy of allowing for such effects. In many cases the GE effects are lower than the partial equilibrium ones. However this need not be the case. Thus, Gallipoli and Fella (2005) show that the impact of an education subsidy on crime is reinforced in General Equilibrium with substantially larger effects.

Considering the general equilibrium effects of a policy is necessarily much more complicated because one has to take a stand on a number of important issues, such as market structure for which the evidence may be scant. In GE models the trade-off between the richness of the model and its tractability can be even more stark than usual. First, comes the problem of having available data on all the required dimensions in a compatible way. Second comes the issue of defining the way agents interact, which, broadly speaking, relates to defining the market structure as well as the role of the government in funding policy interventions. Thirdly comes the issue of potentially dealing with macroeconomic shocks. Inevitably, compromises have to be made.

We illustrate the issues involved in evaluating policy using two similar general equilibrium models chosen to fit US and UK data respectively. In both cases individuals choose labor supply, consumption and education. They face uncertainty on the returns to education. The models are of the overlapping generations type and only steady state equilibria are considered. In other words questions relating to transitional dynamics are not addressed. In the first case, the focus of the model is on analyzing human capital policies. The model and results are drawn from Gallipoli, Meghir, and Violante (2005), and we use this model to illustrate the potential issues of introducing tuition subsidies. The main question is how effective can a policy be, funded by proportional taxation of earnings, in encouraging college education and hence increasing overall education levels and earnings. In the second example we consider a policy affecting individuals later in life, namely a wage subsidy available to individuals at an age following the age when most people would have obtained college education. The results we present are taken from Blundell, Costa-Dias, and Meghir (2003) and illustrate not only the importance of allowing for price changes but also the importance of dynamic incentive effects: Individuals are shown to change their early education choices in response to the future availability of the temporary subsidy. This illustrates, how a program designed to reduce unemployment can in the long run have opposite effects once dynamic incentive and price changes combine. The motivation is to consider issues relating to the New Deal – an active labor market program in the UK designed to help the long-term unemployed back to work. To economize in space, we base our description on the model developed by Gallipoli, Meghir, and Violante (2005); when required we highlight some key differences between the models.

3.1   The Model

We consider a closed economy where a unique good is produced, and it can be either consumed or used as physical capital. Our specification effectively precludes factor price equalization and hence both the interest rate and human capital prices are taken as endogenous to the economy. This is a contentious and important issue that can affect policy in dramatic ways because when prices are exogenous the GE effects we discuss will not take place. However the individual dynamic incentives will still be altered by the policy.

We specify an overlapping generations general equilibrium model. Consumers maximize an intertemporal utility function over their finite life-cycle, with respect to education, labor supply, and consumption/savings. Agents can accumulate assets representing ownership of shares of physical capital. They have a maximum lifetime and they plan to consume all their assets. However, they may die before that, leaving accidental bequests. The maximum possible lifetime is 99 years. Individuals can work up to 65 but not beyond. They can, however, decide not to work before that. Retirement is financed by the accumulated assets. The population consists of 99 overlapping generations ex-ante heterogeneous agents, each with an ex-ante identical distribution of heterogeneity.

Young and old households are not linked in any direct way. Bequests are pooled together and redistributed to all newly born individuals according to the steady state equilibrium wealth distribution. This reflects both inter-vivo transfers for education and actual bequests. We now provide a brief description of the components of the model.

The individual problem: Individuals can live up to a maximum age of 99, but can die earlier with probability given by the US life tables. They maximize an intertemporal utility function of consumption c and leisure l, additive over time but nonadditive between consumption and leisure. They discount the future at a personal discount factor β. Time can be used for education, work or leisure up to age 22 and only for work or leisure after that age. When in education ($d = 1$), individuals have to pay an annual fee; subsidizing this fee will be the policy instrument that we will examine in this paper. Individuals differ by an ability factor θ. This affects the utility cost of education, by changing the time input required for obtaining a particular qualification (high school or college). This same factor also affects the wage the individual can earn in the labor market. Individuals also choose consumption in each period and can invest in a riskless asset at a rate r, which is endogenous to the model. Assets have to be zero at the maximal age of 99. However, individuals may die accidentally, leaving positive or negative assets. As explained above, these are redistributed to those entering the economy. The individual faces uncertainty because of shocks to human capital that are not insurable; these are described below.

The within period utility function is assumed to take the isoelastic weakly separable form

$$u\left(c_i, l_i \mid \mathrm{d}_i = 0\right) = \frac{\left[c_i^\nu l_i^{1-\nu}\right]^{(1-\lambda)}}{1 - \lambda}$$

When in education l_i is set to $f^e(\theta_i)$, reflecting the time costs of education, which depends on ability θ_i. Hence

$$u\left(c_i \mid \mathrm{d}_i = 1, \; l_i = f^e(\theta)\right) = \frac{\left[c_i^\nu f^e(\theta)^{1-\nu}\right]^{(1-\lambda)}}{1 - \lambda}.$$

The individual problem is solved recursively by backward induction. This results in education, consumption, and labor supply choices all as a function of unobserved heterogeneity, human capital prices, the interest rate and the state variables – which include the individual amount of human capital and wealth, as well as consumption/savings decisions. In the model simulations we present here, we have set the intertemporal elasticity of consumption to 0.75 as in Blundell, Browning, and Meghir (1994) and Attanasio and Weber (1993). Given this, a value of $\nu = 0.33$ and hence $\lambda = 2$ leads to a solution that matches the labor supply data very well.

3.2 The Wage Process

A key element of the model is the wage process because it drives both the incentives to obtain education and the uncertainty faced by individuals. The model we use is in effect the Roy model where the sector is identified with level of education and is similar in nature to the model of Heckman and Sedlacec (1985). The wage equations are stochastic, and the shock to wages is the main source of uncertainty in the model. For this we use the well-established specification as in MaCurdy (1981), Abowd and Card (1989) and Meghir and Pistaferri (2004). Thus, the empirical specification we estimate on the PSID data has the form

$$\ln w_{eit} = w_{et} + g_e(age_{eit}) + u_{eit} \qquad (1)$$

where w_{et} represents the log of the aggregate price of human capital for education group e and where $g_e(age_{eit})$ is the education specific age profile of wages. The unobservable component u_{eit} is specified to be

$$\begin{aligned}
u_{eit} &= z_{eit} + m_{it} \\
z_{eit} &= z_{eit-1} + \varepsilon_{eit} \\
z_{ei0} &= \alpha_e \theta_i
\end{aligned} \qquad (2)$$

where α_e represents the effect of ability on initial wages. Consistent with the literature z_{eit} is the (persistent) component of unobserved human capital, which evolves as a random walk. The shock to wages ε_{eit} is drawn from a normal distribution with education specific variance. Thus the model allows for one more important factor influencing education choice, namely that of insurance.

Because individuals are risk averse, they will take into account the different variance of the shocks when making education decisions. Finally, m_{it} represents measurement error, is assumed iid, and does not affect behavior.

The wage process is estimated using the PSID. The variance of wage shocks and of the measurement error are estimated using the variances and autocovariances of residual wage growth after taking out time and age effects based on the PSID data. The approach followed is based on Meghir and Pistaferri (2004). The main difficulty that needs to be addressed, however, is estimating the impact of ability on wages. This is important because it will allow education choice to depend on labor market ability. To deal with this we use an IQ test administered by the PSID in 1972. We thus regress wages on an age polynomial and the IQ score, separately for each education group to obtain the effect of the IQ test on wages. This is then used when solving the individual's problem.

3.3   Uncertainty or Unobservability

An issue of central importance in such models is the real degree of uncertainty. Measured wages vary; however, there is no reason why this variability should represent uncertainty because it may well be that the individual anticipates much of this variability, or because it just reflects measurement error. The model described here strips out measurement error from uncertainty. It also ignores any transitory shocks. Finally, uncertainty is taken to be the set of future innovations to the permanent component of wages. There are two questions: First, what is the extent to which such uncertainty, due to the wage process, is insurable? Second, when does the "innovation" become known to the individual? These are very hard issues to resolve; papers that have gone in that direction are Blundell and Preston (1998), Blundell, Pistaferri, and Preston (2005) and in the context of education choices, Cunha, Heckman, and Navarro (2004). Identifying what is in the information set and what is not at the time of a decision is of course a very hard task, which requires strong identifying restrictions. In the present paper we assume that the variance of the permanent shocks to wages reflect uncertainty. This shock explains just a fraction of the observed conditional cross-sectional variance. This relates to the accumulation of past shocks, already in the information set, as well as measurement error.

3.4   Production Structure

As far as the effectiveness of human capital policy is concerned, the structure of the production function is of central importance. In one extreme, all types of education can be perfect substitutes in the production function, and the only pertinent difference between individuals in this respect is the amount of efficiency units of HC that they possess following their education and given their ability θ. In this case, increasing the supply of say college graduates increases overall human capital but does not affect the relative prices across types, and hence there can be no GE effects. The other extreme is a Leontieff type technology where GE effects will lead to full crowding out of any partial equilibrium effects since the increase in one input has no impact on production unless the other inputs increase by the right proportions. Thus, reliable estimates of the production technology are central to understanding the policy impact of an intervention. We thus specify the production function to be

$$Y = K^\alpha \left[\left(\delta_1 H_1^\rho + \delta_2 H_2^\rho + (1 - \delta_1 - \delta_2) H_2^\rho \right) \right]^{\frac{1-\alpha}{\rho}}.$$

In principle, one could allow different elasticities of substitution between the various skill groups. However, on US data we found these to be of very similar magnitude, and we could not reject that they were in fact equal. In the UK paper on wage subsidies we use a more general specification as described below. Details on estimation are provided in Gallipoli, Meghir, and Violante (2005) and draw from Heckman, Lochner, and Taber (1998a). The key issue is that we do not observe human capital aggregates corresponding to the types of education in the model. Thus we use the relative price series obtained from estimating the wage equation on the PSID to compute efficiency units of human capital for each individual in the CPS, based on their observed earnings. We then aggregate these quantities by education type and use NIPA data to fit the production function using GMM.

The resulting elasticity of substitution based on an estimated ρ of 0.45 (se 0.13) is 1.82. Thus in the aggregate economy there seems to be quite a lot of substitutability between the various types of human capital. This need not reflect the flexibility of technology within firms but could also include the shift of production between different sectors relying on different mixes of these inputs, as relative factors change. The hypothesis of perfect substitutability, however ($\rho = 1$) is clearly rejected; thus changes in the supply of the different types of human capital can lead to changes in their relative prices. However, we do accept the hypothesis that the elasticity of substitution is the same across different pairs of human capital.

3.5   The Effects of a Tuition Subsidy

Given the preference parameters, the estimated wage process, and the production function, the remaining parameters, including the time costs of education $f(\theta)$ are obtained by calibration. The baseline model is calibrated on the basis that direct costs of college education are 30% of median annual income. The model also includes a government sector whose sole role is to raise proportional labor taxes to fund any interventions. In other work we also consider the relative merits of taxes on capital income.

When we solve the model we use the notion of a stationary recursive competitive equilibrium (see Lucas (1980)). In equilibrium, all individual decisions are optimal, input prices are set equal to the marginal product and the goods and asset markets clear.

The model we have set up can address a number of topical policy issues, including the impact of welfare benefits, minimum wages, active labor market programs or of education policies. The key point of course, is that such interventions have effects on the decisions in the entire life-cycle, altering both work incentives and incentives to accumulate human capital. The fact that individuals are *ex ante* different is a central characteristic of these models. It allows for the existence of a group of individuals who justify the existence of the program as an attempt to compensate for low productivity and/or high costs of schooling. It also allows an examination of how a policy affects inequality.

Here we illustrate some of the issues by considering a tuition subsidy for college. This is an interesting policy to consider because it is high on the agenda of many governments. In the UK, for example, there has been extensive debate on how much the subsidy should be, culminating with the introduction of fees covering part of the costs of higher education tuition. In many other European countries no fees are charged and all is paid for through general taxation. In the US there is an extensive loan system as well as a number of scholarship programs. The policy we consider is a very simple one, namely a blanket reduction of college fees by 50% paid for by general taxation. We will consider the effect of the subsidy on overall numbers attending college, how this is distributed by ability groups, what is the impact on between group inequality, and what is the effect on total human capital supplied in each category.

The top panel of Table 10.3 shows the results for the benchmark economy. The panel below shows what happens in partial equilibrium, when prices for human capital do not change. However, taxes must change to fund the tuition subsidy. The underlying wealth distribution and work behavior will also change. Thus even when the prices are taken as exogenous, this dynamic model can give different results from a simple pilot/control group comparison because the need to fund the intervention internally will affect all individuals. The lowest panel shows the general equilibrium results where human capital prices and the interest rates are allowed to change.

In partial equilibrium this universal subsidy leads to an increase of college graduates from 16.7% to 19.1%. Note that in this economy there are no liquidity constraints, and hence the tuition subsidy impact originates from the distortion in education prices alone. There is also a counteracting effect from increased taxation to fund the subsidy. The subsidy leads to large relative increases in college attendance among the second and third ability groups but not among the lowest group who did not even complete high school. It also increases college completion for the highest ability group. The total supply of human capital increases by 14%. The key to what is going to happen next however, is the large decline in the marginal product of college graduates, which declines from 1.413 to 1.294. If we now assume that prices are endogenous, we obtain the results in the lower part of the Table. On aggregate, the increase in the proportion of college graduates relative to the benchmark is less than 1% (17.4% college graduates). Interestingly though, the ones who drop out are primarily the highest ability group. For them the decline in returns has the highest impact; the next largest drop comes from the second highest ability group. Ability group 2 is hardly affected. Whether the policy is judged as effective or not depends very much on the original objectives and on the social welfare function: what has

Table 10.3. *Tuition subsidy simulations with a CES production function*

Groups	The Impact of Tuition Subsidy					
	Edu. Participation (aggr. shares)			Human Capital Aggregates		
	Benchmark (30% of median income)					
All	Less than HS	HS	College	Less than HS	HS	College
	0.251	0.583	0.167	3.312	7.837	2.812
	Edu. Shares by Ability			Marg. Products after Tax. and Depr.		
Ability 1 (lowest)	1.0	0.0	0.0	0.955	1.0	1.413
Ability 2	0.576	0.394	0.03			
Ability 3	0.305	0.595	0.10			
Ability 4 (highest)	0.121	0.615	0.263	% with zero wealth 0.162		
	Partial Equilibrium Results with a 50% Tuition Subsidy					
	Less than HS	HS	College	Less than HS	HS	College
	0.248	0.562	0.191	3.280	7.622	3.207
	Edu. Shares by Ability			Marg. Products after Tax. and Depr.		
Ability 1 (lowest)	1.0	0.0	0.0	0.948	1.0	1.294
Ability 2	0.576	0.379	0.045			
Ability 3	0.303	0.577	0.120			
Ability 4 (highest)	0.116	0.590	0.295	% with zero wealth 0.157		
	General Equilibrium Results with a 50% Tuition Subsidy					
	Less than HS	HS	College	Less than HS	HS	College
	0.250	0.576	0.174	3.324	7.802	2.820
	Edu. Shares by Ability			Marg. Products after Tax. and Depr.		
Ability 1 (lowest)	1.0	0	0	0.954	1.0	1.396
Ability 2	0.568	0.389	0.042			
Ability 3	0.307	0.580	0.113			
Ability 4 (highest)	0.119	617	0.265	% with zero wealth 0.162		

Elasticity of Substitution = 1.5.
Source: Gallipoli et al. (2005).

been achieved is an increase in college completion by lower ability individuals, although the aggregate effects are small. In other simulations we show that in the presence of liquidity constraints the policy impact is larger, and has a strong impact on higher ability individuals who wish to attend college because it offers funding they would otherwise not have. However, here the absence of formal liquidity constraints replaces the funding for college that would in many cases be offered by parents.

To take the policy analysis further, one needs to link individuals to families. One important source of college finance comes from parents. Ability and parental income are correlated – if anything because wealthier parents invest in their children at an early age. Modeling this relationship and allowing for liquidity constraints will allow us to better consider the targeting of the policy and analyze its effects in a possibly more realistic context. However these results, obtained by using parameters estimated from US data, show that standard pilots only contain part of the story. They are more useful as a tool for estimating the impact of incentives on individuals than on the ultimate design of policy. The latter requires us to put together knowledge obtained from a variety of sources and combined with theory and reasonable assumptions. The final outcomes can be dramatically different from those implied by a small-scale pilot study. By the way, this conclusion is also true, at least to an extent, even when prices are exogenous because of the impacts of changes in taxes and because of changes in incentives not directly targeted by the policy, such as, say, work incentives or incentives to train on the job, which have not been modeled here.

3.6   Wage Subsidies, Education and Employment

Using a model similar to the one described above, Blundell, Costa-Dias, and Meghir (2003) analyze the effect of a wage subsidy on employment and education. There has been increased interest in such policies in a number of different countries. Examples include the British "New Deal" introduced in 1998, and the Canadian "Self Sufficiency Program." The impacts of such programs have shown mixed results (see Card and Hyslop (2005) for Canada, and Sianesi (2003) for Sweden). The effectiveness of such policies in terms of increasing wages and hence the longer term impact on employment remains an open question. Certainly in the results we present with the empirical dynamic model, where a time limited program is used, the partial equilibrium results are modest.

However, we wish to bring out both the importance of longer term incentives and the potential divergence between partial and general equilibrium policies. Thus, the key point being emphasized here is that policies that are designed to encourage employment may have substantially different effects in the long run, as incentives for education choice and the attractiveness of unemployment changes.

In the model used by Blundell, Costa-Dias, and Meghir (2003), a period is five years. However, the key difference from the model described in the section above is that education choices can be made throughout the life-cycle, rather than just at the start. Moreover work experience leads to the accumulation of human capital. Thus while an individual is working her/his human capital increases at a rate that depends on individual ability. This feature is important in this model because it allows us to examine the basic premise of active labor markets, namely that once individuals are placed in work, their labor market attachment will improve because their earnings increase. In our model, experience is education type specific and is lost once the individual decides to obtain more education and change type. Heterogeneity in this model is of course crucial because it allows us to define a margin of individuals who are potential clients of a program and who could change their long-term investments as a result of the program's existence. In this model, labor supply is endogenous but does not enter the utility function. It is determined as a function of a fixed cost of work. The utility function is isoelastic in consumption. Hence uncertainty matters and this originates in the stochastic process for wages. Thus the specification described above has been designed to allow the program to have an effect on education choice and also to allow for the possibility that individuals substitute between formal education and on-the-job-training offered by the program, when placed in work through a wage subsidy.

The production sector is a CES between the three types of Human Capital and overall it is a Cobb-Douglas between HC and physical capital – much as in the model before with the difference that this model allows for a different level of substitutability between the three types of human capital. It was found in fact that the elasticity of substitution between college graduates and high school graduates was about 5. However, between the less-than-high-school group and the aggregate of the other two, the elasticity of substitution is 1.0. The different levels of substitutability will imply that GE effects for policies will differ depending on the skill group at which they are targeted.

With this model we consider two policies. One where those unemployed are offered a wage subsidy of 25% the minimum wage and one of 50%. The wage subsidy is only offered to the young, which in this model relates to the first period of five years. We then examine the impact of the policy on those registered in the program. In the baseline, individuals have the choice to work, study or remain unemployed in each and every period. They must also choose their consumption/savings level. The policy is introduced by adding a new option in the first five-year period of life. Under this option the individual may choose to remain unemployed and then will obtain an offer of a subsidized wage as described above. Although our graph depicts both policies, we only discuss the stronger one, which has some discernible long-term impact.

The partial equilibrium results reported in Figures 10.1 and 10.2 are not comparable to the results one would obtain from a small-scale short-run pilot study because it allows individuals to change their work and education decisions (as well as consumption) early on in the life-cycle. The results reported relate to the impact of the program for those who register. The program makes a spell of early unemployment more attractive and education less attractive, particularly for individuals on the margins of ability, enough for them to work or continue with high school in the baseline economy. Such effects are potentially very important but cannot normally be picked up from a standard field trial. An intermediate approach is to run trials to learn about behavior and incorporate this knowledge within the structural model, along the lines we described in the PROGRESA experiment.

As seen in the figures, the partial equilibrium effect of the policy, i.e., where human capital prices are kept constant is to reduce unemployment by 1.5 percentage points. The effect is due to the increased labor market attachment induced by the improvement in productivity, obtained as a result of the program.

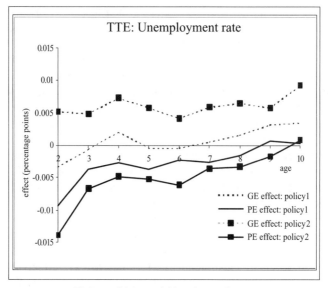

The impact of the wage subsidy on the unemployment rate

Figure 10.1. The impact of wage subsidies on life-cycle employment (Source: Blundell et al., 2005)

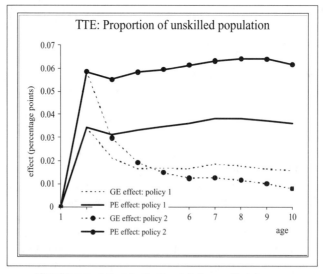

Effect of the wage subsidy on the education rate for those enrolling in the programme

Figure 10.2. The impact of the wage subsidies on education rates (Source: Blundell et al., 2003)

Five years later the effect declines to half the size. At the same time, Figure 10.2 demonstrates that education rates decline, with an increase in the proportion of those with less-than-high school of 6 percentage points. In general equilibrium the effect of the policy is actually reversed. The reason for this at first sight surprising result is precisely the fact that the composition and size of the unemployment pool changes as a result of the policy, initially drawing in individuals who would otherwise not be unemployed. This reduces the price of unskilled labor to such an extent that the policy now ends up increasing long-run unemployment because of the number of people with low ability who prefer to go for the subsidy in period 1 of working life.

In terms of education the GE effect mitigates the adverse impact of the program. Some individuals find it beneficial to invest in formal education once the program period has ended and when they observe the decline in unskilled wages. However, there are still more unskilled workers now relative to the benchmark economy.

The key point to take away from this is that the longer term incentives structure introduced by an intervention designed to reduce unemployment may in fact achieve the opposite and may discourage the accumulation of human capital, ultimately defeating the original aim of the program. What our model shows is that with parameters obtained from data, these concerns can be of practical relevance. More research needs to be carried out to establish the reliability of such models and the sensitivity of human capital prices to changes in domestic supply. Placed in an international context, factor prices may be equalized, in which case some of the effects we have documented will not be relevant. However, even with exogenous prices of human capital, the issue of dynamic incentives is likely to be important, with policies implemented over the long run having very different impacts from the short run returns.

4 CONCLUSIONS

Evaluation has progressed with leaps and bounds in recent years. The progress has built upon the important advances in our understanding of methods as well as by the increasing demands for high quality evaluation by governments and international organizations. In some sense, increasing emphasis has been given to non-parametric, "model free" methods and in particular to randomized experiments. These have been very valuable in establishing the success or otherwise of specific programs, but by their nature they are quite limited in their ability to allow for redesign of programs or for evaluating major interventions, that are likely to affect prices, thus violating a key assumption in the evaluation literature, namely that the control group is not affected.

In this paper we have explored two themes. In the first we considered a simple structural model that is estimated based on data from a randomized experiment but is then used to address issues of how the program could be redesigned. The estimated model is richer than one that would be estimated by traditional observational data, and one could argue that its identification rests on firmer ground than is often the case with such models. However, it uses assumptions from economic theory that may or may not appeal to some; with this combination of data and assumptions, one obtains a tool that can go far beyond the abilities of the simple field trail.

In the second theme we explored the use of general equilibrium models for policy evaluation with heterogeneous agents. In many ways this is quite a new field that requires exploration. Almost inevitably, these models require crucial modeling choices and often heroic assumptions to be made. It is also often the case that the model structure one wishes to impose leads to specifications that are either very difficult to estimate in a rigorous way or for which suitable data is not available, requiring short cuts to be made in the way that parameters are chosen or estimated. Despite all the difficulties however, the results themselves justify the need to explore further and develop these models: GE outcomes can be very different from PE ones both overall and in detail. Thus small pilot studies are frequently incapable of providing even a remotely accurate picture of how a policy will operate when rolled out nationally. One may be justified in being deeply skeptical in certain circumstances about results from GE models; however, these models illustrate that one should also be deeply skeptical about concluding from the results of small scale pilot studies on the effects of major policy interventions that alter long run incentives and that could affect prices.

References

ABOWD, J. M., AND D. CARD (1989): "On the Covariance Structure of Earnings and Hours Changes," *Econometrica*, 57(2), 411–45.

ADDA, J., C. DUSTMANN, C. MEGHIR, AND J.-M. ROBIN (2005): "Career Progression and Formal versus on the Job Training," Mimeo, UCL.

ALONSO-BORREGO, C., J. FERNNDEZ-VILLAVERDE, AND J. E. GALDON-SANCHEZ (2004): "Evaluating Labor Market Reforms: A General Equilibrium Approach," IZA Discussion Papers 1129, Institute for the Study of Labor (IZA).

ATTANASIO, O., C. MEGHIR, AND A. SANTIAGO (2005): "Education Choices in Mexico: Using a Structural Model and a Randomised Experiment to Evaluate Progresa," IFS working paper EWP05/01.

ATTANASIO, O., AND G. WEBER (1993): "Consumption Growth, the Interest Rate and Aggregation," *Review of Economic Studies*, 60(3), 631–649.

BLUNDELL, R., M. BROWNING, AND C. MEGHIR (1994): "Consumer Demand and the Life-Cycle Allocation of Household Expenditure," *Review of Economic Studies*, 61(1), 57–80.

BLUNDELL, R., M. COSTA-DIAS, AND C. MEGHIR (2003): "The Impact of Wage Subsidies on Education and Employment: A General Equilibrium Approach," Mimeo, Institute for Fiscal Studies.

BLUNDELL, R., L. PISTAFERRI, AND I. PRESTON (2005): "Consumption Inequality and Partial Insurance," IFS Working Paper W04/28, November, 2004, revised May 2005.

BLUNDELL, R., AND I. PRESTON (1998): "Consumption Inequality and Income Uncertainty," *Quarterly Journal of Economics*, 113(2), 603–640.

CARD, D., AND D. R. HYSLOP (2005): "Estimating the Effects of a Time-Limited Earnings Subsidy for Welfare Leavers," *Econometrica*.

CUNHA, F., J. HECKMAN, AND S. NAVARRO (2004): "Counterfactual Analysis of Inequality and Social Mobility," Mimeo.

DEARDEN, L., C. EMMERSON, C. FRAYNE, AND C. MEGHIR (2005): "Education Subsidies and School Drop-Out Rates," Institute for Fiscal Studies W05/11, June.

GALLIPOLI, G., AND G. FELLA (2005): "Education and Crime over the Life Cycle," Mimeo.

GALLIPOLI, G., C. MEGHIR, AND G. VIOLANTE (2005): "Education Decisions, Equilibrium Policies and Wages Dispersion," Mimeo, IFS.

HECKMAN, J., H. ICHIMURA, AND P. TODD (1997): "Matching as an Econometric Evaluation Estimator," *Review of Economic Studies*, 65(2), 261–294.

——— (1998): "Characterizing Selection Bias Using Experimental Data," *Econometrica*, 66(5), 261–294.

HECKMAN, J., L. LOCHNER, AND R. COSSA (2003): "Learning-By-Doing Versus On-the-Job Training: Using Variation Induced by the EITC to Distinguish Between Models of Skill Formation," in *Designing Inclusion: Tools to Raise Low-end Pay and Employment in Private Enterprise*, ed. by E. Phelps. Cambridge: Cambridge University Press.

HECKMAN, J., L. LOCHNER, AND C. TABER (1998a): "Explaining Rising Wage Inequality: Explorations with a Dynamic General Equilibrium Model of Labor Earnings with Heterogeneous Agents," *Review of Economic Dynamics*, 1(1), 1–58.

——— (1998b): "General Equilibrium Treatment Effects: A Study of Tuition Policy," *American Economic Review, Papers and Proceedings*, 88(2), 381–386.

HECKMAN, J., AND R. ROBB (1985): "Alternative Methods for Evaluating the Impact of Interventions," in *Longitudinal Analysis of Labor Market Data*, ed. by J. Heckman, and B. Singer. Cambridge: Cambridge University Press.

HECKMAN, J., AND G. SEDLACEC (1985): "Heterogeneity, Aggregation, and Market Wage Functions: An Empirical Model of Self-Selection in the Labor Market," *Journal of Political Economy*, 93(6), 1077–1125.

HECKMAN, J., AND B. SINGER (1984): "A Method for Minimizing the Impact of Distributional Assumptions in Econometric Models for Duration Data," *Econometrica*, 52(2), 271–320.

HECKMAN, J. J., R. LALONDE, AND J. SMITH (1999): "The Economics and Econometrics of Active Labor Market," in *Handbook of Labor Economics, vol. 3A*, ed. by O. Ashenfelter and D. Card. North-Holland.

IMBENS, G., AND J. ANGRIST (1994): "Identification and Estimation of Local Average Treatment Effects," *Econometrica*, 62(2), 467–475.

LALONDE, R. (1986): "Evaluating the Econometric Evaluations of Training Programs with Experimental Data," *American Economic Review*.

LEE, D. (2001): "An Estimable Dynamic General Equilibrium Model of Work, Schooling and Occupational Choice," Ph.D. thesis, University of Pennsylvania.

LEE, D., AND K. I. WOLPIN (2005): "Intersectoral Labor Mobility and the Growth of the Service Sector," forthcoming *Econometrica*.

LUCAS, R. E. (1980): "Equilibria in a Pure Currency Economy," in *Models of Monetary Economics*, ed. by J. Kareken, and N. Wallace. Federal Reserve Bank of Minneapolis, Minneapolis.

MACURDY, T. E. (1981): "An Empirical Model of Labor Supply in a Life-Cycle Setting," *Journal of Political Economy*, 89(6), 1059–1085.

MARSCHAK, J., AND W. H. ANDREWS (1944): "Random Simultaneous Equations and the Theory of Production," *Econometrica*, 12(3/4), 143–205.

MEGHIR, C., AND L. PISTAFERRI (2004): "Income Variance Dynamics and Heterogeneity," *Econometrica*, 72(1), 1–32.

ORCUTT, G. H., AND A. G. ORCUTT (1968): "Incentive and Disincentive Experimentation for Income Maintenance Policy Purposes," *American Economic Review*, 58, 754–772.

ROSENBAUM, P. R., AND D. B. RUBIN (1983): "The Central Role of the Propensity Score in Observational Studies for Causal Effects," *Biometrica*, 70(1), 41–55.

SCHULTZ, T. (2003): "School Subsidies for the Poor: Evaluating the Mexican Progresa Poverty Program," *Journal of Development Economics*.

SIANESI, B. (2003): "Swedish Active Labour Market Programmes in the 1990s: Overall Effectiveness and Differential Performance," *Swedish Economic Policy Review*, 8(2), 133–169.

TODD, P., AND K. WOLPIN (2003): "Using Experimental Data to Validate a Dynamic Behavioral Model of Child Schooling and Fertility: Assessing the Impact of a School Subsidy Program in Mexico," Mimeo, University of Pennsylvania.

CHAPTER 11

Microeconometric Search-Matching Models and Matched Employer-Employee Data

Fabien Postel-Vinay and Jean-Marc Robin

Abstract

The recent advent of matched employer-employee data as part of the labor market scholar's toolbox has allowed a great deal of progress in our understanding of individual labor earnings. A growing number of empirical analyses of available matched employer-employee data sets now combine with the already voluminous literature on empirical wage equations based on individual or household survey data to draw an even richer picture of wage dispersion, individual wage dynamics, and the productivity-wage relationship.

In this chapter we tour the empirical wage equations literature along these three lines and make a case that viewing it through the lens of structural job search models can help clarify and unify some of its recurring findings. Among other things, we emphasize and quantify the role of matching frictions in explaining the share of "residual" wage dispersion that is left unexplained by the reduced-form approach. Secondly, we quantitatively assess the importance of labor market competition between employers relative to non-competitive wage formation mechanisms (namely, wage bargaining) as a theoretical underpinning of the wage-productivity relationship. Thirdly, we show how search frictions, combined with a theoretically founded wage formation rule based on renegotiation by mutual consent, can account for the widely documented dynamic persistence of individual wages. We conclude with a list of questions that are open to further research.

1 INTRODUCTION

Understanding differences between individual wages – both across individuals (wage inequality) and over time (wage dynamics) – is a fundamental motivation of labor economics as a research field. For a very long time, the competitive wage model, whereby individual wages equal the marginal productivity of individual labor supply, was the first and foremost theoretical reference in the empirical literature in sharp contrast with a theory deeply concerned with imperfect information issues and interrogations about the nature of labor market equilibrium.

The Mincer equations estimated in the 70s and the 80s revealed large differences in wages across education and experience groups, which could be interpreted as productivity differences. Panel data sets on wages, which started to be widely available to labor economists in the 80s, permitted a thorough analysis of the residuals of Mincer equations. This analysis further showed that a large part of wage dispersion resulted from unobserved heterogeneity in individual ability and complex accumulation of idiosyncratic shocks. At that point, the competitive view of wages reflecting individual productivity was left essentially unchallenged. Even inter-industry wage differentials were successfully interpreted within the competitive framework of the Roy model (e.g. Heckman and Honoré, 1990): It suffices to allow workers to differ in several dimensions of industry-specific abilities instead of one single, general-purpose ability dimension.

The advent of matched employer-employee data at the end of the 90s brought this nice series of empirical successes to an end. The estimation of wage equations with person and firm effects by Abowd, Kramarz and Margolis (1999) revealed systematic wage differentials both across individuals and across employers. Moreover, a significant fraction of wage dispersion still remained unexplained. This new empirical evidence is difficult to rationalize within a perfect information framework. The idea that there is more wage variability than the Walrasian model can explain is why this model began to gain ground among labor economists, who began to turn their interest toward equilibrium models with imperfect information.

Yet in retrospect, it is still striking to observe how little influence novel theoretical ideas have had on applied work in labor economics over the recent couple of decades. The last twenty years of microeconomic theory, and labor economics is no exception, is all about information imperfections. At the same time, most applied contributions assume competitive markets. Things went very differently in the literature on Industrial Organization. There, oligopolistic competition and auction models received a lot of attention from applied economists. As an example, one can compare the interest that the paper by Berry, Levinsohn and Pakes (*Econometrica*, 1995) stirred up in the profession (464 citations in Google Scholar[1]), with the relative lack of excitement with which the pioneering work of Eckstein and Wolpin (*Econometrica*, 1990: 59 citations; *Review of Economic Studies*, 1995: 26 citations) was received.

In this chapter we review the empirical wage equations literature and make a case that viewing it through the theoretical lens of structural job search models can help clarify and unify some of its recurring findings. While we focus on a particular theoretical paradigm (namely, the theory of job search), our broader and more general hope is that, in the future, more theory will irrigate applied labor microeconomics.

Our main theoretical focus in this chapter will be on the family of sequential auction models, which feature labor markets with two-sided heterogeneity

---

[1] All citation numbers were collected at the time of Econometric Society World Congress in London.

(across workers and across firms). Firms compete for workers' services, but competition is limited by search-information frictions. Between-firm competition forces employers to grant wage raises to their employees, implying that wages monotonically increase over job spells. However, when more productive firms successfully bid workers away from less productive ones, such worker movements are sometimes associated with voluntary wage cuts. We shall also discuss two important extensions of the basic equilibrium-search-sequential-auction model. Firstly, between-firm competition is not necessarily the only force driving wage dynamics (or mobility). The analysis of matched employer-employee data indeed reveals that imperfect between-firm competition falls short of fully explaining the extent of rent sharing in the economy. We thus extend the model by incorporating bargaining as an additional wage setting mechanism. Secondly, between-firm competition cannot alone account for the full extent of within-firm wage variations, both upward and downward. Thus, we next consider match productivity shocks and human capital accumulation. At the end of the day, the sequential auction paradigm proves able to incorporate most empirical features of wage data that those wedded to the purely competitive model consider to be fundamental.

The plan of this chapter is as follows. The first part deals with wage dispersion. The second part deals with wage dynamics. We start by reviewing what we learned on wage dispersion from matched employer-employee data. Then, we explain why equilibrium search models are useful tools to comprehend the different heterogeneity components of wage dispersions. The section on wage dynamics presents ongoing research aiming at establishing that equilibrium search models can also account for the dynamic patterns of wages.

2 WHAT DO WE LEARN ON WAGE DISPERSION FROM MATCHED EMPLOYER-EMPLOYEE DATA (MEE)?

In the past ten years, following Abowd, Kramarz and Margolis's (1999, AKM thereafter)[2] initial push, many matched employer-employee data sets have been constructed in Denmark, Italy, Sweden, Austria, etc., to estimate wage equations. Matched employer-employee data are obtained by merging two different data sources. One needs:

- one panel of worker data with individual index $i \in \{1, \ldots, I\}$ and time index $t \in \{1, \ldots, T\}$,
- one panel of firm data with individual index $j \in \{1, \ldots, J\}$ and same time index $t \in \{1, \ldots, T\}$,
- a matching function $j(i, t) \in \{1, \ldots, J\}$ that defines worker i's employer at time t.

---

[2] 336 citations in Google Scholar.

Worker data are usually register data (employer payroll reports collected for tax purposes). Very often, there is no other information on employers than their administrative identity. Yet in some cases the wage register data can be merged with firm accounting data (value added, EBIT, book value, etc.). Matching with other individual social security or health insurance data has also been done in some countries (Denmark, Sweden).

Wage Equations for MEE Data.   The model considered by AKM (and in subsequent work by Abowd, Kramarz and coauthors) is a standard error–component model with firm fixed effects:

$$w_{it} = x_{it}\beta + \psi_{j(i,t)} + \alpha_i + u_{it}$$

$$= x_{it}\beta + \sum_{j=1}^{J} \psi_j d_{it}^j + \alpha_i + u_{it} \tag{1}$$

where w_{it} is the log individual wage, x_{it} is a vector of time-varying individual characteristics (experience, tenure), $d_{it}^j = \mathbf{1}\{j(i,t) = j\}$ are indicator variables of worker i working at firm j at date t, α_i is a time-invariant worker-specific effect (maybe of the form $\alpha_i = z_i'\gamma + v_i$, where z_i is a vector of observed individual attributes), ψ_j is a firm-specific effect, and u_{it} is some idiosyncratic residual component.

AKM propose to estimate β, person effects $\alpha = (\alpha_1, \ldots, \alpha_I)$ and firm effects $\psi = (\psi_1, \ldots, \psi_J)$ by OLS. An immediate problem with this approach is the huge number of parameters to estimate: $I = O\left(10^6\right)$ and $J = O\left(10^5\right)$. Because of this problem, AKM's initial *Econometrica* (1999) paper only reports approximate OLS estimates. Yet in more recent work, these authors show how one can exploit the sparse structure of the least squares matrices to come up with computationally feasible OLS estimates (see Abowd, Creecy and Kramarz, 2002).[3]

Bias.   For the OLS estimators of β, ψ and α to be unbiased, firm-worker assignment must be strictly exogenous, that is:

$$\left(d_{it}^j\right)_{\substack{t\in\{1,\ldots,T\} \\ j\in\{1,\ldots,J\}}} \perp (u_{it})_{t\in\{1,\ldots,T\}}, \quad \forall i \in \{1, \ldots, I\}.$$

This is an acceptable assumption so long as u_{it} has no impact on workers' job mobility decisions. This implies in particular that workers decide whether or not to change employers based on relative values of firm fixed effects ψ_j.

Then, if mobility is exogenous conditional on firm and worker permanent characteristics, the OLS estimator of β is consistent when I tends to infinity for

---

[3] Sparse matrices should become more common use in applied econometrics as available data sets grow larger. Danilov and Magnus (2005) are currently developing sparse matrix techniques for least squares, apparently more powerful and faster than the currently available MATLAB routines.

fixed T.[4] Lastly, the OLS estimator of α and ψ are consistent when T tends to infinity faster than I and J.

Finite Sample Precision. Estimates of β and firm effects ψ are obtained by applying OLS to the within-transformed model (1):

$$w_{it} - w_{i\bullet} = (x_{it} - x_{i\bullet})\beta + \sum_{j=1}^{J} \psi_j \left(d_{it}^j - d_{i\bullet}^j \right) + u_{it} - u_{i\bullet},$$

where $z_{i\bullet} = \frac{1}{T} \sum_{t=1}^{T} z_{it}$ for an arbitrary variable z_{it}. Inspection of this latter model brings about a new issue: If workers don't change employers, then $d_{it}^j = d_{i\bullet}^j$ for all j and no firm effect can be estimated. In practice, for typical values of T (less than 10 years), few workers will be matched with more than two or three different employers. With such a small amount of worker mobility, regressors are close to colinear and OLS estimates are thus expected to be very imprecise.

OLS estimates of person effects α are then obtained as:

$$\widehat{\alpha}_i = w_{i\bullet} - x_{i\bullet}\widehat{\beta} - \sum_{j=1}^{J} \widehat{\psi}_j d_{i\bullet}^j.$$

This equation shows that any statistical error affecting firm effects is transmitted to worker effects with a sign reversal. We thus expect a spurious negative cross-sectional correlation between $\widehat{\alpha}_i$ and $\widehat{\psi}_{j(i,t)}$ in every year t.

To conclude, in practice, OLS estimates of firm and worker effects in model (1) are likely to be both imprecise and spuriously negatively correlated (across individuals) given the limited time dimension and scant worker mobility that characterize most MEE data sets. Moreover, pointwise estimation of each worker and firm effect is of no intrinsic interest: Only the joint cross-sectional distribution of $\widehat{\alpha}_i$ and $\widehat{\psi}_{j(i,t)}$ is providing useful parameters to interpret (such as its second-order moments, which convey information on wage inequality and firm-worker assortative matching). All this suggests that it would be preferable to develop an estimation protocol, treating α and ψ as random components. Nonetheless, AKM's technique of directly estimating fixed effects to then deduce arithmetic moments of their empirical distribution is straightforward and certainly conveys useful – albeit noisy – information.

Some Results. Table 11.1 shows some results for French and US data. The first column displays the standard deviation of the left-hand side variable and estimated components of the right-hand side of model (1). The remaining seven columns show the corresponding correlation matrix.

Interestingly, no component dominates in the explanation of total log wage variance. For France (resp. the US), experience alone explains 29% of the log

---

[4] Note that J is likely to be a proportion of I (firms are not bigger in China than in the US or France). It should thus make little sense to discuss asymptotics in I for fixed J.

Table 11.1. *Correlations of components of real annual wage rates*

France 1976–1996

	St.D.	w_{it}	$x'_{it}\beta$	$\alpha_i =$	$z'_i\gamma$	$+v_i$	$\psi_{j(i,t)}$	u_{it}
Log real annual wage rate (w_{it})	0.9772	1.0000						
Experience and experience squared ($x'_{it}\beta$)	0.4087	0.5377	1.0000					
Person effect (α_i)	0.5217	0.4569	0.0698	1.0000				
Schooling ($z'_i\gamma$)	0.1522	0.1510	−0.0469	0.2917	1.0000			
Unobservable (v_i)	0.4990	0.4316	0.0872	0.9565	0.0000	1.0000		
Firm effect (ψ_j)	0.4665	0.4287	0.1670	−0.2225	0.0293	−0.2415	1.0000	
Residual (u_{it})	0.5545	0.5675	0.0000	0.0000	0.0000	0.0000	0.0000	1.0000

US 1990–1999

	St.D.	w_{it}	$x'_{it}\beta$	$\alpha_i =$	$z'_i\gamma$	$+v_i$	$\psi_{j(i,t)}$	u_{it}
Log real annual wage rate	0.8941	1.0000						
Experience	0.6965	0.2305	1.0000					
Person effect	0.8434	0.4871	−0.6085	1.0000				
Schooling	0.2317	0.1733	−0.1527	0.2748	1.0000			
Unobservable	0.8110	0.4571	−0.5893	0.9615	0.0000	1.0000		
Firm effect	0.3586	0.4926	0.0635	0.0445	0.0824	0.0228	1.0000	
Residual	0.3614	0.4042	0.0000	0.0000	0.0000	0.0000	0.0000	1.0000

Source: Abowd, Kramarz, Lengermann, and Roux (2003).

wage variance (resp. 5%), person effects alone explain 21% (resp. 24%), firm effects alone explain 18% (resp. 24%) and the residuals alone explain 32% (16%). French and US numbers are similar. Moreover, the correlation between person and firm effects is -0.22 in France and 0.04 in the US, two small numbers, which tend to indicate that there is no sorting of workers by firms.

Whatever the precision of these estimates, it seems relatively clear that no effect dominates the others. After filtering wage distribution from the deterministic effects of individual education, experience and inter-industry differentials, a very significant fraction of wage dispersion remains to be explained. What matched employer-employee data show is that there are systematic differences across workers and across firms that cannot be explained by classical individual or market attributes. What's more, after accounting for worker and firm heterogeneity, there is still a significant share of the wage variance that remains unexplained. This residual component may reflect productivity shocks, measurement error or some genuine wage indeterminacy, as we shall later argue.

Using Firm Accounting Data. The preceding statistical analysis made no use of firm accounting data, which (in France) can be matched with the wage register data. We now want to evaluate the extent to which firm effects reflect differences in labor productivity. To answer this question, we regress log wages w_{it} on employer's mean log productivity (measured by mean log value-added per worker):

$$w_{it} = x_{it}\beta + \alpha_i + \gamma \bar{y}_{j(i,t)} + u_{it}, \quad \text{where } \bar{y}_j = \frac{1}{T}\sum_{t=1}^{T} \ln y_{jt}.$$

We want to think of $\bar{y}_j$ as $\psi_j + \eta_{jt}$. The more noisy $\bar{y}_j$ is as a measure of ψ_j, the less explanatory power it will have.

Table 11.2 shows the results of our own estimation. Experience and experience squared, alone, explain 2% of the log wage variance. Worker effect explains 79%, firm average labor productivity 8% and the residual 18%. The

Table 11.2. *Correlations of log wage with heterogeneity components accounting controlling for firm value added*

	St.D.	w_{it}	$x_{it}\beta$	α_i	$\gamma \bar{y}_{j(i,t)}$	u_{it}
Log real annual labor cost (w_{it})	0.477	1.000				
Experience ($x_{it}\beta$)	0.077	0.139	1.000			
Person effect (α_i)	0.420	0.888	-0.029	1.000		
Firm effect ($\gamma \bar{y}_{j(i,t)}$)	0.022	0.290	0.047	0.269	1.000	
Residual (u_{it})	0.204	0.428	0.000	0.000	0.000	1.000

Sample: French DADS data matched with BRN, 1990–2000, including all private sector employees aged 20–50 in initial year.

estimated correlation between firm ($\gamma \overline{y}_{j(i,t)}$) and worker ($\alpha_i$) effects is again small (27%), even though it is now positive.

Taking Stock.   Statistical issues notwithstanding, the type of exercise just sketched reveals the presence and quantitative importance of firm-specific effects in wage determination. One natural interpretation of this finding is to conclude that the Law of One Price does not hold in the labor market, which in turn implies that one should depart from the competitive paradigm as a description of the labor market.

While the set of alternative theoretical constructs to choose from is potentially rather large, we are looking for a model that is both reasonably realistic and tractable enough to be empirically implementable. Following Mortensen (2003), we argue that equilibrium search models meet these latter two requirements and offer a natural framework in which to analyze the multiform wage dispersion evident in MEE data.

Equilibrium search models rest upon two basic principles:

1. Labor market competition between employers is the fundamental determinant of wages.
2. Competition is limited by search frictions reflecting information imperfection on the location of job offers.

In the presence of search frictions, wages are determined within a bilateral monopoly-type of relationship between employers and workers. While the specific way in which this bilateral monopoly problem is approached varies across particular applications (see the rest of this chapter for a sample), it remains that by varying the intensity of search frictions, the "generic" job search model can be made consistent with a broad array of equilibrium patterns, ranging between the two polar benchmarks of *competitive wage equilibrium* (when all workers can freely force employers into competition and get paid their marginal productivity) and *monopsony wage equilibrium* (when employed job search is infinitely costly and firms offer unemployed workers their reservation wages; Diamond, 1971).

Apart from these two limiting cases, equilibrium search models offer simple explanations of why wages vary both across workers and firms, and why some residual wage dispersion remains once heterogeneity has been accounted for. These explanations are reviewed in the next two sections.

3 A PROTOTYPICAL STATIONARY SEARCH MODEL OF WORKER TURNOVER AND WAGE DISPERSION

Jolivet, Postel-Vinay and Robin (2005, JPR hereafter) examine empirical features of worker turnover and wage distributions across European countries and the US.[5] They conclude that a successful formal description of worker turnover and dispersion should account for the following broad facts:

1. Workers transition from job to job or in and out of employment.
2. Most job-to-job transitions are associated with a wage increase, yet a sizeable fraction of those transitions (20-40%) are associated with a wage cut.
3. Job separation hazards exhibit (slightly) negative duration dependence.
4. Wages are dispersed. Moreover, the distribution of wages in a cross section of employed first-order workers stochastically dominates the distribution of entry wages and is less positively skewed.

JPR then go on to show that the steady-state predictions of a simple (partial equilibrium) search model does a good job of capturing these features. The model that these authors consider builds on a basic set of formal assumptions that are largely common to all the models we shall review in this chapter. We now list these basic assumptions.

Model Description.   Time is continuous. The labor market has a unit-mass of infinitely lived workers who can be either employed or unemployed. The labor market is affected by search frictions in that unemployed workers can only sample job offers sequentially at some finite Poisson rate $\lambda_0 > 0$. Employed workers are allowed to search on the job and face a sampling rate of job offers of $\lambda_1 > 0$. Firm-worker matches are dissolved at rate $\delta > 0$. Upon match dissolution, the worker becomes unemployed.[6]

A job offer is a wage draw w from a sampling distribution F. The wage w stays constant for the duration of the job spell, i.e., until the match is dissolved for exogenous reasons (δ-shock) or the worker quits into another job upon reception of an outside offer. From the workers' viewpoint, jobs are otherwise identical. Hence, a job offer of w is preferred to a job offer of w' if $w > w'$.[7] For simplicity, it is also assumed that any wage draw from F is preferred to unemployment.

In this section, we keep the wage offer distribution F exogenous. For example, wages could be paid a fixed proportion of match productivity, the distribution of which is exogenous. We shall derive it as part of the labor market equilibrium in the next section, as we turn to equilibrium search models.

---

[5] They use data from the European Community Household Panel (ECHP) and the PSID.

[6] All "transition parameters," λ_0, λ_1 and δ will be considered exogenous throughout this chapter. They can be endogenized within a matching model, making a more careful description of labor demand (see Pissarides, 2000, and Mortensen, 2003).

[7] Note that this feature of the model is evidently at odds with the observation that many job-to-job transitions are associated with a wage cut. JPR consider a more general model with reallocation shocks and wage cuts upon job-to-job mobility. We shall return to this at several points below.

Steady-State Equilibrium. The model is solved in steady state. At a steady-state equilibrium, worker inflows and outflows from any given stock balance each other in order to maintain the stock constant. In particular, this holds true for the proportion of unemployed workers, u, and for the cross-sectional distribution of wages across employed workers, G.

- **Unemployment rate, u.** Equality of flows in and out of the stock of unemployed workers writes as:

$$[\text{out}] \quad \lambda_0 u = \delta (1 - u) \quad [\text{in}] \qquad \Longleftrightarrow \qquad u = \frac{\delta}{\delta + \lambda_0}. \quad (2)$$

- **Cross-sectional wage distribution, G.** Equality of flows in and out of the stock of employees paid less than w, $(1 - u) G(w)$, writes as:

$$[\text{out}] \quad \left[\delta + \lambda_1 \overline{F}(w)\right](1 - u) G(w) = \lambda_0 u F(w) \quad [\text{in}]$$

$$\Updownarrow$$

$$G(w) = \frac{F(w)}{1 + \kappa \overline{F}(w)} \qquad \text{or} \qquad F(w) = \frac{(1 + \kappa) G(w)}{1 + \kappa G(w)} \quad (3)$$

where $\kappa = \dfrac{\lambda_1}{\delta}$ is the average number of job offers that a worker receives between two job destruction shocks (index of search frictions), $\overline{F} = 1 - F$.[8]

Estimation and Results. Figure 11.1 is taken out of the JPR paper. Using data from the ECHP and the PSID, they first estimate the density of wage offers, f, from the sample of wages of all employed workers who were just hired from unemployment. They estimate the earnings density, g, from the sample of all employees' wages. An alternative estimator of f can then be constructed from g by differentiating the second equation in (3).[9] We can first verify that the wage offer densities are to the left of earnings densities. Moreover, the distribution of wage offers is systematically less dispersed than the distribution of wages among all employees and is more positively skewed. Finally, the discrepancy between f and g is reasonably well captured by formula (3). We view this last result as strongly supportive of the general structure of job search models: It implies that employed workers accept jobs associated with better wages than unemployed workers, and, what's more, that this selection process is somehow related to the process of job mobility – i.e., the capacity of workers to contact more than one employer at a time – as equation (3) indicates. The extent to which G dominates F is fully characterized by only one parameter, κ, which is estimated from job mobility data, independently of any information on wages.

---

[8] Throughout this chapter, a bar over a cdf will be used to denote the survivor function.
[9] The parameter κ can be estimated separately from job duration data.

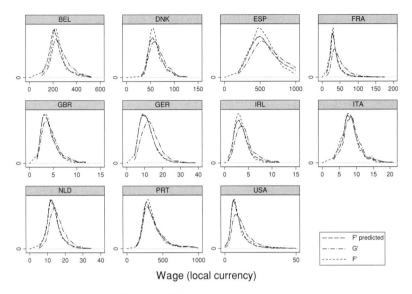

Figure 11.1. Wage densities

While the above results show the model's broad consistency with observations 1 and 4 in the list given at the beginning of this section, JPR also examine the model's rendering of duration dependence in job spell hazards. Because wages are fixed over any given job spell, the hazard rate of a job spell associated with some wage w is constant over time and equal to $\lambda_1 \overline{F}(w)$. The model thus predicts negative duration dependence in a cross section of job spells through wage heterogeneity: Job spells with longer elapsed durations tend to be associated with higher wages, which in turn makes them more likely to last longer in the future. While this prediction is qualitatively consistent with observation 3, it comes at a high price: In the JPR model (and indeed, as we shall see shortly, in wage posting models in general), negative duration dependence hinges on the constancy of wages over any given job spell, which implies that workers only move up the "wage ladder." This rules out not only job-to-job transitions associated with wage cuts (thus contradicting observation 2), but also any within-job wage dynamics. These qualitative shortcomings will be addressed in sections 4 and 5 below. Moreover, the model's quantitative success at predicting negative duration dependence in job spell hazards is more mitigated. JPR indeed show that the source of duration dependence built into the model turns out to be quantitatively weak, if still significant, and conclude that, in most of the countries from their ECHP sample, cross-spell differences in the arrival rates of job offers must be appealed to in order to replicate the observed duration profiles of job spell hazard rates. Such differences arise endogenously in wage posting models when worker search intensity is made endogenous (Christensen et al., 2005).[10]

---

[10] All this refers to "artificial" duration dependence due to heterogeneity. To our knowledge, "true"

Unemployment Rates From Stocks and Flows
(French LFS and US CPS)

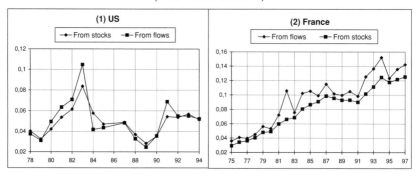

From stocks: Fraction of unemployed in March of year t.
From flows: t/t+1 job destruction rate divided by t/t+1 job destruction rate plus t/t+1 re-employment rate.
Rates are computed by comparing the state in March of year t+1 to the state in March of year t.

Figure 11.2. Unemployment rates from stocks and flows

More on the Steady-State Assumption.   Figure 11.2 depicts the French and US series of unemployment rates as they can be computed from a cross section of employed and unemployed workers and as they can be computed from worker flows in and out of employment and unemployment across two consecutive years. Our data sources are the French labor Force Survey and the US Current Population Survey. Both series are remarkably close.

Perhaps the most intriguing implications of both Figures 11.1 and 11.2 is that the steady-state assumption seems to be a reasonable one. Said more precisely, it seems that observed time series variations mostly reflect variations in predicted steady states.

In the case of the unemployment rate (Figure 11.2), this should not sound too surprising considering the yearly frequency of the data from which Figure 11.2 is constructed and the average duration of an unemployment spell. More precisely, the law of motion of unemployment in the model writes down as:

$$\frac{du_t}{dt} = \delta (1 - u_t) - \lambda_0 u_t, \tag{4}$$

implying a half-life for u_t of $\ln 2/(\delta + \lambda_0)$. Given the very small estimated values for δ, this is well approximated by $\ln 2/\lambda_0$, i.e., 0.7 times average unemployment duration. This number would typically be less than 6 months in continental Europe and around a couple of months in the US. In other words, dynamic adjustments of the unemployment rate are "quick" when the reference period is one year, which explains why the steady-state assumption is a reasonable approximation.[11]

---

duration dependence (i.e., non-stationarity of individual hazards) has so far not been modeled in a job search context. (Yet see below footnote 16.)

[11] Interestingly, Figure 11.2 gives the impression of a slightly better fit in the United States than

Turning to the offered and earned wage distributions, F and G, it is well known that earnings distributions change slowly over time, certainly more slowly than unemployment rates.[12] If this is also the case for the wage offer distribution, then it must also be true for the friction index, which consequently approximately satisfies the equation:

$$\kappa = \frac{F_t(w) - G_t(w)}{G_t(w) \, \overline{F_t}(w)}$$

for all w.

4   STEADY-STATE MARKET EQUILIBRIUM WITH SEARCH FRICTIONS

In the preceding section, we argued that a simple stationary Markovian model of worker turnover based on a reservation wage policy fits the data reasonably well. The model was partial equilibrium in that it kept the distribution of wage offers, F, exogenous. We now want to describe two extensions of the prototypical search models endogenizing the wage offer distribution: Burdett and Mortensen's (1998) wage posting model, and Postel-Vinay and Robin's (2002) sequential auction model.

4.1   Wage Posting Models: Burdett and Mortensen (1998)

Burdett and Mortensen's (1998, BM hereafter) wage posting model builds on the following assumptions about wage formation:

- Firms make take-it-or-leave-it offers to workers. They decide ex ante what wage to offer, then commit to paying the chosen wage for the duration of the job. In particular, they do not counter outside offers.
- Equilibrium wages are a Nash equilibrium of the noncooperative game where firms choose what wage to post, and workers decide what wages to accept.

In the basic BM model, workers and firms are homogeneous, and the production technology is linear in labor.

In this context, Burdett and Mortensen show a very important result. Even though firms and workers are ex-ante identical, the equilibrium wage offer of distribution F is a continuous, nondegenerate distribution. This is because firms play a mixed strategy in the wage posting game's equilibrium. The idea of the proof is very simple. Suppose that a mass of firms were offering the same wage w. Then, each of these firms would gain from offering slightly more because the additional flow of workers that it could attract from the other firms; also,

---

in France. This is consistent with average unemployment duration being about a third in the US of what it is in France.

[12] It is the usual practice to describe changes in inequality across decades.

on-the-job searches would more than compensate the marginal loss in profit per worker.

Although the BM model generates equilibrium wage dispersion among identical firms and workers (and thus potentially explains the residual wage variance left unexplained by the AKM decomposition), the predicted wage density in the homogeneous model is upward sloping, which is at odds with empirical evidence (see Figure 11.1). Fortunately, it is easy to change that by allowing for heterogeneity in match productivity.

BM Model with Heterogeneous Productivity. The BM model can be extended by assuming that firms differ in their (constant) marginal productivity of labor, p. In the sequel we shall refer to p as firm *type*. Upon receiving a job offer, workers draw the type of the firm from which the offer comes from as an (exogenous) sampling distribution, $\Gamma(p)$. Let $F(w)$ denote the corresponding equilibrium sampling distribution of wage offers. For it to be a Nash equilibrium, it must be the case that:

1. Each firm of type $p \in \text{Supp}(\Gamma) = \left[\underline{p}, \overline{p}\right]$ offers a wage $w(p)$ that maximizes the steady-state profit flow $\pi(w, p) = (p - w)\ell(w)$, where $\ell(w)$ is steady-state employment:

$$\ell(w) = \frac{(1 - u)g(w)}{f(w)} = \frac{(1 - u)(1 + \kappa)}{\left[1 + \kappa \overline{F}(w)\right]^2},$$

   and $1 - u = \frac{\lambda_0}{\lambda_0 + \delta}$.

2. The sampling distributions of wages and firm types are equal, i.e., $F[w(p)] = \Gamma(p)$.

The equilibrium solution is such that the firm with the smallest productivity, $\underline{p}$, offers unemployed workers their reservation wage ϕ and hires workers only from the unemployment pool. Moreover, free entry will ensure that $\underline{p} = \phi$. All other firms with productivity p in $\left[\underline{p}, \overline{p}\right]$ offer:[13]

$$w(p) = p - \left[1 + \kappa_1 \overline{\Gamma}(p)\right]^2 \int_\phi^p \frac{dx}{\left[1 + \kappa_1 \overline{\Gamma}(x)\right]^2}. \tag{5}$$

---

[13] This result is a direct consequence of the Envelope Theorem applied to the profit maximisation problem:

$$\frac{d\pi(p, w(p))}{dp} = \frac{\partial \pi(p, w(p))}{\partial p} = \ell(w(p)) = \frac{(1 - u)(1 + \kappa)}{\left[1 + \kappa \overline{F}(w(p))\right]^2} = \frac{(1 - u)(1 + \kappa)}{\left[1 + \kappa \overline{\Gamma}(p)\right]^2}.$$

As free entry further implies that $\pi\left(\underline{p}, \phi\right) = 0$, integration of the above equation leads to:

$$(p - w(p))\ell(p) = \pi(p, w(p)) = \int_\phi^p \frac{(1 - u)(1 + \kappa)}{\left[1 + \kappa_1 \overline{\Gamma}(x)\right]^2} dx.$$

Hence $w(p)$.

Empirical Applications of the BM Model. An appealing property of this version of the BM model is that any observed wage offer distribution F can be rationalized in equilibrium as resulting from a properly chosen underlying productivity distribution Γ, provided that the resulting wage equation (5) defines an increasing function $w(p)$ (an implementability condition that is not prohibitively restrictive in practice). Partly as a consequence of this flexibility, the BM model has received a lot of attention from microeconometricians. Bowlus, Kiefer and Neumann (1995 and so forth) assume a discrete distribution of productivity. This turns out to be very cumbersome if there are too many support points. Van den Berg and Ridder (1998) assume segmented homogeneous markets. Workers differ in productivity across labor markets but not within. Bontemps, Robin and Van den Berg (2000) propose a simple estimation procedure for the heterogeneous productivity version of the BM model. Bontemps, Robin and Van den Berg (1999) have both heterogeneous productivity and heterogeneous leisure costs but impose equal job offer arrival rates for employed and unemployed workers. Christensen, Lentz, Mortensen, Neumann and Werwatz (2005) estimate an extension of the BM model featuring endogenous search intensity (declines with wage). The estimation technique draws on Bontemps, Robin, and Van den Berg (2000). Barlevy (2005) proposes an estimation technique based on record statistics.

The estimation technique developed by Bontemps, Robin and Van den Berg (2000) is very simple and can be applied to other empirical microeconomic equilibrium models. It proceeds in the following steps:

1. Estimate G and g nonparametrically.
2. Estimate κ by maximization of the likelihood of worker job and wage mobility,[14] replacing F by

$$\widehat{F}(w;\kappa) = \frac{(1+\kappa)\widehat{G}(w)}{1+\kappa\widehat{G}(w)}.$$

3. Estimate the inverse wage function (5),

$$p(w) = w + \frac{1+\kappa\overline{F}(w)}{2\kappa f(w)} = w + \frac{1+\kappa G(w)}{2\kappa g(w)},$$

to retrieve the underlying productivity distribution Γ.[15]

Successes and Failures of the BM Model. The main lesson drawn from empirical implementations of the BM model is that, while it fits worker turnover and wage distributions well, the underlying distribution Γ of firm productivity required to achieve that good fit is implausible: It exhibits an exceedingly long

---

[14] The hazard rate of a job spell associated with wage w is $\delta + \lambda_1 \overline{F}(w) = \delta\left(1 + \kappa\overline{F}(w)\right)$.

[15] The aforementioned implementability condition of the BM equilibrium clearly appears here. For the (inverse) wage function to be increasing, it has to be the case that the observed cross-sectional earnings density g does not increase "too steeply" over any part of its support.

right tail. It is easy to understand why. High-productivity firms have a lot of market power in the BM model. This tends to concentrate wages toward the lower part of the distribution. In order to generate the very long, thin tails of observed wage distributions, productivity distributions with much longer and thinner tails are thus necessary.

Finally, as we already emphasized in section 3, a substantial shortcoming of the wage posting model lies in its predicted pattern of individual wage dynamics: The wage posting assumption rules out any within-job wage dynamics by assumption, and further implies that workers can only experience wage gains as they move directly from job to job. Both of these features are counterfactual, which calls for further theoretical thinking about the wage formation process. A very promising line of research has been opened by Stevens (2004) and Burdett and Coles (2003), who analyze posting models where firms post wage-tenure contracts instead of single wages.

4.2   Sequential Auctions: Postel-Vinay and Robin (2002)

One of the reasons why the BM model fails to fit the data is because there is too little between-firm competition. Postel-Vinay and Robin (2002, PR hereafter) propose to temper the monopsonistic inclination of employers by allowing employers to counter the outside offers made to their employees. As we shall see, this alternative hypothesis about wage formation also helps in addressing the issue of wage dynamics.

The model allows for two-sided heterogeneity in match productivity: Firms are heterogeneous as in the BM model and workers now differ in ability parameter ε. The marginal productivity of a match between a type ε worker and a type p firm is $p\varepsilon$ (i.e., workers are perfect substitutes, up to their type ε). As they receive offers, workers draw firms of type p from the same sampling distribution F, whatever their type or labor market status.

Wage Contracts.   Wage contracts are negotiated between employers and employees under complete information: When an unemployed worker contacts an employer, the latter observes the employment status of the worker and his/her ability. When an employed worker contacts an outside firm through on-the-job search, the latter observes the worker's current wage and ability as well as the incumbent employer's type. The worker also informs his/her current employer about the exact type of the poaching firm. Wage contracts can be renegotiated by mutual consent only. Lastly, PR assume that employers make take-it-or-leave-it offers to workers, an assumption that is relaxed in Cahuc, Postel-Vinay and Robin (2006).

Let $V_0(\varepsilon)$ denote the lifetime value of unemployment for a worker of type ε. Let $V(w; \varepsilon, p)$ denote the lifetime value of current wage w for a worker ε in firm p. When an unemployed worker meets a potential employer, the latter offers a wage $\phi_0(\varepsilon, p)$ that is just enough to make the former prefer employment to unemployment. That is, $\phi_0(\varepsilon, p)$ solves the equation:

$$V\left(\phi_0(\varepsilon, p); \varepsilon, p\right) = V_0(\varepsilon). \tag{6}$$

When an employed worker paid w in firm p receives an offer from a firm p', the two employers compete to hire the same worker. They play a Bertand game, the solution of which is such that the more productive firm bids the worker away from the less productive one and pays the value-equivalent of the best wage the latter firm can offer, which equals match productivity: In other words, the worker extracts the full surplus from the less productive employer. For instance, if $p < p'$, then firm p' eventually hires the worker for a mobility wage $\phi(\varepsilon, p, p')$ that solves the equation:

$$V\left(\phi; \varepsilon, p'\right) = V\left(\varepsilon p; \varepsilon, p\right). \tag{7}$$

More precisely, depending on the values of p, p' and the worker's initial wage w, the consequence of the worker receiving an outside offer is one of the following three events:

- If $p < p'$, the worker moves to p' for a wage $\phi(\varepsilon, p, p')$ (possibly lower than w – see below).
- If $p > p'$ and $w < \phi(\varepsilon, p', p)$, the worker stays at firm p but her/his wage is raised to $\phi(\varepsilon, p', p)$.
- If $\phi(\varepsilon, p', p) < w$ nothing happens.

PR further show that equations (6) and (7) can be solved in closed form. Specifically, all wages have the following expression (for a pair $p \le p'$):

$$\phi(\varepsilon, p, p') = \varepsilon \cdot \phi(1, p, p')$$
$$= \varepsilon \cdot \left(p - \frac{\lambda_1}{\rho + \delta} \int_p^{p'} \overline{F}(x)\, dx\right), \tag{8}$$

where ρ is the discount rate and where "starting" wages $\phi_0(\varepsilon, p) = \phi(\varepsilon, b, p)$ (i.e., being unemployed is like working at a firm of productivity $b \le \underline{p}$).

This wage equation highlights two important theoretical predictions of the PR model. First, wages gradually increase over a given job spell as the worker receives outside offers, which her/his employer matches. The PR model thus has non-trivial, if monotonic, within-job wage dynamics. Second, some voluntary job-to-job changes will be associated with a wage cut. Consider a type ε worker employed at a type p firm, who at some point in time is lucky enough to draw an outside offer from a poacher of the exact same type p as her/his current employer. Bertrand competition will then leave the worker with the full rent associated with an (ε, p) match: According to (8), the resulting wage will equal εp, the worker's marginal productivity. Now suppose that this same worker later receives an offer from a more productive firm $p' > p$. According to the mechanism outlined above, the worker will quit his job at firm p to take up the job offered by firm p', with a mobility wage given by (8), which is strictly less than her/his initial wage, εp. This results from a straightforward option value effect: Being paid her/his marginal productivity at firm p, the worker has no hope of seeing her/his wage further raised if s/he stays at firm p. The worker is therefore willing to give up some income today in exchange for the prospect of future wage raises (offered by firm p' only) as s/he moves from firm p to firm p'. Drawing a parallel with the BM model, in which workers only moved toward jobs associated with higher w's, the PR model workers only move up the *productivity* ladder – i.e., they only move toward jobs offered by higher type p firms – even though such moves can be associated with a cut in w.[16]

Overall, the PR model thus predicts qualitatively richer individual wage dynamics than the wage posting models previously reviewed. How far it goes into quantitatively explaining the observed dynamic behavior of wages will be examined in section 5.

Equilibrium Distribution.   Any employed worker is thus paid a wage $w = \phi(\varepsilon, q, p)$, where (ε, p) are the match characteristics and q is the productivity of the employer from which the worker was last able to extract the full surplus in a wage negotiation (this equals b if the last mobility was out of unemployment). Thanks to the perfect substitutability of workers, employers are indifferent to worker ability. As a consequence, the steady-state equilibrium distribution of worker ability ε is the same in all firms, irrespective of their types p (there is no sorting). Further exploiting the balance of inflows and outflows between employment states, between firms and within firms, PR arrive at the following characterization of the equilibrium distribution of the triple (ε, p, q):

1. ε has some exogenous distribution, say H.
2. (q, p) are independent of ε (no sorting).
3. The distribution of p is the steady-state distribution of firm labor productivity across employees, with cdf:

$$G(p) = \frac{F(p)}{1 + \kappa \overline{F}(p)}, \tag{9}$$

where $\kappa = \lambda_1/\delta$ and where F is the sampling distribution of firm types that job seekers face.
4. The distribution of q given p has cdf:

$$q \mid p \sim \left(\frac{\delta + \mu + \lambda_1 \overline{F}(p)}{\delta + \mu + \lambda_1 \overline{F}(q)} \right)^2$$

on $\{b\} \cup [\underline{p}, p]$.

---

[16] This particular implication of the PR model is potentially counterfactual, just as BM's implication of workers only moving up the wage ladder is counterfactual. Yet as p is not directly observed in the data (at the very least, it is arguably less readily measurable than individual wages), this particular implication of the PR model is difficult to assess empirically.

Estimation. PR use the French wage register data (DADS) unmatched with firm accounting data. The only information on a firm is its ID number. Yet, this is enough for identification. Using the steady-state distribution of (ε, q, p) derived in the previous paragraph, one can write down the mean wage paid by a firm of type p to its employees as:

$$y(p) \equiv \mathbb{E}(w \mid p)$$
$$= \mathbb{E}(\varepsilon) \cdot \left(p - \left[1 + \kappa \overline{F}(p) \right]^2 \int_{p_{\min}}^{p} \frac{1 + (1 - \frac{\rho}{\rho+\delta})\kappa \overline{F}(q)}{\left[1 + \kappa \overline{F}(q) \right]^2} dq \right).$$

(10)

Assume that y is an increasing function of p. A job-to-job mobility then only occurs if the mean wage is higher in the poaching than in the incumbent firm. Consequently, Bontemps, Robin and Van den Berg's technique for estimating the BM model can be applied to estimate λ_1 and δ and the distribution of firm-level mean wages (y) among employees, i.e., $G[p(y)]$ where $p(y)$ is the inverse of $y(p)$. In a second step, inverting equation (10), where (9) is used to substitute $F[p(y)]$, identifies $p(y)$ (and thus $F(p)$).

Application. PR apply the model to obtain a log-wage variance decomposition similar to the one produced by AKM:

$$\text{Var}(\ln w) = \text{Var}(\ln \phi(\varepsilon, q, p))$$
$$= \begin{cases} \text{Var}(\ln \varepsilon) & \text{(person effect)} \\ + \text{Var}\,\mathbb{E}[\ln \phi(1, q, p) \mid p] & \text{(firm effect)} \\ + \mathbb{E}\,\text{Var}[\ln \phi(1, q, p) \mid p] & \text{(effect of frictions)}. \end{cases}$$

(11)

The interpretation of the first two terms in the above decomposition as the contributions of, respectively, person and firm effects is rather straightforward. These first two terms directly parallel the contributions of α_i and ψ_j to total log wage variance in the AKM model (1).

As to the third term, it is the share of within-firm wage variance, which is not due to worker heterogeneity in ability ε. This term is the counterpart of the share of wage variance that was left unexplained in the AKM decomposition, i.e., the variance due to the residual term in (1). Within PR's structural model, though, this residual within-firm variance has a clear interpretation: It reflects conditional heterogeneity in terms of individual histories of outside offers. Identical workers employed at identical firms can still earn different wages depending on how lucky they both were in drawing outside job offers.[17] This ex-post heterogeneity arises because of the randomness of the process of outside offers, i.e., because of search frictions, hence the label "effect of frictions" that was attached to it in (11).

---

[17] Formally, recalling that wages are a combination of a triple of random variables (ε, q, p), this residual variance reflects conditional heterogeneity of q given (ε, p).

PR's quantitative results confirm the importance of search frictions in wage determination: The third component in (11) accounts for about 50% of total log wage variance, with little variation across worker categories. The person effect explains 40% of Var $(\ln w)$ for managers and quickly drops to 0 for unskilled categories. These last numbers are in the same ballpark as AKM's result of about 20%, all categories pooled.

4.3   Sequential Auctions and Bargaining: Cahuc, Postel-Vinay and Robin (2006)

Cahuc, Postel-Vinay and Robin (2006, CPR hereafter) extend the PR model to further investigate the wage-productivity relationship. The CPR contribution is two-fold. First, contrary to PR (and AKM), CPR merge the administrative data on wages with firm accounting data in order to obtain direct estimates of the firms' productivity levels. The literature before CPR (including PR) was inferring those productivity levels from observed wages and from the structure of the particular model that was estimated. In other words, it was predicting what the wage-productivity relationship or what the productivity distribution should be, given the model's structure, in order to implement the observed distribution of wages as an equilibrium. Using actual data on productivity removes one degree of freedom and offers a way of testing the theory.

Second, CPR relax the assumption of firms making take-it-or-leave-it offers to workers and give bargaining power to the latter. The PR sequential auction model has it that wages are less than marginal labor productivity, so that non-trivial rent-sharing takes place between workers and employers. Yet, it cannot tell whether sheer competition between employers in the presence of search friction is enough to quantitatively explain the workers' share of value-added observed in linked wage-productivity data. To answer this question, it is necessary to nest the PR model in a more general model allowing for an additional "non-competitive" source of rent-sharing. Bargaining is a natural candidate. In the CPR model, unemployed workers negotiate with a single employer in a conventional way, but when an employed worker receives an outside job offer, a three-player bargaining process is started between the worker, her/his incumbent employer and the poacher. This bargaining process is modeled using a version of the Rubinstein (1982) infinite-horizon, alternating-offers bargaining game.

Labor Productivity.   In order to construct a labor productivity value for each firm j of the sample, CPR estimate the following production function:

$$Q_{jt} = \theta_j \left(\alpha_1 L_{1jt} + \alpha_2 L_{2jt} + \ldots \right)^\xi, \qquad \sum_j \theta_j = 0,$$

where Q_{jt} is firm j's value added at date t (sales minus intermediate costs; available from the firm accounting data), and L_{1jt}, L_{2jt}, etc., are firm j's employment of various occupation categories (secretaries, engineers, etc.) defining different labor markets. Parameters α_1, α_2, ... are the corresponding occupation-wide average ability.

It should be raised at this point that inferring measures of firm productivity from firm-level data on value-added as CPR do requires assumptions about the competitive environment on the product market. For instance, one can assume that all firms produce the same multi-purpose good and that the good market is competitive. In this case, a proper production function is estimated. If, however, firms operate on an imperfectly competitive product market, then a reduced-form firm-revenue equation is estimated. In any case, for the equilibrium sequential auction model to apply, we need this firm-revenue/production function to exhibit constant returns to scale, a property that is confirmed by the firm data that we use to estimate the model. Nevertheless, diminishing (apparent) returns to labor, labor demand, and interactions between labor market structure and goods market structure are definitely important areas to investigate.

In market k, firm j thus has labor productivity $p_{jk} = \alpha_k \theta_j$. CPR estimate p_{jk} for each firm j and each market k.

Wage Contracts. The fact that workers now have some positive bargaining power entails the following changes from the PR wage contracts. Consider two firms with productivity levels p and p' competing for worker ε. The maximum values that these firms can yield to the worker are, respectively, $V(\varepsilon p; \varepsilon, p)$ and $V(\varepsilon p'; \varepsilon, p')$. Suppose that $p' > p$. Then the outcome of the strategic bargaining game exposed in CPR is such that the type p' firm wins the worker and pays a wage $\phi(\varepsilon, p, p')$ such that

$$V(\phi; \varepsilon, p') = (1 - \beta) V(\varepsilon p; \varepsilon, p) + \beta V(\varepsilon p'; \varepsilon, p'), \qquad (12)$$

where $\beta \in [0, 1]$ measures the worker's bargaining power. This outcome is clearly reminiscent of the "generalized Nash solution" to a bargaining problem between a firm of type p' and a worker of type ε where the worker's threat point would be to take up employment at the less productive, type p firm for a wage of εp. Equation (12) has the following closed-form solution:

$$\phi(\varepsilon, p, p') = \varepsilon \cdot \left(p' - (1 - \beta) \int_p^{p'} \frac{\rho + \delta + \lambda_1 \bar{F}(x)}{\rho + \delta + \lambda_1 \beta \bar{F}(x)} dx \right),$$

where the notation is the same as for the PR model. Note that, as expected, the CPR bargaining model confounds itself with the PR sequential auctions model in the case where workers have zero bargaining power, $\beta = 0$.

Application. CPR estimate workers' bargaining power β to equal zero for all low skill categories and to lie between 0 and 0.3 for high skill workers (depending on the industry). CPR's main finding is that between-firm competition alone is essentially enough to explain – or at the very least plays a prominent role in explaining – wage determination in France over the period 1993–2000. Yet although skilled workers are found by CPR to have less bargaining power than is usually estimated, they are still able to capture a substantial share of the job surplus for reasons that cannot be entirely explained by between-employer competition for labor services. This is an interesting result which calls for further research in order to better understand what hides inside the "black box" of the bargaining power parameter β. The game-theoretic model featured in CPR's paper interprets this parameter in terms of different response times for workers and firms and different time discount rates. But empirical evidence on the dependence of these variables on such intuitive candidate determinants as education or trade union density, for example, is still missing.

A glance at the various panels of Figure 11.3 next shows that the model is reasonably consistent with the observed wage-productivity relationship, thus improving on what seemed to be a failure of the BM wage posting model. More specifically, the figure suggests two remarkable stylized facts. One is that the wage paid by the lowest-p firms in all four samples and all categories of workers displayed is always very close to match productivity (solid line) at $\underline{p}$. The other is that profit rates are increasing with productivity: The gap between wages and productivity – which again is near zero at $\underline{p}$ – becomes substantial at higher values of p. CPR's structural model correctly captures this phenomenon, which, incidentally, remained concealed in AKM's reduced-form analysis.

5   WAGE DYNAMICS

The discussion has been thus far focused on "cross-sectional" aspects of the data, namely wage dispersion or the wage-productivity relationship. Yet job search models are inherently dynamic and do have strong predictions about the process followed by individual wages over time. Even though this is not (yet) directly related to matched employer-employee data, it is interesting to ask whether those predictions are sensible, or more generally, if we can learn anything from structural job search models about individual wage dynamics. This is the question that we ask in this final section. We begin by putting twenty years of empirical literature on wage dynamics in a nutshell and then turn back to job search models.

5.1   Empirical Models of Income Dynamics

The literature studying individual labor earnings dynamics, as they are observed from worker panel data, is literally huge.[18] While the "true" earnings process is still to be discovered, a twofold conclusion seems to emerge from that literature. First, earnings shocks are highly persistent over time. Second, it takes a fairly

---

[18] A somewhat arbitrary selection includes the seminal papers by Lillard and Willis (1978), Lillard and Weiss (1979), MaCurdy (1982) and Abowd and Card (1989); the comprehensive comparative analysis of recent developments by Alvarez, Browning and Ejrnæs (2001); Blundell and Preston (1998) for an application to UK data; and Meghir and Pistaferri (2004) as an example of a state-of-the-art paper in this field.

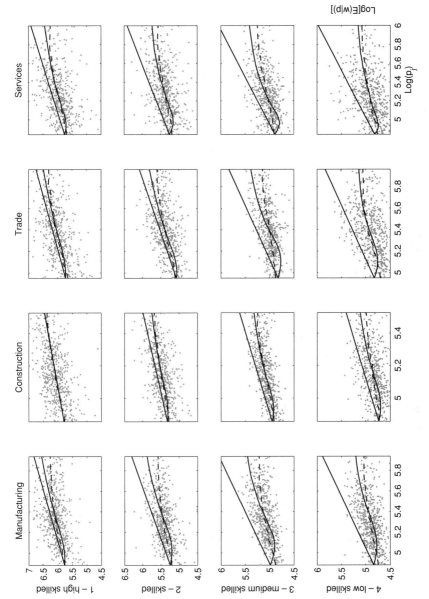

Figure 11.3. The Wage-Productivity Relationship

rich mix of random processes to replicate the intricate autocovariance structure of earnings.

Indeed there is a long tradition of fitting ARMA-type models to individual income trajectories in worker panel data. The archetypal such ARMA-type decomposition of the individual earnings process features a martingale or a highly persistent Markov component, on top of a fixed-effect and a transitory (MA) shock. In its simplest form, it looks like:

$$\begin{cases} w_{it} = \alpha_i + s_{it}^P + s_{it}^T, & \text{with } \alpha_i \text{ a fixed effect,} \\ s_{it}^P = s_{i,t-1}^P + u_{it}, & \text{with } u_{it} \text{ i.i.d.} \\ s_{it}^T = \sum_{\ell=0}^{q} \theta_\ell \varepsilon_{i,t-\ell}, & \text{with } \varepsilon_{it} \text{ i.i.d. and typically } q = 0 \text{ or } 1. \end{cases}$$

(13)

While the dynamic properties of individual earnings – notably persistence – are by now well diagnosed by this kind of decomposition, the economic mechanisms at the root of these properties are still unknown or at least controversial. Progress in this area is once more likely to come from a structural approach. We now turn to job search models as potential structural candidates.

5.2   What Do Job Search Models Have to Say on Income Dynamics?

Probably owing to the analytical difficulty of combining a realistic job search model with individual level shocks, research on individual wage dynamics within structural search models is just taking off, and the contributions reviewed in this section are still somewhat preliminary. Yet they do contain some promising results.

Wage Dynamics in PR's Sequential Auctions Model.   Postel-Vinay and Robin (2002) briefly assess their model's quantitative rendition of individual wage dynamics by comparing the observed and predicted distributions of yearly wage changes among various subgroups of workers. They do so separately for job movers (i.e., workers who have experienced a job-to-job transition within the year) and job stayers (i.e., workers who haven't). Their results are summarized in Tables 11.3 and 11.4.

Table 11.3 reveals that the predicted distribution of wage changes among job movers first-order stochastically dominates the observed one. It does so to a larger extent in its bottom than in its top half, meaning that, while the PR model does have a theoretical mechanism predicting that workers may be willing to take wage cuts as they change employers, this mechanism is not quantitatively strong enough.

Turning to Table 11.4 (which relates to job stayers), one sees that the predicted distribution is clearly much more concentrated around zero wage change than the observed one. The only force governing within-job wage dynamics in the PR model is the sampling of outside job offers by workers: As employers match these offers, workers obtain wage raises. There is thus nothing to cause

Table 11.3. *Distribution of yearly wage changes in the PR model: Job movers*

		Median	% Obs such that $\Delta \ln w \leq$				
Occupation		$\Delta \ln w$	−0.10	−0.05	0	0.05	0.10
Executives, engineers	Data	3.1%	23.6	28.5	38.1	55.1	65.4
	Simul.	3.1%	13.0	22.9	38.8	55.1	65.4
Admin. and sales supervisors	Data	3.7%	21.6	27.1	36.6	54.3	65.2
	Simul.	3.3%	2.7	12.4	35.0	55.8	66.7
Technical supervisors	Data	3.8%	14.0	20.2	32.2	55.5	67.3
	Simul.	2.8%	4.2	10.0	32.2	57.8	71.8
Administrative support	Data	2.2%	21.5	28.7	40.7	60.5	69.2
	Simul.	5.1%	1.1	6.1	24.3	49.7	64.4
Skilled manual workers	Data	0.5%	33.2	37.7	49.2	62.3	72.0
	Simul.	4.5%	1.7	7.5	28.2	51.7	66.0
Sales and service workers	Data	1.4%	31.3	37.7	45.1	58.0	67.5
	Simul.	3.0%	0.2	5.5	31.0	59.1	75.3
Unskilled manual workers	Data	−1.3%	33.5	42.9	54.5	63.4	72.3
	Simul.	3.6%	0.2	4.4	29.4	55.5	70.0

wage cuts within a job spell in the model, and (as the table shows), simulated wages are indeed downward rigid within jobs. What's more, this mechanism of offer matching does not seem to be quantitatively strong enough to account for observed wage increases within jobs.

Overall, failure of the PR model to replicate individual wage dynamics comes mainly from its tendency to predict excessive downward wage rigidity, and indeed total downward wage rigidity within job spells. Now, when comparing PR's predictions to actual data, it should be mentioned that PR's simulations presented in Tables 11.3 and 11.4 are run assuming the absence of measurement error. Yet adding classical (i.e., symmetric) measurement error to the simulation model is unlikely to help much, as the predicted distribution is more skewed than the observed one. Moreover, recent attempts at measuring the actual extent of downward wage flexibility[19] suggest that, even though much of the observed downward wage flexibility is due to measurement error (Gottschalk, 2005; Dessy, 2005), such downward flexibility is still a real phenomenon, even among job stayers. Something thus has to be added to PR's model in order to explain these "genuine" within-job wage cuts.

A clear shortcoming of the PR model is the lack of individual-level pro- ductivity – or "match quality"– shocks. The assumption that individual or firm productivity is fixed over time is certainly an unrealistic one, and, to the ex- tent that wages are related to productivity, wage changes are likely to reflect

---

[19] See e.g. Smith (2000) and Nickell and Quintini (2003) on UK data, Gottschalk (2005) on US data and Dessy (2005) for a multi-country study based on data from the ECHP.

Table 11.4. *Distribution of yearly wage changes in the PR model: Job stayers*

Occupation		Median $\Delta \ln w$	% Obs such that $\Delta \ln w \leq$				
			−0.10	−0.05	0	0.05	0.10
Executives, engineers	Data	2.7%	6.6	11.3	28.5	64.4	80.0
	Simul.	0%	0	0	85.8	93.9	96.6
Admin. and sales supervisors	Data	2.6%	7.9	12.9	28.6	65.2	81.1
	Simul.	0%	0	0	84.7	94.8	97.3
Technical supervisors	Data	2.5%	6.6	11.9	29.6	68.1	85.0
	Simul.	0%	0	0	87.2	95.8	97.9
Administrative support	Data	2.2%	7.9	12.4	30.0	69.8	84.2
	Simul.	0%	0	0	84.9	94.7	97.3
Skilled manual workers	Data	1.9%	7.9	15.0	34.9	69.5	85.1
	Simul.	0%	0	0	85.6	94.5	97.2
Sales and service workers	Data	2.5%	7.4	12.8	31.4	64.5	79.1
	Simul.	0%	0	0	84.0	94.9	97.5
Unskilled manual workers	Data	2.2%	7.7	14.6	32.9	66.4	81.9
	Simul.	0%	0	0	84.5	94.2	96.8

(at least partially) changes in productivity. Moreover, adverse individual productivity shocks line up as a possible cause for within-job wage cuts, hence potentially correcting the PR's model counterfactual prediction of downward wage rigidity within a job spell.

Introducing Individual-Level Shocks. Postel-Vinay and Turon (2005, PT hereafter) investigate the capacity of the PR model with simple i.i.d. match-level productivity shocks to capture the main aspects of observed earnings processes. They thus show how the combined assumptions of on-the-job search and wage renegotiation by mutual consent can act as a realistic "internal propagation mechanism" of i.i.d. shocks. This combination of assumptions, which they take up from the PR model, indeed implies that purely transitory productivity shocks are translated into persistent wage shocks with a covariance structure that they find to be consistent with the data.

Neglecting measurement error to simplify the argument (measurement error is found to explain much, but not all, of the observed downward wage flexibility), the PT model delivers the following dynamic structure for log wages (the model is now in discrete time): $w_{it} = \alpha_i + v_{it}$, where α_i is a fixed effect and v_{it} is a shock such that

$$v_{i,t+1} \mid v_{it} = \begin{cases} v_{it} & \text{with probability } \overline{F}(v_{it}) - \frac{\lambda_1}{1-\delta}\overline{F}(v_{it})^2, \\ v' < v_{it} & \text{with density } f(v'), \\ v' > v_{it} & \text{with density } 2\frac{\lambda_1}{1-\delta}f(v')\overline{F}(v'), \end{cases}$$

(14)

Table 11.5. *Job search vs. ARMA decomposition*

	$\mathrm{Cov}(\Delta w_{it}, \Delta w_{i,t+s})$, $s = \ldots$				
	0	1	2	3	4
BHPS	0.032	−0.009	−0.000	−0.001	0.000
	(0.001)	(0.001)	(0.001)	(0.001)	(0.001)
Simulated	0.035	−0.009	−0.002	0.002	0.001
	(0.001)	(0.001)	(0.001)	(0.001)	(0.001)

	ARMA Parameters			Test of OI Rest.: Test Statistic
	$\mathrm{Var}(u_{it})$	$\mathrm{Var}(\varepsilon_{it})$	θ_1	(df: p-value)
BHPS	0.010	0.011	0.119	65.52
	(0.001)	(0.001)	(0.045)	(52: 0.099)
Simulated	0.011	0.012	0.110	63.76
	(0.001)	(0.001)	(0.039)	(52: 0.127)

where F is the sampling distribution of underlying productivity shocks. Conditional on individual fixed-effects p, PT thus predict that wages follow a first-order, nonlinear Markovian process based on a specific acceptance/rejection scheme of i.i.d. wage innovations.

This particular structure turns out to capture the covariance structure of wages amazingly well. PT estimate the structural model using twelve years of data on highly educated workers of both genders from the BHPS, then simulate a panel of income data.[20] Among other illustrations of their model's goodness of fit, they fit the canonical ARMA process (13) to both real and simulated data. The results are in Table 11.5. Also, for a more direct comparison with the PR model without shocks, we can use the PT simulations to construct a table similar to Tables 11.3 and 11.4, reporting the observed and predicted distributions of yearly wage changes (Table 11.6).

In both tables, the similarity between the results obtained with the simulated and the true BHPS samples is striking (in spite of a slight tendency of the model to over-predict large wage cuts). A particularly intriguing result in Table 11.5 is that, as commonly found in the literature, a significantly positive variance for the innovation of the permanent earnings shock u_{it} is estimated, both for the actual and simulated data. One would, however, wrongly conclude to the presence of a random walk component of the individual earnings process, as we know that, for the simulated data, the fitted ARMA process

---

[20] For lack of space, we do not discuss PT's estimation procedure. Yet it differs quite fundamentally from the methods presented in the previous two sections that were used to estimate the BM or the PR model: While these latter exploit almost exclusively the data's cross-section dimension, PT's estimation technique is based on dynamic moments – as is standard estimation of an ARMA model like (13).

Table 11.6. *Distribution of yearly wage changes in the PT model*

		Median $\Delta \ln w$	\% Obs such that $\Delta \ln w \leq$				
			-0.10	-0.05	0	0.05	0.10
All workers	BHPS	0%	22	34	50	60	73
	Simulated	-1.5%	28	40	51	60	73

is misspecified and the true DGP is stationary. This illustrates the difficulty of numerically distinguishing between a linear process truly exhibiting a unit root and other types of a highly persistent (possibly nonlinear) processes. This point was thoroughly investigated in a related context by Baker (1997), who compares a linear ARMA decomposition of earnings dynamics similar to (13) to a competing "profile-heterogeneity" model featuring individual heterogeneity in (linear) earnings-experience profiles using twenty years of PSID data. Even though he finds evidence of a unit root when fitting the ARMA process to his sample, tests based on specifications nesting the two models lead to rejection of the unit root hypothesis. Overall, Baker (1997) concludes that the evidence favors the "profile-heterogeneity" specification over the unit root model.

The PT model in turn suggests that wage persistence could/should be thought of as the outcome of a specific acceptance/rejection scheme of i.i.d. shocks. Incidentally, a look around existing theories of individual income dynamics reveals that the PT model is not the only one propounding this type of scheme. The process in (14) is indeed formally reminiscent of predictions obtained by Harris and Holmström (1982), Thomas and Worral (1988), or Beaudry and DiNardo (1991) in models of self-enforcing wage contracts designed to allocate risk between a risk-neutral employer and a risk-averse employee faced with uncertainty about match productivity and/or market opportunities.

The PT results thus suggest that job search models potentially offer structural explanations of the widely documented persistence of earnings shocks and can potentially help with the interpretation of observed wage dynamics. In particular, as the rates of transition between labor market states (δ and λ_1) are key determinants of the individual earnings process in (14), the PT results highlight the link between labor market competition (as measured by the probability of raising outside job offers when employed), worker mobility across jobs, and individual earnings dynamics.

What About Human Capital Accumulation?   One serious shortcoming of all the theories reviewed thus far is that they completely overlook human capital accumulation as a potential driving force of the wage process. Ongoing work by Bagger, Fontaine, Postel-Vinay and Robin (BFPR hereafter) incorporates human capital accumulation in a version of the PR model. Assuming piece-rate wages, BFPR derive the following structural log-wage equation:

$$w_{it} = \alpha_i + k_{it} + p_{j(i,t)} - \int_{q_{it}}^{p_{j(i,t)}} \left[1 - \frac{\rho \lambda_1 \overline{F}(x)}{1 - \rho(1 - \delta)} \right] dx,$$

where $p_{j(i,t)}$ and q_{it} are firm productivity levels that evolve along with the occurrence of outside job offers following similar rules as in PR, and where k_{it} is worker i's human capital and follows an arbitrary Markov process. The BFPR wage equation thus not only features human capital with flexible dynamics (two important additions to the PR/PT efforts), but also clearly identified firm effects (which were absent from the PT model). This allows us to go back to matched employer-employee data (as BFPR propose to do, using Danish register data) with a structural model, which is potentially capable of explaining the relationship between wages and productivity, from both a cross-section and a dynamic perspective.

To conclude this section, it seems that the sequential auction model delivers a promising description of wage dynamics both within and between employment spells. Yet, much remains to be done in the way of explaining features of income dynamics such as income persistence, the role of human capital accumulation, experience *vs.* tenure effects, and the role of firm heterogeneity. This now opens the door to a new research agenda, aiming at bridging the gap between the "wage dispersion" (AKM) and "income dynamics" (Abowd and Card) literatures.

6 WHERE DO WE GO FROM HERE?

In this chapter we have given a review – although a partial one – of existing empirical structural models of wage dispersion and wage dynamics, with a particular emphasis on some new empirical properties of wage dispersion and individual wage and employment processes revealed by the most recent descriptions based on matched employer-employee data. We have focused on equilibrium job search models with on-the-job search. The theoretical models feature heterogeneous productivity attributes for both firms and workers, and wage setting mechanisms that include alternative assumptions of wage posting, sequential auctions, and wage bargaining.

This class of models is used to provide new results about the decomposition of log-wage variance into firm effects, worker effects and the effect of labor market frictions. The model can also be used to estimate workers' bargaining power in a general equilibrium model of the labor market with interfirm competition limited by search frictions. It also provides a simple enough framework that allows us to replicate the complex empirical properties of actual dynamic wage processes.

We now list a few desirable extensions.

One richness of this literature is also a drawback. It offers a choice between two alternative wage setting mechanisms: wage posting and sequential auctions. They correspond to different sets of assumptions about the information that is available – or exploitable – to a worker and a firm about each other's characteristics when a matching opportunity occurs. More work is needed to understand which set of assumptions is better suited to describe a particular labor market. It is likely that skill, occupation, and industry are crucial determinants.

The particular equilibrium search models considered in this review assume away any potential source of sorting. Indeed these models predict the absence of sorting as a straightforward consequence of the combined assumption of perfect substitutability between workers within a firm and constant returns to scale. Nevertheless, it is hard to believe that there is no sorting on unobservables (to the econometricians but observables to the interacting agents) in the labor market. Moreover, the no-sorting prediction is at odds with results from the literature on hedonic wage/competitive equilibrium models. More research is thus called for to obtain estimates of the degree of sorting in matched employer/employee data that are robust to the existence of endogenous mobility. In particular, nesting the two theoretical paradigms of job search and hedonic wages is one of the most exciting theoretical and empirical projects for future research in labor economics.

A final desirable avenue for future research relates to macroeconomics and policy analysis. It is possible to use these models to analyze equilibrium effects of policy interventions only if contact rates and job destruction rates are endogenized. Here again, Dale Mortensen opened the way in his 2000 paper, "Equilibrium Unemployment with Wage Posting: Burdett-Mortensen meet Pissarides." Mortensen shows that it is rather easy to incorporate features of equilibrium matching models into the equilibrium search models and thus turn these latter into fully general equilibrium models. While much more work is needed to identify and estimate matching functions using micro data, reasonable calibrations of the additional parameters should still be of great help in the analysis of such large-scale policy measures as the EITC or WFTC for instance.

Still in the field of macroeconomics, and apart from policy, a strong limitation of the models considered in this chapter is that they are only tractable in steady-state equilibrium. It is considerably more difficult to describe out-of-equilibrium dynamics here than in Pissarides's canonical matching model. This is because some of the endogenous variables are distributions, i.e., infinite dimensional parameters, and it is very hard to analyze their dynamics (see Shimer, 2003). Issues about possible analytical solutions, numeric simulations or acceptable approximations, are all very uncertain at the present.

References

[1] Abowd, J. M. and D. Card (1989), "On the Covariance Structure of Earnings and Hours Changes", *Econometrica*, 57(2), 411–45.
[2] Abowd, J. M., R. Creecy, and F. Kramarz (2002), "Computing Person and Firm Effects Using Linked Longitudinal Employer-Employee Data", Cornell University Working Paper (http://www.crest.fr/pageperso/dr/kramarz/note on computation revised.pdf).

[3] Abowd, J. M., F. Kramarz, P. Lengermann, and S. Roux (2003), "Interindustry and Firm-Size Wage Differentials in the United States and France", Cornell University working paper.

[4] Abowd, J. M., F. Kramarz and D. N. Margolis (1999) "High Wage Workers and High Wage Firms", *Econometrica*, 67, 251–333.

[5] Alvarez, J., M. Browning, and M. Ejrnæs (2001), "Modelling Income Processes with Lots of Heterogeneity", CAM discussion paper 2002-01.

[6] Baker, M. (1997), "Growth-Rate Heterogeneity and the Covariance Structure of Life-Cycle Earnings", *Journal of Labor Economics*, 15 (2), 338–75.

[7] Barlevy, G. (2005), "Estimating Models of On-the-Job Search using Record Statistics", Federal Reserve Bank of Chicago Working Paper (http://www.chicagofed.org/publications/workingpapers/papers/wp2003-18.pdf).

[8] Beaudry, P. and J. DiNardo (1991), "The Effect of Implicit Contracts on the Movement of Wages over the Business Cycle: Evidence from Micro Data", *Journal of Political Economy*, 99(4), 665–88.

[9] Berry, S., J. Levinsohn and A. Pakes (1995), "Automobile Prices in Market Equilibrium", *Econometrica*, vol. 63, no. 4, 841–90.

[10] Bontemps, C., J.-M. Robin, and G.-J. Van den Berg (1999), "An Empirical Equilibrium Search Model with Continuously Distributed Heterogeneity of Workers' Opportunity Costs of Employment and Firms' Productivities, and Search on the Job", *International Economic Review*, 40 (4), 1039–74.

[11] Bontemps, C., J.-M. Robin and G. J. Van den Berg (2000), "Equilibrium Search with Continuous Productivity Dispersion: Theory and Non-Parametric Estimation", *International Economic Review*, 41 (2), 305–58.

[12] Bowlus, A. J., N. M. Kiefer, and G. R. Neumann (1995), "Estimation of Equilibrium Wage Distributions with Heterogeneity," *Journal of Applied Econometrics*, 10, S119–31.

[13] Bowlus, A. J., N. M. Kiefer, and G. R. Neumann (2001), "Equilibrium Search Models and the Transition from School to Work," *International Economic Review*, 42 (2): 317–43.

[14] Burdett, K. and M. G. Coles, (2003), "Equilibrium Wage-Tenure Contracts", *Econometrica*, 71, 5, 1377–1404.

[15] Burdett, K. and D. T. Mortensen (1998), "Wage Differentials, Employer Size and Unemployment", *International Economic Review*, 39, 257–73.

[16] Blundell, R. and I. Preston (1998), "Consumption Inequality and Income Uncertainty", *Quarterly Journal of Economics*, 113, 603–40.

[17] Cahuc, P., F. Postel-Vinay and J.-M. Robin (2006), "Wage Bargaining with On-the-Job Search: Theory and Evidence". *Econometrica*, 74, 323–64.

[18] Christensen, B. J., R. Lentz, D. T. Mortensen, G. R. Neumann and A. Werwatz (2005), "On the Job Search and the Wage Distribution", *Journal of Labor Economics*, 23(1), 31–58.

[19] Danilov, D. and J. R. Magnus (2005), "Least Squares in Sparse Systems", work in progress (http://center.uvt.nl/staff/magnus/).

[20] Dessy, O. (2005) "Nominal Wage Rigidity in Europe: Estimates and Institutional Causes", Università di Milano mimeo.

[21] Diamond, P. A. (1971), "A Model of Price Adjustment", *Journal of Economic Theory*, 3, 156–68.

[22] Eckstein, Z. and K. I. Wolpin (1990), "Estimating a Market Equilibrium Search Model from Panel Data on Individuals", *Econometrica*, 58, 783–808.

[23] Eckstein, Z. and K. I. Wolpin (1995), "Duration to First Job and the Return to Schooling: Estimates from a Search-Matching Model", *Review of Economic Studies*, 62, 263–86.

[24] Gottschalk, P. (2005), "Downward Nominal Wage Flexibility: Real or Measurement Error?", *Review of Economics and Statistics*, 87 (3), 556–68.
[25] Harris, M. and B. Holmström (1982), "A Theory of Wage Dynamics", *Review of Economic Studies*, 49, 315–33.
[26] Heckman, J. J. and B. Honoré (1990), "The Empirical Content of the Roy Model", *Econometrica*, 58 (5), 1121–49.
[27] Jolivet, G., F. Postel-Vinay and J.-M. Robin (2005), "The Empirical Content of the Job Search Model: Labor Mobility and Wage Distributions in Europe and the US", in H. Bunzel, B. J. Christensen, G. R. Neumann and J.-M. Robin, editors, *Structural Models of Wage and Employment Dynamics*, Elsevier Science.
[28] Lillard, L. A. and Y. Weiss (1979), "Components of Variation in Panel Earnings Data: American Scientists 1960–1970", *Econometrica*, 47(2), 437–54.
[29] Lillard, L. A. and R. J. Willis (1978), "Dynamic Aspects of Earnings Mobility", *Econometrica*, 46(5), 437–54.
[30] MacLeod, W. B. and J. M. Malcomson (1993), "Investments, Holdup, and the Form of Market Contracts", *American Economic Review*, 83(4), 811–37.
[31] MaCurdy, T. E. (1982), "The Use of Time-Series Processes to Model the Error Structure of Earnings in a Longitudinal Data Analysis", *Journal of Econometrics*, 18(1), 83–114.
[32] Meghir, C. and L. Pistaferri (2004), "Income Variance Dynamics and Heterogeneity", *Econometrica*, 72, 1–32.
[33] Mortensen, D. (2000), "Equilibrium Unemployment with Wage Posting," in H. Bunzel, B. J. Christiansen, P. Jensen, N. M. Kiefer and D. T. Mortensen, eds., *Panel Data and Structural Labor Market Models*, Amsterdam: Elsevier.
[34] Mortensen, D. (2003), *Wage Dispersion: Why Are Similar Workers Paid Differently?*, MIT Press.
[35] Nickell, S. J., and G. Quintini (2003), "Nominal Wage Rigidity and the Rate of Inflation", *Economic Journal*, 133 (October), 762–81.
[36] Pissarides, C. A. (2000), *Equilibrium Unemployment Theory*, 2nd edition, Cambridge, MA: MIT Press.
[37] Postel-Vinay, F. and J.-M. Robin (2002), "Equilibrium Wage Dispersion with Worker and Employer Heterogeneity", *Econometrica*, 70 (6), 2295–350.
[38] Postel-Vinay, F. and H. Turon (2005), "On-the-Job Search, Productivity Shocks, and the Individual Earnings Process", manuscript, University of Bristol and PSE (http://www.ecn.bris.ac.uk/www/ecfybpv/wp/Shocks.pdf).
[39] Rubinstein, A. (1982), "Perfect Equilibrium in a Bargaining Model", *Econometrica* 50, 97–109.
[40] Shimer, R. (2003), "Dynamics in a Model of On-the-Job Search" (paper presented at the SED meeting, Paris, June).
[41] Smith, J. C. (2000), "Nominal Wage Rigidity in the United Kingdom", *Economic Journal*, 110, C176–95.
[42] Stevens, M., (2004), "Wage-Tenure Contracts in a Frictional Labor Market: Firms' Strategies for Recruitment and Retention", *Review of Economics Studies*, 71(2), 247, 535–51.
[43] Thomas, J. and T. Worrall (1988), "Self-Enforcing Wage Contracts", *Review of Economic Studies*, 55, 541–54.

CHAPTER 12

Discussion of 'Dynamic Models for Policy Evaluation' and 'Microeconometric Search-Matching Models and Matched Employer-Employee Data'

Joseph G. Altonji*

1 INTRODUCTION

The papers by Costas Meghir and Fablen Postel-Vinay and Jean-Marc Robin provide useful discussions of developments in two important areas in labor economics and public finance. There is little overlap between the two papers, and so I consider them seperately.

Meghir assesses the relative strengths and weaknesses of policy evaluation based on straightforward experimental designs and on structural models. He makes a strong case that the two approaches are complementary, particularly when dynamics and general equilibrium effects are likely to be important. Below I begin with a short summary of his most important points. I then discuss the potential to utilize more of a continuum of models between a simple experimental or quasi-experimental analysis on the one hand and a dynamic structural model on the other, even in complicated dynamic settings where reduced form analysis is difficult. In particular, I suggest using simulation to derive the reduced form implied by the structural model and then treating the implied reduced form as a baseline reduced form around which to expand.

Postel-Vinay and Robin provide a valuable overview of developments in search/matching models and their application using matched employer/employee data. I briefly supplement their coverage of the literature and their research agenda.

2 DYNAMIC MODELS AND POLICY EVALUATION

Meghir addresses three broad issues of methodology. The first is the role of analysis conducted in a simple "treatment effects" framework in the presence of experimental variation (or plausibly exogenous non-experimental variation) versus analysis based on a structural model. The second concerns the role of structural models in meeting the challenge posed by dynamics in the analysis

* Support from the Economic Growth Center, Yale University and the National Science Foundation under grant SES-0301142 is gratefully acknowledged.

of policy. The third is the importance of accounting for equilibrium effects of large-scale social programs rather than simply extrapolating from the results of a small-scale program. Meghir appropriately stresses the advantages of experimental and "quasi-experimental" variations in providing a transparent source of identification of the causal effect of a specific program. Few assumptions are needed for experimental evaluation of a specific small-scale program on a specific population studied. However, it is hard to extrapolate the results from a specific program to different populations or to alternative programs. It is also difficult to account for "feedback effects" arising through externalities or through the general equilibrium effects of large-scale programs operating through prices, congestion, or other mechanisms.

Meghir argues that there is an important synergy between experimental evaluations and structural modeling. In one direction, the sources of exogenous variation provided by an experiment aid in the identification and the testing of the structural model. In the other, a structural model provides a way to extrapolate from the results of the specific experimental variation to consider dynamic responses and, more importantly, to estimate the impact of alternative policies and to consider effects for populations that differ from the control and experimental groups. Furthermore, it is hard to imagine how a simple experimental or quasi-experimental design could be used to account for general equilibrium effects that operate at the level of a large region or country.[1]

Meghir draws on three of his own studies to illustrate these points. Attanasio, Meghir and Santiago (2005) (hereafter, AMS) reanalyze Mexico's PROGRESA program using a dynamic discrete choice model. They use the model to study the optimal age profile of the subsidy. They show that a budget neutral shift of subsidy from younger to older children would boost impact of PROGRESA on education because secondary school attendance is a key decision point. The experimental results point strongly in this direction, and the age pattern of the response probably did not come as a surprise to those involved in the original design of PROGRESA, which has multiple objectives.[2] However, AMS's structural analysis gives a quantitative guide to what the most cost effective design would be if one wishes to maximize school attendance. One cannot draw such inferences from the experimental analysis.

Meghir is very clear about the costs of structural analyses. The main question is whether the structural model is a good enough approximation to reality to provide a useful guide to how agents would respond to alternative policies. AMS (2005) represents work in progress, and there are a number of issues that could be raised, many of which Meghir or AMS touch on. First, not very much is done to validate the fit of the model, although it is encouraging that it can reproduce the main experimental results by and large. Second, data limitations

---

[1] Miguel and Kramer (2004) and Angrist and Lavy (2004) are recent examples of studies that use experimental design to account for externalities that operate over a small geographic group or within a specific institution (such as a school).

[2] See for example Schultz's (2004) analysis of the effects of PROGRESA on education.

preclude estimation of the returns to education at later ages when considering how monetary benefits influence decisions. AMS simply specify a terminal value for each education level at age 18. Furthermore, wages are not observed for most sample members, and so the opportunity cost of staying in school is specified simply as a function of age, education, and region. The empirical estimates imply that the effects of a subsidy are three times larger than the effect of an equivalent shift in the wage. There are several explanations as to why this might be the case, and a strength of structural analysis in the context of an experiment, is that one can work with less restrictive models. My concern is that the authors lack data on key variables in an economic model of education choice – wages by education level. I would like more discipline to come from the theory of education choice that motivates the structural model, and I wonder how much of the identification of the model is coming from specific functional form assumptions and assumptions about dynamics that are not strongly motivated by theory.

Like Meghir, I view experimental and quasi-experimental designs and structural models as complements rather than substitutes. However, I think that it would be productive for researchers to work with more of a continuum between models that rely almost exclusively on the experimental design at one extreme and a full-blown structural model that makes use of the experimental variation at the other. I have in mind models that impose enough structure to permit one to extrapolate beyond the specific policies and population groups considered in the experiment, as is possible with a structural model. The study of dynamic decisions, such as education choice, makes reduced form analysis difficult because behavior is likely to depend both on past choices and on future values of the exogenous variables and the education subsidy. Nevertheless, there are some possibilities.

2.1   Possibility 1: Reduced Form Dynamic Models with Lots of Restrictions on Interactions and Functional Form

First, it is worth exploring what can be learned from a reduced form dynamic model that heavily restricts interactions among the variables and imposes smoothness restrictions on the link between school attendance and the exogenous variables. Consider the following specification for the probability of school attendance at t.

$$\Pr(Attend_{it} = 1) = F(\mu_i, grant_{it}, \ldots, grant_{i18}, z_{it}, \ldots, z_{i18},$$
$$ed_{it}, t, x_{it}^p, x_{it+1}^p, \ldots, x_{i18}^p, x_{it}^s, \ldots, x_{i18}^s,$$
$$w_{it}(ed_{it}), \ldots, w_{18}(ed_{it})) \tag{1}$$

where $F(\cdot)$ is a cumulative distribution function such as the normal, $attend_{it}$ is an indicator for school enrollment at age t, $grant_{it+j}$ is the size of the grant at age $t + j$, z_{it+j} consists of age $t + j$ variables that capture the cost of schooling, including parental education, and x_{it+j}^p and x_{it+j}^s capture the costs of primary and secondary school and include distance to the nearest school and w_{it}. In the above model the wage at $t + j$ is assumed to depend on education at t. Alternatively, one might evaluate the wage in $t + j$ at the average value of education of persons who remain in school up to $t + j$. The initial condition for ed_{it}, ed_{it_0}, might be treated as in AMS, with

$$ed_{it_0} = f(\mu_i, z_{it_0}, school\_availability_{it_0}). \tag{2}$$

Even if one were to exclude all interactions among the variables from the reduced form model while allowing the coefficients to depend on t, the reduced form would have many, many more parameters than the structural model has. The complexity arises from the fact that future values of the grant, costs of school, and other variables influence the decision at t and that the nature of the intertemporal dependence will vary with t. However, one could proceed by heavily restricting the reduced form. First, one could use AMS's linear specification of the period t gain from schooling to restrict the way that $grant_{it}$, z_{it}, x_{it}^p, and x_{it}^s affect $Attend_{it}$. Second, one could heavily restrict how the coefficients relating variables dated $t + j$ to $Attend_{it}$ vary with t and j. For example, one might restrict the coefficients on $grant_{it+j}$, $w_{it+j}(ed_{it})$, z_{it+j}, x_{it+j}^p, and x_{it+j}^s to equal constants plus simple functions of t and j. Third, one could heavily restrict the interactions among the variables.

An approach that is complementary is related to Ichimura and Taber (2000), which builds on ideas going back to Marschak. In AMS's structural model, $Grant_{it}$ affects behavior by altering the current utility gained from attending school relative to working through the index $\gamma Grant - w_{it}$. Imposing the same restriction on the reduced form model would lead to

$$\begin{aligned} \Pr ob(Attend_{it} = 1) = F(\mu_i, \gamma grant_{it} - w_{it}(ed_{it}), \ldots, \gamma grant_{i18} \\ - w_{18}(ed_{i18}), z_{it}, \ldots, z_{i18}, t, ed_{it}, t, x_{it}^p, \\ x_{it+1}^p, \ldots, x_{i18}^p, x_{it}^s, \ldots, x_{i18}^s). \end{aligned} \tag{3}$$

In practice, one would have to heavily restrict (3) along the lines mention above.

One could use the reduced form to simulate the effects of alternative grant policies. One might also use it as a benchmark with which to assess the fit of the structural model. In particular, one might use the reduced form to assess the dimensions in which the structural model fails to fit the data and to guide modifications to it. One could assess whether or not the specific shortcomings of the structural model undermine its usefulness for the policy evaluations AMS perform.

2.2   Possibility 2: Using the Structural Model
to Shape the Reduced Form Model

As a practical matter, in high dimensional problems reduced form specifications are never completely unrestricted. Furthermore, in an experimental setting with limited variation in the treatment such a model could not be used to evaluate alternative policies. In many settings, one writes down a reduced form model that is linear in most variables, with some interaction terms and nonlinear terms. Such a model can be regarded as an approximation to the true reduced form. One can think of an unrestricted reduced form model with lots of interaction terms and nonlinear terms as an expansion around a baseline reduced form model that contains only main effects and linear terms. An alternative is to make explicit use of the structural model to come up with a "baseline" for the reduced form and expand around that baseline. Why is this appealing? Because the structural model incorporates the prior information that the researcher has about how education choices are made. Indeed, the specification of the structural model is almost always the natural place to impose those priors, particularly in a complicated dynamic setting such as the PROGRESA program. Given this fact, I am proposing that one use the structural model as the starting point for a reduced form model that is heavily shaped by, but less restrictive than, the structural model.

One would proceed as follows. First, one would use the estimates of the structural model to simulate the endogenous variables given the observed distributions of the exogenous variables. From the simulated distribution of the endogenous and exogenous variables, one could arrive at a reasonably parsimonious specification for the reduced form that describes the simulated data well. Let the resulting reduced form be

$$\Pr ob(Attend_{it} = 1) = H(\mu_i, grant_{it}, \ldots, grant_{i18}, z_{it}, \ldots, z_{i18}, t,$$
$$ed_{it}, x_{it}^p, x_{it+1}^p, \ldots, x_{i18}^p, x_{it}^s, \ldots, x_{i18}^s,$$
$$w_{it}(ed_{it}), \ldots, w_{18}(ed_{it}); \hat{\theta}_1)$$
$$ed_{it_0} = h(\mu_i, z_{it_0}, school\_availability_{it_0}; \hat{\theta}_2)$$

where H and h are known up to the parameter vector θ_1 and θ_2. The values $\hat{\theta}_1, \hat{\theta}_2$ are the value of θ_1, θ_2 that best fit the simulated data according to some standard criterion. One might then generalize the restricted reduced form by using the real data to estimate the model

$$\Pr ob(Attend_{it} = 1) = G\{H(\mu_i, grant_{it}, \ldots, grant_{i18}, z_{it}, \ldots,$$
$$z_{i18}, t, ed_{it}, x_{it}^p, x_{it+1}^p, \ldots, x_{i18}^p, x_{it}^s, \ldots, x_{i18}^s,$$
$$w_{it}(ed_{it}), \ldots, w_{18}(ed_{it}); \hat{\theta}_1) + X_{it}'\alpha_1\}$$
$$ed_{it_0} = h(\mu_i, z_{it_0}, school\_availability_{it_0}; \hat{\theta}_2)$$
$$+ X_{i0}'\alpha_2 + error$$

where X_{it} consists of a small subset of the exogenous variables and interactions among them, α_1, α_2 are vectors of parameters to be estimated, and $\hat{\theta}_1$ and $\hat{\theta}_2$ are treated as known. For example, given that AMS are interested in how the effect of the grant depends on age, one might include $grant_{it} \cdot t$ in X_{it}'. The estimates of α_1 and α_2 indicate the dimensions in which the structural model does not capture the relationship between the exogenous variables and school attendance, and might suggest modifications to the structural model.

If such modifications are likely to be difficult to carry out (say, because of computational complexity), one could use the "generalized" reduced form of the structural model to provide an alternative set of estimates of the impact of policy reforms. This is a halfway house between the use of a fully structural model and the use of a complex, poorly estimated, atheoretical reduced form. Even a misspecified structural model might provide a good point of departure for the specification of a parsimonius reduced form model.

2.3   Policy Evaluation and General Equilibrium

Meghir does an excellent job of bringing to the forefront the issue of general equilibrium (GE) effects in most econometric studies of program effects. It is important to note that there is in fact a well-established literature on "applied general equilibrium modeling."[3] Nevertheless, such issues have been largely neglected by the army of empirically oriented labor and public finance economists who focus on estimation of specific "treatment effect" parameters.

Gheallipoli, Meghir and Violante (2004) (hereafter, GMV) use a dynamic GE model of education choice and wages to study the effects of an education subsidy on education choice and inequality. In their model, the response of education to a large-scale program may be amplified by peer effects and dampened by wage responses. Consequently, one needs a GE model to assess the effects of the program. Similar issues arise with other policies, such as the effects of a wage subsidy. GMV incorporate labor supply into a framework that resembles Heckman, Lochner and Taber's (1998) dynamic GE model of human capital investment and inequality in some respects. This addition permits them to assess the effects of taxes used to finance the education subsidy. They also incorporate unobserved heterogeneity that affects non-wage costs of education as well as wages, and use an overlapping generations model to endogenize the wealth distribution. An important omission from the model relative to Heckman, Lochner and Taber is the exclusion of on-the-job training. The authors use a complex estimation/calibration strategy to come up with parameter estimates for the model.

The model is still under development and so the results are preliminary, but they are very interesting. GMV, like HLT, find that subsidies have a large positive effect on educational attainment in a partial equilibrium model, but that GE feedbacks undo most of the effect of the subsidy. The authors raise many questions about the specification of the model and the estimation procedures that underlie these results, and I could add a number of my own. It will be quite some time before GMV and subsequent papers settle the issue of how important GE effects are for the classes of policies the authors consider. However, there is growing evidence that GE effects are a first order issue when considering the effects of large-scale programs.

---

[3] Kehoe, Srinivasan, and Whalley (2005) contains a number of recent contributions to this literature and provides many references.

3 MICROECONOMETRIC SEARCH-MATCHING MODELS AND MATCHED EMPLOYEE-EMPLOYER DATA

Postel-Vinay and Robin (hereafter, PR) ably survey recent developments in the use of search-matching models to study wage inequality, wage dynamics, job mobility, and unemployment. For many questions involving wages in labor economics, one may reasonably abstract from fact that employer and match specific components of wage variation are quantitatively significant. However, labor economists have known for a long time that wages vary substantially across jobs for a given worker. Panel data on individuals indicate that a substantial component of wage variation is specific to the firm and/or the job match. Indeed, one needs only compare the variation in the change in wage rates for jobs stayers and job changers to see this. A number of studies have documented that there is an important variance component of wages associated with jobs and that it is related to job stability and to wage growth over a career. Examples include Abraham and Farber (1987), Altonji and Shakotko (1987), Topel (1986), and Topel and Ward (1992). A large literature examining dislocated workers using household data and using social insurance earnings records shows the same thing. With only panel data on individuals that lack firm identifiers, one cannot distinguish job match specific error components from firm level error components. Studies of employer wage surveys (e.g., Groshen (1992)) show clearly that wages have an important firm specific component. Finally, empirical search models of wages and unemployment suggest that wage variation is substantial.

As PR document, the past ten to fifteen years have brought remarkable advances in our understanding of the role of job search and heterogeneity in wage offers in the distribution of wages, wage dynamics, wage growth over a career, and mobility. The progress stems from three main sources. The first is better data, as PR stress. The growing availability around the world of employer-employee data sets, in some cases with matches to significant amounts of information about the firm and the worker, has lead to an explosion of research in this area, with Abowd, Kramarz, and Margolis's (1999) influential analysis of the French DAS data as the leading example. The advent of additional high-quality household panel data sets with good information on wages, job mobility and unemployment, such as the British Panel and GSEOP, has also been helpful. The second source is a series of important advances in search and matching models, many of which are summarized in the paper. The third is advances in computing power and computational methods that have made implementation of more complex, more realistic models possible.

3.1   Statistical Accounting for Wage Dispersion

PR summarize studies that decompose the variance of wages into a number of factors. Abowd, Kramarz, and Margolis made great progress on this important issue. I don't have much to add to their discussion. Future work needs to pay more attention to sampling error in the estimation of firm effects, person effects, experience slopes, and tenure slopes when examining the importance of various sources of wage dispersion. This should not be very difficult to do.

3.2   Search/Matching Models

After thirty years of steady progress on the theoretical side, search/matching models are approaching a level of realism that will permit them to become workhorse models for empirical labor economists over the next couple of decades. PR mention the theoretical literature and associated empirical studies that demonstrate that even with homogeneous firms and workers an equilibrium wage distribution can emerge. These papers are important from a theoretical point of view but are not very interesting from an empirical point of view given overwhelming evidence that fixed characteristics of workers such as education, test scores, race, and the success of parents have strong links to wages. We also have evidence that firm observables matter for wages. PR note that even the homogeneous equilibrium search model does a reasonable job of fitting wage distributions but misses the right tail. The fact that such models can roughly fit the wage distribution raises questions about how informative such a comparison is.

The evolution of research toward models with heterogeneity in both firm productivity and worker productivity is a critical development. Within this literature, the sequential auction model of PR (2002) is a promising building block. There is an exciting research program here.

There are two directions for future research that I think are particularly important. The first is directed search models, which are briefly mentioned in the paper and are still in an early stage of development. These models are technically challenging, but it is clear that firms and workers target search on the basis of skills and skill requirements. At some point, directed search models will take over the literature. The second is to move beyond wage rates and consider models with multiple job attributes and heterogeneous preferences on the part of workers and firms. Work schedules, health benefits, pension benefits, and location matter to workers, and the costs and benefits of providing these differ across firms. Panel data on job stayers and job changers show that firm effects on hours worked per week or per year are very large (e.g., Altonji and Paxson (1986), Senesky (2004)). There has been some progress in the development of equilibrium search models with job packages, heterogenous firms and/or workers, including Lang and Majumdar (2005) and Dey and Flinn (2004).

3.3   Theoretical Models of Wage Dynamics: Skill Specificity and Employer Learning

PR discuss recent research that seeks to provide a theoretical foundation for statistical models of wage dynamics. There has long been a need to bring more economics into statistical models of wages over a career. Real progress is being made, and rather than recount the developments they cover, I will discuss two additional factors that eventually need to be incorporated into the search/matching models PR discuss. The first is the role of general, industry specific, occupation specific, and firm specific human capital. A large literature quantifies the importance of these types of skills for wages and for mobility. However, much of the analysis of wages is conducted in a single equation framework. It would be much better to incorporate general, sector specific, and firm specific skills into a search/matching model, although it will not be easy. Specificity of skills and comparative advantage on the basis of general skills are reasons why incorporating directed search by firms and workers into models of mobility and wages is important.

The second issue concerns the role played by employer learning about the skills of workers in wage dynamics and job mobility. The studies surveyed by PR abstract from uncertainty about what the productivity of a worker actually is. Harris and Holmström (1982), Farber and Gibbons (1996), and Chiappori, Salanie, and Valentin (1999) explore the implications for wage dynamics of the assumptions that employers learn about the worker productivity over time and information is public. Farber and Gibbons's result that if worker productivity is fixed, employer learning induces a martingale component into the wage process is directly relevant for statistical models of wage dynamics, as they show using NLSY79 data. Altonji and Pierret (2001) and subsequent studies consider the implications for wage models in which employers statistically discriminate on the basis of readily available information but acquire additional information over time. Gibbons, Katz, Lemieux, and Parent (2005) present and estimate a model of wage dynamics and sectoral mobility with public learning and comparative advantage across sectors on the basis of skill. Altonji (2005) considers the implications for employment rates, wages, and occupational attainment of a model in which the sensitivity of productivity to the worker's skills is increasing in the skill requirements of the job and in which employers learn about the worker's skill more rapidly in high skill jobs.

The assumption that employer information about worker skills is public is analytically convenient but very strong. Greenwald (1986), Lazear (1986), Waldman (1984) and others analyze models in which information is asymetric, and the incumbent employer has an information advantage. Recently there have been some promising developments in both theoretical and empirical research on the implications of asymmetric information for mobility and wage dynamics. Gibbons and Katz (1991) and a few subsequent studies examine the implications of private learning for wage losses of workers who are laid off. Pinkston (2005) draws on the second price auctions literature (also used by PR (2002)) to formulate a model of bidding between the incumbent firm and the outside firm in a search environment. His model also allows for public learning. Schoenberg (2005) derives tests for both private and public learning from a two period model of wages, mobility and unemployment. Her findings suggest that private learning is important for college educated workers. Theoretical and empirical work on the implications of public and private learning for wage dynamics within and across jobs and for job mobility is still in an early stage, but is a promising development.

References

Abowd, J. M., F. Kramarz, and D. N. Margolis (1999): "High Wage Workers and High Wage Jobs," *Econometrica*, 67, 251–333.

Abraham, K G., and H. S. Farber (1987): "Job Duration, Seniority, and Earnings," *American Economic Review*, 77, 278–97.

Abraham, K. G., J. R. Spletzer, and J. C. Stuart (1998): "Divergent Trends in Alternative Wage Series," in *Labor Statistics Measurement Issues,* National Bureau of Economic Research Studies in Income and Wealth, Vol. 60, ed. by Haltiwanger, Manser and Topel, Chicago: University of Chicago Press, 293–324.

Addison, J. T., and P. Portugal (1989): "Job Displacement, Relative Wage Changes, and Duration of Unemployment," *Journal of Labor Economics*, 7, 281–302.

Altonji, J. G., and C. H. Paxson (1986): "Job Characteristics and Hours of Work," in *Research in Labor Economics*, Vol. 8, Part A, ed. by R. G. Ehrenberg, Greenwich: Westview Press, 1–55.

Altonji, J. G., and C. R. Pierret (2001): "Employer Learning and Statistical Discrimination," *Quarterly Journal of Economics*, 116, 313–50.

Altonji, J. G., and R. A. Shakotko (1987): "Do Wages Rise with Job Seniority?" *Review of Economic Studies*, 54, 437–59.

Angrist, J. D., and V. Lavy (2003): "Achievement Awards for High School Matriculation: Evidence from Randomized Trials," BREAD Working Paper No. 019.

Attanasio, O., C. Meghir, and A. Santiago (2005): "11 Education Choices in Mexico: Using a Structural Model and a Randomised Experiment to Evaluate Progresa," IFS working paper EWP05/01.

Chiappori, P.-A., B. Salanie, and J. Valentin (1999): "Early Starters versus Late Beginners," *Journal of Political Economy*, 107, 731–60.

Dey, M. S., and C. J. Flinn (2005): "An Equilibrium Model of Health Insurance Provision and Wage Determination," *Econometrica*, 73, 571–627.

Gallipoli, G., C. Meghir, and G. Violante (2005): "Education Decisions, Equilibrium Policies, and Wages Dispersion," Mimeo IFS.

Greenwald, B. (1986): "Adverse Selection in the Labor Market," *Review of Economic Studies*, 53, 325–47.

Gibbons, R., and L. Katz (1991): "Layoffs and Lemons," *Journal of Labor Economics*, 9, 351–80.

Groshen, E. L. (1991): "Sources of Intra-Industry Wage Dispersion: How Much Do Employers Matter?" *Quarterly Journal of Economics*, 106, 869–84.

Heckman, J., L. Lochner, and C. Taber (1998): "Explaining Rising Wage Inequality: Explorations with a Dynamic General Equilibrium Model of Labor Earnings with Heterogeneous Agents," *Review of Economic Dynamics*, 1, 1–58.

Ichimura, H., and C. Taber (2000): "Direct Estimation of Policy Impacts," unpublished paper, Northwestern University.

Kehoe, T. J., T. N. Srinivasan, and J. Whalley (2005): *Frontiers in Applied General Equilibrium Modeling,* Cambridge, UK: Cambridge University Press.

Lang, K., and S. Majumdar (2004): "The Pricing of Job Characteristics," *International Economic Review*, 45, 1111–28.

Lazear, E. (1986): "Raids and Offer Matching," in *Research in Labor Economics* 8, ed. by R. G. Ehrenberg, Greenwich, CT: JAI Press, 141–65.

Miguel, E., and M. Kremer (2004): "Worms: Identifying Impacts on Education and Health in the Presence of Treatment Externalities," *Econometrica*, 72, 159–217.

Pinkston, J. C. (2005): "A Model of Asymmetric Employer Learning With Testable Implications," unpublished paper, US Bureau of Labor Statistics.

Schoenberg, U. (2005): "Testing for Asymmetric Employer Learning," unpublished paper, University of Rochester.

Schultz, T. P. (2004): "School Subsidies for the Poor: Evaluating the Mexican Progresa Poverty Program," *Journal of Development Economics*, 74, 199–250.

Senesky, S. (2005): "Testing the Intertemporal Labor Supply Model: Are Jobs Important?" *Labour Economics,* 12, 749–72.

Topel, R. H. (1991): "Specific Capital, Mobility, and Wages: Wages Rise with Job Seniority," *Journal of Political Economy*, 99, 145–76.

Topel, R. H., and M. P. Ward (1992): "Job Mobility and the Careers of Young Men," *Quarterly Journal of Economics*, 196, 339–479.

Waldman, M. (1984): "Job Assignment, Signaling, and Efficiency," *Rand Journal of Economics*, 15, 255–67.

CHAPTER 13

Field Experiments in Development Economics*

Esther Duflo

Abstract

There is a long tradition in development economics of collecting original data
to test specific hypotheses. Over the last 10 years, this tradition has merged
with an expertise in setting up randomized field experiments, resulting in an
increasingly large number of studies where an original experiment has been
set up to test economic theories and hypotheses. This paper extracts some
substantive and methodological lessons from such studies in three domains:
incentives, social learning, and time-inconsistent preferences. The paper argues that we need both to continue testing existing theories and to start thinking
of how the theories may be adapted to make sense of the field experiment results, many of which are starting to challenge them. This new framework could
then guide a new round of experiments.

There is a long tradition in development economics of collecting original
data in order to test a specific economic hypothesis or to study a particular
setting or institution. This is perhaps due to a conjunction of the lack of readily
available high-quality, large-scale data sets commonly available in industri-
alized countries and the low cost of data collection in developing countries,
though development economists also like to think that it has something to do
with the mind-set of many of them. Whatever the reason, the ability to let questions determine the data to be obtained, instead of the data determining the
questions that can be asked, has been the hallmark of the best work in empirical
development economics and has led to work that has no equivalent in other
fields, for example, Townsend (1994) and Udry (1994).

Two concurrent developments have taken place over the last 10 years. First,
high-quality, large-scale, multipurpose data sets from developing countries have
become more readily available. The World Bank's Living Standard Measurement Surveys and the Rand Corporation Family Life Surveys are two examples

* I would like to thank Richard Blundell, Joshua Angrist, Orazio Attanasio, Abhijit Banerjee, Tim
Besley, Michael Kremer, Sendhil Mullainathan and Rohini Pande for comments on this paper
and/or having been instrumental in shaping my views on these issues. I thank Neel Mukherjee
and Kudzai Takavarasha for carefully reading and editing a previous draft.

of high-quality comprehensive data sets available for many countries. The Demographic and Health Surveys have shorter questionnaires but cover a large number of countries and have generally more than one round per country. Some census data from developing countries are now available on the IPUMS web site, and this collection is growing. Finally, statistical agencies in developing countries have started to make their own surveys, in some cases of excellent quality, available to researchers. These data sources and the wealth of natural experiments available in developing countries have opened a gold mine, which researchers and students have enthusiastically started to exploit. Empirical methods developed in other specialties (notably labor and industrial organization) are now used routinely in development economics. The standards for empirical evidence have risen, putting the field on par with other empirical domains. As a result, studies using an original data set to make an interesting observation not supported by a convincing empirical design are no longer as readily accepted.

Nevertheless, development economists continue with the tradition of doing fieldwork to collect original data: The second development over the last 10 years has been the spread of randomized evaluations in development economics. Randomized evaluations measure the impact of an intervention by randomly allocating individuals to a "treatment" group, comprising individuals who receive the program, and a "comparison" group, comprising individuals who do not, at least for some period of time, receive the treatment. The outcomes are then compared across treatment and comparison groups. Here again, cost is an enormous advantage. While the cost of a good randomized policy evaluation in the U.S. easily reaches millions of dollars, both program costs and data collection costs are much lower in developing countries. This has allowed the practice to generalize beyond a few very well-crafted, major projects to a multiplicity of programs, countries, and contexts. In addition, while some of the well-known randomized evaluations are just that – rigorous evaluations of a particular policy intervention[1] – the tradition of posing the question first and then finding the data to answer it has continued with randomized evaluations.

What many development economists now do is to work closely with implementing agencies – NGOs, private companies, or governments – to develop interventions and evaluate them in a randomized setting. The interventions are designed to answer a specific practical problem in a specific context: for example, how to get teachers to come to school more often, how to help farmers to save more, how to convince parents to get their children immunized, how to fight corruption most effectively. What the economists bring to the table, in addition to evaluation expertise, is prior evidence and theories that help them

---

[1] For example, the Government of Mexico requested an evaluation of its conditional cash transfer program, PROGRESA/Oportunidades. Then, using a combination of the randomization inherent in the program and assumptions from economic theory, researchers were able to recover parameters of interest (Attanasio, Meghir, and Santiago, 2002; Todd and Wolpin, 2004).

to predict what should work – and how – and what should not. The evaluation of the program then serves to test these theories: Randomized evaluations have become, in effect, field experiments – a new and powerful tool in the arsenal of the economist. In this essay, "field experiment" refers to the implementation and evaluation, by comparing different treatment groups chosen at random, of an intervention or a set of interventions specifically designed to test a hypothesis or a set of hypotheses.

There remains a clear need for better evaluations of different policy options. As Banerjee and He (2003) point out, what is lacking among development practitioners are not ideas, but an idea of whether or not the ideas work. Mullainathan (2005) argues that self-serving bias, which is perhaps particularly pervasive among those who are the most motivated to help the poor, contaminates many evaluations. Randomized design can, to some extent, alleviate this problem. Elsewhere (Duflo, 2004; Duflo and Kremer, 2004), I have advocated the systematic use of randomized evaluations as a way to improve policy effectiveness and in Duflo, Glennerster, and Kremer (2005) discussed design issues and technical aspects of running and analyzing randomized experiments. The objective of this paper is different: It is to review the use of field experiments as a tool by development economists and to assess the lessons we have learned from them, the challenges field experiments face and those they pose to core theories in economics, and the areas field experiments leave open for research.

The remainder of the paper proceeds as follows: Section I reviews the substantive conclusions from field experiments in three domains: incentives, social learning, and time-inconsistent preferences. Section II extracts methodological lessons from this experience. It argues that we now need to both continue testing existing theory and to start thinking about how the theories may be adapted to make sense of the results from the experiments. Section III concludes.

1   A FEW THINGS WE HAVE LEARNED FROM EXPERIMENTS

Field experiments have been designed to shed light on core issues in economics, such as the role of incentives or social learning. In recent years, several experiments have tested some of the hypotheses put forward in behavioral economics. A full review is beyond the scope of this paper, but this section reviews what has been learned from field experiments in three domains: incentives, social learning, and time-inconsistent preferences.

1.1   Incentives

The idea that individuals respond to incentives is at the core of much of economics. The poor performance of government workers in developing countries is often attributed to the weak incentives they face and to the fact that incentives that are in place on the books are not implemented. For example, teachers in India can be suspended for not showing up to school, but a survey in rural India showed that this hardly ever happens, despite very high absence rates (Chaudhury et al., 2005).

Accordingly, many experiments have been set up to study how incentives faced by individuals affect their behavior. A fair number of these experiments have been conducted in schools, with incentives provided either to teachers or to students in the form of rewards for improved performance. Answering these questions is important, since this will tell us whether efforts to reform institutions to provide stronger incentives can have a chance to improve performance.

To obtain a sense of the potential impact of providing high-powered incentives to teachers on absence and learning, Duflo and Hanna (2005) evaluated an incentive program that was actually rigorously implemented in the field. Working in conjunction with Seva Mandir, the implementing NGO, they designed and evaluated a simple incentive program that left no space for manipulation and could be strictly implemented.

Seva Mandir runs non-formal, single-teacher primary education centers (NFEs) in tribal villages in rural Udaipur district, a sparsely populated, arid, and hilly region. Tribal villages are remote and difficult to access, which makes it very difficult for Seva Mandir to regularly monitor the NFEs. Consequently, absence rates are very high despite the organization's policy calling for dismissal in cases of high absence rates: in a study they conducted in 1995, Banerjee et al. (2005) found an absence rate of 40 percent, and at the beginning of their study, in August 2003, Duflo and Hanna (2005) found an absence rate of 44 percent.

Seva Mandir selected 120 schools to participate in the experiment. In 60 randomly selected schools (the "treatment" group), they gave the teacher a camera with a tamper-proof date and time function and instructed him to take a picture of himself and his students every day at opening time and at closing time. Teachers received a bonus as a function of the number of "valid" days they actually came to school. A "valid" day was defined as a day where the opening and closing pictures were separated by at least 5 hours and a minimum number of children were present in both pictures. The bonus was set up in such a way that a teacher's salary could range from 500 rupees to 1,300 rupees, and each additional valid day carried a bonus of 50 rupees (6 U.S. dollars, valued at PPP, or a little over a dollar at the official exchange rate). In the remaining 60 schools (the "comparison" group), teachers were paid 1,000 rupees and they were told (as usual) that they could be dismissed for poor performance. One unannounced visit every month was used to measure teacher absence as well as teachers' activities when in school.

The introduction of the program resulted in an immediate and persistent improvement in teacher attendance. Over 18 months, the absence rate was cut by almost half in the treatment schools, falling from an average of 42 percent in the comparison schools to 22 percent in the treatment schools. The program was effective on two margins: it completely eliminated extremely delinquent behavior, and it increased the number of teachers with a perfect or very high attendance record.

The experiment also provided an ideal setting to test the hypothesis of multitasking (Holmström and Milgrom, 1991), in which individuals facing high-powered incentive schemes may change their behavior in such a way that the proximate outcome on which the rewards are based increases, but the ultimate outcome in which the principal is interested remains constant or even decreases. In this case, the incentive was explicitly based only on presence, but Seva Mandir was ultimately interested in improving learning. Teachers may have decided to teach less, once in school. In fact, when in school, the teachers were as likely to be teaching in treatment as in comparison schools, and the number of students present was the same. But, since there were fewer absences, treatment schools taught the equivalent of 88 child-days more per month than comparison schools, a one-third increase in the number of child-days, resulting in a 0.17 standard deviation increase in children's tests scores after one year.

Multitasking did happen, however, in an experiment conducted in Kenya where the incentives provided to teachers were based on the test scores of students in their class (Glewwe, Ilias, and Kremer, 2003). International Child Support (ICS) Africa, the implementing NGO, provided prizes to teachers in grades 4 through 8 based on the performance of the school as a whole on the district exams each year. All teachers who taught these grades were eligible for a prize. Prizes were awarded in two categories: "Top-scoring schools" and "Most-improved schools." Schools could not win in more than one category. Improvements were calculated relative to performance in the baseline year. In each category, three first, second, third, and fourth prizes were awarded. Overall, out of the 50 schools participating in the program, 24 received prizes of some type, and teachers in most schools should have felt that they had a chance of winning a prize. Prizes were substantial, ranging in value from 21 percent to 43 percent of typical monthly salaries of teachers. The comparison of the 50 treatment and 50 control schools suggested that this program did improve performance on the district exams (by about 0.14 standard deviations), but it had no effect on teacher attendance. Instead of attending more often, teachers held more test preparation sessions. This, the authors conclude, was rational based on the (limited) evidence on what is most effective in improving test scores over the short horizon. However, these preparation sessions probably cannot be counted as substitutes for the regular classes: for one, they did very little for long-term learning, as evidenced by the fact that once the program ended, those who had been in the program schools did not outperform students in the comparison schools. In this case, we see teachers responding to incentives in the most cost-effective way possible from their point of view.

Combined, the results of the two experiments make sense. Coming to school regularly is probably the most costly activity for a teacher: there is the opportunity cost of attending, the pressure to dispatch other duties in an environment where nobody strongly expects the teachers to show up every day, and the distance to travel. Once they are in school, their marginal cost of teaching is actually fairly low. Thus, it is not surprising that an effective incentive program rewarding presence does not effectively lead to a reduction in the provision of other inputs when in school. An incentive based on test scores, on the other hand, leaves teachers with ample room (and incentive) to manipulate their way around paying the cost of regular attendance: Rather than coming more often, they find other ways to improve test scores.

The camera experiment shows that a straightforward incentive program, mechanically implemented in a relatively simple environment (a single-teacher school), is a very effective way to reduce absence in schools. But most school systems, being larger, more complicated, centralized hierarchies, do not implement incentive schemes this directly; instead, they rely on the mediation of people in the hierarchy, such as inspectors and headmasters. This experiment suggests that one of the reasons why the incentives may fail in these systems is not so much that people do not react to incentives but that the mediators pervert the incentive system. Indeed, Kremer and Chen (2001), in an experiment they conducted in Kenya in partnership with ICS Africa, found that when implemented by headmasters, incentives tend to lose their power. ICS Africa introduced an incentive program for pre-primary school teachers, and the headmaster was entrusted with monitoring the presence of the teacher. At the end of the term, a prize (a bicycle) was to be given to teachers with a good attendance record. If a teacher did not have a good attendance record, the money would remain with the school, and could be used as the headmaster and the school committee saw fit. In all treatment schools, the headmasters marked the teachers present a sufficient number of times for them to get the prize. However, when the research team independently verified absence through unannounced visits, they found that the absence rate was actually at the same high level in treatment and in comparison schools. It seems that in order to avoid the unpleasantness of a fight, or out of compassion for the pre-school teachers, or because they wanted to give the impression of running a tight ship (after all, ensuring presence was part of their regular duties), headmasters actually cheated to make sure that pre-school teachers could get the prizes. This suggests that whenever human judgment is involved, in an environment where rules are often bent, incentives may be easily perverted, either, as in this case, in an equitable direction or else to favor some specific individuals or groups.

The results of these experiments all conform to the priors most economists would have, namely, that individuals respond to incentives and will try to pervert the incentives if they can do so at little cost. As such, the findings of the camera experiment may not provide immediate policy levers or options for policy action, since they do not tell the policymaker that self-policing using cameras would be possible in the larger government schools that constitute the more general and larger policy concern. But combined with the findings on incentive schemes mediated by headmasters, they do clarify the policy possibilities by telling us that the main, and more general, impediment seems to be in the implementation of incentives schemes rather than in the effectiveness of the approach.[2] Other experiments offering incentives to students to perform well in school (Angrist and Lavy (2002) in Israel; Kremer, Miguel, and Thornton (2004) in Kenya) have also yielded results that accord well with this prior: when provided with rewards to perform well on exams, students increased their performance. The results of the latter experiment, however, are a little difficult to reconcile with the results of the study on incentives for teachers we discussed above (Glewwe, Ilias, and Kremer (2003)). Incentives for students based on test scores led to durable (rather than only temporary) improvement in test scores as well as a reduction in teacher absence, whereas when teachers were rewarded based on test scores, the improvement in test scores was only temporary, and there was no reduction in absenteeism. The argument of multitasking, which made sense in the teacher incentive context, should apply just the same in the student incentive case, which was based on the same type of tests. The multitasking theory alone provides little guidance on why the reaction was different in one context than in the other.

Still, these experiments show that when incentives are expected to matter, they do. But do they matter even when we would not expect them to? Some experiments designed to answer this question have led to surprising results. For instance, Abhijit Banerjee, Esther Duflo, and Rachel Glennerster, in collaboration with Seva Mandir, set up an experiment to test the impact of small incentives for children's immunization. The rate of immunization in the sample at the baseline was abysmally low – only 1 percent of children are fully immunized by the age of 2. This is surprising, given that immunization is provided free of charge at local health centers, and that the individual benefits of immunization for the child are extremely large: it protects the child against deadly diseases that are still prevalent in the area (measles, tuberculosis, tetanus, and so on). But the absence rate at the center is 45 percent (Banerjee, Deaton, and Duflo (2004)). One reason the immunization rate is so low may be that the parents hesitate to travel to the health center because they are not sure that the center will be open. Given the distance, the travel costs, combined with the uncertainty, may be large enough to compensate the existing benefits. To test the hypothesis that it is the travel costs that prevent parents from immunizing their children, regular immunization camps were set up in the 68 randomly selected villages (out of 135 study villages). The camps were held on a fixed day of the month. Villagers were all informed of the camps in a village meeting, and those who had children to be immunized were reminded of the camp by a health worker the day before it was held. The health worker also reminded them of the importance of immunization. The health worker (usually a man) had an incentive to

---

[2] Given the weak incentives provided by formal systems, many have been tempted to propose the use of community monitoring as an alternative to external monitoring. Banerjee and Duflo (2005) review evidence from a variety of field experiments on this topic. Existing evidence is not encouraging for the community model: In all the experiments that have been conducted so far (in education as well as other domains, such as corruption in roads – see Olken (2005)), entrusting communities to conduct the monitoring has been ineffective.

do his job as well as possible, since he was paid as a function of the number of children immunized. In half of these camps, mothers were additionally given a kilogram of lentils (a value of 20 rupees) for each immunization received by a child under 2. (Children under 5 would still be immunized in the camp, but the mother would not receive an incentive for them.) The incentive was small and unremarkable (lentils are a staple of the local diet). If the cost of immunization was the main barrier, immunization rates should immediately increase when the camps are set up, and the incentive should not matter very much. Even though the experiment is still ongoing, the preliminary results very clearly indicate that the story is more complicated. While the camps are well attended, and are indeed associated with an increase in immunization rates, the attendance is more than five times as large in camps where the lentils are distributed. This increase in attendance is due to crowding; people traveling a fair distance from other villages; and to the increase in the probability of being immunized among children in villages hosting the camps. A survey of immunization rates among children 0 to 2 years old conducted on 30 families randomly selected from among families in all 135 villages showed the following: In control villages, 4 percent of the 0- to 2-year-olds are "on target" (i.e., they have received the recommended immunization for their age). In villages hosting the camps, 22 percent are "on target." And in the villages participating in the incentive scheme, over 40 percent are "on target," even though the camps have often not been in existence long enough for all the 0 to 2-year-olds to have "caught up" if they started late. A small incentive associated with an activity that has very high returns in the future leads to a very large change in behavior. Either people are not aware of the benefits of immunization (even after they are informed in one large meeting and reminded of it every month), or, more likely, they tend to delay activities that are a little bit unpleasant in the present (they still need to take a few hours off to take the child to the clinic; immunization makes children cry), even if they have very large returns in the future. For a large number of people, the small but immediate reward is sufficient to solve this problem, whereas a direct subsidy of the activity fails to convince them. Similar results have been found in other contexts. Thornton (2005) finds that very small rewards induce large changes in the probability that someone decides to return to a clinic to find out the results of a (free) HIV-AIDS test. This difference in response indicates that even though individuals are responsive to incentives, they give much more weight to short-term gains. This could be due to a lack of information about what the long-term gains really are, resulting in a very flat indifference curve. Another explanation may be that people have either extremely high discount rates, or more likely, discount rates that are inconsistent over time, with a strong preference for the present. Thus, even when an activity is subsidized to the point where the cost of undertaking it cannot be reduced further, the small, short-term cost does prevent people from participating in it unless the cost is balanced by an equally small reward.

What have we learned from experiments on incentives so far? People seem to be extremely responsive to incentives. They seem particularly responsive to incentives that lead to an immediate reward, relative to large gains in the future, suggesting deviation from the exponential utility model. New experiments should be designed to push this point further. Would people be responsive to delayed incentives if they were given more information or if the incentives were made more salient? Or is it the delayed character of the reward that creates this wedge between a small immediate reward and a large gain in the future?

1.2   Learning and Social Effects

The extent to which people learn from each other is a central question in development economics. In particular, the diffusion of new technologies through social networks (neighbors, friends, and so on) has been, and continues to be, intensively studied. The impact of learning on technology adoption in agriculture has been studied especially carefully. Besley and Case (1994) showed that in India, adoption of high-yield variety (HYV) seeds by an individual is correlated with adoption among his neighbors. While this could be due to social learning, it could also be the case that common unobservable variables affect adoption of both the neighbors. To address this issue, Foster and Rosenzweig (1995) focus on profitability. During the early years of the Green Revolution, returns from HYV seeds were uncertain and depended on adequate use of fertilizer. The paper shows that in this context, the profitability of HYV seeds increased with past experimentation, by either the farmers or others in the village. Farmers do not fully take this externality into account, therefore there is underinvestment in the new technology. In this environment, the diffusion of a new technology will be slow if the neighbors' outcomes are not informative about the individual's own conditions. Indeed, Munshi (2004) shows that in India, in adopting HYV rice, a grain characterized by much more varied conditions, farmers displayed much less social learning than with HYV wheat.

But all these results could still be biased in the presence of spatially correlated profitability shocks. Using detailed information about social interactions, Conley and Udry (2003) distinguish geographical neighbors from "information neighbors" – the set of individuals from whom an individual neighbor may learn about agriculture. They show that pineapple farmers in Ghana imitate the choices (of fertilizer quantity) of their information neighbors when these neighbors have a good shock, and move further away from these decisions when they have a bad shock. Conley and Udry try to rule out the fact that this pattern is due to correlated shocks by observing that the choices made on an established crop (maize-cassava intercropping), for which there should be no learning, do not exhibit the same pattern.

All these papers seek to solve what Manski (1993) has called the "reflection problem": outcomes of neighbors may be correlated because they face common (unobserved) shocks, rather than because they imitate each other. This problem can be solved, however, using an experimental design where part of a unit is subject to a program that changes its behavior. The ideal experiment to identify social learning is to exogenously affect the choice of technology of a group of farmers and to follow subsequent adoption by themselves and the members of their network.

Duflo, Kremer, and Robinson (2005) performed such an experiment in Western Kenya, where less than 15 percent of farmers use fertilizer on their maize crop (the main staple) in any given year, despite the official recommendation (based on results from trials on experimental farms), as well as the high returns (estimated to be greater than 100 percent in these farmers' conditions). In each of six successive seasons, they randomly selected a group of farmers (among the parents of children enrolled in several schools) and provided them with fertilizer and hybrid seeds sufficient for small demonstration plots on their farms. Field officers from ICS Africa guided the farmers throughout the trial, which was concluded by a debriefing session. In the next season, the adoption of fertilizer by these farmers was about 10 percent higher than that of farmers in the comparison group. (Over time, the difference between treatment and comparison farmers declined.) However, there is no evidence of any diffusion of this new knowledge: People listed by the treatment farmers as people they talk to about agriculture (their "contacts") did not adopt fertilizer any more than the contacts of the comparison group. Note that this is very different from what would be obtained if one simply regressed a farmer's adoption on his contacts' adoption. The difference suggests that the omitted variable bias, which many of the studies quoted above worried about, is indeed serious: a farmer who has one more contact that uses fertilizer is 10 percent more likely to use it himself in a given season (and this coefficient is significant).

To understand the lack of learning revealed by these results, it is necessary to "unpack" various reasons that may prevent farmers from learning from each other. Note that the trials gave the farmers the opportunity to experiment with fertilizer on their own farms, but it also provided them with additional inputs: the fertilizer was applied with the help of an ICS field officer, who also visited the farmers regularly and helped the farmers compute their rate of return and gave information on results obtained by others at the end of the intervention. The neighbors did not get the benefit of this information.

To distinguish the effect of learning by doing from the effect of the additional information provided, two additional experiments were conducted. In the first, designed to evaluate the impact of learning by doing, each farmer was provided with a starter kit consisting of either enough fertilizer or enough fertilizer and hybrid seeds for a 30-square-meter plot. Farmers were instructed that the kit was sufficient for this amount of space, and they were given twine to measure two plots of the relevant size. Beyond this, there was no monitoring of whether or not (and how) the farmers used the starter kit. Starter kits have been used elsewhere: for instance, the Malawian government distributed 2.86 million such packs beginning in 1998. In the ICS program, field staff explained how to use the inputs but did not formally monitor or measure the yields. Relative to the comparison group, farmers who were provided starter kits were 12 percentage points more likely to use either fertilizer or hybrid seeds. Learning by doing alone seems to affect fertilizer use by about as much as learning from an experiment conducted in one's own field.

The other component of the agricultural trial was that the demonstrations were conducted on the farmer's own plot. If different plots have different characteristics (soil quality, slope, and so on), the learning gained on one farm may not be as useful for a neighbor as it is for the farmer himself. To evaluate the impact of this component, ICS randomly selected one of the farmer's "agricultural contacts" for an invitation to take part in the key stages of the trial (notably planting, harvesting, and the discussion of profitability). After one season, adoption was 17.8 percentage points higher in the first group. This suggests that the effect of watching a demonstration on someone else's plot is as large as the effect of experimenting on one's own plot. It is possible to learn from others.

This last result suggests that if farmers talked to each other, they would be able to learn from each other's experience: the shocks to a farmer's plot are not so large that they make learning impossible. This did not seem to happen, which suggests that the remaining explanation is either that farmers do not talk very much to each other about agriculture, or that they do not trust each other (and they trust the outside (and impartial) experimenter more). The former hypothesis was corroborated by interviewing farmers about themselves and their neighbors and contacts on key parameters of agriculture (date of planting, whether or not the neighbor uses fertilizer, whether or not the neighbor participated in an agricultural trial), and cross-examining the answer: Most farmers are either unable to answer regarding their friends or neighbors, or give the wrong answer. Farmers do not appear to know much about each other at all.

If there is diffusion in Ghana and India, but not in Kenya, then there may be another type of externality and source of multiple steady states: When there is very little innovation in a sector, there is no news to exchange, and people do not discuss agriculture. As a result, innovation dies out before spreading, and no innovation survives. When there is a lot of innovation, it is more worthwhile to talk to neighbors, and innovations are in turn more likely to survive.

It is worth noting that, given the accumulated evidence about social learning, the "file drawer bias" would have probably led to the burial of the initial results of "no learning" if they had been obtained in a regression, rather than in an experiment. In a non-randomized study, the researchers would probably have concluded they had done something wrong, and there was nothing interesting in these results. Instead, the initial results of "no learning" prompted a series of additional experiments that helped shed light on the finding. The combination of several experiments examining various aspects of the question should, at a minimum, move our priors about the strength of these effects.

An even more surprising result is obtained by Kremer and Miguel (2003). They use a very similar design in the context of a program to fight intestinal worms in Western Kenya. The program was randomly phased in among three groups of schools, where treatment started in different years (Group 1 started the first year, Group 2 the following year, and finally Group 3 the final year).

Because the schools were randomly assigned to each group, conditional on the total number of friends a child had, the number of friends she had in "early treatment" (Group 1 or 2) or "late treatment" (Group 3) schools was exogenous. In 2001 (when the program was just starting in the late treatment schools), the researchers conducted a survey on the number of friends that parents and children in the study schools had in various schools. They then regressed the probability of a child taking the treatment on the number of friends that a child (or her parents) had in the early and late treatment schools, after conditioning on total number of friends the child had and the number of friends she had in her own school. Surprisingly, they found that the more friends a child (or her parents) had in the early treatment schools, the *less* likely she was to take the treatment herself: for each additional social link to an early treatment school, a parent's child is 3.1 percentage points less likely to take the drugs. Further, the effect is too large to be explained by the health externalities effect (if my friend takes the treatment, I do not need to take it). Instead, the researchers attribute it to overoptimistic priors of the family regarding the private health benefits of taking the treatment. When a child's friend takes the medication and does not instantly get much better, the parents actually learn that the medication is less effective than they thought.

Importantly, replicating the usual "due diligence" specifications without using the randomization, produces dramatically different results: when a child's take-up is regressed on average take-up in her school, there is a very significant positive relationship. The correlation is stronger with the take-up in the child's own ethnic group (as in Munshi and Myaux (2002), which uses this strategy as a way to attempt to correct for bias), and there is still a positive correlation between take-up among the child's friends and own take-up. The "effect" is also stronger when more of the child's classmates report a positive experience with the medicine (as in Conley and Udry (2003)), though this difference is not significant.

The experiments reviewed in this section address a very important question for development economics and solve an identification problem that has proved extremely difficult to address with observational data alone. In both cases, the results differ quite markedly from what the observational studies had found, even when using the same "robust" strategies. These two experiments are clearly insufficient to invalidate prior evidence: They took place in a different setting, and they are both consistent with theoretical models where there is social learning in some conditions but not others.[3] The fact that they are able to replicate the results of previous studies in the same population where they

---

[3] Moreover, it is not the case that no experiment finds any trace of social learning: Duflo and Saez (2003), who conducted the first experiment to implement this design, found very strong social effects in the case of 401k participation in the U.S., consistent with previous non-experimental evidence (Duflo and Saez (2002)). In the case of neighborhood effects on teenager schooling and crime in the U.S., however, experimental evidence suggests that they are much smaller (or even perverse as in this case) than non-experimental evidence would suggest (Kling and Liebman (2005)).

find very different experimental results is, however, troubling: Here we cannot argue that it is because the context is different that the results are different. The difference has to come entirely from the methodologies and the assumptions and implies that the identification assumptions made by the other studies would be violated in this context. In order to believe the previous studies, we now need to believe both that the effects are different and that the assumptions that are invalid in one case are valid in the others. While there is a good a priori argument to make about the former, it is much less clear we can convincingly argue the latter: The argument made by Munshi and Myaux (2002) about communication within and across religious groups, for example, could be essentially replicated for schoolchildren of different ethnic groups in Kenya. These experiments make both a methodological point and a substantial point: They cast doubt on the previously "accepted" methodologies and require revisiting the generally agreed upon notions about social learning.

1.3   Time-Inconsistent Preferences; Demand for Commitment and Savings

Behavioral economists and psychologists have extensively studied the phenomenon of time-inconsistent preferences. In particular, lab experiments and survey questions have all shown that individuals are impatient in the present and patient in the future. For example, many people who would refuse to get $110 tomorrow instead of $100 today are happy to get $110 in 31 day versus $100 in 30 days. This phenomenon (short-run impatience, long-run patience) is often modeled as discount rates that vary with horizon. People have a very high discount rate for short horizons (decisions about now versus the future), but a very low one for distant horizons. This is often called hyperbolic discounting (Strotz 1956, Ainslie 1992, Laibson 1997). Banerjee and Mullainathan (2005) propose a different model of time-inconsistent preferences, where the individuals must resist immediate temptation (for example, a cousin is sick and wants money now, and it is painful to refuse, even though saving for your children's school fees is the rational decision to make in the long run). Their model makes it explicit that time-inconsistent preferences may arise from the dynamic social context in which individuals are plunged. Time-inconsistent preferences constitute one of the key theories of behavioral economics, and Mullainathan (2005) makes a very convincing argument that they are likely to be central to our understanding of many problems in developing countries, ranging from education to savings.

Yet, while the existence of time-inconsistent preferences is well established in the lab, and while there are institutions (such as ROSCAs in developing countries, 401k plans with withdrawal penalties and Christmas clubs in developed countries), which are consistent with such preferences, there was until recently a dearth of direct evidence of their practical relevance. A key question when analyzing the consequences of these preferences is whether people are sophisticated or naïve in how they deal with their temporal inconsistency. Sophisticated people would recognize the inconsistency and (recursively) form dynamically consistent plans. In other words, they would only make plans that they would follow through on. Naïve people, on the other hand, would not recognize the problem and would make plans assuming that they'd stick with them, only to abandon them when the time comes. Sophisticated hyperbolic discounters will therefore have a demand for commitment devices, whereas naïve hyperbolic discounters will not.

Two recent experimental studies directly test this prediction. Ashraf, Karlan, and Yin (2006) designed a commitment savings product for a small rural bank in the Philippines. Individuals could restrict access to the funds they deposited in the accounts until either a given maturity or a given amount of money was achieved. Relative to standard accounts, the accounts carried no advantage other than this feature. The product was offered to a randomly selected half of 1,700 former clients of the bank. The other half of the individuals were assigned either to a pure control group or to a group that was visited and given a speech reminding them of the importance of savings.

Relative to the control group, those in the treatment group were 28 percentage points more likely to open a savings account after six months, and their savings increased by 47 percentage points more. The effects were even larger after one year. Prior to offering the products, the experimenters asked the standard hypothetical preference-reversal questions. They found that among women, those who had a greater tendency to exhibit preference-reversal were also the most likely to take up the product. This study leaves some important points somewhat unresolved: First, the effect of the "marketing" treatment (where the clients were just reminded of the importance of savings and could open a regular account) is also positive, quite large, and it is not possible to statistically distinguish the effect of the commitment savings treatment from the effect of the marketing treatment. Second, the fact that the time-reversal questions predict seed take-up for women, but not for men, is not something that was predicted by the theory.

However, this is one of the few studies that links "lab" evidence to real behavior (other studies in a development context include Binswanger (1980) – followed by many similar exercises in other contexts – and Karlan (2005)). Moreover, this is the first study where the real-life outcome that was studied (the take-up of a commitment savings product) was studied in the context of a randomized experiment. In addition to the substantive points (individuals do take up commitment savings products when they are offered to them, and do set up meaningful targets; they save at least as much with those as with a regular reminder, and probably more), the study makes a methodological contribution regarding the usefulness of time-reversal questions. While the conclusion of the authors is that the results do reflect time-inconsistency in preferences, the results for men suggest that they need more probing before they can be widely used in this way.

Duflo, Kremer, and Robinson (2005), as part of the project discussed earlier, also set up experiments to test whether there is a demand for commitment savings for fertilizer use for maize crop in Western Kenya. They observed that many farmers *plan* to use fertilizer in the next season, or later in the season, but very few end up doing it. The reason they give most frequently is that they have no money when the time comes to buy it. Maize crop in Kenya is harvested in two seasons, long and short rain. Fertilizer is administered either at planting (a few weeks after harvest) or at top dressing (a few weeks later, when the maize is knee-high). A farmer needs to save enough between harvest and planting or top dressing to be able to use fertilizer. Over several seasons the researchers worked with ICS Africa to develop, refine, and test in randomized settings a commitment product (called SAFI – Saving and Fertilizer Initiative – *safi* means "pure" in Swahili) for farmers. Each season, a farmer is visited at harvest time, and is given the offer to buy a voucher for fertilizer, valid for whenever he or she wants to redeem it. The voucher can be paid in cash or in maize. The maize is bought at harvest price (a low price), and the fertilizer is sold without a discount. The only advantage to the farmer, in addition to the value of deciding now to use fertilizer later, is that the fertilizer is delivered to his farm, and that the maize is also purchased at his farm.

The final experiment (conducted in 2004) followed a design that allows the testing of several hypotheses. The SAFI program was offered to a group of 420 farmers, randomly selected. In addition, 293 farmers were visited at fertilizer application time. Half of them were offered exactly the same deal. Half of them were offered a 50 percent discount on the fertilizer. Comparing the take-up of the offer to purchase fertilizer in the "visit" group to that in the "SAFI" group allows the researchers to test whether the timing of the decision to purchase the fertilizer is important (as opposed to the free delivery and the ability to sell maize). Comparing the take-up of the offer in the SAFI group to that in the subsidy group lets the researchers benchmark the value of the early purchase relative to a subsidy. In the SAFI group, 40 percent of the farmers bought a voucher for fertilizer. In the subsidy group, 45 percent did. In the visit group, 21 percent did. The impact of an early offer to buy fertilizer at full price is therefore almost as large as the impact of getting the fertilizer at a 50 percent reduced price.

Another feature of the experiment allows the researchers to distinguish whether buying fertilizer when offered at the time of harvest is just another instance of the farmer succumbing to temptation (or because chasing away someone who asks you to buy fertilizer is not pleasant, so if you have the money you may as well just buy it), rather than a rational decision to set aside money for fertilizer use. Before harvest, a field officer visited all farmers to find out when their harvest was. For a group of farmers, they also asked them whether they would be interested in such a product (where ICS Africa sells and delivers fertilizer to them) and if yes, when they should come. This visit takes place in the "hungry season," when farmers have no money. If they just wanted to be nice to the interviewer, but never intended to buy fertilizer (and they knew they would buy it if he were to "tempt" them with it when he arrived at harvest time and they had money), they could tell the interviewer to go away and to come back at planting time. In fact, almost all of the farmers did ask him to come back at some point. However, 44 percent of them asked the field officer to come back at harvest time (rather than at planting time), and most of these farmers eventually bought fertilizer (almost none of the people who asked them to come at planting or top dressing time ended up buying fertilizer). The resulting take-up of the SAFI offer under the "choice of timing" condition was exactly the same as that under the "no choice" condition, suggesting that the decision was a rational one, rather than due to farmers succumbing to pressure at harvest time.

Up to this point, the results seem to vindicate the hypothesis that agents are sophisticated hyperbolic discounters who understand the value of commitment. Interestingly, however, most farmers requested a very rapid delivery of the fertilizer, and ended up storing it for themselves, rather than letting the NGO store it and deliver it when they needed it. Preliminary evidence on adoption suggests that a large fraction of farmers who purchased fertilizer under the SAFI program did use it, suggesting that fertilizer is sufficiently illiquid that once farmers have it, they manage to hold on to it until they use it. Commitment devices help farmers to save and invest, and they are sufficiently aware of this to take up these devices when offered them. But if farmers can just buy fertilizer and hold on to it, and if they know that they might not end up buying it if they don't do it early in the season, why don't they just buy fertilizer on their own immediately after harvest? This seems at odds with the fact that they themselves seem to know that they will not buy fertilizer if it is delivered to them at planting time (since, under the choice condition, almost half of the farmers request a visit at harvest time). Or why doesn't someone (say, a fertilizer seller) decide to woo customers at harvest time, when they are much more likely to buy it? These questions have prompted a new set of experiments, currently ongoing. In one program, farmers are just reminded at harvest time that if they do not purchase fertilizer right away, they probably will never do it. In one program, they are offered a small discount on fertilizer, with a short deadline (valid only during the immediate post-harvest season). The results of these experiments will help disentangle these possibilities.

2 LESSONS

With these three examples, I have tried to show that field experiments have led to substantive learning on key questions of interest to economists. Beyond this, the experience gained in these and other projects has led to methodological insights.

2.1   The Field as a Lab

The fertilizer experiments described above were designed to test well-defined theories (production function, learning, and time-inconsistent preferences). As each set of new results came in, there was a constant back and forth between the questions that should be asked and the answers that emerged, but each new program was guided by theory. These experiments are examples of using the design of programs to answer very specific questions guided by theory. The field is used as a lab where variation necessary to test specific ideas is generated experimentally.

Karlan and Zinman (2005) and Bertrand, Karlan, Mullainathan, Shafir, and Zinman (2005) are two related projects which are excellent examples of using the field as a lab. Both projects were conducted in collaboration with a South African lender, giving small loans to high-risk borrowers, with high interest rates. In both cases, the main manipulation started by sending different direct mail solicitations to different people. Karlan and Zinman (2005) set out to test the relative weight of ex-post repayment burden (including moral hazard) and ex-ante adverse selection in lending. In their setup, potential borrowers with the same observable risk were randomly offered a high or a low interest rate in an initial letter. Individuals then decided whether to borrow at the solicitation's "offer" rate. Of those that responded to the high rate, half were randomly given a new lower "contract" interest rate when they actually applied for the loan, while the remaining half continued to receive the rate at which they were offered the loan. Individuals did not know beforehand that the contract rate might differ from the offer rate. The researchers then compared repayment performance of the loans in all three groups. This design allows the researchers to separately identify adverse selection effects and ex-post repayment burden effects (which could be due to moral hazard or sheer financial distress ex post). Adverse selection effects are identified by considering only the sample that eventually received the low contract rate and comparing the repayment performance of those who responded to the high offer interest rate with those who responded to the low offer interest rate. Ex-post repayment burden effects are identified by considering only those who responded to the high offer rates and comparing those who ended up with the low offer to those who ended up with the high offer. The study found that men and women behave differently: while women exhibited adverse selection, men exhibited moral hazard. This experiment constitutes a significant methodological advance because it shows how simple predictions from theory can be rigorously tested. This is a very powerful design that allows us to quantify the importance of mechanisms that are at the heart of our understanding of credit markets.

Bertrand et al. (2005) apply the same principle (and the same setup) to a broader set of hypotheses, most of them coming directly from psychology. The experiment is overlaid on the Karlan and Zinman (2005) basic experiment: The offer letters are made to vary along other dimensions, which should not matter economically, but have been hypothesized by psychologists to matter for decision making, and have been shown to have large effects in laboratory settings. For example, the lender varied the description of the offer, either showing the monthly payment for one typical loan or for a variety of loan terms and sizes. Other randomizations include whether and how the offered interest rate is compared to a "market" benchmark, the expiration date of the offer, whether the offer is combined with a promotional giveaway, race and gender features introduced via the inclusion of a photo in the corner of the letter, and whether the offer letter mentions suggested uses for the loan. The analysis then compares the effect of all these manipulations. While not all of them make a difference, many do, and some of the effects are large and surprising. For example, for male customers, having a photo of a woman on top of the offer letter increased take-up as much as a 1 percent reduction in the monthly interest rate. In some sense, the juxtaposition of the two experiments may be the most surprising: On the one hand, individuals react as "homo economicus" to information – they are sensitive to interest rates, and bad risks accept highest interest rates (at least among women). On the other hand, these effects are present in the same setting where seemingly anodyne manipulations make a large difference.

The two experiments and many others that have been described in this paper illustrate how development economists have gone much beyond program evaluations to use randomization as a tool and the field as a "lab." Compared to retrospective evaluations (even perfectly identified ones), field experiments, when the collaboration with the partner is very close, offer much more flexibility and make it possible to give primacy to the hypothesis to test, rather than to the program that happens to have been implemented. With retrospective evaluations, theory is used instrumentally as a way to provide a structure justifying the identifying assumptions (this is more or less explicit depending on the empirical tradition the researchers belong to). With prospective evaluations, it is the experimental design that is instrumental. This gives more power both to test the theory and to challenge it.

The set of fertilizer experiments also illustrates how experiments can be used sequentially, with each set of results providing the inputs for designing a new round of experiments. Such a set of sequential experiments is conducted on the sample population, and in part, on the same panel of farmers, interviewed many times over the course of the experiment. In the process, the researcher successively builds a panel data set on farmers spanning many time units. Though this design remains fairly rare, it offers interesting possibilities in that the experiments become more relevant as the underlying theory becomes more pertinent, and the richness of the data collected allows the researcher to use the data in many other ways than conducting a simple test of the theory. An open question is whether the population becomes affected by staying too long in a panel and being subject to several experiments. This may eventually reduce the external validity of these findings. I am not aware of systematic research on this issue, however.

Lab experiments share this flexibility. Where field experiments are different from lab experiments, however, is that they take place in a context where people are making important decisions, with high stakes. Economists are often suspicious of lab experiments, because it is not clear that behavior observed in the lab would still apply when people make "real" decisions, or whether they would persist over time. Despite their interest, this criticism often applies to some "field experiments" conducted in the U.S. because they take place in very specific, unusual contexts or on rather marginal decisions. Field experiments in development (and some in developed countries as well) have not suffered from this criticism. In the case of the Bertrand et al. (2005) study, for example, the loan sizes average one-third of the borrower's income. In the case of Duflo, Kremer, and Robinson (2005), farmers are making agricultural decisions, with which they have plenty of experience. Thus, the lessons from field experiments in development economics are directly relevant to important issues, and also much more likely to generalize.

Working in the field also allows the researchers to calibrate effects against each other. Duflo, Kremer, and Robinson (2005) and Bertrand et al. (2005) quantify the importance of the "non-standard" hypotheses against price effect. They both show that these effects are large. Duflo, Kremer, and Robinson (2005) find that the timing of the offer has almost as large an effect on take-up as that of a 50 percent subsidy. Bertrand et al. (2005) found that any one of the psychological manipulations that had an effect had an effect on take-up of the loan roughly equivalent to that of a 1 percent reduction in the monthly interest rate.

Of course, the fact that the research is conducted with real people facing real decisions also puts limits on what can be done: Ethical considerations play an important role, as does the imperative not to propose programs to people that do not make any sense to them. In this sense, the field has fewer options than the lab. However, the external validity of asking people to make decisions that would not make any sense in reality is in any case limited.

2.2   The Relationship Between Theory and Experiments

Field experiments, like lab experiments, are often criticized for lacking external validity (see Basu, 2005): They may be giving the right answer about the behavioral response to an intervention in a particular population, but this is not sufficient to infer that the response would be the same if the intervention were somewhat different, or if the population were somewhat different. The latter is because the experiments are often quite localized and specific in focus. There is no way to generalize the results without recourse to some theory that is external to the experiment (for example, a sense that the treatment effect would be the same for people with similar observed characteristics). As Banerjee (2005) points out, this is clearly correct, but this does not imply that nothing can be learned from a well-executed empirical exercise: In most of what we do as social scientists, we assume that there is some constancy in nature, so that we can parametrize the contexts according to a limited number of dimensions. This makes it possible (and desirable) to replicate experiments in different contexts. It is always a theory (more or less explicit or well articulated) that will guide the dimensions according to which the experiments will need to be replicated.

To solve both problems of external validity (the specificity in the population and the specificity of the program), several authors, including Mookherjee (2005), have proposed combining experiments with structural models. Attanasio, Meghir, and Santiago (2002) implemented such a strategy on the PROGRESA program. In some sense, the field experiments I have described in this paper subscribe to this approach more radically, since they are generally motivated by the desire to answer one specific well-defined question, and they design the experiment with that in mind. The issue that Attanasio, Meghir, and Santiago (2002) are grappling with in the case of the PROGRESA program is that they are trying to obtain several parameters of interest out of one single experiment, which was really a package of interventions (a conditional cash transfer delivered only to women): They then need the theory to provide them with the additional identifying restrictions ex post. The experiments we describe here were set up not to maximize the effect of an intervention, but with a view to understanding the effect that one isolated manipulation would have. In many cases, a stratified design was used in order to identify more than one such relationship. Several "treatments" and different "treatment intensities" can be combined (Karlan and Zinman (2005), for example, combine different interest rates, both ex post and ex ante) to answer more than one question, calibrate treatments against each other, understand their interactions, and get a sense of the "dose response" function. Yet, even as they can be used to test the conceptual foundations of policies, field experiments do not, in general, evaluate a "package" of policies that may be optimal from a policy design point of view. For example, the particular combination of the conditionality of the cash transfer, the way it varies with the age of the child, the fact that the transfers are given to women, and the sheer size of the transfers have presumably been chosen by the promoters of PROGRESA to optimize its effectiveness. Field experiments can be used to test theories, while "traditional" randomized program evaluations can be used to test the effectiveness of more complex policies, combining a variety of policy levers, which have not necessarily been tested, or even implemented, together in the field. Ideally, the results of field experiments and the theories that underlie them would also inform the design of such "combination" policies, so that the two approaches are both policy relevant and complementary.

In field experiments, the structure is imposed ex ante by the choice of which variations are tested and which are not. However, as we have seen, the results of many of these experiments have challenged the theories they started from and set out to test. There are fundamental reasons why experiments are more likely to generate surprising results than retrospective work. First, as noted previously, randomization frees the experimenter from the need to use theory to justify identification assumptions. Secondly, while it is always possible to reject experimental results on the grounds that the experiment was poorly designed, or failed, when an experiment is correctly implemented (which is relatively easy to ascertain), there is no doubt that it gives us the effect of the manipulation that was implemented, at least in this particular case. It is therefore more difficult to ignore the results even when they are unexpected. An investigator can of course always choose to file the results in a drawer and never mention them again to anyone. It is critical that institutions are developed to avoid this. The FDA requires reporting results of any funded medical trial. Institutions of this type need to be developed for field experiments. Field experiments always start with a proposal that describes the design and the results that are expected. It could (and probably should) be made compulsory for researchers to post their design ex ante and the results corresponding to the design they have posted.

In contrast, non-experimental research designs often leave more room for interpretation and choices, and knowing this, if the initial results accord less well with intuition, a rational Bayesian investigator will give them less weight than she would if they came from an experiment. She will also know that others will be unlikely to believe her study. If she is (like we all are) affected by self-serving biases, she is likely to decide that the initial design was flawed and may choose to change the specifications, the choice of control variables, etc., until the results accord better with her initial prior.[4] This can happen without any manipulation, just by applying the simple rule of stopping the research when the results "make sense." Consider, for example, the case of learning in the deworming drug cases: If researchers had run the usual specifications and found evidence that children are more likely to take the drug when more of the children in their school take the drug as well, they would have been very likely to just accept this result and publish one more paper confirming positive social learning in this new context. Nobody would have been surprised.

2.3   What Theoretical Framework?

Field experiments need theory, not only to derive specific testable implications but to give a general direction of what the interesting questions are. A body of theoretical work allows different results to resonate with each other. Empirical development economists (not only those who conduct field experiments) have greatly benefited from a body of theory that was developed in the 1980s and 1990s, which has been called elsewhere the "poor but neo-classical" paradigm. The "poor but neo-classical" paradigm (starting with the work of Stiglitz) incorporates the insights of the economics of information into development. With imperfect information, moral hazard, limited liability, or adverse selection, poverty radically changes the options that an individual has access to: how much someone can borrow depends on his asset position; when insurance options are limited, poor people may be less willing to take any risks. This means that poverty leads to inefficient outcomes, even if everybody is perfectly rational.

This theoretical framework gave a coherent meaning to the empirical results that had been accumulating at the doorstep of the "poor but efficient" framework (Schultz, 1964) and that had been resisted for some time as being inconsistent

---

[4] Mullainathan (2005) makes this point to highlight that there will be a tendency for evaluation of development programs to find that programs "worked." I think that more generally, researchers will be tempted to find what they want to find. Given the publication bias in the profession (significant results are more interesting to publish), this may be equivalent in most cases.

with theory (for example, the famous farm-size productivity relationship). The initial, theoretical advances opened a new empirical agenda to mainstream economists: The stake was not to accept or reject the hypothesis of "poor but efficient," and with it all the postulates of neo-classical economics; the task of empirical economics shifted to providing evidence for market inefficiencies and the impact of economic policies to alleviate them.

The paradigm "poor but neo-classical" helped define an empirical agenda and structure a vision of the world, even though it often remained implicit in empirical work. It still provides us with a wealth of empirical predictions that could be explicitly tested in the field. Karlan and Zinman (2005), which I discussed above, is a great example of the shape this work can take, but there is little experimental work designed to test these central ideas. The questions are plentiful: How important are dynamic incentives and group lending to the repayment performance in microcredit organizations? If people had access to health or weather insurance, would they undertake riskier, but more profitable, investments? What is the marginal rate of return to capital for small entrepreneurs? Is there evidence of increasing returns to capital over some range? Would increasing the flow of information about prospective borrowers increase lending? Would increased bargaining power of sharecroppers increase agricultural productivity?

One direction in which the work of field experiments needs to go in the future is thus to exploit more fully this powerful theoretical framework to come up with hypotheses to test in the field. However, we also need to deal with the fact that the results of many of these experiments have challenged this framework. In the absence of a well-funded alternative frame of analysis, these rejections appear now as a collection of random results that do not fit very well within any existing theory, and that we don't necessarily fully understand. This makes it difficult to generalize results and give them meaning, as some of the critics of randomized evaluation have pointed out. However, criticizing the experiments on this ground, like many have done, is a little bit like shooting the messenger. One may instead want to accept the message that they deliver: that we need to work on a new theoretical framework that can accommodate these results and predict new ones.

Banerjee (2005) identifies this as the "new challenge to theory." According to him (a central contributor to the "poor but neo-classical" framework), the challenge is to form a new body of theory that can be used as a general framework to make sense of the disparate results emerging from the field. For this, he argues, "We need to give up trying to defend the existing theory (which has been incredibly successful in many ways) against the onslaught of seemingly random results that are coming out of the field experiments." I see these results less as a challenge than an opportunity. It was not the remit of the "poor but neo-classical" framework to explain the entire world, and in this sense, it does not need to be "defended" for not being able to explain everything.

While the empirical work continues to explore the relevance and the limits of the "poor but neo-classical" framework, a direction in which the theoretical work needs to be going is to start working on a theoretical framework that can accommodate the new results; this is exactly what theorists did when the "poor but neo-classical" framework incorporated and replaced the "poor but rational" one. This theory is lacking at the moment. While many experiments use insights gleaned from behavioral economics or psychology to design tests and interventions, the work of organizing these insights into a coherent framework that applies to development has not taken place. Behavioral economics, in particular, has not yet produced a coherent unifying theory. The "theories" to be tested sometimes look more like a collection of anomalies. Moreover, faithfully applying the theories developed for developed countries to the analysis of the decisions of the poor in developing countries would, however, be making the same mistake as the "poor but efficient" proponents and failing to recognize the central insight of the "poor but neo-classical" line of research. Trying to reduce the behavior of a Kenyan farmer who does not use fertilizer and that of an American employee who does not contribute to his 401k to the same model may be as fruitless as trying to convince oneself that Guatemalan farmers are on the efficiency frontier. The same limitation in cognitive ability or self-control that affects the rich may also affect the poor, and has different implications for them. As Mullainathan (2005) points out, the point is not to say that the poor are just particularly irrational, but to recognize that the same failure of rationality may have dramatically different consequences for the poor. Being poor almost certainly affects the *way* people think and decide. Perhaps when choices involve the subsistence of one's family, trade-offs are distorted in different ways than when the question is how much money one will enjoy at retirement. Pressure by extended family members or neighbors is also stronger when they are at risk of starvation.

What is needed is a theory of how poverty influences decision making, not only by affecting the constraints, but by changing the decision-making process itself. That theory can then guide a new round of empirical research, both observational and experimental.

3   CONCLUSION: OPEN QUESTIONS

I'll conclude by briefly outlining two open areas where research (experiments and theory) are particularly needed: These are areas that are both of tremendous practical importance and of great interest to research.

The first can broadly be named the question of behavior change: Why are people not doing things that are obviously good for them or their children (even when they love their children), such as using a condom to protect themselves from HIV/AIDS, taking their TB medicine, immunizing their children, getting free antenatal checkups, using an oven with a chimney to avoid filling up the room with smoke when cooking, etc. This is clearly a phenomenon that is common to developed and developing countries, but the consequences are often so dire in developing countries that this is, to paraphrase Lucas, a problem that it is almost impossible to let go of when one starts thinking about it. Behavioral economists are studying similar problems in developed countries, with particular attention to the question of savings. Their approach has been in some cases akin to the approach we described above. For example, Thaler and Benartzi (2003) developed a financial product, "Save More Tomorrow," which allowed new employees to save a fraction of future increments in their salaries in their 401k. This is precisely a product that would appeal to a hyperbolic discounter. Though it was not evaluated formally (there was no experiment), the program appeared to be extremely successful and has now been adopted by many companies. Many NGOs in developing countries are engaged in trying to solve exactly these problems. Collaborating with them to evaluate their approach or design and evaluate new approaches could help build a body of effective interventions. By being open-minded about what will work (beyond information and incentives), one can make progress both in understanding behavior and in improving lives considerably.

The second area does not involve solving intra-person problems, but interpersonal ones. Development economists have always stressed the importance of institutions, and recently, the study of institutions has re-emerged as one of the central questions in development (see Pande and Udry (2005) in this volume). A central reason for underdevelopment is the lack of institutions that favor cooperation and social behavior. The central practical question then becomes: what to do about poor institutions. Should we just write off those countries which are plagued with (often historically inherited) poor institutions, or should we instead work on ways to get things done in these environments (with a view, perhaps, to arrive at institution change eventually)? Most countries with very poor institutions function to some extent. Absenteeism rates are extremely high in schools and health services, but what may be surprising is that nurses or teachers actually come at all in the absence of any sort of punishment for delinquent behavior (Chaudhury et al. (2005)). Understanding how to harness people's intrinsic motivation and social preferences may help improve the day-to-day functioning of countries where institutions are in disarray. There is nothing in this that is particularly new: As Ray (1998) points out in the introduction to his textbook, development economics is in large part the study of indigenous, informal institutions that emerge to palliate the absence of well-functioning formal institutions. This may just demand researchers to be a bit more imaginative in thinking about what can motivate people.

In all these cases, the economist goes beyond a purely positive role and does not shy from assuming a normative position. This was already advocated by Banerjee (2002). Working in developing countries makes one acutely aware of how much "slack" there is in the world, and how small interventions can make large differences. But if economists are normative, it becomes critical that they rigorously evaluate their propositions, since, like most people feeling around for the light switch, they are likely to make mistakes. This makes the experimental approach indispensable, both as a practical and as a scientific tool.

References

Ainslie G. (1992). *Picoeconomics*. Cambridge: Cambridge University Press

Ashraf, Nava, Dean S. Karlan, and Wesley Yin (2006). "Tying Odysseus to the Mast: Evidence from a Commitment Savings Product in the Philippines," *Quarterly Journal of Economics*, forthcoming

Angrist, Josh and Victor Lavy (2002). "The Effect of High School Matriculation Awards: Evidence from Randomized Trials," NBER Working Paper No. 9389

Attanasio, Orazio, Costas Meghir, and Ana Santiago (2002). "Education Choices in Mexico: Using a Structural Model and a Randomized Experiment to Evaluate PROGRESA," MIMEO, Inter-American Development Bank

Banerjee, Abhijit (2002). "The Uses of Economic Theory: Against a Purely Positive Interpretation of Theoretical Results," MIMEO, MIT

Banerjee, Abhijit (2005). "'New Development Economics' and the Challenge to Theory," *Economic and Political Weekly*, October 1

Banerjee, Abhijit and Ruimin He (2003). "The World Bank of the Future," *American Economic Review, Papers and Proceedings*, 93(2): 39–44

Banerjee, Abhijit, Angus Deaton, and Esther Duflo (2004). "Health Care Delivery in Rural Rajasthan," *Economic and Political Weekly*, 39(9), 944–949

Banerjee, Abhijit and Esther Duflo (2005). "Addressing Absence," *Journal of Economic Perspectives*, forthcoming

Banerjee, Abhijit, Suraj Jacob, and Michael Kremer, with Jenny Lanjouw and Peter Lanjouw (2005). "Moving to Universal Education! Costs and Trade offs," MIMEO, MIT

Banerjee, Abhijit and Sendhil Mullainathan (2005). "Motivation and Poverty," MIMEO, MIT

Basu, Kaushik (2005). "The New Empirical Development Economics: Remarks on Its Philosophical Foundations," *Economic and Political Weekly*, October 1

Bertrand, Marianne, Dean Karlan, Sendhil Mullainathan, Eldar Shafir, and Jonathan Zinman (2005). "What's Psychology Worth? A Field Experiment in the Consumer Credit Market," Yale University Economic Growth Center Discussion Paper No. 918

Besley, Timothy and Anne Case (1994). "Diffusion as a Learning Process: Evidence from HYV Cotton," RPDS, Princeton University, Discussion Paper No. 174

Binswanger, Hans (1980). "Risk Attitudes of Rural Households in Semi-Arid Tropical India," *American Journal of Agricultural Economics* 62: 395–407

Chaudhury, Nazmul, Jeffrey Hammer, Michael Kremer, Karthik Muralidharan, and F. Halsey Rogers (2005). "Teacher Absence in India: A Snapshot," *Journal of the European Economic Association* 3(2–3), April–May

Conley, Timothy and Christopher Udry (2005). "Learning About a New Technology: Pineapple in Ghana," MIMEO, Yale University

Duflo, Esther (2004). "Scaling Up and Evaluation" in *Accelerating Development*, edited by Francois Bourguignon and Boris Pleskovic. Oxford, UK and Washington, DC: Oxford University Press and World Bank

Duflo, Esther, Rachel Glennerster, and Michael Kremer (2005). "Randomization as a Tool for Development Economists," MIMEO, MIT

Duflo, Esther and Rema Hanna (2005). "Monitoring Works: Getting Teachers to Come to School," NBER Working Paper No. 11880, December

Duflo, Esther and Michael Kremer (2004). "Use of Randomization in the Evaluation of Development Effectiveness," in *Evaluating Development Effectiveness* (World Bank

Series on Evaluation and Development, Volume 7), edited by Osvaldo Feinstein, Gregory K. Ingram, and George K. Pitman. New Brunswick, NJ: Transaction Publishers, pp. 205–232

Duflo, Esther, Michael Kremer, and Jonathan Robinson (2005). "Understanding Fertilizer Adoption: Evidence from Field Experiments," Mimeo, MIT

Duflo, Esther and Emmanuel Saez (2002). "Participation and Investment Decisions in a Retirement Plan: The Influence of Colleagues' Choices," *Journal of Public Economics*, 85(1): 121–148

Duflo, Esther and Emmanuel Saez (2003). "The Role of Information and Social Interactions in Retirement Plan Decisions: Evidence from a Randomized Experiment," *Quarterly Journal of Economics*, 118(3): 815–842

Foster, Andrew and Mark Rosenzweig (1995). "Learning by Doing and Learning from Others: Human Capital and Technical Change in Agriculture," *Journal of Political Economy*, 103: 1176–1209

Glewwe, Paul, Nauman Ilias, and Michael Kremer (2003). "Teacher Incentives," MIMEO, Harvard University

Holmström, Bengt and Paul Milgrom (1991). "Multitask Principal-Agent Analysis: Incentive Contracts, Asset Ownership and Job Design," *Journal of Law, Economics and Organization*, 7: 24–52

Karlan, Dean (2005). "Using Experimental Economics to Measure Social Capital and Predict Real Financial Decisions," *American Economic Review*, 95(5): 1688–1699

Karlan, Dean and Jonathan Zinman (2005). "Observing Unobservables: Identifying Information Asymmetries with a Consumer Credit Field Experiment," MIMEO, Yale

Kling, Jeffrey and Jeffrey Liebman (2005). "Experimental Analysis of Neighborhood Effects on Youth," NBER Working Papers No. 11577

Kremer, Michael and Daniel Chen (2001). "An Interim Report on a Teacher Attendance Incentive Program in Kenya," MIMEO, Harvard

Kremer, Michael and Edward Miguel (2003). "Networks, Social Learning, and Technology Adoption: The Case of Deworming Drugs in Kenya," MIMEO, Harvard

Kremer, Michael, Edward Miguel, and Rebecca Thornton (2004). "Incentives to Learn," NBER Working Paper No. 10971

Laibson D. (1997). "Golden Eggs and Hyperbolic Discounting," *Quarterly Journal of Economics*, 62: 443–478

Manski, Charles (1993). "Identification of Exogenous Social Effects: The Reflection Problem," *Review of Economic Studies*, 60: 531–542

Mookherjee, Dilip (2005). "Is There Too Little Theory in Development Economics?" *Economic and Political Weekly*, October 1

Mullainathan, Sendhil (2005). "Development Economics Through the Lens of Psychology," in *Annual World Bank Conference in Development Economics 2005: Lessons of Experience*, edited by Francois Bourguignon and Boris Pleskovic. Oxford, UK and Washington, DC: Oxford University Press and World Bank

Munshi, Kaivan (2004). "Social Learning in a Heterogeneous Population: Technology Diffusion in the Indian Green Revolution," *Journal of Development Economics*, 73(1): 185–215

Munshi, Kaivan and Jacques Myaux (2002). "Social Norms and the Fertility Transition," *Journal of Development Economics*, forthcoming

Olken, Benjamin (2005). "Monitoring Corruption: Evidence from a Field Experiment in Indonesia," NBER Working Paper No. 11753

Pande, Rohini and Christopher Udry (2005). "Institutions and Development: A View from Below," in *Advances in Economics and Econometrics: Ninth World Congress*, edited by Richard Blundell, Whitney Newey, and Torsten Persson. Cambridge, UK: Cambridge University Press

Ray, Debraj (1998). *Development Economics*. Princeton, NJ: Princeton University Press

Schultz, Theodore W. (1964). *Transforming Traditional Agriculture*. New Haven, CT: Yale University Press

Strotz, R. (1956). "Myopia and Inconsistency in Dynamic Utility Maximization," *Review of Economic Studies*, 23:165–180

Thaler, Richard and Shlomo Benartzi (2004). "Save More Tomorrow: Using Behavioral Economics to Increase Employee Saving," *Journal of Political Economy*, 112(1): 164–187

Thornton, Rebecca (2005). "The Demand for and Impact of Learning HIV Status: Evidence from a Field Experiment," MIMEO, Harvard University

Todd, Petra and Kenneth I. Wolpin (2004). "Using a Social Experiment to Validate a Dynamic Behavioral Model of Child Schooling and Fertility: Assessing the Impact of a School Subsidy Program in Mexico," WP 03-022, University of Pennsylvania

Townsend, Robert (1994). "Risk and Insurance in Village India," *Econometrica*, 62(4):539–591

Udry, Christopher (1994). "Risk and Insurance in a Rural Credit Market: An Empirical Investigation in Northern Nigeria," *Review of Economic Studies*, 61(3): 495–526

CHAPTER 14

Institutions and Development: A View from Below

Rohini Pande and Christopher Udry[*]

Abstract

In this paper we argue for greater exploitation of synergies between research on specific institutions based on micro-data and the big questions posed by the institutions and growth literature. To date, the macroeconomic literature on institutions and growth has largely relied on cross-country regression evidence. This has provided compelling evidence for a causal link between a cluster of 'good' institutions and more rapid long run growth. However, an inability to disentangle the effects of specific institutional channels on growth or to understand the impact of institutional change on growth will limit further progress using a cross-country empirical strategy. We suggest two research programs based on micro-data that have significant potential. The first uses policy-induced variation in specific institutions within countries to understand how these institutions influence economic activity. The second exploits the fact that the incentives provided by a given institutional context often vary with individuals' economic and political status. Variations in how individuals respond to the same institution can be used to both identify how institutions affect economic outcomes and to understand how institutional change arises in response to changing economic and demographic pressures.

1 INTRODUCTION

Recent years have seen a remarkable and exciting revival of interest in the empirical analysis of how a broad set of institutions affects growth. The focus of the recent outpouring of research is on exploiting cross-country variation in 'institutional quality' to identify whether a causal effect runs from institutions to growth. These papers conclude that institutional quality is a significant determinant of a country's growth performance.

[*] We have greatly benefited from discussions with Daron Acemoglu, Tim Besley and James Robinson. We are grateful to Orazio Attanasio, Richard Blundell and Tim Guinnane for comments. Finally, we thank James Fenske and Pinar Keskin for fantastic research assistance and Hyungi Woo for editorial assistance. We thank the Yale Center for International and Area Studies for financial support.

These findings are of fundamental importance for development economists and policy practitioners in that they suggest that institutional quality may cause poor countries and people to stay poor. The economic interpretation and policy implications of these findings depends on understanding the specific channels through which institutions affect growth and the reasons for institutional change or the lack thereof. However, for reasons discussed below, we argue that the coarseness of cross-country data limits its usefulness for such research. Instead, a more fruitful research agenda is to exploit the synergies between micro-data based research by development economists and the questions posed by the institutions and growth literature.

North (1981) defines an economic institution as "a set of rules, compliance procedures and moral and ethical behavioral norms designed to constrain the behavior of individuals in the interests of maximizing the wealth or utility of principals" (pp. 201–202). In this paper we adopt his definition of institutions as sets of rules, procedures or norms that constrain behavior but not the notion of agency embodied in this definition. Institutions need not be 'designed,' and even if they are, their actual operation may be quite different than intended. For this reason, we emphasize a research agenda on institutions that pays attention to *de facto* rather than *de jure* institutions and to how changes in resource endowments can cause individuals to alter their economic behavior within a given institutional context. This, in turn, can potentially cause the institution itself to change in the longer run. Such a focus is particularly relevant when thinking about institutions in low income countries – since development, by definition, is about change.

In section 2 we summarize the main insights from the cross-country literature on institutions and growth. This literature has successfully focused attention on the complex interactions between economic growth and institutional development. It has uncovered important correlations across countries between growth and the nature and quality of a core set of economic, political and social institutions. It has also been careful in noting, and accounting for, the fact that institutions and economic growth jointly cause each other. A positive correlation between 'good' institutions and growth may reflect reverse causation; faster growing countries may have 'better' institutions because they can afford them. Faced with the statistical challenge of isolating causal pathways, authors have been extraordinarily inventive in identifying features of countries that are plausibly exogenous to the growth process but that might influence the character of institutional development and thus might serve as instrumental variables. However, we also conclude from our review that this literature has served its purpose and is essentially complete. The set of possible instrumental variables is limited, and their coarseness prevents close analysis of particular causal mechanisms from institutions to growth. Further, the fact that instrumental variables tend to be derived from persistent features of a country's institutional environment (such as its colonial past) limits their usefulness for studying institutional change.

This suggests that the research agenda identified by the institutions and growth literature is best furthered by the analysis of much more micro-data than has typically been the norm in this literature. In section 3 we describe how policy-induced variation in institutional form within a country can be exploited to examine how specific institutions influence economic outcomes. An important advantage of such studies is that information about how such change was implemented across regions in the country and/or differences in the regional incidence of the policy can often be exploited to obtain instruments for specific institutions.

Finally, in section 4 we discuss a different but complementary research focus – close examinations of the economic choices of individuals in a specific institutional context. A given institutional setting can provide a rich variety of incentives to different individuals, depending upon their economic and political standing. The resulting variation in individual behavior can be exploited to identify the economic implications of the given institution. Further, with panel data one can potentially also examine institutional change in response to changing factor endowments. We illustrate this research agenda with an example from Ghana, in which we analyze the effects of a complex land tenure system on investment incentives. We also discuss the historical evolution of that institution and provide some indications of how changes in economic environment may cause individuals to take actions that have the potential to transform the institutional environment.

2   CROSS-COUNTRY ANALYSIS

In this section we summarize the important recent contributions to the empirical institutions and growth literature, and then discuss reasons why we believe this literature to be essentially complete. In Table 14.1 we list five widely cited papers in this literature, which we term 'Core Papers.' These are the papers which were the first to use (and often develop) influential institutional quality measures or instrumental variables to address the endogeneity of institutional measures. We then describe 'Papers citing core papers.' These are articles which cite at least one core paper and are published or forthcoming (that we could identify) in the following journals: *American Economic Review*, *Econometrica*, *Journal of Development Economics*, *Journal of Economic Growth*, *Quarterly Journal of Economics*, *Journal of Political Economy* and *Review of Economic Studies*. We restrict attention to papers with at least one cross-country regression, which consider a measure of the country's growth performance (or well-being of the population) as the outcome variable of interest, and include a measure of institutional quality as an explanatory variable.[1]

For each paper, Table 14.1 describes the outcome variable of interest, the institutional measure, the instrumental variables used and the paper's main

---

[1]   Our focus implies that we exclude a vital literature in economic history that explores the interconnections between institutions, factor endowments, technology, and economic growth (Engerman and Sokoloff (1997, 2005)). We also leave largely unexamined a related literature on the impact of institutional quality on policy outcomes, such as the size of government (Laporta et al. (1999)).

Table 14.1. *Institutions and growth: Literature review*

| | | | Institutions | |
Article	Dependent Variables	Measures	Instrument	Key Results[1]
CORE PAPERS				
Acemoglu, Johnson & Robinson (2001)	Log GDP per capita (1995)	Protection against expropriation risk[2] (1985–1995)	Settler mortality[1]	One standard deviation (SD) increase in protection against expropriation risk (1.5) increases GDP per worker by 118% (OLS) and 309% (IV)
Hall & Jones (1999)	Log output per worker[1] (1988)	Index of social infrastructure[2] which combines: i. index of government antidiversion policies[3] ii. index of country's openness[4]	I. Distance from equator[2] II. English speakers[3] III. European-language speakers[4] IV. Predicted trade share[5]	One SD increase in index of social infrastructure (0.25) increases output per worker by 128% (OLS) and 261% (IV)
Knack & Keefer (1995)	I. Annual GDP per capita growth (1974–1989) II. Private investment/GDP (1974–1989) (all averages)	I. ICRG index[5] II. BERI index[6]	No IV estimates.	One SD increase in ICRG index (13.50) increases annual per capita income growth rate by 1.24 (OLS)
LLSV(1999)	Dependent variables are classified in five groups (data from 1990s): I. Interference with private sector II. Efficiency	I. Ethnolinguistic fractionalization II. Legal origin III. Religion	No IV estimates.	A French legal origin country (relative to others) has 42% more infant mortality (OLS)

Study	Dependent variables	Institutions	Instruments	Results
	III. Output of public goods IV. Size of public sector V. Political freedom			
Mauro (1995)	I. GDP per capita growth (1960–1985) II. Investment/GDP (1960–1985) III. Investment/GDP (1980–1985) (all averages)	I. Index of institutional efficiency[7] II. Index of bureaucratic efficiency[8]	Ethnolinguistic fractionalization[6] (1960)	One SD increase in index of bureaucratic efficiency (2.16) increases average growth of GDP per capita by 0.6% (OLS) and 2.3% (TV)
PAPERS CITING CORE PAPERS				
Acemoglu, Johnson & Robinson (2002)	I. Log GDP per capita (1995) II. *Urbanization*[2] (1995)	I. Current institutions: i. protection against expropriation risk ii. executive constraints in 1990[9] II. Early institutions: i. executive constraints in 1900 ii. initial executive constraints[10]	Settler mortality	One SD increase in expropriation risk (1.5) increases GDP per capita by 118% (IV), controlling for urbanization in 1500
Acemoglu & Johnson (2005)	I. Log GDP per capita (1995) II. Av. investment/GDP (1990s) III. Private credit/GDP (1998) IV. Average stock market capitalization[3]/GDP (1990–1995)	I. Contracting institutions: i. legal formalism[11] II. Property rights institutions: i. executive constraints ii. protection against expropriation risk	I. Settler mortality II. *Log of indigenous population density in 1500*[7] III. Legal origin[8]	One SD increase in expropriation risk (1.47) and legal formalism (1.24, using "check measure") together increase GDP per capita by 189% (OLS) and 523% (IV)

(cont.)

Table 14.1. *Institutions and growth: Literature review*

Article	Dependent Variables	Measures	Institutions Instrument	Key Results[1]
Aghion, Howitt & Mayer-Foulkes (2005)	Average growth rate of GDP per capita (1960–1995) relative to the United States	I. Private credit[12] II. Liquid liabilities[13] III. Bank assets[14] IV. Commercial–central bank[15]	I. Legal origin II. *Settler mortality*	One SD increase in private credit (0.28) increases steady-state GDP by 21% in Belgium[2]
Alcala & Ciccone (2004)	Log GDP per capita (1995)	Index of institutional quality[16]	I. *Settler mortality* II. European-language speakers III. Predicted trade share (AC)[12]	One SD increase in index of institutional quality increases GDP per capita by 35% (IV) (controls include log real openness[3])
Bockstette, Chanda & Putterman (2002)	I. Log output per worker (1988) II. Average GDP per capita growth (1960–1995)	I. Index of social infrastructure II. ICRG index	I. Distance from equator II. English speakers III. European-language speakers IV. Log predicted trade share V. State antiquity[9]	One SD increase in index of social infrastructure (0.25) increases output per worker by 126% (OLS) and 229% (GMM-IV)
Clague, Keefer, Knack & Olson (1999)	I. Annual per capita GDP growth (1970–1992) II. Output per worker (1988) III. Capital per worker (1988) IV. Years schooling per worker (1985) V. TFP (1988)	I. Contract-intensive money[17] II. ICRG index III. BERI index	I. Colonial origin[10] II. Ethnolinguistic homogeneity[11]	One SD increase in contract-intensive money (0.14) increases growth by 94.5 (OLS) and 1.739 (TV), controlling for log GDP per capita in 1970

Study	Dependent variables	Explanatory variables	Instruments	Results
Djankov, La Porta, Lopez–de Silanes & Shleifer	I. Deaths from (i) intestinal infection (ii) accidental poisoning II. Quality standards (no. ISO 9000 certifications) III. Water pollution IV. Unofficial economy: (i) size/GDP (ii) employment V. Product market competition	Number of different procedures that a start-up has to comply with in order to obtain a legal status, i.e., to start operating as a legal entity.	No IV estimates	One SD increase in number of procedures (4.37) increases deaths from intestinal infection by 4.588% (OLS), controlling for log per capita GDP in 1999
Esfahani & Ramirez (2003)	I. Growth of GDP per capita II. Growth rates of telephones and power production per capita	I. Adverseness of policy environment[18] II. Indices of democracy and centralization[19] III. Indices of contract repudiation, bureaucratic quality and corruption[20] IV. Ethnolinguistic fractionalization	No IV estimates	One SD increase in contract enforcement (0.24) increases GDP per capita growth by 5.8% (OLS) (includes other institutional quality measures as controls)
Glaeser, La Porta, Lopez–de Silanes & Shleifer (2004)	I. Log GDP per capita (2000) II. Growth rates of GDP per capita 1960–2000, overall and by decade III. Years schooling IV. Political institutions (III and IV are 5-year change)	Executive constraints	I. Settler mortality II. Legal origin III. Log indigenous population density in 1500	One SD increase in constraints on executive (0.185) decreases GDP per capita by 6% (IV), controlling for population in temperate zone (1995) and years of schooling

(cont.)

Table 14.1. *Institutions and growth: Literature review*

Article	Dependent Variables	Institutions		Key Results[1]
		Measures	Instrument	
Jones & Olken (2005)	Change in annual growth rate of real GDP per capita comparing 5-year growth averages before and after leader deaths	Index of democratization[22]	No IV estimates	One SD increase in democratization increases annual growth by 2.1% (OLS) after the deaths of leaders in autocratic regimes
Knack & Keefer (1997)	I. Average annual growth in per capita income (1980–1992) II. Investment/GDP (1980–1992)	I. Trust[23] II. Civic norms (civic cooperation)	I. Ethnolinguistic homogeneity II. % Law students 1963	One SD increase in trust (0.14) increases annual per capita income growth by 1.1% (OLS) and 1.2% (IV) (includes other controls)
Kogel (2005)	Annual average growth rate of TFP (1965–1990, panel data of 5-year averages)	Index of social infrastructure	I. English speakers II. European-language speakers III. Predicted trade shares IV. Distance from equator V. State antiquity	One SD increase in index of social infrastructure (0.25) increases annual average TFP growth rate by 91.7% (TV), controlling for initial log TFP
Masters & McMillan (2001)	Log output per worker (1988)	Index of social infrastructure	I. Distance from equator II. Predicted trade share III. English speakers IV. European-language speakers	One SD increase in index of social infrastructure (0.257) increases output per worker by 680% (IV) for "tropical" countries (average frost days <5 per month in winter)

Study	Dependent variable	Institutions	Instruments	Results
Rodrik (1999)	Average dollar wages in manufacturing (1985–1989)	I. Political institutions: i. two rule of law indicators[24] ii. two democracy indicators[25] II. Labor market institutions: i. unionization rate ii. number ILO workers' rights conventions ratified	I. Dummy for oil exporter II. Colonial origins III. *Each measure of democracy as an instrument for the other*	One SD increase in freedom house index (0.33) increases average dollar wages in manufacturing by 19.8% (OLS) and 37.62% (TV) (includes controls)
Rodrik, Subramanian & Trebbi (2004)	Same as Clague, Keefer, Knack & Olson (1999), except they use GDP per capita (1995)	Rule of law index[26]	I. *Settler mortality* II. *European-language speakers* III. *Predicted trade shares*	One SD increase in rule of law index (0.94) increases GDP per capita by 112% (OLS) and 205% (TV), controlling for distance from equator

Notes to Table 14.1 are in the Appendix to this chapter.

finding. Typically, we report the estimates for the most basic specification in the paper.

2.1   Observations

The resurgence of the cross-country literature on institutions and growth is clearly linked to two factors – the availability of comparable measures of institutional quality for a large set of countries, and the use of instrumental variable techniques to deal with the endogeneity of institutions. This is a rich and active literature with much debate about the suitability of empirical strategies adopted by the different papers, the validity of their identification assumptions and the relative magnitudes of the effects of different kinds of institutions on growth outcomes. From Table 14.1 we pull together some observations about this literature.

A. Institutions Matter

Almost without exception, the papers listed in Table 14.1 find a robust positive correlation between growth outcomes and an array of measures of institutional quality. Looking across countries, the literature argues that improvements in the quality of contracting institutions, better law enforcement, increased protection of private property rights, improvements in central government bureaucracy, improved operation of formal sector financial markets, increased levels of democracy, and higher levels of trust are all correlated with higher economic growth.

B. Comparable Institution Measures Are Coarse and Urban-Based

This literature has mainly used aggregate measures of institutional quality, and one of its strengths is the broad range of such measures that it examines. Many of the papers rely on indicators generated by organizations whose primary purpose is to provide assessments of the various forms of political risk or of the contractual environment in countries around the world. These sources (for example, Political Risk Services, Business Environmental Risk Intelligence, or the Economist Intelligence Unit) have the important advantage of being expressly designed to be comparable across countries. For example, a 'protection against expropriation' score of 7 from Political Risk Services is supposed to mean the same thing in any country of the world. Most measures relate to institutional quality as faced by businesses and individuals in the more formal urban sector. It is also the case that this literature, almost by definition, has to treat 'institutions' coarsely. The fundamental problem is that the dimension of the vector of institutions that we believe influences growth is extremely large. Because some dimensions are unobserved (by nature, or because of data problems) and because the number of countries is small, regressions never include this whole vector of institutions as independent variables.

C. Instruments Are Rare

There is widespread recognition of the fact that economic performance may determine institutional form. In Table 14.1 we see that a very small number of variables have been called upon to identify the causal effects of the wide range of institutions examined in the literature. The key instrumental variables have been based on geography (distance from equator and predicted trade share, oil exporter) and colonial and pre-colonial history (settler mortality, legal origin, ethnic and linguistic composition, pre-colonial population density, state antiquity). The paucity of plausible instruments arises from the fact that there are few variables that are important determinants of the current form of a particular economic institution and affect growth only through that institution.

Another striking feature is that the same variable is often used in different studies as an instrument for different indices of institutions and interpreted in varying ways. Consider settler mortality. It is used to instrument for: (i) protection against expropriation risk; (ii) executive constraints; (iii) measures of financial depth such as private credit; (iv) a rule of law index; and (v) the overall index of institutional quality.[2]

D. Persistent Institutional Effects

The instruments that dominate the literature are based on geography and colonial and pre-colonial history and exploit long-term persistent institutional features of a country. The IV strategy purges the estimates of the effect of any institutions that change along the path of development because these are clearly endogenous to the growth process. This, however, implies that the IV strategy by design is not able to identify the consequences of institutional change for growth.

E. IV Estimates Typically Exceed OLS Estimates

IV estimates of the institutions growth relationship are always significantly larger than the OLS estimates. Given that endogeneity concerns would suggest an upward bias in the OLS estimate, a common interpretation is attenuation bias in the OLS due to measurement error.

2.2   The Limits of Cross-Country Analysis

Based on the above observations, we suggest that the general approach of this literature may not allow us to explore the channels through which institutions affect economic development, or to identify the precise magnitude of the impact of institutions on growth. Our concerns relate to the construction of commonly

---

[2] Another remarkable fact is that almost all the instrumental variables were introduced in one of the five core papers as instruments or institutions. That only state antiquity, the oil exporter dummy and the proportion of postsecondary law students in 1963, have been introduced in the 16 papers that follow is further indication of the difficulty of finding suitable instruments for endogenous institutions.

used institutional measures and to heterogeneity across countries in both how an institution operates and how it is affected by the instrumental variable.

The use of coarse institutional measures implies that cross-country regressions are typically unable to isolate the causal effect of any single institution. Further, the inability to include the entire array of institutions that impinge on, say, growth as independent variables (often due to the small set of available instruments) raises the possibility of omitted variable bias. A different source of potential bias is heterogeneity across countries in how the same institution affects economic outcomes and in how the institution responds to the instrumental variable at hand. Both omitted variables and heterogenous treatment effects may induce an upward bias in the IV estimate, an issue of some concern since IV estimates in the cross-country literature typically exceed the OLS. Some of our arguments, especially the problems with using measures based on a country's colonial past to instrument for specific institutions, have already received attention in the institutions and growth literature; for a very complimentary analysis see Acemoglu (2005).

A. Coarseness of Institutional Measures and Instruments

The cross-country literature has largely relied on broad indices of institutional quality. A first concern is that the construction of these indices requires subjective valuations of what belongs in the index. Typically, the information that underlies the indices is not fully public and reflects the subjective judgments of analysts at the risk assessment organization. For example Political Risk Services (PRS) constructs the widely used ICRG measures. The ICRG provides a number of indicators, most of which rely on a combination of objective information about the country and subjective assessments of PRS analysts and their research team (moreover, different papers combine these indicators in different ways). PRS reported to us that to construct the commonly used 'protection against expropriation risk' index,

> We 'infer' the risk involved from the degree of accountability of the government, the freedom of the judiciary, the level of application of the rule of law, and the level of apparent corruption. (personal communication 15 July 2005)

We have no reason to doubt the competence or judgment of those who construct the indicators, and indeed, the fact that investors are willing to pay for this information shows that the indicators are associated with something that investors care about. However, the opacity of construction of these indicators limits open debate about these judgments. Other measures of institutional development used in these papers are subject (to greater or lesser degrees) to the same difficulty.[3]

---

[3] These include the BERI index, the Economist Intelligence Unit's indices of bureaucratic efficiency and institutional efficiency, the Freedom House democracy index, and (to a much lesser degree) executive constraints and the index of democracy (from Polity III and Polity IV). Obviously, some

A second concern relates to arbitrary choice of weights to combine the underlying sub-indices (the most common index is an unweighted average of the sub-indices – the notes to Table 14.1 describe the construction of the different indices of institutional quality). This makes interpreting the estimated impact of institutional quality, and relating this estimated impact to the true effect of the underlying institutions, problematic. To see this more clearly, consider the basic model used in this literature

$$y_i = \beta_0 + \beta x_i + v_i, \tag{1}$$

where y_i is growth and x_i an index of institutional development. Of course there are multiple control variables, but we exclude these for clarity (though their choice and treatment is essential). In most cases, the literature recognizes that x_i is endogenous and relies on a first stage

$$x_i = \gamma_0 + \gamma z_i + \xi_i \tag{2}$$

for some instrument z_i. Again, this might include various control variables, and sometimes it is placed into a panel data context.

Suppose, however, that the correct model is

$$y_i = \beta_0 + \beta_1 x_{1i} + \beta_2 x_{2i} + \varepsilon_i \tag{3}$$

where x_1 and x_2 are two different institutions that matter. Instead of estimating their separate effect, papers in the cross-country literature use an aggregate index of institutional quality, such as the ICRG index, of overall institutional development, defined as

$$x_i = \alpha_1 x_{1i} + \alpha_2 x_{2i} \tag{4}$$

with the weight α_k defined by a Political Risk Services analyst. The actual equation estimated is (1), which is equivalent to imposing the restriction that $\alpha_1 \beta_1 = \alpha_2 \beta_2$. If this restriction is incorrect, what are we actually estimating? The instrument z in (2) is related to the underlying x_k by

$$x_{1i} = \gamma_{10} + \gamma_1 z_i + \xi_{1i}$$
$$x_{2i} = \gamma_{20} + \gamma_2 z_i + \xi_{2i}.$$

So we have

$$x_i = \alpha_1 \gamma_{10} + \alpha_2 \gamma_{20} + \left[\alpha_1 \gamma_1 + \alpha_2 \gamma_2\right] z_i + \alpha_1 \xi_{1i} + \alpha_2 \xi_{2i}. \tag{5}$$

The probability limit of the IV estimator is

$$plim\ \hat{\beta}_{IV} = \frac{\beta_1 \gamma_1 + \beta_2 \gamma_2}{\alpha_1 \gamma_1 + \alpha_2 \gamma_2}. \tag{6}$$

Three key problems are readily apparent.

---

measures of institutional development are not subject to this concern. For example, the index of trust (Knack and Keefer 1997) is based on survey responses to a specific question; readers can make their own judgment regarding the suitability of the measure.

First, our estimate of the effect of institutions on growth depends on the arbitrary weights α_k used to weight the various components of the index of institutional development. Therefore, $\hat{\beta}_{IV}$ cannot estimate a structural feature of the underlying economies.

Second, the coarseness of our measures of institutions implies that we estimate a 'composite' effect of multiple institutions on growth. $\hat{\beta}_{IV}$ depends on the underlying structural relationship between specific institutions and growth, but not in a simple fashion. While institutional measures are correlated, it is clear that the economic interpretation of, say, 'executive constraints' and 'private credit' differ. We would, therefore, want to distinguish between their effects on growth. However, our measures of institutions do not permit rich disaggregation.[4]

Third, even with more disaggregated measures of institutions, there is a clear paucity of plausible instruments that can serve to identify the causal effects of institutions on growth. There are few variables that are important determinants of the current form of a particular economic institution and that do not have effects on growth other than through that institution. Hence, important as these variables might be as determinants of a particular institution, an IV strategy can rarely isolate the causal pathway. Since these broad underlying features of an economy (e.g., settler mortality, colonial history, position on the earth's sphere) have myriad effects on the institutions and economic organization of a society, they are not valid instruments for any particular institution. Indeed, there is a real danger that the instrument may have different relationships with the underlying institutions; that is, that γ_k might have opposite signs. In this case, the estimated $\hat{\beta}_{IV}$ can fall outside the range of the underlying β_k. One context in which this might happen is where there is a trade-off between the institutions, where improving one institution might be at the cost of worsening another. This should arise most commonly when the construction and development of institutions involves negotiation or cost trade-offs.

B. Omitted Variables

We noted earlier that, in every case, an IV approach strengthens the positive effect of institutional quality on growth performance. There is no doubt that the measures of institutions are afflicted by classical measurement error. However, because of the unquestionable ubiquity of omitted unobserved variables, it is worth considering their effect on the IV estimates as well.

---

[4] The composite nature of the estimated $\hat{\beta}$ is not a consequence of the IV strategy. If υ_i is uncorrelated with x_i, then the probability limit of the OLS estimator of (1) is

$$plim\ \hat{\beta} = \frac{\alpha_1\beta_1\sigma_{x_1}^2 + \alpha_2\beta_2\sigma_{x_2}^2 + (\alpha_2\beta_1 + \alpha_1\beta_2)\sigma_{x_1x_2}^2}{\alpha_1^2\sigma_{x_1}^2 + \alpha_2^2\sigma_{x_2}^2 + 2\alpha_1\alpha_2\sigma_{x_1x_2}^2}.$$

While this parameter can give a broad-brush picture of the relationship between institutions and growth, it will be hard to say anything about the relative importance of the components of the composite indicators. If these components are negatively correlated, then the estimated $\hat{\beta}$ may even fall outside the range of $[\beta_1, \beta_2]$.

Consider the simplest form of omitted variables bias. Despite the use of very broad indices of institutions, other institutions are unmeasured and left out of the estimated equation. That is, (4) is constructed using $\alpha_1 = 1$ and $\alpha_2 = 0$. The probability limit of $\hat{\beta}_{IV}$ is now

$$plim\hat{\beta}_{IV} = \beta_1 + \beta_2 \frac{\gamma_2}{\gamma_1}. \tag{7}$$

This leads to an overestimate if the correlations between the instrument and the different institutions have the same sign. Indeed, since

$$plim\hat{\beta}_{OLS} = \beta_1 + \beta_2 \rho_{x_1 x_2} \frac{\sigma_{x_2}}{\sigma_{x_1}}, \tag{8}$$

the IV estimator can have a larger upward bias than the OLS estimator.

Indices of institutions used in the cross-country literature are very strongly biased towards measuring the institutional environment facing urban, formal sector agents. In some cases this is explicit: Political Risk Services attempts to gauge the "risk of expropriation of foreign private investment by government." Other measures focus strongly on *de jure* procedures that may or may not govern actual behavior. The 'index of legal formalism,' for instance, measures the number of formal legal procedures needed for collecting on a bounced check. Some might argue that the institutions facing agents in the formal sector are the most salient for the overall growth prospects of a country. However, the possibility that the *de facto* environment within which the majority of the population lives is at least as relevant suggests that omitted variable bias can be serious.

C. Heterogenous Treatment Effects

A different concern relates to within country heterogeneity in the characteristics and operation of particular institutions.[5] For instance, any measure of 'trust' will vary across communities and individuals within communities. Mechanisms of contract enforcement differ across rural and urban entrepreneurs. The institutional framework within which corruption occurs is likely to operate very differently for multinational corporations and small-scale traders.

More formally, differences across and within countries in individual responses to institutions can significantly affect the appropriateness of an IV strategy (Imbens and Angrist (1994), Heckman and Vytlacil (2000) and Manning (2004)). IV estimates capture the impact of the institutional variable on the growth outcomes of those countries in which instrumental variables affect the institutional outcome. Interpretation of the IV estimate as the average effect of the institution on growth relies on assumptions on both how countries respond to the institution and on how the institution responds to the instrument.

---

[5] Brown and Guinnane (2005) discuss the deleterious consequences of analysis that obscures internal heterogeneity in the well-known European Fertility Project.

A simple version of the model is

$$y_i = \beta_0 + \beta_{1i}I_i + \varepsilon_i \qquad (9)$$

and we have available an instrument

$$I_i = \gamma_0 + \gamma_{1i}z_i + \upsilon_i. \qquad (10)$$

In this case both stages of the IV are characterized by heterogeneous effects. We know that (after we make the helpful assumptions that β_{1i} and γ_{1i} are independent of ε_i, υ_i and z_i, that $E(\gamma_{1i}) \neq 0$ and that $E(\upsilon_i|z_i) = E(\varepsilon_i|z_i) = 0$):

$$\hat{\beta}_1^{IV} \to^p \frac{E(\beta_{1i}\gamma_{1i})}{E(\gamma_{1i})}. \qquad (11)$$

If β_{1i} and γ_{1i} are independent of each other, then $\hat{\beta}_1^{IV} \to^p E(\beta_{1i})$, which may be what we want. However, consider the following plausible form of heterogeneity. Suppose $\beta_{1i} = \beta_1 + \beta_2 x_i$, where x_i is some unobserved omitted variable that influences the effect of the institution on growth. For concreteness, assume x_i is some unobserved dimension of pre-colonial history (such as security of land tenure) that changes the effect of formal credit market expansion on growth. We normalize x_i to have mean zero and assume $\beta_2 > 0$ – better tenure security increases the effect of credit markets on growth.

At the same time, of course, $\gamma_{1i} = \gamma_1 + \gamma_2 x_i$, because the same omitted feature influences the degree to which current institutions (I_i) depend on our observed instrument (say, settler mortality). If γ_2 is also positive, the IV estimator will exceed the true causal effect. Specifically,

$$\begin{aligned}
\hat{\beta}_1^{IV} \to^p \frac{E(\beta_{1i}\gamma_{1i})}{E(\gamma_{1i})} &= \frac{E(\beta_1 + \beta_2 x_i)(\gamma_1 + \gamma_2 x_i)}{E(\gamma_1 + \gamma_2 x_i)} \\
&= \frac{\beta_1\gamma_1 + \beta_2\gamma_2 var(x)}{\gamma_1} = \beta_1 + \frac{\beta_2\gamma_2 var(x)}{\gamma_1} > \beta_1 = E(\beta_i).
\end{aligned}$$

This simple example suggests that IV estimation techniques in the presence of hetereogeneity in institutional form across countries can cause the IV to overestimate the true effect. Below, we use the example of land law in Africa to demonstrate that such within-country heterogeneity is commonplace in many low income countries.

2.3   The Limitations in Practice

We now provide two illustrations of the empirical relevance of concerns related to potential omitted variable bias and heterogenous treatment effects.

A. Institutions and Poverty

The typical institutions regression has GDP per capita as the dependent variable. As development economists, however, we should be at least as interested in the determinants of poverty. What can we learn by replacing GDP with a poverty measure, the head count ratio, in this canonical regression?

There is reason for some skepticism. As institutional measures tend to focus on the urban and formal sector, we would expect them to have less impact when we consider poverty, which depends particularly strongly on features of the rural and informal economy.

Table 14.2 reports these regressions. Our measure of institutional quality is 'Protection against Expropriation Risk' and we use log settler mortality as the instrument. Following Acemoglu, Johnson, and Robinson (2001) we start with the sample of 64 ex-colonies with settler mortality data. We have poverty data for 43 of these countries. Our poverty measure is the head-count ratio, defined as the percentage of the population living in households with consumption or income per person below the global poverty line, defined as one dollar per day (Source: PovCal Net, World Bank). We use the median head-count ratio value, over 1981–2001 (typically, this ratio is reported at three-year intervals). We also report results where we include the four OECD countries, which were ex-colonies and set their head-count ratio to zero.

Panel A provides OLS results. We observe a strong and significant negative correlation between protection against expropriation risk and the head-count ratio. A one standard deviation increase in institutional quality reduces the percentage population that is poor by 10% in our base specification. This estimate is relatively unchanged by the inclusion of a geography control and continent dummies. Panel B provides 2SLS estimates, and Panel C the corresponding first stage regression. Excluding controls, the 2SLS estimate is twice the size of the OLS (column (1)), while with controls the 2SLS estimate is four times the size of the OLS estimate (column (3)). If we were to take the column (3) estimate seriously it would suggest that a one standard deviation increase in institutional quality would move the country from the 75th to the 25th percentile of the distribution of the head-count ratio. This is a much more dramatic effect than is observed in the corresponding growth regression, where a one standard deviation increase in protection against expropriation leads to a 2.7-fold increase in income, which corresponds approximately to a move from the 25th to the 50th percentile of the distribution of income per capita. It is very likely that settler mortality is correlated with other, unobserved, features of the rural environment that are much more important for poverty outcomes than the protection that foreign investors have against expropriation by the central government. These same omitted features of the rural environment may also be associated with a stronger treatment effect of improved security of formal property rights on rural poverty. In both instances, the IV estimator will overestimate the effect of these institutions on poverty.

B. Land Law

Aggregate formal sector-based indices of institutional quality are unlikely to capture institutional quality as faced by the average person in developing

Table 14.2. *Institutions and poverty: Cross-country evidence*

	Base Sample (1)	Base Sample without OECD Countries (2)	Base Sample (3)	Base Sample without OECD Countries (4)	AJR Base Sample (5)
Panel A: Ordinary Least Squares (Dependent Variable: Median Head Count Ratio)					
Protection against expropriation risk (1985–1995)	−9.99	−12.61	−8.65	−11.14	
	(1.78)	(2.48)	(2.14)	(2.32)	
Distance from equator			−7.21	−36.32	
			(20.16)	(23.38)	
Asia dummy			11.82	−14.76	
			(7.14)	(7.01)	
Africa dummy			16.52	17.26	
			(5.53)	(5.36)	
Other continent dummy			13.81		
			(13.24)		
Panel B: Two-Stage Least Squares (Dependent Variable: Median Head Count Ratio)					
Protection against expropriation risk (1985–1995)	−18.30	−19.88	−32.79	−44.82	
	(3.95)	(7.54)	(18.92)	(31.29)	
Distance from equator			79.71	−9.02	
			(77.87)	(64.68)	
Asia dummy			14.79	26.10	
			(14.62)	(20.67)	
Africa dummy			−1.41	−0.64	
			(17.68)	(21.31)	
Other continent dummy			64.59		
			(47.10)		

Panel C: First Stage (Dependent Varibale: Protection Against Expropriation Risk (1985–1995))

	(1)	(2)	(3)	(4)	(5)
Log settler mortality	-0.59	-0.30	-0.27	-0.20	-0.34
	(0.13)	(0.13)	(0.18)	(0.17)	(0.18)
Distance from equator			2.77	0.29	2.00
			(1.42)	(1.65)	(1.38)
Asia dummy			0.07	0.28	0.46
			(0.50)	(0.47)	(0.50)
Africa dummy			-0.39	-0.28	-0.25
			(0.44)	(0.41)	(0.40)
Other continent dummy			1.67		1.04
			(0.95)		(0.84)
R^2	0.30	0.10	0.42	0.13	0.33
Number of observations	47	43	47	43	64
	1%	25%	50%	75%	99%
Percentiles of median head count ratio	0.28%	5.56	18.94	36.45	87.60

Notes: The dependent variable is the median head count index (1981–2001) given by % population living in households with consumption or income per person below the poverty line, defined as living on $1 a day ($32.74 per month at 1993 PPP), from Povcal Net, World Bank. Protection against expropriation risk (1985–1995) is the risk of expropriation of private investment by government, scaled from 0 to 10, where a lower score means more risk, from Acemoglu, Johnson, and Robinson (2001). Panel A reports OLS estimates. Panel B reports two-stage least square estimates, where we instrument for protection against expropriation risk using log European settler mortality, which is log of estimated mortality for European settlers during the early period of European colonization (before 1850), from Acemoglu, Johnson, and Robinson (2001). In Panel C, we report the corresponding first stage. In columns (3) and (4) where we include continent dummies as controls, the dummy for America is omitted, following Acemoglu, Johnson, and Robinson (2001). Standard errors are given in parentheses.

Our base sample is limited to 47 countries which were excolonies and for which we have head count, expropriation risk and settler mortality data. To create the sample, we set the median headcount value to zero for four OECD countries which were ex-colonies: Australia, Canada, New Zealand, and USA assuming there is no one living under $1 poverty line in these countries. AJR base sample in column (5) refers to the largest sample of ex-colonies used by Acemoglu, Johnson, and Robinson (2001).

countries. Further, heterogenous treatment effects may be a real concern in developing countries where social and ethnic networks remain an important constraint on individual decision-making.

To illustrate these concerns we describe property rights in land in four African countries. We choose the African countries with the highest and lowest value of the expropriation risk index used by Acemoglu, Johnson, and Robinson (2001). These are Gambia and the Democratic Republic of Congo (formerly Zaire, henceforth DRC). In addition we choose Ghana, a country we study in more detail below, and its neighbor Cote'd Ivoire. These two countries offer an interesting contrast of neighbors, which were ruled by different colonial powers. The legal origins variable codes Ghana and Gambia as having English law, and DRC and Cote'd Ivoire as having French Law. Table 14.3 describes property rights in land for these four countries.

(i) De Jure *and* De Facto *Land Rights: The Importance of 'Customary' Law*

Measures of 'institutions' in the cross-country literature are typically based on either formal rules and procedures or perceptions of those working in the urban business sector. It is immediate from Table 14.3 that what matters for rural land rights is the country's community-based mechanisms as exemplified by customary law. The use of almost all land in these four countries is governed by customary tenure arrangements, not formal sector rules. The influence, if any, of the formal legal system introduced by colonial powers on land rights as experienced by households is indirect. It is clear that any exercise examining the effect on economic activity of property rights as they are actually experienced by agents cannot restrict attention to the *de jure* legal system.

We observe a stark contrast between *de jure* and *de facto* property rights in these countries. French authorities typically did not recognize land ownership by traditional chiefs. In contrast, in colonies without significant white settlement, the British policy of indirect rule included (the colonists' interpretation of) customary land tenure rules. In terms of *de jure* laws, this is reflected in a more limited recognition of customary law in French colonized countries (DRC and Cote'd Ivoire). However, there is no close correspondence between 'legal origins' and *de facto* land tenure rights in these four countries. In the French colonized countries war seems to have played a more important role in defining the security of property rights. Further, a central tenet of customary law that, for most part, individuals cannot sell land on which they have user rights, remains relevant in the rural sector of all countries, save Cote'd Ivoire (for Gambia, see Freudenberger (2000); for Ghana, see Berry (2001); and for DRC, Moyroud and Katunga (2002)).

Equally, there is no clear relationship between 'average protection against expropriation' and the actual likelihood that a cultivator controls his or her land. While Gambia is a clear outlier in this group of four, categorized as having much higher protection against expropriation, use rights in some Gambian areas are

Table 14.3. *Land rights in four African countries*

	Gambia	Ivory Coast	Ghana	DRC
Coding of Institutions Expropriation Risk	8.27	7.00	6.27	3.50
Legal Origin	English	French	English	French
Urbanization	26%	46%	44%	30%
Overview of Land Tenure	Urban land legislation only applies to Banjul and Kombo (St. Mary State Lands Act (1990)). Under this, land is state-owned except if held in "fee simple" or subject to grants. Customary land occupiers hold a 99-year renewable lease. The Lands (Provinces) Act 1946, which recognizes customary law, holds elsewhere else, and district tribunals may apply Islamic law.	Land tenure is in a state of confusion. The 1998 law 98–750 on Rural Land Tenure initiated a transition to private ownership, but tenure issues have become linked with political upheavals since the early 1990s. Critically, more than a third of the population consists of foreigners, and most conflict is over the status of both Ivorian and non-Ivorian migrants.	Land tenure derives from tradition and English Common Law. Five types of interest are recognized – allodial, customary freehold, common law freehold, leasehold and customary tenancy. The 1986 Land Titling Registration Law applies only in a few urban areas. Most of the country is governed by a mix of customary rules and legislation (e.g. the 1992 constitution and the 1962 State Lands Act).	The 1973 General Property Law makes all land state property. At the local level, customary rules apply where state power is weak; less than 1% of land in the DRC is registered. In much of the country the dominant factor in determining access to land has been war, which has brought armed occupation and population displacement.
Customary Sector Extent	99% (i.e., outside Banjul & Kombo)	98% of land	80–90% of Ghanaian land	97% of land (*de facto*)
De Jure Status	Authority under the Lands (Provinces) Act is given to the District Authorities, who are the head chiefs (seyfos) under 1990	Customary tenure has limited legal stature. The 1998 land law allows only the state, public institutions and native Ivorians to own rural	Customary law has limited recognition. The 1992 Constitution recognizes chiefs' authority over stool and skin lands, and of families over family	Customary arrangements are not recognized by law.

(*cont.*)

Table 14.3. *Land rights in four African countries*

	Gambia	Ivory Coast	Ghana	DRC
	Laws of Gambia. District Tribunals may administer customary and Islamic law, so long as these are not "repugnant to justice."	land. Though intended to create individual tenure, it makes customary rights the basis of claims, Communities registered as village cooperatives or associations have had their rights upheld by the courts.	lands. Several laws, including article the 1992 Constitution (giving Land Commissions a veto over land transactions) and the 1994 Office of the Administrator of Stools Land Act circumscribe chiefs' authority.	
De Facto Status	The state has given customary law legal legitimacy.	A "truly muddled and ad hoc system" has resulted from combined assertion of government contol and tolerance of customary systems. Though a 1962 law vests all land in the state, the president refused to enact a 1963 law that abolished customary tenure.	Though several attempts have been made by the government to centralize control over land, for the most part they defer to customary authorities.	Elites have used legal uncertainty due to failure of 1973 presidential decree to secure customary tenure to appropriate untitled land. Though required to advertise lease of 'vacant' land, the state has allowed Bamis (local chiefs) to retain their leasing powers in return for political support. Local people, through chiefs and elders, have "*de facto* veto over the acquisition process" and "droit de regard" – an informal management right.
Variation	Gambian customary tenure is complex and diverse; a community may have multiple types of property regimes, and these will change over time. Where all parties to a dispute are Muslim, District Tribunals may apply	There are over 20 ethnic groups. The Agni and Baoule in central and eastern provinces are matrilineal. The king allocates land to lineages. The Agni redistribute land annually, whereas the Baoule keep the same parcels of land over	There are broad regional differences between the southern coast scrubland, the cocoa-growing rainforest of the southern interior, and northern savannah. Ethnic differences also exist. Among the Ashanti, Dagomba and Gonja, paramount chiefs have ultimate	There are over 250 ethnic groups spread across the central and northern rainforests, the northern and southern savannahs, and the eastern Rift Valley highlands. Population is concentrated in areas such as the Kinshasa region,

	several years. Among matrilineal Senoufi, Lobi and Koulango, the senior male of the founding lineage allocates land; in patrilineal Malinke the senior male in the oldest lineage does this.	authority over land. "Traditional" tenure systems have survived more in the relatively land-abundant North.	Islamic law. Approximately 90% of the country is Muslim, and the Mandinka Fula, Wolof, Jola and Serahuli account for more than 90% of the total population.	Banundu, and the Kivus. Other areas are sparsely inhabited. Strictness of a tenure regime increases with population density (particularly in Kivu, Bas-Congo, and near cities).
Land Ownership	Land may be owned by lineages, families or individuals. Allocation practices vary, but for the most part land is allocated by a king, lineage head, or senior male.	Individuals, families/communities represented by stools and skins, Tendamba (original settlers) and clans own customary land. Ideologically, a community and its ancestors own the land. Allodial title is the highest proprietary interest (analogous to freehold interest in English common law). It is invested in chiefs on behalf of their subjects in stool and skin areas. In some areas tendamba and chiefs assert competing claims to this title. Whether family and stool/skin lands face the same regulations remains ambiguous.	Customary tenure is patrilineal and based on original village settlement (unless trumped by conquest). The male household head allocates land within the family and mediates land disputes. The seyfo (head chief) holds land in trust for the community. There is some confusion about the relative powers of seyfos, alkalos (village chiefs), families and lineages which dates back to at least the early colonial era.	Groups or clans own land. A family may "own" land, but cannot sell it, since the land "belongs" to the central government. Where there is a strong chieftaincy (especially in the East), the Mwami (king) owns the land, and distributes it "through a sophisticated system of reward and punishment." This connects land to political power. Individual families may directly control family land, and individuals often own trees. Customary authorities' power is particularly great where rebel authorities are seen as illegitimate.
Right to Transfer Land	Sales are common, though the seller may retain some use rights and have to approve any resale. Local communities have developed their own contracts, often recorded in writing as "petits papiers" and endorsed by several "headmen and sub-prefects, and even some judges." The state system is of no use, since ownership can only be	Land sales are restricted and require chiefs' or elders' permission. Non-transferable allodial title resides in the community and freeholds cannot be granted from stool and skin lands. The Lands Commission must approve land grants to outsiders. Customary freehold is secure and transferable, but cannot be acquired by	Land sales are generally restricted; extended families "own" cultivated land (including fallow land), but cannot alienate it. Founding families have usufruct rights, and can transfer land by inheritance, gifts, trades and loans, Some private property exists in the customary sector. Trees and wells are usually planters' private	Sales of land are generally restricted; customary tenure usually involves inalienable group land rights. A community cannot sell land, but can cede it to other villages or rent it to strangers. In Masisi, after promulgation of the 1973 law it became impossible to buy or sell land without the permission of the Hunde chiefs; this encouraged

(cont.)

Table 14.3. *Land rights in four African countries*

	The Gambia	Ivory Coast	Ghana	DRC
	property. Lineage and household heads often exercise significant control over land transfers. Alienation outside the lineage is usually disallowed (less effective around Banjul). Most primary rights transfers are through inheritance.	established by a certificate that does not yet exist. Conflicts have erupted between purchasers and return migrants who have claimed that the land is inalienable.	non-Ghanaians. An allodial title holder can sell or gift a common law freehold and grant leaseholds. Land can be purchased or gifted, but community leaders must agree if it is to an outsider. Leaseholders can grant lesser rights (e.g., abusa and abunu sharecropping). The land market is informal, most transactions are unrecorded, and those documented are rarely noted by the state.	clientelism as they profited from selling large parcels.
Inheritance	"Primary rights," gained through original settlement or direct allocation, include permanent occupation, control of land use, and inheritance without interference; this is similar to western ownership. Women borrow land from their husbands to cultivate vegetables and rice, though some own land that is passed from mother to daughter.	In 1964 customary inheritance rules, other than patrilineal systems, were outlawed, but this is not usually enforced. Children of immigrants do not have established inheritance rights. A tenant who selects an heir without his tuteur's permission may lose his rights. Women inherit nothing from husbands but have recently gained the right to hold land given by their fathers. For land pledged to a creditor, the creditor's rights are inheritable for outstanding debt.	Inheritance rules are matrilineal in Akan-speaking areas and patrilineal in the north, and among the Volta and Ga. The matrilineal system is flexible, allowing for a variety of possible heirs and ways to inherit land. Patrilineal areas in the south suffer from fragmentation into parcels too small to be economically viable.	Rules vary between communities; the Kongo are matrilineal, while the Zande Vungara are patrilineal.

User Rights	Owners can reclaim borrowed land in land scarce areas. Use rights (rights to build a house/other structures, control water, and plant fruit trees) are more common than to rent or lend out land. Those who sell land usually have all other land rights. Primary right holders can grant "secondary" rights (usually exclude ability to plant trees). Pastures, mangroves, streams and most forests are commons available for hunting and gathering. Common-property regimes are frequent, but not open-access ones. Alkololu (local chiefs) and seyfolu (head chiefs) can determine a tongo – a seasonal prohibition on activities such as harvesting mangoes.	Women can usually only access land through their husbands. A mix of contracts exist that can give owners and non-owners varying cultivation rights; these include tutorat, busan, bugnon, troukatalan, rental, surveillance or guardianship, and pledging.	Chiefs can grant lesser interests to members of the community. These are typically customary freehold, or usufruct, and give members use rights. The interest is indefinite so long as the land is not abandoned.	Individual rights to the harvest are usually protected. Women may only have access to land through men. The Kivus and Ituri were depopulated during the war. Many squatters arrived from Rwanda and the rest of the DRC, setting up on ranches from 1999–2003. With the return of the original landowners, some have been evicted, while others have stayed under the protection of armed groups.
Right to Improve Land	Women and borrowers have fewer land rights than owners; they cannot plant trees or must receive permission (because these are associated with permanent rights). Improvement rights are stronger for durable improvements. A long-term borrower attempts to strengthen his or her rights by investing in wells, trees or fencing can spark conflict with the landowner.	Individuals can lose land, but retain ownership over any trees they have planted. In the case of coffee and cocoa trees, this has been a source of conflict.	The Regional Lands Commission must approve any "development or disposition" of stool or skin lands. Families are reluctant to tie up capital in orchard production; thus, young family members often remit a portion of their crop to their families in return for taking land out of general use.	State policy under Mobutu demanded obligatory production of certain crops, contributing to food insecurity. Often poor land is used for this, causing environmental degradation.

(cont.)

Table 14.3. *Land rights in four African countries*

	The Gambia	Ivory Coast	Ghana	DRC
Rights of Non-Community Members	Land is often lent, usually on a seasonal basis but sometimes longer, to settlers from other ethnic groups. Payments may be symbolic or actual tribute, depending on land scarcity. Incomers acquire land from chiefs or founding families. Secondary rights are transferred through borrowing, pledging, rental, and sharecropping. District tribunal members may grant land to newcomers, in contravention of Lands (Provinces) Act's vesting of power in District authorities. Individuals only have this power if they gain lineage consent.	Relations between indigenous cultivators and migrants are the most important aspect of Ivorian tenure. The 1998 law bars non-Ivorians from owning rural land. Non-Ivorian farmers can at best hope for a long-term lease from the certificate-holder or the state. The Houphouët-Boigny government encouraged migrants, who obtained land mainly through "tutorat," whereby one remits to a local patron or "tuteur". Foreigners, especially the Burkinabe, have been particularly vulnerable under the 1998 law.	Strangers (non-subjects) must obtain the chief's permission to reside in an area. After this is granted, he acquires land from a landowner or the chief, for example as an "abusa" or "abunu" sharecropper. Abusa has also come to be used by local landless to acquire land. In forest areas, migrants are often in the majority. Here, chiefs act as landlords. Tenancy is less common in the north, as land is more abundant, and migrants may obtain land for free.	Strangers have insecure tenure, or none at all. In some areas of the Kivus, Rwandan Hutu prisoners are used as forced laborers. Congolese have been forced into camps, while Rwandan settlers are brought in to take their land.
Formal Sector Individual Acquisition	The State Lands Act, operating only in Banjul and Kombo St. Mary, converts all customary tenure into 99-year leases if the occupant applies for a title by a specified deadline; if he does not, he becomes a tenant that can be evicted by the state.	In 1963 Houphouët-Boigny declared "la terre appartient a celui qui la met en valeur" (the land belongs to those who develop it). This has since changed – in 2001, one minister declared that land belongs to the owner, not the farmer. Under the 1998 law, land holders must obtain a land certificate within 10 years, and after another 3 years individual registration and private property will be enforced. Only	The 1986 Land Titling Registration Law allows for registration of land, in order to produce secure tenure and reduce fraud in sale. This applies only in Accra, Tema, and Kumasi and is generally inaccessible to peasants. Squatter rights are not recognized by law. Though public land is officially available to all Ghanaians, getting a land lease is time-consuming and expensive, so political and	Individuals can gain land rights through "perpetual" or "ordinary" concessions from state and must improve land during lease. This "mise en valeur" principle implies a concession can be sold or bequeathed, but the state is the proprietor and can revoke the concession if the parcel is abandoned, not improved, or transferred without approval. Only a Congolese can have a perpetual

	N/A	12 hectares can be individually owned; the rest comes in a 25-year lease from the state, which may be sold, mortgaged, inherited, and renewed. The length and expense of the process implies most land remains under community-based tenure.	economic elites have benefited most.	concession. The concessionaire pays a license fee or rent and effectively occupies the land for many years. All children (born in and out of wedlock) must divide equally three-quarters of the deceased's estate as inheritance. Land rights cannot be transmitted through death without a judge's approval.
State Acquisition and Involvement	The 1998 law vests all unregistered land in the state. Though a 1962 law asserted state ownership over all land, the government allowed farmers to retain land used in production. Government attempts to delineate mining, forest and tourist lands have been ineffective. Politicization of the land question has become part of the larger politics of Ivorianness.	The 1994 coup of Yayeh Jammeh maintained the status quo on tenure issues. All land not in freehold in Banjul and Kombo St. Mary is vested in the state, as are resources such as forests, watercourses and expropriated land. Acquisition Act permits government appropriation of land for a broad range of "public purposes," including defense, conservation, and planning.	"Public land" categories in Ghana are (i) land compulsorily acquired (under the 1962 State Lands Act), and (ii) land invested in the president (1962 Administration of Lands Act). The State Lands Act allows the state to acquire any land "in the public interest." Outstanding compensation claims on the government are more than $100 million USD, with some claims dating back to the 1970s.	The 1973 General Property Law made all lands, including forest resources, state property. Edict 81-013 of 1981 and Constitution Article 10 make the under-soil, including mineral and petroleum wealth, state property. The Mobutu "kleptocracy" encouraged land tenure "informalization" which allowed favored groups and individuals to expropriate land. The political deadlock between Mobutu and parliament in the early 1990s prevented legal redress to resolve the agricultural crisis or land-related issues.
The Role of War During the 1990s	The 1998 law 98750 on Rural Land Tenure has not been effectively enacted. Article IV of the Linas-Marcoussis Agreement (2003) reaffirms this law and charges the Government of National Reconciliation with	N/A	N/A	Land conflict between Hema and Lendu in Ituri has a long history. 'Zairianisation' involved transferring several foreign concessions to Hema, and conflicts over these concessions are frequent. Violence since 1999 has

(cont.)

Table 14.3. *Land rights in four African countries*

The Gambia	Ivory Coast	Ghana	DRC
	implementation. The Accra III agreement of July 2004 specified changes to land tenure laws in the Linas-Marcoussis Agreement were to be implemented by August 2004. This deadline was not met.		displaced half a million people from Ituri; killed 50,000 and caused the state to lose control of several areas. Forced migration, crop theft by armed forces, and short-run gains to mining coltan, gold and diamonds led many to abandon food production. Illegal resource exploitation by foreign armed groups has affected locals' land access.
Sources: Toure, 2003; Knox, 1998; Chavas, Petrie and Roth, 2005; Freudenberger, 2000. (Urbanization data from 2005 World Population Data Sheet, Risk of Expropriation from Acemoglu, Johnson and Robinson, 2001, originally from the IRIS-3 data set, legal origin from The International Institute for Corporate Governance at the Yale School of Management, and ethnic and religious data from the CIA World Factbook)	*Sources:* Chauveau, 2000; Chauveau, 2002; Furth, 1998; Conte, 2004; Crook, no date; Human Rights Watch, 2004; Linas-Marcoussis Agreement, 2003; USDA Foreign Agricultural Service, 2004, Kone, 2002. (Urbanization data from 2005 World Population Data Sheet, Risk of Expropriation from Acemoglu, Johnson and Robinson, 2001, originally from the IRIS-3 data set, and legal origin from The International Institute for Corporate Governance at the Yale School of Management)	*Sources:* Toure, 2003; Wily and Hammond, 2001; Kasanga and Kosey, 2001; Asiama, 2003; Ministry of Lands and Forestry, Ghana, 2003; Amanor, 1999; Manama, 2003, Knox, 1998. (Urbanization data from 2005 World Population Data Sheet, Risk of Expropriation from Acemoglu, Johnson and Robinson, 2001, originally from the IRIS-3 data set, and legal origin from The International Institute for Corporate Governance at the Yale School of Management)	*Sources:* Huggins et al., 2005; Leisz, 1998; Aide et Action Pour la Paix, 2004; African Development Fund, 2004; Hart and Ducarme, 2005; Vlassenroot and Huggins, 2004; Moyroud and Katunga, 2002. (Urbanization data from 2005 World Population Data Sheet, Risk of Expropriation from Acemoglu, Johnson and Robinson, 2001, originally from the IRIS-3 data set, and legal origin from The International Institute for Corporate Governance at the Yale School of Management)

less well established than those in much of Ghana (in particular, use rights are very secure in Ghana's cocoa-producing areas). Protection against expropriation in the DRC is rated as extremely poor relative to that in Côte d'Ivoire, but tenure security in less war-affected areas seems to be quite similar in the two countries.

(ii) Land Rights Are Heterogeneous Within Countries

Customary law has nearly full legal recognition in Gambia (Freudenberger 2000) and none in the DRC Leisz (1998). In Ghana and Côte d'Ivoire it has only partial recognition. Further, the complexity of *de facto* land rights hinders the interpretation of "secure property rights." Customary law tends to view land and resources as inalienable, such that property rights cannot be wholly ceded by those to whom the land has been allocated (Bruce and Migot-Adholla 1994b). As a consequence, in none of the four countries is anything approaching freehold tenure common in agriculture. In Côte d'Ivoire, land sales are generally permitted by customary law (Kone 2002), which could appear to be an indication of more secure tenure than exists in most of Ghana. However, usufruct rights are generally secure in most of Ghana while the land is under cultivation (even including tree crops) (Amanor 1999), while the usufruct rights of the large population of non-Ivoirian migrants in Côte d'Ivoire are very insecure (Chauveau 2000). Apparently, property rights over land are more secure in Ghana than in Côte d'Ivoire for some individuals, while for others the opposite is true. Within any of the countries listed in the table there is a distribution of tenure security; clearly, the usefulness of summarizing that distribution with a single index is sensitive to the context and the economic model.

Further, the same piece of land can be subject to multiple claims, which relate to the ways in which it is used by separate groups and individuals at different levels. For example, one individual may have the right to cultivate annual crops on a plot, while another retains rights to the tree crops that exist on the same land. An elder might have the right to allocate a plot to a family member for temporary use but not the right to rent the plot to an outsider on a commercial basis. Property rights are typically multidimensional and collapsing this down to a single index might be misleading in important ways.

(iii) Political and Contractual Institutions Are Intertwined

A common distinction in the cross-country institutions literature has been between political institutions (as measured by, say, expropriation risk) and institutions which determine contractual form (as measured by, say, legal origins). However, the real world is much more complicated, and, in particular, this distinction is treacherous when considering land rights in Africa. Indigenous tenure principles are implemented and arbitrated by authorities (chiefs, lineage heads, elders) whose legitimacy is typically drawn from a local political process. Their authority over land allocation is political power, since it enables them to give or refuse a farmer the right to cultivate or to settle. "By allowing or forbidding newcomers to settle and by fitting them, from the outset, within a network of alliances, the land chief regulates the process where a local community is constituted" (Raynaut, 1997, 289–290). Thus, political and contractual institutions seem to be fundamentally intertwined for land tenure processes in Africa. Importantly, the nature of such intertwining varies significantly across countries. This again suggests heterogeneity in the effect of institutions across countries.

We conclude that the extraordinary diversity of institutional practices across and within countries places natural constraints on the usefulness of cross-country analyses for understanding the specific channels through which institutions affect economic outcomes, and how these institutions, in turn, respond to economic, demographic, political, and social forces.

3   WITHIN-COUNTRY INSTITUTIONAL VARIATION

Recent years have seen an explosion in empirical research in development economics. One of the most fruitful research avenues has been program evaluation studies in developing countries. These studies typically combine household or regional level data with detailed information on the implementation of a particular institution or policy in the country to estimate its economic impact. In this section we discuss how such research can both complement and advance the research agenda suggested by the institutions and growth literature.

Table 14.4 lists some recent papers which study potential within-country counterparts of the main institutions studied in the cross-country literature.[6] While our literature review is non-exhaustive, it is clear from the table that many synergies exist between the cross-country and within-country literatures.

Relative to cross-country analyses, an important advantage of within-country studies is the relative homogeneity of the institutional and constitutional setting across the units of analysis. This potentially helps us better disentangle the economic impact of institutions from unobserved heterogeneity across the units of analysis. In addition, concerns of heterogenous treatment effects are likely to be more limited in the context of a single country. Finally, and we would argue most importantly, the scope for identifying credible instruments for particular institutions is much greater in the case of within-country studies. The reason is that institutional change is typically implemented at the country (or sub-country) level. This opens up the possibility of exploiting specific features

---

[6] For the journals considered in the cross-country literature review we did a Google Scholar search with the keywords institutions and development. We also manually reviewed the *American Economic Review*, *Quarterly Journal of Economics* and *Journal of Political Economy* for 2002-2004. For this set of papers, we then used our judgment to identify studies that provide a within-country counterpart to the main institutions covered in the cross-country review. In a couple of cases we have augmented the list with recent unpublished papers.

Table 14.4. *Institutions and development: Within country evidence*

Institutions in Cross-Country Literature	Within Country Counterpart		Findings – An Illustration
	Country	Institution Measure (Paper)	
Protection against Expropriation Risk; Index of Government Antidiversion Policies; ICRG Index	Indonesia China (importer) Hongkong (exporter)	Political connections (Fisman) Evasion gap: Difference between reported exports to a country and imports reported by receiving country (Fisman and Wei)	Fisman exploits differences in share price reactions to "news about former President Suharto's health" of firms with varying degrees of political exposure to show that political connections can account for up to a quarter of a firm's share price.
Index of Country Openness	India Colombia Brazil	Tariff changes (Topalova) Tariff changes (Pavcnik and Goldberg)	Topalova uses variations in exposure of Indian districts to trade liberalization to show that districts which witnessed the largest reductions in trade protectionism saw the least fall in poverty.
Intellectual Property Rights	India	Assessment of patent protection (Chaudhuri, Goldberg and Jia)	Without price regulation or compulsory licensing, total annual welfare losses to the Indian economy from withdrawal of 4 domestic product groups in the fluoroquinolone sub-segment would be about 118% of the entire sales of the systemic anti-bacterials segment of pharmaceuticals in 2000.
Legal Formalism; Contract Repudiation	India	Debt relief tribunal (Visaria) State court efficiency (Chemin)	Visaria exploits variation in spread of debt tribunals, and in which firms were affected by it, to shows that tribunal establishment reduced loan repayment delinquency in loan by 3–10 percent.

(*cont.*)

Table 14.4. *Institutions and development: Within country evidence*

Institutions in Cross-Country Literature	Within Country Counterpart		Findings – An Illustration
	Country	Institution Measure (Paper)	
Privatization	Argentina	Privatization of water services (Galiani, Gertler, and Schargrodsky)	Galiani, Gertler, and Schargrodsky exploit time-series variation in the privatization of water services across Argentinian municipalities to show that water privatization improved access, expanded service, and reduced child mortality.
	China	Community Public Firm (Jin and Qian)	
Financial Intermediation	Mexico	Savings institution (Aportela)	Burgess and Pande exploit the introduction and subsequent removal of a branch licensing program in India which constrained branch openings in already banked areas and increased branch opening in rural unbanked areas to show that rural branch expansion significantly lowered rural poverty, and increased non-agricultural output.
	India	Rural bank branch expansion (Burgess and Pande)	
		Change in eligibility for formal sector loan (Banerjee and Duflo)	
		Financial development (Bell and Rousseau)	
	South Korea	Financial restraints (Demetriades and Luintel)	
Labor Market Institutions	India	Labor regulation (Besley and Burgess)	Regulating labor market in a pro-worker direction lowers investment, employment, productivity and output in registered manufacturing. Pro-worker amendments to the Industrial Disputes Act increase urban poverty.

Ethnolonguistic Fractionalization	Kenya	Ethnolinguistic fractionalization (Miguel and Gugerty)	Variation in ethnic diversity across schools is used to show that such diversity lowers primary school funding and worsens school facilities.
Democratization	India	Political representation and decentralization (Foster and Rosenzweig; Bardhan and Mookherjee; Pande, Chattopadhyay and Duflo; Besley, Pande and Rao; and Faguet)	Pande exploits quasi-random variation in mandated political representation for disadvantaged groups to show that it increased targeted redistribution towards these groups.
Trust	Ghana Taiwan	Kinship patterns (La Ferrara) ROSCAs (Kan)	La Ferrara shows that about 67 percent of the total amount borrowed is borrowed from potential kinsmen, and suggests this is because membership in a dynastically linked community shapes individual incentives in economic transactions
Land Rights		See Table 5	

of how institutional change was implemented across regions in a country or across different population groups to obtain instruments for the institutional variable of interest. In contrast, both the choice and implementation of public policies varies significantly across countries. Hence, using any single country's experience with institutional change to identify instruments for a cross-country analysis will typically not yield an instrument with sufficient power across a large number of countries. Hence, the reliance on relatively crude instruments such as settler mortality.

A common approach in this literature is to use panel data for households or regions, which spans years both before and after the policy change. Having a long period of pre-program data allows the investigator to confirm that before the policy change the evolution of economic outcomes in regions (or households) that were differentially exposed to the policy was similar. The studies typically exploit cross-sectional variation in the extent of policy-induced institutional change for identification. Such variation may arise due to timing differences in policy implementation across different regions within the country, or because the extent of institutional change was explicitly related to underlying economic features of the regions. The canonical regression in this literature takes the form

$$Y_{st} = \alpha_s + \beta_t + \gamma I_{st} + \phi Z_{st} + \epsilon_{st}$$

where s denotes regions within a country and t time. Y_{st} is the outcome of interest and I_{st} the relevant institution. The inclusion of regional fixed effects (α_s) accounts for permanent differences between regions and time fixed effects (β_t) for shocks that affect all regions. Finally, Z_{st} is a set of conditioning co-variates, which control for observable time-varying region specific variables, which may influence the outcome variable of interest.

This regression specification cannot, in itself, allay the concern that the institutional variable and the economic outcome of interest are both affected by some omitted time-varying region-specific variable. That is, $E(I_{st}, \epsilon_{st}) \neq 0$ (Besley and Case (2003)). One may also be concerned about the external validity of such a study – a study which focuses on institutional change within a country may not be informative of the true average effect of the institution (that country may, for instance, be much poorer than the average country in the world).

We discuss the ability of within-country studies to address these concerns in the context of single country studies, which examine how private land rights affect economic outcomes. Table 14.5 provides a non-exhaustive summary of papers analyzing the economic impact of land titling and registration, organized by country.[7] These studies span numerous countries and a multitude of different economic settings. Thus, while any single study may have limited external validity, a comparison across studies in different regions suggests the following

---

[7] The selection of papers is aimed at depicting the richness of country experiences with land titling programs.

Table 14.5. *Impact of land-titling and registration programs: Micro evidence*

Country (Paper)	Outcome of Interest	Data Set	Policy	Findings
Empirical strategies used in the papers are in the notes below.				
PANEL A: AFRICA				
GHANA Besley (1995)	i. Land Rights ii. Productivity	Year: Not given Region: Wassa and Anloga Unit: 334 households with 1568 fields	None	Having a deed has a significant positive effect on land rights that require approval in Wassa. In Anloga, the correlation is negative, suggesting lineage sanctions and title are substitutes. Land rights increase productivity.
GHANA, RWANDA & KENYA Migot-Adholla et al. (1991) (hereafter MA) Place and Hazell (1993) (PH)	i. Credit Use ii. Inputs iii. Investment iv. Yields	Year: 1987–1988 Region: 10 rainfed agriculture regions Unit: Farm surveys	None	No clear relationship between land registration and productivity (MA). PH focus on land rights. Effects of land rights on credit are mixed. Land rights did not significantly affect input use. Strongest positive relationship between land rights and investment was for long-term investments in Rwanda; elsewhere mixed results. Insignificant relationship between land rights and yield.
KENYA Migot-Adholla Place and Oluoch. Kosura (1994) (hereafter MPO) Place and Migot-Adholla (1998) (hereafter PM)	i. Investment ii. Output iii. Determinants of Title iv. Access to Credit	Year: 1988 Region: Nyeri and Kakamega Unit: 406 households with 463 parcels	Registered Land Act (1963): individualizes land rights while giving land committees considerable control over land transactions.	Land title and land rights have limited effect on farm investments, and none on yield (MPO). Rights are "more comprehensive" on titled and registered parcels, but absence of titles and indigenous tenure systems restrict sales or mortgages. Registered parcels are slightly more subject to litigation. Title does not affect credit use, but title ownership by close relatives and credit access are weakly positively correlated. Male household head and no previous subdivision increases title and registration. Predicted title has no effect on yield (PM).

(cont.)

Table 14.5. *Impact of land-titling and registration programs: Micro evidence*

Country (Paper)	Outcome of Interest	Data Set	Policy	Findings
KENYA Cartier, Wiebe and Blarel (1994)	i. Input Use ii. Output	Year: Not given Region: Njoro division Unit: 109 households (plot-level data)	i. Squatter Settlement Scheme: opened forest reserve to settlement, redistributed ex-European land. ii. Fourth Development Plan (1979–1983): approved *de facto* subdivisions of land.	"Untitled" farms produce 20% less than titled ones. Titled farms are more productive but note this may be due to correlation between titling and farmer/farm characteristics. In fixed effect regressions, mixed results for output with no evidence of security-induced demand for inputs.
KENYA & TANZANIA Pinckney and Kimuyu (1994)	i. Access to Credit ii. Investment iii. Land Market iv. Inequality	Year: 1991–1992 Region: Murang'a (Kenya) and Moshi (Tanzania) Unit: 230 households	Land registration in Kenya, abolition of private title in Tanzania.	No land-secured loans in Tanzania and only two in Kenya, so titling has not increased credit use. There is more investment in Kenya, but this is due to cash-crop policy, not titling. Differences in inequality are due to differing practices of land partition at inheritance, not land policies.
SENEGAL Golan (1994)	i. Investment ii. Credit Access	Year: 1987 Region: Unit:	1. 1900 Re d'immatriculation: allowed some to apply for registration.	Very few original registered titles, and these were owned by the elite. No surviving investments on titled land but title is used to obtain credit. Areas more affected by the Law of National Domain have greater tenure insecurity.

SOMALIA Roth, Unruh, and Barrows (1994)	i. Perceived Benefits ii. Land Value iii. Tenure Security iv. Credit Access v. Investment	Year: 1987–1989 Region: Kigezi District Unit: 148 registered and unregistered smallholders and registered largeholders with 226 parcels	Agricultural Land Law (1975): sets out registration procedures; individuals can apply at the local district level, though officials are sometimes instructed to find unregistered land for "outsiders."	Registered and unregistered farmers perceive registration increases tenure security, the propensity to sell or lease land, credit access and investment. The marginal effect of registration on land value is 44 300-57 300 SSh. Title has a weak negative effect on perceived tenure security (significant for small-holders with high-quality land) and a weak positive effect on access to credit.
UGANDA Roth, Cochrane and Kisamba-Mugerwa (1994)	i. Investment ii. Perceived Benefits	Year: 1987 Region: Kigezi District Unit: 228 households with 505 parcels	Rujumbura Pilot Land Registration Scheme (1958)	Households compelled to register their parcels receive less cash income and remittances, and are significant coffee producers. Those with voluntarily registered parcels own more productive capital. Dispute incidence is lower for registered land. Registration significantly increases farm investments, with the effect more widespread for voluntary (relative to compulsory) registration.
PANEL B: ASIA				
INDIA Banerjee, Gertler and Ghatak (2002)	i. Productivity	Year: 1979–1993 Region: West Bengal and Bangladesh Unit: District	Operation Barga (1977), which gave tenure security to registered sharecroppers	Relative to Bangladesh, the program raised sharecropper productivity in W. Bengal by 51%. Fixed-effects estimate suggests the program boosted sharecropper productivity by 62%.

(cont.)

Table 14.5. *Impact of land-titling and registration programs: Micro evidence*

Country (Paper)	Outcome of Interest	Data Set	Policy	Findings
INDIA Pender and Kerr (1999)	i. Credit Use ii. Investment iii. Land Use	Year: 1993 Region: Aurepalle and Dokur, Andhra Pradesh Unit: Survey of 291 households with 563 plots.	No specific policy; most land is held in formal title, "assigned" land has been granted to poorer residents who receive non-transferable usufruct rights.	Assigned land has a negative effect on supply and demand for moneylender and institutional credit. Adult males increase investment on assigned plots but decrease it on titled plots. Effect of household characteristics on investment is greater on titled plots. Share of land subject to sales restrictions has no effect on decision to cultivate in Aurepalle, and a negative effect in Dokur.
THE PHILLIPINES Friedman, Jimenez and Mayo (1993)	Land Value	Year: 1983 Region: Manila	None	Formal sector units are worth more than squatter units, and this difference shrinks with age of squatter unit. Concrete foundations, several stories or locating in richer area signals low eviction risk, even in absence of title. A ten-year-old residence sells for 25% more if it is in the formal sector.
THAILAND Feder and Onchan (1987)	i. Investment ii. Credit Access	Year: 1987 Region:- Lop-Buri Nakhon Ratchasima and Khon-Kaen Provinces Unit: 48 compounds	Land Code (1954), which created both title deeds and utilization certificates for private land.	Titles increase capital accumulation, except in Lop-Buri, where there is ample non-institutional credit, more commercialization, and lower-risk cash cropping. Investment in bunding of land and clearing of stumps is positively affected by land title, but effects are insignificant in Lop-Buri.

THAILAND Pagiola (1999)	i. Program Benefits ii. Rate of Return iii. Credit Access	Year: 1991–1992 and 1995–1996 Region: National	Land Titling Project, Phase 2, 1991–1994	Credit use increased faster in provinces where the program was implemented. This increase was greatest in provinces that were poorest at the outset. Results for productivity were too sensitive to model specification to be useful. Anecdotal information suggests titles increase land values. The estimated rate of return from the program is 34%.
VIETNAM Do and Iyer (2003)	i. Investment ii. Productivity iii. Credit Access iv. Land Transfers	Year: 1992–1993 and 1997–1998 Region: Unavailable Unit: 4000+ household panel. Provincial LUC issuance data	Land Law (1993), which allows for transferable leases from the state implemented using Land Use Certificates (LUCs)	Titled households increase proportion of multi-year crops by 7.5% relative to untitled farms, at the expense of annuals. Titled households increase irrigated area by 20% and labor inputs by 4.5 weeks. Impact of title on credit access is insignificant, but it does have a positive effect on land transfers.

PANEL C: LATIN AMERICA

BRAZIL Alston, Libecap, and Mueller (2000)	i. Violent Conflict	Year: 1991–1994 (Conflict), 1985 Region: Para Unit: 105 Municipos	Formal Settlement Programs organized by the government agency INCRA	Squatting, forest clearing and large farms weaken property rights, contributing to violent conflict. Value is significantly related to conflict, and "higher land values encourage invasions and evictions."
BRAZIL Alston, Libecap, and Schneider (1996)	i. Supply and Demand for Title ii. Land Value iii. Investment	Year: 1940–1970 (Para) and 1870–1985 (Parana) Region: Para; Parana Unit: 206 households	No specific policy; titling is administered by state governments.	Title has a positive and significant effect on land value, independent from its impact on investment, which decreases with distance. The increase in land value predicted by the value regressions has a positive but less significant impact on title acquisition. Title increases investment.
ECUADOR Lanjouw and Levy (2002)	i. Land Value ii. Tenure Security iii. Ability to Transfer Land	Year: 1996 Region: Guayaquil Unit: 400 households (1921 individuals)	1992 Titling project initiated by Municipality of Guayaquil	Title increases perceived market value of property by 23.5%.

(cont.)

Table 14.5. *Impact of land-titling and registration programs: Micro evidence*

Country (Paper)	Outcome of Interest	Data Set	Policy	Findings
GUATEMALA Pagiola (1999)	i. Program Rate of Return	Year: Not given Region: Peten	Land Administration Project	The estimated rate of return is 12.3%, and the profitability of the program is robust to several changes in assumptions.
HONDURAS Lopez (1996)	i. Productivity ii. Investment iii. Access to Credit	Year: 1983–1994 Region: Santa Barbara and Comayogua Unit: 450 farm households	Project funded by USAID, initiated in 1983.	Average investment for USAID-funded farmers was twice that of others. A greater proportion of these farmers received credit, and in larger amounts. The difference in yields between the two groups was statistically significant in 1993 but not 1983. Rate of return to the titling project was 17%.
NICARAGUA Deninger and Chamorro (2003)	i. Investment ii. Land Value	Year: 1996 and 1999 Region: National Unit: 2476 households (3212 plots)	Programa Nacional de Catastro, Titulacion y Registro, since 1992, which encourages titling and registration	Full registration increases investment; title without registration has an insignificant impact. Registration affects plot-level, not household-level, investment, suggesting credit access is unaffected. Registration increases land values by 30%.
NICARAGUA Broegaard et al. (2002)	i. Land Title Registration ii. Tenure Insecurity iii. Land Use iv. Land Values v. Credit vi. Agricultural Production	Year: Not given Region: National Unit: 921 households with 975 plots of land	1997 legislation sanctioning ownership by beneficiaries of Sandinista redistribution	Complete formal documents improve tenure security. Formal title deeds increase probability of public registration and permanent crop cultivation, and reduce perceived future tenure conflict. Formal title has a small positive effect on land value and none on credit. Land-reform documents increase registration and tenure security, but effects are smaller than the impacts of formal title. Further, they do not affect permanent crop cultivation.

Study	Topic	Program	Year/Region/Unit	Results
NICARAGUA de Laiglasia (2004)	i. Investment ii. Determinants of Registration iii. Credit Access	Programa Nacional de Catastro, Titulacion y Registro, since 1992, which encourages titling and registration	Year: 1996 and 1999 Region: National Unit: 2476 households (3212 plots)	Land registration increases the probability of land-attached investment by 35% – the specific type of title (excluding indigenous forms) is unimportant. No link between credit and land registration.
PARAGUAY Carter and Olinto (2000)	i. Investment ii. Credit Access	No General Progam: Land can be either "Titled" or "Formal" but untitled.	Year: 1987 Region: Paraguari, San Pedro and Itapua Unit: 48 compounds holding 351 parcels	Legal security improves attached capital and has a negative impact on movable capital. Positive impact of title on investment weaker for liquidity-constrained farms, and reductions in movable capital are not offset by increases in attached capital for small farms. Below 3 hectares no effect on credit rationing probability.
PERU Antle, Yanggen, Valdivia, and Crissman (2003)	Investment	Proyecto Especial de Titulacion des Tierras (Special Land Titling Project), encourages farmers to obtain titles.	Year: 1997–1999 Region: Cajamarca Unit: 847 parcels	Accounting for endogenous titling increases the mean probability of terracing from 25.8% to 32.4%.
PERU Field (2003); Field and Torero (2004)	i. Labor Supply (Field) ii. Credit Access (Field and Torero)	i. Committee for the Formalization of Private Property ii. Decree 424: Law for Formalization of Informal Properties (1996): over 1.2 million urban households given formal property titles between 1992–1997.	Year: March 2000 (middle of the program) Region: Urban Unit: 2750 households	Untitled households work 17% fewer hours than those with titles and are 47% more likely to work inside the home. Titled households are 28% less likely to engage in child labor (Field). Untitled households are 10% less likely to be approved for formal sector loans. Titling does not affect private sector approval rates, but lowers the interest rate by 9% (Field and Torero).

Notes to Table 14.5 are in the Appendix to this chapter.

generalizable lessons:

- Land titling and registration typically increase agricultural productivity and farm investment. However, the extent of increase depends upon the details of the titling program and the pre-existing land tenure system.
- There is a weaker, but usually positive, effect on credit. The impact of titling on credit is very limited in situations with less developed credit markets.
- There is some evidence that land value rises, but this remains very preliminary.

To identify the economic impact of tenure security, it is common to exploit the passage of land titling or registration programs, which take land claims out of the realm of informal lineage, community land ownership, or informal 'squatter' rights and making them legal, formal, and individual (Binswanger, Deninger, and Feder 1995). It is clear that endogenous uptake of land titles presents a serious concern for empirical evaluations and that not all papers address this concern adequately. However, we would argue that the potential for using the institutional details of the land titling intervention to identify credible instruments for exposure to land titling far exceeds that available in the context of a cross-country study. A good example is Field (2003), who analyzes the value of increased tenure security (as measured by his/her labor supply response) associated with obtaining a property title for a squatter household in Peru. Over a five-year period a national titling program in Peru issued formal property titles to more than a million urban households. Field uses two sources of variation in program influence to isolate the effect of titling: neighborhood program timing and program impact based on prior household ownership status. In particular, staggered regional program timing enables a comparison of households in neighborhoods already reached by the program with households in neighborhoods not yet reached. She combines these facts with data on past and future title recipients (collected half way through the titling program) to identify a natural set of comparison groups composed of treated and yet-to-be-treated households. A comparison of the labor supply behavior of these two sets of households can be interpreted as reflecting the causal effect of land titling. Similar empirical methods are used by Banerjee, Gertler, and Ghatak (2002) in the context of India, and Iyer and Do (2004) in the context of Vietnam. The absence of a unifying institutional environment implies that such studies could not be undertaken at the cross-country level.

On the other hand, even more strongly than in a cross-country setting, the use of local variation in program implementation for identification requires that migration or cross-region/market effects be negligible. Often significant linguistic differences or differences in ethnic makeup across areas makes this a valid assumption (Gugerty and Miguel (2000), (Burgess and Pande (2005)). In other cases, program benefits are restricted to long-term residents in the area, and migration as a response to the program is potentially less of an issue (Field

(2003)). Another solution is to explicitly model the changes in the demographic composition across areas. Two further concerns with difference-in-difference estimates such as those described in Table 14.4 are substitution and general equilibrium effects. In the Peruvian land titling example, substitution would arise if the labor supply increase of those who got a title was substituting for the labor supply of those not exposed to the titling program. General equilibrium effects would arise if the program is wide enough to affect wages through changes in the supply of labor. One solution is to use a diversity of comparison groups who will be affected differentially by these types of indirect effects to obtain some indication on the importance of such biases (Blundell, Dias, Meghir, and Reenen 2004). However, it remains clear that the above remain areas in which more work is required.

4   WITHIN INSTITUTION VARIATION: INSECURE PROPERTY RIGHTS IN GHANA

A given institution can provide a variety of incentives to different individuals, depending on their endowments. This makes it possible to use data on the behavior of individuals within a given institutional setting to explore the consequences of an institution for behavior, and potentially of changing factor endowments for institutional form. In this section we use household survey data from Ghana to provide one example of such research.

Over 60 percent of the Ghanaian population is in the agricultural sector, and land distribution is mostly governed by customary law. Under customary law, land is often regarded as a common asset and resource. Individual ownership is recognized for standing crops but not for the soil itself. Rather, ultimate title over land is vested in corporate groups, in particular in the lineage, and individuals gain access to land via membership in such groups. There are multiple potential claimants to any particular plot; competing claims are negotiated and certain members of the community are recognized as having the power to arbitrate such conflicts. Land rights in the study area are complex, ambiguous, and highly negotiable (Goldstein and Udry 2005). Those who hold political office are responsible for land allocation and, by virtue of this, have more secure property rights on their own land.

The typical concern in examining how tenurial security affects productivity is that both variables are potentially jointly determined by a third variable, e.g., farmer ability. A first advantage of using very detailed household and plot-level data is the possibility to directly control for many potential determinants of farm profits. A second advantage is that one can directly derive credible instruments for tenurial security from a political economy model. Being able to provide theoretical underpinnings for the structural equation of interest improves one's ability to interpret the point estimates. It also allows us to derive alternative specifications and thereby check the robustness of the exclusion restrictions. Finally, detailed farm data imply that we are able to identify the economic impact of a specific channel through which tenurial security affects profits – increased fallowing.

Below we examine how micro-data can be used to understand the implications of this land tenure system for investment and agricultural productivity. We also explore the potential of using micro-data to examine institutional change. Specifically, we examine how changing factor endowments in Ghana have affected the cost of having insecure property rights and the consequent responses of political actors and citizens.

4.1   The Investment and Productivity Effects of Land Rights

Our data comes from a two-year rural survey in the Akwapim South District of the Eastern Region of Ghana conducted by Goldstein and Udry.[8]

The main farming system is an intercropped mixture of maize and cassava, which is cultivated for both home consumption and sale through a well-developed marketing system. Land productivity is managed primarily through fallowing; cultivation is periodically stopped in order for nutrients to be restored and for weeds and other pests to be controlled. An element of the land tenure system that plays a key role in the evolution of its agricultural economy is that cultivators have historically had very secure rights over their growing crops (both tree crops and annual crops). Wilks (1993) summarizes the principle as "afuo mu yε deε, asase yε ohene deε " ("the farm is my property, the land is the stool's").

However, the lineage leadership may reallocate fallow land to other members of the lineage. The details of this allocation process are unique to the local context, but many of its broad features arise frequently in African (particularly West African) land tenure systems.[9] In our study area land is held by the *abusua*, which is defined by matrilineal descent, on the authority of the paramount chief (or *stool*). The leadership of the matrilineage is locally based and is responsible for allocating use rights within a village to members of the matrilineage.[10] The allocation of land within the matrilineage is rooted in local politics and social relations.[11]

Land allocation is, thus, a political process that operates at the level of the local matrilineage. Cultivators on the margins of local political power – those who hold no form of local political office – are less confident of their rights over land than those who have local political office. Table 14.6 presents evidence of this difference in confidence. [12]

Goldstein and Udry (2005) use these survey data to establish that insecurity of land tenure is associated with lower investment in land and hence reduced

---

[8] For survey description and data, see www.econ.yale.edu/˜cru2/ghanadata.html.

[9] Fred-Mensah (1996); Biebuyck (1963); Bruce and Migot-Adholla (1994a); Binswanger, Deininger, and Feder (1995); Bassett (1993); Bruce and Migot-Adholla (1994a); and Bromley (1989).

[10] In our sample, leaders tend to be male and older than other members of our sample, but no more likely to be educated.

[11] Berry (2001, 145).

[12] There is a wide variety of local political offices held by individuals in our sample. Typical offices include lineage or village head or elder.

Table 14.6. *Perceptions of land rights*

	Percent of Cultivated Plots on which Respondent Claims Right to			
	Determine Inheritance (1)	Rent Out (2)	Lend Out (3)	Sell (4)
Non-officeholders	6	22	32	15
Officeholders	26	53	60	32
t-test for equality	6.41	6.74	5.83	4.34
Number of observations	575	576	576	575

Notes: See Goldstein and Udry (2005) for details on the data set.

agricultural production. Table 14.7 summarizes the main consequences of this difference in tenure security for fallowing behavior and hence for output. Conditional on observed characteristics of the plot, officeholders leave plots fallow for approximately 2 years longer than non-officeholders, and each additional year of fallowing is associated with an increase in plot profits per-hectare of over 300 thousand cedis (compare this magnitude with the mean gross output per hectare of about 1.2 million cedis, or to per capita GDP of approximately 700 thousand cedis). Goldstein and Udry (2005) estimate the magnitude of the loss associated with this inefficient fallowing to be approximately one-third of output.[13] Some plots are obtained through commercial transactions (about half through fixed-rent contracts, and half through sharecropping), rather than through the allocation of matrilineage land. If we look (in column (3)) at fallow duration by form of land allocation we observe that commercially obtained plots are fallowed for longer (slightly over half a year). Further, officeholders and non-officeholders exhibit similar behavior on commercial plots. In column (4) we continue to observe increased fallowing of commercial plots when we compare across different plots cultivated by an individual farmer.

4.2   The Evolution of Land Rights

In Pande and Udry (2005) we provide an account of the historical emergence of this land tenure system. The principle that all members of a local corporate group are entitled to cultivate land has ensured that no substantial disenfranchised

[13] See Goldstein and Udry (2005) for full details of the econometric procedures. These estimates are all conditional on household*year fixed effects (except column (4), which uses finer individual fixed effects) because imperfect factor markets in these villages imply variation across households in the shadow costs of factors of production. Each also includes spatial fixed effects (with neighborhoods defined as a distance of 250 meters) to better account for unobserved variation in land characteristics. Estimates are also conditional on a set of plot characteristics, including deciles of plot area, indicators of soil type, and toposequence.

Table 14.7. *Fallow duration, profits, and political office*

	Fallow Duration (Years)	Plot Profit (1000 cedis)	Fallow Duration (Years)	Fallow Duration (Years)
	OLS (1)	IV (2)	OLS (3)	Individual F.E. (4)
Fallow duration		314 (182)		
Female	−0.430 (0.54)	143 (426)	−0.921 (0.36)	
1 if resp. holds trad. office	1.950 (0.80)		3.085 (0.64)	
Commercially obtained plot			0.633 (0.34)	0.698 (0.24)
Office*Commercially obtained			−0.407 (0.78)	
1 if first of family in town	0.290 (0.64)			
Years family/resp. lived in village	0.010 (0.01)			
Number of wives of father	0.520 (0.23)			
Number of father's children	−0.020 (0.05)			
Parity of mother in father's wives	−0.420 (0.36)			
1 if fostered as child	0.350 (0.61)			
Size of inherited land	−0.520 (0.57)			
1 if mother had any education	0.960 (1.05)			
1 if father had any education	−0.980 (0.63)			

Notes: All regressions include plot controls (deciles of area, indicators of soil type, toposequence, and location), full set of plot characteristics, full set of family background variables, and household and spatial fixed effects. All regressions also include spatial fixed effects, with radius of 250 meters. Standard errors, corrected for spatial correlations as in Conley (1999), are given in parentheses.

group of landless persons has ever emerged in Ghana.[14] However, insecurity of land tenure in this farming system is associated with a very large cost of lost output. Here, we provide some preliminary evidence of forces towards institutional change.

---

[14] Only two households in our sample have no land; in both cases the husband has an office job and the wife is a trader.

Table 14.8. *Fallowing, networks and abusua resources*

	(1) Last Fallow Duration Parameter Estimate	(2) Last Fallow Duration Parameter Estimate
Female	−0.66	−0.69
	(0.35)	(0.60)
Office	3.88	−2.44
	(0.63)	(2.21)
Households in *abusua*/ha	−0.23	−0.63
	(0.05)	(0.58)
Office*Households in *abusua*/ha		3.38
		(1.37)
Number of observations	368	368
Quintiles of population density	50%	75%
Households in *abusua*/ha	1.91	2.60

Notes: All specifications include full set of plot characteristics, full set of family background variables, and household fixed effects. All regressions also include spatial fixed effects, with radius of 250 meters. Standard errors, corrected for spatial correlations as in Conley (1999), are given in parentheses.

The *abusua*-based land tenure system emerged during conditions of land abundance, with fallow periods far longer than needed to maintain soil fertility. Under such conditions, uncertainty regarding one's ability to re-establish cultivation on a fallowed plot has no effect on land productivity. However, as population density increases and fallow periods decline, the efficiency losses documented above emerge. Indeed, this pattern can be observed in the survey data. As matrilineage land resources become more scarce (relative to the matrilineage population), the efficiency cost associated with insecure property rights of the rank and file members of the matrilineage grows. In column 1 of Table 14.8, we see, unsurprisingly, that fallow durations are, in general, shorter in more densely populated matrilineages. More interestingly, the gap between the fallow durations of non-officeholders and officeholders is larger in matrilineages in which land is more scarce. In column 2, we observe that the difference in fallowing by officeholders and others rises with population density in the matrilineage. The interquartile range of the number of households per hectare in a matrilineage is approximately 1.5. These estimates imply that officeholders in a 'poor' matrilineage (at the 75th percentile of households/hectare) have a fallow duration about 5 years longer (relative to other households in the matrilineage) than households in a 'wealthy' matrilineage at the 25th percentile of households/hectare.

To summarize, it appears that the flexible system of allocating temporary usufruct rights through a political process at the matrilineage level has enabled land reallocation, helping avoid the emergence of a class of destitute landless in the villages. We also find evidence that this system is inefficient, with the cost of inefficiency mainly borne by those not holding political office. Finally, we find the efficiency cost of this system of insurance is apparently increasing with population density.

The transition away from a system of insecure property rights may take many forms. We begin by noting that as land gained value over the course of the early 20th century, both the courts and the chieftaincy councils maintained two principles that checked the opportunism of the contemporary generation of matrilineage leaders. First was a strict prohibition on the sale of land to outsiders without approval from higher-level authorities. All land under the control of a particular matrilineage was granted to it by a higher-level chief (called a 'stool') who retained a superior form of ownership: "... what we may call inferior ownership meant that a lineage owned its land subject to continued performance of its members' obligations as subjects, and acknowledgement of the ultimate and reversionary claim of the village headman or stool which had originally granted it the land" (Austin, 2004, 101). (Also see (Berry, 2001, 146–7).) It was the obligation of the stool to ensure that land remained available for the use of his subjects; therefore, only he had the right to sell land to outsiders. There is no question that a number of stools have sold land to outsiders, particularly in urban areas, but in general, such sales have been rare and when attempted have often resulted in the destoolment of the chief Berry (2001). Second was a resistance to granting permanent rights to land to local individuals. Current leaders could not guarantee cultivators the right to restart cultivation after fallowing. The most visible mechanism used to inhibit the transfer of long-term rights was the prohibition on permitting land to move outside the matrilineage via patrilineal inheritance. In most lineages the leadership carefully monitored allocated land to ensure that it was not passed down from father to son. This was often a source for land disputes because fathers were generally permitted to 'lend' matrilineage land to their sons for brief periods (Austin, 2004, 174).

In effect, these two restrictions have acted as formal barriers to *abusua* leaders using their powers to create more permanent property rights. Pervasive imperfections in capital markets have also limited this transformation. The large inefficiencies associated with the uncertainties of tenure security imply the existence of substantial gains if the matrilineage leadership could guarantee long-term tenure security. However, the benefits from this transformation would be spread far into the future, over a period of decades. With imperfect capital markets, the cultivators receiving long-term tenure security would not be able to pay the present value of this long-term gain. Nor could they commit to a long-term stream of future payments, for the same limited commitment reasons that long-term capital markets are so imperfect in these villages.[15]

The barriers to movement towards long-term security of land tenure are substantial. Nevertheless, we do observe cross-sectional evidence that villagers

---

[15] Binswanger and Rosenzweig (1986) use this same argument in their discussion of the development of freehold tenure in land abundant agriculture.

Table 14.9. *Responses to land scarcity*

	Nonfarm Activity (Hours/Day) (1)	Cultivation of Commercially Obtained Plots (% of total cultivated area) (2)
Office	−4.169	−0.219
	(1.078)	(0.143)
Abusua land per household	−2.415	−0.392
	(0.978)	(0.122)
Office * *abusua* land per household	5.534	0.489
	(1.418)	(0.319)
Number of observations	325	222

Notes: All specifications include full set of plot characteristics, full set of family background variables, and household fixed effects. All regressions also include spatial fixed effects, with radius of 250 meters. Standard errors, corrected for spatial correlations as in Conley (1999), are given in parentheses.

find ways around these barriers where they are particularly costly. In column 1 of Table 14.9, we show that individuals in matrilineages that have particularly intense population pressure on matrilineage land spend more time on non-farm activities than individuals in less densely populated matrilineages. Officeholders are exempt from this pattern – their security of tenure permits them to maintain their level of farm activity even as population density increases. The general population shifts time to non-farm activities in those matrilineages in which the fallowing behavior of officeholders and others differs the most.

In column 2 of Table 14.9, we show that farmers in more densely populated matrilineages are more likely to use commercial transactions to obtain land. Recall that in Table 14.7, we showed that fallowing choices on commercial land are independent of officeholder status, and that (within individuals) fallow periods on commercially obtained plots are substantially longer than on *abusua* land. Therefore, we see that in those matrilineages in which *abusua* land is under more severe population pressure (and that have shorter fallow periods, as seen in Table 14.8), a larger proportion of cultivated land is obtained through commercial fixed-rent and sharecropping contracts. Officeholders, on the other hand, do not respond to population pressure by moving towards cultivating commercially obtained land because they use their control over the land allocation process to mitigate the consequences of that pressure.

These results must be considered tentative because they depend on variation at a given moment in time across a very limited number of matrilineages. However, they are suggestive that population pressure is inducing actions that may have the long-term consequence of transforming the land tenure system of the study area.

5 CONCLUSION

Gross correlations between institutional development and growth observed in cross-country data have provided a persuasive case that long-run growth is faster in countries that have higher quality contracting institutions, better law enforcement, increased protection of private property rights, improved central government bureaucracy, smoother operating formal sector financial markets, increased levels of democracy, and higher levels of trust.

This literature also suggests that understanding the channels of influence, and why such extreme variation in institutional quality persists, are research questions of central importance. However, the scope of using cross-country data for identifying the channels of influence is limited. The measurement of 'institutions' at the country level is necessarily coarse and obscures important dimensions of heterogeneity. Even more important, there are very few plausible sources of exogenous variation in country-level institutions that can serve to identify the causal effect of institutions on growth. It is this fact that in the end most severely limits the range of questions that can be addressed with this methodology. For instance, a paper which relies on institutional persistence to obtain instruments for institutional quality will be hard pressed to identify institutional evolution. Further, we argue that due consideration must be given to the appropriate unit of analysis when considering the relationships between institutions and economic activity. A unit smaller than a country may provide a more homogeneous environment for a given institution, and therefore reveal more about the causal role of that institution.

These observations lead us to point to the empirical research based on micro-data in development economics and suggest that the research methodologies pursued in this literature can help make progress on the above issues. One such opportunity is presented by country-specific policies that implement institutional change. Exploiting within-country variation implies a focus on a more homogenous environment. Further, it is often possible to exploit features of the policy implementation process to obtain instruments, which can help isolate the effect of a specific institution.

A given institutional setting can provide a rich variety of incentives to different individuals, depending upon their economic, social, or political position. In section 4 we provide an example from Ghana. We describe the complex land tenure system that exists in one region of Ghana. In this system, individuals have very different levels of tenure security, depending upon their position in a local political hierarchy. We show how this variation in the degree of security can be exploited to identify the implications of tenure security for investment in land. We also discuss the historical evolution of this land tenure system and provide some evidence regarding actions that individuals are currently taking to mitigate the dramatic inefficiencies associated with tenure insecurity. Our evidence suggests that these actions have the potential to transform the land tenure system of the region, and suggests that a close examination of individual actions may help us understand how institutional change is initiated in economic environments facing changing economic and demographic pressures.

Appendix: Notes to Table 14.1 and Table 14.5

Notes to Table 14.1

Outcome Variables:

1) Output per worker: Output calculated as GDP minus value added in the mining industry (which includes oil and gas).
2) Urbanization: % population living in urban areas with a population of at least 5,000 in 1995. Source: World Bank, World Development Indicators.
3) Stock market capitalization: Market value of all traded stocks as a % of GDP, average over 1990–1995. Source: Beck, Demirgüç-Kunt, and Levine (2003).

Institution Measures:

1) Protection against expropriation risk: A measure of risk of expropriation of foreign private investment by government, from 0 to 10, where a higher score indicates less risk. Originally used by Knack and Keefer (1995). Source: IRIS Center, also known as Political Risk Services.
2) Index of social infrastructure: Institutions and government policies that provide incentives for individuals and firms in an economy.
3) Index of government antidiversion policies: Created by averaging five indicators following Knack and Keefer (1995) for 1986–1995. Two categories relate to government's role in protecting against private diversion: (i) law and order, and (ii) bureaucratic quality. Three categories relate to government's possible role as a diverter: (i) corruption, (ii) risk of expropriation, and (iii) government repudiation of contracts. The index takes values from zero to one (higher is better). Source: Political Risk Services.
4) Index of country's openness: Sachs-Warner index which measures fraction years between 1950 to 1994 that the economy has been open, measured on a 0–1 scale. A country is open if it satisfies the following criteria: (i) nontariff barriers cover less than 40% of trade, (ii) average tariff rates are less than 40%, (iii) any black market premium was less than 20% during 1970s and 1980s, (iv) country is not classified as socialist by Kornai (1992), and (v) government does not monopolize major exports. Source: Sachs and Warner (1995).
5) ICRG index: Combines (i) protection against expropriation risk, (ii) rule of law, (iii) repudiation of contracts by government, (iv) corruption in government, and (v) quality of bureaucracy. Source: International Country Risk Guide (ICRG) data set, Political Risk Services.
6) BERI index: Combines (i) contract enforceability, (ii) infrastructure quality, (iii) nationalization potential, (iv) bureaucratic delays. Source: Business Environmental Risk Intelligence.
7) Index of institutional efficiency: Combines nine indices of institutional efficiency: political change, political stability, probability of opposition group takeover, stability of labor, relationship with neighboring countries, terrorism, legal system, red tape, and corrupton. Indices are integers between 0 and 10, higher values indicate that country has "good" institutions. All indices are simple country averages for the period 1980–1983. Source: Business International (BI), now part of Economist Intelligence Unit.
8) Index of bureaucratic efficiency: Combines three indices used for institutional efficiency measure: judiciary system, red tape and corruption indices.
9) Executive constraints: 1–7 category scale, higher score means more constraints on the executive. Equals one if country not independent. Source: Polity III data set, Gurr (1997).
10) Initial executive constraints: Executive constraints in the first year that country appears in the Gurr's (1997) Polity III data set. Source: Polity III data set, Gurr (1997) .

11) Legal formalism: Measures number of formal legal procedures necessary to resolve a simple case of collecting on an unpaid check or evicting a non-paying tenant (from 1 to 7). "Check measure" and "Eviction measure" from Djankov, La Porta, Lopez–de Silanes, and Shleifer (2003). Source: Djankov, La Porta, Lopez–de Silanes, and Shleifer (2002, 2003).

12) Private credit: Value of credits by financial intermediaries to the private sector, divided by GDP.

13) Liquid liabilities: Currency plus demand and interest-bearing liabilities of banks and nonbank financial intermediaries, divided by GDP.

14) Bank Assets: Ratio of all credits by banks (but not other financial intermediaries) to GDP.

15) Commercial-central bank: Ratio of commercial bank assets to the sum of commercial plus central bank assets, which has been used by others.

16) Institutional quality: Combines bureaucratic quality, law/order, and property rights protection indices. Source: Political Risk Services; similar to Knack-Keefer (1995), Hall-Jones (1999).

17) Contract-intensive money: Ratio of noncurrency money to total money supply. An objective measure of enforceability of contracts and the security of property rights based on the citizens' decisions regarding the form in which they choose to hold their financial assets.

18) Adverseness of policy environment: Measured by black market premium on the foreign exchange rate. Source: Barro and Lee (1994).

19) Index of democracy: Average of 8 indicators ranking policymaker selection process and the constraints on them. Index of centralization: Geographic devolution of state decision-making authority, values of 1 and 3 assigned to federal and unitary systems, respectively, and 2 to intermediate categories. Source: Polity III data set, Jaggers and Gurr (1996).

20) Index of contract repudiation: Risk of a modification in a contract taking the form of repudiation, postponement, or scaling down due to budget cutbacks, indigenization pressure, a change in government, or a change in government economic and social policies. Higher scores indicate lower risks. Index of bureaucratic quality: Autonomy from political pressure and strength and expertise to govern without drastic changes in policy or interruption in government services as well as the existence of an established mechanism for recruiting and training. Higher scores indicate higher quality. Index of corruption: Indicator of the degree of "improper practices" in the government. The higher the indicator, the lower the degree of corruption. Source: International Country Risk Guide (ICRG) data set, Political Risk Services.

21) Index of institutional quality: Measured by scores for corruption, law and order, and bureaucracy for 1990. Three different measures are scaled from 1 (worst) through 6 (best). They have followed Rodrik in employing a rescaled unweighted average of the three measures. Source: International Country Risk Guide (ICRG) data set, Political Risk Services.

22) Index of democratization: Measured using the "polity" variable in the Polity IV data set. Autocrats are defined as having a polity score less than or equal to 0. Democrats are those leaders with a polity score greater than 0.

23) Trust: The question used to assess trust in a society is: "Generally speaking, would you say that most people can be trusted, or that you can't be too careful in dealing with people?" Trust indicator used by the authors is the percentage of respondents in each nation replying "most people can be trusted" (after deleting the "don't know" responses).

24) These indicators are: (i) ICRG (Knack and Keefer (1995)) and (ii) bureaucratic efficiency (Mauro (1995)).

25) These indicators are: (i) Freedom House Index (a composite index of democracy for the 1970s, constructed from the indicators of political rights and civil liberties

with a scale from 0 to 1 where 1 indicates a fully democratic system) (ii) Polity III (Gurr (1995))

26) Rule of law index: Composite indicator of multiple elements that capture the protection afforded to property rights and the strength of the rule of law. This is a standardized measure with range -2.5 (weakest institutions) and 2.5 (strongest institutions). Approximates for 1990s institutions. Source: Kaufmann, Kraay, and Zoido-Lobaton (2002).

Instruments:

1) Settler mortality: Log estimated mortality for European settlers during European colonization (before 1850). It is calculated from the mortality rates of European-born soldiers, sailors and bishops when stationed in colonies. It measures the effects of local diseases on people without inherited or acquired immunities. Source: Curtin (1989).

2) Distance from equator: Center of county or province within a country that contains the most people. Source: Global Demography Project, University of California, Santa Barbara.

3) English speakers: Fraction of the population speaking English at birth.

4) European-language speakers: Fraction of the population speaking one of the five principal languages of Europe (English, French, German, Portuguese, or Spanish) at birth.

5) Predicted trade share: Log value, based on a gravity trade model that only uses a country's population and geographical features. Source: Frankel and Romer (1999).

6) Ethnolinguistic fractionalization: Measures probability that two randomly selected persons from a given country will not belong to the same ethnolinguistic group. Source: Taylor and Hudson, World Handbook of Political and Social Indicators (1972).

7) Indigenous population density: Population density is calculated as total population divided by land area usable for agriculture. Source: McEvedy and Jones (1978).

8) Legal origin: Legal origin of the company law or commercial code of each country (French Commercial Code versus English Common Law Origin) Source: La Porta et al. (1999).

9) State antiquity: Index for the depth of experience with state-level institutions. Scales from zero to one.

10) Colonial origin: Dummy variable indicating whether country was a British, French, German, Spanish, Italian, Belgian, Dutch or Portuguese colony. Source: La Porta et al. (1999).

11) Ethnolinguistic homogeneity: Percentage of a country's population belonging to the largest ethnic group. Each ethnolinguistic group is identified by religion, race, or language depending on which of these appears to be the most important cleavage in the given community. Source: Sullivan (1991).

12) Predicted trade share (AC): A geography-based instrument for trade. They used exactly the same approach as Frankel and Romer (1999), except that they employ more bilateral trade data than Frankel and Romer (1999).

Key Results:

1) IV results reported in our table use all the instruments in 'Instruments for Institutions' column except those *italicized*. 2) Belgium is the (estimated) converging country with the smallest level of private credit. 3) Real openness: Log imports plus exports in exchange rate US$ relative to GDP in purchasing-power parity US$.

Notes to Table 14.5 (Empirical Strategies)

Alston, Libecap, and Mueller (2000)	Conflict incidence estimated as a function of settlements, squatting, forest clearing, farm size, value, and number of establishments. Instrument for settlements are federal versus provincial jurisdiction, distance from state capital, and area of projects receiving institutional credit.
Alston, Libecap, and Schneider (1996)	Census and survey data for land value and investment, survey data for determinants of land-titling, land value and investment. Expected change in value and landholder characteristics are used as instruments for title.
Antle, Yanggen, Valdivia, and Crissman (2003)	Impact on terracing on title with farm size and years of ownership as instruments for obtaining land title.
Banerjee, Gertler and Ghatak (2002)	Difference-in-differences comparisons of yield per acre using district panel data with West Bengal as treatment and Bangladesh as a control group. Exploit over time variation in sharecropper registration rates in West Bengal for fixed effects model.
Besley (1995)	Effect of transfer rights on productivity using title deed as instrument for transfer rights.
Broegaard et al., (2002)	Titles are instrumented using wealth and education.
Carter and Olinto (2000)	Simulated maximum likelihood to separate liquidity constrained and unconstrained households. Impact of title status on attached and unattached capital estimated using OLS first-differences.
Cartier, Wiebe and Blarel (1994)	Compare farms with and without titles. Plot level regression with farm fixed effects for 26 farms with plots under a variety of arrangements.
de Laiglesia (2004)	Investment from 1996 to 1999 as a function of tenure status. Household fixed effects are used to deal with unobserved heterogenity, and endogeneity is controlled for by repeating the regression only for households participating in legalization and by instrumenting registration with documents held.
Deninger and Chamorro (2003)	Probit for the effect of title on investment occuring and tobit for the amount of investment. The impact on land values uses household fixed effects.
Do and Iyer (2003)	Differences-in-differences approach, with provincial LUC rates used to measure the probability that a household benefited. Registration rates do not appear endogenous.
Dowall and Leaf (1991)	Simple regressions, not controlling for endogeneity, and comparison of average land prices.
Feder and Onchan (1987)	Regressions of capital stock on titles, with father's landholdings instrumenting for quality-adjusted amount of land. Logit estimates for the adoption of land improvements, without instrumentation.
Field (2003), Field and Torero (2004)	Uses differences across regions induced by the timing of the program, and differences across target populations in the level of pre-program tenure security.

Friedman, Jimenez and Mayo (1993)	Logit estimations of determinants of squatting. Hedonic regressions of dwelling value.
Golan (1994)	Compare survey data from two villages differentially affected by the law of National Domain (no regressions).
Lanjouw and Levy (2002)	Linear regression where dependent variable was what the respondent thought would be the change in land value if he or she were to gain or lose title.
Lopez (1996)	In addition to comparing descriptive statistics, factors that were statistically similar between USAID and non-USAID farmers in 1983 and dissimilar in 1993 were identified. Yield was insignificantly different in 1983, but significantly different in 1993.
Migot-Adholla et al. (1991)	Details are not available (table information is based on a description in Feder and Nishio (1998)).
Migot-Adholla, Place and Oluoch-Kosura (1994)	Estimate effect of title on (i) fourteen types of farm investment and (ii) yield
Pagiola (1999)	For Thailand, he takes results from other studies about the benefits of land-titling in Thailand before producing a cost-benefit analysis, while for Guatemala he uses observed willingness to pay to measure benefits.
Pender and Kerr (1993)	Maximum likelihood switching regressions are used to separate the effects of title on credit demand and supply. Because of the simultaneous occurrence of land use and investment, and possible dependence on previous investment a "simultaneous tobit-probit" model was created for this paper.
Pinckney and Kimuyu (1994)	Comparison of two samples (no regressions).
Place and Hazell (1993)	Household fixed effects are used to deal with unobservables, but no instruments are available to tackle endogeneity.
Place and Migot-Adholla (1998)	Comparison of descriptive statistics. Predicted title is used as an explanatory variable in the credit and investment equations; due to lack of variation in predicted title, error-components GLS was used.
Roth, Cochrane and Kisamba-Mugerwa (1994)	Estimate effect of registration on six types of investment.
Roth, Unruh, and Barrows (1994)	Regressions with land value and investment demand as outcomes. Do not account for endogenous registeration.

References

Acemoglu, D. (2005). Constitutions, Politics and Economics: A Review Essay on Persson and Tabellini's "The Economic Effect of Consitutions." *Journal of Economic Literature*.

Acemoglu, D., and S. Johnson (2005). Unbundling Institutions, *Journal of Political Economy*, 113(5), 949–995.

Acemoglu, D., S. Johnson, and J. A. Robinson (2002). Reversal of Fortune: Geography and Institutions in the Making of the Modern World Income Distribution. *Quarterly Journal of Economics*, 117(4), 1231–1294.

Acemoglu, D., S. Johnson, and J. A. Robinson (2001). The Colonial Origins of Comparative Development: An Empirical Investigation. *American Economic Review* 91(5), 1369–1401.

Acemoglu, D., S. Johnson, and J. A. Robinson. The Colonial Origins of Comparative Development: An Empirical Investigation. *NBER Working Paper No. 7771.*

African Development Fund (2004). *Democratic Republic of Congo: Agricultural and Rural Sector Rehabilitation Support Project in Bas-Congo and Bandundu Provinces (PARSAR) Appraisal Report.*

Aghion, P., P. Howitt, and D. Mayer-Foulkes (2005). The Effect of Financial Development on Convergence: Theory and Evidence, *Quarterly Journal of Economics*, 120(1), 173–222.

Aide et Action pour la Paix (2004). *Ce Qu'il Faut Connaitre Sur le Sol en Droit Congolais.*

Alston, L. J., G. D. Libecap, and B. Mueller (2000). Land Reform Policies, the Sources of Violent Conflict, and Implications for Deforestation in the Brazilian Amazon. *Journal of Environmental Economics and Management*, 39, 162–188.

Alston, L. J., G. D. Libecap, and R. Schneider (1996). The Determinants and Impact of Property Rights; Land Titles on the Brazilian Frontier. *Journal of Law, Economics and Organization*, 12(1), 25–61.

Amanor, K. S. (1999). *Global Restructuring and Land Rights in Ghana: Forest Food Chains, Timber and Rural Livelihoods.* Vol. 108. Uppsala: Nordiska Afrikainstutet.

Antle, J., et al. *Endogeneity of Land Titling and Farm Investments: Evidence from the Peruvian Andes.* Bozeman, MT: Department of Agricultural Economics and Economics, Montana.

Aportela, F. (1998). *Effect of Financial Access on Savings by Low-Income People.* Massachusetts Institue of Technology.

Aryeetey, E., J. Harrigan, and M. Nissanke (2000). *Economic Reforms in Ghana: The Miracle and the Mirage.* Oxford: James Curry; Accra, New Town, Ghana: Woeli Publishing Services; Africa World Press.

Asiama, S. O. (2003). *Comparative Study of Land Administration Systems: Case Study – Ghana.* UK Department for International Development.

Austin, G. (2004). *Labour, Land, and Capital in Ghana: From Slavery to Free Labour in Asante, 1807–1956*, Vol. 18. Rochester, NY: University of Rochester Press.

Banerjee, A. V. (1997). A Theory of Misgovernance, *Quarterly Journal of Economics*, 112(4), 1289–1332.

Banerjee, A. V., P. J. Gertler, and M. Ghatak (2002). Empowerment and Efficiency: Tenancy Reform in West Bengal. *Journal of Political Economy* 110(2), 239–280.

Barro, R. J. and J. Lee (1999). Data Set for a Panel of 138 Countries. Available from http://post.economics.harvard.edu/faculty/barro/data.html.

Bassett, J. T. (1993). Cartography, Ideology, and Power: The World Bank in Northern Côte d'Ivoire. *Passages: A Chronicle of the Humanities.*

Bates, R. H. (1981). *Markets and States in Tropical Africa: The Political Basis of Agricultural Policies.* Berkeley: University of California Press.

Beck, T., A. Demirguc-Kunt, and R. Levine (2003). Law, Endowments, and Finance. *Journal of Financial Economics*, 70(2), 137–181

Bell, C. and P. L. Rousseau (2001). Post-independence India: A Case of Finance-Led Industrialization? *Journal of Development Economics*, 65(1), 153–175.

Benneh, G. (1988). The Land Tenure and Agrarian System in the New Cocoa Frontier: Wassa Akropong Case Study. In *Agricultural Expansion and Pioneer Settlements*

Chattopadhyay, R. and E. Duflo (2004). Women as Policy Makers: Evidence from a Randomized Policy Experiment in India. *Econometrica*, 72(5), 1409–1443.

Chaudhuri, S., P. Goldberg, and P. Jia (2004). *Estimating the Effects of Global Patent Protection in Pharmaceuticals: A Case Study of Quinolones in India*. Yale University.

Chauveau, J. P. (2002). La Loi Ivoirienne de 1998 sur le Domaine Foncier Rural et L'agriculture de Plantation Villageoise: Une Mise en Perspective Historique et Sociologique. *Land Reform: Land Settlement and Cooperatives*, 1, 62–79.

Chauveau, J. P. (2000). Question Foncière et Construction Nationale en Côte d'Ivoire. Les Enjeux Silencieux d'un Coup d'Etat. *Politique Africaine*, 17, 94–125.

Chavas, J. P., R. Petrie, and M. Roth (2005). Farm Household Production Efficiency: Evidence from the Gambia. *American Journal of Agricultural Economics*, 87(1), 160–179.

Chemin, M. (2004). Does the Quality of the Judiciary Shape Economic Activity? Evidence from India. mimeo., LSE.

Clague, C., P. Keefer, S. Knack, and M. Olson (1999). Contract-Intensive Money: Contract Enforcement, Property Rights, and Economic Performance. *Journal of Economic Growth*, 4(2), 185–211.

Conte, B. (2004). *Côte d'Ivoire: Clientélisme, Ajustement et Conflit*. Université Montesquiteu–Bordeaux IV: Centre d'Economie du Developpement.

Côte d'Ivoire (2003). *Linas-Marcoussis Agreement*.

Crook, R. C. *Civil War in Cote d'Ivoire; Behind the Headlines*.

Curtin, P. D. (1989). *Death by Migration: Europe's Encounter with the Tropical World in the 19th Century*. New York: Cambridge University Press.

de Laiglesia, J. R. (2004). *Investment and Credit Effects of Land Titling and Registration: Evidence from Nicaragua*. LSE.

Demetriades, P. O. and K. B. Luintel (2001). Financial Restraints in the South Korean Miracle. *Journal of Development Economics*, 64(2), 459–479.

Deninger, K., and J. S. Chamorro (2004). Investment and Equity Effects of Land Regularization: The Case of Nicaragua. *American Journal of Agricultural Economics*, 30, 101–116.

Djankov, S., et al. (2003). The New Comparative Economics. *Journal of Comparative Economics*, 31(4), 595–619.

Djankov, S., R. La Porta, F. Lopez-De-Silanes, and A. Shleifer (2002). The Regulation of Entry. *Quarterly Journal of Economics*, 117(1), 1–37.

Dowall, D. E., and M. Leaf (1991). The Price of Land for Housing in Jakarta. *Urban Studies* 28(5), 707–722.

Duflo, E., and A. V. Banerjee (2004). *Do Firms Want to Borrow More? Testing Credit Constraints Using a Directed Lending Program*. Massachusetts Institue of Technology.

Engerman, S. L. and K. L. Sokoloff (1997). Factor Endowments, Institutions, and Differential Paths of Growth among New World Economies. In *How Latin America Fell Behind*, edited by S. H. Haber. Stanford, CA: Stanford University Press.

Engerman, S. L., and K. L. Sokoloff (2005). "Colonialism, Inequality and Long-run Paths of Development." NBER Working Paper No. 11057.

Esfahani, H. S., and M. T. Ramirez (2003). Institutions, Infrastructure, and Economic Growth. *Journal of Development Economics*, 70(2), 443–477.

Feder, G., and T. Onchan (1987). Land Ownership Security and Farm Investment in Thailand. *American Journal of Agricultural Economics* 69(2), 311–320.

Field, E. (2003). *Entitled to Work: Urban Property Rights and Labor Supply in Peru*. Harvard University.

Field, E. (2003). *Fertility Responses to Urban Land Titling Programs: The Roles of Ownership Security and the Distribution of Household Assets*. Harvard University.

Institutions and Development: A View from Below

in the Humid Tropics, edited by Walther Manshard and William B. N
United Nations University.

Berry, S. (2001). *Chiefs Know Their Boundaries: Essays on Property, I
Past in Asante, 1896–1996*. Portsmouth, NH: Heinemann.

Berry, S. (1993). *No Condition Is Permanent: The Social Dynamics of Ag*
in Sub-Saharan Africa. Madison: University of Wisconsin Press.

Besley, T. (1995). Property Rights and Investment Incentives: Theory and I
Ghana. *Journal of Political Economy*, 103(5), 903–937.

Besley, T. and A. Case (2003). Political Institutions and Policy Choices: F
the United States. *Journal of Economic Literature*, 41(1), 7–73.

Besley, T., R. Pande, and V. Rao (2005). Participatory Democracy in A
Evidence from South India. *Journal of the European Economic Associ*
648–657.

Besley, T. and R. Burgess (2004). Can Labor Regulation Hinder Economic I
Evidence from India. *Quarterly Journal of Economics*, 119(1), 91–134.

Biebuyck, D., ed. (1963). *African Agrarian Systems*. Oxford: Oxfor
Press.

Binswanger, H. P., K. Deninger, and G. Feder (1995). Power, Distortions
Reform in Agricultural Land Relations. In *Handbook of Development*
Volume III, edited by J. Behrman and T. N. Srinivasan. Amsterdam: Elsel

Binswanger, H., K. Deininger, and G. Feder (1995). *Handbook of Devel*
nomics, Vol. 3. Amsterdam: North-Holland.

Binswanger, H. and M. Rosenzweig (1986). Behavioral and Material Dete
Production Relations in Agriculture. *Journal of Development Studies*, 22

Bloch, P. and J. Foltz (1999). *Recent Tenure Reforms in the Sahel;*
and Suggestions for Redirection. University of Wisconsin-Madison: L
Center.

Blundell, R., M. Costa Dias, C. Meghir, and J. Van Reenen (2004). Eva
Employment Impact of a Mandatory Job Search Assistance Program.
European Economic Association.

Bockstette, V., A. Chanda, and L. Putterman (2002). States and Markets: The
of an Early Start. *Journal of Economic Growth*, 7(4), 347–369.

Boozer, M. and M. Goldstein (2003). *Poverty Measurement and Dynamics*. L
of Economics: Yale University.

Broegaard, R. J., R. Heltberg, and N. Machlow-Moller (2002). *Property I*
Land Tenure Security in Nicaragua. Center for Economic and Business
Copenhagen.

Bromley, D. (1989). Property Relations and Economic Development: The C
Reform. *World Development*, 17(6), 867–877.

Brown, J. and T. Guinnane (2005). Regions and Time in the European Ferti
sition: Problems in the Princeton Project's Statistical Methodology. *Explo*
Economic History.

Bruce, J. W. and S. E. Migot-Adholla, eds. (1994). *Searching for Land Tenure*
in Africa. Dubuque, IA: Kendall/Hunt.

Burgess, R. and R. Pande (2005). Do Rural Banks Matter? Evidence from tl
Social Banking Experiment. *American Economic Review*, 95(3), 780–795.

Carter, M. R. and P. Olinto (2000). *Getting Institutions 'Right' for Whom: Cr*
straints and the Impact of Property Rights on the Quantity and Compositi
vestment. University of Wisconsin-Madison.

Cartier, M. R., K. D. Wiebe, and B. Blarel (1994). Tenure Security for Whom? I
tial Effects of Land Policy in Kenya. In *Searching for Land Tenure Security i*
edited by John W. Bruce and Shem E. Migot-Adholla. The World Bank.

Field, E., and Torero, M. (2004). *Do Property Titles Increase Credit Access Among the Urban Poor? Evidence from a Nationwide Titling Program.* Harvard University.

Firmin-Sellers, K. (1996). *The Transformation of Property Rights in the Gold Coast: An Empirical Analysis Applying Rational Choice Theory.* New York: Cambridge University Press.

Firmin-Sellers, K., and P. Sellers (1999). Expected Failures and Unexpected Successes of Land Titling in Africa. *World Development*, 27(7), 1115–1128.

Fisman, R. (2001). Estimating the Value of Political Connections. *American Economic Review*, 91(4), 1095–1102.

Fisman, R., and S. J. Wei (2004). Tax Rates and Tax Evasion: Evidence from "Missing Imports" in China, *Journal of Political Economy*, 112(2), 471–496.

Foster, A. D., and M. R. Rosenzweig (2001). *Democratization, Decentralization and the Distribution of Local Public Goods in a Poor Rural Economy.* University of Pennsylvania.

Francisco, A. and A. Ciccone (2004). Trade and Productivity. *Quarterly Journal of Economics*, 119(2), 613–646.

Frankel, J. A., and D. Romer (1999). Does Trade Cause Growth? *American Economic Review*, 89(3), 379–399.

Frankel, J., and A. Rose (2002). An Estimate of the Effect of Common Currencies on Trade and Income. *Quarterly Journal of Economics*, 117(2), 437–466.

Fred-Mensah, B. K. (1996). *Changes, Ambiguities and Conflicts in Buem, Eastern Ghana.* Johns Hopkins University.

Fred-Mensah, B. K. (1996). Changes, Ambiguities and Conflicts in Buem, Eastern Ghana. Ph.D. diss., John Hopkins University.

Freudenberger, M. S. (2000). *Tenure and Natural Resources in the Gambia: Summary of Research Findings and Policy Options.* Vol. 40. University of Wisconsin-Madison: Land Tenure Center.

Friedman, J., and E. Jimenez, and S. K. Mayo (1988). The Demand for Tenure Security in Developing Countries. *Journal of Development Economics*, 29, 185–198.

Furth, R. (1998). Ivory Coast Country Profile. In *Country Profiles of Land Tenure: Africa, 1996*, edited by John W. Bruce. University of Wisconsin-Madison: Land Tenure Center.

Galiani, S., P. Gertler, and E. Schargrodsky (2005). Water for Life: The Impact of the Privatization of Water Services on Child Mortality. *Journal of Political Economy*, 113(1), 83–120.

Glaeser, E. L., R. La Porta, and F. Lopez-de-Silanes, and A. Shleifer (2004). Do Institutions Cause Growth?, *Journal of Economic Growth*, 9(3), 271–303.

Golan, E. H. (1994). Land Tenure Reform in the Peanut Basin of Senegal. In *Searching for Land Tenure Security in Africa*, edited by John W. Bruce and Shem E. Migot-Adholla. Washington, DC: The World Bank.

Goldberg, P. K. and N. Pavcnik (2003). The Response of the Informal Sector to Trade Liberalization. *Journal of Development Economics*, 72(2), 463–496.

Goldstein, M. (2000). *Intrahousehold Allocation and Farming in Southern Ghana.* UC Berkeley.

Goldstein, M. and C. Udry (2005). *The Profits of Power: Land Rights and Agricultural Investment in Ghana.* mimeo Yale.

Gugerty, M. K. and E. Miguel (2000). *Community Participation and Social Sanctions in Kenyan Schools.* Harvard University.

Guyer, J. (1981). Household and Community in African Studies. *African Studies Review*, 24(2/3), 87–137.

Guyer, J. I. (2004). *Marginal Gains: Monetary Transactions in Atlantic Africa.* Vol. 1997. Chicago: University of Chicago Press.

Hall, R. E. and C. I. Jones (1999). Why Do Some Countries Produce So Much More Output per Worker than Others? *Quarterly Journal of Economics*, 114(1), 83–116.

Hart, T. B. and R. Ducarme (2005). Forestry and Conservation Activities During a War Fought over Land and Resources in the Democratic Republic of Congo. *ETFRN News*, 42–44.

Hayes, J., M. Roth, and L. Zepeda (1997). Tenure Security, Investment and Productivity in Gambian Agriculture: A Generalized Probit Analysis. *American Journal of Agricultural Economics*, 79, 369–382.

Heckman, J. J. and E. J. Vytlacil. (2000). Local Instrumental Variables. In *Nonlinear Statistical Modeling: Essays in Honor of Takeshi Amemiya*, edited by C. Hsiao, K. Morimune and J. Powell. Cambridge: Cambridge University.

Hill, P. (1963). *The Migrant Cocoa-Farmers of Southern Ghana; A Study in Rural Capitalism*. Cambridge: Cambridge University Press.

Hoeben, H. C. (2001). *Human Rights in the D.R. Congo: 1997 Until the Present Day; the Predicament of the Churches*. Germany.

Huggins, C., et al. (2005). *Land, Conflict and Livelihoods in the Great Lakes Region: Testing Policies to the Limit*. Vol. 14. Nairobi: African Center for Technology Studies.

Human Rights Watch (2004). *Côte d'Ivoire: Accountability for Serious Human Rights Crimes Key to Resolving Crisis*.

Hussein, K. and D. Gnisci (2005). *Land, Agricultural Change and Conflict in West Africa: Regional Issues from Sierra Leone, Liberia and Côte d'Ivoire Phase I: Historical Overview*. Sahel and West Africa Club/OECD.

Imbens, G. and J. Angrist (1994). Identification and Estimation of Local Average Treatment Effects. *Econometrica*, 62, 467–475.

Iyer, L. (2005). History Institutions and Economic Performance: The Legacy of Colonial Land Tenure Systems in India. *American Economic Review*.

Iyer, L. and Q. Do (2004). Land Titling and Rural Transition in Vietnam. *mimeo, Harvard Business School*.

Jansen, K. and E. Roquas (1998). Modernizing Insecurity; The Land Titling Project in Honduras. *Development and Change*, 29.

Jin, H. H. and Y. Y. Qian (1998). Public versus Private Ownership of Firms: Evidence from Rural China. *Quarterly Journal of Economics*, 113(3), 773–808.

Joachim, A. D. *Conflits Ethniques en Côte d'Ivoire*.

Johnson, N. L. (2001). Tierray Libertad: Will Tenure Reform Improve Productivity in Mexico's Ejido Agriculture? *Economic Development and Cultural Change*, 291–309.

Jones, B. F. and B. A. Olken (2005). Do Leaders Matter? National Leadership and Growth Since World War II. *Quarterly Journal of Economics*.

Kan, K. (2000). Informal Capital Sources and Household Investment: Evidence from Taiwan. *Journal of Development Economics*, 62(1), 209–232.

Kasanga, K. and N. A. Kosey (2001). *Land Management in Ghana: Building on Tradition and Modernity*. London: International Institute for Environment and Development.

Kaufmann, D., A. Kraay, and M. Mastruzzi (2004). Governance Matters III: Governance Indicators for 1996, 1998, 2000, and 2002. *World Bank Economic Review*, 18(2), 253–287.

Knack, S. and P. Keefer (1995). Institutions and Economic Performance: Cross-Country Tests Using Alternative Institutional Measures. *Economics and Politics* 7, 207–227.

Knack, S. and P. Keefer (1997). Does Social Capital Have an Economic Payoff? A Cross-Country Investigation. *Quarterly Journal of Economics*, 112(4), 1251–1288.

Knox, A. (1998). Gambia Country Profile. In *Country Profiles of Land Tenure: Africa, 1996*, edited by John W. Bruce. University of Wisconsin-Madison: Land Tenure Center.

Knox, A. (1998). Ghana Country Profile. In *Country Profiles of Land Tenure: Africa,*

1996, edited by John W. Bruce. University of Wisconsin-Madison: Land Tenure Center.

Kogel, T. (2005). Youth Dependency and Total Factor Productivity. *Journal of Development Economics*, 76(1), 147–173.

Kone, M. (2002). *Gaining Rights of Access to Land in West-Central Côte d'Ivoire*. London: International Institute for Environment and Development.

La Ferrara, E. (2003). Kin Groups and Reciprocity: A Model of Credit Transactions in Ghana. *American Economic Review*, 93(5), 1730–1751.

La Porta, R., F. Lopez–de Silanes, A. Shleifer, and R. Vishny (1999). The Quality of Government. *Journal of Law Economics & Organization*, 15(1), 222–279.

Lanjouw, J. O. and P. I. Levy (2002). Untitled: A Study of Formal and Informal Property Rights in Urban Ecuador. *The Economic Journal*.

Leisz, S. (1998). Zaire Country Profile. *Country Profiles of Land Tenure: Africa, 1996*, edited by John W. Bruce. University of Wisconsin-Madison: Land Tenure Center.

Lopez, R. (1996). *Land Titling and Investment in Honduras*. Department of Agricultural and Resource Economics, University of Maryland, College Park, MD.

Mahama, S. (2003). *The Ghana Land Administration Project: The Process and Challenges*. Marburg, Germany: Philipps-University.

Mamdani, M. (1996). *Citizen and Subject: Contemporary Africa and the Legacy of Late Colonialism*. Princeton: Princeton University Press.

Manning, A. (2004). Instrumental Variables for Binary Treatments with Heterogenous Treatment Effects: A Simple Exposition. *Contributions to Economic Analysis & Policy*, 3(1), 1273.

Masters, W. A. and M. S. McMillan (2001). Climate and Scale in Economic Growth. *Journal of Economic Growth*, 6(3), 167–186.

Mauro, P. (1995). Corruption and Growth. *Quarterly Journal of Economics*, 110(3), 681–712.

McEvedy, C. and R. Jones (1978). *Atlas of World Population History*. New York: Facts on File.

Miceli, T. J., C. F. Sirmans, and J. Kieyah (2001). The Demand for Land Title Registration: Theory with Evidence from Kenya. *American Law and Economics Review*, 3(2), 275–287.

Migot-Adholla, S. E., F. Place, and W. Oluch-Kosura (1994). Security of Tenure and Land Productivity in Kenya. In *Searching for Land Tenure Security in Africa*, edited by John W. Bruce and Shem E. Migot-Adholla. Washington, DC: The World Bank.

Migot-Adholla, S., P. Hazell, B. Blarel, and F. Place (1991). Indigenous Land Rights Systems in Sub-Saharan Africa: A Constraint on Productivity? *World Bank Economic Review*, 5, 155–175.

Ministry of Lands and Forestry (2003). *Ghana: Emerging Land Tenure Issues*. Accra, Ghana.

Moyroud, C. and J. Katunga (2002). Coltan Exploration in Eastern Democratic Republic of the Congo (DRC). In *Scarcity and Surfeit*. Nairobi: African Centre for Technology Studies.

North, D. C. (1981). *Structure and Change in Economic History*. New York: Norton & Co.

Pagiola, S. (1999). *Economic Analysis of Rural Land Administration Projects*. Economics Working Paper Archive at WUSTL.

Pande, R. and C. Udry. Institutions and development: A View from Below (Working Paper). MIMEO *Economic Growth Center*.

Pande, R. (2003). Can Mandated Political Representation Increase Policy Influence for Disadvantaged Minorities? Theory and Evidence from India. *American Economic Review*, 93(4), 1132–1151.

Pender, J. L. and J. M. Kerr (1999). The Effects of Land Sales Restrictions: Evidence from South India. *Agricultural Economics*, 21, 279–294.

Persico, N. and A. Lizzeri (2004). Why Did the Elites Extend the Suffrage? Democracy and the Scope of Government, with an Application to Britain's Age of Reform. *Quarterly Journal of Economics*, 119(2), 705–763.

Peters, P. E. (1994). *Dividing the Commons: Politics, Policy, and Culture in Botswana*. Charlottesville: University Press of Virginia.

Pinckney, T. C. and P. K. Kimuyu (1994). Land Tenure Reform in East Africa: Good, Bad or Unimportant? *Journal of African Economies*, 3(1), 1–28.

Place, F. and P. Hazell (1993). Productivity Effects of Indigenous Tenure Systems in Sub-Saharan Africa. *American Journal of Agricultural Economics*, 75(1), 10–19.

Place, F. and S. E. Migot-Adholla (1998). The Economic Effects of Land Registration on Smallholder Farms in Kenya: Evidence from Nyeri and Kakamega Districts. *Land Economics*, 74(3), 360–373.

Quisumbing, A., J. B. Aidoo, E. Payongayong, and K. Otsuka (2001). Agroforestry Management in Ghana. In *Land Tenure and Natural Resource Management: A Comparative Study of Agrarian Communities in Asia and Africa*, edited by Keijiro Otsuka and Frank Place. Baltimore: Johns Hopkins University Press.

Raynaut, C. (1997). *Sahel Diversitè et Dynamiques des Relations Société Nature*. Edited by C. Raynaut, E. Grégoire. Routledge.

Rodrik, D. (1999). Democracies Pay Higher Wages. *Quarterly Journal of Economics*, 114(3), 707–738.

Rodrik, D., A. Subramanian, and F. Trebbi (2004). Institutions Rule: The Primacy of Institutions Over Geography and Integration in Economic Development. *Journal of Economic Growth*, 9(2), 131–165.

Roth, M., B. Carr, and J. Cochrane (1996). *Land Rights, Intra-Household Employment and Resource Use in the Peri-Urban Areas of Banjul, the Gambia*. University of Wisconsin-Madison: Land Tenure Center.

Roth, M., J. Cochrane, and W. Kisamba-Mugerwa (1994). Tenure Security, Credit Use, and Farm Investment in the Rujumbura Pilot Land Registration Scheme, Uganda. In *Searching for Land Tenure Security in Africa*, edited by John W. Bruce and Shem E. Migot-Adholla. Washington, DC: The World Bank.

Roth, M., J. Unruh, and R. Barrows (1994). Land Registration, Tenure Security, Credit Use, and Investment in the Shebelle Region of Somalia. In *Searching for Land Tenure Security in Africa*, edited by John W. Bruce and Shem E. Migot-Adholla. Washington, DC: The World Bank.

Sachs, J. D. and A. Warner (1995). Economic-Reform and the Process of Global Integration. *Brookings Papers on Economic Activity*, 1, 1–95.

Sjaastad, E. and D. Bromley (1997). Indigenous Land Rights in Sub-Saharan Africa: Appropriation, Security and Investment Demand. *World Development*, 25(4), 549–562.

Sullivan, M. J. (1991). *Measuring Global Values*. New York: Greenwood.

Taylor, C. L. and M. C. Hudson (1972). *World Handbook of Political and Social Indicators*. Ann Arbor, MI: ICSPR.

Topalova, P. (2005). *Trade Liberalization, Poverty, and Inequality: Evidence from Indian Districts*. NBER.

Toure, M. D. (2003). *Rural Land Tenure and Sustainable Development in the Sahel and West Africa; Secure Land Tenure Problems in the Sahel and West Africa: Nine Years After PRAIA; Regional Summary Report*. Bamako, Republic of Mali: Permanent Interstates Committee for Drought Control in the Sahel.

USDA Foreign Agricultural Service (2004). *Cote d'Ivoire Solid Wood Products Annual, 2004*. Vol. IV4013.

Visaria, S. (2005). *Legal Reform and Loan Repayment: The Microeconomic Impact of Debt Recovery Tribunals in India*. MIMEO Columbia University.

Vlassenroot, K. and C. Huggins (2004). Land, Migration and Conflict in Eastern D.R. Congo, *Eco-Conflicts*, 3(4), 1–4.

Wilks, I. (1993). *Forests of Gold: Essays on the Akan and the Kingdom of Asante*. Athens: Ohio University Press.

Wily, L. A. and D. Hammond (2001). *Land Security and The Poor in Ghana: Is There a Way Forward? A Land Sector Scoping Study*. UK.

The World Bank (2005). *2005 World Development Indicators*. Washington DC.

Name Index

(continued from page iii)

Eric Ghysels, Norman R. Swanson, and Mark Watson, Editors, *Essays in econometrics: Collected papers of Clive W. J. Granger* (Volume II), 0 521 79207 X, 0 521 80407 8, 0 521 79649 0, 0 521 79697 0

Cheng Hsiao, *Analysis of panel data*, second edition, 0 521 81855 9, 0 521 52271 4

Mathias Dewatripont, Lars Peter Hansen, and Stephen J. Turnovsky, Editors, *Advances in economics and econometrics – Eighth World Congress* (Volume I), 0 521 81872 8, 0 521 52411 3

Mathias Dewatripont, Lars Peter Hansen, and Stephen J. Turnovsky, Editors, *Advances in economics and econometrics – Eighth World Congress* (Volume II), 0 521 81873 7, 0 521 52412 1

Mathias Dewatripont, Lars Peter Hansen, and Stephen J. Turnovsky, Editors, *Advances in economics and econometrics – Eighth World Congress* (Volume III), 0 521 81874 5, 0 521 52413 X

Roger Koenker, *Quantile Regression*, 0 521 84573 4, 0 521 60827 9

Charles Blackorby, Walter Bossert, and David Donaldson, *Population issues in social choice theory, welfare economics, and ethics*, 0 521 82551 2, 0 521 53258 2

John E. Roemer, *Democracy, education, and equality*, 0 521 84665 X, 0 521 60913 5

Richard Blundell, Whitney K. Newey, and Torsten Persson, Editors, *Advances in Economics and Econometrics – Ninth World Congress* (Volume I), 0 521 87152 2, 0 521 69208 3